A Commentary on Kant's
Critique of Practical Reason

By
LEWIS WHITE BECK

The King's Library

Phoenix Books

THE UNIVERSITY OF CHICAGO PRESS
CHICAGO & LONDON

This book is also available in a clothbound edition from
THE UNIVERSITY OF CHICAGO PRESS

The University of Chicago Press, Chicago & London
The University of Toronto Press, Toronto 5, Canada

© 1960 by The University of Chicago. All rights reserved. Published 1960. First Phoenix Edition 1963
Fourth Impression 1966. Printed in the United States
of America

Foreword

Odd though it may be, the *Critique of Practical Reason* is a neglected work. There is no study of it in any language that can be compared favorably with the commentaries on the *Critique of Pure Reason* by Kemp Smith, Paton, or Vaihinger. Not even briefer commentaries like those of Cohen, Ewing, or Weldon on the first *Critique* exist in English for the second; there seems to be only one (that of Stange) in German. Nothing like the uncompleted commentary on the *Critique of Judgment* by Baeumler has been published to give the full historical background for the development of Kant's ethical theory. H. W. Cassirer, who has written commentaries on the first and third *Critique*'s, has not done so for the second. So far as I have been able to discover, no book even with the title of commentary has been published on the *Critique of Practical Reason* since the eighteenth century.[1] Every book on Kant in general and on his ethics in particular, of course, deals with some of its contents; and surveys and abstracts of it as a connected whole appear occasionally as chapters in larger works. But no one, I believe, has essayed on a large scale to study the *Critique of Practical Reason* as a literary unity and integral philosophical treatise.

There are at least two reasons for this comparative neglect of one of Kant's greatest works. First, a commentary is not so absolutely indispensable to the study of this *Critique* as it is to that of the others. The book has few of the stylistic difficulties and philosophical obscurities of the other *Critique*'s. In contrast to the bewildering complexity of the first and the third, most of the second *Critique* is straightforward and almost simple. Or at least it appears to be on first reading, which is perhaps the only reading most people give it.

The second reason lies in the understandable preference that many readers have for the *Foundations of the Metaphysics of Morals*. This

[1] Unless one excepts August Messer's *Kommentar zu Kants ethischen und religionsphilosophischen Hauptschriften* (1929), in which he attempted to cover all the principal treatises and succeeded in giving little more than paraphrases. The title, of course, is not the important thing. Barni's *Examen . . .* (1851) is a commentary in most senses of the word, though it neglects to explore historical and literary connections. Barni says that "it is not meant to be a sterile commentary but an advanced and fruitful criticism," though its analytical chapter "will offer at least an exact and useful commentary" (pp. vi, vii).

small work has had three English commentaries (those of Duncan, Paton, and Ross) in the last ten years and is perhaps the most widely read of all Kant's works in England and America, existing in no less than five current English translations (by Abbott, Beck, Friedrich, Manthey-Zorn, and Paton). The *Foundations* does not, at least in its first two parts, presuppose knowledge of the rest of Kant's writings and is directed to those not involved in, or committed to, the Kantian system. As a contribution to moral philosophy it must stand on its own internal merits, and this fact makes it pedagogically more useful than the larger *Critique*. While there are topics discussed in the *Critique* which are omitted from the *Foundations*, there is also much overlapping. In these overlapping areas, preference has almost always been given to the simpler exposition in the *Foundations*, and the more obviously systematic and in part divergent treatments in the *Critique* have been regrettably overlooked. Only the teachings of the *Critique* which have no counterpart in the *Foundations* find their way into most expositions and criticisms of Kant's work. It has been wittily remarked that if a reader of books on Kant noticed the few isolated passages from the *Critique of Practical Reason* which are repeatedly cited, he might conclude that the *Critique* was a lost work, only a few fragments of which have survived.

Nevertheless, as a part of the system of the critical philosophy, the *Foundations* does not have the full merit of the larger work to be examined here. For it is only in the *Critique* that all the various strands of Kant's thought are woven together into the pattern of his practical philosophy. This pattern, in turn, can be understood only in the entire fabric of the critical philosophy, and that rich design can be clear only to those who have understood each of its three principal parts, which are the three *Critique*'s and not shorter and more popular works like the *Prolegomena* and the *Foundations*.

The absence of a commentary is a sign, in part an effect but perhaps in part also a cause, of neglect of the *Critique*. It is my hope here to take a step toward removing this cause. The commentary has a twofold purpose. First, as a hermeneutic study, it will seek to place the *Critique of Practical Reason* in the context of Kant's philosophy and of the moral philosophy of the eighteenth century insofar as it was the body of thought to which Kant responded and which he wished to modify. The *Critique* was written as a technical, professional work by a philosopher who saw, and who insisted that his readers should see, the way in which every part involved the others. Kant's architectonic has been much derided as a pedantic crotchet of the aging baroque philosopher. But it is a mistake to believe that what is of utmost importance to an author can be justly neglected by the reader. Parallels and differences in content and structure and terminology between this *Critique* and the others cannot be passed over in silence if we are to penetrate below the surface of any of them. In attempting to show how this treatise stands out against a background often discerned only vaguely by the reader, I shall have to recall again and again the doctrines of Kant's contemporaries and the revolutionary theses in other parts of his own work, knowledge of which was tacitly assumed when he came to write this *Critique*. I hope to provide this basic information with sufficient brevity and accuracy not to drive away the Kant-scholar—a man known in the legends of scholarship for the vastness of his learning and the shortness of his temper, a trait which has given a notorious acerbity to Kant-literature for nearly two centuries. But I hope also to be able to provide it with sufficient fulness and simplicity to throw light on the text needed by those to whom memory of the first *Critique* gives, at best, only wavering illumination and uncertain guidance. I cannot flatter myself into thinking that I may not at times offend either the Kant-adept or the beginner; I hope only that if I tire or irritate the former, I shall not, on the same page, puzzle or discourage the latter.

My second purpose is to examine the contents of this work on their philosophical merits. We seem to be going through one of the periods —the third in English philosophy, the second in American—in which the study of Kant provides stimulation and sustenance to new and creative work in philosophy. In the past few years there has been a noteworthy increase in the amount and improvement in the quality of studies devoted to Kant in France, England, Italy, and America; there seems to be a heightening of interest in Kant even in Germany, where the number and quality of Kant-studies have always been high. It seems as if a period of thought in which the creative and critical work and spirit of David Hume are dominant (as in America and England) is to be followed by one in which Kantian criticism and reconstruction— perhaps not recognized as such—revive. In this book, therefore, exposition of Kant may well be combined with philosophic estimation insofar as the latter does not require a whole treatise to itself.

But the first task is to find out what Kant said, how he said it, and why. Only then can evaluation have before it a firm object, not an amorphous mass that varies in shape with the degree of sympathy or hostility with which it is approached; too often in the past, debates on whether Kant was right or wrong have been vitiated by lack of the most rudimentary agreement as to what he actually said and meant.

It is a genuine pleasure to record my thanks to those who made it possible for me to write this book. The University of Rochester allowed me to be free of all academic duties during 1957–58 so that the book could be completed. That year was spent in Germany and Italy under a fellowship from the John Simon Guggenheim Memorial Foundation and with the generous assistance of the Committee on Grants in Aid for Research of the College of Arts and Science of the University of Rochester. During the time I was in Germany, I was guest of the Philosophical Seminar of the Albertus Magnus University in Cologne and used its extensive facilities. Members of my family and colleagues gave encouragement, advice, and assistance; each of them will see, on page after page, evidence of my indebtedness. I am particularly grateful to Professor C. B. Earp, of Wake Forest College, for help with the eighteenth-century Latin authors.

The Frontispiece is by Heinrich Wolff, and was first published in the bicentenary memorial volume for Kant issued by the University of Königsberg.

L. W. B.

SAN DOMENICO, FIRENZE

Note on the Citations

References to the *Critique of Practical Reason* are given as follows. The first number refers to the page in the edition of the Königliche Preussische Akademie der Wissenschaften, Berlin, Volume V (2d ed., 1913), edited by Paul Natorp. The second number, in parentheses or brackets, refers to the Abbott translation, sixth edition, reprint of 1954. When no book title is given but only page numbers, they always refer to these two editions of the *Critique*. If the reader be annoyed by what may no doubt appear to be an excessive number of specific page references to the *Critique*, let him be reminded that they have not been heaped up in this quantity out of any desire to document and redocument the obvious, but to make Index I, to passages in the *Critique*, full enough to be useful to anyone who wishes to survey all my comments on any specific passage.

References to the *Foundations of the Metaphysics of Morals* refer to the Akademie edition, Volume IV, with the number in parentheses or brackets referring to the Abbott translation in the single-volume edition containing the *Critique*, as mentioned above.

Since my own translations of the *Critique* and *Foundations*, from which quotations are drawn (with occasional, but not indicated, modifications), include the Akademie pagination, it is not necessary to cite the pages in these editions for the benefit of those who may wish to use them in preference to Abbott's.

References to the *Critique of Pure Reason* indicate pages in the first edition by the letter "A" and in the second edition by the letter "B." The translations are those of Norman Kemp Smith, occasionally modified.

References to the *Critique of Judgment*, in many cases, cite only the paragraph number. When it is necessary to indicate a specific page, the first number given refers to the page in the Akademie edition, Volume V, and the number in parentheses or brackets refers to the translation by J. H. Bernard in the edition of the "Hafner Library of Classics."

Kant's other works, with very few exceptions, which are clearly noted, are cited by giving the title or a short title and a paragraph number or the volume and page in the Akademie edition. If an English translation is easily available, this is indicated by giving the title in English and, after the Akademie reference, the name of the translator and the page in the translation. Full bibliographical data on the translations thus cited will be found in the Bibliography, Section III.

Occasionally it has been necessary to cite passages which, because there is not yet an index, I have been unable to find in the Akademie edition; these references are made self-explanatory.

All references to Kant's *Lectures on Ethics,* prepared for publication from students' notes, are exclusively to the translation by Louis Infield.

Kant's correspondence is cited by stating the addressee and date of each letter and its location in the second Akademie edition, Volumes X–XIII, and in Volume XXIII, first (only) edition.

Kant's fragments (*Reflexionen*) are identified only by their number in the Akademie edition, except those taken from Volumes XX and XXIII. In these volumes the fragments are not numbered, and they are cited by volume and page number. For specific places in long, numbered fragments, I have also added the Akademie pagination.

References to works not by Kant are generally given by short title with a minimum of bibliographic information. The Bibliography, Section IV, supplies the information needed on these titles. Other works touching on only a specific point and having little or no bearing on the whole of the present study are cited in the notes with sufficient bibliographic information. Authors named in the footnotes are listed in Index, II; authors listed only in the bibliography are not indexed.

Table of Contents

xi

BIBLIOGRAPHY

INDEXES

Part I

I

The Writing of the
"Critique of Practical Reason"

§ 1. INTRODUCTION

Few substantial philosophical treatises have been written in the haste in
which the *Critique of Practical Reason* was composed. The book, however, shows few of the signs of hurry that marred some of Kant's other
works. Indeed, the short time he devoted to thinking it out as a single
self-contained book and to its actual writing may be responsible for a
virtue singularly lacking in the *Critique of Pure Reason*, which he med-
itated on for twelve years and "brought to completion in some four or
five months,"[1] presumably by making more or less judicious use of
manuscripts composed at various times during the twelve-year period.
For, unlike the first *Critique*, the second adheres to one single straight
line of argument, developed without exploring blind alleys and without getting almost lost on tangents. In it, we do not, as it were, listen to
Kant thinking aloud or watch him trying first this and then that way
of making himself understood. The book has the magisterial tone and
direct style that come to a man who has thought out all he wants to say
before he puts one word on paper.

By Kantian standards, at least, it is an exceedingly well-written book.
To many, this may seem damning with the faintest praise possible. Certainly Kant's style is not to everyone's liking, not even to his own. But
few men have had juster estimates of their own style than Kant had of
his, and his decision not to try to write in a popular way was justified
by the nature of the materials he was dealing with and by the demands
he rightly made of him who ventures to read philosophy.[2] And it can

[1] To Garve, August 7, 1783; to Mendelssohn, August 16, 1783 (X, 338, 345). The
last part of this sentence does not commit one to the "patchwork theory" (cf. H. J.
Paton, *Kant's Metaphysics of Experience* [London, 1936], I, 41).

[2] For an explicit caveat, see *Prolegomena*, end of Introduction. In an undated
note (5040), he says: "If, like Hume, I had the power to embellish my work, I would
hesitate to use it. It is true that some readers will be frightened away by its dryness.
But is it not necessary to frighten some of them away, with whom the matter would
come into bad hands?"

be excused, if an excuse is needed, by the urgency which marked his literary activity in his old age. The fastidious reader should remember that all the best-known works of Kant were written in excusable haste by an old man who had first discovered his message to the world late in life and who was never robust but carried (by modern university standards) a crushing load of academic duties.

Given the circumstances, what is surprising is how well the book is written. Style cannot be considered apart from content, and the strongly masculine, *sachlich,* and encyclopedic style of Kant's thinking permits and perhaps requires[3] the often condemned Kantian style of writing, which Schopenhauer called "brilliantly dry." It does not exclude occasional eloquence and poignancy of expression, and it never allows the tone to be less than elevated. Unfortunately, however, these high virtues do not entirely exclude the vices of pedantic distinctions followed by carelessness in their use, overcondensation[4] alternating with repetitiousness, and lack of the art of perspicuous paragraphing.

These weaknesses cannot be denied, but they are frequently exaggerated by philosophers who write no better. It is often remarked by Kant-scholars that when, after dogged effort, they come to the root of some perplexing sentence or paragraph, they find that the complexities of the writing cannot always be attributed to the ineptitude of the writer, but more often to the demands of the thought expressed. They often realize that it would be very difficult, if not impossible, to say better exactly what Kant was saying and that any simplification of style would almost inevitably involve oversimplification of the thought. Attempts at simplification have usually produced only faint and distorted echoes of Kant's meaning, and most of them, if they succeed in making him seem simple, do so only by making his views seem silly.

Except in a few passages, simplification of style is not needed in the *Critique of Practical Reason.* There are few passages in which the attentive reader will experience any real difficulty in discerning what Kant means. Diagramming of sentences, often said in the legends of

---

[3] Cf. *Critique of Pure Reason,* A xviii–xix.

[4] Kant could appreciate a joke about his own style, at least this aspect of it. Zelter told the following anecdote to Goethe and said that Kant had been amused by the event reported. Wlömer, a banker, told Kant that he had read some of his works and would have read more if he had had more fingers. "How so?" inquired the philosopher. "Well, my friend," replied the banker, "your way of writing is so rich in parentheses and conditional clauses which I have to keep my eye on that I put one finger on this word, a second on that, and so on for the third and fourth. Before I get to the end of the page all my fingers are used up" (Vorländer, *Immanuel Kant: Der Mann und das Werk,* II, 99).

scholarship to be prerequisite to understanding the *Critique of Pure Reason*, is not called for here.

We do not know much about the actual writing of the book. But in the light of evidence about to be adduced, it is probable that the book was begun in the spring of 1787, brought nearly to completion by June, and finished by September. I speak only of the actual writing; most of the contents of the book had been clear in Kant's mind at least as early as 1785. But the plan of writing a *Critique of Practical Reason* as a single, integral work did not slowly mature. The book was not long anticipated, and Kant came suddenly, and presumably with reluctance, to the decision to write it.

In order to understand this decision, it is necessary to go back toward the beginning of Kant's literary career to see what the book was that he did want and plan to write.

§ 2. THE DEFERRED PLAN TO WRITE A METAPHYSICS OF MORALS

Kant's writings in the 1750's and 1760's were almost all in the field of the natural sciences. But his interest in them was genuinely philosophical, and he was concerned most of all with questions of the method and scope of the sciences. Even in these works, however, when occasion offered, he commented freely upon ethical and religious questions which had become involved in the cosmological speculations of the day. This direction of his thinking is especially clear in his most important scientific work, the *Universal Natural History and Theory of the Heavens* (1755).

The so-called *Prize Essay: An Inquiry into the Evidence of the Principles of Natural Theology and Morals*, published by the Berlin Academy in 1764, is the first of his works which deals more than incidentally with questions of moral philosophy. Even here, as is seen from its title, it was the foundations and methods of ethics that were in the center of his interest. This essay, often interpreted as manifesting a commitment to the moral-sense theory of Shaftesbury and Hutcheson, and hence to empiricism in ethics, ends with a query the answer to which gives direction to all his subsequent work in moral philosophy. He says there that "it is still a question to be settled whether it is simply the cognitive faculty or whether it is feeling . . . which decides the basic principles of practical philosophy."[5]

Metaphysics is regarded in the *Prize Essay* as a "philosophy of the ultimate grounds of our knowledge," as philosophy "applied to the more universal rational insights." While rejecting the alleged identity

---

[5] *Prize Essay*, II, 300 (Beck, 285).

of the methods of mathematics and those of metaphysics—an identity almost definitive of the dominant metaphysics of the time—Kant believed that metaphysics, following its own method of analyzing experience, could find indemonstrable propositions as certain as those of mathematics.[6] The basic indemonstrable propositions of metaphysics would be self-evident rational principles, though not definitions or intuitively certain axioms as in mathematics. He thought metaphysics to be possible as a rigorous science, and already to exist in natural theology. The metaphysical foundations of morals, however, were yet to be found: "The primary grounds of morals are not yet, in their present state, capable of all requisite evidence."[7]

Kant must soon have felt capable of supplying this lack. In a letter to Lambert the next year, he announced a fateful plan that, in one form or another, was to attract, even almost to haunt, him throughout his mature life. It was the plan to write a work "on the metaphysical foundations of practical philosophy."[8] The title of this work and a report on his progress with it were given in a letter to Herder in 1768, in which he said that he was then at work on a "Metaphysics of Morals" and that he hoped to complete it within a year.[9]

We can only speculate on what would have been the contents and structure of this work, had it been completed at that time. But we do not need to make any conjectures about it for our present purposes.

---

[6] It was in this spirit that he favorably compared Rousseau to Newton, for both discovered "the hidden law the observation of which justifies providence" (*Bemerkungen zu den Beobachtungen*, XX, 58–59). Similarly, he esteemed the work of Shaftesbury, Hutcheson, and Hume as containing the method by which "the abiding nature of man" can be discerned in the variety of his empirical appearances. This, he said, is "an excellent discovery of our days," and accordingly he promised to evaluate historically and philosophically what happens before showing what *ought* to happen (*Nachricht von der Einrichtung seiner Vorlesungen in dem Winterhalbjahr von 1765–1766*, II, 311). Each of these passages indicated the analytical method he was to use, beginning with observations and rising by abstraction from empirical to metaphysical concepts. The passage in the announcement of his lectures, however, does not indicate that Kant at this time thought a descriptive, merely empirical, ethics to be possible, though it has been interpreted as evidence for this by some writers.

[7] *Prize Essay*, II, 298 (Beck, 282).

[8] To Lambert, December 31, 1765 (X, 56).

[9] To Herder, May 9, 1768 (X, 74). The book itself was announced as forthcoming by the publisher Kanter, under the title "Critique of Moral Taste." The term "metaphysics of morals" was little used before Kant. It seems to have originated with Canz, *Disciplinae morales omnes* (1739), according to Max Wundt, *Die deutsche Schulphilosophie im Zeitalter der Aufklärung* (Tübingen: Mohr, 1945), p. 223. Cf. also *ibid.*, p. 251, on A. F. Hoffmann's conception (*Vernunftlehre* [1737]) of metaphysics and moral philosophy, which was closer to Kant than to Wolff.

For though Kant's thoughts on ethics were undoubtedly undergoing changes during this period, the most important change at this time occurred in his view of the nature of metaphysics itself. His views on this, unlike his ethical views at this time, can be documented and described with confidence.

These changes were clearly shown in his *Inaugural Dissertation: The Forms and Principles of the Sensible and Intelligible World,* published in 1770 on the occasion of his accession to the professorship in Königsberg. This is a brief systematic treatise on metaphysics. It not only distinguished but also sharply separated the sensible and the intellectual elements in knowledge, and it discussed the "real use" of the intellect in metaphysics whereby truths are discovered, contrasting it with the "logical use" in merely drawing inferences from given judgments. It contained a clear, though later surrendered, claim on the proper method and realm of metaphysics as knowledge of an intelligible world, with nothing borrowed from sensible knowledge of phenomena. Metaphysics, as pure knowledge dealing with concepts not derived from experience but "given by the pure intellect itself," was held to be possible and valid only when pursued according to a rule for preventing the principles of sensibility from "passing their boundaries and meddling with the intellectual."[10] Such a rule, of course, depended upon a clear and systematic discernment of the roots of our concepts—a discernment that he believed he had achieved and which he never seriously revised, even when he later concluded that metaphysics, as envisioned in this work, was impossible.

Metaphysics of morals thereafter took on a very different look. Whereas "metaphysics" had previously meant hardly more than the most general conceptual knowledge issuing from an analysis of experience, it now came to mean systematic philosophy containing nothing empirical but referring to a world beyond experience.[11] Metaphysics is knowledge of things as they are, and concepts of the appearances of things, i.e., space and time, do not belong within it. A metaphysics of morals, therefore, could not be a continuation of the empirical-anthropological investigations of Shaftesbury; thenceforth Kant invariably made clear the independence of metaphysics of morals from all anthropology, even from "pragmatic anthropology," which deals with how men should conduct themselves in the ordinary affairs of life. Rather, metaphysics of morals had to have its basis in a Platonism of a nonphenomenal world. "Moral philosophy, so far as it supplies the first principles of moral judgment, is known only through the pure under-

---

10 *Inaugural Dissertation,* § 24 (Handyside, 73).
11 Cf. *Critique of Pure Reason,* A 843 = B 871.

standing, and itself belongs to pure philosophy," i.e., metaphysics.[12] It contains no empirical concepts of human nature.

That he was satisfied with this new path to metaphysics and with its goal, at least for a while, is shown by a letter of the same year to Lambert, in which he says he planned "this winter to complete my investigations concerning pure moral philosophy and . . . the metaphysics of morals,"[13] in which there would be no empirical principles. Contrary to this fond hope, however, the *Inaugural Dissertation* marked the beginning of the "silent decade" in which he published almost nothing but during which the herculean labor of writing the *Critique of Pure Reason* was performed, while the "Metaphysics of Morals," still repeatedly promised, was delayed again and again.

Less than a year later he wrote Marcus Herz that he was at work on a book to be titled "The Boundaries of Sensibility and Reason"—the book the world now knows as the *Critique of Pure Reason*. The book as then planned was to contain not only a theory of appearances ("Phenomenology") but also the essentials of a theory of morals, taste, and metaphysics.[14] On February 21, 1772, he described, again to Herz, his plan for this book. It was to contain a section on metaphysics, one part of which was to give "the ultimate grounds of morality," and it was to be published within three months.[15] In 1773, in still another letter to Herz, he announced his plan to complete "my transcendental philosophy, which is really a critical examination of pure reason,"[16] and then "to get to metaphysics, which has only two parts, the metaphysics of nature and the metaphysics of morals, the latter of which I shall finish first, and towards which I am looking forward with pleasure."[17]

The letter of 1772 shows Kant's dissatisfaction with the method of the *Dissertation* in establishing the possibility of a priori knowledge of a

---

[12] *Inaugural Dissertation*, § 9 (Handyside, 49). Moral concepts, though confused, are not sensible or empirical but are known by the pure intellect itself. Earlier rationalistic philosophers had thought of "sensible" and "confused" as corollaries in descriptions of modes of cognition, and the obscurity of ethical principles had therefore led them to combine, in a most astonishing manner, empiricism in ethics with rationalism in their philosophy as a whole. Kant shows in the *Dissertation* that this confusion no longer troubles him, that he has now outgrown it, if he ever had fallen into it.

[13] To Lambert, September 2, 1770 (X, 97).

[14] To Herz, June 7, 1771 (X, 123).

[15] To Herz, February 21, 1772 (X, 132).

[16] Literally, "Critique of Pure Reason," though probably these words were not meant then as a title of the book.

[17] To Herz, end of 1773 (X, 144).

purely intelligible world; but there was not yet any sign of his having to give up the hope and expectation of being able to establish speculative metaphysics on a solid ground. After the letter of 1772, however, Kant's "recollection of Hume" awakened him from his "dogmatic slumber," and he gave up forever the dream of a speculative metaphysics of the intelligible world. Still, the transcendental philosophy or critical examination of pure reason, as elaborated in the *Critique of Pure Reason*, did provide the prerequisites, in Kant's opinion, for a "Metaphysics of Morals" in two senses: a systematic presentation of the a priori laws of morality, and a practical rather than a speculative answer to traditional metaphysical questions.

So in the *Critique of Pure Reason*, as it was at last published in 1781, Kant still spoke of the metaphysics of morals. He distinguished two parts of philosophy: critique, or propaedeutic philosophy, which "investigates the faculty of reason in all its pure a priori knowledge," and metaphysics, or the "system of pure reason" which "exhibits in systematic connection the whole body . . . of philosophical knowledge arising out of pure reason." "Metaphysics," he continued, "is divided into that of the speculative and that of the practical employment of pure reason, and is therefore either metaphysics of nature or metaphysics of morals."[18] The entire faculty of reason, including the practical, was subjected to critique; that is, the *Critique of Pure Reason* was meant to be propaedeutic to metaphysics in both its divisions.[19]

In spite of mentioning the metaphysics of morals as a division of pure philosophy, in the first edition of the *Critique of Pure Reason* Kant did not promise to write such a work; he projected only a "Metaphysics of Nature."[20] Transcendental philosophy, which is the system of all principles of reason so far as it concerns knowledge of objects, contains only pure a priori concepts and principles, and thus it excludes ethics. For though the highest principles of ethics were said even then to be a priori and intellectual, "in the construction of a system of pure morality empirical concepts must necessarily be brought into the concept of duty."[21]

[18] *Critique of Pure Reason*, A 841 = B 869.

[19] *Ibid.*, A xii, note.

[20] *Ibid.*, A xxi.

[21] *Ibid.*, B 29. The *Critique of Pure Reason* excludes moral philosophy from transcendental philosophy, not because the former is not pure, but because the latter is concerned solely with the cognitive (cf. A 801 = B 829). Kant tacitly widened the concept of transcendental philosophy (as he narrowed that of metaphysics) until it is hardly distinguishable from critique itself; and though he never explicitly included moral philosophy in transcendental philosophy, we shall see the

Instead of a "metaphysics of morals," therefore, we have in the *Critique of Pure Reason* a "Canon of Pure Reason," i.e., a statement of the a priori principles of the correct employment of pure reason. This employment is entirely and exclusively practical, not speculative. The Canon does not answer the practical problem as such, viz., "What ought I to do?" but the problem he calls both theoretical and practical, to wit, "What may I hope if I do my duty?" Thus was introduced the discussion of the immortality of the soul and the existence of God, which are Ideas of pure theoretical reason, dialectical and empty for theoretical cognition. It is only in relation to man's will that these Ideas have any necessary use, as guides or regulative principles for the pursuit of happiness through becoming worthy of it.[22]

Again, Kant did not long remain satisfied with a mere Canon of Pure Reason. He soon returned to the long-deferred plan, not mentioned in the *Critique* itself, to write a systematic work on ethics, presumably to include a metaphysics of morals, for he referred in 1783 to being at

---

full apparatus of transcendental philosophy in discussions included in the *Critique of Practical Reason*.

The tacit inclusion is due not merely to a widening of the scope of transcendental philosophy, however; it is also to be attributed to a deepening of the level of moral analysis itself. Thus the passage just quoted says that in a system of moral philosophy empirical concepts will have to be brought into the *concept of duty*, whereas in A 15, the corresponding passage in the first edition, he had said, with less caution, that "the concepts of pleasure and pain, and of desires and inclinations, etc. will have to be presupposed." In both editions he distinguished between the doctrine of virtue, or applied ethics, and pure ethics, the former of which alone is in part dependent on empirical or psychological principles (A 54-55 = B 79). The *Critique of Practical Reason* and the *Foundations of the Metaphysics of Morals* are meant, of course, to be pure ethics in the sense of this passage, even though in the *Critique* he makes use of definitions of psychological concepts needed in the concept of duty and in depicting the relation of man to the moral law, which requires no psychological concepts for its formulation. But in actual composition of the second *Critique* and even of the *Metaphysics of Morals,* as we shall see (below, p. 53), Kant made no very consistent effort to separate discussion of pure from applied ethics, or metaphysics from critique, or either from system.

We shall see that the ascribing of something very like, if not identical with, transcendental status to practical principles was one of the factors leading to the decision to publish the second *Critique* on the same level with the first and not subordinate to it, as a metaphysics of morals would have been subordinate to it. Later Kant came to regard the first *Critique* as not a sufficient propaedeutic to all metaphysics, and he indicates this implicitly in constantly referring to the first *Critique* not by its correct title but by such expressions as "the critique of speculative reason," as in the first paragraph of the second *Critique* (3[87]).

[22] *Critique of Pure Reason*, A 806 = B 834. It is not quite accurate to say that this is their *only* use; for they are also regulative of inquiry, but they contribute nothing substantively to knowledge.

work on "the first part of my ethics."[23] We do not know whether he was referring to the *Foundations of the Metaphysics of Morals* or not. But when the *Foundations* was published in April, 1785, he again mentioned his plan, now twenty years old, for a "Metaphysics of Morals" to which the *Foundations* was only preliminary.[24]

The *Foundations* differs sufficiently from the Canon of Pure Reason to make it easy to explain Kant's decision to write the *Foundations* as still another propaedeutic to the ever receding "Metaphysics of Morals." The Canon presented a view of moral problems without the concept of autonomy and independent of the solution of the problem of freedom that had already been worked out in the first *Critique*—the two foundation stones on which all his later work in practical philosophy was to be based.

Fragment 6 of the *Lose Blätter*,[25] which I think must have been written between 1781 and 1784, shows the transition to the new position in asking of practical judgments the question that the *Critique of Pure Reason* raised with respect to theoretical judgments: How are synthetic judgments a priori possible? For he realized at this time that morality requires synthetic a priori judgments, that these judgments cannot be justified in exactly the same way that their theoretical counterparts had been justified, and that to justify them requires a more positive concept of freedom than that used in the Canon. Justification of synthetic a priori judgments everywhere in Kant requires what he invariably calls a "Deduction," not a canon of use. And the proper place for a deduction is a critique.

But, instead of a critique, in 1785 Kant presented the *Foundations of the Metaphysics of Morals*. And yet:

There is, to be sure, no other foundation for such a metaphysics of morals than a *Kritik* of pure practical reason, just as there is no other foundation for a metaphysics than the already published *Kritik* of pure speculative reason. But, in the first place, a *Kritik* of pure practical reason is not of such extreme importance as that of speculative reason, because the human reason, even in the commonest mind, can easily be brought to a high degree of correctness and completeness in moral matters, while, on the other hand, in its theoretical but pure use it is entirely dialectical. In the second place, I require of a *Kritik* of pure practical reason, if it is to be complete, that the unity of the practical reason and the speculative be subject to presentation under a common principle, because in the final analysis there can be but one and the same reason, which must be differentiated only in applica-

---

[23] To Mendelssohn, August 16, 1783 (X, 346–47).

[24] *Foundations of the Metaphysics of Morals*, 391 (6).

[25] *Reflexion* 7202.

tion. But I could not bring this to such completeness without bringing in observations of an altogether different kind and without thereby confusing the reader. For these reasons I have employed the title, *Foundations of the Metaphysics of Morals*, instead of *Critique of Pure Practical Reason*.[26]

Notwithstanding this, the third section of the *Foundations* is entitled "Final Step from the Metaphysics of Morals to the Critical Examination [*Kritik*] of Pure Practical Reason." Presumably all that he regarded as essential in a critical examination of pure practical reason was given here, for in a letter to Schütz written five months later he said that he would immediately begin writing his "Metaphysics of Morals."[27]

Yet it appears a bit odd that a metaphysics of morals has been developed in Section II of the *Foundations* and that a transition is made from it to a "Critical Examination of Pure Practical Reason." The explanation of it is this. In the first and second sections of the *Foundations*, Kant's method had been analytical, i.e., he began with the "moral facts" and analyzed them to find what must be true if they were not illusory. The moral imperative and the esteem for the good will are chimerical unless the thought of duty can be a motive to action; and it can be so only if the will is free. But is the will free? This is a question which can be answered only by a synthetical method, i.e., a deduction of its possibility. Only this can justify any categorical statements about morality; without it, all our statements must be hypothetical and problematic. Hence the *Foundations* is, as a whole, propaedeutic to a "Metaphysics of Morals," even though the internal structure which a metaphysics of morals must have is achieved long before the end of the book; the last section is aimed at justifying the assertion of what was only entertained in the first two sections.

Some scholars[28] have offered the hypothesis that at this time Kant planned next to write his "Metaphysics of Morals" and *then* a "Critique of Pure Practical Reason," which would complete his system by proving what neither the *Foundations* had shown nor what a yet-to-be-written "Metaphysics of Morals" would show, to wit, the unity of theoretical and practical reason. But the evidence for this hypothesis seems to me to be utterly unconvincing. It seems much more likely that the *Foundations* constituted, in Kant's mind, precisely what its title indicates and that no other "Critique" was planned. Even as late as April, 1787, when the *Critique of Pure Reason* had been revised, Kant spoke

---

[26] *Foundations of the Metaphysics of Morals*, 391 (6–7).

[27] To Schütz, September 13, 1785 (X, 406).

[28] E.g., Paul Natorp, in the Akademie edition notes to the *Critique of Practical Reason* (V, 496), and A. R. C. Duncan, *Practical Reason and Morality*, pp. 23, 35, 132.

of saving time for his "proposed scheme of providing a metaphysics of nature and a metaphysics of morals"[29] and makes no mention of the work that was actually to occupy him that summer—the writing of the *Critique of Practical Reason.*

§ 3. THE DECISION TO WRITE THE "CRITIQUE OF PRACTICAL REASON"

In 1786 a preliminary work on the metaphysics of nature (*Metaphysische Anfangsgründe der Naturwissenschaft*) was published, and Kant turned to the heavy labor of preparing the second edition of the *Critique of Pure Reason.* It was begun by April, 1786, and completed by April, 1787. With his usual optimism in such matters, he had estimated that the revision would take six months. He told Bering that his "System of Metaphysics" would be delayed by two years, because he was also planning a "System of Practical Philosophy" to be published before the book on metaphysics proper.[30]

What was this "System of Practical Philosophy"? We do not know, but we may presume that it was the "Metaphysics of Morals," so often promised, so long postponed. Certainly it was not the *Critique of Practical Reason;* Kant almost always distinguished between the words "critique" and "system" and "metaphysics," even though their scopes in fact overlap to a large extent. So, as late as April, 1786, we know that the *Critique of Practical Reason* was not planned as such.

We first hear of a "Critique of Pure Practical Reason" as a specific literary project on November 8, 1786. Born, in a reply to a letter from Kant not now extant, spoke of the new work as an addition to the *Critique of Pure Reason.*[31] The *Allgemeine Literaturzeitung* (Jena) on November 21, in an announcement of the future publication of the second edition, said: "To the Critique of pure speculative reason contained in the first edition, in the second there will be appended a critique of pure practical reason."[32]

---

[29] *Critique of Pure Reason,* B xliii. In the Preface to A, only a "metaphysics of nature" was promised.

[30] To Bering, April 7, 1786 (X, 441). Bering, in his reply of May 10 (X, 445) regretted the delay and expressed the wish that he could talk with Kant. "Perhaps soon," he wrote, "our aeronauts will make their trips less expensive and dangerous, and then a trip of 140 miles [*sic*—from Marburg to Königsberg] will be a trivial thing."

[31] Born to Kant, November 8, 1786 (X, 471).

[32] The notice is reprinted in Ak. III, 556. That this information came from Kant himself, or at least that it did not originate with the editor (Schütz), is made clear in Schütz's letter to Kant of November 3, 1786 (X, 469). Kant had written to Born and Schütz on the same day (May 26) and may have mentioned his plan to them at that time, for Born clearly had the information before it was published by Schütz. Unfortunately, the letters of May 26 are not extant.

During 1786 and 1787, therefore, Kant must have entertained at various times the following plans: (*a*) to write a "Metaphysics of Morals" based on the *Critique of Pure Reason* and the *Foundations;* (*b*) to write a "System of Practical Philosophy" as soon as he had completed the revision of the *Critique of Pure Reason;* (*c*) to append a "Critique of Pure Practical Reason" to the new edition of the *Critique of Pure Reason;* (*d*) to write the *Critique of Practical Reason,* as we know it today. The first two projects were no doubt substantially identical.[33] What interests us is the shift from *a* and *b,* considered together, to *c,* and the final decision to go forward with *d.* As we shall see, Kant did not go directly from *c* to *d.*

The step from *b* to *c* represents the magnitude of development in Kant's views from the Canon of Pure Reason to the *Foundations.* The *Critique of Pure Reason,* when it was written, was regarded as a propaedeutic to both divisions of metaphysics; but by 1785 the proper basis of a metaphysics of morals was located in the concept of autonomy, a concept not so much as mentioned in the first *Critique.* But plan *c* was dropped, not at first in favor of *d* but because of a return to *a* or *b,* as shown in the Preface to the second edition of the *Critique of Pure Reason.*

Some of the reasons for dropping it must have been external. The success of the *Foundations* had created a demand for a new edition of the first *Critique,* and there was considerable urgency in meeting it. By November, 1786, the "six months" that Kant had estimated for the revision had already elapsed, and the work was still six months from completion; and, even so, all the revisions were in parts which have little or no direct bearing on questions of practical philosophy. He left untouched the rest of the Dialectic (with the exception of the Paralogisms) with the surprising explanation that he had not found any serious misundersanding of the other parts[34]—misunderstandings which he found in plenty when he came, in 1787, to deal with the critics who had charged that the *Critique* and the *Foundations* were incompatible. The differences between the teachings of the Canon and of the *Foun-*

[33] The two divisions of work, when it was no longer a question of two different literary projects, were later distinguished from each other in the statement that a "system of practical philosophy" would contain anthropological data and would presuppose a metaphysics of morals, which would take nothing from anthropology (*Metaphysik der Sitten,* Einleitung, § ii [VI, 216-17]). In actual execution, however, the *Metaphysik der Sitten* is more like the projected "system." The manifold changes in Kant's conception of what "metaphysics of morals" should contain are traced by Georg Anderson, "Kant's Metaphysik der Sitten—ihre Idee und ihr Verhältnis zur Ethik der Wolffschen Schule," *Kant-Studien,* XXVIII (1923), 41-61.

[34] *Critique of Pure Reason,* B xli.

dations were too great to add an architectonic paraphrase of the latter to the former; there would have had to be extensive rewriting as well, and the architectonic structure of the Methodology of the first *Critique* would have been completely destroyed. His solution of this problem was to provide a new and extensive Preface to the second edition, which showed his thinking on the ethical problem, while leaving the Canon unchanged.

Furthermore, the original *Critique* was too long to add another major work to it, even if it could have been fitted into its shape; the revisions he did make added another thirty to its original 850 pages. Again, the winter of 1786–87 was a time when Kant was rector of the University, and on this occasion, at least, this was not simply a sinecure or position of honor. There were the ceremonies attendant upon the death of Frederick the Great in August, 1786, and the accession of Friedrich Wilhelm II later in the year, in all of which Kant had a major role to play.[35] All these facts help explain Kant's desire to restrict the revisions of the *Critique of Pure Reason* to the absolutely essential, and we know his impatience to get on with plan *a* or *b*, now deferred nearly twenty years.

We may then suppose that the plan to write a separate *Critique of Practical Reason* as a separate work was formed later than April, 1787, the date of the Preface to the second edition of the first *Critique*, replacing the plan mentioned there for going ahead with a "Metaphysics of Morals." What reasons led to this final, fateful, decision?

I shall suggest several. The first was Kant's acknowledgment, even in 1785, that a complete critical examination of practical reason was not given in the *Foundations*. Two fundamental topics were not dealt with in that work, and at least one of them was a topic both intrinsically important and fascinating to Kant's turn of mind: the proof of the ultimate unity of theoretical and practical reason. The second was the connection between the moral law, applicable to rational beings in general, and man, a connection not to be based upon anthropology but on an a priori connection that Kant discerned between will and feeling. This transition to specifically human reason was adumbrated in the *Foundations*, but it was essential to plans *a* and *b* that it be fully elaborated. Thus arose the necessity for what we now have as chapter iii of the Analytic of the second *Critique*.

Another must have been the desire, natural to Kant and welcome to his audience, to develop more systematically his concept of "the key-

[35] It should perhaps be remembered also that Joseph Green died in 1786, and Kant's earliest biographers, e.g., Jachmann, tell us how much this event affected the philosopher and the daily course of his life.

stone of the whole architecture of pure and even speculative reason" (3 [88]), i.e., the concept of freedom. This concept had been established only as a possibility, i.e., as not self-contradictory, in the first *Critique;* discussion of it in its full depth was ruled out as being unnecessary in practical philosophy as such; and it had been explored, but not systematically, in the third section of the *Foundations;* but it needed full encyclopedic and critical treatment.

Fourth, there was the objection that in the *Foundations* Kant had gone against the injunctions made against speculative knowledge in the first *Critique.* This was a charge made by a man he respected (Pistorius), which, if valid, threatened the entire critical philosophy, in both its theoretical and its practical parts. It was a charge that had to be met at all costs.[36] The method of postulates, used in the Canon, easily led to such criticisms; but the development of an antinomy and its successful resolution was always Kant's way of exposing illicit pretensions, and he could not renounce the opportunity to develop an antinomy in the concept of the highest good as a way of showing that he was not, in fact, advancing speculative claims.

Very closely related to all these reasons was Kant's desire to answer the critics who had raised still other objections, before building on foundations that had been widely challenged.

Finally, I think Kant saw an opportunity to strengthen the conviction that he had sought to establish in the first *Critique* by writing another book, from another point of view, which would lead to some of the same conclusions by a different route. The second *Critique* is not a continuation of the first, though the Preface to it may make the reader forget that it is not. The second *Critique* made an entirely fresh beginning in another realm of experience; and Kant warned repeatedly against self-consciously trying to avoid discussions already completed in the first and against keeping the first so much in mind that the natural path of the second would be affected by extraneous considerations (7, 106 [92, 201]). The first point of fruitful contact between the two books was reached only in the Deduction. At that place it was essential to Kant's argument that the *independence* of the two works be granted; the argument required that there be a common focus from two quite different angles, and, at the end of the Analytic, Kant insisted, perhaps more than was justified, upon this independence of the two works—as if the common focus were a gratifying surprise to him because "their agreement was by no means sought after" (106 [201]). Such a "confirmation," however specious it may seem to a reader who

---

[36] *Critique of Practical Reason,* 6–7 (91–92): "Only a detailed *Critique of Practical Reason* can set aside all these misconceptions."

is not convinced that there can be such single-mindedness in any man's work on a single part of a larger whole,[37] was one that could not even have been proposed in a work that was either a part of the *Critique of Pure Reason* (plan *c*) or in a metaphysics of morals based on the first *Critique* (plans *a* and *b*).

These and perhaps still other reasons determined Kant, after April, 1787 (the date of the Preface to the second edition of the *Critique of Pure Reason*), to undertake the new and unannounced book. On June 25 of that year he wrote Schütz that the *Critique of Practical Reason* was nearing completion and would be sent to the publisher within a week. We do not know when it was actually finished, though in September he wrote that it was in the hands of the publisher.[38] There was a delay in getting a font of new and sharper type for it, but it was delivered to Kant in December, with the publication date given as 1788. Even this book, however, he called only preliminary to a "Metaphysics of Morals" (161 [260]).

Taking all the evidence in hand, the book cannot have taken more than fifteen months to write; and this maximal estimate is based on the supposition that he actually worked on plans *a, b,* and *c* and that he worked on them at the very same time that he was making the very heavy revisions, in quite other topics, of the first *Critique*. The second supposition conflicts with all we know of Kant's working habits; and if the first is correct, there is no evidence of it in any "stratification" or "patchwork" structure of the completed book. Moreover, this maximal estimate leaves quite unexplained Kant's silence on plans for such a book in April, 1787. Apart from the initial incredibility of supposing that a man could do such a feat, it is in best accord with all our definite evidence to conclude that the book was begun not earlier than April, 1787, and finished before September. The initial incredibility weighs little, however, when we remember that the *Critique of Pure Reason* was "brought to completion" in an equally short interval.

Such was the long series of deferred plans, evolving through more than thirty years from the *Prize Essay* to the final *Metaphysics of Mor-*

---

[37] And it will appear especially unconvincing to one who remembers that Kant said that it was practical concerns that led to the distinction between phenomena and noumena, and his remark that the foundation of the critical philosophy lay in the concept of freedom, in considering the imputability of actions (cf. *Lose Blätter zur Preisschrift über die Fortschritte der Metaphysik*, XX, 335; Reflexion 6339). In the *Fortschritte der Metaphysik* itself (XX, 311), however, he does modify this and state that there are "two angles" around which metaphysics or critique (it is not possible to tell which is the antecedent of *sie*) turns: the theory of the ideality of space and time and the reality of the concept of freedom.

[38] To Schütz, June 25, 1787 (X, 490); to Jakob, September 11, 1787 (X, 494).

als, and having almost as by-products the *Critique of Pure Reason,*[39] the *Foundations of the Metaphysics of Morals,* and the *Critique of Practical Reason.* Even if the *Metaphysics of Morals* were not an intrinsically important and interesting work, it is one for which we should have a feeling of gratitude. As a goal, it inspired Kant to labors which produced other and greater masterpieces. Had the promise to Herder been kept earlier, the loss to moral philosophy would have been very great indeed.

[39] Cf. *Lose Blätter zur Preisschrift über die Fortschritte der Metaphysik,* XX, 335. That this was indeed the lay of things is the thesis of Richard Kroner's *Kant's Weltanschauung* (Chicago: University of Chicago Press, 1956).

II

The Limits of Theoretical Reason

More than half the Preface of the *Critique of Practical Reason* is concerned with issues that had been raised and, in Kant's view, settled in the *Critique of Pure Reason* or deals with objections that had been made by readers who detected what they regarded as inconsistencies between the first *Critique* and the *Foundations of the Metaphysics of Morals*. Since the *Critique of Practical Reason* was to repeat and elaborate some of the doctrines of the *Foundations*, Kant regarded it as essential to his purposes to show that his doctrines here and in the *Foundations* were consistent with those of the first *Critique* and, indeed, that they gave additional support to his findings there. While the full proof of consistency and mutual support could be given only in the body of the *Critique*, there are many assertions in the Preface that can hardly be appreciated unless the main conclusions of the earlier *Critique* are kept in mind. In writing this book, Kant certainly assumed familiarity with the former work. Yet he explains the fact that "concepts and principles of the pure speculative reason are now and again reexamined in this work"; only in this way, he says, can the "old and new," i.e., the theoretical and the practical, uses of the "concepts of reason" be compared and connected, so that the "new path" of the *Critique of Practical Reason* can be "clearly distinguished from the previous one."[1]

In this chapter I shall attempt to give a summary statement of the argument and conclusions of the first *Critique*, sufficient only to make the Preface easily comprehensible. From time to time in later parts of this commentary it will be necessary to study specific parts of the earlier work in order to provide the proper background for understanding specific parts of this one. The reader who is generally familiar with the *Critique of Pure Reason* will not need to go through this entire chapter but is advised to go directly to § 6, which is more directly concerned with the text of the Preface.

---

[1] *Critique of Practical Reason*, 7 (92); cf. Reflexionen 5019, 5036.

The *Critique of Pure Reason* is a sustained effort to determine sys-tematically the answer to the question "What can I know?" The an-swer is "I can know the truths of mathematics and of the sciences of nature, but I cannot know the objects of traditional speculative meta-physics."

This answer is reached by examining the presuppositions of knowl-edge. In this examination, it is found that the ground which makes it possible for us to have knowledge in mathematics and science does not extend to the alleged knowledge of metaphysical objects. This ground is the givenness of the objects of knowledge to our sensibility, or to what Kant calls "intuition."

All our knowledge and alleged knowledge is expressed in one of three kinds of judgments.

i) A judgment may be analytic, such as "Every red object is col-ored" or "Every body is extended in space." Such a judgment is called "analytic" because its predicate is found by analysis of the concept of the subject. Such judgments are certain, and they are important in or-ganizing and articulating our knowledge. But an analytic judgment does not extend our knowledge; such a judgment does not tell us more than we already know, at least implicitly, in entertaining the concept of the subject. Moreover, it does not tell us anything whatsoever about the existence of the subject it mentions. "A triangle has three angles" is absolutely true and would be just as true if no triangle had ever ex-isted in the world; "God is a perfect being" is such a judgment, and we do not need to know whether God exists in order to know that the concept of God contains the concept of perfection as one of its predi-cates.

ii) A judgment is synthetic if the predicate is not logically included in the concept of the subject. Thus "This girl is young" and "All men are less than two hundred years old" are synthetic judgments. Whether they are true or false must be found out by experience; they are based upon experience and refer to experience if they are true. Even if true, however, such a judgment is not *necessarily* true; it is quite conceivable that the girl is not as young as she looks and that human life might extend beyond two centuries. Such synthetic judgments, whose truth can be judged only in the light of experienced facts, are called "a pos-teriori," in distinction to the analytic judgments, which are a priori.

iii) Kant believed, however, that there are some synthetic judgments which are necessarily true and therefore can be based neither upon ob-servation and induction from experience nor upon a merely logical analysis of the concepts they contain. These are synthetic a priori judgments. He held that mathematical judgments, such as the theorems of mathematics, and the principles of a "pure science of nature," like "Every event has a cause," are a priori synthetic. Hume, as Kant tells us (13, 52 [99, 142]), regarded mathematical judgments as analytic because he recognized that they were a priori, and he believed that scientific principles like that of causation were a posteriori because they were not analytic. The consequence of regarding the causal principle as merely a product of custom or habit, built upon induction and therefore a posteriori, is skepticism in science as well as in metaphysics; and Hume, Kant says, was saved from universal skepticism only by retaining the apriority of mathematical knowledge, which he saved from skepticism only because he mistakenly believed that it was analytic.

It is easy enough to explain the possibility of judgments of the first two kinds. Previous philosophers had not even noticed that the third kind of judgment existed; for Kant, however, they are essential even for synthetic a posteriori judgments, since any judgment based on experience, such as "The sun warms the stone," presupposes an a priori synthetic judgment of the connection of one event to another as cause to effect. The problem of the *Critique of Pure Reason* is, therefore, How are synthetic a priori judgments possible?

§ 3. THE "COPERNICAN REVOLUTION"

The answer to the question is vividly described in what has been called Kant's "Copernican Revolution" in philosophy. In a justly famous passage in the Preface to the second edition of the *Critique of Pure Reason*, Kant compares his new theory of knowledge to the Copernican system in astronomy. The predecessors of Copernicus had had difficulty in explaining the apparent motions of the planets on the assumption that they all revolved around the earth. Before Kant, it was similarly impossible in philosophy to explain how there could be a priori knowledge of things on the assumption that knowledge is a passive conformity to an object. "Failing of satisfactory progress in explaining the movements of the heavenly bodies on the assumption that they all revolved around the spectator," Kant says, Copernicus "tried whether he might not have better success if he made the spectator to revolve and the stars to remain at rest."[2] By analogy, Kant did the same thing. If the phenomenal characteristics of objects, the way they appear to us, are explained in terms of the conditions of our knowing them, it is possible to see how knowledge of these characteristics can be a priori, because they are dependent in part at least upon the functions of the spectator. Then it becomes necessary, of course, to make a clear dis-

[2] *Critique of Pure Reason*, B xvi.

tinction between the phenomenal and the real characteristics of objects, just as Copernicus, in rejecting the Ptolemaic epicycles, had to make a clear distinction between the real and the apparent planetary motions. Let the things in themselves be as they may, the objects of knowledge, which are their appearances to us, must conform to the structure and synthetic activity of the knowing mind.

The faculties of the knowing mind which make knowledge of phenomena possible are sensibility, or receptivity to data, which presents the sensations for our conceptions and through which our conceptions are related to actual objects, and understanding, which connects the conceptions into synthetic judgments about objects. The a priori forms of the data, to which they must all conform, are space and time. Therefore, all objects that we can know must be spatiotemporal. The a priori rules for the synthesis of concepts into judgments about objects are twelve categories of the understanding, which are derived from the forms of judgments in formal logic.

Both the forms of intuition and the categories may be called "subjective" in the sense that they are forms of our experience, not of metaphysical realities or things in themselves. But they are "objective" in the sense that they are not personal, psychological features of this or that mind, but are rules for the conduct of experience from the reception of data to the establishment of knowledge of public objects in one space and time, the same for all observers. They are thus the foundation for the kind of objectivity that characterizes knowledge and distinguishes it from mere fancy and error, to wit, objectivity as universality and necessity, producing a standard for all knowing minds and underlying agreement among various observers about their common objects.

Both sensibility or intuition and understanding or concepts are necessary to knowledge. Intuitions without concepts are blind, a blooming, buzzing confusion. Concepts without intuitions are empty, an unearthly ballet of bloodless categories.

From this it follows that we can have knowledge only of a phenomenal world, for we have no intuition of things as they are. Since intuition is necessary to knowledge and touches only on things in space and time, what is metaphysical, in the literal sense of the word as that which lies beyond physics, is not attainable by human knowledge.

Thus we can say that that which makes objective knowledge of nature possible, namely, the a priori forms of intuition, is lacking in alleged metaphysical knowledge, and this lack makes metaphysics impossible. Hume rejected metaphysics, rightly, but on the wrong grounds, for his grounds of rejecting metaphysics forced him also to reject necessary judgments in science too. Kant, through the doctrine of the a priori form of intuition, saved science from Humean skepticism and, by the same device, destroyed traditional metaphysics.

The knowledge we have of nature is real knowledge, not a subjective substitute for it, even though the objects of our knowledge are not things in themselves. The phenomena we know through intuition and the conceptions we have of their connection through the synthesis guided by the categories are not just thoughts in our minds; they are a system of phenomena under law, identical with what is meant by "nature." This systematic organization of experience is what the scientist is talking about when he talks about nature. It is not something in my head, different from what is in your head; it is sticks and stones, sealing wax, cabbages and kings, stars and atoms, and nebulae not to be seen until we have a larger telescope. The "metaphysics of nature," of which Kant often spoke, is the systematic development and exposition of all the a priori principles involved in our knowledge of nature, independent of what specific discoveries are made about what is in nature.

§ 4. THEORETICAL AND SPECULATIVE REASON

Besides sensibility and understanding, knowledge also requires reason. Reason is the faculty of systematic thought, of providing a wherefore for every therefore. In reasoning, we press on from partial knowledge toward complete knowledge. Nature comprises series of phenomena in space and time, and these series can and must be infinitely extendable, for every phenomenon has other phenomena before it and after it and beside it, all of which determine its spatiotemporal position and empirical character. Every cause is likewise effect, and every law seems to be a special case of a more general law. It is this aspect of our experience that it is the office of reason to explore.

Theoretical reason, as we see it at work in science, attempts to organize our knowledge into a logically rigorous system which will give parsimonious explanations for phenomena. The most successful scientific theory is one which explains the most facts with the fewest assumptions. But in our sciences of nature there are always assumptions; the fundamental propositions are fundamental only because we do not yet know how to explain them. No final answers can be found in nature to the questions we ask of her; science only defers the time when we have to say, "This is the way things are; they might have been otherwise, and I cannot say why they are not."

If we are to satisfy our demand for final answers, philosophers have always thought that we must go outside or beyond our knowledge of nature. The attempt to do so is the work of the speculative metaphysician. To complete the work of theory, theoretical reason must become speculative reason and must leave physics in order to try to get answers from metaphysics. Metaphysics is the product of speculative reason, and it consists of alleged knowledge of things as they are which will explain why things appear as they do.

Speculative reason, in going beyond phenomena, must cut off the line tethering knowledge to the world of experience; but, since it is a way of thinking, it still must use the categories of thought. The result is the emptiness of thought without perceptual contact with things. It is not knowledge, for a category can be applied in a definite way to an object only through a sensuous representation. The categories, therefore, while permitting us to think of supersensible objects, do not permit us to know them.

Our thinking of them is not, however, idle fantasy. The categories themselves and the demand for systematic unity determine what concepts of objects must be used in order to complete, or to attempt to complete, the search for ultimate principles which will explain everything. We are not just permitted to think of the soul, God, and the world as a whole as being explanatory of things in our experience; we are compelled to do so if we follow out into the supersensible realm the principles which function within experience. The categories, freed of their anchorage in experience, become Ideas of reason. Ideas are concepts to which no object in the senses can ever be adequate; but they are not useless. They regulate the orderly pursuit of the whole. But if it is erroneously thought that the Ideas refer to objects as they really are, as the categories refer to objects of the senses, there arise various kinds of illusions which it is the business of critique to expose.

The *Critique of Pure Reason* is, therefore, a negative critique and rejection of the pretensions of traditional metaphysics, in which, it had been believed, we had knowledge of objects beyond the scope of science. Speculative metaphysics is not a legitimate part of knowledge; the only metaphysics which is possible is "immanent metaphysics," i.e., the systematic exposition of the a priori principles within experience and of the regulative Ideas.

§ 5. THE THIRD ANTINOMY[3]

Kant was not content to "prove" that knowledge of the supersensible world is impossible by showing that it lacked one of the conditions, viz., sensibility, that he held to be necessary for there to be knowledge. Such an argument would be a *petitio principii* which would convince

---

[3] This is fully discussed in chap. xi.

no rationalist, who held that sensibility is only the lowest form of knowledge and not a necessary condition of all knowledge. Kant tried to show directly that such knowledge was in fact impossible, by exposing errors involved in all arguments designed to prove the existence of God or the existence and immortality of the soul. More dramatically, he attempted to uncover an "antinomy" in speculative reason by showing that for every synthetic a priori judgment it produced, an equally good and necessary argument could prove its contradictory. For reasons we are about to see, Kant called the antinomy "the most fortunate perplexity" into which pure reason could ever fall (107 [203]).

An antinomy is a pair of contradictory statements, each of which is validly proved and each of which expresses an inescapable interest of reason. There are four in the first *Critique*. We shall here be concerned only with the third, that between freedom and natural causation.

The antinomies strictly limit theoretical reason to the world of space and time, nullifying all speculative flights from the results of science and all attempts to use scientific hypotheses in speculations beyond the limits of sense. But their resolution permits an altogether different use of reason; their occurrence and resolution indicate reason's broader competence as a faculty not exclusively devoted to cognition.[4]

This is very clear in the third antinomy. This arises from the conflict in the idea of causality—if every single thing must have a cause, then all causality is in time under the law of nature; but if all things have a cause, there must be a cause which is not an event in time under the law of nature. Each of these is essential if we are to give absolute validity to the causal principle; yet both of them, it seems, cannot be true.

The resolution is this: The thesis, which asserts the reality of causes not subsumed under the law of nature, and the antithesis, which asserts that all causation is under the laws of nature now known or yet to be discovered, may each be true if their respective scopes are distinguished.[5]

The field of application of each is defined by the nature of the argument supporting it, and neither can be validly employed beyond the area to which the respective proofs extend. The proof of the thesis pre-

---

[4] Actually, Kant had discovered the antinomy before he had fixed the final lines of his theory of knowledge, and it was probably the discovery of the later antinomies which led him to retreat from the position taken in the *Inaugural Dissertation* that metaphysical knowledge was possible. He told Garve that the discovery of the antinomy was the beginning of his critical philosophy (September 21, 1798 [XII, 257]).

[5] This is strictly true only of the third and fourth antinomies, as pointed out in *Critique of Practical Reason*, 104 (199).

sents the interest of reason, which requires a sufficient cause for each and every phenomenon. The sufficient cause cannot be found within phenomena, because every phenomenal cause is itself the product of prior causes and hence not, by itself, a sufficient explanation of subsequent phenomena. The proof of the antithesis, on the other hand, presents the claim of the understanding in applying the law of natural causation to all members of a series of events in space and time. The argument shows that the assumption of a free cause (i.e., of a cause that is not itself an effect) within phenomena would disrupt the reign of law required by our conception of nature. The counterargument, however, shows that if we do not assume a free cause, we cannot assume a first cause, and therefore that we cannot give a *complete* causal explanation of anything, regardless of how much progress we may make in knowledge.

The antinomy is resolved by showing that the thesis can be applied to the relationship between noumena (things in themselves) and phenomena, and the antithesis is restricted to relations among phenomena. These separate and distinct but compatible applications are all that is legitimized by the two proofs. The solution is attained by a distinction between the world of appearance and a noumenal world. *This dualism is a necessary presupposition of Kant's ethical theory* and is the principal conclusion of his criticism of speculative metaphysics.

By this dualism, science is limited in two respects: a boundary is fixed beyond which scientific knowledge cannot aspire, and the possibility is established that natural law is not the only formula of causality. But beyond the scope of science, there may be another use of reason. "I have therefore found it necessary," says Kant, "to deny knowledge in order to make room for faith."[6] If this denial of knowledge had not been effected—and effected on solid epistemological grounds and not by human wish and obscurantism—it would be morality and not science that we should have to surrender.

§ 6. TRANSITION FROM THE PROBLEMATIC TO THE ASSERTORIC JUDGMENT OF FREEDOM[7]

Note that only the possibility of another kind of causality with its own law is established by the resolution of the third antinomy. Nothing is said (except incidentally) in the *Critique of Pure Reason* to show that freedom as a mode of causality is actual or that there is an a priori law for such causality. If there is not such a causality, however, the at-

---

[6] *Critique of Pure Reason*, B xxx.

[7] This transition is fully discussed in chap. x.

tempt of theoretical reason to establish in principle a complete system of causes is condemned to failure; even theoretical reason needs such a concept for its own completion, but cannot establish it. Without such a conception, however, the very being of theoretical reason is endangered, and its lack may "plunge it into an abyss of skepticism" (3 [88]).

Such a concept can be established only by showing that it alone can do for some realm of experience what the principle of natural causation does for the sciences of nature. That is, there must be some realm of experience which, upon analysis, shows the necessity of some a priori synthetic judgment which is possible only if free causes are asserted actually to exist. The *Foundations of the Metaphysics of Morals* and the *Critique of Practical Reason* show that there is an unconditional necessity in the moral law. The moral law is an a priori synthetic practical proposition, and these two works show that it is possible. It is possible if and only if the will is a free cause. "There really is freedom, for this Idea is revealed by the moral law." The moral law is the *ratio cognoscendi* of freedom, and freedom is the *ratio essendi* of the moral law (4 n. [88 n.]).

Nevertheless, we thereby have no knowledge of freedom. A category, that of causality, is applied to a supersensible object, viz., ourselves as noumena. We *think* ourselves free, though in another context (nature) we *know* ourselves as phenomena under the law of nature. The contradiction between what we must think and what we know is resolved just as the third antinomy was resolved: we distinguish our reality from our phenomenal appearance. We thereby gain no knowledge which has been interdicted by the *Critique of Pure Reason*, but likewise, if we properly understand the meaning of practical reason,[8] we involve ourselves in no contradiction.

In the Dialectic of the first *Critique*, Kant considers two other Ideas, viz., that of the soul as substance characterized by immortality and that of God as a perfect being. He refutes arguments for each, but not to prove that the soul is not immortal or that God does not exist. He proves only that theoretical proof of each is impossible. Each is a necessary object of thought, playing a regulative role in the guidance of our search for completeness in theory; but neither is an object of knowledge.

The *Critique of Practical Reason* converts the problematic judgments of the *Critique of Pure Reason* (such as "The soul may, for all

[8] *Critique of Practical Reason*, 6 (90): "This must have seemed an inconsistency so long as the practical use of reason was known only by name," i.e., so long as it was thought that practical reason was only a special kind of cognitive faculty.

we know, be immortal and God may exist") into assertoric judgments. They were "mere Ideas, . . . unsupported by anything in speculative reason," but they now "attach themselves to the concept of freedom and gain, with it and through it, stability and objective reality" (4 [88]). This they do by being shown to be conditions of a necessary object that must be possible if the law is not to be vain and delusive, namely, the *summum bonum* (4 [89]).

But neither do these assertoric judgments, employing the categories beyond the limits of experience, express or add to our knowledge. They are postulates of a practical but rational faith, necessary because, without them, moral experience could not be made fully intelligible. There is nothing in them of a subjective will to believe or an emotional need.[9] They are rational, but not cognitive.

[9] In the Preface, Kant is mainly concerned to deny the accusation that he has treated these judgments as if they gave knowledge. Later (143 n. [242 n.]) he deals with the opposite criticism that, since they are not cognitive, they must be arbitrary and subjective.

III

Thought, Action, and Practical Reason

§ I. TWO ASPECTS OF CONDUCT

That thought and action are intimately related in Kant's philosophy is
evident from the very title of the book. "Practical reason" is not now
a widely used term, and it has connotations which do not recommend
it to many recent writers in moral philosophy. Yet that which is named
by this term in the philosophy of Kant is an important and obvious
element of human action. I shall try to describe it, eschewing at first
Kant's somewhat perplexing terminology. We shall then see that many
features of Kant's view of thought and action are not markedly different from those of the legendary man in the street, always assuming that
this exemplary figure is not wholly un-introspective and that he knows
a little psychology.

Human behavior presents two quite different faces to human beings:
it is Janus-like and never seems to the person who is acting exactly like
what it seems to the person who is watching the action. We may look
upon a man's action in the way a psychologist does, as a series of events
whose connection illustrates highly complex descriptive laws. Given
the whole set of conditions, constitutional and environmental, it is supposed by the psychologist that a man's behavior can be predicted. The
viewpoint of the psychologist who makes this assumption and who attempts to make specific predictions under it is the viewpoint of a spectator or observer. He seeks to understand and to predict behavior, but
he does not actively participate in it. Granted that the requisite laws are
not yet known in full; granted, indeed, that they may never be known
exhaustively; granted that the laws so far discovered have only low
statistical validity compared to those of the sciences of inanimate nature; granted, finally, that for even the best established of these laws
the factual data necessary for their application to an individual case are
usually lacking at the time they are most needed—granted all this, nevertheless and in principle, most psychologists would agree with Kant[1]

[1] ". . . If we could exhaustively investigate all the appearances of men's wills,
there would not be found a single human action which we could not predict with
certainty, and recognize as proceeding from antecedent conditions. . . . It is only in

29

that human behavior might be predicted with the same certainty as an eclipse of the sun or moon (99 [193]).

What the content of the necessary laws would be—whether like that of the laws of physics or physiology or economics—must be determined by the success with which each kind of attempt at formulating them will be rewarded. But that there are such laws is a necessary presupposition of a psychology or anthropology that claims to be a science.

The other aspect of human behavior is one seen by the person involved in the action. All the facts seen from one point of view may be needed in and present to the other, but the entire *mise-en-scène* is different. In the second mode of regarding and understanding conduct, one deals with his own behavior as the actor, but not as an actor who routinely runs through a fixed role in the human drama, a role well known to the outward observer. No; human beings are actors who do not quite know what is expected of them by the audience. The actor's considering his act is itself one of the determining causes of the specific action he ventures upon, and, until his consideration is carried through, he does not know what his action will be. Though it may be true that the spectator, as a professional psychologist or wise *Menschenkenner*, might foretell the precise effect that the actor's concern with his own action will have upon his conduct, this specific cause-effect relation is not known to the actor himself. The taking thought of his action is one of the causes of his action; but, until he himself has taken thought and thereby reached his own decision, the specific direction of the action that will issue from his taking thought cannot be known to him. To him, the act of taking thought is not so much a cause of a particular action, related to it by causal laws, as it is a search after a ground or good reason which will lead him to choose a specific act. The action is a product of choice or decision which is reached just in this process of taking thought. That much of the taking thought is a rationalization may be insisted upon by the observer and suspected even by the actor. After the choice is made, laws may be adduced to show that the actor could have been expected to do as he in fact did; they may be adduced by a behaviorist who might refuse to consider seriously what the actor's thoughts and inner struggles were; indeed, they may be adduced even by the actor himself, who, with growing sophistication about himself and his own quirks and turns of mind, may discover that his action falls into a pattern that applies to men in general.

---

the light of this [empirical] character that man can be studied—that is to say, we are simply *observing*, and in the manner of anthropology seeking to institute a physiological investigation into the motive causes of his actions" (*Critique of Pure Reason*, A 550 = B 578).

Even before the event, the psychologist may be able to say that such and such a percentage of men brought up as his subject was and placed in the situation in which his subject is found could be expected to delay their action for a day, saying that they wanted to think it over before deciding, and then that a specific percentage of them would do precisely so and so. A certain number of men will try to decide whether they should continue smoking when their physician advises them not to, and they will try to decide in long deliberations whose outcome they do not know. But the psychologist, armed only with statistics on past cases, might be able to say, "Whatever they think, x per cent will go right on smoking and cite y as a good ground for doing so."

But none of this perhaps frightening knowledge, even supposing that the psychologist had it and gave it to the actor, in the least serves as a sufficient condition for the actor's making up his mind in a particular way. He does not know whether he will belong to the fraction of men who will do this predicted so and so or whether he will belong to the other group; and the only way for him to find out is to do the considering and decide the issue, which should, in principle, have been predicted by the observer. The actor may know the statistics and be wise to the little hypocrisies and rationalizations he practices; but he must *decide*, and not merely know, whether he will be guided by this knowledge to do what rationalization suggests he will do or whether he will do the other, precisely because he recognizes rationalization for what it is. If it were merely a matter of knowing, so that he could predict his behavior with the same certainty that the perfect psychologist could have, the experience of deliberation, taking thought, and deciding would not be just illusory, as the observer may believe it to be; it would not even occur.

In a word, from the point of view of the actor making a decision, there is the experience that deliberation is effective, that thinking makes a difference, that one is free and not wholly determined by causes beyond his control. From the spectator's point of view, this may be an illusion: *"Du glaubst zu schieben und du wirst geschoben,"* as Mephistopheles said.[2]

Kant's theory that man's actions are both free and predictable is, apart from its metaphysical explanation, a report on the distinction between the two points of view and the assumptions which define each of them. When wishing to avoid having to "prove freedom in its theoretical aspect," Kant avails himself directly of the different assumption necessary in the attitude of the actor, and he says: "The laws

[2] *Faust*, Part I, Walpurgisnacht.

which would obligate a being who was really free would hold for a being who cannot act except under the idea of his own freedom"[3]— and all of us are such beings whenever we face a choice. Put more generally and without restricting it to the Kantian problem, we may say that those considerations without which a person cannot act deliberately must be included in a full account of his behavior. In acting deliberately, a person does not need to show that these considerations are really psychological causes effective in his behavior; he does not even need to know, in advance, whether he will in fact be able to carry out his decision when once it is made (15 [101]). All this concerns only the observer; and if the observer's knowledge of this is made available to the actor, this new knowledge is just one more factor to be taken into account in the process of deciding. For what the actor is concerned with is this: Are the reasons I have for making this choice sound reasons? It is not this: What makes me decide to do x or y, and will the causes which make me *decide* to do x suffice to make me do x in fact? Decision on the soundness of doing x is an entirely different matter from the cognitive or theoretical decision that the causes exist which justify the prediction that x will be done or that the actor will decide to do x. The cognitive prediction belongs to the observer, the practical decision to the actor.

Every time we act deliberately, we evaluate the soundness of reasons. The psychological causes why these reasons occur to us and why we assign to each the specific weight we do assign to it are matters which it is very important for us to know; self-knowledge consists in this knowledge, and such knowledge may moderate our dogmatism and prevent our fanaticism about them. But to make use of the reasons we have for doing something, in mathematics as in morals, does not require that we know the psychological facts underlying our awareness of them and the effectiveness that they have in the guidance of our behavior. The principles themselves, not the psychological causes of our acceptance of them, are what deliberating human beings do almost invariably consider. The attitude of the spectator is, in comparison with it, artificial, difficult to maintain, and coldly indifferent to the issues to be adjudicated in periods of painful indecision and more painful decision.

§ 2. CONATIVE AND COGNITIVE ELEMENTS IN ACTION

The actor in a situation demanding decision can discern in himself two very different but interrelated factors. The first is impulse. There is, as a dynamic moving factor, some want, need, desire, or wish. Pre-

[3] *Foundations of the Metaphysics of Morals,* 448 n. (67 n.).

sumably animals are conscious of this; certainly men feel pushed or pulled in this way by their wants, needs, desires, passions.

But it is equally certain that a man in full possession of his powers does not observe in himself that these wants always appropriate his entire resources and lead automatically to the action which the need seems to demand. Action is deferred; the need may be denied. Sometimes, of course, a reflex or an uncontrollable force from some importunate need may, as it were, seize him and force upon him or wring from him some action against which thoughts of wisdom and prudence are impotent. When this occurs, the person is no longer an actor; he no longer even seems to himself to control his actions, and he disclaims responsibility for them. He is like the spectator of a person in a drama (who happens, tragically, to be himself) swept along without effective deliberation, choice, conscious purpose, decision, or responsibility by forces either unknown to him or uncontrolled by him.

Happily, however, the more usual situation is one in which behavior is not automatically triggered by impulse, but one in which impulse is moderated, directed, redirected, and sometimes thwarted by our taking thought of the meaning of the impulse or spur to action. Perhaps "meaning" is not an entirely suitable word for this phenomenon, and whence the phenomenon itself comes—from the ego or superego, from some overarching sentiment, from the prefrontal lobes, from some plan of life projected by reason—may well be disputed. Yet the phenomenon is indisputable, even if the taking thought which goes into the phenomenon is itself just a necessary part of our psychological makeup.[4] It may be decried by the cynic who doubts that man deserves the honorific name of *Homo sapiens;* but the *soi-disant Homo sapiens* feels it keenly, poignantly, and often painfully.

In saying that the meaning of an impulse is a factor in conduct, I refer to two closely related facts. First, a person regards the dynamic factor which pushes or pulls him as being a certain *kind* of push or pull. It is not just a vague and amorphous restlessness, which could call forth nothing worth the name of action. And, second, a person has a conception of the *kind* of response which is appropriate to it. For instance, I have a feeling which began as a vague discomfort but which I easily recognize and classify as thirst; and I have a conception, perhaps vague around the edges but with a nucleus of clarity, of what sorts of action would quiet this need and end this discomfort, e.g., drinking water or beer certainly would, wine might, milk or coffee would not. In the course of our experience, not only do the internal drive and the responses to it become associated together through trial and error in

[4] Cf. *Critique of Pure Reason,* A 803 = B 831.

matching this response to that need, but they each become generalized. Such generalization is the essential step in learning. Such association and generalization occur in animals, and they occur below the level of consciousness in us men. But when a situation is complex and highly novel and problematic, a conscious effort must be made toward identifying the stimulus and the possible responses, toward determining the boundaries of the two generalizations, and toward accumulating the factual knowledge needed in order to associate the most effective class of responses with each class of needs. In this process the impulsive element must be held back while the cognitive exploration goes ahead and even issues forth in tentative experiments. All this is what I mean to suggest when I say that an intelligent being is able to discriminate, conceptualize, formulate, and act in the light of the meanings of his needs. These meanings appear as habits in his behavior and as rules of his conduct.

The spectator has to deal with all this; in fact, the previous paragraph is a typical "spectator paragraph." He knows the habit or disposition of a particular person who discovers particular meanings and who adopts specific lines of action in the light of these meanings. Psychological laws can be formulated which will help predict behavior even this complex. Such laws will hold whether they are known to the actor or not; indeed, they can best be discovered by observing cases in which the actor does not know them. The actor is seen as illustrating these laws, not as really obeying them; I no more need to know the laws of habit formation in order to act in accordance with them than the planets need to know Kepler's laws.

What the actor has and what the planets lack, however, is a *conception* of the connection of things and events; and for our present analytical purposes, it does not matter at all whether this conception is accurate or not. This conception may be hardly more than an association of ideas such as the barely conscious "Things that look like that usually taste good." It may be a conception of an objective law of nature, which will lead the actor to act in accordance with his belief that if he jumps from a certain height, he will be injured. It may even be a conception of what is right, such as the moral precept that, when tempted to lie, one should not do so. In any of these cases, the judgment may be correct or incorrect, and its truth or falsity is irrelevant to the initiation of the actual behavior predicted by the spectator as that which could be confidently expected of a man with this or that conception or misconception.

But that it should be a correct conception is of utmost importance to the actor, and he acts on the assumption that his conception is a correct one. If the action is not an automatic response to a stimulus and there is time permitted for deliberation, there is always some conception of the kind of thing or situation which he must handle, of the kinds of promises or threats of future experience which will eventuate from the alternative actions, and the proper rule for choice among them.

What the thing promises, what it means in future experience, may be so different from what it seems to be in its present impact upon us that the action we undertake in the light of its meaning can be painfully antagonistic to the impulses salient at the moment. When I submit myself to present pain in the interest of avoiding future pain, I have this experience of allowing, or rather of making, the meaning of the present situation dominate over its *hic et nunc* character in the determination of my behavior. In the light of what I think is knowledge of myself and of the way of the world, as a being whose thought is to be effective in conduct, I act on a policy and not on an impulse, though the impulse is always there.

This is possible only because impulse, through the medium of meaning, can be integrated into and controlled by interest. Though interest has a dynamic character which comes from impulse,[5] it also has a dispositional governing character which is sustained by putative knowledge of the meaning of situations and of the consequences of alternative actions. Interest is impulse conceptually weighed and in part conceptually directed. Intelligent action is action whose motive is an interest guided by appropriate conception and not a blind and naked impulse. Impulse leads to trigger-happy action or outbursts, to the jerks and twitches that come and go with passing moments; interest leads to actions directed according to policies and plans. Only a being having the power to reason can act from an interest. "Interest is that by which reason becomes practical, i.e., a cause determining the will. We therefore say only of a rational being that he takes an interest in something; irrational creatures feel only sensuous impulses."[6]

I may put the policy in favor of an interest into words and try to live according to it. Policies may be formulated in very specific rules which may express a specific habit, as I may say, "I make it a practice to write my name on the flyleaf of all my books." They may be expressed in general maxims that cover a wide variety of different behaviors, such as *Carpe diem*. They may be highly artificial and only

[5] Up to this point Kant would, I believe, agree with our general account of action. But he would assert that this definition of interest is too narrow, for there is an interest which is not derived from impulse, though always associated with it in some way (cf. below, § 4).

[6] *Foundations of the Metaphysics of Morals*, 459 n. (80 n.); cf. *Critique of Practical Reason*, 79 (172), and *Critique of Judgment*, § 2.

slightly effective good New Year's resolutions. They may represent a settled policy of life which can perhaps be clearly formulated only by one's biographer or psychiatrist. Finally, and most important for our purposes in moral philosophy, they may represent a consciously chosen or invented aspiration for a life integrated by respect or reverence for an ideal value, an aspiration that remains even when actual life repeatedly falls below it and mocks it with failures.

A person who tries to act on a policy of any of these kinds, which Kant summarily groups under the name "conception of a law,"[7] is said by him to have a will. A voluntary action differs from an impulsive action in that there is in it some control through a policy supposedly based upon knowledge of ourselves, our circumstances, and the consequences of our acts. "The will is never determined directly by the object or by our conception of it," he says (60 [151]). "Rather, the will is the faculty which makes a rule of reason [i.e., the conception of a law of the connection of these meanings] the efficient cause of an action which can make an object real." Policy, expressed in these rules or conceptions of laws, gives direction and stability to a complex life that could not long subsist upon the vagaries of passion. Only a being who claims knowledge of the connections of acts with one another and with consequences and sees them all in the context of a pattern of life can be said to have a will. Such a conception of laws and patterns, which are not mere tracings of past experience, is the product of our ability to reason. It is this simple thought that Kant had in mind when he identified will with practical reason.

One hears little of "practical reason" in present-day psychology, because behavior can be described by the spectator without reference to will, which seems to many psychologists to be a "ghost in the machine" or a relic of an obsolete faculty psychology. This should not disturb us, however, or make the moral philosopher apologetic to his scientific colleagues when he is concerned in action or in evaluating the actions of others. It should certainly not have the effect, which it may in fact have had, of occasioning a neglect of the peculiarities of voluntary action because of the greater psychological respectability and acceptability of concepts of impulse and emotion. Give it any name we wish in order to placate the behaviorist in his own field, the phenomenon of responding to meanings according to conceptions of rules and laws and of mobilizing our resources to withstand the importunities of momentary impulse is the essential, though often agonizing, kernel in consciousness of the kind of action which makes us men.

---

[7] *Foundations of the Metaphysics of Morals*, 412 (29); *Critique of Practical Reason*, 60 (151); *Critique of Judgment*, §§ 4, 10.

While psychology has vastly deepened our knowledge of the impulsive in its many and mysterious ramifications in normal life, neurosis, art, religion, politics, philosophy, and even science, Kant was primarily concerned with the cognitive or conceptual factor in willing. What he has to say about this has been, I think, little affected except in terminology by recent science. For science is developed from the spectator's point of view, from which the cognitive condition of action is likely to be sometimes tacitly assumed and at other times overlooked or even denied.

§ 3. PRACTICAL REASON AND WILL

Though Plato had distinguished willing from mere desiring, Aristotle was the originator of the distinction between practical reason (*nous praktikos*) and theoretical reason (*nous theoretikos*).[8] The Schoolmen translated the former as *intellectus practicus*,[9] and they also used the terms *intellectus activus*[10] and *ratio practica*.[11] The Wolffians did not use these terms in their Latin works or give literal translations in their German works, but nevertheless they maintained the distinction in their terminology of *cognitio movens* and *cognitio iners*[12] and recognized the cognitive as well as the conative elements in volition in such terms as *appetitus rationalis*.[13] Kant originated the term *praktische Vernunft* in 1765.[14]

---

[8] *De anima* 433 ᵃ 15 ff.; cf. *Politics* 1333 ᵃ 18 ff.

[9] Thomas Aquinas, *In decem libros ethicorum Aristotelis ad Nicomachum expositio* § 1132.

[10] Thomas Aquinas, *Summa theologica*, Prima, Q. 79, art. 11; Secunda secundae, Q. 179, art. 2. A fourteenth-century translation (*Middle High German Translation of the Summa theologica*, ed. B. Q. Morgan and F. W. Strothmann ["Stanford University Publications in Language and Literature," Vol. VIII, No. 1 (1950)], p. 371) renders *intellectus practicus* as *daʒ würkliche verstan*. Cf. also M. Grabmann, *Mittelalterliches Geistesleben* (Munich, 1926), p. 434.

[11] *Summa theologica*, Sec. sec., Q. 83, art. 1, ad 3.

[12] Baumgarten, *Metaphysica*, §§ 669, 690.

[13] Wolff, *Psychologia empirica*, §§ 880 ff.; cf. also *Vernünftige Gedancken von den Kräfften des menschlichen Verstandes*, § 15, where the term *lebendige Erkänntnis* is used.

[14] *Nachricht von der Einrichtung seiner Vorlesungen im Winterhalbjahr von 1765–66* (II, 312); at least, no earlier *Beleg* is given by Grimm. Mellin (*Kunstsprache der Kantischen Philosophie* [1798], p. 283) says: "The expression *praktische Vernunft* was not usual before Kant; one spoke only of *Verstand* and *Wille*." (I am indebted to Professor Paul Schrecker for calling Mellin's remark to my attention.) I can find no English use of the words "practical reason" before Richard Burthogge's *Organum vetus et novum, or Discourse on Reason and Truth*, sec. 61 (1678). The term does not, I think, occur in any of the British moralists Kant knew, with the exception of Reid, *Essay on the Active Powers of the Mind*, Book III, Part iii, sec. 2; but this was published in 1788, after the *Critique*.

Even the words used give some indication of the progress that Kant had made beyond the Wolffians in the conception of the will. In making his distinction between reason and understanding,[15] Kant ascribed to reason the task of going beyond the order of things, as given, to an ideal order of systematic connection of experience, a systematic connection that is never passively found in knowledge but must be striven for according to regulative Ideas. Reason is spontaneous in formulating Ideas that can never be adequately represented in our sense experience of the actual, even though this is categorized by the understanding. The understanding is, of course, spontaneous, but its spontaneity is restricted to a re-working of what is or can be given in perception. Though Kant acknowledged a practical function of the understanding (23, 55 [109, 145]), in making reason the prime practical faculty he did three things. First, he called attention to the manner in which it is theoretical knowledge in its systematic and ideal integrity that is relevant to the act of voluntary choice, and not some isolated bit of experience or rule of thumb. Second, he called attention to the fact that in practice we sometimes demand an unconditional certainty comparable to that which reason alone is supposed to afford us in our theoretical occupations. Third, and most important, through the connection asserted between reason and will, he prepared the way for a new definition of will itself, with all the moral consequences to be drawn from this conception.

Will is the faculty of acting according to a conception of *law*, which is not a product or discovery of understanding but of reason. In contrast, his predecessors had thought of will as only rational desire, i.e., the faculty of acting according to a clear (rational) representation of the object of desire.[16] They could discern a difference only between the lower and higher faculties of desire and were never able, according

15 Wolff translates *ratio* as *Vernunft* and defines it as "insight into the connection [*Zusammenhang*] of truth," and hence as the art of inference; *intellectus* is translated as *Verstand* and is the faculty of clearly representing the possible. Pure understanding (*intellectus purus*) is understanding separated (*abgesondert*) from senses and imagination, but human understanding is never completely pure (cf. *Vernünftige Gedancken von Gott, der Welt und der Seele des Menschen* [1736], §§ 368, 381, 277, 282, 285). Logically, this corresponds very well to Kant's distinction between reason as the faculty of inference and understanding as the faculty of concepts; but the important Kantian distinction between the real and the merely logical use of reason and understanding and the equally important theory of the generic difference between sense and the discursive faculties are not anticipated.

16 Cf. Wolff, *Vernünftige Gedancken von Gott, der Welt, und der Seele des Menschen*, § 492, and *Psychologia empirica* (1737), § 880; Crusius, *Entwurf der nothwendigen Vernunftwahrheiten* (1753), § 445. The gradualistic conception of the distinction between *ratio* and *intellectus* is fundamental to this.

to Kant, to single out the unique feature of willing and, a fortiori, of moral willing. For these reasons, Kant rejects, as inadequate to ethics, their conception of a universal practical philosophy and, as inconsistent with their own views, their attempt to distinguish in any ethically significant way between the lower and the higher faculties of desire (22 f. [109 f.]).

Yet there are two puzzles which arise from Kant's way of speaking of the relationship among will, practical reason, and theoretical reason, and these must be cleared up before we come to the most important of his doctrines, to wit, that pure reason can be practical.

First, Kant identifies will with practical reason, but he often confuses the reader by speaking of reason as the determiner of the will. Theoretical reason, which demands an order in the totality of the data of possible experience, is practical when, through the order it projects as possible if such and such an action is executed, it becomes a determinant in behavior whose dynamic component is provided by impulse or desire. That is, theoretical reason provides the knowledge of the law which can be applied in the satisfaction of desire, and, insofar as it does so, it is practical reason. Thus far, at least, there are not two reasons, a theoretical and a practical, but one reason—the faculty of formulating laws and principles—which has two applications. One gives knowledge of things as they are (or appear); the other gives direction to the changes we introduce into this natural order by means of voluntary action. The following two sentences therefore mean the same thing: (*a*) Will is impulse guided by reason; and (*b*) Will is practical reason. From *a* it is easy to move to another sentence, (*c*) Reason can determine the will, which seems to be incompatible with *b*, for *b* identifies them. But, properly understood, *b* and *c* are not incompatible. The last sentence means simply: (*c′*) Reason determines the action by which impulse is to be satisfied; when it does so, it is called "practical reason," and the action chosen is called an "act of will."

Second, another puzzle is presented by Kant's often speaking of practical reason as a cognitive faculty[17] and as a faculty of desire.[18] He mentions the danger of taking the words "practical reason" as if the "object" of practical reason were comparable to an object of theoretical reason, i.e., as an epistemological object and not as an object of de-

---

[17] *Critique of Pure Reason*, A 633 = B 661: "The practical use of reason is that through which it is known a priori what ought to take place"; also draws distinction between theoretical and practical knowledge. *Critique of Practical Reason*, 66 (157): pure practical concepts are directly cognitions, not having to wait upon, or be applied to, intuition.

[18] *Critique of Practical Reason*, 24 (111); *Erste Einleitung in die Kritik der Urteilskraft*, XX, 245-46; *Critique of Judgment*, Introduction, III (V, 177 [13]).

sire or volition.[19] We should be warned by this against taking "practical reason" to denote merely the faculty by which we gain knowledge of right and wrong, though we should not forget that practical reason does have this cognitive function. It provides the cognitive factor in the guidance of action whose *dynamis* is impulse. The sentences of theoretical reason or understanding, such as "A is the cause of B," become the practical proposition or cognition of practical reason, "If you desire B, do A" (26 n. [113 n.]). The latter proposition might better be called a cognition of technical or practical understanding when B is some specific, well-defined object or situation. A prudent policy of life, on the other hand, as an allegedly unconditional ground for choice not only of means to happiness but also and more importantly of the genuine composition of such an ideal, could properly be called the object of a cognition of practical reason, as its pursuit is undertaken because of a maxim of practical reason. We should then retain the name "cognition of pure practical reason" for knowledge of the moral law and of the highest moral aims.

§ 4. PURE PRACTICAL REASON

If practical reason can hold before us a law valid for practice but not derived from our experience of the way things go in the world when we attempt to satisfy some specific desire, this would be a law of a kind entirely different from those of interest in theory. The relevance of the latter kind of law, though essential for intelligent practice, is always contingent upon there being some experienced situation by reference to which we choose, from all the actual laws of nature, those which are concerned with the causes of the object of the specific desire. Such laws in their theoretical formulation may be necessary; but, when formulated as practical rules, they are always contingent upon there being in us the desires which can be satisfied through successful application of our knowledge of them. If there is an unconditional practical law, it could be discovered only by a reason that is intrinsically practical, and not by a theoretical reason which is only extrinsically and contingently practical, i.e., one issuing laws which may or may not be applicable in practice, depending upon the desires and the situation. Such an intrinsically practical reason is called *pure* practical reason.[20]

---

[19] *Critique of Practical Reason*, 5 (90). We shall see later, in chap. ix, Kant's justification for referring to both as objects.

[20] Kant uses the word "pure" to refer to both cognitions and faculties. In the former usage it refers to (*a*) cognitions which are independent of experience and (*b*) cognitions in which there is no empirical content. Meaning *a* is equivalent to a priori, and Kant said later (not quite accurately) that the *Critique of Pure Reason*

That pure reason can be practical is the chief thesis of the Kantian moral philosophy; it is equivalent to the assertion that there are unconditional practical laws. Kant rejected the Aristotelian thesis[21] that reason alone cannot move us and the Humean thesis[22] that reason is and ought to be the slave of the passions. Reason is concerned not with the choice among ways to some end projected by desire; this is its merely logical use. It establishes the goals of action through the formulation of an intrinsically practical and unconditional law. This is its real use.[23]

Pure reason, in its real use, is always concerned with unconditioned conditions. Pure practical reason is the faculty of providing an unconditioned condition for voluntary action, which is a law demanding direct obedience without a *quid pro quo*. As Kant is to show in the early parts of the *Critique of Practical Reason*, such unconditioned conditions cannot be found in or by an empirically practical reason, which is indeed the slave of the passions. If pure reason is practical, however, there is some intrinsically practical law and some motive independent of the contingent and empirically discovered human desires. This motive must be our knowledge of the law itself through the respect that it creates in us. An action having this motive is moral, and a being which acts from this motive has a good will. The *Foundations of the Metaphysics of Morals* stated, in this way, the requirement that an action must meet if it is to be counted moral, and it concluded that pure reason must be practical if morality is not a mere chimera.

But can pure reason, in its real use, be practical? Or is this analysis of morality an analysis of a vain and empty delusion? To show that pure reason can be practical, we are told in the first paragraph, is the prime task of the *Critique of Practical Reason*.

---

was concerned only with "pure" in this sense (*Über den Gebrauch teleologischer Prinzipien in der Philosophie*, VIII, 183–84). When used in reference to a faculty, "pure" indicates that the faculty is a priori legislative (*Critique of Judgment*, V, 179 [15]). It is important not to confuse these two meanings, though they are closely related. The moral law is pure in senses *a* and *b;* the concept of duty is pure only in sense *a;* practical reason is pure, or may be pure, in the sense that it is an a priori legislating faculty, giving the moral law.

21 *De anima* 433 ᵃ 23.

22 *Treatise of Human Nature*, Book II, Part III, sec. iii (Selby-Bigge ed., p. 415). Kant was not the first in his time to state that reason is both the necessary and the sufficient condition of action; in this he was anticipated by a critic of Hutcheson's, namely, John Balguy (*The Foundation of Moral Goodness* [1728] [Selby-Bigge, *British Moralists*, II, 92–93]), and by Price (*Review of the Principal Questions of Morals* [1758], chap. viii). There is no evidence that Kant knew of Balguy or Price.

23 For this distinction cf. above, p. 7.

IV

Name, Purpose, and Structure of the "Critique"; Commentary on Preface and Introduction

The Preface of the *Critique of Practical Reason* discusses the following topics: the title of the book, its purpose, and its relation to other works; and it gives a preliminary exposition of Kant's theory of freedom and a defense of his views against his critics. A major part of the Preface deals with criticisms that had been made of the first *Critique* and of the *Foundations of the Metaphysics of Morals;* by answering his chief critics, Kant hoped to show better the consistency among the various parts of his philosophy. In addition, there are brief replies, or anticipations of replies to be given later, to isolated criticisms of specific points in his ethical theory.

The Introduction again discusses the title of the book and its purpose, and then proceeds to a description of the structure and organization of the new *Critique*.

In this chapter, I shall deal with these matters as follows: In § 2, I shall discuss the title of the book and Kant's reason for choosing it; § 3 will discuss the purposes of the book as stated here and elsewhere; and §§ 4 and 5 will deal in more detail with two of these purposes. Then I shall take up, in § 6, the relation of this work to the *Metaphysics of Morals;* § 7 will be concerned with the organization of the *Critique;* and, finally, in § 8, I shall review the polemics of the Preface, laying primary emphasis upon their historical occasion, since most of their philosophical import can be better discussed in the more systematic and less historical studies to follow.

§ 2. TITLE OF THE BOOK

Even before he planned to write this book, Kant referred to the "critical examination [*Kritik*] of pure practical reason," as we have seen in chapter i. Yet when the book was written, he called it simply *Critique of Practical Reason,* though, as he says in the first paragraph, "the parallelism between it and the critical examination of speculative reason seems to demand" the longer title (3 [87]).

In interpreting this first sentence, we meet with a difficulty that exasperates all translators of Kant: in what sense is the word *Kritik* being used? It may be part of the title of a book, in which case it should be rendered as *Critique*. It may mean merely a critical examination of something. It may mean that formalized division of philosophy that he called the propaedeutic to the development of a system of reason; in this case, it should be translated as *critique*. The typographical practices of the eighteenth century and the fact that all nouns are capitalized in German make it impossible to base a decision on the letter of the text. One must try to understand what Kant meant at each particular place where he used the word *Kritik*. It is obvious that in the first paragraph the words *Kritik der praktischen Vernunft* refer to the book in hand and that the words *Kritik der spekulativen Vernunft* refer to the *Critique of Pure Reason*, though they do not properly state its title, nor do they give an entirely correct intimation of its contents.

Kant here suggests that there is a parallelism between two *Critique*'s. But when he added the second *Critique* to the corpus of the critical philosophy, he surrendered a belief that he had had when he wrote the first; for the first was to give a critical examination of the entire faculty of reason, both theoretical and practical. When he wrote the *Foundations*, he referred to the "critical examination of pure practical reason" as doing for practical reason what the "critical examination of pure speculative reason" (*sc. Critique of Pure Reason*) did for metaphysics, in the sense of transcendental philosophy and the metaphysics of nature.[1] In 1785, therefore, Kant recognized a parallelism of function of the two "critical examinations," one of which had already been written and the other one of which was not even at that time a separate literary project. In 1787, however, though mentioning the parallelism and suggesting that it might seem to justify the use of the title mentioned in 1785, he was more intent upon denying the parallelism of the function of the two works. For the first *Critique* was concerned with denying the pretensions of pure theoretical reason, while the second is concerned with denying those of empirical practical reason.

In both the first paragraph of the Preface and in the second and third paragraphs of the Introduction he says that pure practical reason requires no critical examination. All that is required is to show that pure reason can be practical, and, in order to show this, it suffices to

[1] *Foundations of the Metaphysics of Morals*, 391 (6).

examine practical reason in general. It is discovered, in such an examination, that only the empirically conditioned practical reason, not the pure practical reason, "presumptuously overreaches itself," as pure theoretical (*sc*. speculative) reason does (3, 15–16 [87, 101–2]).

This justification for the title, however, is not coercive. For there is a duality of meaning in the word *Kritik* as a name for a division of philosophy, and this equivocation is bound to make any such decision somewhat arbitrary. That the word *Kritik* even in the title of the first book has various meanings is shown by the fact that its object, what it is a critique *of*, is variously given by the following descriptive but inaccurate titles: "Critique of Reason," "Critique of Theoretical Reason," "Critique of Speculative Reason," and even "Critique of Pure Understanding."[2]

Kant formally defines *Kritik* as "a science of the mere examination of reason, its sources and limits,"[3] and it is propaedeutic to a system of pure reason. There are two functions of *Kritik*. Negatively, *Kritik* fixes the boundaries of the competence of reason; this is its "police" function[4] in preventing or exposing the dialectical illusions of speculative metaphysics. Positively, *Kritik* is to secure to reason the "sure path of science" against the import of skepticism from regions where it is justified (speculative metaphysics) into those where it is not justified (science and morals). *Kritik* in the negative sense is Kant's answer to rationalistic metaphysicians; *Kritik* in the positive sense is his answer to skepticism based on empiricism.

Since Kant favors the title *Critique of Practical Reason*, he seems to be using the word here primarily in its negative sense and to have as his chief aim the limiting of the claims of practical reason based on empirical motives. But in the negative sense of *Kritik*, there is not, as we have seen, a parallelism between the two works, since it is *pure* speculative reason and *empirical* practical reason that stand in need of negative criticism.

Yet negative critique of practical reason *as such* is not, in fact, the entire purpose of the work before us. Even pure practical reason has its dialectic. This dialectic is not a conflict between sensuously determined and pure practical reason but a conflict among the Ideas of pure practical reason itself. Hence pure practical reason also stands in need of negative critique.

On the other hand, if we take the word "critique" in its positive

---

[2] *Critique of Judgment*, Introduction, III (V, 179 [15]).

[3] *Critique of Pure Reason*, A 11 = B 25.

[4] *Ibid.*, B xxv.

sense, an equally good justification for calling this book "Critique of Pure Practical Reason" can be given. For only as pure can practical reason be legislative, and though the yet-to-be-written "Metaphysics of Morals" would have the task of spelling out that legislation, the fundamental constitutional law of moral experience must be given in critique, just as the fundamental principles of theoretical reason, which "gives the law to nature," are uncovered in the *Critique of Pure Reason*. Accordingly, he says that the *Critique of Practical Reason* "gives an account of the principles of the possibility of duty, its extent and limits . . ." (8 [94]), and this is critique of pure practical reason in the positive sense.

In view of these arguments and counterarguments, it seems to me that equally good grounds can be found for either decision. For the actual choice the decisive ground seems to have been the importance he attached to critique in the negative sense, which he made his first task in the book. Once the title was chosen, a historical accident was responsible for the first paragraph of the Preface. Kant means that the parallelism seems to demand the following pair of titles: "Critique of Pure Practical Reason" and *Critique of Pure Reason*. But it does not. The correct parallels would be either "Critique of Practical Reason" and "Critique of Speculative [or Theoretical] Reason" or "Critique of Pure Practical Reason" and "Critique of Pure Theoretical [or Speculative] Reason." There is no book with the title of "Critique of Speculative Reason" (where "speculative" means "pure theoretical"); yet Kant suggests that his readers may expect the present book to have a different title from the one he gave it, all because of a fancied parallel with a title he had not used for another work!

But the historical accident was this. There was a parallelism in titles used in the announcement of the new edition of the *Critique of Pure Reason* in 1786. There it was said that "to the critique of pure speculative reason" there would be added a "critique of pure practical reason." When, finally, for reasons that I have suggested were not particularly convincing, he chose the shorter title, the first paragraph was necessary to tell his readers that this was indeed the work they had been expecting since 1786. Either Kant had a very different conception of the work in 1786, or at the time of the announcement he had not formulated a very clear conception of what its contents would be. I suspect that the latter was the case.

§ 3. THE PURPOSES OF THE BOOK

In the preceding section, when evaluating Kant's reasons for having chosen the title, we have had to mention some of its purposes as he states them in the Preface and Introduction. The purposes may be stated more systematically as follows:

1. To examine reason's entire practical faculty so as to show
   a) That pure reason can be practical,[5]
   b) That empirically affected practical reason makes presumptuous claims and must therefore be restricted to its proper bounds (16 [102]),
   c) And that pure practical reason makes no claims that are interdicted by the *Critique of Pure Reason* (5, 6 [90]). But
2. Without collusion of the two *Critique*'s, to establish the reality of certain Ideas needed even by theoretical reason, which theoretical reason could show only to be logically possible but not to be really possible or to have actual objects.[6]
3. To establish the principles of the possibility of duty, as laws of pure practical reason, so that they can be applied to man as a particular kind of empirically discovered being, in the "Metaphysics of Morals" to which the *Critique* is a propaedeutic (8 [93–94]).
4. To resolve an inevitable dialectic in the judgments of pure practical reason (16 [102]).

In addition, two other purposes of at least major parts of the book are not explicitly mentioned in the Preface. They are:

5. To investigate and justify the fact that moral philosophy must have precisely the systematic form it does have and no other (89 [182]).
6. To determine the way in which we can secure to the laws of pure practical reason access to the human mind and an influence on its maxims (151 [249]).

[5] *Critique of Practical Reason*, 3, 15, 45 (88, 101, 134); Reflexion 7201. The answer to the question as to how reason can determine conduct is erroneously ascribed to metaphysics, not critique, in *Foundations of the Metaphysics of Morals*, 426 (44).

[6] *Critique of Practical Reason*, 3, 5 (87, 89). This is shown with respect to freedom in the "credential of the moral law" at *ibid.*, 48 (137), from which the reality of the other Ideas is inferred. Thus the *Critique of Practical Reason* "accomplishes something I denied to speculative reason" (to Schütz, June 25, 1787 [X, 490]), viz., the step to a "practical-dogmatic metaphysics" as a part of a metaphysics of nature. Such a practical-dogmatic metaphysics must be distinguished from the metaphysics of morals as a "moral-practical science of reason" (*Fortschritte der Metaphysik*, XX, 293). Purposes 2 and 3 may accordingly be restated as follows: (2') to provide a propaedeutic for a practical-dogmatic metaphysics of God, freedom, and immortality and (3') to provide a propaedeutic for an immanent metaphysics of morals as a system of all a priori principles of morality.

To these reasons must be added two others that are not mentioned in the Preface or Introduction, but which have been stated in the *Foundations* to require a critical examination of pure practical reason. Since these purposes are among the most important that Kant had in writing this book, it is astonishing that they are not given a prominent and, indeed, dominant position here at the beginning of the book. These purposes are:

7. To show the unity of the speculative and practical reason under a common principle, because "in the final analysis there can be but one and the same reason which must be differentiated only in application."[7]

8. To show that a synthetic use of pure practical reason is possible, i.e., to show how a synthetic a priori practical proposition is possible.[8]

We shall consider purposes 7 and 8 before proceeding further into the text of the Preface.

§ 4. THE UNITY OF THEORETICAL AND PRACTICAL REASON

The unity of theoretical and practical reason is asserted in the *Critique* (121 [217]), and almost the entire book can be considered an elaboration of this. Yet one can only regret that at no point in the book does Kant, as it were, take the reader by the hand and say, "Now I shall show you precisely why I think theoretical and practical reason differ only in being two applications of the same faculty." And in one place he writes as if he does not have a proof that satisfies him; for he says that comparison of the structures of the two *Critique*'s "correctly occasion the expectation of being able some day to bring into one view the unity of the entire pure rational faculty (both theoretical and practical) and of being able to derive everything from one principle" (91 [184]).

Still it is fortunately not difficult to state what may have been this "one principle," even though Kant did not and perhaps at this time could not spell it out. Kant is concerned, in his mature ethical treatises, to show that there are no moral concepts or practical principles that have any basis other than the "legislation of pure reason." Reason is the faculty of principles, and it brings all that is thought by the understanding under the highest unity of thought. Now if there are valid practical principles whose necessity is not derivable from universal

[7] *Foundations of the Metaphysics of Morals*, 391 (7).

[8] *Ibid.*, 445 (64). This is, of course, closely related to task 1*a*.

and necessary principles conceived only by reason, then the internal unity of practice would itself be nonexistent or, at best, contingent. Only reason can supply universal and necessary principles, whether to knowledge or to conduct.

Kant's effort, through the first parts of the *Foundations* and much of the *Critique*, is to show that non-rational grounds for decisions to act are neither internally consistent, necessarily binding, nor universal in application. Practically, they are divisive instead of unifying; no "moral order" can be constructed on their foundation (35 [124]). But reason serves the same function in the practical that it does in the theoretical realm, that of systematizing, integrating, universalizing, and rendering necessary what appears prima facie to be contingent.

While, in the theoretical realm, the Ideas used for these purposes are only regulative and provide mere maxims for the conduct of inquiry without determining its outcome or being necessary (for inquiry itself is not necessary) (5 [89]); in the practical, the Idea of freedom is constitutive of the experience to which it applies, for the experience is of what ought to be (as defined by the Idea) and not of what happens to exist independently of it. We may and do mistake the function of theoretical reason and think that its Ideas are constitutive of an intelligible world—of the world of things as they really are and not as they appear. When we make this mistake, transcendental Ideas become transcendent, and philosophical thinking falls into antinomies, paralogisms, and other fallacies exhibited and eradicated in the Dialectic of the first *Critique*. The same reason, following our demands for unconditional conditions for every motive and for the unity of motives in a pattern of life, is, on the contrary, an immanent reason, actually producing the objects to correspond to its Ideas. These objects, produced by us in acting in accordance with the demands of these Ideas, are not things in the outer world, which we may have or lack the power to effect; they are motives or states of mind or decisions of will which directly express in actual experience the Idea of freedom, of which the moral law is a necessary consequence. Edward Caird has excellently said of the transition from theory to practice: "Just because reason cannot find its ideal [of necessary and universal systematic unity] realised in the world, it seeks to realise that ideal for itself."[9] Reason becomes practical, generating an Idea of a world that, through our actions and attitudes, may be established with immanent completeness, order, and systematic unity, whether it can be actualized in

---

[9] *The Critical Philosophy of Immanuel Kant*, II, 164.

the products of human skill or not.[10] Theoretical reason, unless these Ideas are established, vainly pursues an ever receding goal.[11]

Still, if one remembers the discussion in the *Foundations* on "The Extreme Limit of All Practical Philosophy," one may doubt that the question as to why reason is practical can be answered. To show how reason can be practical, he there tells us, is as impossible as (and essentially the same as) to explain how freedom is possible. Like the question as to why we intuit objects only in space and time, these questions cannot be answered with an answer derived from any higher principle. We show that they must be as they are because they are necessary presuppositions for something that is actual; we do not comprehend them, but we can at least comprehend their incomprehensibility.[12]

Nevertheless, an explicit answer to this question is given, not in the *Critique of Practical Reason*, where, if anywhere, one might expect it, but in the *Critique of Judgment*.[13] He tells us that reason always makes a demand to find the unconditioned condition for all conditions. In experience, this demand cannot be met, and it leads to theoretical speculation about an unconditioned thing in itself, an unconditioned substance, and an unconditioned cause. But in speculation these Ideas are only assumptions, not cognitions, and no theoretical conclusions can be drawn from the fact that we assume them for the guidance of inquiry. In the practical realm, the unconditioned necessity is reason's own causality, under the name of freedom, and this is revealed to us, as a fact, in our awareness of the claims of duty. What is commanded by reason's imperative, however, may not take place in the phenomenal world. We therefore draw a distinction between what does and what ought to happen. Practical reason establishes the latter concept, theoretical reason the former. There seems to be an unbridgeable conceptual chasm between them, even if, in fact, what ought to be can be made actual by an act of will and the ensuing behavior.

This conceptual distinction, however, is drawn by reason only be-

[10] Cf. *Critique of Pure Reason*, A 548 = B 576; *Critique of Practical Reason*, 15 (101).

[11] *Critique of Pure Reason*, A 796 = B 824.

[12] *Foundations of the Metaphysics of Morals*, 463 (84); cf. *Critique of Pure Reason*, A 393.

[13] § 76. The idea is put forward in *Critique of Pure Reason*, A 816 = B 844, that the unity of the two legislations is to be based on the regulative Idea of God as the author of both types of law, the theoretical and the practical.

cause of a peculiarity of the human mind. If our reason were an autonomous sufficient cause of its objects, the distinction between what is and what ought to be would never arise, just as in a world in which reason had the power to produce objects by merely thinking of them, the distinction between the necessary, the actual, and the merely possible would have no place. It is only owing to the subjective constitution of our minds—that reason as a cognitive faculty is applicable to objects only under the condition that we passively receive sensible data, while as a pure practical faculty it is independent of what is given by the senses, since it is not in the least a faculty of knowing objects[14]—that we do not immediately see that there is a single reason in two different relations. For a differently constituted intellect, an intuitive understanding, the distinction would not arise. It is a contingent fact that our reason is discursive, i.e., that it must begin with data and move to universals, and is not capable of producing data simply by thinking of them. This fact is as contingent and inexplicable as the fact that we experience objects only in space and time. We can imagine another kind of mind, for which pure reason would directly give knowledge of objects, and of objects as they are and not as they appear to us. We have no grounds for supposing that there is such an intellect, but we do not need to assume its existence; its mere possibility is sufficient to render intelligible to us the way in which a distinction which seems at first to be absolute can, in fact, be thought of as only a difference in relation. From the possibility of an intuitive intellect and from the fact that our intellect is not intuitive, we can see that it is only for us (and, so far as we *know*, all actual minds) that there is a distinction between what is and what ought to be, between the necessary and the possible, between the mechanically and the teleologically caused.

So far from there being an opposition between theoretical and practical reason, therefore, Kant believes that there is one reason that carries out the same function in two different applications—this function being to supply unconditioned conditions for all that is empirically

---

[14] The practical counterpart of the intuitive intellect as a possible cognitive faculty is the holy will (*Critique of Practical Reason*, 82 [175]). Each is possible (conceivable), but we have no reason to think that either of them exists, except insofar as we have reason to believe that God exists. But each is an important conception, for, by comparison with it, Kant brings out more clearly the peculiarities of the human cognitive or practical faculty. For a holy will, the concept of duty would have no application, since duty presupposes that there are other grounds of choice, different from and in conflict with the legislation of reason. For it, the difference between what is willed and what ought to be willed would not arise. Similarly, for an intuitive intellect the distinction between the actual and the necessary would not arise.

conditioned. But the *Critique of Practical Reason* is very much concerned with the apparent opposition between practical and theoretical reason, because this felt opposition is the setting for the concept of duty, respect for law and virtue, and the distinction between knowledge and faith.

§ 5. HOW IS A SYNTHETIC A PRIORI PRACTICAL PROPOSITION POSSIBLE?

This question is different from that of task 1 (*a*), which is to show that pure reason can be a directly determining ground of will and have a direct influence upon conduct. It also differs slightly from the formulation in the *Foundations of the Metaphysics of Morals,* where Kant asks, How is a synthetic use of pure practical reason possible?[15] The question as stated here does not occur in the *Critique* but first appears in print in the *Metaphysics of Morals.*[16] But that Kant knew that the question needed an answer is shown by its formulation in Fragment 6.[17] In view of the prominence given to the analogous theoretical question in the *Critique of Pure Reason* (especially in the second edition) and in the *Prolegomena,* it is a bit strange that it is not even mentioned in the second *Critique,* where one would expect it to have a programmatic position.

The first two sections of the *Foundations* examine the phenomena of morality in order to discover what would be its formula for action; and this formula is presupposed by the *Critique* (8 [93]). This inquiry issues, in the first part of the *Foundations,* in the statement that morality is solely a matter of will or motive, not of circumstance or consequence, and that a good will is a will that acts from the motive of doing an action because it is the right action, though any will may in fact do the right *action* from other motives. A good will is one which does the action from respect for law, not from the desire for this or that consequence, though there is always some desire to effect some change in the world by any action voluntarily undertaken. In Part II, this examination leads to the formula of the categorical imperative as the presupposition of and the criterion for a motive which could be considered morally good.

But the first two sections, though containing many statements that can be most readily interpreted as asserting real facts and expressing

[15] *Foundations of the Metaphysics of Morals,* 445 (64). My translation, in the Chicago edition (p. 101) is in error. The penultimate sentence of the last paragraph of Section II should read: "But we must not venture on this [synthetical] use without first making a critical examination of this faculty of reason."

[16] *Metaphysik der Sitten,* Rechtslehre, § 6 (VI, 249).

[17] *Reflexion* 7202 (XIX, 282).

valid moral commands, also contain statements that remind the reader that the purpose of these sections is analytical and that their conclusions are put forth problematically; they give the structure of morality, whether or not such a thing is real. The principles are enunciated as those which must be true "if duty is not a vain delusion and a chimerical concept,"[18] and their conceptual correctness is independent of an answer to the question as to whether "true virtue can be found anywhere in the world."[19]

In bringing these principles to light, Kant has followed an analytical method in beginning with "common rational knowledge of morals" and "popular moral philosophy" assumed as the *prius*, just as in the *Prolegomena* he assumed the validity of mathematics and natural science and asked what must be true if they are valid knowledge. But just as the *Prolegomena* is a grand *petitio principii* if taken as an answer to skepticism in isolation from the *Critique of Pure Reason*, the first two parts of the *Foundations* are a *petitio principii* if taken in isolation from the third part or the *Critique of Practical Reason*. (Or it would be better to say that they would have been a *petitio principii*, had not Kant kept clearly in mind throughout that they constitute an exposition of a concept, not an argument.)

It does not follow that the analytical method will lead only to analytical judgments, and, indeed, it there leads to the formulation of the categorical imperative, which Kant calls an "a priori synthetic practical judgment." Synthetic propositions cannot be justified by analysis, though they may be discovered in this way; and if they are a priori, they cannot be justified by any appeal to the facts of experience. They must be justified, if at all, by a critical inquiry like that of the *Critique of Pure Reason*. We must ask, How are such judgments possible? What right do we have to assert such propositions? Only when we have answered this question satisfactorily can a synthetical use of the principles be made; only then can we know that the formula of a *possible* moral command is the formula of a *real* and legitimately issued command.

When Kant thus states the problem of Section III of the *Foundations* and reverts to it in the *Critique* (89 [182]) in a passage that he especially urges in the Preface (8 [93]) upon the reader's attention, he is saying that the *Critique of Practical Reason* has the task of showing (*a*) that pure reason does have a real use in practice, not a merely logical use in the hypothetical analysis of a possible phenomenon of morality

[18] *Foundations of the Metaphysics of Morals*, 445 (64).

[19] *Ibid.*, 407 (24).

and not a merely logical (technical) use in organizing our experience for the sake of pragmatic success,[20] and (*b*) that the synthetic a priori judgments found in the analysis of morality are actually justified. Purpose *a* is accomplished in the Analytic as a whole, and purpose *b* is assigned to that part of the Analytic called the Deduction.

§ 6. RELATION TO THE "METAPHYSICS OF MORALS"

I have already discussed some of the historical relations between this book and the *Metaphysics of Morals*, and in § 8 I shall have to return to some of them in explaining the polemics of the Preface. In this section, I shall consider one paragraph and one footnote in which Kant speaks of the relation of the *Critique* to the "system of science" (8 [94]) and to the "metaphysics of morals" to which the *Critique* is only a preliminary (161 [260]).

We are told that this *Critique* is not to give us a classification of the practical sciences, as the first *Critique* did of the theoretical sciences, for the division of theoretical sciences there (into mathematics, natural science, and metaphysics) is said to be entirely a priori, while the division of practical sciences (into the Doctrine of Right and the Doctrine of Virtue) requires empirical knowledge of man for the specific definition of duties as human duties. Such knowledge is not a part of the critical examination of practical reason but presupposes both critique, the elaboration of its a priori principles, and empirical knowledge concerning human nature.

Yet the footnote, in answering a possible criticism of his general position that it was based on the alleged facts of psychology, gives definitions of life, faculty of desire, and pleasure, as the *Critique of Pure Reason* said would be necessary,[21] and declares that these are all the definitions or facts that he needs that are empirical in character. Even these facts are not introduced as direct evidence but, as it were, obliquely, in order to show that psychology does not need to define these concepts in such a way that pure practical reason would be impossible.

But even this much empiricism seems to be incompatible with the purposes of a critical examination of pure practical reason, and it raises the following question: Just how "pure" can moral philosophy be? Kant is not very explicit or consistent in his answer to this question; he seems always to have been striving for a degree of purity which could be obtained only in the emptiness of Wolff's "universal

20 This is equivalent to purpose 1*a*.
21 Cf. above, p. 9, n. 21.

practical philosophy." But we may discern at least five levels of purity involved in the articulation of Kant's total plan:

1. Moral philosophy independent of the peculiar nature of human reason[22] (e.g., that we do not have an intuitive understanding) and dependent only upon the fact of pure reason, which is not an empirical fact (31 [120])—metaphysics of morals as envisaged in the *Foundations*.

2. Moral philosophy dependent upon level 1 and upon the three definitions drawn from psychology, which give the ground for the concepts of imperative, respect, and duty—*Critique of Practical Reason*.

3. Moral philosophy as the systematic development of principles in 2, independent of, but applicable to, human nature in the variety of its forms as empirically known—metaphysics of morals in the book with that title.[23]

4. System of practical philosophy ("system of the science") as systematic exposition of 3, along with the empirical facts—repeatedly mentioned, but never written.

5. Moral and pragmatic anthropology—episodic elaboration of practical rules—*Lectures on Ethics* and *Anthropology*.

So the sharp line separating critique and system is blurred, if not breached. And the book *Metaphysics of Morals* is much more like 4 than like 3. The only metaphysics of morals that Kant ever wrote, in fact, was the *Critique of Practical Reason*, for only it is "a system of knowledge a priori from mere concepts"—if, indeed, it is that.

Kant never wrote, or at least never completed, the "metaphysics of nature" to which the *Critique of Pure Reason* was propaedeutic; all he published in this direction was still another propaedeutic, the *Metaphysische Anfangsgründe der Naturwissenschaft*. Metaphysics that could "come forth as science" had already come forth in the *Critique*'s themselves. The two metaphysics and systems were ever receding ideals, and any further metaphysics, strictly conceived, after the *Critique*'s would have been supererogatory,[24] though they might have

---

[22] *Foundations of the Metaphysics of Morals*, 412 (28).

[23] *Metaphysik der Sitten*, VI, 216–17.

[24] As critique grew and system receded, Kant once denied that the *Critique of Pure Reason* was propaedeutic and stated that it was itself system (*Erklärung in Beziehung auf Fichtes Wissenschaftslehre*, XII, 370–71). This statement, I believe unique in Kant, can best be explained by his pique at Fichte, who claimed to have completed the work which his teacher had only begun, and probably it does not represent any fundamental surrender of his own architectonic ideal. It nevertheless expresses an opinion to which one is brought by examination of the actual contents of the "critical" and the "systematic" works.

given Kant occasion to do what he had repeatedly said would be a pleasure he had to refrain from—the systematic, analytic, or encyclopedic unrolling of consequences from his a priori principles and concepts.

§ 7. THE STRUCTURE OF THE BOOK

In this section I shall deal with the over-all structure of the *Critique*. Details of the various subdivisions will be discussed as they are reached in the course of the commentary.

Kant's architectonic has been treated sometimes with amusement, often with contempt, and almost always with impatience. It has been argued that, had he not held to the rigors of his architectonic schemes, his works could have been organized in a less forbiddingly scholastic pattern and could have been made shorter, since his ideal of completeness of articulation led him to write whole chapters (e.g., at the end of the first *Critique*) in which he had little interest and little to contribute.

The *Critique of Practical Reason* is almost wholly free from excessive architectonic zeal; only two parts may seem to owe their origin to a forced parallelism with the first *Critique,* and in the course of this commentary we shall find reason to believe that they are integrally necessary parts of the organic structure of this work.

The organization is easily grasped but presents some interesting features that call for discussion. There are two statements of the plan of the work (16, 89–91 [102, 183–84]). In the latter statement there is a comparison of the structure of the two *Critique*'s; but, in making this comparison, Kant incorrectly recalled the division of the first *Critique.* This error is itself instructive. The accompanying tabulation presents the structure of the relevant parts of the first *Critique* in fact, their structure as Kant recalled it, and the structure of the corresponding parts of the second *Critique.*

Actual Structure of First *Critique*	Remembered Structure of First *Critique*	Structure of Second *Critique*
Transcendental Aesthetic	Transcendental Analytic	Logic
Transcendental Logic	Transcendental Aesthetic	Analytic
Analytic	Transcendental Logic	Of Principles
Of Concepts	Analytic of Concepts	Of Concepts
Of Principles	Analytic of Principles	
		"Aesthetic"
Dialectic	Dialectic	Dialectic

The first column, showing the actual scheme of the *Critique of Pure Reason*, gives a division according to the cognitive faculties involved, viz., sensibility, understanding, and reason. The second, showing the scheme as he remembered it in 1787, is a division according to the objects of knowledge, with the Analytic including the Aesthetic because both are involved in the knowledge of phenomena and both are set apart from the Dialectic, which deals with alleged knowledge of noumena. In one respect, the division in the second column represents the more important division of the material as a critical ontology[25] of two realms, one theoretically valid and one theoretically invalid, the second to be given practical validity in the second *Critique*.[26]

§ 8. THE POLEMICS OF THE PREFACE

I have suggested that the reviews of Kant's earlier works contributed to his decision to write the *Critique of Practical Reason*. Certainly, they are among the first things he takes up, and large parts of the book can be interpreted as responses to the criticisms mentioned in the Preface. Kant's views were not discernibly modified by any criticisms; the parts of the *Critique of Pure Reason* which were surrendered when he came to the second were not surrendered because of any external criticism of those parts but because of his own development and self-criticism. There was little dialectical play between Kant and his critics. Yet their statements were vivid in his mind when he set about to write this book, and it will be worthwhile to consider them, if not as philosophically significant, yet as stimuli to some of the particular turns of his mental operations in 1787.

Immanuel Kant was not a contentious man,[27] and in his long career of over forty years few of his works can properly be called "polemical." Yet he was bent upon making himself understood and was repeatedly disappointed to discover how little he had succeeded in his

---

[25] *Critique of Pure Reason*, A 247 = B 303: the proud name of "Ontology" must give way to that of mere "Analytic." But Analytic is called "Ontology" in *Fortschritte der Metaphysik*, XX, 260.

[26] For the meaning of "Analytic" and the reasons for the parts of the Analytic being taken in an order the reverse of that in the first *Critique*, see chap. v, §§ 1 and 2. On the concept of an "aesthetic" of practical reason see chap. xii, §§ 1 and 2. On the term "dialectic" and the structure of the Dialectic of Pure Practical Reason, see chap. xiii, §§ 1 and 2.

[27] At least, this seems to have been his estimate of himself (cf. letter to Reinhold, December 28 and 31, 1787 [X, 514]). His biographers frequently remarked on his dislike of contradiction and argument, though he valued stimulating interchange of different opinions. But as he grew older, they said, he became less and less able to enter sympathetically into any views not his own.

efforts. We today ought to have a certain sympathy for those poor men who were given the task of writing the first reviews of his difficult books, which were far more puzzling then than now, when we have the benefit of the work of generations of expositors, critics, and commentators. Kant himself, however, usually responded to the reviewers, not with the sympathy that can be expected from few authors but with impatience and occasionally with justified contempt. He was held back from more frequent explicit replies only by the importunities of his friends, who saw better uses for his time and who took most of the polemical burdens on their own shoulders.[28]

But inasmuch as one could not go forward in the critical philosophy without understanding what had already been accomplished, Kant in the *Critique of Practical Reason* (7 [92]) and in other works felt constrained, from time to time, to "re-examine" the "concepts and principles of pure speculative reason" which, he learned from the reviews, had been misinterpreted. Granting the need for answers to them, he spoke of the *Critique* as being "better than all controversies with [his reviewers] Feder and Abel."[29] Yet the reviews of the *Foundations* and the rankling he continued to feel at the Garve-Feder review of the *Critique of Pure Reason* certainly affected the work he did in 1787; and it is possible to show in detail what these effects were and to discover their causes.

The *Critique*, though born in controversy, is not, however, explicitly polemical after the Preface, with the exception of one passage; it is dialectical (in a non-technical sense), in that it presents a struggle among opposing ideas, but not forensic, as a struggle between opposing men. The Preface, however, is in large part polemical, for he pays personal attention to his reviewers; and the objections to which he replies and the way in which he replies to them indicate the situation which underlay the decision to write the *Critique* and which are responsible for some of the major parts of the book.

The polemical issues referred to in the Preface may be divided into two kinds. The first concerns the criticisms repeatedly made which permitted no specific answer because of their blanket character. Such were the criticisms of those who boasted of knowledge that Kant had

---

[28] Cf. letters from Biester, June 11, 1786; from Schütz, March 23, 1787; and from Bering, May 28, 1787 (X, 457, 480, 488); also *Critique of Pure Reason*, B xliv.

[29] To Schütz, June 25, 1787 (X, 490). Schütz had written on March 23: "It is fine that you hold yourself back from refutations, and plan to follow your own path undisturbed" (X, 480). Cf. also the letter to Reinhold accompanying the gift of the book, December 28 and 31, 1787 (X, 514).

declared and, he believed, proved to be impossible.[30] To this class belong also the criticisms by those who could not believe that ethics required so subtle a foundation as Kant had supplied,[31] who charged unspecified inconsistencies in the critical philosophy, who blamed Kant for inventing "a new language" with "far too frequent use of abstract terminology" in which to enunciate "in incomprehensible language long-known things as if they were new."[32]

A second group of criticisms dealt with in the Preface provide a more specific target and often show more philosophical acumen. They concern issues which Kant mentions in the Preface, but the full answer to all of them except the last is found only in the body of the *Critique* itself. There are four such criticisms, and we shall deal briefly with each.

a) The alleged inconsistency involved in "the denial of the reality of the supersensible use of the categories in speculation" and the assertion of their validity "in respect to the objects of pure practical reason" (5 [90]). This "most weighty of the criticisms of the *Critique* [*of Pure Reason*]" (6 [91]), involving also the questioning of the distinction between the noumenal and phenomenal selves, was made by H. A. Pistorius, in his review[33] of the *Foundations* and of Schultz's *Erläuterungen über des Herrn Prof. Kants Kritik der reinen Vernunft*.[34] It is like-

[30] "They wish to prove; very well, let them prove, and the critical philosophy will lay down its weapons before them as victors" (5 [89]). The allusion is to Horace *Satires* 1. 1. 19. This is an echo of the challenge to Garve and Feder in *Prolegomena*, IV, 278, 368 (Beck, 25, 117). Certain turns of phrase here and in the review of J. A. H. Ulrich's *Eleuthereologie* (VIII, 453–60) published by Kraus on the basis of extensive notes prepared by Kant lead me to conjecture that Ulrich may have been one of the targets of this paragraph, though the *Eleuthereologie* was apparently (but not certainly) published too late for Kant to have read it when writing the Preface. We must remember, however, that Kant saw many books before publication and that he undoubtedly knew Ulrich's somewhat similar *Institutiones logicae et metaphysicae* of 1785 (cf. Ulrich's letter to Kant, April 21, 1785 [X, 402–3]). Vaihinger, the discoverer of the Kantian provenance of the Kraus review of Ulrich's book, studied this controversy but did not suggest that Ulrich may already have been in Kant's mind as an opponent to be answered in the Preface (cf. Hans Vaihinger, "Ein unbekannter Aufsatz Kants über die Freiheit," *Philosophische Monatshefte*, XVI [1880], 192–209).

[31] These criticisms were reported to Kant, but not indorsed, by Jenisch in his letter of May 14, 1787 (X, 485–87); they seem to be alluded to in the paragraph beginning on Ak. 8 (93) of the *Critique*.

[32] *Critique of Practical Reason*, 10 (96), and the important footnote on "formula" at *ibid.*, 8 n. (93 n.), directed against G. A. Tittel, *Über Herrn Kants Moralreform* (Frankfort and Leipzig, 1786). Cf. also *Critique of Pure Reason*, A 831 = B 859, and *Critique of Practical Reason*, 105 (200).

[33] *Allgemeine deutsche Bibliothek*, LXVI (1786), 447–63.

[34] *Ibid.*, pp. 92 ff.

wise present, in less pointed form, in the criticisms by J. F. Flatt.[35] Kant refers to Pistorius as "truth-loving and acute, and therefore worthy of respect,"[36] and it is to his criticism that it is not permissible to apply the categories to the noumenal that Kant makes the statement quoted earlier: "Only a detailed *Critique of Practical Reason* can set aside all these misconceptions" (6–7 [91–92]). Few other topics occupy a larger part of the *Critique* proper. It is the central theme of Section II of chapter i of the Analytic, "Of the Right of Pure Reason to an Extension in Its Practical Use Which Was Not Possible to It in Its Theoretical Use."[37]

b) The alleged circularity in the relationship of freedom and the moral law in the *Foundations*. It had been said by Flatt[38] that each was used to prove the other and that this was a vicious circle. Kant mentions and replies to this in a very concise and effective manner in the Preface (4 n. [88 n.]), and the full refutation of it occupies the main

---

[35] *Tübinger gelehrte Anzeigen,* May 13, 1786. Kant returned to deal with Flatt, one of the critics of whom he was most contemptuous, in *Metaphysik der Sitten,* VI, 207.

[36] *Critique of Practical Reason,* 8 (94). This "truth-loving critic" is even more fulsomely praised in *Opus postumum,* XXI, 416. Contrast with the contempt for Flatt in *Critique,* 14 (100).

[37] Pistorius' review must have been known to Kant when he wrote the Preface to the second edition of the *Critique of Pure Reason.* But he said there (B, xli) that he made no changes after the first chapter of the Dialectic "because I have not found among competent and impartial critics any misapprehension of the remaining sections." Yet Pistorius' questions did concern the status of the Ideas and the noumena-phenomena distinction. I do not know what may have been Kant's intentions with respect to the Pistorius criticism in April, 1787. Perhaps the review by Pistorius was in part responsible for his rewriting the section on the Paralogisms, though credit for this is generally given to the Garve-Feder review, with its accusations of idealism. Whatever the cause, only a few weeks later he found that the understanding of the Dialectic as a whole was so inadequate that it had to be explained again in the second *Critique.* It may be worth noting that Kant praises Pistorius both times (cf. n. 36 above) in the context of criticism (*c*) instead of (*a*).

[38] Kant himself had mentioned the apparent circle in the argument (*Foundations of the Metaphysics of Morals* 450 [69]), and he explained it again to Kiesewetter (letter of April 20, 1790 [XI, 155]). But in the *Foundations* he pointed out a somewhat different route of escape. There he emphasized that there is in the experience of thought itself an awareness of free spontaneity, and this is independent of the question of the validity of the moral law. Even if one denied the reality of freedom in words, he would be expressing his freedom as the precondition for his argument's having any legitimate claim to validity. This argument is repeated in the review of Schulz's *Sittenlehre* (VIII, 13) but is absent from the second *Critique.* The thought was an enduring one, however, and the term "autonomy" is extended finally to cover theoretical as well as practical reason in *Opus postumum,* XXI, 93, 100.

portion of Section I of chapter i of the Analytic, "Of the Deduction of the Fundamental Principles of Pure Practical Reason."

c) The error, alleged again by Pistorius, that "the concept of the good was not established before the moral principle."[39] This is admitted, and it is defended in chapter ii of the Analytic.

d) The alleged discovery that "there can be no a priori knowledge at all" (12 [97]). This was the view of Feder,[40] who had revised the review submitted by Garve of the *Critique of Pure Reason*. By this time, of course, Kant knew to what extent Feder was guilty and Garve was innocent of the worst features of that review, to the stimulus of which we owe so much of the *Prolegomena*. So Kant allowed himself to indulge in bitterness and irony in dealing with this alleged discovery.[41]

In reply to this, Kant takes the following course. He first shows that it is inconsistent, for what we know by reason is a priori, and to prove that we have no a priori knowledge would be to prove by reason that reason is not valid. Next he criticizes the Humean conception[42] of causation, on the ground that its substitution of common human consent for the a priori principle is inexplicable if the concept is "fundamentally false and a mere delusion of thought," which he believes is the correct inference to be drawn from Hume's premises. But, third, he exculpates Hume from the absurdity of the doctrine of attempting to prove by reason that there is no reason, by pointing out that Hume, unlike the unnamed critic Feder, did not make his empiricism so universal as to include mathematics in his strictures. Mathematics escaped, however, only because of Hume's error in regarding mathematical

39 *Critique of Practical Reason*, 8–9 (94–95); cf. 62–64 (154–55).

40 *Über Raum und Caussalität* [*sic*] *zur Prüfung der Kantischen Philosophie* (Göttingen, 1787). Kant identifies Feder as his target in the letter to Schütz, June 25, 1787 (X, 490).

41 With his characteristic and unvarying admiration for Hume, Kant first distinguished between the genius who made the original discovery and the epigone who reduced it, in his opinion, to an absurdity, and he reserved his scorn for the latter. The note at the end of the passage (13 n. [100 n.]) is a defense against mislabeling Hume a "genuine empiricist"; but in this defense Kant could not resist making one more indirect rejoinder to Feder's having labeled *him* an idealist (cf. the comparable footnote in *Prolegomena*, IV, 375 n. [Beck, 124 n.]). The allusion to William Cheselden (1688–1752) refers to the physician who cured a blind man and whose report on his adjustment to seeing was repeated by Herder (*Vierter Wald* [1769], *Werke* [Suphan ed.], IV, 49) and thus, probably, passed on to Kant.

42 I see no reason to think that Tetens was the opponent whom Kant had in mind here, as asserted by Cay von Brockdorff, *Die deutsche Aufklärungsphilosophie* (Munich, 1926), p. 105.

judgments as analytic. But though Hume was wrong in holding them to be analytic,[43] what is important here is that he correctly held them to be a priori and thus maintained an internal standard of criticism for other forms of knowledge. Genuine empiricism is not just skeptical of philosophical speculation but would destroy both mathematics and morality, and on these two counts it is not, according to Kant, to be taken seriously, since here a philosophical theory, itself speculative, directly collides with the "highest evidence."

A lesser man might have spent his limited time in extended debate with his critics or (at his own expense) have ignored their objections and misunderstandings. But it is one of the marks of Kant's greatness that he was able to deal systematically, if not sympathetically, with other men's errors and misunderstandings and out of the bits and pieces of scholarly journalism to take materials to be built into the permanent edifice of philosophy. It is to this aspect of his talent that we owe much of the *Critique of Practical Reason*. The signs of it are scattered throughout his work, but they are concentrated here in the Preface.

[43] In *Enquiry concerning Human Understanding*, Sec. VII. Elsewhere (*Critique of Practical Reason* [53 (143)]) Kant says Hume's views lead "inevitably to skepticism" even with respect to mathematics. This might refer to Hume's actual, though passing, skepticism of geometry in the *Treatise*, while the remark in the Preface refers to the *Enquiry*. But it is more likely that the judgment does not pretend to state a historical fact, but means only that empiricism, once on the skeptical path, stops neither at the "chief branches of knowledge" nor at "ordinary reason," which was the refuge of the common-sense philosophers, who wished to be skeptical of rationalistic metaphysics while remaining credulous of other kinds of knowledge that would be destroyed in a genuine and thoroughgoing skepticism.

Part II

V

Survey of the Analytic of Practical Reason

Throughout the *Critique*, Kant uses the word "analytic" as though it were entirely familiar to his readers. But we must refer back to the first *Critique* if we are to understand precisely what he means by this word and why he chose this name.

General logic, he there tells us, contains an analysis or resolution of the formal procedure of understanding and reason into their elements and exhibits them as principles of a logical criticism of knowledge; as general logic, it entirely abstracts from all content of our judgments and concepts and deals exclusively with their formal relations.[1] Transcendental logic, on the other hand, does not disregard the important distinction between a priori and a posteriori knowledge and is concerned with the grounding and structure of concepts and judgments known a priori. Transcendental logic, therefore, contains only rules of the a priori thought of objects, and hence it excludes other concepts and judgments which are formally identical with them as respects their logical interrelations but which, as regards their cognitive content, are drawn from experience.[2] The analytical part of transcendental logic resolves the a priori or "transcendental" operations of understanding and reason into their elements, and thus it serves as the standard of criticism for all our knowledge of objects, including even empirical knowledge. The transcendental analytic, therefore, is a "logic of truth" and not, like the analytical part of general logic, a logic of mere formal consistency. Transcendental analytic consists in the "dissection of our a priori knowledge that pure understanding of itself yields"; the concepts and principles which it exhibits must be pure and not empirical, intellectual and not intuitive, simple and not composite, fundamental and not derivative, systematically complete and not rhapsodically aggregated.[3]

[1] *Critique of Pure Reason*, A 60 = B 84.

[2] *Ibid.*, A 56 = B 60.   [3] *Ibid.*, A 64 = B 89.

Except that it is practical reason and not understanding or theoretical reason that is here under examnniation, the term "analytic" has the same meaning in the present *Critique*. The analytic is the "rule of truth" in practical philosophy, and its most important tasks are the differentiation between the (empirical) doctrine of happiness and the (pure) doctrine of morality (92 [186]) and the systematic exposition of the a priori principles and concepts of the latter.

§ 2. THE STRUCTURE OF THE ANALYTIC

Kant says: "We begin with principles and proceed to concepts, and only then, if possible, go on to the senses, while in the study of speculative reason we had to start from the senses and end with principles" (16 [102]; 90 [184]). There are two points to be examined here: the causes of the reversal of the order of the parts of the Analytic, and the presence or absence of an Aesthetic.

a) *The order of the parts.*—Two slightly different reasons are given for the reversal of the order: (i) Since we are here dealing with a will and not with knowledge of objects, the determination of the will by principles and not by concepts of objects must first be established (16 [102]). This follows from the definition of will. (ii) It is easy to establish the principles, since there is in every natural human consciousness a recognition of the principle as a law completely a priori and independent of the senses (91 [185]), and therefore independent of concepts of objects and of the givenness of objects to the senses.

The concepts of the objects of practical reason (either empirical, as the concept of the object of some specific desire, or the pure concepts of the objects of a pure practical reason, which, as we shall see, are the moral good and evil) cannot be given prior to, or independently of, this principle. If it were, either we should have no a priori knowledge of good and evil (as we have no a priori knowledge of empirical objects of desire or of the empirical characteristics of objects of empirical knowledge), or else we should have to have a moral sense, as a kind of a priori intuition of moral value. But Kant asserts that the principle is the prius of the concept, for the concept can be drawn only from a principle or from an intuition like that of the alleged moral sense; and he denies the cognitive validity of the so-called moral sense.[4] The relation of the principle to the concept is accordingly compared with that of the major to the minor premise in a syllogism and not to that of generalization to fact of observation (90 [184]).

---

[4] *Critique of Practical Reason*, 38–39 (129): Such an intuition would have to be a "feeling for law as such" and would "regard as an object of sensation what can only be thought by reason."

b) An aesthetic of pure practical reason?—Transcendental Aesthetic, in the *Critique of Pure Reason*, has nothing to do with the theory or judgment of beauty but is "a science of all principles of a priori sensibility."[5] It is concerned with intuition, the faculty by which our concepts are brought into relation with their objects. It is a peculiarity of the human intuition that it is always sensible, sensibility being the mode in which we are affected by the objects.[6] Hence the forms of our sensible intuition, which are space and time, are necessary in our knowledge of objects as appearances. A critique of knowledge must contain an analysis of the a priori principles or forms of sensibility, and, since sensibility furnishes objects for our concepts and principles, such an analysis appropriately precedes the Analytic as a part of Transcendental Logic.[7]

Practical reason, however, is not concerned with the relation of knowledge to objects which may be given to us, but with the bringing into existence of objects which are not passively given to us. Hence it is not surprising that there should be nothing in practical reason exactly corresponding to the Transcendental Aesthetic and that anything analogous to it should come after the discussion of the principles and concepts, not before it. So Kant says that, after establishing the principle and the concepts, he will, "if possible, go on to the senses." "Only then could the last chapter [of the Analytic], dealing with the relation of pure practical reason to sensibility and with its necessary influence on it, i.e., the moral feeling which is known a priori, close [the Analytic]" (90 [183]).

There are two things to be noted here: (i) We are concerned not with the effect of objects on the sensibility, since we are not concerned with relating our concepts to given objects as objects of knowledge, but with the effect of reason itself and its principles and concepts upon our sensibility. The problem is that of the subjective determination of the will, the subjective factor being provided by sensibility or feeling and the determining factor by the principles of practical reason. The analogous problem in the *Critique of Pure Reason* is perhaps that of the pure imagination, which represents in the sensibility the synthetic operations of the understanding. (ii) The mode of sensibility which is

[5] *Critique of Pure Reason*, A 21 = B 35.

[6] *Ibid.*, A 19 = B 33.

[7] We have noted above that in the *Critique of Pure Reason* the Aesthetic precedes and is not a part of the Logic, of which the Analytic is the first part, whereas in the *Critique of Practical Reason* the part analogous to Aesthetic is made a part of Analytic but is still separated from the Logic, which is only a subdivision of the Analytic (cf. chap. iv, § 7).

relevant here is not sensation, referred to outer objects, but feeling, which is without cognitive function.

The concepts of pure theoretical reason do not apply directly to individual sensuous representations. That which mediates between them and makes the application of the categories to experience possible is the schema of the concepts. There is something analogous to this mediating function in pure practical reason in what Kant calls the "type of pure practical judgment." The analogy between the typic and the proper function of an aesthetic is perhaps closer than that between the chapter on incentives and the Aesthetic of the first *Critique*. But the closest analogy is between the discussion of typic and the discussion of the schematism; and, since Kant himself uses the word "aesthetic" to refer to the material of chapter iii instead of that at the end of chapter ii of the Analytic, we shall follow his suggestion.

§ 3. THE PROBLEMS OF THE ANALYTIC

If morality is not to be declared "a vain and chimerical notion," Kant must solve three problems. They are as follows:

I. To formulate the law the knowledge of which could, independently of impulse, be a motive for action.

II. To prove that pure reason can be practical, i.e., the conception of the law formulated in answer to Problem I can indeed be a motive for action.

III. To bring to light, in the nature of a rational being in general and in man as a rational being sensuously affected, those factors which make it possible that knowledge of this law can in fact be a motive for action.

Kant's solutions to these problems constitute the main body of the Analytic. Since the problems are not isolated from one another, he attacks first one and then another, using partial solutions to the one in order to gain a foothold in approaching the others, in such apparent confusion that the entire Analytic has sometimes seemed to be a lifting by transcendental boot-straps. But this apparent confusion is a consequence of the actual relations existing among the problems; each one is so intimately related to the others that a full answer to any one implicitly contains answers to all of them. Roughly speaking, however, chapter i gives his solution to Problems I and II, though chapter ii continues the solution of Problem I, reformulated as a question concerning what concepts can legitimately enter into a law the knowledge of which is to be a motive for action. Chapter iii constitutes the main answer to Problem III.

While it is hazardous to press analogies between the first and second

Critique's further than Kant himself, the great analogizer, carried them,[8] it is interesting to observe a parallelism that Kant does not point out between these three problems and those of the Analytic of the first *Critique*. We shall find that every one of the three principal questions has its counterpart in clearly separated problems of the first *Critique*.

Problem I is a problem formally like that of the Metaphysical Deduction of the Categories, i.e., that part of the Analytic which shows what the pure concepts of the understanding are and hence indirectly determines the a priori principles of understanding and the Ideas of reason. Here there is likewise a "metaphysical deduction" of the principle of pure practical reason, i.e., a specific a priori definition of it and of its concepts.

Problem II is a problem formally like that of the objective Transcendental Deduction of the Categories, namely, the problem of showing that the categories which are discovered in answering Problem I do have objective validity. In the second *Critique*, there is a "transcendental deduction" which shows that pure reason can be practical, not merely what its law would be if it were practical.

Problem III has some resemblances to that of the so-called Subjective Deduction of the Categories in the first edition of the *Critique of Pure Reason*, i.e., to show what mental operations are necessary if pure concepts are to be applied in experience. I have already pointed out that this problem might also be compared with that of the schematism. But, inasmuch as Kant compares it with the problem of the Transcendental Aesthetic, it is perhaps well to maintain this analogy.

§ 4. DIVISION OF THE COMMENTARY ON THE ANALYTIC

In this commentary we wish to separate out the various strands of Kant's arguments and to present his conclusions as specific answers to these specific problems. The Commentary on the Analytic is therefore divided as follows:

Problem I.—Chapters vi and vii present an analytic of practical reason in general and, more specifically, an analytic of an empirically affected practical reason, in order to show the characteristics of its maxims and their relation to moral laws. These chapters are primarily commentary on chapter i, §§ 1–6, of the Analytic.

Chapter viii gives the derivation of the one principle of pure practical reason and is, accordingly, entitled "The 'Metaphysical Deduction' of the Moral Law." This chapter continues the commentary on §§ 1–6, and moves forward into §§ 7 and 8.

Chapter ix, "Pure Practical Concepts and Judgment," is, in sub-

---

8 Cf. the remark at *Critique of Practical Reason*, 91 (184).

stance, a continuation of the "metaphysical deduction," though it interrupts the serial movement of the analysis of the argument as Kant gives it, by being devoted to an interpretation of chapter ii of the Analytic. The reasons for this interruption will be made clear in chapter ix.

Problem II.—Chapter x discusses Kant's solution to this problem and is accordingly entitled "The 'Transcendental Deduction' of the Principle of Pure Practical Reason." It is commentary on §§ 8 and 9 of chapter i and on the section entitled "On the Deduction of the Principles of Pure Practical Reason."

Chapter xi, "Freedom," examines Kant's theories on this concept, as expounded here and in other places. Because this concept is used so extensively here and in most of his other books, it is not feasible to give exclusive attention to the treatment in any specific section of the *Critique of Practical Reason;* but chapter xi deals fully with two parts of the Analytic, namely, "Of the Right of Pure Reason to an Extension in Its Practical Use . . ." and "Critical Examination of the Analytic of Pure Practical Reason."

Problem III.—Chapter xii, following the suggestion made by Kant, is entitled "The 'Aesthetic' of Pure Practical Reason" and is a commentary on chapter iii of the Analytic and on the Methodology.

§ 5. SUMMARY OF CHAPTER I, §§ 1–8

We have set out three problems of the Analytic but pointed out that these problems are so intimately entwined that Kant does not take up and finish one and then move, in stately fashion, to the next. In almost every section he is concentrating on one but keeping the others in mind, and he constantly directs his readers' attention to the ramification of each answer into the spheres of the others. Any attempt to isolate the problems, therefore, involves some artificiality, an artificiality that must jeopardize the exegetical work before us unless the reader is prepared to see the context from which the artificial abstractions have to be drawn for the sake of microscopic examination. To aid in this, I give now, in conclusion, a brief running account of Kant's exposition in its printed form.

"Practical propositions" are those propositions the knowledge of which plays a part in determining the will to make a specific choice among possible actions. They are called "principles" if they are general, i.e., if they express a general determination of the will and if other practical propositions, called "rules," are subsumable under them or derived from them in their application to specific circumstances. A principle is called a "maxim" if the motive which is involved in obedience to it is a motive only for the person who actually embraces this maxim as expressing his own policy in life. A principle is an "objective law," however, if the motive which it formulates and to which it gives expression is recognized as proper to the will of every rational being.

Every principle to some extent constrains the person who acknowledges it. Even if my principle is a mere maxim that holds only for myself, such as the maxim of not allowing any wrong done me to go unavenged, it constrains me, at least sometimes, to bring my momentary impulses (e.g., fear) into line with this general purpose or determination of the will. Even such a principle, therefore, can give rise to rules which determine what I, with this motive, ought to do and would do if I (*a*) had this policy and (*b*) were completely rational in the choice of actions with respect to this policy. Such rules are called "imperatives" for a being who, like man, does not always willingly and spontaneously do what is prescribed by reason as necessary for the carrying-out of the purpose. It is only by reasoning that we know what we ought to do in order to carry out the policy expressed in the maxim, but no one is so rational that he does what he ought without more or less frequent conflict with his inclinations.

If a principle is really a maxim, so that the motive for action in accordance with it is some subjective condition, the corresponding imperative, which tells us what a reasonable man would do in order to satisfy this desire if he had it, is a "hypothetical imperative." It commands, or rather counsels, a man only if he has the desire in question. The conative, dynamic factor in obedience to such an imperative is desire or impulse; the cognitive factor is a theoretical cognition or some belief about the relation of means to end.

A law, on the other hand, such as "lying is wrong," is not, at least prima facie, addressed just to a man who wishes for honor or some other specific goal. The imperative which expresses this law to a man who does not obey it by nature is a categorical imperative. It does not tell us to avoid lying if we would obtain a good reputation; it tells us not to lie, period. It seems to be addressed to rational beings generally, not just to those men having specific desires that can be satisfied through obedience to it.

All principles based on any object of desire apply only to those who actually have the desire. All such principles are mere maxims, not laws. They cannot be laws even for those beings who do have the desire in question, such as the desire felt by all men for their own happiness. A law must have objective necessity, recognized by reason; but the presence or absence of a specific desire can be known only empirically. Furthermore, a law must give rise to imperatives which are definite and specific, yet universal in application; but the diversity of desires is so great that even if they are all subsumed under the general desire for happiness, they do not issue forth in anything more than general counsels, proverbs, and good advice which is sensitive to the variety of men and circumstance.

Every principle or rule which presupposes, for its application, some specific desire falls under the general principle of self-love or the desire for one's own happiness; for a state of happiness is one in which there is continuous satisfaction of all desires. Those philosophers who make the desire for happiness the proper motive for morality cannot derive from it any universal precepts, for each man's conception of happiness differs from that of others, and any one man's conception varies from time to time according to the state of his specific desires. No rule derived from the desire for happiness is more than a hypothetical imperative, and it therefore lacks the a priori necessity characteristic of law.

It follows from this that if a rational being regards his maxims as universal laws, as he does when he says that some action that he does is the kind of action that all men (or other rational beings) should do, it cannot be by virtue of the material of the maxim, which refers to the object or the purpose of his will. This is true even if the maxim should fortunately, in a person of benevolent or sympathetic disposition, be a desire for the general welfare or the happiness of others. If the material or goal of desire is presupposed in a principle, whatever it may be, there is no universality in the principle, and the corresponding imperative is not categorical.

Besides the material of the maxim, however, there is only its form. The form of the maxim as expressed in an imperative is "ought," just as the form of every theoretical proposition is some mode of "is." As form, it is independent of any specific desire, which constitutes the content of specific maxims. If we abstract from an imperative all content by virtue of which it is addressed to a person motivated by a specific subjective desire, we are left with only the form, the skeletal "ought." What is derivable from this, unlike what is derivable from any specific content, is addressed to all rational beings who act, and the rules derived from it are fitted to be universal in application. That is, the form of a maxim and not its content determines whether it is a law or a mere maxim.

If a principle is a law, its form must be such that it applies to all rational beings, and the corresponding imperative must be directed to all rational beings who do not, by nature, observe the law automatically. Thus only a law can generate a categorical imperative. The categorical imperative tells a partially rational being to act on a maxim that a wholly rational being would act upon without being commanded to do so. If a rational being can decide upon his actions under a maxim simply because the maxim is a law valid for all rational beings, this being can obey a categorical imperative, and pure reason can be practical.

Assuming that a person can obey a categorical imperative, Kant shows that the will of this person must be free in the strict, transcendental sense. That is, it cannot be entirely determined by the person's conception of his sensuous impulses, for this would make his actions only an effect of natural phenomena. Only reason can present the conception of a universal law as a motive, and of a being that acts upon this motive we say that his will is "free."

Conversely, if we assume that the will is free from the mechanism of nature, the will must be determined by the form and not by the content of the maxim or law. It must be determined by some conception of some law, for otherwise it would not be will but mere caprice. And if it were determined by the content, i.e., what the law held before the person as a way of satisfying one of his desires, the will would not be free from the mechanism of empirical nature.

Hence the concept of freedom and that of a universal practical law reciprocally imply each other. We are not directly aware of freedom, but we are directly aware of the binding quality of a universal law, for we have it presented to us in our consciousness of the moral law. The moral law thus leads us inevitably to assert the existence of freedom; it is the *ratio cognoscendi* of freedom, while freedom is the *ratio essendi* of the moral law.

The moral law is this: A purely rational being acts only on maxims that he would will to be maxims for all rational beings, i.e., only on maxims that could be willed to be principles universally binding on all such beings. For men, who are not completely rational, this is expressed in the categorical imperative: "So act that the maxim of your will could always hold at the same time as the principle for giving universal law."

Only pure reason could be the source of such a law and imperative. Reason discovering sensuous motives and the laws of nature by which they might be managed or satisfied would not be able to formulate any laws having the universality and necessity that we find in the moral obligation we experience. This law is not derived from any observation of empirical fact; it is not a theoretical law of what is. It is a practical law that pure reason itself prescribes as the ground of its own actions. Thus pure practical reason, as the source of its own law, is autonomous or self-legislating in a way in which an empirically conditioned practical reason could not be.

The principles of the empirically affected will are based upon the

contingent fact that certain desires are felt and upon our knowledge of
the way in which they may be satisfied in the course of nature. They
are not, therefore, products of the autonomous lawgiving of reason,
and they are not, consequently, absolutely binding or obligatory. All
moral systems except the one based upon pure reason as providing the
motive are heteronomous and are unable to account for the absolute,
unconditional, universal, and necessary constraint that we experience
in moral obligation. Either we must explain away these characteristics
of moral obligation by showing them to be illusory products of a psychological mechanism, or we must accept the thesis that pure reason
can be practical, i.e., can give a law the knowledge of which can and
should be a sufficient motive for action.

VI

The Analytic of Empirical Practical Reason
I. Formal Considerations; Commentary
on Section 1

§ 1. EMPIRICAL PRACTICAL REASON

"Practical reason" and "will" generally, for Kant, mean the same thing. We have already discussed in chapter iii this identification of the two concepts. It suffices, therefore, to remind ourselves here that reason in its logical use is the faculty of drawing inferences and of systematizing knowledge, of finding a "wherefore" for every "therefore," and that in its real use it posits certain a priori synthetic propositions or principles which are supposed to state the unconditioned conditions for all that is found in experience. If the then-clause in an inference is a statement that a certain action should be done or an imperative or a decision to do it, the reasoning that leads to this conclusion is an inference of practical reason. Reasoning as thus determinative of an action does what the common man believes his will to do, the will being thought of as an almost palpable organ for decision and execution, often warring with a recalcitrant or weak flesh.[1]

Yet the terms "practical reason" and "will" are not in every respect synonymous; they are so little synonymous that one is, I believe, surprised when he learns that Kant identifies them. There often seems to be something especially *un*reasonable about will, so much so that Schopenhauer could easily see them in ineluctable conflict. If one does not follow Schopenhauer in thinking that there is unceasing opposition be-

[1] Especially in the early parts of the *Critique* but also quite generally elsewhere, Kant uses two words which are ordinarily translated as "will": *Wille* and *Willkür*. Though they are later distinguished and the distinction becomes important, I cannot see much consistency in Kant's choice between them. Roughly speaking, we may surmise that practical reason is *Wille*, and what I have called "the almost palpable organ for decision and execution" is *Willkür*. We shall attempt later (pp. 176 ff.) to clarify the distinction as Kant subsequently drew it; but nothing, I think, is gained by insisting upon it here. The words seem to be meant as synonyms in § 2.

tween them, one can still discern a great difference in the connotations of the two words. "Will" suggests more directly the dynamic impulse involved in action; "practical reason" suggests something cold and deliberate and without any "push." Such difference in connotation must have been present also in Kant's mind, for we have seen how he often speaks of reason as determining the will, as if there were two factors here in opposition to each other.

However little he is justified by his own definitions in speaking in this way, it is easy to understand why he did so. In acts of will, there are two distinguishable factors: a want, which I have called the "dynamic" or "conative" factor, and what we recognize as that which we ought to do, the recognition of which I have called the "cognitive" factor. What I want appears as an incentive, and it speaks to my inclination, impulse, drive, and propensity. What I ought to do in order to achieve what I want is discerned by reason. Reason may discover a rule for what ought to be done if we are to obtain what we want; in this respect, Hume was right in calling reason the slave of the passions; but it is an intelligent slave, which, while serving its master, nevertheless guides, disciplines, and in part controls the master for the master's own best interests. When the conative factor is the condition which makes a specific rule of action relevant to choice, the reasoning involved in formulating or picking out and applying the rule to the specific situation is based on empirically given data of two kinds: the present data (feeling), which indicate the existence of a particular wish or want, and the facts of past experience, which indicate how this wish or want can be satisfied.

Reasoning functioning in this way is called "empirical practical reason." The analytic of empirical practical reason is the study of the fundamental principles and rules of the conduct of reasoning in this concurrence with desire, whereby blind pushing desire is converted into interest. Such a study to be undertaken here has two parts: a study of the formal aspects of such reasoning (in the present chapter) and a study of the dynamic factors and the specific kinds of volitions resulting from them (in the following chapter).

§ 2. PRACTICAL PRINCIPLES

Practical propositions "assert [*aussagen*] an action, through which, as a necessary condition, an object becomes possible."[2] The term "practical proposition" therefore refers to all sorts of rules of action,

---

[2] *Vorlesungen über Logik,* § 32.

such as directions for a construction in geometry, a recipe, a counsel, or any statement of a means to an end. Any proposition which is effective through being entertained in deliberation on action is a practical proposition, even though its content may be the same as that of a theoretical proposition expressing mere knowledge without direction for use.[3] The familar theoretical proposition, "Alcohol causes drunkenness," becomes, when related to a want, a practical proposition, "Drink alcohol" or "Don't drink alcohol," depending upon the direction of the specific want that makes theoretical knowledge of the effect of alcohol practically relevant. Not every theoretical proposition, of course, has a practical counterpart; a practical proposition concerns only what is possible through will, and it states what, in some sense, ought to be done instead of what is done.

The first definition in § 1 is that of a species of practical propositions, viz., principles (*Grundsätze*). "Practical principles," we are told, "are propositions which contain a general determination of the will, having under it several practical rules." Practical propositions are thus of different levels of generality, from a specific command like "Shut the door now" or a general precept like "Do not take unnecessary chances when driving an automobile" to a general policy of life such as "Do not permit any offense to go unavenged." Kant wishes to preserve the name "principle" for those on the third level of generality. This is in keeping with the requirement, implicit in the word *Grundsatz*, that principles must be basic, not derived from more fundamental propositions. In the *Lectures on Logic*,[4] he restricts the word "principle" even further to propositions which are a priori synthetic. At this stage of his exposition in the *Critique of Practical Reason*, however, he is not prepared to assert that there are any practical principles in this strict sense;[5] here he means by "principle" only a proposition expressing a

---

[3] Practical propositions differ from theoretical propositions only in their *Vorstellungsart*, not in their *Inhalt*, with the exception of practical propositions which concern freedom under laws (*Erste Einleitung in die Kritik der Urteilskraft*, XX, 196). The statement above, therefore, is true of "technically practical propositions" but not, according to Kant, of "morally practical propositions." This is not quite correct, however. If we maintain, more successfully than Kant did, the distinction between imperative and law, a morally practical imperative (i.e., the categorical imperative) will correspond to the moral law, which is a theoretical statement about the freedom of rational beings in general.

[4] *Vorlesungen über Logik*, § 34 (IX, 110); cf. also *Critique of Pure Reason*, A 149 = B 188.

[5] They would be laws, and he is not yet in a position to assert that there are any practical laws.

determination of the will which is not regarded as being taken for the sake of some prior commitment or policy.[6]

Fundamental practical propositions, then, are propositions which contain a general determination (*Bestimmung*) of the will, having under it several practical rules. What is a general determination of the will? The word *Bestimmung* is one of Kant's favorite words, and he overuses it. Among the English words needed to translate it are "definition," "determination," "predicate," "decision," and "motive." Here it seems to have the following meanings: a determining cause of an action, in which sense it means "motive" (*Bestimmungsgrund*), and a decision that is taken,[7] by virtue of which the will is not indefinite volition but a specific or determinate volition with a specific direction and goal. The essential point in "general determination of the will," therefore, is that the practical fundamental principle must contain or express a lasting policy or settled disposition of will, not a capricious resolve or a variable rule of thumb.

Also in the first sentence the word "contain" requires brief comment. *Enthalten* is a curious word here; one might say that a proposition "contains" terms, but hardly that it "contains" a determination of the will. One would be tempted to translate *enthalten* as "asserts," but this would disjoin the proposition too much from the determination of the will and make it merely theoretical. I think Kant means this: the practical proposition formulates what the determination of the will is, gives expression to it, and does not merely refer to it. It is a proposition the knowledge or entertainment of which is itself a factor in the will's decision.

The question for an analytic of empirical practical reason is this: What principle or principles exist which do indeed contain general determinations of the will, so far as these determinations can be found in experience? The question for an analytic of practical reason in general is this: Are there any fundamental principles in the strict sense of a priori synthetic propositions which contain a determination of the will; and, if so, what are they?

---

[6] Having formally introduced the word *Grundsatz*, Kant in characteristically regrettable fashion frequently ignores it. (It has been said of Kant that he succeeded in being technical without being precise.) Almost invariably in its stead he uses the word *Prinzip*, which, though declared synonymous with *Grundsatz* (*Vorlesungen über Logik*, § 34), is much looser in meaning. Thus a rule or precept (*Vorschrift*) is often called a *Prinzip*, while a genuine *Grundsatz* is also called *Prinzip* (e.g., in § 4, p. 27 [114]). Where necessary for the sake of clarity, I shall refer to *Grundsatz* in the strict sense as a "fundamental principle," even though this is strictly pleonastic.

[7] For example, *Critique of Practical Reason*, 90, four lines from end of page (184, l. 18).

§ 3. RULES

Kant gives no formal definition of "rule," and his usage is highly variable. Sometimes it means "law,"[8] sometimes "imperative,"[9] and sometimes merely a precept or common maxim which guides us in dubious cases—the kind of rule that serves as a "go-cart for the stupid" who do not trust themselves to act wisely in the complexity of particular cases and who therefore fall back upon some simple standard commonplace.[10]

In the Remark on § 1, however, he shows us that he means a rule to be concerned with the empirical contingent character of action in specific situations, given the general determination expressed in the principles. Rules are thus distinguished from fundamental principles which express an actual policy of life (maxims) and from fundamental principles (if there are any) which are universally valid.[11] Rules express what is, on the average, right under a general principle, but they do not hold necessarily and without exception. They require healthy common sense and good judgment for their wise application, and they cannot be applied automatically by appeal to a general policy.[12]

Kant does not say that the rules fall directly under the principles, as if they were logically contained in them. They are contained, he says, in the general determination of the will, not in the principle. Thus rules may be identical when principles are different, and different when principles are identical; two men can aim at the same end and achieve it by following different rules. It is important to note that Kant must insist upon this loose relationship between rule and principle; otherwise he could not distinguish, within a single type of action, those cases of it that are moral from those that are merely legal. Precisely this important loose relationship is what is overlooked in some of the most common criticisms of Kant's ethics, those which insist that uniformity in moral actions is overemphasized by Kant.

Kant is not asserting the universal applicability of any rules. The uni-

---

[8] *Ibid.*, 31 (119). They are confused also in the first *Critique;* cf. Paton, *Kant's Metaphysic of Experience,* I, 493.

[9] *Critique of Practical Reason,* 20, second paragraph (106).

[10] Reflexionen 5235–8; cf. *Critique of Pure Reason,* A 134 = B 173.

[11] *Foundations of the Metaphysics of Morals,* 389 (4), distinguishes rule from law by reference to the empirical conditions involved in the former. But the proper dichotomy is between rule and principle, and under principles it is necessary to distinguish laws from mere maxims; then rules fall under both maxims and laws.

[12] The same is true of rules of theoretical judgment (cf. *Critique of Pure Reason,* A 133 = B 172).

versality he insists upon is not that of a rule but that of a principle, which permits latitude in the choice of rule. But his failure to abide by his terminological distinction between "rule" and "principle" and his tendency to regulate his own life by "maxims" (really rules, as described by his acquaintances who wrote biographies of him) perhaps led him into the error of sometimes thinking of rules as valid without regard to circumstances, as in *On an Alleged Right To Lie from Altruistic Motives* written in reply to Benjamin Constant.[13]

A rule is always a "product of reason," for only reason (as the faculty of thought in general, not as one of the three cognitive faculties) can give us the knowledge of the relation of the means to an end which is expressed in a rule. Because a rule has a cognitive component that is invariant with respect to the purposes which may be served by using the knowledge it expresses, Kant calls a rule for the use of a means to an arbitrary end a "technical principle" (*Prinzip;* should, of course, be *Satz*) and not a practical principle.[14] A technical rule is *objectively valid* as a statement of what ought to be done by a rational being who has the general determination under which the rule falls. But it is *subjectively practical,* i.e., actually relevant in the determination of behavior only for a being who has the general determination in question. We may therefore properly call rules which prescribe means to ends "conditional rules," even though they embody knowledge independent of the subjective condition of its use.

We cannot answer the general question, "What are the conditional rules of an empirical practical reason?" The answer would be too compendious to state: it would include all practical art, all applied science, and all knowledge of the ways of the world. But we must ask, in an analytic of practical reason generally, "Are there any unconditional practical rules which follow directly from unconditional principles?" And the answer to this question would have to be given in an analytic of pure practical reason.

§ 4. MAXIMS

Practical principles are then classified as maxims or as laws, as subjective or objective. Kant's formulation of this division is peculiar, how-

---

[13] Recent studies have convincingly shown the relevance of circumstances to rules in Kant's ethics; cf. especially H. J. Paton, "An Alleged Right To Lie: A Problem in Kantian Ethics," *Kant-Studien,* XLV (1954), 190–203, and "Kant on Friendship," *Proceedings of the British Academy,* XLII (1956), 45–66; Marcus G. Singer, "The Categorical Imperative," *Philosophical Review,* LXIII (1954), 577–91; and W. I. Matson, "Kant as Casuist," *Journal of Philosophy,* LI (1954), 855–90.

[14] *Critique of Practical Reason,* 26 n. (113 n.). In *Critique of Judgment,* Introduction, I, they are called "technically practical" as distinct from "morally practical."

ever, because the *principium divisionis* is not whether the principle itself is regarded as objective or subjective but whether the *condition* is valid for the individual only, or for every rational being. And, furthermore, it is a logically faulty division, because "maxim" is broader than "law" and, in fact, includes "law" as one of its species. We must examine each of these peculiarities.

What is meant by "condition" (*Bedingung*)? Most simply, we can say that it means the same as "determination" (*Bestimmung*) in the sense of a general setting of the will.[15] But why, then, in this paragraph setting forth the formal definitions, where precision and elegance are called for, did not Kant repeat the word "determination"? The reason lies in his logical terminology. It was his practice to call the major premise in a syllogism of the first figure a *principle* (sometimes a rule), and its middle term (the subject of the principle) he called the *condition*.[16] In the light of this usage, we can say that "condition" means that which is involved in the maxim as the general determination of the will, and thus it becomes the middle term in a practical syllogism:

To avenge a wrong is always my purpose—Maxim or principle.
To tell this lie would avenge a wrong—Rule.
Therefore, I purpose to tell this lie—Decision.[17]

"To avenge a wrong" is the condition, and it may be held only by myself or ascribed to all rational beings.

I turn now to the relation between maxim and law. The term "maxim," like "condition," is also taken from logic, deriving from *sententia maxima*, the name of the first major premise in a polysyllogism. Logically, then, "maxim" and "principle" have the same meaning, and law is only a species of them. In fact, however, Kant seems to distinguish sharply between them; in the *Foundations*,[18] he says that a maxim states how we do behave and a law prescribes how we ought to behave. Instead of this dichotomy, however, he is interested in establishing the following possibilities: (*a*) a rational man acting according to some maxim while holding it to be valid only for him, and for him only because its condition is the actual state of his own motives; (*b*) a rational man recognizing a condition valid for, though not necessarily effective in, all

---

[15] Indeed, Käubler (*Der Begriff der Triebfeder in Kants Ethik*, p. 41) suggests that *Bedingung* is a typographical error for *Bestimmung;* and *Bestimmung* is used in this sense in *Metaphysik der Sitten*, Einleitung (VI, 212).

[16] *Vorlesungen über Logik*, § 57 (IX, 120); *Critique of Pure Reason*, A 322 = B 378, A 300 = B 357; cf. *Critique of Practical Reason*, 90 (184).

[17] *Critique of Practical Reason*, 90 (184); *Metaphysik der Sitten*, VI, 437–38.

[18] *Foundations of the Metaphysics of Morals*, 420 n. (38 n.).

rational beings; (*c*) a rational man recognizing a condition as present and effective in all rational beings as such and therefore as valid for and applicable to himself. There is thus a trichotomy, not a dichotomy, to wit: (*a*) mere maxim, (*b*) law, (*c*) law which is also a maxim.[19]

The questions requiring an answer are these: (1) What is the supreme maxim or maxims of an empirically practical reason? (2) Are they laws, or mere maxims? (3) Can a law itself be a maxim? The first of these questions must be answered in the light of empirical facts about man and will concern us in the next chapter. The third question belongs in the analytic of pure practical reason. The formal question in an analytic of empirical practical reason is the second.

§ 5. ARE THERE EMPIRICAL PRACTICAL LAWS?

Kant answers that they are mere maxims, and he supports this answer with many arguments. In this section, however, we shall be concerned only with the answer insofar as it is based upon purely formal or epistemological considerations; the other arguments properly fall within the scope of the next chapter.

A mere maxim must depend upon conditions which reflect individual differences among rational beings. These differences are differences in their desires, in the conative and not in the cognitive components of their volitions. A law, on the other hand, might seem to depend upon what all men do, in fact, have in common, and this need not necessarily be something common to their cognitive faculties but might be something lying in their conative makeup. In fact, Kant believes that all men do have a common desire, namely, the desire for happiness. Why, then, are we not, in Kant's opinion, able to state a practical law based upon this putative empirical fact—or, indeed, upon any other alleged fact, if we are able to find some other common conative component in all men?

A law cannot be based upon *any* actual features inductively discovered in the generality of mankind. For let us suppose that one desire, upon examination of a fair sample of mankind, turns out to be present in them. We might then make the statement, "All men have desire D," in which D would be a general determination of their wills. But, even so, D would not issue in a law that all men should act so as to satisfy D. For let us see what would happen if we found a man in whom D was absent, as we might always possibly find one by continuing our induction. The fact that everyone else had D would not constitute the slightest reason why he should do actions called for by D, or should feel any shame for lacking D; it would, in fact, provide a ground for rejecting

[19] Cf. *Critique of Pure Reason*, A 812 = B 840.

the generalization. The generalization is a posteriori, but a law, says Kant, must be universal and necessary, that is, a priori. This, he says, is true of laws in natural science as well.[20]

Few would agree with Kant in this sweeping statement. There is an element of brute fact in what seem to us to be the supreme "laws of nature," and they might, for all we know, have been quite different. It is just a brute fact about our universe that bodies attract each other; yet we call the description of this attraction a "law."

It is nevertheless clear that Kant is here pointing out an important distinction in morals which depends upon our different responses to an exception to an alleged law. There is no possible logical inference from how men do, in fact, behave to how they ought to behave. No empirical generalization can do anything but surrender in the face of a well-authenticated exception. An a priori principle or law, on the other hand, can "condemn" an apparent exception, and it does so even in natural science. A body that does not fall according to Galileo's law— and none does—is simply not a freely falling body. We do not revise the law when we find an "exception" to it; we reclassify the object. The law which can be held in spite of apparent exceptions is accordingly not a mere summary of experience; it is prescriptive, not merely descriptive, even though experience may have suggested its form and may, in fact, corroborate it. There are such laws in science; there seem to be such laws for men's practical conduct.

A law is prescriptive, whether it is a theoretical or a practical law. (Perhaps it would be better to say that a law is prescriptive but that it may prescribe for theory-construction, in which case we call it "theoretical" even though it represents a practical decision, or it may prescribe for conduct, in which case we call it "practical.") Kant, therefore, in warning against allowing any empirical principle to be called a law is calling attention to "the most important distinction which can be considered in practical investigations" (26 [114]), to wit, that between factual generalizations and practical[21] prescriptions. No logical inference between them is possible. There are, therefore, no empirical laws of practical reason, but only empirical maxims (21 [108]). If there are any laws, they are not empirical.

[20] *Critique of Practical Reason*, 26 (114); *Critique of Pure Reason*, A 159 = B 198.

[21] "Practical" is here taken in a sense broad enough to include the practical (prescriptive) aspect of even theoretical systems. In the *Critique of Pure Reason* Kant often speaks of *maxims* for the conduct of speculative inquiry and inquiry in natural science; a maxim is such a rule which is subjectively necessary for the conduct of inquiry but has no direct objective validity (cf. *Critique of Pure Reason*, A 666 = B 694).

Kant's point can perhaps be made clearer if we avoid the use of the term "a priori," which seems to belong only to theoretical knowledge, or at least to be univocal in meaning only when applied there. His point is the essentially simple one that practical laws must be prescriptive, and empirical laws, which are a posteriori, are not prescriptive. By exclusion, then, he can call practical laws, if there are any, a priori.

§ 6. HYPOTHETICAL IMPERATIVES

Rules are formulated in the imperative mood. In an almost casual manner, down in the Remark to § 1, Kant reintroduces one of his most significant distinctions, that between an imperative and a law,[22] and then the no less important, but more celebrated, distinction between two types of imperatives.

As an excuse for this apparent casualness, let it be said that the second of these distinctions, so elaborately developed in the *Foundations*, really plays only a comparatively minor role in the remainder of the *Critique*. The reason for this is that the analytical method of the *Foundations* begins with the phenomenon of moral constraint, while the synthetic method of the *Critique* commences with the principles, and the imperative is only the appearance of such principles to a less than perfectly rational being, to one not *ipso facto* determined by the rational law. The doctrine of imperatives is therefore at most a corollary to the investigations of the *Critique*. It is the discussion of imperatives and the formula of the categorical imperative that is presupposed in the *Critique*. For this reason, it is appropriate to refer to the fuller discussion of these matters in the *Foundations*.

Any practical proposition is a product of reason. For a being like man, who is not wholly guided by his reason, a practical proposition is presented as a command of reason and is expressed in the imperative mood. It is objectively valid and thus differs from a mere maxim; but it need not express a law in the sense of being unconditional in its practical function. It may be objectively valid as an imperative only for a being with a specific condition of volition. We must, therefore, distinguish between a law which is necessarily binding on a rational being as such, which gives an unconditional imperative to all partially rational beings, and a law which is merely the objectively valid cognitive component in the determination of choice by a rational being affected in a particular empirical way. The latter kind of law is a theoretical proposition functioning as a practical proposition only under the condition

22 A distinction he repeatedly ignores; cf. *Critique of Practical Reason*, 21, 30 (107, 119); *Foundations of the Metaphysics of Morals*, 420 and n. (37, 38 n.); *Critique of Pure Reason*, A 802 = B 830; *Metaphysik der Sitten*, Einleitung, VI, 222–23.

of the subject's volition, which makes some among the myriad of theoretical propositions practically relevant in the determination of his conduct. An imperative to take an action, so far as it is determined by the actual condition of the subject's will and by a theoretical component based upon knowledge of fact, is one that commands hypothetically, or is a hypothetical imperative.

In the *Foundations* two types of hypothetical imperatives were distinguished: the problematic or technical[23] imperative and the assertoric or pragmatic. The difference between them is that in the former the condition is not asserted but mentioned only hypothetically (e.g., "If you want to make bread . . ."), while in the latter it is asserted (e.g., "Since you want to . . ."). The former are also called "rules of skill"; the latter, "counsels of prudence." The distinction between the two types of hypothetical imperatives is ignored in the *Critique*, but a central problem of the *Critique*, to which the next chapter will be devoted, is to determine what condition it is that is asserted in all hypothetical imperatives of the second kind.

An analysis[24] of a hypothetical imperative would make the following components explicit:

a) In the protasis:
  (I) A conative element, directed to something, *B*, which is the purpose of the commanded action, *B* being an object or state of affairs the representation of which is one of the causes of its existence as an effect of action undertaken by the subject; this is expressed in the imperative by "If I want *B*" or "Since I want *B*."
  (II) A cognitive element: knowledge of the causal relation between the action commanded, *A*, and the purpose, *B*; equivalent, under condition I, to the statement "*A* is a means to *B*."
  (III) A tacit premise or rule of practical inference: "If I fully will the effect [*B*], I also will the action [*A*] required for it."[25]
b) The apodosis: "Do *A*."

In the technical imperative, *B* may be the object of any desire; and in many cases there are well-established laws of nature (II) which tell us how we can achieve *B*. In the pragmatic imperative, *B* is one specific object which Kant thinks we can assert and not merely entertain as possibly desired; we *have* the desire for happiness. But in this case, the con-

---

23 *Erste Einleitung in die Kritik der Urteilskraft*, XX, 200 n., criticizes the term "problematic imperative" and substitutes "technical imperative" for it. *Metaphysik der Sitten*, VI, 222, distinguishes only between technical and categorical.

24 The full analysis is given in my contribution to the *Paton-Festschrift*, "Apodictic Imperatives," *Kant-Studien*, XLIX (1957–58), 7–24, and the remainder of this section is taken largely from that essay.

25 Cf. *Foundations of the Metaphysics of Morals*, 417 (34).

tent of *B* is so vague and the knowledge of the world and its ways is so inadequate that we cannot state universal rules that will permit us to count on achieving *B*. Therefore, the range of the conative component and the certainty of the cognitive component seem to vary inversely: where the end in view is highly specific, real laws of nature may enter at II, and where it is a vague end, like well-being or happiness, the cognitive component is likely to be empirical knowledge not worthy of the name of law but mere belief and opinion.

Kant tells us that the possibility of these imperatives is easy to establish, since they are, "in what concerns the will," analytical.[26] This is correct, but it requires a little analysis to see what it means and why it is true.

It is not entirely clear in what sense an imperative is the kind of judgment that can be either analytic or synthetic. Imperatives are not judgments with a subject and predicate, and thus they do not fall under Kant's explicit division of the types of judgment. And though for any imperative a set of indicative statements (not necessarily factual; they may be value-judgments) may be formulated from which the imperative could be reached merely by a syntactical change of mood, in the case of hypothetical imperatives some of the corresponding indicative judgments are themselves hypothetical, and hence they do not fall under Kant's official rubric for distinguishing analytic from synthetic judgments. It is not entirely pedantic to insist upon these niceties; but the minor infelicities of expression should not excuse us from finding the important and correct point that Kant is insisting upon.

If we take the statements of the conditions under which the apodosis is regarded as being binding and phrase them in declarative statements, e.g., "Under conditions *C* a rational being will do *A*," then the proposition "A rational being will do *A*" will follow analytically from this and another factual proposition, "A rational being is under condition *C*." By "follow analytically" I mean that a denial of the conclusion will contradict the joint assertion of the premises; hence to deny the proposition corresponding to the apodosis will contradict the propositions which are its premises. Since the apodosis is connected analytically with the protasis, Kant says the imperative is analytic.

[26] *Ibid.*, 417 (34). I overlooked the following point in my paper presented to Paton. Actually, Kant says that only the technical imperative is analytic "in what concerns the will," while the pragmatic imperative would be analytic "if it only were easy to give a definite concept of happiness" (*ibid.*, 417 [35]). But in this distinction between the two imperatives, Kant is incorrect. "In what concerns the will," both are analytical in the sense to be described; in what concerns the understanding, i.e., the cognitive content in the choice of particular means to the end in view, both are synthetic.

But it is analytic in this broad sense only "in what concerns the will." That A is necessary to B is not known analytically and that the rational being is under condition C is not known analytically. All that is analytical is component III, and this concerns the form of the volition and not the specific contents willed. Component III merely specifies the relation between A and B as variables. Kant should say, therefore, not that the hypothetical imperative is analytic, but that its formal principle, which is III, is analytic. It alone concerns the will of a rational being independently of the cognitive content and the contingencies of human desire. Not to accept III is to fail to be a rational being concerned with desires; but we fail, in varying degrees, to follow through in our obedience even to this formal principle. We will health, but we will acts that jeopardize it, and we fail to be prudent men.

The conclusion of the hypothetical imperative is reached only through component III. Because of its formal character, even hypothetical imperatives can be objectively valid; they are not persuasive or emotive but rational, even though they are relevant to action only under specific conditions which need not be true of rational beings as such. The conditions that they are concerned with are conditions of him to whom the imperative is directed, not of him who issues the command.

Since beings like us do not, in fact, always will the means necessary to their ends, even when they know the means, the hypothetical imperative expresses a constraint of reason upon impulse. If we were completely rational beings, the maxim of doing whatever is necessary to the end in view would be easy to follow. But since we are not, even our desires and wishes can create constraints and not mere lures and enticements. Pleasure itself, it has been ruefully discovered, can be a hard mistress.

Kant's treatment of imperatives, under the supposition that the hypothetical-categorical distinction taken over from formal logic is definitive of two sharply distinguished kinds of constraint (the prudential and the moral), has led to some unfortunate interpretations of his ethical doctrine. These misinterpretations would not have arisen, perhaps, if he had followed one of his own suggestions that the distinctions of modality of judgments rather than the distinctions of their form should be used in distinguishing among imperatives. A hypothetical imperative is defined by its form: "If you wish so and so, then do this or that," and a categorical imperative is defined by its form: "Do this or that." It would appear from this that all imperatives having moral import must be categorical imperatives, and Kant regularly states the moral imperative in categorical form. This in turn has led to the view that for Kant in moral decision we should ignore *all* circumstances which would be expressed in the antecedent of a hypothetical judgment or imperative, and this has given rise to one of the interpretations of Kant that can be considered only silly.

The important point is not that a moral imperative must have a specific grammatical or logical form different from that of a prudential or technical imperative. There are morally valid imperatives that are hypothetical in form: "If you have promised to return the book, do so"; and categorical imperatives which do not have any moral import or claim: "Shut the door." What we must do if we are to remain faithful to Kant's purpose in drawing the distinction is to see that no imperative is morally valid if it is directed merely to the man who has a specific desire, whether it is in the form of "If you wish to be warm, shut the door" or in the categorical form, "Shut the door." We must be able to discern that condition of will which must be present in a man if it is intelligent to direct an imperative to him at all; this is the condition that he be a person with a practical reason. Assuming only this and the fact that he does not by nature do what the law would require either for the achievement of some specific purpose or for intelligent action in the pursuit of any purpose whatsoever, the imperative is directed to him as a practically rational being regardless of his specific desires; under this condition, the imperative is apodictic whether it is formally hypothetical or categorical. In contrast to it there are assertoric imperatives— imperatives relevant to a man of whom it can be empirically asserted that he does, as a matter of fact, have such and such a maxim which can be carried out in the way stated in the imperative. In an apodictic imperative, hypothetical conditions may enter into the determination of the specific action required, but not into the determination of the one condition that renders the imperative valid for everyone instead of valid only for an individual who just happens to have the desire that could be satisfied through obedience to this imperative. For example, making a promise creates an obligation, and one can say (categorically), "Keep your promise" or (hypothetically) "If you promised to return the book, do so." But the hypothetical imperative, "If you want to be able to borrow another book, keep your promise," cannot be put into a categorical form that is apodictically necessary; such an imperative, whether categorical or hypothetical, is only assertoric in modality.

§ 7. CONCLUSION

In this chapter we have studied the formal structure of practical reason as employed in satisfying any conative or dynamic urge whose existence in us is empirically discoverable. In so doing, we have raised questions that cannot be answered by purely formal considerations but require knowledge of human nature and of the moral phenomenon. We want to know:

1. What principle or principles are there which express a general determination of the will so far as this can be discovered empirically?

2. Are these principles mere maxims, or laws, or both maxims and laws?

3. Are there any principles which express a general determination of the will independently of empirically discoverable dynamic or conative factors?

The next chapter will answer questions 1 and 2 by tracing Kant's theory (*a*) that all principles which express an empirically discovered condition of will are "principles of self-love or private happiness" and (*b*) that they are mere maxims and do not have the force of law. Chapters viii and ix will then study Kant's affirmative answer to the third question and show how such principles, which are the only laws, are discovered and what they are.

VII

The Analytic of Empirical Practical Reason
II. Material Considerations; Commentary
on Sections 2, 3, and Part of 8

§ 1. INTRODUCTION

Empirical practical reason is reasoning used in the guidance of behavior for the sake of satisfying some desire. In chapter vi we examined the formal aspects of this guidance as exercised through principles, maxims, rules, and imperatives. In this chapter we shall be concerned with the moving forces in such conduct, with its efficient and final causes instead of its formal causes. This will require us to try to understand Kant's views of and terminology in psychology or, as he would say, anthropology. We must understand what he means by desire, pleasure, pain, interest, and happiness in their empirical, psychological setting. We shall then follow Kant's argument that these concepts and the principles employing them are not competent to fill the office ascribed to moral concepts and principles.

§ 2. DESIRE

Desire is the faculty of a being, through its ideas (*Vorstellungen*, representations or "ideas" in the Lockean sense), to cause the reality of the objects of these ideas.[1] This succinctly indicates the two factors in desire that we have already distinguished: the cognitive factor, or idea, and the dynamic or conative factor. The latter is sometimes called "desire proper" (*Begierde*); when it is of a settled dispositional character, Kant calls it "inclination" (*Neigung*); often the name "impulse" (*Antrieb*) or "incentive" (*Triebfeder*) is applied to it.[2]

---

[1] *Critique of Practical Reason*, 9 n. (94 n.); *Metaphysik der Sitten*, VI, 211. Following Wolff and Baumgarten, the faculty of desire (*Begehrungsvermögen*) is distinguished from that of aversion (*Abscheuungsvermögen*) at *Critique of Practical Reason*, 58 (148), but no further use is made of this formal distinction, and nothing is lost in Abbott's not speaking of faculties at all in this passage.

[2] The usage of *Neigung* to refer to settled disposition is not always observed. It generally means any inclination and is approximately equivalent to *Triebfeder* ex-

90

Interest is that by which reason determines the will.[3] But since practical reason is identical with will, it is more accurate to say that interest "indicates an incentive of the will as it is presented by reason" (79 [172]). In a dependent will, i.e., one not wholly rational, there is always an interest which is expressed in a maxim; unless it is so expressed, and thus subject to intelligent inspection, we do not have a will but only blind impulse. Will differs from mere desire in that in the latter there is an image of an object which is the target of behavior; while in willing, on the other hand, there is also guidance by knowledge of a law or principle which relates the action objectively to what it is that is desired. Thus animals have desires, but only rational beings can have a will.

The objects of the ideas—the objects being the final causes of action, the ideas being among the efficient causes—are also called "objects of interest or of inclination."[4] The objects are the purposes of the action, since purpose is defined as the concept of an object considered as the cause of the reality of the object.[5] The idea is one of the efficient causes of the object by virtue of being one of the factors which determine the

---

cept when *Triebfeder* refers to the moral incentive or motive. Abbott translates *Triebfeder* as "motive" or "spring." "Spring" follows a usage going back to the early seventeenth century, but not common now. There is good etymological justification for it, since *Feder* refers, e.g., to the mainspring of a watch. "Motive" is a less fortunate choice, because Kant carefully distinguished between *Triebfeder* and *Bewegungsgrund* (= "motive") in the *Foundations of the Metaphysics of Morals*, 427 (45). Yet the fault is Kant's, not Abbott's, for in this chapter of the *Critique* he is using *Triebfeder* in the sense in which the *Foundations* defined *Bewegungsgrund*. Picavet translates it as *mobile*, Capra as *movente*, Born (following a Kantian parenthesis) as *elater*. I have followed the translation suggested by Greene and Hudson in their rendition of *Religion within the Limits of Reason Alone*. But I have done so with growing dissatisfaction, for the meaning of *Triebfeder* is obvious to a German, while *incentive* must be explained to a reader of English. It does not seem possible to find an entirely suitable English equivalent, and I suspect that the reason for this is that Kant himself did not use the word univocally. On the terminology and its variations see Käubler, *Der Begriff der Triebfeder in Kants Ethik* (1917).

[3] *Foundations of the Metaphysics of Morals*, 459 (80 n.); *Metaphysik der Sitten*, VI, 212-13; *Critique of Judgment*, §§ 2, 3.

[4] "Object of inclination" and "object of interest" must be distinguished from "object of practical reason." It is only the latter that is defined as the good or evil. "Object of choice [*Willkür*]" is used by Kant in the legal sense, referring to that which I may dispose of as I choose, i.e., property (*Metaphysik der Sitten*, VI, 246) as well as in the sense of "that which I choose" (e.g., *Critique of Practical Reason*, 36 [125]).

[5] *Critique of Judgment*, V, 180 (17).

person's action which, in turn, will produce the object. An object is a purpose if we ascribe its realization to a chain of causes one member of which is an idea or conception of the object which determines the person's behavior in actually producing the object.

The word "object" denotes two quite different things. It may mean an actual state of affairs, a physical thing and its psychological effects that can be brought into existence by action. The production of such an object requires empirical knowledge of its causes and skill in applying this knowledge. It is in this sense only that the word "object" is to be used in analyzing an empirical practical reason. But the word has another, quite unusual, meaning. It may refer to an internal setting of the will, to an act of decision itself without regard to the causality of will in bringing its object (in the first sense) into existence. This is the meaning that the word will have in the analysis of pure practical reason.[6]

§ 3. PLEASURE

Kant's theory of desire is hedonism. "To wish for something and to have satisfaction in its existence, i.e., to take an interest in it, are identical."[7] Desire is always directed to something—its object—the existence of which is expected to give pleasure.

The converse, however, does not hold. While his theory of desire is hedonistic, his theory of pleasure is not exclusively conative. For it is possible to experience pleasure without antecedent desire. Pleasure can arise from the mere contemplation of an object or from the experience of an idea in imagination. Such pleasure is called "contemplative pleasure" and is best seen in the enjoyment of beauty, where the pleasure is characterized as being disinterested. Pleasure which is the goal and re-

---

[6] *Critique of Practical Reason*, 15 (101). Similarly, *Foundations of the Metaphysics of Morals*, 432, l. 22. (Abbott [50, four lines from bottom] paraphrases and misses the word "object.") It is essential for Kant to use the word "object" in this unusual way, for otherwise moral action as such would have to be declared without object, i.e., without interest or purpose. When he says that there is an interest present in all action but that interest need not be assumed as the determining cause of all action, he is referring to interest in the existence of the object, which is the first sense. But there can be an interest in making the right decision whether the decision can be rendered effective in the world or not. The latter is the moral interest, and its object is a certain setting of the will to act from a certain motive (cf. *Foundations of the Metaphysics of Morals*, 413 n. [30 n.], and *Critique of Practical Reason*, 33 [122]). This is the sense of "object" in chap. ii of the Analytic, when Kant is discussing the object of pure practical reason, and it will be discussed in chapter ix of this commentary.

[7] *Critique of Judgment*, § 4 (V, 209 [43]).

ward of action, however, is called "practical pleasure"—practical pleasure is an "interest of inclination."[8]

Both kinds of pleasure may be defined by reference to the subjective state of the person. Pleasure is the consciousness of the causality of an idea to keep the subject in the state in which he is having this experience. This is true even of disinterested aesthetic pleasure. Pain is, by corollary, our consciousness of an effect that an idea has in making us try to, or wish to, change our subjective state.[9] Pleasure is present when there is harmony or facilitation of function; Kant calls it the idea of the agreement of an object or action with the subjective condition of the person (desire)[10] or with the work of our perceptual and imaginative capacities (as in the disinterested pleasure of art). It would perhaps be clearer to say that pleasure is the feeling produced by such agreement. Pain is the spur to activity to bring about such agreement and is thus connected with desire.[11]

The faculty or capacity for experiencing pleasure and pain is feeling. Feeling is one species of the general affection of the sensibility (*sensatio*), the other species being sense proper (*Sinn*).[12] If the content of our sensory experience is of such a kind that it can be related to an object of knowledge and thus, notwithstanding its dependence upon the subject's psychological constitution, can become a component in knowledge of the object, the content is called "sensation." Receptivity to it is sense proper. The color green, for instance, is a sensation and is subjective, since it depends upon the person; yet it is related to the object in such a way (by means of an a priori synthesis under the category of subsistence and inherence) that one can correctly say that the object is green. This objective attribution cannot take place with feelings, and hence they are subjective in a double sense.

There are only two elementary feelings—pleasure and pain. All other feelings, such as the feeling of the sublime, the beautiful, and respect are defined by the accompaniments, contexts, causes, or "objects" of the pleasure or pain we feel. Whether the origin of the pleasure lies in some physical stimulation, the physical fulfilment of a desire, or some

---

[8] *Metaphysik der Sitten*, VI, 212.

[9] *Anthropologie in pragmatischer Hinsicht*, § 60.

[10] *Critique of Practical Reason*, 9 n. (94 n.), in the definitions drawn from psychology.

[11] *Anthropologie*, § 60.

[12] *Metaphysik der Sitten*, Einleitung, I; *Critique of Practical Reason*, 23 (109); *Erste Einleitung in die Kritik der Urteilskraft*, XX, 226. Pleasure is referred to "inner sense." This is not the inner sense of the *Critique of Pure Reason* but the inner sense or capacity of feeling as described in *Anthropologie*, § 15.

idea held in contemplation, the feeling is always an effect upon our sensibility. In a hedonistic calculus, there is no place for qualitative differences (23 [110]).

A feeling of pleasure or pain, we have seen, cannot be ascribed as a property to an object. It cannot even be related to the existence of an object by a necessary rule. For whether a feeling of pleasure or pain will arise in the presence of an object can be learned only in the actual experience. All our action aimed at the satisfaction of desire, i.e., at pleasure in the existence of an object, is therefore based upon experience; all knowledge of the pleasurableness of any existing state of affairs is, therefore, a posteriori. From this it follows that no law, i.e., no necessary principle valid for all rational beings, can be based upon any maxim for the realization of practical pleasure.

§ 4. THE LOWER FACULTY OF DESIRE

The distinction between the lower and the higher faculties of desire (22 [109]) is the scholastic distinction between *appetitus sensitivus* and *appetitus rationalis*, which, in turn, derives from the classical distinction between passion and will.[13] The paragraphs before us are directed primarily against "the otherwise acute men," the Wolffians,[14] who, while drawing this distinction, did not sharply distinguish between the sensitive and the rational faculties in general. In Wolff's doctrine, desire has as its condition the knowledge of a perfection.[15] If this knowledge is obscure or confused, corresponding to the lower faculty of sense, the desire can mislead us into erroneous or bad conduct; if it is clear and distinct, coming from the higher cognitive faculty of under-

[13] Thus Hutcheson (*Essay on the Nature and Conduct of the Passions and Affections* [Selby-Bigge, *British Moralists*, I, 400 n.] which existed in a German translation of 1765) quotes the scholastic definition of *appetitus rationalis:* "A constant natural Disposition of Soul to desire what the Understanding, or these sublimer Sensations, represent as Good," and adds, "This many call the Will as distinct from the Passions." On the concept of "passion" and Kant's views of its relation to feeling and reason, cf. Karl Bernecker, *Kritische Darstellung des Affektbegriffes von Descartes bis zur Gegenwart* (Diss., Greifswald, 1915).

[14] Wolff, *Psychologia empirica*, § 584; Baumgarten, *Metaphysica*, § 689; Baumeister, *Philosophia definitiva*, §§ 849, 852, 891.

[15] *Op. cit.*, §§ 887–90. Pleasure necessarily accompanies the awareness of a perfection, according to Wolff. This is denied by Kant (*Erste Einleitung in die Kritik der Urteilskraft*, XX, 226). But Wolff is not, at least by his own profession, a hedonist, for the perfection is desired because it is good and not because its achievement gives pleasure (cf. *Vernünftige Gedancken von der Menschen Thun und Lassen*, §§ 14, 139; *Psychologia empirica*, §§ 511, 558–59). Many of Wolff's followers did not observe this nice distinction, which resembles Butler's, and were easy targets for Kant's criticism here.

standing, the will is rightly guided to choose a real perfection. Hence the work of reason or understanding in morals, as elsewhere in the rationalistic philosophy, is to bring our ideas to clearness and distinctness, for the difference between a sensuous and a rational concept is a difference only in clarity and not in kind. Hence the Wolffians, Kant tells us, should not have distinguished between two faculties of desire. For them, consistency would require only one faculty, and only he is able properly to distinguish two. The Wolffians should have admitted:

If the determination of the will rests on the feelings of agreeableness or disagreeableness which [one] expects from any cause, it is all the same to him through what kind of notion [whether intellectual or sensible] he is affected. The only thing [one] considers in making a choice [if Wolff is correct] is how great, how long lasting, how easily obtained, and how often repeated this agreeableness is [23 (110)].

But the essential epistemological premise that Kant had held since the *Inaugural Dissertation* was that there is a generic difference between sensibility and understanding. The corresponding ethical thesis here is that there is a generic difference between any sensuous desire, no matter how refined, with its maxim, no matter how clear and distinct, and a higher faculty of desire and its principle, which is not determined by desire for pleasure at all. In fact, this distinction is even sharper in Kant's ethical writings than in his epistemology, since knowledge is always the joint product of sensibility and understanding, whereas morality depends solely upon the determination of conduct by the rational faculty. Empirical practical reason is always concerned with the satisfaction of the lower faculty of desire. If there is a pure practical reason, it must be the higher faculty of desire which is not just a refined Epicurean version of our empirical and animal nature. The higher faculty of desire must, of course, have an entirely different structure and function from the lower faculty.

§ 5. MAXIMS OF THE LOWER FACULTY OF DESIRE

Our next task is to follow Kant's argument that the lower faculty of desire cannot give rise to laws, but only to mere maxims. If he can show this and if he can demonstrate that the moral law is a law in the strict sense of the word, he will thereby show that an ethical system cannot be based on an empirical foundation in the nature of the human lower faculty of desire.

Theorem I is as follows: "All practical principles [*Prinzipien*] which presuppose an object (material) of the faculty of desire as the determining ground [*Bestimmungsgrund*] of the will are, without exception, empirical and can furnish no practical laws" (21 [107]). It will follow from this that all imperatives which constrain us or require action for the satisfaction of the lower faculty of desire are hypothetical imperatives.

Before studying the proof of this theorem, let us examine for a moment the word "material." "Material" here seems to be equated with "object of the lower faculty of desire," but the connotations of the two words are distinct, and the distinction is of great importance. "Material" is also contrasted with "form" and "formal," and Kant means here: All practical principles which figure as the cognitive component in volition because of their content, i.e., their reference to an object of desire, and not because of their form, are empirical. It is of the utmost importance not to fall into the common misapprehension of this theorem and to conclude that Kant means that the presence of a desire and hence of a material disqualifies a maxim from being a law. He says explicitly that there must be an object of desire if there is to be action at all (34 [123]). The theorem disqualifies only those maxims which are chosen to guide conduct *because* of their content, i.e., because of their reference to an object of desire (material) as the determining factor. All maxims have material; but only the latter are material maxims. Content (object of desire) without form is blind impulse; form without object of desire is practically ineffective—this is as true of Kant's ethics as the corresponding sentence in the first *Critique* is of his theory of knowledge.

I now give Kant's proof of the first part of the theorem, i.e., down to the last six words. If the desire for an object is the condition for enunciating the proposition expressing the determination of the will to realize this object, the practical proposition is empirical. This is because desire for the object is the ground for determination, desire for the object being desire for the pleasure expected from its existence; and knowledge that the object will give pleasure is merely empirical and hence, at best, only probable. Therefore, the maxim which calls for such action is valid only under the empirical and therefore uncertain condition that the object will in fact give pleasure.

Kant's proof can be strengthened, so as to make it independent of the debatable hedonistic theory of desire, by considering the rules involved in such an action. A rule for the realization of any object can be learned only empirically. Therefore, a determination of the will and its train of specific rules guiding action is doubly uncertain: it is uncertain whether the production of the object will satisfy the desire (whatever it is), and it is uncertain whether the object will be produced by the action initiated and guided by the acceptance of the maxim.

The second paragraph gives the proof of the last part of the theorem, to wit, that such material principles can furnish no practical laws. It would have been better to say, "cannot be practical laws," since his own wording suggests that laws are related to principles in the way in which a rule is related to them and thus creates the supposition that there are a priori rules of morality.

A principle is a law when the condition of the general determination of the will is correctly regarded as a condition of the will of every rational being as such. But whether the object will give pleasure is contingent upon the condition of the subject, and this condition is known only empirically and cannot be known to be necessarily and universally present in rational beings. To hold as a practical law, the condition underlying the principle would have to be known to be necessarily valid for rational beings as such, and this knowledge cannot be got by any observation. When a theoretical proposition is made into a practical proposition because of our interest in its content, the practical proposition is never a law; it is, at best, a mere maxim or a rule practically relevant on the assumption of the maxim.

With the proof of Theorem I, the stage is set for the analytic of pure practical reason, which begins at Theorem III. Theorem II and Remark II of § 8, however, are parts of an analytic of empirical practical reason, and to them we now turn.

§ 6. HAPPINESS

Theorem II is "All material practical principles [*Prinzipien*] are, as such, of one and the same kind, and belong under the general principle [*Prinzip;* should be *Grundsatz*] of self-love or one's own happiness" (22 [108]). In this section, we shall be concerned with the theorem only in so far as it expresses the doctrine of hedonism and shall reserve for later treatment those aspects of it concerned with the ethics of egoism.

A rational being's consciousness of the agreeableness of life which without interruption accompanies his whole existence is happiness. That a being who desires pleasures desires happiness, and conversely, follows from this. Therefore, any practical proposition which is based on the desire for pleasure (a material principle) falls under the fundamental principle of making desire for happiness the supreme motive in action and choice. The desire for happiness, however, is not merely the aggregate of our desires for pleasures. Happiness, unlike pleasure, is a concept belonging to understanding, not to feeling; it is not itself a direct object of any one impulse. Its pursuit, therefore, is guided by a maxim of higher order than the rules for the pursuit of a particular pleasure and is therefore under the regulation of a general fundamental principle, while maxims or rules for the pursuit of particular pleasures can hardly be called "principles" at all. But as happiness is our concept of a systematic whole of pleasures, the maxims for the pursuit of pleasures are under the restrictive condition of a general principle which regulates their relations to each other. In this sense they "belong to" the general principle (*Grundsatz*) of happiness.

From this is derived the corollary that all material practical principles place the motive in the lower faculty of desire and that, if all our principles were of this kind, there would be nothing worthy of the name of the higher faculty of desire (22 [109]).

The second Remark in § 3 discusses further the insufficiency of the desire for happiness as supplying a practical law (25 [112]). The desire for happiness is admitted to be necessary in any rational being endowed with feeling and to be one, though not always an effective, determinant of the being's interests. But because happiness is merely the "general name for subjective grounds of determination" and since these grounds vary from person to person and from time to time within one person, the principle cannot be a law, which must be the same for all rational beings. The diversity of interests summed up under the abstract name of happiness, even supposing that all men consistently follow the maxim of trying to achieve happiness as they conceive it, for themselves or even for others, would lead necessarily to conflicts in conduct.[16]

Kant's argument at this point leaves much to be desired in cogency. He is placing a demand upon hedonism that his own theory cannot meet, to wit, that identity of principle should lead to identity of rule and action. While the *Critique* does not make it as clear as does the *Metaphysics of Morals*, there can be a variety of rules of action even under the moral law itself. To require that the desire for happiness should issue in identical and universally applicable specific rules and to conclude that, because it does not do this, it is an inadequate foundation for law is to demand too much of any principle. Kant's own formulation of the law would not pass this test, though he seems to have thought, in his oversimplified examples, that it could. The moral law requires that we should seek the happiness of others; but it does not require that all benevolent men should do the same action, for the happiness of others is at least as variable as my own. That my concept of happiness can issue only in contingent rules, therefore, does not show that this principle is not a law and does not provide a basis for destructively criticizing it.

The more valid argument that an empirical principle cannot be or

---

[16] *Critique of Practical Reason*, 28 (115–16); cf. also *Versuch den Begriff negativer Grössen in die Weltweisheit einzuführen*, II, 181–82, versus Maupertuis.

furnish a law is given in the second paragraph of Remark II under § 3. This argument, which is formal in character, has already been discussed in chapter vi, § 5.

Objectionable as the argument in the Remark to § 3 may be from the standpoint of fairness to his opponents, however, we should not overlook it in favor of the purely formal argument, for in it Kant is enunciating a richer principle for the moral imperative. He is saying that a maxim must be universalizable in the sense not only that it must not be self-contradictory or contradictory to the purposes of the person who accepts it in a particular instance but that the actions which it dictates must be compatible with each other. It is not really essential that the actions be identical, though he implies that it is. It is essential, however, that the actions which one man undertakes under a maxim not be incompatible with the actions which I or another man undertakes under the same maxim; and if they are, then the maxims cannot be instances of a single law. In a fragment he says this more clearly than anywhere else: "The regulative principle of freedom: that [the actions] do not conflict; the constitutive principle: that they reciprocally promote each other [for the] purpose of happiness."[17]

If we apply this richer principle to the case in point, I could without logical contradiction will that each man should strive only for his own happiness. If I do so, I am willing that each man should follow a self-consistent maxim but, at the same time, that he should follow a maxim that will produce incompatible and mutually frustrating actions. This maxim cannot be a law, because a law must be a unifying and not a divisive factor in the world; it must make a system of ends possible.[18]

In § 3 Kant is thinking too narrowly of a logical criterion of law, where logic admits of only identity and difference in terms. But his theory requires him to think in terms also of real repugnance and harmony, and not merely of difference and identity. His brief and pointed statements and examples usually illustrate the latter concern, even when some of the former concern is presupposed. In the *Metaphysics of Morals*, however, the former principle comes into its full rights, though it has been made explicit in the concept of a realm of ends in the *Foundations* and that of a moral commonwealth in *Religion within the Limits of Reason Alone*.[19]

---

[17] Reflexion 7251.

[18] This is the principal component in the doctrine of the type of the moral law (cf. below, chap. ix, § 10).

[19] *Foundations of the Metaphysics of Morals*, 430 (49); *Religion within the Limits of Reason Alone*, VI, 98 (Greene and Hudson, 90).

§ 7. EGOISM

Kant equates the principle of hedonism with that of egoism. To seek happiness and to seek one's own happiness are tacitly identified in Theorem II.

Self-love is "predominant benevolence towards oneself (*philautia*)" and is also called "selfishness."[20] Interest in one's own happiness is perfectly natural and inescapable, and to seek one's own happiness is at least indirectly a duty, since its lack is a rich source of temptation against the perfection of one's self.[21] There is a joy in the apprehension of one's own perfection, or at least in recognizing one's progress toward it. This may properly be called the moral feeling; but any theory which places the worth or criterion of morality in the pleasure of this feeling reduces to a eudaemonistic, egoistic theory that Kant thinks is patently false, since the acknowledgment of what is right must precede and be independent of the enjoyment of our possession of it (38 [128]).

With apparently no apprehension that he is being inconsistent, Kant admits that an interest in the happiness of others can be a part of our nature and that such directly altruistic actions can occur without any moral constraint to them. Such an interest is present in at least some men as a sympathetic disposition.[22] We cannot suppose the interest or disposition to be present in all men, and certainly not in all rational beings as such. The reason we have a duty to consider the happiness of others is entirely independent of the fact that some men do naturally consider it.

[20] *Critique of Practical Reason*, 73 (165). There is a difference between Kant's concept of self-love in § 3 and that in later parts of the *Critique* and in the *Lectures on Ethics*. In chap. iii of the *Critique* and in the *Lectures*, Kant is most directly concerned with what I shall call an "egoism of the will," while here his target is "egoism of the feelings." By "egoism of the will" I do not mean the selfish preference of one's own happiness to that of others, which is what is ordinarily meant by selfishness and which is the meaning it has in § 3. The principle of self-love expressive of the egoism of the will is "the propensity to make the subjective grounds of one's choice into an objective determining ground of will in general" (*Critique of Practical Reason*, 74 [166]), and Kant calls it "moral self-love" and "an inclination to be satisfied with one's perfections" (*Lectures on Ethics*, 135). No doubt the two vices go together, and if Kant is correct in Theorem I, they must go together; but they are, nevertheless, different vices. The egoism of will approaches moral conceit and arrogance and is a much more serious vice than mere preference for one's own happiness to that of others.

[21] *Critique of Practical Reason*, 93 (186); *Foundations of the Metaphysics of Morals*, 399 (15).

[22] *Lectures on Ethics*, 194: "We have an instinct to benevolence, but not an instinct to righteousness."

The inconsistency between saying that all material maxims are maxims of self-love and that some men have a direct and even general interest in the happiness of others, therefore, does not mean that there is an inconsistency in Kant's *ethical* theory. Whether we have or have not a duty to consider our own happiness or that of others is not affected by a decision as to whether we do, in fact, treasure the happiness of others only insofar as it contributes to our own. But a serious inconsistency in his psychological theory and in the analytic of empirical practical reason is present.

This inconsistency was often present in the writers whom Kant most admired. Butler, whom Kant presumably did not know as a writer on ethical subjects,[23] had been able to point the way to making it psychologically intelligible that men could have, and indeed sometimes do have, a direct sympathetic or benevolent interest in the welfare of others. For philosophers like Butler and his opponent Hobbes,[24] who based their (different) ethical theories upon their (different) conceptions of human nature, it was of the utmost importance to know whether men could possibly be genuinely unselfish. For Kant, on the other hand, to whom the facts about human nature (whatever they might be) do not suffice to determine man's duty, the dispute between the egoists and the altruists lies this side of the ethical question. The ethical question is independent of questions of human nature. But it is nonetheless regrettable that Kant did not clarify his own thinking about human nature in this important respect.

Let us not, with some other writers on Kant, exaggerate the importance of this error. It has been said that, in order to break the hold of pleasure (especially of one's own) on the faculty of desire and to find maxims which are not selfish and hedonistic, Kant had to leave the empirical realm altogether and base his ethics upon what amounted to an actual renunciation of human nature. The conclusion is accordingly drawn that if Kant had had a more adequate psychology, like that of Butler, he would not have had to reject so completely the conception of human nature as a basis for morals.

---

[23] But he might have found the same thing in Wolff, *Vernünftige Gedancken von der Menschen Thun und Lassen*, § 139, and in Hume, *Inquiry concerning the Principles of Morals*, Appendix II.

[24] Because Kant distinguished, as we have seen, between practical pleasure and contemplative pleasure, he is not guilty of the oversimplification of the hedonists and egoists criticized by Butler. What Butler says of pleasure in general, Kant says only of pleasure in moral action: there is a pleasure in the action, but the interest in the moral action is not an interest in the pleasure itself (*Critique of Practical Reason*, 116, 160 [212, 258]; *Metaphysik der Sitten*, VI, 378).

This, however, is incorrect. Butler's analysis of desire may refute Hobbes or Mandeville not only in psychology but in ethics putatively based upon an analysis of human nature; but it does not touch Kant in any essential point. For Kant's argument against the principle of private pleasure is not that it is selfish in any morally repugnant sense, and his argument that we should concern ourselves with the happiness of others is not predicated upon the alleged fact that we do so concern ourselves. Precisely the same infirmity in the moral argument for selfishness is found in the moral argument for altruism, when each is based upon real or alleged facts of human nature.[25] Neither desire—that for my own happiness or that for the happiness of others—can found a duty to seek either.

§ 8. HETERONOMY

All action directed to the satisfaction of an interest in an object of desire is action according to rules which fall under the material of some maxim. If constraint is necessary in order that these actions rather than others take place, the action is commanded by a hypothetical imperative. In actions under a hypothetical imperative, we have seen that there are always two laws which are relevant. One of them comes from reason itself and is the formal principle of hypothetical imperatives. The prudent man accepts this principle in the choice of actions for the satisfaction of *any* desire. The other is a law of nature, or at least some more or less trustworthy generalization about facts of experience, and states a connection between causes and effects. It supplies the values, as it were, for the variables of the formal principle, so that the prudent man not only decides to do that which will, in principle, lead to his goal but decides what it is that will, in fact, lead to it. The second of these laws does not come from reason itself but is borrowed from experience.[26] In content, it is a theoretical proposition; only the choice of a specific end by the acting person gives it practical relevance.

In following a hypothetical imperative, reason is thereby acting under one law which it has not itself prescribed; it chooses a law, prescribed as it were by nature to the person who has, as a matter of empirical fact, the goal which can be achieved by use of this theoretical knowledge. Kant borrows from politics his name for this mode of action: he calls it "heteronomy" and distinguishes it from autonomy or self-legislation. A reason which is the slave of the passions, a will which follows the promptings of desire and chooses laws of nature as its

---

[25] *Foundations of the Metaphysics of Morals*, 398 (14); *Critique of Practical Reason*, 34 (123).

[26] *Foundations of the Metaphysics of Morals*, 435–36 (54).

guide in satisfying them, a principle or a maxim whose content is the condition of an act of choice, and the imperative[27] which directs this choice of a specific action—all these can be called "heteronomous," even if the laws are laws of nature or even of God (38, 152 [127–28, 250]).

Remark II of § 8 contains (40 [129]) what Kant claimed was an exhaustive classification of all material practical principles which had been proposed as a basis for morality, together with a summary criticism and rejection of each. By such criticism and rejection, he claims to have established the necessity for there being a purely formal law under which and through which the will can be autonomous.

Kant was fascinated by such classifications, and there exist, in addition to the one he chose finally for the *Critique*, at least four others.[28] In the *Foundations*, the classification is the following:

I. Empirical principles, drawn from the principle of happiness
   1. Physical feeling
   2. Moral feeling
II. Rational principles, drawn from the principle of perfection
   3. Ontological concept: perfection as a possible result of action
   4. Theological concept: an independent (antecedent) perfection, viz., the will of God.

---

[27] Kant does not apply the adjective "heteronomous" to imperatives, but its use in this connection is suggested by Manfred Moritz, *Studien zum Pflichtbegriff in der Kantischen Ethik*. The important point here is not, however, terminological but substantive; an imperative that is heteronomous in origin may nevertheless be categorical in form (cf. my "Apodictic Imperatives," *Kant-Studien*, XLIX [1957], 7–24).

[28] They appear in Reflexionen 6631 and 6637, *Lectures on Ethics*, 12 ff., and *Foundations of the Metaphysics of Morals*, 441 f. (60 f.). The Reflexions are undoubtedly early, and the classifications given include Kant's own theory. They were written before he had clearly formulated the distinction between heteronomy and autonomy, which does not make its appearance prior to the *Foundations*. The theory he was later to espouse appears in them as "truth," as the source from which moral principles are derived. By "truth" he refers to the character of those maxims which are objective and necessary, as shown by the fact that they can be "openly admitted": "That the maxim of which can be openly admitted is good. Consequently everything morally bad is against the truth, because it tacitly assumes a different maxim from the one it professes" (Reflexion 6642). The language is that of Samuel Clarke. Here is one of the earliest anticipations of the categorical imperative and the "maxim of publicity" in *Perpetual Peace*.

The classification of the empirical principles in the *Lectures* is the same as in the *Critique*, though Mandeville is cited as representing the doctrine of physical feeling and Hobbes as the representative of "government." The intellectual principles classified in the *Lectures* also include Kant's own theory that the "inner nature of the action as comprehended by the understanding" is the valid principle. Because his own theory is included, these early attempts at classification are not, strictly speaking, classifications of heteronomous principles alone.

This classification, however, would no longer serve after Kant had established, in Theorem II, that all material principles, including the rational ones, were under the general principle of happiness or self-love. Both principles I and II are derived from this fundamental principle, as he explicitly states in the penultimate paragraph of the Remark. In improving upon this classification, he goes back to the *Reflexionen* and the *Lectures* and takes over the internal-external (i.e., natural-conventional) distinction employed in them and thus creates a new genus, "external subjective principles," and puts concepts 1 and 2 into the same genus as being both subjective and internal. There then results the following classification:

I. Subjective
  A. External
    1. Education (Montaigne)
    2. Civil constitution (Mandeville)
  B. Internal
    3. Physical feeling (Epicurus)
    4. Moral feeling (Hutcheson)
II. Objective
  A. Internal
    5. Perfection (Wolff and the Stoics)
  B. External
    6. Will of God (Crusius and other theological moralists)

The major criticism of these tables is the at least partial arbitrariness of ascribing the views to specific thinkers; Kant, who has already complained of the injustice of labels in philosophy (13 n. [100 n.]), here applies labels to his opponents. The arbitrariness is made clear in the difference in the positions assigned to the same thinkers in different versions of the table. Thus in Reflexion 6637 and in the *Lectures*, Mandeville and Helvetius are classified under what, in the *Critique*, is given as physical feeling; and Hobbes in the *Lectures* is taken as representing the political principle, since, in his view, the sovereign power may permit or prohibit any action and thereby make it right or wrong. The attribution of this view later to Mandeville may no doubt be justified by citing his aphorism that "moral virtues are the political offspring which flattery begot upon pride."[29] Montaigne is described, in the *Lectures*, as "basing himself on examples and pointing out that in

---

[29] "It is visible, then, that it was not any heathen religion or other idolatrous superstition, that first put man upon crossing his appetites and subduing his dearest inclinations, but the skillful management of wary politicians; and the nearer we search into human nature, the more we shall be convinced, that the moral virtues are the political offspring which flattery begot upon pride" (*An Inquiry into the Origin of Moral Virtue* [1723], in Selby-Bigge, *British Moralists*, II, 353).

matters of morality men differ with their environment, and that the morality of one locality is not that of another."[30] There is, of course, only a short step from "custom" to "education," especially when education is as fallible and variable (because not guided by an ideal of universal validity) as Montaigne regarded it.[31]

The criticism of Epicurus has already been given in Kant's general condemnation of the hedonistic foundation for ethics, though he admires the consistency of the Epicurean doctrine, which he holds to be higher than that of the moral-sense theory (24 [111]). In the *Inaugural Dissertation*, § 9, Kant had placed Epicurus and Shaftesbury together in reducing "the criteria of morals to the feeling of pleasure or unpleasantness," and for this he was criticized by Mendelssohn, who rightly saw that there was a difference in saying, with Epicurus, that pleasure is what makes good things good and in saying, with Shaftesbury, that there is a particular pleasure in the contemplation of the good which serves as a mark of its presence.[32] In now separating them, Kant criticizes the moral-sense theory because, to the degree to which it tries to distinguish the pleasurableness of the moral feeling from that of physical feeling,[33] it must already presuppose that the concept of the good is held in mind, conformity to which could give the special feeling of moral pleasure. Feeling itself has no cognitive value; we have "no feeling for law as such"; for consciousness of the law is a product of reason and, without it, conformity to law would bring no pleasure (38 [129]).

But Kant is clearly wrong in this argument. He erroneously thinks that, by showing the pleasure of the moral sense to be like all other pleasures, he has a right to say that the moral-sense theory "reduces everything to the desire for one's own happiness" (38 [128]). This confuses two very different things that the British philosophers had kept properly separate, viz., the disinterested pleasure we experience in doing something righteous or in contemplating a righteous action, whatever it may be that makes it righteous, and the interest we have in the pleasure accruing to us if we do or contemplate a certain action,

---

[30] *Lectures on Ethics*, 12.

[31] Montaigne characteristically says: "Whatsoever is told us, and whatever we learn, ever remember: it is a mortal hand that presents it, and a mortal hand that receives it" (*Essays*, Book II, chap. xii). Kant must have known that this did not represent the whole point of Montaigne's thought on morals, however, for the same essay gives an extensive criticism of the *variability* of customs.

[32] Mendelssohn to Kant, December 25, 1770 (X, 114).

[33] But it cannot do so; cf. *Critique of Practical Reason*, 23 (109); *Metaphysik der Sitten*, VI, 376–77.

which may be righteous or unrighteous.[34] If the former pleasure is disinterested, as Kant might hold when he developed his views on moral contentment (117 [214]), its presence could serve as a mark of ethical value, comparable to the hedonic mark of beauty, without committing him to the view that pleasure derived from the moral sense is the goal of the action itself. If this feeling arises from the immediate apprehension of the fittingness of actions without the need of an antecedent concept of this fittingness, which would be the concept of virtue, then the sentence beginning "One must already value the importance of what we call duty" (38 [128]) begs the question against the theory of the moral sense. To the assumption that we pursue virtue for the sake of the accompanying pleasure, both Hutcheson and Price anticipate Kant in making precisely this objection.[35]

In spite of his objections to it, however, Kant prefers the moral-sense theory to an outright and consistent hedonism because "it pays virtue the honor of ascribing the satisfaction and esteem for her directly to morality, and does not, as it were, say to her face that it is not her beauty but only our advantage that attaches us to her."[36]

Perfection as an ontological concept is rejected as empty and indefinite.[37] When made specifically moral perfection, it is circular to argue that perfection is the source of the moral predicates, which must have been added to it.[38] In the *Critique* he distinguishes transcendental and metaphysical perfection from practical perfection, which is "fittingness or sufficiency of any thing to any kinds of ends." This, however, is insufficient to define more than the highest form of talent and skill, which are ethically neutral. Thus Wolff's concept of perfection suffers from the same weakness as his universal practical philosophy,[39] to wit, it is so general that nothing specifically ethical can be derived from it. Ends must be given, and, if ethical perfection is here in question, ethical ends defined by some other principle than mere perfection or a mere general will must be presupposed. The concept of perfection, however, is esteemed by Kant more than any of the other heteronomous

[34] Cf. Hutcheson, *Inquiry concerning the Original of Our Ideas of Virtue or Moral Good*, Introduction (Selby-Bigge, *British Moralists*, I, 72).

[35] Cf. *Ibid.*, sec. II; and *Review of the Principal Questions of Morals*, chap. i, sec. iii (Selby-Bigge, *British Moralists*, I, 92; II, 124).

[36] *Foundations of the Metaphysics of Morals*, 443 (61).

[37] As already recognized in the *Lectures on Ethics* (pp. 24, 26, 39) in his criticism of Baumgarten, Wolff, and Cumberland that moral rules drawn from the concept of perfection are "tautologous."

[38] *Foundations of the Metaphysics of Morals*, 443 (62).

[39] *Ibid.*, 390 (5). Wolff's conception of perfection is given in *Ontologia*, § 128.

principles, since it does preserve morality from all contamination with empirical concepts.[40]

Finally, there is the external perfection represented by the will of God as the putative source of ethical principles.[41] The same objections apply to this as to internal perfection, but even more strongly, since the consequences of this error are much more damaging. Either Crusius surreptitiously introduces ethical predicates into the concept of divine perfection,[42] with the result that theological perfection no longer grounds the moral principle but presupposes it; or a hedonistic motivation is postulated as the ground of obedience to God, whereby the "concept of the divine will is made up [only] of the attributes of desire for glory and dominion combined with awful conceptions of might and vengeance,"[43] to the detriment and, indeed, destruction of both ethics and religion.

But every one of the heteronomous principles, thus banished from the foundations of moral volition, re-enters the moral scheme of things, once the purity of the source of morals has been secured. The external subjective grounds return not as grounds of duty but as the duty of decorum[44] and obedience to authority. We have a duty to cultivate moral feeling, a feeling of satisfaction or contentment in the performance of duty.[45] We have at least an indirect duty to achieve happiness if possible, both in this life and in the next.[46] The will of God is a symbol of the holiness of will, which is an ideal to be striven for (32 [121]); our own moral perfection is one of the ends which are also a duty.[47] In rejecting heteronomy, therefore, Kant does not reject the moral, political, social, religious, and physical goods which the philosophers of heteronomy had rightly commended. They are all affirmed, but under the condition that their pursuit be regulated by a formal principle.

[40] *Foundations of the Metaphysics of Morals*, 443 (62).

[41] Crusius, *Anweisung vernünftig zu leben* (1744), § 174.

[42] On relation of conscience to obedience to God, *ibid.*, §§ 132–33.

[43] *Foundations of the Metaphysics of Morals*, 443 (62).

[44] *Anthropologie in pragmatischer Hinsicht*, § 14.

[45] *Metaphysik der Sitten*, Tugendlehre, Einleitung (VI, 399–400); *Critique of Practical Reason*, 38 (129).

[46] *Foundations of the Metaphysics of Morals*, 399 (15); *Critique of Practical Reason*, 93 (186).

[47] *Metaphysik der Sitten*, VI, 385 f. Wolff, on the contrary, in making happiness the mere consciousness of perfection, had included the perfection of others in the end which is also a duty (cf. *Philosophia practica universalis*, II, § 28).

Believing, then, that he has not only proved, in Theorem II, that, *in principle*, no empirical motive can give a moral law, but that in Remark II on § 8 he has shown that no proposed empirical principle does, *in fact*, provide a law in spite of the pretensions of other moralists, Kant concludes that "the formal practical principle of pure reason" is the only one that can furnish categorical imperatives, i.e., "practical laws which enjoin actions as dutiful" (41 [130]). To the positive derivation and defense of this principle we now turn.

VIII

The "Metaphysical Deduction" of the Moral Law; Commentary on Sections 4, 5, 6, 7, and Part of 8

§ 1. THE IDEA OF A "METAPHYSICAL DEDUCTION"

Chapter i of the Analytic of Concepts of the *Critique of Pure Reason* is entitled "The Clue to the Discovery of All Pure Concepts of the Understanding." In that chapter Kant argues that the table of judgments, taken, with slight modification, from classical logic, provides a table of categories for knowledge. For there to be knowledge of objects, which are not given to consciousness *in propria persona*, there must be a synthesis of the representations we have of objects, since only the connection between our representations makes it possible for different ones of them to have a common focus in the object which is the source of each of them. Synthesis of representations, of course, may be mere psychological association of ideas; but this synthesis is only subjective and holds only for the individual who happens to associate this representation with that. For there to be knowledge, this synthesis must be governed by rules which are valid for all knowers, so that we can judge that an object has such and such properties and not merely say that I happen to associate one representation with another. Knowledge arises in the synthesis of representations and issues in judgments of objects. The kinds of judgments that constitute the corpus of knowledge, therefore, are a clue to the kinds of synthesis which are necessary to knowledge. The categories, or pure concepts of the understanding, are the concepts or rules of these syntheses, and to each form of judgment there corresponds a category.

In a passage added in the second edition, Kant refers to this chapter as the "metaphysical deduction." The adjective "metaphysical" refers to the pure a priori conceptual knowledge which this chapter is supposed to provide. The metaphysical deduction is distinguished from the transcendental deduction. The latter has the responsibility for showing that the categories do enable us to have a priori knowledge of objects. The metaphysical deduction is Kant's effort to discover what the categories are; the transcendental deduction is his effort to show that they are valid. The two deductions are, in principle, independent of each other, though they both have the same starting point in the doctrine that knowledge requires synthesis and is always expressed in judgments. Had the metaphysical deduction in some way discovered other categories than those it did in fact discover, the transcendental deduction need not have been affected in any significant way. The specific categories derived in the metaphysical deduction are used only illustratively in the transcendental deduction. The essentials of the metaphysical deduction were clear in Kant's mind long before he even realized the need for a transcendental deduction.

In the *Critique of Practical Reason* and even more clearly in the sharply demarcated divisions of the *Foundations of the Metaphysics of Morals*, there is an analogous separation of tasks. Kant first sets out to discover what the moral law must be if the concept of duty and therewith all morality are not spurious. Then he attempts to show that the law thus discovered is valid and not just an empty conception.

Yet the separation is not so clean-cut in the second as in the first *Critique*. The reader himself must draw the boundaries between them, and the boundary is not a single straight line but a wandering line that weaves its way in and out of the various sections.[1] There are several reasons for this lack of formal neatness, which is elsewhere one of the most characteristic marks of organization in Kant's larger works. The moral law, he says, is in no need of "justifying grounds," for it speaks with authority even to the commonest intelligence. Human beings, he believes, acknowledge its validity even when they could not begin to state it in formally exact terms. To formulate, in Socratic manner, and not to teach and defend, as it were, from the outside is the method to be followed in practical philosophy. Hence Kant often permits himself to speak as if the moral law had been established (that is, transcendentally deduced) when, in fact, at those points he has only succeeded in formulating it (i.e., metaphysically deduced it).

Moreover, the fact that there is for Kant only one moral law makes it more difficult, simply as a stylistic matter, to separate the task of formulating it from that of defending it. In the first *Critique*, he had twelve categories, any of which he might choose, from time to time, for purposes of illustration, since the specific justification of any one of the twelve, in the metaphysical deduction, was easily distinguished from the grounds of justification of any category whatsoever. Hence

---

[1] He is more careful to preserve the distinction between the two tasks in *Foundations of the Metaphysics of Morals;* cf. 426, 445 (44, 64).

illustration and justification were easily distinguished. But here it is only one principle that is under examination, and it is one that he thinks is already given with full authority, needing only to be worked out and brought to clear consciousness. Consequently, the formulation and the defense of the principle can hardly be so clearly separated as in the earlier work.

Nevertheless, he is aware of the dual nature of his task, and he points it out explicitly in his distinction between the "exposition" and the "deduction" (46 [135]). We could, in fact, as well speak of the "metaphysical exposition" as of the "metaphysical deduction" in each of the first two *Critique*'s, for by "exposition" he means "the clear, though not necessarily exhaustive representation of that which belongs to a concept; the exposition is metaphysical when it contains that which exhibits the concept as given a priori."[2] But the established position of "metaphysical deduction" in Kant's architectonic makes me prefer this name for the material about to be examined.

Still, too much must not be expected from the proffered analogy to chapter i of the Analytic of the first *Critique*, in spite of its obvious existence. For there is no ready-made table of formal distinctions to serve as a clue to the discovery of the principle of pure practical reason. There is nothing in the *Critique of Practical Reason* comparable to the synthetic procedure of the metaphysical deduction in the first. Yet there is a parallelism between the larger movements of thought that underlie the formulations in each work. For Kant himself says: "We come to know pure practical laws in the same way we know pure theoretical principles, [to wit] by attending to the necessity with which reason prescribes them to us, and to the elimination from them of all empirical conditions, which reason directs" (30 [118]).

In spite of the differences in appearance, the argument of the *Critique of Practical Reason* in its discovery and formulation of the moral law is comparable to that of the *Foundations* and the *Prolegomena*. In all three of these works, Kant begins with a problem presented by ordinary experience to philosophical analysis, and he reaches his conclusion by attempting to demonstrate that only one principle or theory is capable of rendering the problematic experience intelligible. In the *Foundations* and in the second *Critique* it is practical experience in general and moral experience in particular. Our task in this chapter is, with Kant, to "attend to the necessity" which is experienced in moral concern, to show how this necessity requires the elimination, or at least the transcending, of empirical conditions, and then to show what remains as the formal principle of a pure practical reason.

[2] *Critique of Pure Reason*, B 38. It is interesting to observe that the Analytic of the *Critique of Judgment* is formally divided into "exposition" and "deduction."

§ 2. PRINCIPAL FEATURES OF THE MORAL EXPERIENCE

In the analytical method employed here and in the first two parts of the *Foundations*, Kant begins with an experience and regresses upon those presuppositions without which it would have to be declared unintelligible or spurious. When the analytical method is employed at the behoof of a metaphysical deduction or exposition, the presuppositions are found as organizing concepts, principles, or forms of the experience examined. The result of this regression upon the formal conditions is the statement of the principle reached in the first two parts of the *Foundations* and presupposed here (8 [93]).

There is no difficulty, he tells us,[3] in discerning the possibility (i.e., in discovering the principles) of hypothetical imperatives. Granted that men have desires that may be satisfied only by the application of their knowledge of the world and granted that they are not sufficiently rational in the pursuit of their aims always readily to do those actions indicated by their knowledge as being necessary, it is obvious that they will experience a constraint to do them, the constraint being expressed in a hypothetical, conditional, heteronomous imperative.

The facts and principles which make heteronomous imperatives so easily explicable, however, are wholly inadequate to account for some of the central and characteristic features of moral experience. An ethics which does not acknowledge the sharp and radical distinction between prudence and morality and which thereby makes morals heteronomous simply leaves unexplained, or explains away, certain obvious characteristics of moral concern. Perhaps they should be explained away; it is conceivable[4] that they may be spurious. Whether they are spurious or not is the decision that must be made in the light of the success or failure of the transcendental deduction. But, first, the sensible thing to do is to discern what principles must be presupposed if we take moral experience at its face value, though provisionally, until we come to the deduction. The most important of these features which require a different set of presuppositions from those involved in heteronomy are the following.

a) *The objective necessitation of the action.*—In moral concern there is a felt constraint to do a certain action, and this constraint has a quite different tone from that which I experience when called upon to do some action for the sake of some even long-range goal I have before me. The latter is a constraint predicated upon a desire I have; the former seems to be independent of and often in conflict with all my

---

[3] *Foundations of the Metaphysics of Morals*, 417 (34).

[4] *Ibid.*, 407 (23–24).

desires. This kind of constraint is called "duty," the objective necessitation of an action that is not subjectively necessary but subject to my free choice to commit or omit it.

The difference between being constrained to do something because of my needs or wishes and being constrained to do it irrespective of them is perhaps most easily discerned in the parallel distinction between being "obliged" to do something and being "obligated" to do it. To be, or to feel, obliged to do something is quite different from being, or believing myself to be, obligated to do it. For instance, I am obliged to put my name in my books, since I do not want them to be borrowed and not returned; but I am obligated to return borrowed books, no matter how much I desire to keep them as my own. It makes perfectly good sense to say, "I had an obligation to tell the truth, but to get out of that scrape I was obliged to lie." To be obliged to do something means that, to accomplish a given purpose, I have to do something I don't particularly want to do, or dislike doing. To be obligated to do something means to be under the necessity of choosing to do something without consulting my desires. In each case my cognitive intelligence (for Kant, reason) must decide what it is that I ought to do; but, in the former case, one of reason's premises is a desire, while, in the latter, desire is not a premise (though, of course, if the phenomenon of morality is in general spurious or in a particular case is only an instance of hypocrisy and cant, it is a cause).

b) Motives as the object of moral judgment.—In passing a moral judgment, I do not pass on the success or failure of an action in leading to the object of some desire. I need not await the issue of an action to decide whether it was good or bad; I need only know the motive which led to it. In making a moral decision, I do not first need to know whether the action I undertake will succeed or not; I do not even need to know whether, in fact, I have the power to produce the effect.[5] But in acts of skill and prudence, success is everything, and motives are of importance only indirectly, if at all.

But, even more obviously, I do not morally judge actions themselves so much as decisions to act. Though Kant often writes as if an action is the object of moral judgment and is itself good or bad, it must be remembered that action is not merely an item of external behavior (e.g., the emitting of certain sounds) but includes, as its definitive component, the motives, intentions, and decisions which lead to it. The complex act of making a decision for certain reasons and not for others is what we attend to in moral judgment; but in matters of skill and prudence, it is the act and its outcome that count.

[5] *Critique of Practical Reason*, 15, 45, 68 (101, 135, 160).

c) The universality of moral judgment.—Moral judgment is no re-specter of persons. Though Kant admits in his discussions of imperfect duties that circumstances make legitimate differences in the specific acts by which moral responsibilities are met, there is always in moral judgment an appeal to a disinterested forum which makes no allowance for the one thing pre-eminently important in questions of prudence, viz., what one happens to desire. Not only is moral obligation inde-pendent of my desires; it is independent of specific desires that any men may have. I can and do make moral judgments of beings that are not men (e.g., God); and though perhaps only men experience obliga-tion, we hold a holy will to the same objective standard of right that we apply to ourselves.

It must always be carefully noted that the universality of moral judg-ment has nothing to do with the variability of custom and the variety of moral judgments current in various societies and in different ages. The fact that moral judgment varies from time to time and from place to place has nothing to do with the kind of universality that Kant is speaking of here. Regrettably, he never explained the precise sense in which he meant, and the precise sense in which he did not mean, that moral judgments are universal. Fortunately, he did so in his treatment of aesthetic judgment,[6] and we can easily apply his discussion of that to moral judgment. Kant was not so blind to the fact that aesthetic judgment is highly variable as he is sometimes believed to have been to the variability of judgment on moral questions. When he insists that, in passing an aesthetic judgment, we are making a judgment that claims (though it does not receive) universal assent, he is distinguishing between what we may call "normative" universality and "social" uni-versality: an aesthetic judgment has, or claims to have, the former but neither has, nor claims to have, the latter. Similarly, moral judgments are normatively universal, but Kant, who knew as much about folkways as perhaps anyone in the eighteenth century, was not concerned with them in the analysis of moral judgment itself. Whether what I believe to be universally valid is in fact universally valid is one question and an important one; whether what I believe to be universally valid is in fact universally believed to be valid is a quite different question and one so easy to answer in the negative that it is of no importance at all. But the obvious negative answer to the second question does not imply that one must in principle give a negative answer to the first question. It is not even a premise for an answer to the first question. Sometimes one must answer the first question in one way, sometimes in another; and Kant is attempting, in this part of the *Foundations* and the *Critique*,

[6] *Critique of Judgment,* § 7.

to find the criterion by which it must be answered. But even prior to the erection of this criterion, it is essential to recognize that moral judgment makes a universal claim of a kind not made by the expression of a wish or a liking.[7]

d) Direct interest in the action.—In all actions done for the sake of some desired consequences, our direct interest is in the consequences, the existence of the state of affairs desiderated; and we have only an indirect interest in the action itself. Though all actions voluntarily undertaken do have consequences and are intended to have consequences, in which there is some kind of interest,[8] Kant denies that the actions necessarily occur because of this interest in the object.[9] He asserts that in moral action there is an interest in the action itself, meaning by "action" the whole complex of motive and decision as well as outward conduct. In modern terminology, Kant is saying that moral value is an intrinsic value and that it interests us because we recognize its intrinsic value. Success and failure in achievement are not moral categories, but concepts of technique and prudence; worthiness to be happy and culpability are the corresponding moral categories, and their applicability is wholly independent of success or failure.

Other characteristics might be added to this list. For instance, Kant speaks of the difference between mere regret and repentance as distin-

---

[7] The reader who is interested in the bearing of the facts of comparative anthropology on a universal moral criterion like that of Kant is advised to read A. Macbeath's *Experiments in Living* (London: Macmillan & Co., Ltd., 1952). On the basis of a wide collection of data, Mr. Macbeath concludes that folkways and customs alone do not establish an acknowledged standard in the consciousness of members of a group until a claim to universality and a bearing upon the general welfare of the group (which is a step toward universalization) are present. He thus finds something comparable to a categorical imperative present as a cultural invariant in all systems of folkways, defining for each the difference between the customary and the moral. Also relevant to the question of universalization is the level of abstractness of the rule or principle being tested. The "exceptions to moral rules" which are paraded by ethical or cultural relativists are not relevant to the evaluation of a universalistic ethics like Kant's unless they can be expressed, for instance, in such a form as "It is sometimes right to act from bad motives" or "It is sometimes right to treat others merely as means," and not merely "It is sometimes right to take property that does not legally belong to you."

[8] *Critique of Practical Reason*, 34 (123). The interest need not be an empirical interest in some sensuous satisfaction resulting from the satiation of a need. In moral action the empirical interest cannot be denied to exist and need not necessarily be frustrated in action; only "no regard must be given to the interest in the object" when we are trying to decide whether an action is morally right. Cf. *ibid.*, 93 (186); *Foundations of the Metaphysics of Morals*, 413 n. (30 n.); *Über den Gemeinspruch* . . . , VIII, 278.

[9] *Foundations of the Metaphysics of Morals*, 413 n., 459 n. (30 n., 80 n.).

guishing two kinds of failure[10] and of the specificity and clarity of moral commands, which he contrasts with the vagueness that is an inescapable infirmity of counsels of prudence.[11] But this latter is certainly an oversimplification of the facts, as Kant fully realized in the *Metaphysics of Morals*. Since it not only is wrong but plays no part in the derivation of the law, it need not be further discussed here. It should be pointed out, however, that this alleged feature of moral principles does play a very great role in the transcendental deduction. There it is not any longer a question of the clarity of specific moral commands in contrast to the obscurity of prudential counsels, but only of the clarity of the moral principle itself, by virtue of which one readily recognizes the difference between what is right and what is only advisable, without having to feel easily assured that some specific act really is the right one in given circumstances.

§ 3. FIRST APPROXIMATION TO THE PRINCIPLE

From these salient features of moral concern, judgment, and action, Kant draws four conclusions concerning the principle involved in moral action.

a) The principle must be a law and not a mere maxim. Only a law can necessitate, and only a law can be universal in application. Such universalizability is essential for normativity. A mere maxim, even if it did express the condition of the will of every man, would not be necessary for any of them, would not obligate any of them.

b) The principle must be a law by virtue of its form and not of its content. The content is always some object of interest in that which is to be achieved by following the law taken as a maxim; but such an interest is neither universal, nor obligation-creating, nor directed to the action as such.

c) But the law must be capable of being a maxim, i.e., of being an expression of the actual condition of a will. Otherwise, the law or the action's conformity to it could not interest us, and knowledge of it would be practically ineffective except under the contingent condition of an interest in the object of the maxim. Knowledge of the principle itself must provide the motive to act in accordance with it, and, when it does so, the action is not only done in accordance with it but because of it, i.e., out of respect for it. Otherwise reason is only the slave of the passions.

---

[10] *Critique of Practical Reason*, 37 (127). The remark on Priestley's view of repentance (*ibid.*, 98 [192]) refers to *The Doctrine of Philosophical Necessity* (1777), pp. 86 ff. (note taken from Natorp in Akademie ed.).

[11] *Critique of Practical Reason*, 36 (126); *Über den Gemeinspruch . . .* , VIII, 286.

d) The law must ground a categorical imperative, though it must be distinguished from the imperative. It must be a law of how a rational being as such would necessarily act. Only such a law can be a categorical imperative to a partially rational being like man, who does not by nature act in accordance with his conception of law. The "would" of the moral law must be expressed as the "should" of the imperative, but distinguished from it.[12] The "should" of this imperative, unlike that of the hypothetical imperative, is not contingent upon there being an interest in the object of the action, or even upon there being an interest in the moral law and its reign, as if those who felt no interest in it were absolved of all blame for transgressing it.[13]

Not every formally categorical imperative, however, is based upon this law, for any imperative can be put into categorical form. Only those imperatives which are "practically right" (21 [107]) are here in question, and these are imperatives which are unconditional or apodictic, even though they may be hypothetical in form.[14] That an imperative can be apodictic in authority, yet not categorical in form, is a nicety that Kant seems to have overlooked, with unfortunate consequences for his concept of the universal application of the moral law. It permitted him to write as if the categorical imperative allowed no room for considerations of contingencies that would appear in the antecedents of hypothetical, but still necessary, imperatives.[15]

§ 4. THE THREE MAXIMS IN MORAL DECISION

In chapter vi, § 6, I analyzed action undertaken because it is believed to lead to a desired end. In the hypothetical imperative, fully expanded, we discovered a material maxim, a theoretical law or cognition of the causal relation of an act to its consequences, and a formal principle that a rational being who fully wills an end also necessarily wills the means believed to produce it.

Analysis of moral action in this chapter shows that if morality is not to be declared chimerical, a specific action must be decided upon in-

---

[12] *Foundations of the Metaphysics of Morals*, 449 (68). Strictly speaking, of course, there is no "should" in an imperative. A sentence "You should do *X*" is not an imperative to do *X*. But both this sentence and the imperative proper are related to the law "A rational being as such does *X*" in the same way; each is directed to a rational being who does not by nature do *X* because of the law.

[13] Thus, while there is no duty to have a moral interest, a being who does not is condemnable not as morally evil but as falling outside the scope of moral concepts altogether (cf. *Metaphysik der Sitten*, VI, 400).

[14] E.g., "If you have made a promise, keep it," is hypothetical in form but apodictic in modality; "Shut the door" is categorical in form but problematic in modality.

[15] Cf. above, pp. 87 f.

dependently of whether there are actual desires that can be satisfied by the action and independently of whether we know and can master the means by which the object of desire can be realized. Kant must accordingly show how a specific action can be decided upon and undertaken without presupposing a specific desire to be satisfied by the action. If this cannot be shown, all actions would have to be analyzed in the manner given on page 85 above, and the universality, necessity, and intrinsic value of moral action would have to be declared illusory. For if the determining maxim is the material one, like I, A, in that analysis (a specific setting of the will to produce a certain end, which can be achieved only by the use of knowledge given in I, B), the imperative cannot be categorical, and the corresponding principle is a mere maxim.

Yet we cannot simply eliminate I, A, and leave moral action unmotivated. Kant rightly recognizes that something at least analogous to I, A, is necessary to all action. "It is certainly undeniable," he says, in a sentence which seems to have been overlooked by many of his critics,[16] "that every volition must have an object and therefore a material." But, he adds, "the material cannot be supposed for this reason to be the determining ground and condition of the maxim" (34 [123]). Kant must find a principle, not to replace I, A, but to control it.[17]

The control of one maxim by another is nothing strange. Material maxims themselves stand in a hierarchy. My desire for money may be expressed in one maxim; my desire to live slothfully in another; and one of these can control the expression of actions done under the aegis of

[16] The most notable of those who have fallen into this error is Max Scheler (*Der Formalismus in der Ethik und die materiale Wertethik*, [Halle, 1916]; also in *Jahrbuch für Philosophie und phänomenologische Forschung*, Vols. I and II). Scheler's Kant-criticism is that, for Kant, the a priori must be empty because it is purely formal. But since ethical principles are also, for Scheler, a priori, there must be an a priori which is material, i.e., given in an intuition of material value-essences. In this way, Scheler believed he could avoid the "subjectivity" and "intellectualism" of Kant's ethics, which are consequences, he held, of Kantian "empty formalism." But this criticism misses the main point of Kant's distinction between the object of the will, which is always present, and the object of the will as its determining ground, which is present only to empirical practical reason. Scheler, in his own constructive work, is left with no rational criterion for material principles, which is what the formal principle supplies in Kant's theory. In the schema introduced below, Scheler locates the a priori at *a*, Kant at *b*. But while *b* is purely formal, it is not therefore empty; *its content is* a.

[17] Cf. Reflexion 6633 (*ca.* 1770): "The supreme principles of moral decision are rational, but they are only formal principles. They determine no purpose, but only the moral form of every purpose. Therefore, according to this form *in concreto* primary material principles occur [*vorkommen*]." On the control of one maxim by another see Paton, *The Categorical Imperative*, pp. 136–37.

the other. This is the sense in which the maxim of self-love is regarded by Kant as the *supreme* material maxim. But, since even this maxim can ground only hypothetical imperatives and the *explicatum* here is unconditional obligation, the maxim he seeks cannot be governing by virtue of its material. The supreme maxim must select from among the material maxims those which should be permitted in our practical syllogisms,[18] and it must do so by virtue of being a criterion of maxims with respect to their form and independent of their content. That is what Kant means when he says that the principle he is seeking must be purely formal; that is his obscure way of saying that it must be a principle regulating conduct through controlling the form of permissible maxims.

In the analysis of moral action, therefore, we must add one more principle to the two practical principles uncovered in our analysis of hypothetical imperatives. We must distinguish the following:

a) A material maxim setting forth some general condition of my will.

b) A principle (law) which determines whether *a* is subject to morally permissible execution and which is itself a maxim.

c) The formal principle of the hypothetical imperative, which is the condition of the choice of acts necessary to attain the end set forth in *a*, the actual means being discovered by the cognition of causal connections between acts and consequences.

For instance, my purpose (*a*) may be to promote the happiness of others. The law (*b*) authorizes me to act upon this maxim. The principle (*c*) selects from among my empirical cognitions those that make specific actions incumbent upon me, granting the legitimacy of *a*. The law (*b*) forbids certain types of maxim (*a*), allows some, and requires still others.

The easiest case to discern in Kant's discussions is the first, so much so that it is often taken as the only one. He is often interpreted[19] as believing (i) that the moral law is only a criterion for the admissibility of material maxims and (ii) that there is always a conflict between natural, spontaneous material maxims and the law. This interpretation is only partially correct and must be supplemented in what follows. But the reason why this half-correct interpretation is so easy lies in Kant's realistic and unsentimental estimate of human character. Where a mate-

[18] This is said in *Foundations of the Metaphysics of Morals*, 432, 444 (50, 63): a will which made a material maxim its law would need still another law to give it the proper universality.

[19] If, that is, the objector has given up the still more common error of believing that Kant thought that *b* had nothing to do with *a* at all.

rial maxim leads to action which does in fact accord with the law, any-one with our philosopher's sense of hard fact and hatred of cant will naturally regard the material as the motive and will distrust its embel-lishment as duty (154 [252]). So that the role of each can be distin-guished, Kant preferred to deal with the extreme cases in which the two things, duty and desire, work at cross-purposes.[20] Hence his ethics seems to be more an ethics of prohibition and of repression of the nat-ural man than one of the celebration of spontaneous good nature. Un-doubtedly, this semblance is based in part on Kant's own personal *habitus* (at least by the time he reached the writing of this book); but even more it is based upon many readers' failure to remember the polemical situation in which Kant found himself, one in which he had to separate and set apart and seem to set in opposition those things that had been confused and even identified by others.

The most significant case, however, is that in which the moral law requires me to act on certain maxims, whether they express an ante-cedent condition of my will or not. If we are to justify the alleged di-rect interest in moral action, the moral principle must become a maxim with its own material. This material is not empirical, like happiness, but is the morally good, which is defined by the principle itself and not de-sired antecedently to it. Only if the formal principle can itself be taken as a maxim, so that we strive to instill in ourselves a certain readiness to act in a given way regardless of whether we have an antecedent dispo-sition to these actions, can we say that pure reason, the exclusive source of *b*, can be practical.

---

[20] Cf. *Critique of Practical Reason*, 92–93 (186), where he compares his procedure to that of a chemist in separating a compound into its elements. Kant's examples in the *Foundations* are of this type. They concern, for instance, the man without sym-pathy who acts from "practical love." If the purpose Kant had in devising these examples is remembered, one can see the error of interpreting him as a proponent of "sour duty." He is simply insisting that *a* and *b* be distinguished and that we not attribute *moral* value to *a* alone but to *a* only when it is instilled in us or acted upon because of *b*; what other values *a* may have is not being discussed here at all, but the specific moral value is being made salient by contrast, i.e., by choosing cases of *a* in which the only prima facie value is the moral one. These are not examples for imitation but examples for illustration. We shall return to this matter in chap. xii when we discuss the relations between Kant and Schiller. It is a pity that the ques-tion must be discussed so fully, but it is necessary because Kant did not make the purpose of his examples absolutely clear with repeated statements that could not be overlooked even by his opponents. Had he done so, the quantity of writing against his ethics would have been halved and its quality raised immeasurably. I have dis-cussed the misinterpretation of the examples which arises from neglect of the polemical context in "Sir David Ross on Duty and Purpose in Kant," *Philosophy and Phenomenological Research*, XVI (1955), 98–107.

But we have not yet seen what this law is which requires that our maxims have a certain form and which has an object that cannot be derived from our natural desires.

§ 5. DEFINITION OF THE PRINCIPLE

The supreme formal principle states that a purely rational being would act on no material maxim that could not be accepted as itself a law for all rational beings. All maxims of a rational being as such are independent of the differences between them, i.e., their desires; the maxims of a rational being as such are, therefore, laws. The imperative, which is the formula of this law's constraint on a partially rational being, is that a maxim should be followed only if it is a maxim that I could will that all rational beings should follow. The imperative serves as a criterion for maxims that may function in morally permissible actions.

Since, however, to be moral and not merely legal, there must be a direct interest in the action, the principle must not be merely a negative test for an antecedent maxim, as the previous paragraph makes it seem. The principle must be something positive, something commanding us to establish maxims in our hearts that are recognized as valid for us as rational beings *because* they are valid for rational beings generally or willed to be the maxims that all rational beings should follow. In this positive, constitutive sense, contrasted with the previous negative and regulative sense of the principle, knowledge of the principle must itself be a ground for action. We must not merely act on maxims that do pass the test, but our supreme maxim must be to act upon them because they do pass it.

It is very easy to emphasize the negative, regulative aspect and to neglect the positive, constitutive aspect of the principle and then to suppose that Kant is refuted by showing that there are maxims which could be universalized but which do not obligate me.[21] For instance, I can easily will that everyone should write his name in his books, but this has no effect on my duty. In the negative, regulative function, there are, as it were, two volitions: a desire to do something, but *only if* I can desire others to do it too. In the positive, constitutive function there is a more intimate relation between them: I desire (or will) to do something *because* I can will it for others too. Only if I will it for myself because I can will it for others, does the supreme moral maxim free

[21] This error is attributed to Kant by, among others, C. D. Broad, *Five Types of Ethical Theory* (London, 1930), p. 128. For an analysis of the logic of this controversy see Austin Duncan-Jones, "Kant on Universalization," *Analysis*, XVI (1955), 12–14. It will be discussed more fully in chap. ix.

itself from antecedent material maxims. This is, I think, intended in Kant's statement of the imperative, in the words italicized: "So act that the maxim of your will could always hold *at the same time* as the principle of a universal legislation."[22]

This is stated by Kant to be the sought-for moral law, or supreme principle of pure practical reason. In fact, however, it is not a law, but an imperative; and though he has distinguished between law and imperative, he nowhere in the *Critique* states the law in proper form. He does so only in the *Foundations,* and there incidentally: "An absolutely good will is one whose maxim can always include itself when regarded as a universal law," which is an a priori synthetic proposition.[23]

§ 6. AUTONOMY

A law is a principle that is universally valid for all rational beings. As a principle, it must contain a general determination of the will. We have been attempting to understand what this principle is, considered as a practical proposition.

In the section immediately following upon his formulation of the principle, however, Kant begins to use the word "principle" in another sense. "Principle" has hitherto meant a basic, fundamental synthetic a priori judgment; now it means the actual *prius* or condition that is formulated by this judgment. The principle he now speaks of is not a judgment but a condition of will or the "general determination" itself. And he says: "The autonomy of the will is the sole principle of all moral laws and of the duties conforming to them. . . . The moral law expresses nothing else than the autonomy of pure practical reason, i.e., freedom" (33 [122]).

In §§ 5 and 6 of the *Critique* (28–29 [116–17]) Kant shows that a formal (synthetic) maxim is sufficient to determine the will only if the will is not wholly determined by the material of its maxims. If a rational being follows a formal (synthetic) principle, he does so because his will is free from empirical determination. This is freedom in the negative sense. And since a will requires some law for its determination, such a being must follow a law not given to it by nature; this can only be a law given completely by reason itself and not by reason working

---

[22] *Critique of Practical Reason,* § 7 (30 [119]). The notion that there are two volitions—one for my own action and another for the universalization of the maxim of the former volition—has not even any apparent verbal justification in later formulas of the categorical imperative in the *Foundations.* Cf. especially the statement of the "principle of autonomy"; "Never choose except in such a way that the maxims of the choice are comprehended *in the same volition* as a universal law" (*Foundations of the Metaphysics of Morals,* 440 [59]; italics added).

[23] *Foundations of the Metaphysics of Morals,* 447 (66).

on the data of experience. Hence the will must be free also in a positive sense, i.e., as self-determining.

Thus Kant concludes that a free will, a moral will, and a pure practical reason are identical. If reason were not capable of prescribing the law to itself, it would have to borrow the law from nature, and such a law can support only a heteronomous imperative. Only a law given by myself as a member of the intelligible world can interest me directly as a member of the empirical world; all other laws and actions under them can interest me only indirectly.

Only a self-given law, therefore, can support the phenomena of morality described above in § 3; and a self-given law of a rational being must have the formula stated by Kant. With it, the metaphysical deduction of the principle is complete, though we shall continue, in the next chapter, to follow Kant in matters corollary to it.

Before turning to these parts of the exposition of the concept, however, it is well to consider Kant's conclusions reached thus far, especially in the light of his philosophy of theoretical law. Some writers have remarked on what they call the "paradox of Kantian ethics," the paradox of his having begun with the most complete subjection of self to law in the history of modern ethics and having ended with the complete subordination of the law to the self. His central moral phenomenon is the restricting of the self by law; its explanation is the lawgiving of the self, or autonomy.

But there is no paradox here, and Kant's thought is a development of an older concept in the light of his previous theoretical development of the concept of the law in general. Wolff and other rationalists had made the law of nature sovereign over man and had regarded reason as man's moral mentor, since only reason could discover nature's law.[24] That obedience to the law of nature would bring men to perfection and happiness was obvious to them; but happiness was not, they thought, the reason why men should obey the law of nature. Obligation followed simply from an analysis of the concept of perfection.[25]

Kant, however, was not, during the critical period, any more taken in by this concept of natural obligation than by that of natural purposive-

---

[24] Cf. Wolff, *Vernünftige Gedancken von der Menschen Thun und Lassen*, § 137: The laws of nature require that we do that which contributes to our perfection. Our conscience requires that we act according to the laws of nature. The laws of nature are the laws of morality and of reason, which discovers them. Similarly, Crusius, *Entwurf der nothwendigen Vernunftwahrheiten*, §§ 133, 137: There is an inborn idea of natural law, placed in us by God and recognized by conscience, which is not a theoretical cognition but a *Grundtrieb* or has as its basis a *Trieb* of the will.

[25] In this they were followed by Kant in the *Prize Essay*, II, 299 (Beck, 283).

ness as a ground for morals. He saw that laws of nature are without moral import and that they can be guides to action only if some purpose is presupposed. The only purpose he could find which could be served by our knowledge of natural law was happiness and all its pleasurable components. Hence he concluded that Wolff's practical philosophy, though ostensibly an ethics of law, was really an ethics of desire, unable to ground the authority of the law it celebrated.

Kant was not willing to surrender one jot of the authority of moral law. His theoretical philosophy provided the clue to his concept of the source of law. In his theoretical philosophy, reason is the source of the law of nature; the laws of nature are not passively recorded but are conditions we place upon experience as criteria of its objective significance. Only because of their origin can they have the necessity denied by Hume or explained on the assumption that they are intrinsically and self-evidently rational or revealed as the laws of God—explanations he contemptuously rejected.

But if the source of the objective necessity of the theoretical laws of nature lies in us as rational beings, it is easy to see how Kant could also locate the source of moral law in autonomous reason and guarantee its objective necessity at the same time. The only significant difference between them is that the former laws have a sensuous condition and are therefore restricted to what is, where "is" means "is for us men, under the sensuous condition of our experience and in accordance with the second Postulate of Empirical Thought." The latter, on the other hand, are not restricted to this sensuous condition and are regarded as laws of a world we do not know actually to exist, but one which we know ought, by our actions, to be brought into existence. Reason does not find its demands for rationality fully satisfied in what is presented as actual; its demands for complete rationality can be met only in a world not actually given to us. The discrepancy between what reason demands and what experience presents—this unsatisfied demand of theoretical reason—appears as the practical interest in the reign of a rational law that does not actually reign in nature.

To a being like man, who legitimately uses existence only as a category of what is presentable to the senses, such a law prescribes what ought to be, not what is. Its claim on him lies in the fact that it is not only a law for him but a law by him. If the law sprang from another source, be it God himself, its claim on man would be only conditional. It could be effective only through a system of reward and punishment working upon his desires. The purity of morals would be destroyed. Only autonomy can unite the two conceptions which are inherent in Kant's ethics: that man is independent of everything outside him in the determination of duty and yet that in the moral struggle we are commanded, and we are not "volunteers" (82, 85 [175, 178]).

Kant's ethics, historically, represents a transition between two great conceptions of the relation of man to the world. Against the eighteenth-century position that man is a part of nature and ought to be subservient to her laws, Kant reacted by inverting the order and making nature what she is because of how she appears to us. Then he transcended even this Copernican venture by daring to weigh nature in the scales of reason and to declare that she is wanting and does not contain the destiny of man. The practical—what man ought to be and how he ought to transform his existence—in this conception takes precedence over what nature is and what she demands of man as part of her order. Nature produced man but brought him to the stage where he can finally assert his independence of her.[26]

Continuance of this development of the theory of the creative self is found in romanticism. For the romanticists, man stands above nature as her author and judge; but the judge has lost his law. The universality of law, which is Kant's heritage from the rationalists and naturalists of the seventeenth and eighteenth centuries, was maintained and even magnified by him, though he anchored it in the abstractly personal, in the *res cogitans*. But with Herder and others, this was only a halfway point, an unstable mixture of rationalism and subjectivism. The development was to be completed, they thought, only by seeing the concretely personal, historical man as the source of law.

But, of course, under this dispensation law is no longer rational and universal, and its necessity is only historical. It is only an expression of feeling and history, of *Zeitgeist*, *Volksgeist*, and *Schwärmerei*. To those who wished to take this last step, Kant addressed his essay on "Orientation in Thinking": "Men of intellectual power and broad minds! I honor your talents and love your feeling for humanity. But have you considered what you do, and where you will end with your attacks on reason?"[27]

With acute foresight, Kant told them what would be the end of those attacks. But the attacks have continued, and we have seen their consequences, and they are as Kant foretold.

[26] Cf. *Idea for a Universal History*, Thesis III (VIII, 19).

[27] *What Is Orientation in Thinking?* VIII, 144 (Beck, 303).

IX

Practical Concepts and Judgment; Commentary on Analytic, Chapter II

§ 1. INTRODUCTION

Chapter ii of the Analytic, "The Concept of an Object of Pure Practical Reason," follows the Deduction. Logically, it should have preceded it and come immediately after the establishment of the formula of the supreme principle in § 7. Because of the difficulty in some of its parts, however, one can well imagine that Kant wished the reader to become thoroughly familiar with the basic principle and its ramifications before undertaking the work on concepts and moral judgment. While its position after the Deduction permits Kant to speak in it sometimes in the context of the law as having been deduced (established as valid), and not merely as formulated, at other places he recognizes that this chapter is a part of the Exposition, or what I have called the "Metaphysical Deduction." In one place, indeed, he writes explicitly as if the (transcendental) Deduction were yet to come.[1] While a few passages can best be interpreted in the light of this Deduction as having been accomplished, as a whole this chapter seems best understood as an elaboration and application of the formula, quite independently of the warrant that the formula gains from the (transcendental) Deduction.

Stylistically, the chapter is very uneven. In its early parts it is one of the clearest and most straightforward sections of the *Critique*. Its middle part, on the other hand, is the most difficult and obscure in the entire book. It is often regarded as merely a specimen of Kant's "vicious

---

[1] *Critique of Practical Reason*, 67 (158): The sentence beginning "Finally, the categories of modality . . ." even suggests that at one time, in the course of writing, the order of the parts may have been reversed. There are internal reasons which require that the Analytic of Principles should follow the Transcendental Deduction of the Concepts in the first *Critique*. But there is no good reason why the study of concepts and judgments should follow the Deduction in the second *Critique*, even though it is necessary that the *formulation* of the principle should precede that of the concepts.

architectonic" and as having no integral place in the argument of the book as a whole. Even the most charitable interpretation of it must admit that it is cryptic and poorly constructed and, unlike the corresponding part of the first *Critique*, left largely unexploited in the further development of Kant's doctrine. The very obscurity and ineptness of the construction, however, speak against this section as having been an expression of a merely crotchety interest in architectonic; for when Kant did follow this penchant, his tables had an elegance and polish sorely missed here. It is at least arguable that he was here exploring entirely new ground, ground which he did not succeed in neatly cultivating. The last part of the chapter is again clear; though it deals with a difficult and subtle topic, anticipations of it in the first *Critique* and in the *Foundations* adequately prepare the reader for its difficulties.

§ 2. PRINCIPLE, CONCEPT, AND JUDGMENT

Kant speaks twice (16, 90 [102, 184]) of the fact that the Analytic of this *Critique* has the same parts as that of the first but in reverse order. The *Critique of Pure Reason* first formulates and justifies certain pure concepts (categories) that cannot have an empirical origin but must apply to empirical objects if we are to have any knowledge of them. Second, it shows how these concepts are to be applied in experience, i.e., how occasions for the application of the categories are found and distinguished within experience. This is performed in the chapter on "Schematism," which is concerned with the faculty of transcendental judgment, i.e., the faculty of subsuming intuitions under concepts which are independent of intuition. Finally, it is shown how these concepts can be synthesized a priori into principles, which are the laws given to nature by the understanding. This is the subject matter of the Analytic of Principles. If the concepts are not restricted to the conditions of experience, they are called "Ideas of Reason,"[2] and the Transcendental Dialectic shows that no synthetic a priori judgments or principles can be justified when the categories are treated as Ideas of non-sensuous objects.

In the *Critique of Practical Reason*, however, the start is made from principles and not from concepts. The reason for this is clearly stated in chapter ii,[3] but it is implicit in the whole spirit of the Kantian ethics. The moral fact—the phenomenon to be explained and rendered in-

[2] Another, more positive, conception of the Ideas also appears in the *Critique of Pure Reason* and passes over into the *Critique of Practical Reason;* it will be fully discussed in chap. xiii.

[3] In answer to Pistorius, *Critique of Practical Reason*, 62–63 (154).

telligible—is the consciousness of obligation to carry out the terms of the moral law. We have no independent faculty of intuition or moral sense to give us the concept of the good as something to be achieved; the mode in which moral concern first arises is obligation, expressed by the law and its imperative, and not intuition or even a judgment that something or other to be achieved by or realized in action is good.[4] Moral concepts—indeed, all practical concepts—are to be derived from principles, and not conversely. If the reverse order is attempted, that which is called "good" would have to be discerned by a receptivity (feeling), and thus heteronomous principles would be derived. Accordingly, the original moral phenomenon of absolute constraint, which requires an autonomous principle, would be left unexplained. Hence Kant says that we should not beg the most important question in moral philosophy by choosing a procedure that dictates its answer, as beginning with concepts would entail heteronomy of principle. We should at least leave open the possibility (and explore it) that principle determines concept.

In his discussion of the difference between the order of topics, however, Kant omits discussion of the mediating role of the faculty of judgment. Yet it has this mediating role, whether the principles and concepts in question be those of theoretical or of practical reason. This is easily seen in the analysis of syllogisms that Kant gives in each *Critique*.[5] In each, the subsumption of facts or acts in the world under the principle or major premises is a task ascribed to judgment (*Urteilskraft*). Transcendental philosophy, in its doctrine of judgment, specifies a priori the instances to which the principle or concept is to be applied. "It must formulate by means of universal but sufficient marks

---

[4] It is correct to insist with Paton (*The Categorical Imperative*, p. 45; cf. *In Defence of Reason*, pp. 157–77) that the concept of the good is basic to that of duty in Kant's ethics. We have no obligation to do anything except under the idea that it is good to do it. Duty is only the form in which the good appears to beings like man who do not necessarily desire the good and must be constrained to seek it. But this does not imply that the *concept* of good is basic to the moral *principle*. The concept of duty can be derived from either, but the principle is basic to the definition of the concept.

[5] *Critique of Pure Reason*, A 304 = B 360–61; *Critique of Practical Reason*, 90 (184). Elsewhere (*Metaphysik der Sitten*, VI, 438) Kant ascribes to reason the responsibility for drawing the conclusion of the practical syllogism, but in this passage he is obviously referring to the logical, rather than the real, use of reason. In this passage he calls practical reason in its real use (in the establishment of the principle or major premise) the "practical understanding." In *Foundations*, 412 (29), he says that, since reason is required for the derivation of actions from laws, will is nothing else than practical reason. Here also we have to do with reason in its logical use, and this follows Wolff's terminology in *Psychologia rationalis*, §§ 494, 528.

the conditions under which objects can be given in harmony with these concepts."[6] Similarly, in the practical syllogism it must decide what object or act falls under the principle which defines the good and state the ground of this decision in the form of a rule of judgment, so that moral judgment and possible facts and acts of experience can be brought together in such a manner that the latter can be estimated.

But, though formally similar, the two syllogisms are quite different in their epistemic or transcendental function. The concepts of pure understanding or categories are applied to intuitions a priori, and the intuitions are the "third thing" that mediates between concepts so that an a priori synthesis of them is possible. But they do not apply directly to intuitions; they apply only to certain formal patterns or structures of them, which are isomorphous with the intellectual synthesis whose rule is given in the corresponding category. These formal structures are the schemata of the concepts. For instance, it is only because "cause" and "effect" are both referred to intuitions in a specific temporal relationship that we are able to make synthetic a priori judgments of causality that apply to experiences. But the concept of the moral good is an Idea that cannot be schematized; we cannot find a structure of intuition that corresponds to it. The concept of lawgiving, which is that of freedom in one of its senses, is the concept of a cause that does not exist in time, and therefore the schema of causation does not apply to moral decision and its expression in action with the same epistemic consequences that it has in theoretical knowledge. Still, the concept of the good, though defined by the principle, is to be applied to particular acts or objects that can be created by our free choice in the world of experience. The principle itself must be, as it were, schematized (68 [160]), so that it does not remain empty and inapplicable in the practical experience of the guidance of choice.

The chapter, accordingly, falls into three clearly distinguishable parts. The first thirteen paragraphs define the concepts of good and evil as the concepts of objects of practical reason. The next four paragraphs develop the categories of practical reason in the light of the principles. The last section prescribes the condition for the application of these concepts and principles.

§ 3. THE CONCEPTS OF GOOD AND EVIL

An object of practical reason is an effect possible through freedom (57 [148]). In this definition, two words require preliminary comment. "Object" must be taken in a sufficiently broad sense to cover two things: states of affairs produced by action and action itself. It

---

[6] *Critique of Pure Reason*, A 136 = B 175.

must not be thought that "object" means only a thing in the world created by action. "Freedom" in this definition is freedom of choice (*Willkür*) and not necessarily transcendental freedom, since the object need not be an object of a pure and autonomous will which is transcendentally free. Since a will is never directly determined by an object of desire, but only by a concept of an object and a rule which the acting person takes as ground for a decision pro or con, freedom in the sense of this sentence is characteristic of voluntary choice, regardless of whether we are concerned with the "free will," which is moral, or only with "free choice," which is characteristic also of intelligent choice and technique.[7] No question concerning transcendental freedom need be raised in the interpretation of this chapter, though, because it follows upon the Deduction, Kant permits himself from time to time to use this deeper concept of freedom.

The concept of the object of practical reason is the object's representation regarded as an efficient cause of the action that is to produce the object. Object of practical reason and purpose of the will are thus identical.[8] Moreover, the material of a practical principle in contrast to its form is the same as its object (27 [114]). It is essential, however, to distinguish between the material *of* a principle and a material principle. All principles have a material because all volition has an object (34 [123]); but a principle is called a "material principle" only if its material is the condition of the action directed or elicited by the principle. If there are laws of practical reason, Kant has shown that there must be principles which are not material principles; but this part of the chapter is devoted to finding out what the material of such a non-material principle can be.

To say of an object that it is an object of practical reason is to envision it in the causal nexus of free action, which, under a law or rule, produces it. This is analogous to the condition under which we say of any conception that it refers to an object. For our theoretical understanding, to refer a datum to an object is to hold that there is a rule according to which this datum is synthesized with others in one spatiotemporal system and thus given the status of evidence of an object as a "permanent possibility" of other data; a "wild datum" is one not synthesizable with others under a rule and hence is not evidence of an object. Object of experience is to theoretical understanding what object of practical reason is to the faculty of rational choice;

---

[7] *Critique of Practical Reason*, 60 (151); cf. *Critique of Pure Reason*, A 802 = B 830, A 548 = B 576; *Über den Gemeinspruch* . . . , VIII, 282; *Metaphysik der Sitten*, VI, 381.

[8] *Critique of Practical Reason*, 57 (148); *Metaphysik der Sitten*, VI, 381, 384–85.

mere sensation is to theoretical understanding what mere object of desire is to rational choice. Object of experience or object of practical reason is that to which our conceptions apply when they stand in necessary synthetic relationships to each other and not merely in casual relationships of associations of ideas.

A rational being acts so as to produce an object only under the thought that the object is or would be, in some sense, good; and it acts to avoid a state of affairs only if it thinks that it is in some sense bad or evil.[9] Hence, Kant says, the only concepts of objects of practical reason as such are the concepts of good and evil.[10] There are, however, three senses of good and evil. Something may be good for some arbitrary purpose (e.g., cyanide is good for suicide), for some actual purpose (e.g., health is good for happiness), or for some obligatory and necessary purpose to be held by a rational being as such. Kant accordingly distinguishes between *bonitas problematica, bonitas pragmatica,* and *bonitas moralis,* corresponding to the three kinds of imperative.[11] In each of these kinds of good, and not merely in the third, there is a necessary relation of the object to the will, necessary as determined by some rule of reason.

Granted that suicide is the end proposed, then every man who is rational and not merely he who is bent upon this act must necessarily recognize the goodness of cyanide for this purpose. The necessary relation of an object to a will which judges it to be good in this way is only a hypothetical necessity, but, even so, it makes a necessary claim on the assent of a rational being. However irrational it may be

---

[9] I am not able to identify the "old formula of the schools" (*Critique of Practical Reason,* 59 [150]) as Kant states it, but the sense (and some of the words) are in Wolff (*Psychologia rationalis,* §§ 880, 881, 892) and in Baumgarten (*Metaphysica,* §§ 661, 665). Baumgarten makes the mistake that Kant points out in the text, putting the anticipation of pleasure in the object in the determining position. He writes: "If I foresee something as pleasing, which is possible by my effort, I strive for it. . . . Hence I am able to strive after many goods, and turn from many evils, *sub ratione* [*boni et*] *mali*" (*ibid.,* § 665). Kant, of course, thinks Wolff is guilty of this error, too, since perfection is a material principle to the extent that it has any moral import at all, and all material principles are ultimately hedonistic. But Wolff himself denies this, holding that perfection is the object of striving and that pleasure is only an accompaniment of its attainment.

[10] *Critique of Practical Reason,* 57 (148). Kant wrote: "By a concept of practical reason I understand the idea [*Vorstellung*] of an object as an effect possible through freedom." Vorländer inserted the words "of an object" after "concept," and this emendation was adopted in my translations.

[11] *Lectures on Ethics,* p. 15. They correspond to the three kinds of necessity in the *Vorlesungen über Metaphysik* (Pölitz ed.), p. 186.

to say "Suicide is good," "Cyanide is good for suicide" expresses an objective decision of reason.

This is easy enough to see when we are concerned only with means to ends. But Kant argues at length that even such a judgment as "Suicide is good" must likewise present a claim to reason. If it were good, it would not be because a despairing man desires it but because it would have some necessary claim to the assent of reasonable beings. Otherwise it would suffice merely to say, "I desire to commit suicide" or perhaps "I desire to commit suicide; would that you did too." It is this necessary relation to rational assent that Kant investigates here.

There are two possible relations between the principle or maxim of a will and its object. The object can determine the concept through the principle, or the principle can determine the concept of the object. The question is Which is the prior notion, the good or the principle?

With respect to *bonitas problematica sive pragmatica*, the concept of what is good is determined by the principle that we have called the "formal principle of a hypothetical imperative." But *what* is good—the denotatum of the concept—is not determined by this principle. That which makes a good thing good in either of these senses is the pleasure we have or expect to have in its existence or the causal relation between something we do and the existence of this pleasurable state. Neither of these is decided by principle or definition. Yet so intimate is the connection in the *bonitas pragmatica* between what is good according to principle and the pleasure that the hedonist identifies the two concepts. Kant challenged this identification; even common usage, he says (like a twentieth-century philosopher) opposes the identification of the good with the pleasant.[12] Good is a communicable, rational concept, and pleasure is merely a private affection of the inner sense.[13] The good is judged by reason, not by private feeling, even though the judgment may have a feeling as its premise. Reason judges what is desirable; feeling decides what is desired. But the good is a normative concept, cor-

---

[12] *Critique of Practical Reason*, 58 (149); *Critique of Judgment*, § 4 (V, 208 [42]). The Stoic at whom Kant says we may laugh (*Critique of Practical Reason*, 60 [151]) for (tacitly) drawing the distinction between the two meanings of "evil" during the sharpest paroxysm of the gout was Poseidonius (Cicero *Tusculan Disputations* ii. 25).

[13] The merely pleasant represents the object simply in its relation to inner sense or feeling; it is therefore contingent. The pleasant can be brought under principles of reason by having applied to it the concept of purpose; then it is the good in one of the senses of this term, and the good necessarily satisfies by virtue of the universal concept involved in the effectuation of a purpose (cf. *Critique of Judgment*, § 4). If something is judged to please without a concept, yet necessarily, it is not good but beautiful.

responding to the desirable and not to the merely desired. So the hedonist, who avoids the erroneous identification of "good" with "pleasure," yet who wishes to maintain a necessary relation between them, comes to mean by "good" that which, according to the judgment of reason, leads to pleasure. In this way, "good" denotes an object that stands in a necessary relation to choice as judged by reason and is identical in meaning with "the useful." The sense in which pleasure is good is then quite different from that in which the means to pleasure are good.

"Good," then, has two quite distinct meanings, even if one denies the main thesis of the Kantian ethics that there is a *bonitas moralis* wholly distinct from *bonitas pragmatica*. It may mean *das Gute* as a characteristic of actions, maxims, and character as judged by reason (even if judged by reason to be good only because it leads to a desired end). Or it may mean *das Wohl* ("well-being") which is decided by each person according to his own feeling and without a necessary relation to reason. To decide whether something is *das Wohl* or a part of it requires an answer to the question Is the end to be achieved actually pleasant in such a way that it is an ingredient in happiness? To decide whether an action is good in the sense of *bonitas pragmatica* (*das Gute* in one of its three subsenses) requires reason to give an answer to the question Will this act lead to the achievement of the end, which is happiness? The answer to each of these questions, though it can be given only by reason (in a broad sense) working on the data of experience, is empirical and only probable. Hence no principle derived from concepts of the good as an object (*das Wohl*) can be a law, and no imperative to seek a previously and independently defined good can be categorical.

On the other hand, it is possible that the principle might determine what objects are good. This must be the actual case, in fact, if there is any reason to choose a principle other than by reference to the empirical object of the maxim or rules subsumed under it. If there is a law which expresses an absolute obligation, it must do so by virtue of its form and not its object. Since every principle of volition, however, has a material or an object, this is to say that the form of the principle, which is one of categorical obligation, must determine the concept of the good.

In making this determination, we do not have to inquire whether the object, i.e., what is desired, be it an action of a certain kind or its consequent end-state, will be pleasant, or whether it is physically possible for us to achieve it in fact. The "moral possibility" of willing it takes precedence over the psychological possibility of having a direct inclination to it and the practical feasibility of reaching it. When deciding on an object of pure practical reason, we consider only the possibility of rationally willing it—whether, that is, if reason completely determined our choice, we would choose it. "Good" in this sense is defined as that which it is necessary to will by a law of reason whose applicability is independent of actual physical capacity of achievement. Hence "good," in the only sense in which anything can be absolutely good—good independent of the state of my private desires and the ways of the world—refers only to actions, the maxims that lead to them, the will that produces them, and the character that supports them as their subject. This is the only good that can be commanded universally; the others can be recommended only "to whom it may concern." The necessary relation of this willing to the good is categorical, not hypothetical; it is apodictic, not problematical.

Thus the connection between action and its object is much more intimate for pure practical reason than for practical reason in general. One might say, though Kant does not say it here,[14] that virtue is its own reward (object). What he does say is that the good characterizes actions directly and not derivatively (though it must be remembered that action means not merely external behavior but the inner setting of the will to behave in a certain way). The object that is absolutely good can be obtained only in and by acting in a certain way—not as if it were an end to be achieved by the use of certain means, the circumstances being favorable. It can be obtained only in and by acting in a certain way because acting in a certain way is the first thing—in fact, the only thing—commanded by an imperative based on a law. The form and the object, so far as the object is the moral good, of the maxim coincide. The object of pure practical reason is not an effect of action but the action itself; the good will has itself as object.[15] The morally good object is not a thing in space and time, but its concept is a supersensuous Idea of a supersensuous nature. It is not a nature to be produced as an effect by a certain kind of action but a nature that is at least partially realized in the mode of action itself (43 [132]). The good is not transcendent to moral action but is immanent within it.

Nonetheless, the good will is not by itself sufficient to determine a specific action. Every volition has an object, though the object need not itself be an unqualified good, something absolutely and in every respect good. The categorical imperative, which commands the pursuit

14 Though he does say it in *Metaphysik der Sitten*, VI, 377.

15 Cf. *Foundations of the Metaphysics of Morals*, 437 (56): "Act according to maxims which can at the same time have *themselves* as universal laws of nature *as their object*" (italics added).

of the immanent moral good, always presupposes maxims which have a material and which it controls, as we have seen.[16] Hence devotion to the moral good does not require renunciation of other goods; it requires only that, in determining what our duty is, we take no account of our desires, which determine directly or indirectly the other kinds of goods.[17] Some desires are compatible with devotion to the good or can be made compatible with it. They should be cultivated and need not be thwarted or eradicated by a single-minded devotion to moral good.[18] The desire for our own happiness may be of this kind, and "reason has an inescapable responsibility to attend to [this] interest and to form maxims with a view to the happiness of this, and where possible, of a future life."[19] To secure one's own happiness is at least indirectly a duty (93 [186]). But my own happiness can be rationally willed only under a law which likewise holds the happiness of others as an object before me (34, 85 [123, 178]).

To be sure, a state of universal happiness might conceivably have been produced by natural mechanisms not guided by reason or by the grace of God working in wondrous ways. But something of inestimable value would be lost in such an arrangement. The immanent object of pure reason is something that only it could realize, at the cost of often failing to realize it. In an Aristotelian vein, Kant here repeats an argument of the *Foundations*[20] that each of our faculties has its own proper function and that of pure practical reason is "to consider . . . what is good or evil in itself, which pure and sensuously disinterested reason alone can judge, and furthermore to distinguish this estimate from a sensuous estimation and to make the former the supreme condition of the latter" (62 [153]). As the perfection of rational nature, this also is an end or object completely determined by pure practical reason and is an object which it is our unrestricted duty to pursue.[21]

Object, in this sense, is not a terminus of action, not something to be gained only through the use of means guided by a knowledge of causal

---

[16] Cf. above, chap. viii, § 4.

[17] *Über den Gemeinspruch* . . . , VIII, 278–79; *Critique of Practical Reason*, 93 (186).

[18] In agreement with Rousseau (cf. *Mutmasslicher Anfang der Menschengeschichte*, VIII, 117).

[19] *Critique of Practical Reason*, 61 (152). Kant has been interpreted as denying this, or at least of having no right to assert it, and is accused therefore of being the proponent of "sour duty" (cf. *Metaphysik der Sitten*, VI, 214, and above, p. 120, n. 20).

[20] *Foundations of the Metaphysics of Morals*, 395 (10–11).

[21] *Metaphysik der Sitten*, VI, 385–87.

law, not something to be hoped for only in the indefinite future when just men shall have been made perfect, the crooked straight, and the rough places smooth. No; the object is a will of a certain disposition, a disposition to act in accordance with and out of respect for law. The only purpose of moral action as such is to secure the reign of law, and every moral action in part accomplishes this aim. It is in this sense that Kant says that what the moral law requires of us can always be accomplished; its object is achievable, however unsatisfactory the state of the world may be, because the object it holds before us and the action that is to achieve it are at least partially identical.

§ 4. THE CATEGORIES OF PRACTICAL REASON

If the reader of the *Critique of Practical Reason* has been lulled into a feeling of easy familiarity by the no doubt interesting, but certainly not surprising, development of the relation between principle and concept, between law and the good, in the beginning of chapter ii, he will be suddenly shocked at the marked change in style and direction of the argument at the beginning of the fourteenth paragraph. A fog seems suddenly to settle over a road along which one expected to make good time. This paragraph and the three succeeding ones are strikingly unexpected, original, and obscure. They require, because of their difficulty, exegesis of each sentence. Without further ado, let us move forward, slowly and cautiously, into the darkness:

Since the concepts of good and evil, as consequences of the a priori determination of the will, presuppose a pure practical principle and thus a causality of pure reason, they do not (as determinations of the synthetic unity of the manifold of given intuitions in one consciousness) refer originally to objects, as do the concepts of the understanding or categories of the theoretically employed reason [65 (156)].

Here Kant is speaking explicitly of the moral good and evil, not of good and evil in the broad sense defined at the beginning of this chapter of the *Critique*. Yet, as an introduction to the further development, it is essential that "good and evil" be taken in the more general sense. In the limited (moral) sense, they do not refer to perceptual objects at all. In the broader sense, they do not refer to objects *simpliciter* but only to objects in the context of the causality of their production by an act of will. "Good and evil," therefore, do not even seem, like the theoretical categories, to apply to objects as they are given in their own right, so that knowledge of them can be connected in one conscious act of theoretical judgment. Nor do they, as the theoretical categories do, actually make these objects possible by being rules for the synthesis of the representations in one consciousness and one spatiotemporal system:

Rather, they presuppose these objects as given, and they are without exception modes of a single category, that of causality, so far as their determining ground consists of reason's idea of a law of causality which, as a law of freedom reason gives itself, showing itself to be a priori practical [65 (156)].

Again, this is explicitly restricted to moral good. But, in the light of what follows later and especially in the light of the first clause of the sentence, we must interpret Kant as still concerned with the more general usage of the concepts. The concepts of good and evil, he says, are not constitutive of objects of experience, as the theoretical concepts are. Rather, they presuppose that the objects of experience to which they are to be applied are already given under the theoretical categories. When we say of an object that it is good, in addition to all the other categories that make it an object *überhaupt*, we use the category of causation to relate the object to its cause which lies in an act of the will. When we say of a given object that it is good, we call attention to the fact that, as good, it is given under the mode of causality by virtue of which it is "an effect possible through freedom" (57 [148]), i.e., that it stands in a causal relation to an act of choice. As an existing or possible thing in nature, it is given by virtue of the synthesis of empirical intuitions under the category of natural causation; but, as something good, it has a necessary relation to a specific cause, an act of will.

On the one side, the actions are under a law of freedom instead of a natural law and thus belong to the conduct of intelligible beings, and on the other side as events in the world of sense they belong to [the world of] appearances; so that the rules of a practical reason are possible only with respect to the latter and consequently in accordance with the categories of the understanding [65 (156–57)].

Here it is clear that he is speaking of practical reason in general and not just of pure practical reason. Kant tells us that any object is called "good" only if it is made an object of practical reason by an act of free choice. Yet free choice is possible only under the condition that the object chosen is possible according to the rules (categories) of sensuous experience. (Thus it is not open to me to make a square circle the object of my will, however much I might desire to accomplish the feat of constructing one.) But a pure practical reason can decide on its object independently of whether I possess the capacity actually to produce the possible object or not. The practical possibility presupposes the theoretical possibility. No principle of practical reason, therefore, can conflict with the conditions of the natural possibility of things, for the objects of a practical reason in general must be possible objects of natural experience.

These rules, however, contribute nothing to the theoretical use of the understanding in bringing the manifold of the (sensuous) intuitions under one consciousness a priori, but only to the a priori subjection of the manifold of desires to the unity of consciousness of a practical reason commanding in the moral law, i.e., [to the unity of] a pure will [65 (157)].

"The rules of practical reason" must be taken very broadly to include principles (maxims as well as laws). Now these "rules" determine what objects in the world of sense are good and evil. But when we know that an object is good, we have not thereby added one bit to our theoretical understanding of it. The object as a cognized object is presupposed in the judgment that it is good, but "It is good" is not a theoretical statement that adds another natural predicate to it.

Yet these "rules" have a role analogous to that of the theoretical categories.[22] The categories (and their schemata) are rules for the synthesis of intuitions not only into representations of objects but into representations for one consciousness. The "I think" must be able to accompany all my representations, and the theoretical categories are the modes in which I can think these representations as related in one consciousness of a single object or realm of objects and events in one space and time. I do not say of any representation that it is of an object unless it stands in a determinate relation to other representations according to rules which are the theoretical categories. A single object presupposes a single integral consciousness, and conversely. Similarly, I do not denominate any object "the good" except insofar as it stands in a necessary relation to the faculty of desire. I do not identify the pleasant with the good, because a pleasant thing does not have this necessary relationship. My desires are manifold and conflicting; the pleasures of the table conflict with those of sport, those of this life perhaps with the hope of those of another. But if I can call anything "good," I mean that it is an object which would necessarily be desired by a rational man whose reason controlled his desires or at least controlled the choice he makes among his desiderata. Hence "I desire, rationally" is like the "I think": it must be able to accompany all my representations of an object as good. Only if "I desire rationally" accompanies all the representations I have that I desire anything *simpliciter,* can I be said to have achieved the integral state of a completely rational personality, to be possessed of a holy will. But though I can desire many things that are not good, i.e., are not desirable but yet are desired, as a rational being I can restrict my choices to those things which are rationally desired, and the state of doing this is not holiness of will, which I cannot achieve, but virtue, or "moral disposition in conflict" (84 [178]).

[22] As pointed out in Fragment 6, i.e., Reflexionen 7202 and 7204 (XVIII, 278, 284).

The statement "I desire X" is a statement of fact, and at any moment I may actually desire X and things I know to be incompatible with it. But "I desire X rationally," i.e., "I will X, under a rule of reason that I regard as valid not only for myself but for others" means "X is good." This judgment can be a constraint on my wayward desires for those things not compatible with X. The judgment "X is good" is a rational estimate, believed to be objectively valid, and is distinguished from the sensuous estimate of X, viz., "X would be pleasant" or "X would be fun." Only a rational being can judge "X is good"—whether, in fact, X does meet the requirements for being good or not—but an animal can desire X. The manifold of desires is synthesized by reason according to practical principles or rules, and their common focus is the object called "good":

These categories of freedom—for we wish to call them this in contrast to the theoretical concepts which are categories of nature—have a manifest advantage over the latter. The latter categories are only forms of thought, which through universal concepts designate, in an indefinite manner, objects in general for every intuition possible to us. The categories of freedom, on the other hand, are elementary practical concepts which determine the free faculty of choice [*einer freien Willkür*]. Though no intuition exactly corresponding to this determination can be given to us, the free faculty of choice has as its foundation [or: the determination of the free faculty of choice has as its foundation] a pure practical law a priori, and this cannot be said for any of the concepts of the theoretical use of our cognitive faculty [65 (157)].

Before exploring and identifying this "manifest advantage," we must pause a moment to consider what Kant has already said. "These categories of freedom"—earlier called "categories of practical reason" (11 n. [96 n.])—what are they? The "these" indicates that they are the "rules" previously mentioned; yet in the table itself it will appear that Kant has not yet decided whether "rule" or "concept" is the better name for them. Still, there is nothing wrong or even surprising in sometimes referring to a category as a rule and sometimes as a concept.[23] A category, though a concept, contains (like any concept) a rule for the synthesis of representations. (This is true not only of categories but of every concept: the concept of "cat," for instance, though a posteriori, is a rule for the synthesis of our perceptual and imaginative representations which are necessary for us to say, on the occasion of one or more of them, "There is a cat.") The elementary practical concepts are just the concepts of good and evil in general; and the rules spell out their use in the synthesis of desires, observance of these rules being necessary for the conversion of desire into rational desire, or will.

---

[23] On the general problem of the relation of category to rule, cf. Vaihinger, *Commentar zu Kants Kritik der reinen Vernunft*, I, 222.

Next, Kant tells us, the categories of freedom are forms of determination of choice and therefore of the objects of rational choice, i.e., of the good as object. They are not forms of objects *simpliciter*, which would require that intuitions be synthesized; this would constitute them objects of knowledge, not of practice. This independence from intuition is the "manifest advantage" of the practical over the theoretical categories. Of any category that functions in the determination of an object, it must be possible to exhibit an intuition or pattern of intuitions which corresponds to it; otherwise the concept is empty, and only analytical judgments can be made upon it. The good and evil, however, have no corresponding intuitions, and no intuition can be given corresponding to the determination of choice, while the determination of an object of knowledge occurs through the schematization of the concept.

What is actually given to keep the concepts of good and evil from being empty is not an intuition, the source of empirical factuality, but a principle which Kant elsewhere[24] calls the "fact of pure reason." That is to say, knowledge of the principle itself gives content to the practical concepts, whereas in the theoretical case the concepts must be established with respect to intuition before synthetic principles can be formulated with them. This constitutes the advantage of the practical over the theoretical categories. Theoretical concepts can be synthesized only by grace of intuition, which is wholly different from and independent of the thought formulated in the categories.[25] Practical con-

[24] *Critique of Practical Reason,* 31, 42 (120, 131); cf. below, chap. x, § 3.

[25] Thus practical concepts have a wider significance than theoretical concepts in their cognitive function. See the remarkable statement that can hardly be understood apart from the present context, though it occurs in the *Foundations* (411-12 [28]): speculative (theoretical) philosophy makes its principles depend upon "the particular nature of human reason," where "human reason" refers to our entire cognitive faculty for which intuition is always sensible, not intellectual. All principles of practical philosophy, on the other hand, depend solely upon pure reason alone, in the strict sense of "reason." This, however, hardly seems compatible with the earlier view in the *Critique of Pure Reason* that excluded practical philosophy from transcendental philosophy, in spite of the fact that its principles were pure (cf. above, p. 9, n. 21). But in the second edition, as we have seen, Kant pointed out that empirical concepts were needed for defining the *concept of duty*. What Kant means can best be stated as follows: The determination of the moral principle is independent of the particular constitution of the human mind and is valid for all rational beings, whether their reason be discursive, like ours, or intuitive and whether their will be holy or only virtuous. But the concept of duty presupposes that there are desires, and hence the concept of duty is not independent of our mental constitution. Concepts of objects used in our cognition are likewise dependent in their cognitive use upon the fact that they are rules for the synthesis of intuitions which, for us men, are given independently of the concepts.

cepts, on the other hand, are justified by the fact of pure reason, without needing any appeal to empirical or pure intuitions or feelings of pleasure. Accordingly (omitting one sentence just paraphrased), Kant continues:

> Since in all the precepts of the pure will it is only a question of the determination of the will and not of the natural conditions (of practical ability) for achieving its purpose, it thereby happens that practical concepts a priori in relation to the supreme principle of freedom thereby become cognitions, not needing to wait upon intuitions in order to acquire a meaning. This occurs for the noteworthy reason that they themselves produce the reality of that to which they refer (the intention of the will)—an achievement which is in no way the business of theoretical concepts [66 (157)].

These sentences explicitly concern only the pure will and are true only of it. "Practical concepts a priori" are direct cognitions of what ought to be, because they are consequences of a primordial fact, the law of pure practical reason that a rational being as such necessarily wills to act in such and such ways. Their object is directly given (as what ought to be, not as what is): the concept itself is a cognition, not needing to await the schematization of the concept or its exhibition or construction in intuition.

Here, then, we have the one instance in the whole of knowledge where thought can create its object directly, and not by being a cause of a series of events which may terminate in an object. (This object is respect, which is a necessary corollary of knowledge of the law.)[26] But the knowledge thus gained is not knowledge that its object exists; that would be theoretical knowledge requiring intuition. The knowledge thus gained is knowledge that something ought to be, and the recognition of this is a necessary condition of its actual existence as an instance of the good. Kant would go even further and say that the concept creates the existence of the object,[27] since the object is a certain setting of the will:

> Freedom is regarded as a kind of causality (not subject to empirical grounds of determination) with reference to actions possible through it, which are appearances in the world of sense, and ... consequently [freedom] is referred to the categories of the possibility [of actions] in nature, while, however, each category is taken so universally that the determining ground of the causality can be placed beyond the world of sense in freedom as the property of an intelligible being [67 (158)].

[26] Cf. below, chap. xii, §§ 6, 8.

[27] There are many expressions of this, e.g., *Critique of Practical Reason*, 66, 92, 153 (157, 186, 251); *Foundations of the Metaphysics of Morals*, 404 (20).

Freedom is a kind of causality in which the cause of an action is not another phenomenal event. This kind of causality cannot be understood by us; we can understand cause-effect relations only when both members of the nexus are in one spatiotemporal series. Yet a category is a pure concept of the understanding. It owes nothing to sensibility, and, though we can use it to give knowledge only in its connection with sensibility, we can and must think with it even when we are thinking of that which can never be given to the senses. Since, however, one member of the nexus is in nature and thus occurs under the schematized theoretical categories, we can think of freedom of the cause under the categories of the possibility of its effects in nature. We thereby gain no knowledge of the cause, but we are enabled in this way to think of freedom in definite and specific ways with respect to events that we do know in nature. Thus, to take a simple illustration, every causal change is the change in the accidents of some substance, which is permanent. In practical action, every act must be thought of as the expression of a single unchanging subject to which the action is imputed, and this subject is the person. Hence in thinking of free actions, we must think them in relation to a person as an agent, though we can have no theoretical knowledge of this substance.

Thus far, Kant may seem to have been repeating—on a repellently technical level, of interest only to Kantian adepts—the conclusion of the more straightforward exposition of the concept of the moral good. But suddenly he bewilders the reader by then remarking that the categories to which such remarkable prerogatives have been ascribed are categories of practical reason in general. (We have, however, taken this into account in the preceding exegesis.) The categories

proceed in order from those which are as yet morally undetermined and sensuously conditioned to those which, being sensuously unconditioned, are determined only by the moral law. . . . The categories of modality initiate the transition . . . from practical principles in general to those of morality.[28]

The puzzle presented by the last sentence here can be resolved, if at all, only after we have examined the Table of Categories. Before leaving this section, however, I must again point out the source of most of its difficulties, to wit, a confusing shift of attention back and forth from the categories of pure practical reason to those of empirical practical reason and practical reason in general. Had the section been written so

---

[28] This citation is a conjunction of two sentences, one on p. 66 (157) and one on p. 67 (158); they are here combined by omitting the parts which are prima facie incompatible with each other. In their full form and relation to each other, they will be discussed below, when the examination of the table has been completed and there can be some expectation of understanding their relationship to each other.

that the categories of practical reason in general had been first elaborated and then those of pure practical reason introduced as a subclass, the section would have been much more lucid. I shall now attempt such a rewriting of the section in its most important parts.

Since the concepts of good and evil presuppose a causality exercised by reason through a principle, they do not refer, as originating and constitutive concepts, to objects which are to be given; this is the task performed by the theoretical categories and their schemata, which make the objects first possible. Rather, the concepts of good and evil presuppose the objects as given in possible experience. They refer only to the specific mode of causation by grace of which they are judged to be good or evil. This is their causal origin in an act of will, which takes place under the guidance of reason's conception of some law. The concepts of good and evil, therefore, implicitly refer to the cause of the actions or objects called "good" or "evil," and a principle for decision on the goodness or evil of an action or a thing is a principle which bears upon the specific causality of the action or thing.

The actions of the will and their consequences are in nature, and therefore are under the theoretical categories of their possibility. In order to understand them, as natural events, we do not need the concepts of good and evil or any principles of practical reason. Theoretical concepts and principles suffice.

The principles of practical reason, however, have an analogy to theoretical principles and categories. They bring the manifold of desires to the unity of practical reason and give rise to acts and decisions of will, just as the theoretical categories bring the manifold of intuition to the unity of self-consciousness and give rise to judgments of objects of experience. The principles of practical reason may therefore appropriately be called "categories of practical reason," or, as modes of the causality of practical reason, "categories of freedom."

They have a manifest advantage over the theoretical categories. The latter have a relation to objects of every intuition possible to us and must await intuition before they have a definite constitutive use in knowledge of any object. The former, however, are in themselves cognitions, because they arise from the same reason as that which presents the fact to be rendered intelligible, viz., the consciousness of the principle of practical reason. They thus produce the reality of that to which they refer, namely, an intention of the will, and do not need to await intuitions to determine whether they refer to something real or not. Theoretical categories can never do this in a mind like ours, for which understanding is discursive instead of intuitive.

The categories of practical reason or of freedom are of two kinds.

Practical reason may have for its material some actual desires which it synthesizes under a principle. The principle is, of course, a priori, but the intention of the will based upon it is contingent upon the presence of the specific and empirically known desires. Such principles and the corresponding concepts of good and evil may be called principles and concepts of empirical practical reason. On the other hand, the principle of the will may be wholly independent of any desire, and such a principle will be one of pure practical reason. There should, therefore, be morally undetermined, but sensuously conditioned, categories and also sensuously unconditioned, but morally determined, categories.

§ 5. THE TABLE OF THE CATEGORIES OF FREEDOM

After giving his table, Kant says: "I add nothing here to illuminate the table, for it is sufficiently understandable in itself." No one has ever granted him this claim. Even Schütz, one of his most faithful disciples, felt called upon to suggest to the master a way in which it could be improved.[29] Since, unlike the table of theoretical categories, almost no further use was made of it[30] in spite of Kant's statement that "such a division based on principles is very useful in any science, for the sake of both thoroughness and intelligibility" (67 [158]), we can read back into it very little that can make *it* more intelligible. Most commentators have ignored it; only Mellin has wrestled with its many difficulties, and, though some of his suggestions are shrewd and valuable, on some points he was, I think, definitely in error. My own ingenuity is quite insufficient to interpret all parts of it consistently with the *ipsissima verba*. Nevertheless, the main features of it are not unintelligible.

Before embarking upon an interpretation of what Kant actually performed here, let us consider what we might legitimately expect him to do in formulating a table of the categories of freedom.

First, we should expect him to set out in a systematic order the abstract and logically constant features of practical judgments. We should expect some kind of systematization of various distinctions that he has

[29] To Kant, June 23, 1788 (X, 541); cf. Ak., XIII, 219.

[30] One might have expected the whole *Metaphysics of Morals* to be organized with respect to it, as *Metaphysical Foundations of the Natural Sciences* was organized according to the table in the first *Critique*. A few fragments suggest that the *Metaphysics of Morals* may have been thought of in this way (cf. *Vorarbeiten*, Ak., XXIII, 218, and the [unsent] letter to Jung-Stilling written after March 1, 1789 [XXIII, 495]). Once in the *Foundations* (prior to the construction of the table) he made explicit use of the categories of quantity (436 [55]), and in the *Metaphysics of Morals* he later made use of those of relation (*Rechtslehre*, § 4). Some (rather fancy) use of the table is involved in *Religion within the Limits of Reason Alone*, VI, 101–2 (Greene and Hudson, 93).

already made: laws and maxims, material and formal principles, categorical and hypothetical imperatives, imperatives of perfect and of imperfect obligation, legal and moral judgments, laws and imperatives, etc.

Second, we should expect him to set up concepts (categories) of good corresponding to each of the kinds of judgments. We should then have a table of judgments or rules and a corresponding table of concepts.

But he does not proceed in these ways. He assumes that the important formal features of practical judgments are identical with those of theoretical judgments, and thus he avails himself of the division of categories arising from the table of judgments in the first *Critique*. And he does not clearly distinguish between the judgments and the concepts, so that in the table we find sometimes one and sometimes the other.

Some of the difficulty is undoubtedly due to the fact that each of the headings is, as it were, imbedded within the single category of causality. We are never told precisely what is meant by a "mode of a single category," and we are left to imagine what is meant by the quantity, quality, relation, and modality of the single category of causation.

Other difficulties arise from the fact that the categories of practical reason are not purely formal like those of theoretical understanding, but always have a content in the peculiar causality (freedom) which is the *ratio essendi* of the moral good. The categories of good and evil do not owe their origin solely to the forms of practical judgment, as the logical organization of the table suggests, but to the classes of causes or effects which are specified in various practical judgments. We can expect to find, therefore, purely logical distinctions mixed up with those of the practical in general and with distinctions belonging to ethics proper.

In order to interpret the table, I shall make one change in it. I shall distinguish principle or rule from category or concept of the good; where Kant states one, I shall try to supply the other.

§ 6. THE CATEGORIES OF QUANTITY

Practical judgments are either principles or rules. We are here concerned only with principles. Principles are either mere maxims or laws. Maxims are maxims either of an individual or of the generality of mankind. Laws are distinguished from mere maxims of either kind by being universally valid and by the requirement that wills under law should coexist in the all-comprehensiveness of a total system of ends.[31]

We have, then, the following principles and categories:

[31] *Foundations of the Metaphysics of Morals,* 438 (57).

1. Mere maxim of individual	Subjective, good for the individual
2. Maxim of human beings generally (precepts)	Objective, good for the generality of men
3. Laws as maxims	Good for rational beings as such, both objective and subjective

Three comments are called for by Kant's own listings. First, he erroneously contrasts maxim and principle. A maxim is a kind of principle. Second, he explicitly makes the third a synthesis of the first two, and thus interprets laws as maxims for individuals. He is able to do this under the judgment of totality, by virtue of the concept of a realm of ends as an organic unity of various rational beings.[32] Third, there is a radical difference between the good in the first two and in the third categories, a difference which is not adequately shown as a difference in quantity.

What kind of good is Kant talking about? Perhaps the first two are *das Wohl*, the third *das Gute*. But this is not a quantitative difference. If we follow Kant in saying that *das Gute* in a heteronomous system means that which leads to the end (*das Wohl*), then all three are equally objective as judged by reason, though in Kant's table only the second and third are called objective.

Here and elsewhere[33] Kant makes it clear that, under the category of quantity, the transition to a strictly moral concept is reached with the third category of this group.

§ 7. THE CATEGORIES OF QUALITY

Theoretical judgments, with respect to quality, are either affirmative, negative, or infinite; the corresponding categories are reality, negation, and limitation.

Practical judgments are, with respect to quality, either rules (in a loose sense) of commission or of omission (counsels or commands to do something or to leave something undone) or permissions to make some exception to a rule of the former kind. Hence the judgments and categories of quality are as follows:

1. Rules of commission	The good as that which is commanded.[34]
2. Rules of omission	The good as that which is to be achieved through the avoidance of certain actions

[32] *Ibid.*, 436 (54–55); cf. *Critique of Practical Reason*, 28 (115).

[33] *Critique of Practical Reason*, 67 (159); *Foundations of the Metaphysics of Morals*, 436 (55).

[34] We are not here concerned with the source of the commands or counsels. They may be arbitrary fiats, civil laws, moral commands, or recipes for making sauces.

3. Rules of exceptions

The good as that which is appropriate in obedience to a general precept

Rules of exception correspond to infinite judgments in theory, in that they exclude certain actions from the scope of one of the earlier rules. They are formally affirmative but have a negative predicate in their theoretical formulation;[35] in their practical form, we might refer to them as "but-rules" which include both a positive and a negative element, viz., "Do so and so, but. . . ." They are to be distinguished from *leges permissivae*.[36] Such rules of exception are present in commands of imperfect obligation.

It should be noted that, while the transition from one kind of category to the other is clearly marked in those of quantity, no one of the subcategories of quality seems to be specifically moral. Even in prudence and skill it is necessary to distinguish among these three kinds of judgment.

§ 8. THE CATEGORIES OF RELATION

Matters become a bit more obscure when we reach the categories of relation. All rules or principles of practical reason state, implicitly at least, a relation of the act and locate the good in a relatum of the act. According to the relations of judgments as categorical, hypothetical, and disjunctive and the corresponding categories of subsistence-inherence, cause-effect, and reciprocity, we have the following categories of relation:

1. The rule that all acts be judged as acts of a subject

The good as the character of the person; moral good; dignity

2. The rule that all acts be judged as having consequences for the state of the person

(For these categories, see the text, below)

3. The rule that in a moral community the acts of one person be decided upon and judged as they affect the state of another, and conversely

The good as justice or equality under a common law; the moral community

The first of these categories corresponds to that of subsistence and inherence in the first *Critique* and is sufficiently clear. Just as substance is that which is the cause of and is preserved through change in its accidents, the person is an intelligible substance to be preserved in con-

[35] *Critique of Pure Reason*, A 72 = B 97.

[36] Cf. *Perpetual Peace*, VIII, 347 n. (Beck, 9 n.).

duct. Accordingly, the person is an end in itself as a setter of all ends, and moral values are always values of a person.

The proper interpretation of the second category is a matter of considerable difficulty. It is subject to at least three interpretations, each of which can be supported by citing Kant's variable usage of the word "state" or "condition" (*Zustand*). "State" may have reference to moral condition, physical condition, or the state of well-being and its opposite. The three interpretations are as follows:

a) The moral rule does not issue from personality as an abstract entity, but from a person in a particular moral condition, a condition of "heart" that requires self-knowledge for its estimation.[37]

b) While our duties of perfect obligation are the same to all men, the modes of their application differ according to the condition of men, such as their age, their sex, their social position, their health.[38]

c) "Condition" may mean merely the state of happiness or unhappiness[39] [60 (151)].

The following are permissible interpretations of the second category:

2*a*) The rule that an action be judged as issuing from a person in a certain moral condition	Goods of action as derivative from specific goods of character, e.g., the courageous, the magnanimous
b) The rule of taking account of the condition of those affected by an action	The good as the suitable to the patient of the act
c) The rule that acts be judged by their consequences for the welfare of the person	The good as the prudent

The third of the categories of relation, in which actions of one are to be judged in relation to their effects on the state of the other, is likewise subject to several interpretations according to the meaning of "state," but the third of the possible meanings is perhaps the most plausible.[40]

---

[37] *Metaphysik der Sitten*, VI, 441. This is relevant in the imputation of merit (cf. *ibid.*, 228).

[38] *Ibid.*, 469.

[39] All three meanings seem to be combined in Reflexion 7211 (XIX, 286), where Kant says that the "unity of will [*Willkür*]" is "conditioned according to the degree of capacity and happiness of one person with respect to another."

[40] Professor Paton, in a personal communication, has proposed the following elegant interpretation of the categories of relation. They are (*a*) relation to *homo noumenon* (personality) under the imperative of autonomy; (*b*) relation to *homo phaenomenon* (person) under the imperative of the end in itself; (*c*) relation of actions of different persons in a kingdom of ends.

§ 9. THE CATEGORIES OF MODALITY

Before considering the specific moments of the category of modality, it is necessary to return for a moment to the last sentence before Kant introduces his table. He says: ". . . The categories proceed in order from those which are as yet morally undetermined and sensuously conditioned to those which, being sensuously unconditioned, are determined merely by the moral law" (66 [157]). This sentence is developed, in the last paragraph of this section, by specific reference to the categories of quantity. The sentence just quoted seems to say that in each group of categories there are two which apply to objects of an empirical practical reason, while the third applies to the moral good. But the sentence just quoted could not have been illustrated with the categories of quality or relation. The question before us is Does it apply to the categories of modality, or do they have some peculiar relation to this transition?

Before answering this question, we must first remind ourselves of some of the peculiarities of the modal categories. The categories of modality in theoretical knowledge "concern only the value of the copula in relation to thought in general" and "contribute nothing to the content of the judgment."[41] By analogy, we can say that the modality of practical judgments tells us nothing of what is the good to which the judgments are related, but only tells us the practical weight to be assigned to their copula, the "ought," and, per corollary, to the corresponding good. The modality of the concept tells us whether what it is about is possibly, really, or necessarily good, where "good" has been previously defined under the other categories. The relevant judgments would be problematic, assertoric, and apodictic imperatives.

Disappointingly, Kant does not seem to follow this apparently simple clue to the modal concepts,[42] though the first of the categories suggests that he is about to do so:

1. The rule that certain actions are to be judged as allowed and certain ones as forbidden with respect to the accomplishment of some arbitrary purpose	The permitted and the forbidden; the possibly good and that which cannot possibly be good on the assumption of an arbitrary purpose[43]

[41] *Critique of Pure Reason*, A 74 = B 99–100.

[42] Though at *Critique of Practical Reason*, 11 n. (96 n.), he suggests that he does so. This would give rise to the three already recognized concepts of the good, *bonitas problematica, pragmatica,* and *moralis.* There is much to recommend this division, in spite of what I judge to be Kant's failure to carry it through; indeed, it is so much to be recommended that others, as we shall see, have actually found it here.

[43] The permitted and the forbidden (*unerlaubt*) are defined *ibid.,* 11 n. (96 n.); *Foundations of the Metaphysics of Morals,* 439 (58); and *Metaphysik der Sitten,* VI, 222.

The second pair of categories corresponds to the theoretical pair: existence and non-existence. It is as follows:

2. The rule that certain actions are required or forbidden by an actual law lying in reason as such

Dutiful actions and actions contrary to duty; the actual moral good and evil

The proper interpretation of the second pair of modality categories is disputable. Mellin[44] interprets "a rule lying in reason as such" to mean a rule that prescribes an action by which an actual end, which is always happiness, is to be achieved. This interpretation makes it possible to regard the three pairs of modal distinctions as corresponding to the three kinds of imperative and to the three species of the good. But, as he admits, it requires him to interpret the concept of duty in a non-moral sense; and this seems to me to be a fatal objection to his view, quite apart from the fact that "a rule lying in reason as such" could hardly refer to the supreme principle of hypothetical imperatives, viz., the maxim of self-love.

Schütz[45] interprets the pair to correspond to "that which is really commanded" and "that which is not really commanded." This gives the contradictories: "duty" and "not-duty" instead of the contraries listed by Kant, "duty" and "contrary to duty." I accept this as the most reasonable way of reading the table, though it conflicts with the *ipsissima verba* of the author.

On either interpretation, a real surprise awaits us in the third pair. Whereas, before, the third category has been an almost Hegelian synthesis of the first two,[46] the third category here arises from a logical division of the second.[47] Of anything that is actual, we can say that it is either necessarily or contingently actual. Of an actual duty, Kant says —by a very tenuous analogy—that it is a duty of perfect or of imper-

---

[44] *Encyklopädisches Wörterbuch zur kritischen Philosophie*, IV, 534; the same interpretation had been given by Bendavid, *Vorlesungen über die Critik der praktischen Vernunft*, p. 29.

[45] To Kant, June 23, 1788 (X, 541–42). Schütz in this letter also reports on and criticizes the effort by A. W. Rehberg in *Allgemeine Literatur Zeitung*, III (1788), 353 ff., to improve the table of modalities by making the three moments: (*a*) the permitted and forbidden, (*b*) the dutiful (*pflichtmässige*) or the virtuous and its contrary, and (*c*) the holy and unholy. Rehberg's article is abstracted in Ak., XIII, 219.

[46] *Critique of Pure Reason*, B 110.

[47] If Mellin is correct, the third appears to be a logical division of duty, but "duty" must then have a moral or juridical meaning lacking in Mellin's interpretation of the second category. Bendavid attempted to make the third a synthesis of the first two, but failed completely.

fect obligation. Thus, corresponding to the contrast between the apodictic and contingent judgments, we have the following:

3. The rule that certain *actions* are made necessary by virtue of the actual rule lying in reason as such and	Perfect duty; an action directly commanded; the necessarily good
The rule that, while a certain *maxim* is necessary for rational beings, there is permissible latitude in the choice of actions under it[48]	Imperfect duty; an action not fully determined by the actual rule taken abstractly, but falling within the scope of the rule as determined by sound judgment using the rule of exceptions; the contingently good action under a necessarily good maxim

The distinction of duties of perfect and imperfect obligation follows that adopted in the *Foundations*, though it diverged from the "usage of the schools."[49] A perfect duty is an act that can be directly commanded or one whose maxim requires a certain act, since the contradictory

[48] Mellin (*op. cit.*, p. 537) interprets only perfect duty as moral, thus diverging from Kant's meaning. Hence the order of the categories in his rendition is as follows:

2. Actually dutiful actions, as those conforming to a law actually lying in reason as such; and actions opposed to this law

3. Duties conforming to a law necessarily lying in reason as such
  a) Duties by a necessary law, required by an apodictic imperative, the law being the moral law (e.g., the duty to tell the truth) = perfect duties
  b) Duties under a contingent imperative which corresponds to "a contingent law (rule) lying in reason as such" (e.g., the duty of a philosopher to teach the truth) = imperfect duties

The scheme proposed here is:

2. Actions which are, in fact, dutiful or opposed to duty; the legally correct or incorrect actions

3. Actions which are necessary *because* they are dutiful; the morally good action
  a) Actions or duties of perfect obligation
  b) Actions or duties of imperfect obligation

The best evidence for the latter interpretation is that it conforms to the doctrine of perfect and imperfect obligation in the *Metaphysik der Sitten*, where both are treated as apodictically necessary and differ only in what is commanded (a certain action, action under a certain maxim).

[49] *Foundations of the Metaphysics of Morals*, 421 n. (39 n.); cf. Reflexionen 7214, 7264, 7270. The distinction of the schools was that perfect duties could be enforced by external legislation, while imperfect duties could not. This is only a corollary of Kant's distinction and appears again in the parallel distinction between *Rechtspflichten* and *Tugendpflichten*. By internalizing the concept of legislation as autonomy, the emphasis is shifted from the aspect of enforcibility.

maxim is self-contradictory when made into a law. An imperfect duty is one in which the rule of exceptions may apply, in order to prevent obedience to one rule from conflicting with another. Moral duties are always imperfect; legal duties are perfect:

> If the law can command only the maxims of the action but not the actions themselves, this is a sign that it leaves open to obedience a certain latitude for free choice. . . . Under a broad [imperfect] duty there is no permit to make exceptions from a maxim of actions, but only a permit to limit one maxim of duty by another. . . . Such imperfect duties are only duties of virtue [and not duties of law or jurisprudence].[50]

Despite all these puzzles, the most puzzling thing in the account that Kant gives of modality is not in the listing of the specific categories but in the statement he makes of the relation of modality to the other categories. "Finally," he says,

> the categories of modality initiate the transition, though only in a problematical way, from practical principles in general to those of morality; and only later will it be possible to establish the principles of morality in a *dogmatic* form through the moral law [67 (158)].

How can this sentence possibly be reconciled with the one that says that the transition occurs within each group of categories?[51]

Perhaps the *principles* of modality in the first *Critique*, instead of the categories of modality in the first *Critique*, can supply an answer. For we are here dealing with a question of real possibility, not merely logical possibility. And in these questions it is principles of modality that are important. The second Postulate of Empirical Thought in General is "That which is bound up with the material conditions of experience, that is, with sensation, is actual."[52] If all our thought of duty and of the good is not to be merely a logical exercise in the analysis of perhaps empty thoughts which are only logically possible, then some actual "material conditions of experience" must be given with which these concepts can be "bound up." This material condition, of course, cannot for practical reason be sensation, but it must be something that could make the same contribution to the practical categories that empirical intuition (sensation) makes to the theoretical. This material condition, or rather this analogon of a material condition, is presented by the "sole fact of pure reason," the direct consciousness of the moral law to which Kant appeals in the Deduction.[53]

Thus interpreted, the two sentences are not inconsistent. In each

---

[50] *Metaphysik der Sitten*, VI, 390.

[51] Cf. above, p. 142.

[52] *Critique of Pure Reason*, A 218 = B 265–66.

[53] *Critique of Practical Reason*, 31 (120); cf. below, chap. x, § 2.

family of categories he meant that the transition occurs from the concepts of practical reason in general or empirical practical reason to those of pure practical reason, though we have seen grounds to doubt that this actually occurs except in respect to quantity. But there is not yet given any warrant for saying that *any* experience requires to be judged in the light of the categories of pure practical reason. The transition is made (or attempted) in each of the first three groups; yet this transition as a logical development is given weight by the categories of modality which relate the copula in every practical judgment to "thought in general" without adding any new internal form or content to the judgment.

Even so, it is not quite correct to say that the categories of modality initiate this transition problematically. They show what are the three possible relations of the "ought" to the totality of practical experience, and in this sense they prepare the way for it. The actual transition, however, is not made by or within the table, but by our being directed, by the categories of modality, to the "fact of pure reason" which will tie all of them to the "material condition" of practical experience. (It must be remembered that "material condition" here means the fact of pure reason, not the material of a practical judgment in the sense in which "material" refers to an actual empirical desire.) By reference to the experience of choice, all the logical distinctions drawn in the table become prescriptive of possible meanings of the concept of the good; by reference to the fact of pure reason, some one or more of each group comes to be the formula for a moral obligation or the concept of the moral good.

This ends our tedious examination of the table of categories. It is presented with hesitation, and it contains more questions than answers, more conjectures than decisions. We regret that Kant did not work it out with his accustomed architectonic skill. Something comparable to it—I make no extravagant claim for my own version—is surely needed to bring the doctrine of principles and the doctrine of concepts together. It is perhaps symptomatic of the poor construction of the table, or at least of its obscurity, that little use was made of it in the book that it should have served to organize. The cause of the failure may well be that Kant was here approaching the principles of a philosophy of action that he never achieved, which we in the twentieth century do not yet have in the formalized manner that Kant was accustomed to give to all his deepest work. He failed to achieve it not merely because of the inherent difficulty of the task but because he carried over into practical philosophy a theory of logical form that was not adequate to elucidate all practical judgments. Even today we are still seeking a complete theory of the forms of decision and valuation; interesting work has been done, but more important work remains to be done, on such notions as the "quantity" of imperatives.[54]

The "metaphysical deduction" of the principle of pure practical reason lacked the elegance of the Metaphysical Deduction in the first *Critique* because there was no sound "logical clue" in the table of judgments suitable to the purposes of the second *Critique*. The attempt subsequently made to use this table of judgments in elaborating a theory of practical categories was therefore destined from the beginning to be a hazardous operation, and we have sufficient evidence to justify the verdict that in fact the results were somewhat artificial and arbitrary, without the completeness and elegance and necessity claimed for the categories of theoretical reason. All the manifold objections made to the listing and derivation of the categories of theoretical reason seem to apply, a fortiori, to those of practical reason. This verdict must stand, I think, until some Kant-scholar has been able to give a more convincing exposition of them than I have achieved here.

§ 10. THE TYPIC OF PURE PRACTICAL JUDGMENT[55]

Judgment (*Urteilskraft*) is the art or faculty of applying a concept or rule to a particular case.[56] Kant shrewdly remarks that a weakness

---

[54] Cf., for example, R. M. Hare, *The Language of Morals* (Oxford, 1952), pp. 187–92. If few efforts have been made by Kant-exegetes to make sense of the table of categories, even fewer have been made to construct a better one in the spirit of Kant's works. The only such attempt I have seen is by J. Stilling, "Über das Problem der Freiheit auf Grund von Kants Kategorienlehre," *Archiv für die Geschichte der Philosophie*, XXI (1908), 518–34, XXII (1909), 1–27. Stilling says that his work (which leads to sixteen "categories of freedom") is an elaboration of Albrecht Krause's *Die Gesetze des menschlichen Herzens dargestellt als formale Logik des reinen Gefühls* (Lahr, 1876), a book I have not seen.

[55] I take this occasion to call attention to the error in the Chicago edition of my translation (p. 176), where the section title is incorrectly given as "Of the Typic of Pure Practical Reason." Barni made the same mistake in his French translation.

[56] Judgment is also the art of finding a rule for a case presented. This is called "reflective judgment," in contrast to "determinative judgment" (*Critique of Judgment*, V, 179 [15]). In the *Critique of Practical Reason* Kant is concerned excusively with determinative judgment: the principle being given, find the case to which it applies. That this is a fundamental insufficiency in his ethical theory is argued by M. C. Nahm, " 'Sublimity' and the 'Moral Law' in Kant's Philosophy," *Kant-Studien*, XLVIII (1957), 502–24. The creative venturesomeness of private moral judgment, which may lead from new moral insights to new moral principles, is an important aspect of moral life that does not receive proper attention in the *Critique*. For Kant, moral concern lies in the application of known principles to given cases, not in eliciting new principles from problems of conduct. Note Kant's remark (*Critique of Practical Reason*, 8 n. [93 n.]) that no one would want to be the inventor of a new moral principle.

in this talent, which he ascribes to mother wit, cannot be perfected by the learning of still other rules, since this talent would again be required for the proper application of them. Thus a man learned in medicine may possess sound theoretical principles and know the rules, but only practice which perfects a native gift can make him a skilful physician.[57]

When the judgment or rule to be applied is a priori, as in the case of theoretical categories, the role of judgment is the same. But it is more difficult to understand how it functions because the concept did not arise from the kind of experience to which it is to apply. Kant holds that it is easy to see how one can say, "This plate is circular," since the empirical concept of plate includes the geometrical concept of circle, or at least has been associated with it in experience; and we can both think and intuit a circle. It is more difficult to see how one can say, "The sun causes the stone to become warm," since, as Hume showed, there is no intuition or datum of cause from which the concept has been abstracted and to which it ostensively applies.

Kant's solution is presented in his doctrine of schematism. A schema is a representation that is homogeneous with both an intuition and a concept, so that the concept can refer to it directly and thence indirectly to the specific intuitions. The schema of an empirical concept is a kind of generic image which contains as its core the defined properties of the *definiendum* but covers also a range of variation that makes it resemble all the members of a class.[58] There can be no image, however, for an a priori concept. Its schema is not an image but the representation of the procedure of the imagination in synthesizing from possible data of intuition in such a way that this synthesis is homogeneous with the conceptual synthesis whose rule is the category itself. The schema is both a rule of this procedure and its product, which is the required formal structure of intuition to which the category is applied. Thus the category of causation is the concept of the dependence of the existence of one thing upon that of another. But Hume showed that we have no intuition of such dependence. Yet we do apply the concept to intuition under one condition, to wit, the regular succession of phenomena according to a (putative) rule. The schema of cause, therefore, consists not in some (impossible) image additional to the images of two events but in the "succession of the manifold [of intuitions] in so far as that succession is subject to a rule."[59] Whether a specific succession *is* subject to a rule, of course, is a question for empirical research to decide. But the schema exhibits

[57] *Critique of Pure Reason,* A 133 = B 172.
[58] *Ibid.,* A 141 = B 180.   [59] *Ibid.,* A 144 = B 183.

the concept of cause in such a way that it can be applied to these sequences which do fall under the rule and can be withheld from those which do not. Without the schema, we could not move from the concept of mere logical dependence, which is analytical, to real dependence, which is synthetic.[60]

An analogous problem arises in judgments which are to subsume actions under practical rules or concepts, where subsumption may mean the estimation of a particular action in the light of a general rule or the decision that a particular action would satisfy the rule and should, therefore, be performed. To decide whether a particular act possible in the sensuous world falls under the principles which define the good requires the power of judgment. The problem of practical judgment, when it is a matter of skill and even of prudence, is not essentially different from that met with in theoretical judgment, since all the practical propositions of skill and prudence have theoretical correlates and since the criteria of a successful technique and of a satisfactory mode of life are to be found in experience.

With pure practical judgment the problem is more difficult, since the law is a law of reason, not of understanding, and no intuition can be adequate to it. We can never be sure, in any experience, whether the full terms of the moral law have been observed. It therefore seems absurd, Kant says, to wish to find a case in experience, which stands under theoretical categories, to which the moral law applies so that the ideal of moral good can be exhibited *in concreto*.[61] Similarly, the

---

[60] I do not wish to appear to be falling into the error of thinking that the forms of judgment which generate the categories are forms of analytical judgment only. Certainly I can say "Ghosts cause miracles," and this is a synthetic judgment. But unless intuitions are supplied, corresponding to the concepts of ghosts and miracles, and unless they follow the schema of causation, such a synthetic judgment cannot be justified. The only kind of dependence that can be known purely conceptually is analytical dependence; intuitions for the schema are necessary if the asserted dependence is to be synthetic. Yet the hypothetical judgment and the category of causation are meant to apply, respectively, to synthetic (causal) judgments and to the synthetic connection of phenomena whereby the occurrence of one is dependent upon the occurrence of the other.

[61] *Critique of Practical Reason*, 68 (159). In *Critique of Pure Reason*, A 425 = B 453, however, Kant states that moral philosophy, like mathematics, "can present its principles, together with their practical consequences, one and all *in concreto*, in what are at least possible experiences." But the contradiction between the two passages is more apparent than real, as can be seen from the context of the latter passage. Kant is there trying to show that the "skeptical method," i.e., the method of the antinomies, is especially serviceable in speculative philosophy but useless in natural science, mathematics, and morals, for none of these "lay claim to insight into what is beyond the field of all possible experiences." The moral philosophy which presents its cognitions *in concreto* is a philosophy already armed with a type

morally good is not a natural property of an act standing in causal or other categorical relations to others. Yet pure practical concepts and principles must be applied, and they are applied even by the "commonest mind" with often more skill than by the moral philosopher.

The questions are: How is it done? What is it that will bridge the conceptual gap between what ought to be and what is, so that the concepts of the former may be applied in a definite way to, or withheld from, at least parts of the latter so as to show that they are, or are not, as demanded by the moral imperative? Without an answer to these questions, the normative-descriptive distinction, upon which Kant lays such enormous weight (26 [114]), marks an uncrossable chasm which is incompatible with the very notion of the ought and which is not, in fact, present in our ordinary moral concern as something uncrossable; we cross it every time we make a moral decision or pass a moral judgment.

Kant's answer to these questions is his theory of the type or typic of practical judgment.[62] Discussion of this has a place in the second *Critique* analogous to that of the schematism in the first.

A practical principle does not, as such, give knowledge of any empirical fact. While a practical judgment presupposes that what is commanded or counseled is possible in the empirical world, this possibility is established by pure cognitive (theoretical) procedures. But that an action possible for me in the world of sense is an action that is morally possible[63] requires a different kind of judgment. We are not concerned, in practical decision as such, with an action to which a specific practical principle applies descriptively by virtue of its cognitive component or correlate; we are concerned only with the decision

---

of judgment (though, of course, the typic was formulated after the passage in question). The *summum bonum*, on the other hand, cannot be presented *in concreto* as a cognition of practical reason, and there the method of the antinomies again comes into its own.

62 Type: "That by which something is symbolized or figured; a symbol, emblem" (*Shorter Oxford English Dictionary*). For full discussion of the meaning of this term see Paton, *The Categorical Imperative*, pp. 160–61. Neither the *New English Dictionary* nor Grimm's *Wörterbuch* recognizes the use of "typic" (*Typik*) as a noun; but it is clear that Kant wishes to distinguish between the type of moral judgment (*Typus*) and the theory of the type (*Typik*). On symbol and schema cf. *Fortschritte der Metaphysik*, XX, 279–80, and *Critique of Judgment*, § 59.

Kant uses the terms "type of the concept" and "type of the principle" as equivalent (*Critique of Practical Reason*, 70 [162]).

63 *Critique of Practical Reason*, 57 (148): "To decide whether or not something is an object of pure practical reason is only to discern the possibility of willing the action."

as to what action ought to be done among all those that are theoretically possible. We have, therefore, an analogy: a schema of a case occurring according to a law is necessary for knowledge of the case, while a schema of the law itself[64] is necessary to connect, in practice, possible events in sense experience with a cause under a law which is not a law of natural connection. Because the schema of a case has an intuitive component, it is always cognitive in function. But no intuition is available to a practical law of what ought to be, for two reasons: (*a*) it is a law of what ought to be, not of what is, and (*b*) only one member of the moral motive-act nexus is within nature. A schema of the law itself must be provided by the understanding or the faculty of thought and not by intuition or imagination.

Just as a schema was the "third thing" that could mediate between pure concept and pure intuition, the type must be a third thing that can mediate between the concept of nature, all that is, and the concept of what ought to be. The third thing in the practical judgment is the concept of law itself as definitive of a realm or kingdom.[65] Nature is phenomena under law, and natural law provides a type or model[66] by which we can think the practical law *in concreto*.

We ask ourselves, in face of temptation, "What sort of world would this be if everybody acted the way I wish to act? Would I be willing to create such a world, or to live in it if it existed?" But the desire to live in a world in which, for example, everyone developed his talents is not the reason why I should develop mine; it is not the motive[67] of my efforts at improving myself, for the obvious and simple reason

---

[64] Kant points out the danger of the expression "schema of the law" (*ibid.*, 68 [160]). He uses the word "schema" in a broader sense in Reflexion 5612; in *Metaphysik der Sitten*, § 45 (VI, 468) it means hardly more than example. In the *Foundations* neither "schema" nor "type" is used, but there is a brief reference to the problem under the name "canon of moral estimation" (424 [41]). Similarly, *Zum ewigen Frieden in der Philosophie*, VIII, 420: "canon of morally practical reason." Reflexion 7260: "analogon."

[65] *Foundations of the Metaphysics of Morals*, 433 (51).

[66] *Perpetual Peace*, VIII, 372 (Beck, 37): Natural law is a "model" for constitutional construction.

[67] *Critique of Practical Reason*, 69–70 (161). Failure to recognize the difference between the type of moral judgment and the motive of moral action has led some critics to say that in the categorical imperative Kant has committed himself to a utilitarian or even egoistic doctrine (cf., for example, Mill, *Utilitarianism*, chap. i). But Kant did not fall into this confusion, which he warns against. He was quite well aware of the fact that if I lie, it does not mean that all other men will lie, and therefore the fear of the consequences of my lying does not include the fear of the consequences which would follow from the existence of a world in which everyone lied. Cf. especially *Foundations of the Metaphysics of Morals*, 438 (57).

that I am not the creator of a world, and in this world I know, all too well, that not everyone is going to act the way I do, be it for good or ill. But implicit in the notion of a moral order is that of an order of interacting wills (the third category of relation), and the best model we have for such a world is the order of nature under law.[68] That is, what would not be possible in an order of nature under law is not morally possible, though what is actual in nature (a matter which empirical intuition must decide) has no judicative function in the abstract determination of what is morally possible and necessary.[69]

"The order of nature under law" means two things, one of which, as Paton points out,[70] is largely forgotten today. First, it means a uniform sequence of phenomena under causal law, and its distinguishing feature is the universal uniformity of nature. Nature, as a mechanical system, was believed, in the eighteenth century, to be "governed" by such laws having universal application. Before passing to the second of the meanings of the "order of nature," we must inquire into the practical significance of this concept of uniformity.

The first test of a maxim is the mere universalizability of the maxim, i.e., the interpretation of it as a descriptive universal principle. Of some maxims, Kant says that they destroy themselves if made universal.[71]

[68] From time to time Kant pushed the analogy very far. Thus he early compared the good will in Rousseau to the force of gravity in Newton, seeing in each an organizing principle in an orderly realm (*Träume eines Geistersehers*, II, 330, 335; Reflexion 5429). He told Mendelssohn (April 8, 1766 [X, 72]) that this did not express a serious opinion but was only an example of how far one could go in *Erdichtung* where data are lacking for knowledge. But the thought evidently had a certain fascination for him, for we find it again in *Metaphysik der Sitten*, Tugendlehre, § 24 (VI, 449) and *Opus postumum*, XXI, 35.

[69] Though, of course, it has a contributory function, since every action is predicated upon empirical knowledge, which provides the content for the abstract principle of choosing means suitable to a given end.

[70] *The Categorical Imperative*, pp. 150 ff., 161 ff. I hesitate to follow Paton in only one point in his definitive and exemplary exposition: I do not think that he is correct in asserting (p. 149) that only the second of these conceptions of the order of nature plays a part in the typic. The concept of causal uniformity does have, I think, at least a minor role, as I try to show in the text.

[71] Kant says this repeatedly. In the *Critique*, however, he speaks also of actions as being universalizable. (Note that in the first and second formulas in the *Foundations* [421 (38, 39)] he speaks of universalizable maxims, while in the typic it is the universalizability of the action itself which is mentioned.) This is an inaccuracy in the *Critique*. If lying were universal, we would be able to get along far better than in this world, where it is only frequent; we should simply interpret affirmative sentences negatively and negative ones affirmatively. But if the *maxim* is to deceive another person, the best way of doing it is by sometimes telling the truth and sometimes not.

That is, the effectiveness of such a maxim is dependent upon the fact that it does not correspond to a universal, or even general, description of human behavior. It is not possible to will rationally that such a maxim should be universal, even though the proposition "All men should lie" is not logically self-contradictory. A maxim like "I should lie" depends for its effectiveness upon the fact that it is not universal, that its theoretical correlate "I lie" is not universalizable into a judgment, "All men always lie"; for, if it were, there would be no such thing as a lie at all.[72] One's lies show mendacity and cleverness only because they are exceptions to a general rule. But general rules which have exceptions are not laws of nature; the latter have no exceptions.

Attention should here be called to a matter already discussed above (p. 121). The universalizability of a maxim is a negative test of its validity as a law. But many maxims can in fact be universalized which do not have the status of law. In this way, the type of the moral law as a universal and uniform natural law is only a negative criterion for moral judgment.

The second meaning of the order of nature is one according to which all the laws and the phenomena under them are in such a relation that nature as a whole can be interpreted as an organic unity,[73] which suggested to the natural theologian that it had been designed by a wise creator. For Kant, the inference to a wise creator is logically invalid; but the thought of a teleological organization is required as a regulative principle in our search for as yet unknown causal connections. Natural theology and natural teleology regard the world of nature as such a realm, though for Kant only the Idea of it is a valid methodological assumption. Moral teleology, on the other hand, sees such a realm as an ideal to be achieved in action;[74] it is a regulative Idea for practice and not for knowledge only. This Idea is that of a realm of ends, organized by the third category of practical relation, that of community of persons under common law, the whole being

[72] This is said independently of the logical problem of the Epimenides paradox. Let it be supposed that all men except Epimenides did, in fact, invariably lie. The logical paradox would not then ensue, but the practical effectiveness of lying would disappear. We should simply say that Epimenides said "Yes" when other men said "No," and no one would be deceived, and if Epimenides willed that all other men should lie, there would be no sense or purpose in his lying. Hence the maxim would be "self-destructive" just as surely as his statement about *all* men was paradoxical.

[73] The moral significance of this conception has already been touched upon lightly (cf. *Critique of Practical Reason*, 27–28 [115], and above, p. 99).

[74] *Foundations of the Metaphysics of Morals*, 436 n. (55 n.).

a *corpus mysticum* of rational beings.[75] Such a world is archetypal, and the Idea of it "determines our will to impart to the sensuous world the form of a system of rational beings" (43 [132]).

This regulative conception of nature, believed by almost all eighteenth-century scientists and philosophers to describe the actual cosmos, is the model for our thought of the moral realm. I do not merely ask myself whether a realm of nature consisting of rational beings acting uniformly in the way I propose to act would be possible, i.e., if the maxim could be a universal law and accomplish the ends I have and express in the maxim; I ask, further, whether I, as a creator of the world in which every part should have its natural place and function, would will that certain maxims should have the force of law. Would it be a world in which the natural ends of things would be systematically thwarted? If so, though such a world is possible as a territory[76] of uniform event-sequences, it would not be a realm which could be rationally desired by a being who consistently traced out the implications of his desires. That is, when I will an immoral action, one that would sow discord among rational beings, I will according to the maxim of the act and also will (tacitly) that my maxim *not* be universal. And such a maxim is not then analogous to a law of nature.

Here it is necessary to point out an easy and frequent error in Kant-interpretation. In the third example in the *Foundations*, Kant is said[77] to have committed himself to the view that the motive of the

[75] *Critique of Pure Reason*, A 808 = B 836.

[76] On territory and realm cf. *Critique of Judgment*, Introduction, II.

[77] E.g., by Ross, *Kant's Ethical Theory*, p. 47. Can the statement (*Critique of Practical Reason*, 70 [162]) that the maxims of a will determined only by the maxim of helping itself serve as a "very adequate type for the morally good" be reconciled with the other statement (28 [115]) that "though elsewhere natural laws make everything harmonious, if one here attributed the universality of law to this maxim there would be the extreme opposite of harmony, the most arrant conflict, and the complete annihilation of the maxim itself and its purpose"? Yes, if we consider the words "If this will made itself into a universal law," for then the freedom of each is restricted by that of the others (cf. 34–35 [123–24]). That such a conception of the mutual restriction of wills, if put into practice, would necessarily lead to the greatest happiness is asserted in *Critique of Pure Reason*, A 809 = B 837, where it is called an "Idea of reason." This is the Idea of a realm of ends, a legitimate moral motive, since our maxims would be legislative for such a realm. But the Idea of universal happiness is only the type of such a realm. In the quotation from p. 28 (115) it may be supposed that Kant is referring to the universalization of each man's selfish maxim as a law of nature and not to the maxim as it must be modified and restricted if it is not to lead to "arrant conflict," while the sentence on p. 70 (162) refers to the maxim as thus refined and restricted.

benevolent action is the desire for benefits from the recipients of my helpfulness. This is not only a misinterpretation of what Kant said and meant; it is a very poor foundation even for enlightened selfishness, human gratitude being the delicate flower that it is. The question is not What do I stand to gain by being altruistic? The question is Can I, standing frequently in need of help from others in carrying out my own purposes, consistently will a maxim to be universal according to which I could not *in principle* expect or demand such help? It is not that by acting unkindly I cut myself off from their kindness; this may or may not happen. It is a question of whether, among all my maxims, I can include one which, made universal, would thwart my efforts to carry out the terms of the others. If my will is good, the expected or hoped-for help from others is not the motive of my action; but if my will is rational, I must consider the consistency of willing both my private purposes and a state of affairs in which the likelihood of satisfying them would be reduced to nothing.

The type of moral judgment, thus interpreted, does not require uniformity of actions but only mutual interaction under a common maxim. This interpretation is certainly favored by the wording in the *Critique* which requires the universalizability of the maxim but allows "variety in the rule" (20 [106]), but is not consistent, in its full implications, with the wording of the Typic (69 [161]), which requires the universalizability of the actions themselves. Only against the latter formulation is the criticism of Hegel[78] and others valid that some actions, e.g., almsgiving, cannot be universalized. As a rule, of course, "Give alms" cannot be universalized; there must be some people who cannot give alms if anyone is to give them. As a principle, however, of helping others in distress, this maxim of imperfect obligation can be universalized.

At the end of this chapter, Kant fully develops the meaning of the type as nature considered as a realm of ends to be made actual by our actions in it. Nature herself, and not merely her law, is considered as a type or symbol but not as the realm of moral ends. Accordingly, Kant warns against the error of Wolff and others who confused the realm of nature and the realm of ends in their doctrine of perfection.[79] This error is empiricism in morals,[80] which is inevitably heteronomy

[78] *Lectures on the History of Philosophy*, trans. Haldane and Simson (1895), III, 460.

[79] Cf. *Vernünftige Gedancken von der Menschen Thun und Lassen*, § 137.

[80] *Critique of Practical Reason*, 70, 94 (162, 188); *Critique of Pure Reason*, A 474 = B 502.

and thus destructive of the purity of morals. And he warns also against taking a type of the realm of ends as if it were a schema of a transcendent intuition and thus confusing the mere ideal thought of a realm of ends with an alleged intuition of an actual, ready-made, realm of ends.[81] In either direction, theory of what is (either of the world of phenomena, in the former, or of the transcendent world, in the latter) pre-empts the place of autonomous theory of what ought to be. All these theories ascribe to judgment a role that can properly be filled only by reason, which alone can supply the universal principle needed by judgment in the guidance of conduct.

[81] *Critique of Practical Reason*, 85–86 (179). This is fanaticism (*Schwärmerei*) in morals and is related to mysticism (*ibid.*, 71 [163]).

X

The "Transcendental Deduction" of the Principle of Pure Practical Reason; Commentary on Section 7 and Ak., 42–50 (Abbott, 131–40)

§ 1. INTRODUCTION

It has been noted that the structure of Kant's exposition in §§ 1–6 and in chapter ii is analytical and problematical. These pages inquire into what would be the form of the law if the hypothesis is correct that reason of itself alone can give an a priori practical law. While there is a categorical finality in Kant's statements about the character of practical reason as such, he is proceeding only analytically in §§ 1–6 with respect to pure practical reason. He is asking only: If pure reason is practical, what is its law and what is the nature of the will that can obey this law?

Nevertheless, a man who believes as firmly as Kant did that the moral law is a law of pure reason cannot keep this belief entirely under cover. There are several places where his belief in the reality of pure practical reason is obvious, before he has reached the place in his treatise where these assertions are systematically justified.[1] Even in the *Critique of Pure Reason*, which does not pretend to show that freedom is real but only that it is possible, he often breaks through this logical reticence and comes out with assertions such as this: "I am justified in making the assumption [that moral laws a priori can determine the will] in that I can appeal not only to the proofs employed by the most enlightened moralists but to the moral judgment of every man, in so far as he makes the effort to think such a law clearly."[2] The "moral judgment of every man" is the true starting point of the Kantian moral philosophy, and this fact should not be forgotten, however synthetic, rather than analytical, the structure of the second *Critique* is meant to be.

[1] E.g., *Critique of Practical Reason*, 19, 27, 29 (105, 115, 117).

[2] *Critique of Pure Reason*, A 807 = B 835.

Kant's readiness to appeal to what the ordinary man thinks in moral matters does not strike the twentieth-century reader as being startling, for to us this is the only place to begin. But the sharpness of the reply to Tittel[3] shows that there was a spirit of novelty (at least in Continental philosophy) in going into moral problems from this direction, instead of in the more usual way of erecting a world system that might subsequently be used to explain, or often to explain away, ordinary moral phenomena. In this procedure, Kant is indebted to Rousseau[4] and to the conscientiousness of pietism, which manifested itself in the profound but simple-minded righteousness of his parents, whom he openly revered all his life. Yet this moral consciousness may be illusory; duty may be a "vain delusion and a chimerical concept."[5] We do not know that true virtue can be found anywhere in the world, even if the concept is valid; and no examples can prove that it does exist.[6]

The tone of Kant's argument suddenly changes in § 7. He no longer attempts to restrict himself to hypothetical statements about what would be true if pure reason were practical, but boldly asserts: "Pure reason is practical of itself alone, and it gives (to man) a universal law, which we call the moral law."[7] To show the contrast between the analysis and the assertion, compare the following two passages:

Sometimes we find, or at least believe we find, that the ideas of reason have in actual fact proved their causality in respect to the actions of men, as appearances.[8]

[3] *Critique of Practical Reason*, 8 n. (93 n.); cf. *Critique of Pure Reason*, A 831 = B 859: "Do you really require that a mode of knowledge that concerns all men should transcend the common understanding and should only be revealed to you by philosophers? Precisely what you find fault with is the best confirmation of the correctness of these assertions."

[4] "By inclination I am an inquirer. I feel a consuming thirst for knowledge, the unrest which goes with desire to progress in it, and satisfaction in every advance in it. There was a time when I believed this constituted the honor of humanity, and I despised the people, who know nothing. Rousseau corrected me in this. This blinding prejudice disappeared and I learned to honor man. I would find myself more useless than the common laborer if I did not believe that this attitude of mine [as an inquirer] can give worth to all others in establishing the rights of mankind" (XX, 44).

[5] *Foundations of the Metaphysics of Morals*, 402 (18).

[6] *Ibid.*, 407 (23–24).

[7] *Critique of Practical Reason*, 31 (120). Here appears the confusion between law and imperative which we have already noticed occasionally. Kant should have said: "It gives a universal law which we call the 'moral law,' valid for all rational beings, and to man it issues a corresponding categorical imperative."

[8] *Critique of Pure Reason*, A 550 = B 578.

One need only analyze the sentence which men pass upon the lawfulness of their actions to see in every case that their reason, incorruptible and self-con-strained, in every action holds up the maxim of the will to the pure will, i.e., to itself regarded as a priori practical [32 (120)].

What is it that authorizes Kant to make this change in the status of the hypothesis that pure reason can be practical? A change in mood does not of itself constitute a step in argument.

There are two reasons for it: the alleged "fact of pure reason" and the somewhat equivocally titled "deduction" of the principle.

§ 2. THE "FACT OF PURE REASON"

What was previously only a methodological standpoint, the assump-tion of moral consciousness, now functions as an actual premise of the argument, in spite of Kant's having acknowledged that it might be illusory. He says:

The consciousness of this fundamental law may be called a fact of reason, since one cannot ferret it out from any antecedent data of reason and since [the law] forces itself upon us as a synthetic proposition a priori based on no pure or empirical intuition [31 (120)].

In order to regard this law without any misinterpretation as given, one must note that it is not an empirical fact but the sole fact of pure reason [31 (120)].

This Analytic proves that pure reason can be practical, i.e., that of itself and independently of everything empirical it can determine the will. This it does through a fact wherein pure reason shows itself actually to be practical. This fact is autonomy in the principle of morality.[9]

The moral law is given, as an apodictically certain fact, as it were, of pure reason, a fact of which we are a priori conscious.[10]

---

[9] *Critique of Practical Reason*, 42 (131). In the next paragraph, this fact is said to be identical with the consciousness of the freedom of the will.

[10] *Ibid.*, 47 (136). Note that this sentence says that it is "as it were a fact." On pp. 6, 31, 42, 43 (91, 120, 131, 132) Kant calls it a "fact"; and on pp. 47, 55, 91, and 104 (136, 145, 185, 199) it is called a "fact, as it were," or some similar qualification is made. (Abbott omitted this qualification on his pp. 136 and 185.) This has suggested to some that Kant was uncomfortable with this unusual use of the word "fact" and became cautious after its earlier use. But though this is the most plausible interpre-tation of the difference, his caution departed when he had finished the *Critique*, for we find the following: *Critique of Judgment*, § 91 (V, 468 [320–21])—freedom is the fact; *Metaphysik der Sitten*, Rechtslehre § 6 (VI, 252)—practical law of freedom is a fact; *Vorarbeiten zur Tugendlehre*, XXIII, 378—"It is *res facti* that this law is in us and is indeed the highest"; *Opus postumum*, XXI, 21—the categorical impera-tive is the fact of moral-practical reason.

Critique of Pure Reason, B xxii and xviii, speaks of "practical data of reason" and practical principles as "a priori data of reason." Reflexion 7201 (i.e., Duisburg Frag-ment 6) introduces the concept, perhaps for the first time, but without the word "fact." But the moral law is here compared to a priori representations of space and time as givens,

With respect to these famous but obscure passages, we must ask two questions: (*a*) What is the alleged fact of reason? and (*b*) Is it a valid foundation for that which Kant attempts to build upon it?

a) What is the fact of pure reason? Kant himself does not seem to have made up his mind on the best way of expressing it. The text shows the following meanings: in the first quotation, it is consciousness of the law; in the second and fourth quotations, it is the moral law itself; in the third quotation, it is autonomy. Since Kant identified freedom as autonomy with the moral law (33 [122]), perhaps the second and third may be allowed to stand as one. But a prima facie distinction exists between "consciousness of the moral law," which can certainly be said to exist as a fact (whether we wish to call it a "fact of reason" or not), and the law itself, of which we are conscious (whose "factuality" is *sub judice*).

If this prima facie distinction is finally valid, Kant's argument refuses to move, except in a circle. For everyone will grant that the "fact" in the first sense exists, but it does not imply the "fact" in the second of the senses. Yet it is the second of the facts that is essential to Kant's argument.

b) Is it really a "fact" in the sense required? That the fact in the second of the senses admittedly cannot be explained is, in itself, no reason to reject it.[11] Some facts must be unexplained; but why this one, instead of some other that might be incompatible with it? Perhaps we have a fundamental intuition or insight into its truth? I think that Kant undoubtedly believed that we do, though he would not have called it an "intuition"; but fundamental insights and intuitions do not seem to be any different from the kind of evidence that Kant has already admitted might be wrong. An appeal to insight or intuition is a confession of failure to find an argument or premise from which some truth can be derived and an unwillingness to surrender it in spite of that. In principle, some kind of intuition is indubitably necessary, but that does not mean that some particular intuition is either necessary or indubitable; it may indeed be wrong. Perhaps the moral law is the kind of fact that must be assumed if we are to explain and render intelligible our moral experience?[12] But if this is the meaning

---

[11] *Critique of Practical Reason*, 31, 47 (120, 136).

[12] The Deduction proper does not strictly follow the second of these paths but adduces an independent warrant for the principle from the need of theoretical reason to assume freedom. Hence it falls outside the scope of the censure of this sentence (cf. below, pp. 173 f.). That the moral law is a "fact" in the sense in which, say, mathematics and natural science are "facts" and therefore subject to the same kind of justification is the interpretation of Hermann Cohen, *Kants Begründung der Ethik*, p. 224, and his Marburg followers.

here, it hardly deserves the name of fact but only of assumption, for the experience it is supposed to organize is itself *sub judice* and could, perhaps, be equally well organized in terms of some other assumptions, e.g., those of psychoanalysis.

Thus if we permit the prima facie distinction between the two alleged facts to stand as a fundamental duality, Kant cannot make a transition from the undisputed fact (that we are conscious of a moral law[13]) to the disputed fact (that there is a law that can come only from pure practical reason). Yet it is the latter whose factuality is to be shown if the moral law is to be justified.

I believe, however, that this duality of meaning of "fact" does not represent Kant's premises properly. There are two intimations of this. First, there is his assertion that this fact (whatever it is) of pure reason is the *sole* fact; and I do not think Kant means that it just *happens to be* the only fact of pure reason. I think there is something about this fact that makes him regard it as a priori unique. Second, there is the difficult and obscure hint that was never developed but is the clue to the interpretation I shall present here. "Freedom and unconditional practical law reciprocally imply each other," Kant says (29 [117]). "I do not here ask whether they are actually different, instead of an unconditional law being merely the self-consciousness of a pure practical reason, and thus identical with the positive concept of freedom," i.e., with the concept of autonomy.

To explore this possibility, we need to draw still another distinction in the meaning of "fact of pure reason." "Fact of pure reason" may mean a fact known by pure reason as its object, *modo directo*. Or it may mean the fact that there is pure reason, known by reason reflexively. These may be distinguished as "fact for pure reason" and "fact of pure reason."

When we think of the moral law as a fact for pure reason, i.e., as an object of a particular and unique insight or intuition, the very uniqueness of this fact is at least a ground of suspicion. The first *Critique* showed that there are not any facts known by pure reason without sensuous intuition. Facts are given to reason only by and through intuition. Should there be any fact "for" pure reason, it would be only a fact "as it were." If he is speaking of the fact "of" pure reason, on the other hand, this is not subject to the suspicion we

[13] If it should be argued that "to be conscious of" is like "to know" and therefore must refer to a true proposition or actual object, then even the first of the facts is not indisputable. It should then be stated: "We believe that there is a moral law," and this states a fact but does not imply, even in ordinary speech, that there is a moral law,

feel about the fact "for" reason. Kant's point is that in *any* willing there is a principle which is purely rational,[14] and "if pure reason is actually practical, it will show its reality and that of its concepts in action."[15]

Only a law which is given by reason itself to reason itself could be known a priori by pure reason and be a fact for pure reason. The moral law expresses nothing else than the autonomy of reason (33 [122]); it is a fact for pure reason only inasmuch as it is the expression of the fact of pure reason, i.e., of the fact that pure reason can be practical. That is why the moral law is the sole fact of pure reason and for pure reason.

If this seems to be a rather tricky argument, let us turn to the moral phenomenon which it represents. A moral principle is not binding upon a person who is ignorant of the principle or law. On the other hand, if a person believes that an imperative is valid for him, then it is in so far forth valid for him, and he shows that reason is practical even in the awareness of this aspect of a valid claim. This is true whether the imperative expresses a claim that is in fact valid or not. Only a being with an a priori concept of normativity could even make a mistake about this. To argue against it is to appeal to normative grounds and is as ridiculous as to attempt to prove by reason that there is no reason (12 [97]). "I say that every being that cannot act otherwise than under the Idea of freedom is thereby really free in a practical respect."[16] But the Idea of freedom is expressed in the moral law; hence to be conscious of moral constraint, i.e., of the law— this is the fact of pure reason—*ipso facto* validates the practical claim of a moral law, which is the fact for pure reason. It is indeed a very odd kind of fact, and Kant is right in calling it a "fact, as it were."

To recapitulate: moral consciousness, consciousness of duty, is an undisputed fact. Prima facie, it does not justify the assertion that duty is not an illusory and chimerical concept. (If I believe, for instance, that there is a God and that duty is determined by the will of God, and if there is in fact no God, then it may remain a fact that I feel the

[14] This is confirmed by the analysis of even hypothetical imperatives, chap. vi, § 6. But Kant goes even further and says that we become conscious of the moral law whenever we construct maxims for the will. By this I think he means that in every decision on a policy of life there is a putative rationality in the rules subsumed under the principle, which, if fully elaborated, would require the rationality of the motive as well as that of the means to its satisfaction (cf. *Critique of Practical Reason,* 29 [117]).

[15] *Critique of Practical Reason,* 3 (87). Cf. *Critique of Pure Reason,* B 430–31, which must have been written only shortly before the second *Critique.*

[16] *Foundations of the Metaphysics of Morals,* 448 n. (67 n.).

call of duty, but it is not a fact that duty is an objectively valid constraint.) But because the moral law—the fact for pure reason—expresses nothing but the lawgiving of reason itself, the fact of pure reason is reflected in the fact for pure reason. For a being who thinks that there is some obligation, there is some valid law. The metaphysical deduction has shown what this law must be; it is the fact *for* pure reason.

§ 3. THE DEDUCTION

In the *Critique of Pure Reason*, Kant says: "Jurists, when speaking of rights and claims, distinguish in a legal action the question of right (*quid juris*) from the question of fact (*quid facti*) and they demand that both be proved. Proof of the former, which has to state the right, they entitle the deduction."[17] This is, at least in part, the sense in which Kant uses the word "deduction" here. It is not a disputed fact that men use the concept of causation and that they believe themselves to be under legitimate moral constraint. But the question of the right to use these concepts is a different one from that of the fact of their use.

A legal deduction is one in which a jurist makes a syllogism: "X is right because X is A, and the Constitution says, 'A is right.'" But a Kantian transcendental deduction does not have this neat structure. There are not any principles implanted in men's minds from which the principles of causality or morality could be shown to be logical consequences and therefore permissible or necessary. Such a principle would not be a bit more obvious than the concept of cause or ought itself and would be subject to the same challenge that Hume brought to the principle of causation. If we attempt to deduce, in this sense, the moral law from some other fact for reason, such as man's natural desire for happiness, that which is thereby derived is not a necessary law. There are no better-established principles from which moral principles can be syllogistically deduced.

The process of transcendental deduction is not that of linear inference from a premise to its logical consequence. It is a process of taking some body of alleged fact (e.g., mathematics or science) which has been challenged and showing (*a*) what its necessary presuppositions are and (*b*) what the consequences of denying these presuppositions are. Thus, for example, the objective validity of mathematics had been challenged by those who held that its propositions were based upon experience and so lacked necessity (Hume in the *Treatise*) or were analytical and so lacked objective application (Hume in the *Enquiry*). The *Critique of Pure Reason* attempted to show that, if mathematics is empirical, not only is it uncertain but the space which

17 *Critique of Pure Reason*, A 84 = B 116.

it treats of can be neither finite nor infinite. That is, an empiricistic mathematics is self-contradictory. Kant then formulates another theory as to what space is, in which the antinomy can be avoided, and then shows that one of its consequences is the necessity of mathematics. This deduction is not undertaken for the sake of mathematicians in their own work, for they had got along very well (in Kant's opinion) with quite erroneous views of space. It was performed to keep them from drawing unwarranted conclusions concerning the nature and limits of their science and to prevent skeptics from deriving spurious aid and comfort from erroneous opinions about mathematics.[18] Similarly, Kant attempts to answer Hume's challenge to the concept of causation. But he does not do so "by taking for granted that which Hume doubted"[19] in order to initiate a syllogistic linear inference to a conclusion that Hume rejected. He does so by trying to show that if causation is only a subjective association of ideas, sanctioned by custom, then even the data from which we might make an induction to an emaciated "causal" generalization would not be available, since only in a causal system can we distinguish between an objective order of events from which an induction might be made and a subjective sequence of representations which is too variable to support an induction.[20] That is, only if some consequence of the causal conception is already available, can Hume's reconstruction of the principle on his own grounds be undertaken.

In its broad outlines, Kant's procedure here is comparable to that in the first *Critique*, though, strangely enough, Kant so emphasizes the differences that he denies, in spite of the title of the section, that there can be a deduction of the principle of pure practical reason (47 [136]). He does not do this, however, until he has already availed himself of the "fact of pure reason" and asserted that the principle needs no deduction.

Before describing what Kant actually does in the remainder of this section, which seems prima facie to be sadly misnamed, let us consider what we might reasonably have expected him to say in a deduction. We should expect him to introduce here a notion very prevalent now, that of "moral experience" as a realm to be analyzed, articulated, and established.[21] A critical regression upon its presuppositions would lead him to one or more synthetic a priori propositions. Their justification would not lie in a claim that they are "firmly established in themselves"

[18] *Ibid.,* A 87 = B 120-21.   [19] *Prolegomena,* IV, 258 (Beck, 6).

[20] *Critique of Pure Reason,* A 196 = B 241.

[21] Cf. *ibid.,* A 807 = B 835.

but by proof that they are principles without which the experience in question, as the *prius*, would be unintelligible. If it be argued that this would be a *petitio principii*, at least the answer could be returned that in any argument one assumes the universe of discourse of the premises. The argument would have made no headway against a critic who stubbornly refused to concern himself with moral phenomena, just as the *Critique of Pure Reason* would make no dent in the armor of a silent skeptic who refused to assert or deny that $7 + 5 = 12$. "Moral experience" here would have the same status that "possible experience" had in the first *Critique*, and both these realms must be assumed at least problematically if epistemological or ethical analysis is to have anything to work upon.

Yet this is not Kant's way here. The moral principle neither has nor needs a deduction. To understand the peculiarity of the method of the *Critique of Practical Reason*, we must return for a moment to the *Foundations of the Metaphysics of Morals*.

In the *Foundations*, Kant's argument takes somewhat the form expected. The concepts of an absolutely good will and a universally legislating will are synthetically related to each other. If necessarily related, they must be related through some third pure cognition (like pure intuition in the theoretical *Critique*). The third cognition is furnished by the positive concept of freedom and is the idea of an intelligible world as the archetype for the sensuous world insofar as it is subject to our will. The intelligible or supersensuous world is nothing else than the world of nature considered under the autonomy of pure practical reason (43, 44 [132, 133]). This seems to be as close as Kant came to the notion of a "moral world" or a system of moral experience as the justification of the moral principle.

In the *Critique*, by having said that the principle needs no deduction, he apparently stands the argument of the *Foundations* on its head. He uses the moral law, the fact of reason, as the *prius* to deduce something else, namely, freedom, which is its *ratio essendi*.

The argument, in spite of Kant's denial that it is a deduction of the moral law, is formally like the deduction of any other synthetic a priori principle in the first *Critique*. The concept of freedom is called upon to play a role analogous to that of intuition. If there were an intuition of freedom, the parallelism of the two arguments would be perfect; but there is not. To show that an Idea of reason (freedom) can be a substitute for intuition in a deduction requires us once again to recall the abstract structure of the deduction in the first *Critique*, for the notion we are examining will otherwise seem completely bizarre and incredible.

The deduction of the categories requires that the objects of knowledge to which the categories apply be given in possible experience. It was necessary, therefore, to begin with a study of the way in which they are given (intuition) and then to follow with a study of the concepts and judgments by which the objects of intuition are thought. In the second *Critique*, however, we cannot begin with intuitions but must begin with principles which are the "given." Instead of holding our concepts to intuitions, as theoretical knowledge requires, we must sharply separate them and hold the concepts up to principles. In the course of the elimination of the intuitively or empirically given (30 [118]), the paths of the two *Critique*'s diverge. When we eliminate the empirical material in the former, we are left with a pure intuitive form; when we do so in the latter, we are left only with the mere form of "ought." Since synthetic theoretical judgments are possible only by reference to the pure form of intuition, which, as it were, bridges the gap between the concepts of their subjects and predicates, it would seem that no synthetic pure judgments would be possible in moral philosophy at all. Yet they are possible and are actually given as the "fact for pure reason."

"A good will [*sc.* a pure practical reason] has as its maxims only universal laws" is claimed to be a synthetic a priori judgment, for "by analysis of the concept of an absolutely good will, that property of the maxim cannot be found."[22] How, then, can it be confirmed? Not by finding an intuition (which would be the obvious step in theoretical philosophy) *but by adducing some substitute for intuition.*[23] It must be purely intellectual, and therefore a moral sense will not suffice. It must be a priori, for otherwise the synthetic judgment would not be a priori. And it must, like intuition, have an *independent warrant;* that is, it must not be just a product of the thought it is to justify. This third thing, this substitute for intuition, is the Idea of freedom. And freedom is not given at all! Only its Idea is given.

Here the argument takes a truly astonishing turn. Since the synthetic a priori judgment that one expected to see Kant deduce needs no deduction and can have none, it is used for the deduction of the Idea of freedom itself. Fortunately, however, the "deduction" is not a linear inference; and, while the moral law serves as a ground for the deduc-

---

[22] *Foundations of the Metaphysics of Morals,* 447 (66).

[23] Kant does not use the expression "substitute for intuition." But that freedom has this function is made perfectly clear in the analogies he draws between the methods of justifying a priori synthetic theoretical judgments (by means of intuition) and that of justifying a priori practical judgments; the analogy is best drawn in *Opus postumum,* XXI, 420–22.

tion of freedom, the concept of freedom is made to serve also as the "credential" of the moral law. It is such a credential because of the independent warrant that this concept has. Only this independent warrant makes it possible for Kant to break out of the circle of using freedom to establish the moral law and the moral law to establish freedom. The independent warrant of the moral law, which is the *ratio cognoscendi* of freedom, is the fact of pure reason. The independent warrant of the concept of freedom, the *ratio essendi* of the law, is found in its theoretical use:

This kind of credential for the moral law, namely, that it is itself demonstrated to be the principle of the deduction of freedom as a causality of pure reason, is a sufficient substitute for any a priori justification, since theoretical reason had to assume at least the possibility of freedom *in order to solve one of its own needs* [48 (137); italics added].

In order to solve one of its own needs, a theoretical need. This is the need to avoid an irresolvable contradition or incompleteness in theoretical reason itself: "[Speculative] reason showed freedom to be possible only in order that its supposed impossibility might not endanger reason's very being and plunge it into an abyss of skepticism" (3 [87]). This refers us back to a peculiarity in the solution of the third antinomy. Not only did that, like all the antinomies, have to be resolved in order to avoid blatant self-contradiction; it had to be resolved by showing that both thesis and antithesis were true. If the thesis were false and the palm of victory given to the antithesis, the contradiction would, of course, have been resolved, but theoretical reason's interest[24] in thinking a connected world would have been thwarted. Reasoning demands a totality of conditions, and if a cause which is not also an effect were shown to be impossible, this demand could not be met in either the phenomenal or the noumenal world. The concept of freedom could not then even be a valid regulative Idea of reason as we push our thought from the conditioned back to the conditions and conditions of conditions. Theoretical reason, in that event, would be in as hopeless a plight as if the direct logical contradiction had not been removed at all.

Theoretical reason thinks that freedom is possible not merely because it can discover no valid logical evidence against it; it *requires* us to think of freedom as possible.[25] But this alone does not show that we know it to be real. Any evidence that would justify our claim to know

[24] *Critique of Pure Reason,* A 474 = B 502–3.

[25] Speculative reason must assume freedom only if it wishes to complete its function in speculation, and this is an arbitrary need, hypothetical and without the status of law (*Critique of Practical Reason,* 5 [89]). Though a problematic concept, it is absolutely indispensable to speculative reason (*ibid.,* 7 [93]).

that it is real would fix "the keystone of the whole arch of the system of pure reason and even of speculative reason." This evidence is that of pure practical reason, which substantiates transcendental freedom "in the absolute sense needed by speculative reason in its use of the concept of causality" (3 [87]). The concepts of pure practical reason, such as freedom, are accordingly "not like the props and buttresses which usually have to be put behind a hastily erected building, but are rather true members making the structure of the system plain, and let the concepts, which were previously thought of only in a problematic way, be clearly seen as real" (7 [92]).

The *Critique of Practical Reason*, therefore, does not begin with a mere permit to occupy the "empty space" left by the first *Critique*, with no indication of how it is to be filled. The space, empty for knowledge, has a shape determined by the demands all around it for knowledge of what can indeed be known. The vacant place, into which the concept of natural causality cannot enter, is suited for only one kind of tenant: "Pure practical reason now fills this vacant place with a definite law of causality. . . . This is the moral law."[26]

What, we may ask at the end of this circuitous route, has been gained for the principle of pure practical reason? The fundamental principle, already asserted as a "fact," is not left a naked and isolated assertion or an assertion surrounded by a closed, circular, and empty system. It is supported in that it is precisely of the form required if the dialectic of theoretical reason is not to be irresolvable.

The *Critique of Pure Reason* said that if an irresolvable conflict between our knowledge of nature and our moral principles arose, it would be the latter that would have to be surrendered.[27] But, recognizing the essentiality of the concept of freedom, it also said that if the antinomy could not be solved, *both* would be jeopardized.[28] Now, because the Idea of freedom was required but not confirmed by theoretical reason, yet is confirmed practically through the fact of pure reason, there is no danger of conflict. Rather, there is mutual support, which far surpasses the evidential value of mere consistency. The independent warrant of the concept of freedom—to wit, that it is needed also by theoretical reason—makes it serve as a systematic credential for the reality of pure practical reason.

[26] *Critique of Practical Reason*, 49 (139); *Critique of Pure Reason*, A 288–89 = B 344–45; A 255 = B 310; A 259 = B 315; *Foundations of the Metaphysics of Morals*, 462 (83), etc. This is one of Kant's favorite metaphors, and there are many imaginative variations upon it.

[27] *Critique of Pure Reason*, B xxix, A 536 = B 564.

[28] *Ibid.*, A 543 = B 571.

XI

Freedom

§ 1. INTRODUCTION

Discussions of freedom are so frequent in Kant's works that the full compass of the concept and its attendant problems cannot well be surveyed in a running commentary on passages taken seriatim. In this chapter, therefore, I shall attempt to examine Kant's ideas on freedom, following an order which will be made clear in the second section.

Some of the difficulties in interpreting the *Critique* become more manageable when we realize that its central doctrine of freedom of the will involves two different concepts of freedom and two different concepts of the will. Each of these pairs of concepts had a long and troubled history before Kant, and each was used in his own earlier work. His most important contribution in the second *Critique* was to show that what is sound in each involves the other. But he did not help the reader see that this is what he was doing, because he did not first establish, or even define, the two pairs of concepts and then bring them together; the unwary reader may not realize that Kant was using two sets of concepts, because he shifts from one to the other without notice and his language does not often indicate directly which he is using. Furthermore, it is by no means certain that he was himself at all times aware of the duality of his concepts and of the problem he was working on.

We must take the confusing fabric he wove, trace out the various threads which form two patterns, and then, if at all, try to find a single larger pattern composed of both. This program of work is summarized in § 2 and occupies §§ 3–12, and it should be judged only in the light of these later sections; §§ 13 and 14 discuss two points which are independent of the major hypothesis of this chapter.

§ 2. TWO CONCEPTIONS OF WILL AND FREEDOM

In the *Critique of Practical Reason*, the concept of will, which has freedom as its attribute, is equivocal. Theories of freedom of the will which do not seem to be consistent with one another are presented side by side, but they are actually theories about different things and answer different questions. The *Critique* is the meeting place of two different, but not explicitly distinguished, conceptions of the will and its freedom, one of which comes chiefly from the *Critique of Pure Reason,* the other of which is a heritage from the *Foundations.* The two conceptions are explicitly distinguished only in the later works, after their interdependence has been shown in the *Critique of Practical Reason.* We must see the *Critique,* therefore, as a bridge where the tangled paths of the earlier works converge and then for the first time clearly separate on the other side.

From the *Critique of Pure Reason* there is inherited the concept of freedom as spontaneity, the faculty of initiating a new causal series in time. From the *Foundations* there is taken the concept of freedom as autonomy, as lawgiving, and hence as independence from any pregiven law. The two faculties are generally called by one name, "will," and discussed under the name of one problem, that of "freedom of the will." Only later did Kant give the reader any help in distinguishing between them, when he "officially" called the former faculty *Willkür*[1] and the latter *Wille.* He had often before used these words, sometimes to indicate a tacit distinction and sometimes apparently interchangeably; but at no time had he intentionally and consistently restricted himself to one of the topics to the exclusion of the other. Even in the *Metaphysics of Morals,* where the attempt is made to draw a good distinction and to avoid confusing them, he does not often succeed in keeping discussion of one of them from interrupting discussion of the other.

---

[1] There is so much dispute about the exact meaning and proper translation of *Willkür* that I shall frequently leave it in German. Born translated it as *arbitrium,* following Kant's own suggestion, and thus distinguished it from *voluntas.* Barni translated it as *arbitre* and Picavet as *libre choix;* on the French words cf. Khodoss, *Kant: La Philosophie pratique,* Glossary, p. 242. Capra's translation is *libero arbitrio.* Abbott used *will* or *choice* or *elective will;* Beck added *free will* and *faculty of choice* to this imposing list. The term *Willkür* was used by Wolff, *Vernünftige Gedancken von Gott, der Welt und der Seele des Menschen,* § 519: "Freedom of the soul is the faculty of the soul to choose, through its own *Willkür,* between two equally possible things the one that pleases it more"; the "Erstes Register" (Glossary) of this work translates *Willkür* as *spontaneitas,* and Baumeister, *Philosophia definitiva* (1768), § 911, following Wolff, in turn defines *spontaneitas:* "est principium, sese ad agendum determinandi intrinsecum." A distinction suggesting that between *Wille* and *Willkür* is drawn by Wolff, *Psychologia empirica,* § 882: "The very act of willing [*actus volendi*] is called *volitio* in opposition to *voluntas,* since the latter denotes a faculty of mind or a power or possibility of eliciting that act." Similarly, Baumgarten, *Metaphysica,* § 690: "A rational act of desiring something is a *volitio.* Therefore I have a faculty of willing [*volendi*] or a will [*voluntas*]." Baumeister, *op. cit.,* § 893: "Volitio est ipse actus volendi. . . ." *Volitio* does not exist in classical Latin in this sense.

His formal definitions of will are drawn up as if will were a faculty or combination of faculties which can be observed and of which we have a direct awareness. Will is the faculty of determining our causality through a conception of rules (32 [120]), and, since for the derivation of an action from a rule or law reason is required, will is nothing but practical reason. It is the relationship between understanding and the faculty of desire (55 [145]). The faculty which makes a rule of reason the efficient cause of an action through which the object is to be made real is will; the will is never determined directly by the object or our conception of it, but always by a rule of reason (60 [151]). That the will is, in this sense, free from direct sensuous necessitation is an empirical fact.[2] This conception of will, as a faculty of desire guided by a rule of reason taken as a maxim, later becomes more specifically *Willkür*, the faculty of choosing an object which is left incompletely determined by the maxim itself. It has, therefore, an incentive (*Triebfeder*) for action in addition to the law, while *Wille* has no *Triebfeder*.[3] *Willkür* may or may not be free, according to the kind of law it puts into the maxim or the degree to which the maxim and not the momentary representation of the object determines the action. It does not give rise to laws but only to maxims, but it may, and when moral it must, make laws its maxims.[4]

In contrast to this, there is a concept of will not as the direct determiner of action but as the lawgiver to the maxims which will determine action. In this sense, Kant says, not quite accurately, that laws determine what ought to happen and maxims determine what does happen.[5] But the point made is sound enough: reason is necessary to the formulation of a law, but a maxim determines behavior directly. In the formulation of a law, we have to do with the *real use* and not with the mere logical use of reason;[6] by the "real use" is meant the establishment of an a priori synthetic proposition, and by the "logical use" is meant merely the inferring of actions from a rule. Pure practical reason has

[2] *Critique of Pure Reason*, A 802 = B 830, there called *Willkür*. It is illustrated, but not defined, by reference to the faculty of choice known empirically (*Metaphysik der Sitten*, VI, 226).

[3] *Vorarbeiten zur Tugendlehre*, XXIII, 378.

[4] *Ibid.*, 383; *Metaphysik der Sitten*, VI, 226.

[5] *Foundations of the Metaphysics of Morals*, 420 n. (38 n.).

[6] On the general distinction between the real and the logical use of reason, cf. above, pp. 7, 75. An empirical practical reason is always merely logical in its use. Kant draws the distinction in *Critique of Pure Reason*, A 800 = B 828, by calling the logical use the "regulative use" of pure practical reason and contrasting it with the "constitutive use" by which reason gives the law.

nothing to do with the logical derivation of actions from given rules. There is little or no verbal justification in calling such a pure practical reason a "will" at all. But it makes perfectly good sense to speak of it as determining the will (*Willkür*) and of its doing so freely, independently of sensuous conditions.

If practical reason determines the will (*Willkür*), then we can say that the latter is free in the psychological or comparative sense (96 [190]), even though there may be a natural law connecting the conception of practical reason with the action and even if conceiving this law is itself a naturally caused event in the inner life and even if the law is a practical translation of a natural law. But to think that this is freedom in the sense needed by ethics seemed to Kant to be a "miserable subterfuge." If all the causes of action are internal to man, not external, if they are intellectual and not sensuous, and if the laws of their connection with action are psychic and not physical (97 [190–91]), still the corresponding concept of freedom, regarded as adequate by Kant's predecessors and by himself in the *Nova dilucidatio* (1755),[7] is inadequate to the needs of ethics.

A new conception of freedom is called for. A law which is given for moral obedience must not be a law of the connection of means to a desired end and hence what I have called the "practical translation of a natural law." It must be a law given by reason to a nature to be made real, not one taken from a nature already realized. A will or *Willkür* which can obey such a law must be independent of the mechanism of nature, in which all connections are among phenomena, for a law which demands absolute and not contingent obedience must be purely formal, commanding by virtue of its form which is known by reason, and not its phenomenal content. This independence of the mechanism of nature is "freedom in the strictest sense" or transcendental freedom, whose logical possibility was established in the first *Critique* (29 [116]).

But what of the origin of the law itself? Kant's most important discovery is that the law is not a mere restriction on freedom but is itself a product of freedom. Precisely this conception marks the chief advance of the second over the first *Critique*. This is the Copernican Revolution in moral philosophy. The *Critique of Pure Reason* saw reason as that which set bounds to a freedom which is itself without law,[8] but it did not show how it does so; it established neither the provenance of the law nor the mechanism by which it is effective.

The law is a product of the freedom of *Wille* as pure practical rea-

---

[7] *Nova dilucidatio*, Proposition ix (England, 231).

[8] *Critique of Pure Reason*, A 569 = B 597.

son, not of *Willkür*. (Though one must complain sometimes that Kant writes *Wille* when *Willkür* would be correct, I do not believe he ever used *Willkür* to refer to *Wille* as pure practically legislative reason.) We cannot say that the actions of *Wille* are free, because *Wille* does not act.[9] It gives only a law for the submission of *Willkür*, which does act. Yet it is free in that its decree follows from its own nature. It does not mediate laws of nature to *Willkür* bent upon the satisfaction of some arbitrary purpose; that is the function of practical reason in its logical use. It does not counsel, but commands, and it commands as a principal, not as an agent. Through submission to it, *Willkür* supplements its negative freedom with a positive freedom which comes from submission to its own idealized nature as purely rational will. Using a political metaphor, as he so often did in speaking of the realms and territories of the legislation of reason, Kant says it is autonomous, free in itself,[10] i.e., free in the positive sense. *Willkür* participates in this autonomy to the degree that its negative freedom vis-à-vis nature is exercised in adherence to the law of pure practical reason. Pure practical reason spontaneously creates an Idea of a *natura archetypa*,[11] and *Willkür*, taking this as its object, can become an efficient cause of giving to the world of nature the form of such an intelligible world.

But we must never suppose that there are two faculties related to each other in some external, coercive way. There is only one, but it has prima facie two kinds of freedom, though one of them will eventually be shown to be the perfection or logical form of the other. *Willkür* is fully spontaneous only when its action is governed by a rule given by pure practical reason, which is its legislative office. It is very hard to avoid speaking as if there were two faculties without falling into the opposite error of failing to distinguish between the two roles and the two meanings of freedom. But unless we are to make Kant more difficult and obscure than he already is, we must be on our guard against both an oversimple identification of function and a "two-faculty theory."

Freedom in the positive sense is not so fraught with problems as that in the negative sense. If we could presuppose freedom, Kant says, the law would follow analytically from it (31 [120]), and a will (in this

---

[9] *Metaphysik der Sitten*, VI, 226.

[10] *Vorarbeiten zur Tugendlehre*, XXIII, 383. Its autonomy is contrasted with the heteronomy of *Willkür;* the freedom of *Willkür*, which is independence of material of desire, is freedom in the negative sense, while the legislation, or autonomy, of *Wille* is freedom in the positive sense (*Critique of Practical Reason*, 33 [122]).

[11] *Critique of Practical Reason*, 43 (132); cf. *Critique of Pure Reason*, A 548 = B 576.

sense) and a free will are identical. The freedom of *this* will is demonstrated by the fact that there are absolute obligations, which could not
be so if all the laws of practical reason were empirical, i.e., if practical
reason were not pure, i.e., autonomous. Though the two conceptions
of will and freedom are inextricably bound together, the metaphysical
difficulties are found mostly on the side of freedom in the negative
sense, where it comes into contact with the natural necessity of the
phenomenal world.

§ 3. KANT'S RECAPITULATION OF THE ARGUMENT OF THE FIRST "CRITIQUE"

The "Critical Examination of the Analytic of Pure Practical Reason"
and "Of the Right of Pure Reason to an Extension in Its Practical Use
Which Is Not Possible to It in Its Speculative Use" give a brief résumé
of the contributions which the *Critique of Pure Reason* made to the
theory of freedom. We may well use these sections as a preliminary
guide through what Kant himself called the "thorny paths" of that
work.

As in the *Prolegomena*, where he credits Hume with having awakened him from his "dogmatic slumber," Hume appears also here as the
chief instigator of Kant's critical labors. Hume, working on the principle that there can be no legitimate idea that does not arise from impressions, failed to find an impression of necessary connection and thus
concluded that "the concept of cause [i.e., of necessary synthetic connection of events in time] has been acquired surreptitiously and illegiti-
mately" or, more drastically, "it can never be acquired or certified because it demands a connection in itself void, chimerical, and untenable
before reason, a connection to which no object could ever correspond"
(51 [141]; cf. 56 [146]).

Granting the validity of Hume's inference from its premises, Kant
finds the only error to lie in Hume's premise that objects of experience
are things in themselves (53 [143]). It perhaps sounds strange to attribute this premise to Hume, who is generally thought of as a phenom-
enalist or subjectivist with reference to the objects of knowledge. But
if we understand Kant correctly, we see that this is indeed Hume's
premise, though it can be less startlingly formulated in non-Kantian
terminology. Kant means that Hume believed that the objects of
knowledge, though called "impressions," are known as they are and in
the order in which they are given, without our actively participating
in their generation and synthesis. But of things as they are (whether
they be impressions or Lockean substances), we cannot understand
why, if one is given, another must also be given. The concept of causal-

ity arises neither from reason (53 [143]), for the connection between a cause and an effect is not one whose denial is self-contradictory, nor from experience, for connections known only in this way are not known to be necessary. If Hume is correct, it is a "bastard of the imagination impregnated with experience."[12]

The first *Critique*, however, with its Copernican Revolution, saved the necessary connection among events by showing that, though it is necessary for knowledge of objects, it gives knowledge only of objects of experience; for they are only phenomena synthesized by rules, not things in themselves, of which we have no knowledge. The rules for the synthesis are necessary in a way in which Hume's synthesis by custom is not. (Since the rule is not derived from knowledge of objects [experience] but, on the contrary, makes it possible, the rule must have its seat and origin in pure understanding.) Because of its purely intellectual origin, it would appear that the concept and rule are applicable also to things which are not objects of possible experience but lie beyond its boundaries (54 [144]). And this is correct, but with a very important proviso that distinguishes Kant from his rationalistic predecessors. If the concept were empirical in its origin, it could not even be used to think of objects beyond experience; but it does not follow that, since it is not empirical in origin, it can be used in order to know them. The restriction of its use in thought falls away, but a Hume-like restriction on its use in knowing remains.

That which made causal knowledge of nature possible is precisely that which is lacking in our thought about things beyond experience, to wit, intuition. Intuition, givenness to sense, is indispensable if there is to be any synthesis of concepts. All necessary connection between pure concepts is analytical; but concepts can refer to intuitions, and thus, through reference to a necessary third thing, can be brought into necessary, but synthetic, relation to one another. Our intuition is sensuous, i.e., it presents things to us only as they affect and appear to us, not as they are in themselves. But when we try to know things as they are in themselves and apply the categories to them, the intuitive condition is missing because we have no intellectual intuition (31 [120]).

This lack, however, does not prevent us from using the categories to think of things as they are in themselves. Such thought may even be valid, but it is not a cognition of things in themselves. If there is any reason why this application of categories should be made, then the purely non-empirical origin of the categories enables us to make the application, which would not be possible if Hume had been right about the origin of these concepts (55 [145]).

[12] *Prolegomena*, IV, 257–58 (Beck, 5, 6).

At this point, Kant's recapitulation diverges in a very important way from the actual argument of the *Critique of Pure Reason* and from his more accurate estimate of it elsewhere in the *Critique of Practical Reason*.[13] For he tells us here that it is not a theoretical purpose but only a practical purpose that makes necessary the application of the concepts beyond the limits of empirical knowledge.[14] For a full development of this important difference, we must turn to the first *Critique* itself.

§ 4. FREEDOM AS A THEORETICAL IDEA

A category freed from the limitations to possible experience and handed over to reason for use in a complete synthesis of all experience is called an "Idea."[15] All synthesis of representations by the understanding is only partial; but reason demands a total and unconditioned synthesis, i.e., reason's Ideas always have reference to a whole which is unconditioned but which contains all conditions of its parts (107 [202]). The principle of reason is that if the conditioned is given, the entire sum of its conditions must also be given, and therefore the absolutely unconditioned, which is either this sum or some member of it, must be given. In carrying out the inquiry into the unconditioned, there are as many Ideas as there are categories of conditionality. In this section, however, we shall concern ourselves only with the category of causality and its corresponding Idea.

In respect to the causal dependence of one thing upon another, we apply the principle just enunciated that if the conditioned is given, the unconditioned must likewise be given, else the conditioned, which can occur only when the totality of its conditions is given, would not oc-

---

13 E.g., *Critique of Practical Reason*, 3, 48 (87, 137) and as already elaborated in chap. x, § 3.

14 Still, Kant says, not only is the theoretical purpose subordinate to the practical, but all purposes of reason are ultimately practical (*ibid.*, 121 [218]; *Critique of Pure Reason*, A 816 = B 844). But the point here is that a theoretical purpose is served by a concept of reason, not that the theoretical purposes themselves are subordinate to the practical.

15 *Critique of Pure Reason*, A 409 = B 435-36. This is the theory of the "cosmological Ideas" and differs markedly from the more general theory (A 299 = B 356) which finds the origin of the Ideas solely in the category of relation and in the forms of syllogism. The two theories exist side by side in the *Critique*, and Kemp Smith (*Commentary on Kant's Critique of Pure Reason*, p. 478) argues that the former is an "early" theory. The footnote added in the second edition, B 395, suggests the pre-eminence of the deduction of the Ideas from syllogism. In both theories, fortunately, the Ideas of God, the soul, and freedom have a place, and, interestingly enough, the place of the treatment of freedom is the same whichever of the two theories is used —it arises in the third antinomy, corresponding to the category of causation and to the hypothetical syllogism.

cur. In searching for this unconditioned, or at least in forming a clear concept of it, even though it is the concept of something that cannot be given directly in any single experience, we have two alternatives before us: (1) We can suppose that the series of conditions is infinite, so that no member of the series is unconditioned, while the series as a whole is unconditioned. (2) We can suppose that the series is finite and that there is an unconditioned member (the first member) in it. The first is equivalent to supposing that natural causation, the relation of one temporal event (cause) to another (effect), is the only kind of causation; and, since no event in time can be found that is not also the effect of an earlier one, we commit ourselves to the doctrine of an infinite series of events as the condition of any given event. The second is equivalent to assuming that the natural causation is not the only kind, since in an infinite series the unconditioned cannot be found. And this is equivalent to assuming another kind of causation, a "causality of freedom," i.e., a causality that is absolutely spontaneous, "whereby a series of appearances, which proceeds in accordance with laws of nature, begins *of itself*."[16]

Neither of these is an arbitrary supposition. In spite of their contrariety, each must be supposed, and thus theoretical reason necessarily falls into an antinomy. The opposition between the two in the antinomy is not just a curiosity of philosophy but is an inescapable opposition between two not-to-be-gainsaid interests of mind. It is an opposition that must be resolvable by the instrumentality of reason, since it is produced by reason; and it is not an opposition that philosophy could calmly accept with resignation, because its own interests are so deeply involved in each side and in their reconciliation.[17]

Let us recount briefly the demonstration of each of the conflicting theorems. The thesis is this: "Causality in accordance with the laws of nature is not the only causality from which the appearances of the world can one and all be derived. To explain these appearances it is necessary to assume that there is another causality, that of freedom." The proof is largely a repetition of the Aristotelian-Thomistic proof of the impossibility of an infinite series of causes and hence of the necessity of a first cause, i.e., of a cause that is not itself an effect and hence is free in the sense defined. That is, in a series of conditions and conditions of conditions, there is never a first condition; but the law of nature is that nothing occurs without a condition that is a priori sufficient. Hence, granting that something does occur, the law of nature is self-contradictory when taken in unlimited generality. Therefore, nat-

---

[16] *Critique of Pure Reason*, A 446 = B 474.

[17] *Ibid.*, A 480 = B 508; cf. *Critique of Practical Reason*, 3 (88).

ural causation, causation under the law of nature, is not the only kind, etc.

The antithesis is as follows: "There is no freedom; everything in the world takes place solely in accordance with the laws of nature." The proof is this: If there is a spontaneous cause or an absolute beginning in the natural causal series, the later members of the series are independent of the earlier, and thereby the "unity of experience," which depends upon the lawfulness of events in time, is made impossible, and thereby no criterion of empirical truth or objectivity is possible.[18]

The thesis is ascribed to dogmatists (e.g., Plato) and the antithesis to empiricists (e.g., Epicurus).[19] In general, the moral and religious interest is on the side of the thesis, which is the interest of pure reason;[20] the interest of science in its unending search for causes within experience is in the antithesis. The latter interest is not, indeed, incompatible with the moral interest except when empiricism itself becomes dogmatic, that is, when it is not content with the unending investigation of phenomena but extends its claims and methods into metaphysics and thereby causes "irreparable injury . . . to the practical interests of reason."[21] The former practical interest is not necessarily incompatible with the scientific, but there is the danger that, while "supplying excellent practical principles, it permits reason to indulge in ideal explanations of natural appearances . . . to the neglect of physical investigation."[22] There is, however, one clear advantage on the side of the thesis: the antitheses of all the antinomies "render the completion of the edifice of knowledge quite impossible. . . . The architectonic interest of reason, the demand not for empirical but for pure a priori unity of reason, forms a natural recommendation for the assertion of the thesis."[23] The interest of speculative, and not merely of practical, reason therefore lies on the side of freedom.[24] But if it were not for the antinomy, metaphysics

---

18 *Critique of Pure Reason*, A 451 = B 479, remark on the antithesis.

19 *Ibid.*, A 466 = B 494, A 471 = B 499.

20 This is not, however, the whole story. The real interest of morality is not on the side of dogmatism but on that of freedom, which the dogmatists defended (cf. *Critique of Practical Reason*, 146 ff. [244 ff.] and below, chap. xiii, § 7). Let there be no guilt by association in moral philosophy.

21 *Critique of Pure Reason*, A 471 = B 499.

22 *Ibid.*, A 472 = B 500.   23 *Ibid.*, A 474 = B 502–3.

24 This is the sense in which Kant says that reason in its theoretical employment requires the concept of freedom (*Critique of Practical Reason*, 3, 7, 48 [87, 93, 137]). One might say that reason's first interest is the removal of the antinomy, but Kant does not call this its "interest" but says it is merely the condition of there being any reason (*ibid.*, 120 [216]).

would be only an extension of physics, i.e., the dogmatization of the antithesis. The antinomy which prevents this is, therefore, the "most fortunate perplexity" into which pure reason can fall.[25]

§ 5. RESOLUTION OF THE THIRD ANTINOMY

The principle which generated the antinomy was as follows: If the conditioned is given, the entire series of its conditions is given; the conditioned is given, therefore the unconditioned is given. But, Kant says, there is a fallacy here, in that the major premise takes "conditioned" in the sense of a pure category, while the minor takes it in the empirical sense of a concept of understanding applied to appearances. But, in appearance, not all conditions are given as phenomena; they are not *gegeben*, but *aufgegeben*—not presented as a gift but assigned as a task. The conditioned within the phenomena is the prescribed object of inquiry. The antithesis is correct when "conditioned" is taken in the sense of a temporal condition of a phenomenon, for there is no first phenomenon. On the other hand, the thesis is correct when "conditioned" is taken in the sense of the major premise, which does not restrict it to the temporal.[26] If "conditioned" were taken in the same sense in the two premises, the antinomy would be irresolvable, i.e., we could show that the conditions would have to form both an infinite homogeneous series and a finite heterogeneous series (95 [189]). But now we can see that the antithesis not only can, but must, be true of phenomena in time, while the thesis can and must be true of things in themselves in their relation to phenomena. Kant then says that the antinomy and its resolution afford indirect proof of the ideality of appearances, the Transcendental Aesthetic having given the direct proof.[27]

The Idea of a totality of conditions, therefore, is not a constitutive Idea in experience for which we could find a corresponding experience

---

[25] *Ibid.*, 107 (203); cf. *Critique of Pure Reason*, A 464 = B 492.

[26] *Critique of Pure Reason*, A 499 f. = B 527 f.

[27] *Ibid.*, A 506 = B 534. Kant wrote Garve (September 21, 1798; XII, 257) that the discovery of the antinomy was what led to the conclusion that space and time were only forms of appearance (cf. also *Critique of Practical Reason*, 107 [203]). It should be noted, however, that the proof of the antithesis presupposes the validity of the Kantian doctrine of the phenomenality of nature, and especially that of the second Analogy of Experience. The proof of the thesis, on the contrary, is a typical rationalistic argument that does not depend upon any exclusively Kantian doctrines. The antinomy alone cannot, therefore, be used as a premise for the phenomenality of the natural order, but it may well have suggested it to Kant. The fact that the proof of the thesis is independent of the Kantian doctrine of space and time is of considerable importance in evaluating the use that Kant made, or could have made, of his doctrine of freedom (cf. below, § 8).

of an object. It is a regulative Idea or a "rule prescribing a regress in the series of given appearances, and forbidding [reason] to bring the regress to a close by treating anything it may arrive at [in experience] as absolutely unconditioned."[28] This we may call the "Regulative Idea of Causal Mechanism," and by it we are enjoined from introducing free causes into our study of nature but are directed to find the condition of every phenomenon in still other phenomena. If, however, we regard the phenomena as things in themselves, this regulative Idea must be regarded as constitutive, and we run into the antinomy in such a way that *neither* freedom *nor* natural causation can be saved.[29]

Kant next attempts to show that if there is any reason to assert the existence of free causality, this does not involve any contradiction with natural mechanism. He does so by asserting that the effects of free causality would be in the phenomenal series and thus in the order of natural mechanism. Every appearance is the appearance of a reality; its appearance is connected with other appearances under the causal law of nature and is predictable with certainty. But in its relation to that which is not appearance, i.e., the noumenon, and not a member of the temporal series, it is an effect of a freely acting cause, where freedom is defined as the power of being a cause without being an effect. Hence, in principle, *every* event in the world is a product of both natural and free causation. We do not understand it in its latter relation; all our knowledge is knowledge of the connections of phenomena among themselves. We cannot apply the category of causation to things in themselves so as to have knowledge of them; but we can apply the category by analogy[30] to the relation of noumena to phenomena and think of the former as a free cause of the latter without infringing on the principle of mechanical causation so far as our possible knowledge is concerned.

In doing this, however, we must be careful not to claim more than we can perform. Kant hedges in this right to think freedom. We cannot know the free causality of a thing in itself;[31] we cannot think of the thing in itself as acting at various times and places (for it is not in

[28] *Critique of Pure Reason*, A 509 = B 537; cf. also *Critique of Practical Reason*, 48 (138).

[29] *Critique of Pure Reason*, A 543 = B 571. Causality in nature cannot be saved because we cannot determine a synthetic necessary connection except insofar as it is prescribed by theoretical reason, and theoretical reason can prescribe only for the realm of phenomena. ("Theoretical reason" is here used in a broad sense, and includes also the understanding and intuition.)

[30] *Ibid.*, B 431–32.

[31] *Ibid.*, A 540 = B 568; *Critique of Practical Reason*, 133, 134 (231 f.).

space and time);[32] we cannot use our concept of freedom as a supplement to our concept of natural causation when we are ignorant of how the latter should be applied in a particular case; and we cannot expect the course of nature to be any different when we admit free causes from what it would be, were they denied.[33] All that Kant says he has accomplished is to show that "causality through freedom is at least not incompatible with nature" and that his intention was not to establish either the (real) possibility or the reality of freedom.[34] Freedom, therefore, is only a problematic concept.

§ 6. PRACTICAL FREEDOM

At this point it is well to consider a peculiarity of the proof of the thesis of the third antinomy. I mentioned earlier that Kant's argument is an adaptation of the Aristotelian argument for the existence of a first cause. What, then, is contributed by it to the establishment of freedom? Kant says, in the Observation on the Thesis:

> The necessity of a first beginning, due to freedom, of a series of appearances we have demonstrated only in so far as it is required to make an origin of the world conceivable. . . . But since the power to spontaneously begin a series in time is thereby proved, it is now also permissible for us to admit within the course of the world different series as capable in their causality of beginning of themselves, and so to attribute to their substances a power of acting from freedom.[35]

One may well say, then, that the demonstration, if successful, accomplishes entirely too much. It seems to justify the concept of freedom, if anywhere, then everywhere. Every phenomenon has the two dimensions of relations, one to previous phenomena, one to noumena. The second dimension or relation is not what is meant by freedom in any interesting sense, because it is indiscriminately universal. Freedom as a universal predicate is of no interest. The concept of noumenal causation is empty unless we could know either (*a*) the substance in question or (*b*) a noumenal law of its activity. In the case of a stone, for instance, we know neither, and therefore we have to be content—and are easily contented—with knowledge of the phenomenal relations of phenomenal stones. In the case of one's own self, however, though we do not know ourselves except as appearances, we do know the law of

[32] *Critique of Pure Reason*, A 541 = B 569; *Critique of Practical Reason*, 99 (192).

[33] *Critique of Pure Reason*, A 550 = B 578; cf. also *Idea for a Universal History*, Introduction (VIII, 17–18).

[34] *Critique of Pure Reason*, A 448 = B 476; cf. *Critique of Practical Reason*, 3 (87).

[35] *Critique of Pure Reason*, A 449–50 = B 477–78.

the noumenal action, for that is nothing other than the moral law. Kant appeals to noumenal causation, therefore, only where there is some reason to go beyond the phenomenal causation, and these are found only in human volition; even when morality is not in question, there is this occasion for use of the concept of noumenal causation:

In lifeless, or merely animal nature, we find no ground for thinking that any faculty is conditioned otherwise than in a merely sensible [mechanical, phenomenal] manner. Man, however, who knows all the rest of nature solely through the senses, knows himself also through pure apperception, and this indeed in acts and inner determinations which he cannot regard as impressions of the senses.[36]

Now the "interest of pure reason," which Kant said at the beginning is on the side of the thesis, comes into its own. The practical concept of freedom, he says, is based on the transcendental Idea of freedom, and without it cannot stand.[37] Freedom in the practical sense is the independence of *Willkür* from coercion through sensuous impulses. In man, there is a power of self-determination which is independent of nature. Practical freedom presupposes that, although something has not happened, it ought to have happened, i.e., that the cause in the field of appearance was not so determining that it necessarily excluded a causality of our will. Though everything that we might will might be due, indirectly, to sensuous impulse, the impulses and all phenomena under the law of nature cannot give rise to the concept of "ought," which entails a concept of free causation and not of natural causation. "No matter how many natural grounds or how many sensuous impulses may impel me to *will*, they can never give rise to the '*ought*,' but only to a willing which, while very far from being necessary, is always conditioned; and the 'ought' pronounced by reason confronts such willing with a limit and an end,—nay more, forbids or authorizes it."[38] The thought of "ought" is impossible if all laws are natural laws;[39] the thought of "ought" implies the thought of a free "can," and if pure reason is actually effective in the control of conduct, then there is free causation in the transcendental as well as in the practical sense. Thereby, also, transcendental freedom ceases to be an all-embracing and hence empty concept.

Kant is insistent, in both *Critique*'s, on the necessity of transcenden-

---

[36] *Ibid.*, A 546 = B 574; cf. *Critique of Practical Reason*, 49, 99, 100 (139, 193, 194).

[37] *Critique of Pure Reason*, A 534 = B 562.

[38] *Ibid.*, A 548 = B 576.

[39] *Ibid.*, A 547 = B 575: "We cannot say of anything in nature that it ought to be other than what it actually is in all its temporal relations."

tal freedom if practical freedom is to be real.[40] There is an empirical freedom, which Kant calls "comparative," which is not absolute or transcendental spontaneity but one which is empirically found in some of our acts, e.g., those in which we exercise what common sense calls self-control, but not in others, e.g., in acts springing from rage or lust. In comparative freedom, the determining causes are internal to the agent and not compulsion from without. This is the freedom of a projectile, which, once started on its trajectory, follows it necessarily but from its internal momentum. Even if the internal causes are intellectually thought reasons and not impulses, this freedom is still only the freedom of a well-run machine like a clock.[41] Empiricists (and here Kant is no doubt thinking of writers like Ulrich and Schulz) think this comparative concept of freedom is an adequate condition for ethics; but this is a mistake. The concept of freedom is the "stumbling block of all empiricists" (7 [93]), whose own concept of freedom is a "wretched subterfuge" (96 [189]).

Immediately this question arises: Does not Kant's doctrine, as over against that of the empiricists, infringe on the mechanism of nature? And if it does not, is it one bit more adequate to ethics than the empiricists' concept is? Kant says freedom in his concept does not in-

[40] In asserting that inward rational determination, which can be empirically exhibited, is not sufficient to morality, Kant is disagreeing with almost all his predecessors and contemporaries and with his own earlier view (*Nova dilucidatio*) that such acts are free because they express the activity and not the passivity of reason.

Section i of the Canon of Pure Reason is often regarded as having asserted that practical freedom is independent of transcendental freedom and as therefore being in this respect out of harmony with the "critical teaching" and hence as "early." Though the Canon was probably one of the earliest parts of the *Critique of Pure Reason* to be written, I beg to differ with this interpretation. The context should be sufficiently explanatory of the apparent discrepancy between Kant's statements for us not to have to suppose that he changed his mind on this central point during the course of writing the book. By a "canon" Kant means "the sum-total of the a priori principles of the correct employment of certain faculties of knowledge" (A 796 = B 824). The last paragraph of Section i does not say that practical freedom could stand if transcendental freedom were not real; it says merely that this question does not concern us in the practical field or in a canon where we "demand of reason nothing but the rule of conduct" and do not require that this rule be shown to be irreducible to a law of nature. "This problem does not come within the province of reason in its practical employment." This does not say that it is of no concern to a critical examination of practical reason; it says only that it is a theoretical, not a practical, problem. This is repeated even in the *Foundations of the Metaphysics of Morals*, 448, n. 456 (67, n. 76), and in the review of Schulz's *Sittenlehre*.

[41] *Critique of Practical Reason*, 96–97, 98, 101 (190–1, 195). The allusion to Leibniz' *automaton spirituale* has reference to *Theodicy*, §§ 52, 403. Kant perhaps knew of Vaucanson's automata through La Mettrie, *L'Homme machine*.

fringe on the laws of nature, and yet it is a basis for moral imputation. To show this, he draws a distinction between the intelligible character, the noumenal or transcendental subject, which is a *causa noumenon*, and the empirical character, which is only its appearance in space and time.[42] The former is free, the latter is under the law of nature. The former is thought (not known) as an unchanging substance in which nothing *happens* (because it is not in time); the latter is its unrolling in time under causal conditions of nature. We infer the nature of the former from that of the latter; we punish or reward the latter in the belief that it is a manifestation of the freedom of the former. The freedom of the empirical character is at first to be understood only negatively, as not being necessitated by things in nature. The freedom of the former is positive, for it originates a series of events in the world which would not have happened, had the intelligible character been different.[43] Every event in human conduct can be seen, therefore, in two ways: as a necessary consequence of preceding events and as directly determined by the intelligible character.

§ 7. CRITICISM OF THIS DOCTRINE

This is hard doctrine, and Kant admits that judgments under it "seem at first glance to conflict with equity" (99 [193]). But is it only "at first glance"? Why should a man repent the wrong he has done (98 [192])? How can we hold a man responsible for his actions and yet say, at the same time, that "before ever they have happened, they are one and all predetermined in the empirical character?"[44] That if we knew all the empirical facts and the natural laws of their connection so

---

[42] *Critique of Practical Reason*, 97 (190); *Critique of Pure Reason*, A 545 = B 573; Reflexion 5608. *Critique of Practical Reason*, 98, 100 (191, 194), however, speaks of our consciousness of having freely created our empirical character, and in this respect it seems hardly to fall under natural law or to fit into the reality-appearance rubric.

[43] *Critique of Pure Reason*, A 554 = B 582, A 556 = B 584; cf. the very similar passage in *Critique of Practical Reason*, 99 (193). Hence it must not be simply assumed that the intelligible-empirical distinction coincides with that between *Wille* and *Willkür*. The intelligible character acts timelessly, manifesting its acts in the conduct of the empirical character. The *Wille* does not act but legislates for (is a law for) the *Willkür*. Kant also speaks of personality (intelligible personality) as an archetype the respect for which constitutes the motive for the *Willkür* (ibid., 87 [180]). The freedom of *Wille* is distinguished from that of *Willkür* as *libertas noumenon* from *libertas phaenomenon;* yet the latter is not to be defined empirically (cf. *Metaphysik der Sitten*, VI, 226; and *Opus postumum*, XXI, 470), for this gives only a comparative or psychological sense of freedom. Kant's statements are so cryptic that it is hard to know whether he is entirely consistent or not.

[44] *Critique of Pure Reason*, A 553 = B 581.

that "his future conduct could be predicted with as great a certainty as the occurrence of an eclipse," we could nevertheless still assert that the man is free" (99 [193])? This requires us to accept a secularized version of the classical theological quandary of man's freedom and God's foresight, and it seems no more intelligible in structure and equitable in outcome than that hoary mystery.

If by "freedom" we mean noumenal causation and assert that we know no noumena, then there is no justifiable way, in the study of phenomena, to decide that it is permissible in application to some but not others of them to use the concept of freedom. The uniformity of human actions is, in principle, as great as that of the solar system; there is no reason to regard statements about the freedom of the former as having any empirical consequences. If the possession of noumenal freedom makes a difference to the uniformity of nature, then there is no uniformity; if it does not, to call it "freedom" is a vain pretension.

There seems to me to be only one way out of the dilemma. There are faint suggestions of it in two widely separated works of Kant, but he never fully developed them. He does not seem to have felt the paradox in his own views that all his critics and most of his disciples felt.

The first suggestion is this: Instead of regarding the world as consisting of two realms—a phenomenal under one set of laws and a noumenal under another—can we not think of one world under two aspects, the aspects to be defined methodologically with reference to the purposes we have in holding these two perspectives on a common world, and not ontologically? Kant intimates such a two-aspect theory, instead of the more commonly known "two-world theory," in his contrast between the observing, theoretical attitude and the acting, practical attitude[45] and in his statement that "supersensuous nature is nothing else than nature under the autonomy of pure practical reason" (43 [132]).

The other suggestion, necessary to the full development of the preceding one, is his conclusion in the third *Critique*[46] that the distinction between natural and moral law is dependent on the peculiar nature of our understanding. We can read these passages as a suggestion to regard the two kinds of laws as co-ordinate, not one as subordinate to the other in constitutive authority in experience. The only evidence we have that Kant entertained such a view is in § 70 of the *Critique of Judgment*, where he speaks of the thesis of the complete mechanical determination of nature, in its antinomic relation to that of teleological causation, as a regulative Idea even in respect to nature. It would be easy to extend this to the antinomic relation between freedom and nat-

[45] *Critique of Pure Reason*, A 550 = B 578; cf. chap. iii, above.

[46] *Critique of Judgment*, §§ 70 and 76.

ural causation. The Idea is expressed as a maxim: "All production of material things and their forms must be judged to be possible according to merely mechanical laws."

Had Kant said, in the solution to the third antinomy in the first *Critique*, that the true meaning of the antithesis is that it is a maxim for procedure and not a constitutive principle of nature, then we would have had two maxims: "Always (in science) search for mechanical causes and allow no non-natural causes to enter into the explanation of natural phenomena," and "Always (in ethics) act as if the maxim of the will were a sufficient determining ground of the conduct to be executed or judged." Neither of these is a declarative a priori statement; they tell us, rather, what we must do in order to be a spectator or an actor, but one cannot be both at the same time and with respect to the same item of conduct.[47]

It may well be that we would, under these rules, sometimes hold a man responsible for actions that he could not have avoided doing, for human freedom is far more limited, I think, than Kant held it to be. In this event, we are simply unjust judges. It may well be that we give an abstract, schematic causal explanation to some event which did not, in fact (though we shall never possibly know it), have a sufficient natural cause; in this event, we are dogmatic (unavoidably so) in our scientific work. But the alternative to sometimes being unjust is that of always being unjust when we hold a man responsible for any of his actions when, if Kant is correct, none of them could have been left undone in the course of nature and history as constituted by natural law.

The solution proposed here involves reading back into the Transcendental Analytic of the first *Critique* some of the conclusions of the Transcendental Dialectic. Specifically, it requires that the sharp distinction between constitutive category and regulative Idea be given up, that even the categories be regarded as devices for the regulation of experience and not as structures necessarily given in a fixed constitution of our experience of nature, and that the Analogies of Experience, which Kant called "regulative" in a very modest sense,[48] be reinterpreted as regulative in the full sense of the Dialectic.[49]

[47] Cf. above, chap. iii. The second of the maxims need not be interpreted in the manner of the fictionalists, i.e., on the assumption that the "as if" introduces a contrary-to-fact condition. There is no more need to assume that the latter is any more fictional than the former or that the former is constitutive while the latter is merely regulative.

[48] *Critique of Pure Reason,* A 179 = B 222.

[49] Such an interpretation of the Transcendental Analytic, in fact, can be recommended on purely epistemological grounds, though it no doubt distorts Kant's own estimate of the relation of the functions of understanding and of reason.

If we undertake to make these revisions, we are allowed to regard the moral or practical realm as a perspective of the realm of experience, which, through other regulative ideas (categories), is seen as the realm of nature. We will then no longer have to think of science as dealing with appearances (in some ontologically pejorative sense) and morals as dealing with noumena (in some epistemologically pejorative sense). Both can keep their a priori structures intact; both will claim to cover all the relevant experience;[50] but each will be carried out for different purposes and only occasionally will come into conflict with each other —a conflict to be settled by moral scrutiny sensitive to all the myriad facts of life—instead of invariably doing so, as, according to the ortho- dox Kantian theory, they must. That one of these realms is a limiting case of the other, that the categories of one of them can be derived from those of the other, is a view, classically developed by Fichte and strongly represented in both idealism and pragmatism, which goes far beyond anything Kant said or probably would accept, though the germ of it is present in the third *Critique*.

§ 8. FREEDOM AS AN ACTOR-CONCEPT; SPONTANEITY

That we have a right and even find it necessary to make use of the concept of freedom in our actions, regardless of how the antinomy is resolved and whether freedom is compatible with natural causation or not—in short, that the actor in a moral situation must act as if he were free and thereby shoulder all the responsibilities that he would have if it were theoretically proved that he is free—is shown by Kant in several ways. It is not shown, however, by appealing to what Kant calls com- parative freedom, i.e., empirically observed relative independence from outward stimuli and inward impulse through the exercise of intelligent foresight. It is shown only through an elaboration of the inward phe- nomenon of choice and a regression upon its conditions.

In the second edition of the *Critique of Pure Reason* there emerges a conception of one's own existence which is not present, at least so explicitly, in the first edition. It is the conception that we have a direct experience of our own spontaneous activity as a substance.[51] This ex-

---

[50] Cf. *Critique of Judgment*, Introduction, II: The realm of theoretical reason and that of practical reason do not limit each other in their legislation, but they per- petually do so in the world of sense.

[51] *Critique of Pure Reason*, B 157–58 n.: "I cannot determine [i.e., know categor- ially] my existence as that of a self-acting being; all that I can do is represent to myself the spontaneity of my thought, that is, of the determination; and my existence is still determinable only sensibly, that is, as the existence of an appearance. But it is owing to this spontaneity that I entitle myself an intelligence." Similarly, *Founda- tions of the Metaphysics of Morals*, 451 (71); *Critique of Practical Reason*, 56 (147).

perience is neither a sensuous intuition[52] nor an abstract thought. Kant never tells us what its epistemic character is, but that it occurs is a fact to which the epistemology of the *Critique of Pure Reason* does scant justice.

Such self-awareness of one's spontaneity and the attendant presupposition of freedom is found even in the act of theoretical thinking, though we can use this conception of the self as a thinking substance in no theoretical explanation of the inner life.[53]

But the clearest evidence of one's spontaneous freedom—sometimes said to be the only evidence[54]—is one's awareness of obligation, which is a necessitation of a wholly different kind from all natural necessitation and which produces a unique kind of feeling (92 [185]). It has this revelatory function when, in fact, the moral law is not obeyed but only acknowledged.[55] As wholly different from natural determination, it cannot be understood in theoretical terms. The freedom that can be understood, he says in his review of Ulrich, is of no use in eth-

[52] When Kant, in the precritical period, believed that there was an intellectual intuition, it was to this faculty that he ascribed consciousness of the self (see *Reflexionen* 4228, 4336, 6001). With the denial of intellectual intuition to man, no so-to-speak official position is taken on knowledge of one's own spontaneity, but the experience is not denied. On the whole question, with a collection of sources, cf. Heimsoeth, *Studien zur Philosophie Immanuel Kants*, pp. 245 ff., and Ingeborg Heidemann, *Spontaneität und Zeitlichkeit*, pp. 173 ff.

[53] The theoretical uselessness of this conception is the main point in the Paralogisms of the first *Critique;* even there the practical importance of the concept is recognized and preserved (B 431–32). Cf. *Foundations of the Metaphysics of Morals*, 448, 451–52 (67, 70–71), on the awareness of spontaneity. In *Besprechung von Schulz's Sittenlehre* (1785), VIII, 13, Kant remarks that the determinist in metaphysics claims freedom for himself in the conduct of his own thinking and a fortiori in his action. Cf. also *Beantwortung der Frage: Ist es eine Erfahrung dass wir denken?* (Cassirer ed., IV, 519–20), where it is denied that the awareness of thinking is an *Erfahrung*, and it is called merely "transcendental consciousness"; similarly *Critique of Pure Reason*, A 117 n.

[54] *Critique of Pure Reason*, B xxxiii, B 430–31; *Critique of Practical Reason*, 42 (131).

[55] The pair of examples in the *Critique of Practical Reason*, 30 (118), brings out this contrast between natural necessitation, which is effective, and a moral necessitation, which may or may not be effective. The first example, concerning the man who says his lust is uncontrollable, resembles one in Rousseau: "Let us suppose the maddest of men, the man who has his senses least under control; let him see the preparations for his death; let him realize that he will certainly die in torment a quarter of an hour later; not only would he from that time forward be able to resist temptation, he would even find it easy to do so" (*Émile*, Book IV ["Everyman" ed., pp. 289–90]). The second example anticipates one to be used in the Methodology (155–56 [254]).

ics, and the freedom needed in ethics cannot be understood.[56] All that we can do is to comprehend its incomprehensibility[57] and accept it as guaranteed by the fact of pure reason, the moral law which reveals it to us.[58]

With this argument, that the consciousness of the moral law itself proves the reality of freedom,[59] we are brought to a somewhat different conception of freedom, which we must now examine.

§ 9. FREEDOM AS SUPREME LEGISLATION; AUTONOMY

Let us suppose that the *Critique of Pure Reason* has proved that it is not self-contradictory to say that there is in man a *causa noumenon* or a faculty of initiating a new causal series in the world. This faculty would be called "freedom in the negative sense"[60] or freedom from nature. But freedom is not lawless caprice, any more than it is lawless in its effects found in nature and history. But what limits freedom and renders it lawful? The *Critique of Pure Reason* says that reason places a limit on freedom,[61] but how it does so is left unexplored and unexplained.

To answer this question is one purpose of the *Foundations of the Metaphysics of Morals*. The problem is to determine a law that the will can obey without losing its freedom through that very act of obeisance to law. The will can "obey" laws of nature in the sense of intentionally using them, in the form of means-end statements, in seeking men's goals in nature. But to be free even from the importunities of the desire for happiness—a goal given by man's natural existence—requires that the law of reason be not such a law borrowed from nature and hence, indirectly, leaving action under the domination of nature. The law must be given by reason. Just as the will (*Willkür*) considered as a faculty in man may be free in the negative sense of spontaneous activity, practical reason is spontaneous in the sense of giving law instead of subject-

---

[56] Ak., VIII, 458.

[57] *Foundations of the Metaphysics of Morals*, 463 (84).

[58] Cf. above, chap. x, and *Critique of Practical Reason*, 31 (120).

[59] It is likewise taken as a route to the consciousness of self, independent of empirical conditions, and thus serves to supplement the failures of rational psychology as a doctrine of the soul, though without making any contribution to theoretical knowledge (cf. *Critique of Pure Reason*, B 430–31; *Critique of Practical Reason*, 105–6 [200–201]).

[60] *Ibid.*, A 553 = B 581; *Critique of Practical Reason*, §§ 5, 6, 8 (29, 33 [116–17, 122]).

[61] *Critique of Pure Reason*, A 569 = B 597. It exercises this control even in issuing hypothetical imperatives, i.e., in its logical as well as in its real use (*ibid.*, A 548 = B 576).

ing itself to an alien law. It gives a law to *Willkür* which it has freely legislated—legislated by the necessity of its own nature. The faculty of lawgiving is will in the sense in which pure practical reason is will, and its legislation is "freedom in the positive sense," or autonomy. In the choice of this language, Kant, as so often, thinks in political metaphors and analogies, and especially in terms of Rousseau's political theory.

This meaning of freedom is quite different from the one we have been examining heretofore. Here it is not a question of whether the acting subject can initiate a new causal series, but it concerns the source of the law which the subject follows in such an initiation. The consciousness of the moral law, and not obedience to it, is the evidence of freedom in the positive sense (47 [136]). Freedom and unconditional law reciprocally imply each other; the latter is the *ratio cognoscendi* of the former, the former the *ratio essendi* of the latter (4 n. [88 n.]). Freedom *analytically* pertains to reason.[62] The moral law reveals to me a "marvelous faculty," a purely intellectual principle for the determination of my existence.[63]

Here we may appropriately notice one of Kant's best-known arguments for freedom, in which he says that a being that cannot act except under the Idea of freedom is really free in a practical respect and is obligated by the laws which follow from that Idea, regardless of whether we can prove theoretically that he is free or not.[64] Which freedom is warranted by this argument? Not the freedom of spontaneous action, for consciousness of this could be illusory. Everyone, including the fatalist or determinist, acknowledges, with Mephistopheles, that "Du glaubst zu schieben"; yet the fatalist or determinist adds, "aber du wirst geschoben." The argument applies to freedom in the sense of obligation-creation, not obligation-execution. For we are not directly obligated to *do* anything, to initiate a specific causal series in time. We are obligated directly and unexceptionally only to take up and act upon a certain maxim and to reject the maxims and actions which are incompatible with it, and even this thought shows a legislation of reason which is not derived from nature, since nature presents no "ought." To think one's self obligated to do something is to be really obligated to do something (though we may not be, in fact, obligated to do precisely that which we thought we were obligated

---

[62] *Critique of Practical Reason*, 31 (120): the moral law "would be analytic if the freedom of the will were presupposed." Cf. *Foundations of the Metaphysics of Morals*, 420 n., 426 (37 n., 44).

[63] *Critique of Pure Reason*, A 431–32.

[64] *Foundations of the Metaphysics of Morals*, 448 n. (67 n.).

to do).[65] The thought of obligation is, therefore, self-guaranteeing in a way in which the feeling of spontaneity is not self-guaranteeing. Hence one can say that freedom in the sense of legislation is real, even though he admits that in the entire history of mankind no free *action* may ever have been performed.

§ 10. THE SYNTHESIS OF THE TWO CONCEPTIONS

Kant regrettably did not single out these two conceptions and then formally show their relationship to each other. He deals with them together, without clearly showing, at any moment, which it is that he is talking about. Had he followed a truly synthetic method, he would have set up the two concepts and then related them. As it is, however, we have to find the relationship between them by an analysis of the complex mixture. Fortunately, it is not difficult to do so, and Kant himself does it, all but explicitly, in § 6 (29–30 [116–17]). I shall now paraphrase this passage, using the two conceptions of will and of freedom, in order to show the synthetic or bridging function of this important section.

Granted that human beings have a free will (*Willkür*)[66] in the practical and phenomenological sense, as a faculty of spontaneously initiating a new causal series in nature, what is the law of its action? A law must have a content, which may be taken from nature, and a form, the form of universality, which can be prescribed only by reason.[67] If the *Willkür* obeys a law because of its content, it can be free in the practical sense, for will shows its freedom even in obeisance to hypothetical imperatives and, indeed, in actions which are evil. But if it is to be determined necessarily, i.e., irrespective of the desires which are the material cause of its willing, as it is if there is duty, it must be determined not by the content but by the form of law. The form of law is universality, fitness for universal legislation. In giving such a law, reason is not responding to the promptings of nature. It is therefore a spontaneous legislator and is free.

Hence a free, i.e., spontaneous, *Willkür*, when it is good, is determined by a free, i.e., autonomous, *Wille*, or pure practical reason, which gives it a law.[68] It can obey only this law without jeopardy to

---

[65] A prima facie obligation can be abrogated only by another prima facie obligation or real obligation. It cannot be simply denied, leaving a kind of moral vacuum.

[66] Kant should have used the word *Willkür* in this section, but he did not.

[67] This is true of both natural and moral laws (cf. *Critique of Practical Reason*, 26 [114]).

[68] *Foundations of the Metaphysics of Morals*, 455 (74): The good will is a law for the bad will as a member of the world of sense. Unfortunately, Kant used *Wille* for each in this passage.

its freedom. Indeed, it gains in freedom, by now being an autonomous as well as a spontaneous will. Thus is added to the negative concept of freedom (spontaneous independence of foreign laws) the positive concept of freedom (autonomous self-legislation). There is a loss only of lawless freedom: "Where the moral law speaks there is no longer, objectively, a free choice [*Wahl*] as regards what is to be done."[69]

The *Willkür* can obey the law of *Wille* without losing its own freedom only because they are not two faculties externally related to each other. They are two aspects of practical reason, differing as the legislative and executive functions. The former function binds the latter; the former is the pure form of the latter. It gives a law that the latter *would* obey, were it a holy will, i.e., if the *Willkür* fully realized its potentialities of purity. The law is found not by seeking something outside the *Willkür* but by a regression upon the conditions of its full freedom, conditions that are not actually realized in the natural man. Thus, Kant explicitly says, we find *Wille* by a regression upon the conditions of *Willkür*.[70]

That the will of man—because of the fact that it is not a simple notion and has two distinguishable aspects—can be both obligation-creating and obligation-executing is one of the most dramatic theses in Kant's philosophy, as dramatic as, and analogous to, the Copernican Revolution in his theoretical philosophy. So long as the origin of law was ascribed to nature or experience or God, no matter how rigoristic and certain it might be, obedience to it had to be heteronomous and restrictive of freedom. That the moral law was rational and was to be discovered a priori and was in some way binding on man quite apart from the rewards that were believed to accompany obedience to it— all this was well-known doctrine in the German academic philosophy of Kant's time. But, because of the abstract ontology of perfection, no specific law seemed derivable from the putative sources of the moral law, and obedience to it was always in danger of being explained only eudaemonistically. Because Kant discovered the law in the concept of rational will (not abstract perfection or "will in general")[71] and was able to derive its formula from the concept of its source and because this source was an idealization of the will as a faculty of spontaneity in man, Kant did not have to seek any outward motivation for obedience to it. Rational personality as lawgiving expressed an "is" which is *ipso facto* an "ought" for partially rational beings; the law and its

---

[69] *Critique of Judgment*, §5 (V, 210 [45]).

[70] *Metaphysik der Sitten*, VI, 221; cf. *Critique of Practical Reason*, 30 (118).

[71] *Foundations of the Metaphysics of Morals*, 390 (5).

imperative and the conditions necessary to obedience to it have a common source which Kant's predecessors never found—indeed, never even sought. They were consequently never able to convert their formalistic ethics into a practical doctrine without jeopardizing or destroying the alleged formality of the principle.

The doctrine of autonomy was anticipated only by Rousseau, for only Rousseau saw the essential connection between law and freedom, while others in the eighteenth century saw law only as a restriction on freedom. Though Rousseau worked out their essential connection only in politics and had his doctrine there adopted with little change by Kant, the doctrine of self-government through law by free citizens is deepened into a moral and metaphysical doctrine by Kant. With Rousseau, Kant can then say that obedience to a law that one has himself prescribed is the only real freedom.[72]

Obedience and prescription are and remain, however, quite different functions. Can our human will be autonomous as well as spontaneous? The question can be answered affirmatively on several grounds. First, it cannot be spontaneous without being autonomous,[73] unless it is to be lawless and, accordingly, useless to morals as well as incompatible with science. Second, reasoning in the opposite direction, it can be spontaneous because, under autonomy, it ought to be.[74] If the awareness of our duty placed impossible demands upon us, as it would if our *Willkür* were not potentially free, then the thought of duty would be illusory. How do we know that it is not? Only because of the positive evidence of the fact of pure reason[75] and the resolution of the third antinomy—the latter making it possible, the former making it actual. Third, Kant believes that the empirical nature of man is such that arguments from human nature which would show autonomy to be impossible can be shown to be false.

[72] "Obedience to a law which one has prescribed to himself is freedom" (Rousseau, *The Social Contract*, Book I, chap. viii).

[73] Even the evil will is autonomous in the sense that the person who does moral evil freely incorporates an incentive into his maxim and makes it (what it is not in itself) a rule in accordance with which he will conduct himself (*Religion within the Limits of Reason Alone*, VII, 24 [Greene and Hudson, 19]; cf. below, § 12).

[74] One of Kant's most famous "statements"—"Thou canst because thou shouldst" —does not exist in his writings in this neat form (cf. David Baumgardt, "Legendary Quotations and the Lack of References," *Journal of the History of Ideas*, VII [1946], 99–102, and L. W. Kahn, "Legendary Quotations," *ibid.*, VIII [1947], 116). But statements that express this inference less succinctly abound, e.g., *Critique of Practical Reason*, 30 (118–19); *Critique of Pure Reason*, A 807 = B 835; *Über den Gemeinspruch . . .*, VIII, 287; *Metaphysik der Sitten*, VI, 380; *Streit der Fakultäten*, VII, 43–44; *Vorlesungen über Metaphysik* (Kowalewski ed.), p. 600; *Opus postumum*, XXI, 16.

[75] This is discussed in chap. i of the Analytic and in chap. xii of this commentary.

It has often been objected that there are two paradoxes in Kant's ethics: (1) Kant is, or is reputed to be, "individualistic" in his ethics, while the moral person is, for him, only an abstraction that is meant in some way to dominate and restrict the individual person. (2) Kant's ethics is so autonomous that the social or universalistic aspect of morality is left unfounded because it is an outward restriction on the freedom he insists upon.[76]

Quite apart from the fact that these two alleged paradoxes cancel each other out, it is possible to show that neither is valid and that both arise from a misinterpretation of the point we are now discussing. Each, if fully expanded, would entail the supposition that in Kant's doctrine there are two wills, and which paradox is drawn depends upon the critic's belief concerning which is the more important to Kant (which happens always to be the one that is less important to the critic—for such are the ways of philosophical polemics). (1) If the *Wille* or pure practical reason as an abstract epistemic or moral concept is emphasized, then the individual human *Willkür* is restricted and is not free. (2) If the legislation is thought of as issuing from an individual *Willkür*, it is not possible to see how the laws issued will meet the requirements of social universality and harmony.[77]

But there are not two wills. There is one will with its formal condition, which is universally valid reason, and its material condition arising from the specificity of its involvement in the world at particular times and places. And the two paradoxes are not paradoxes of Kant's ethics so much as manifestations of the human predicament in which we find in ourselves individualized manifestations of universal mandates and injunctions. Man is the only being in the world that not only is a manifestation of some universals but ought to be an instance of others; he is an individual that gives no valid laws to others that he does not lay upon himself, that gives no privileges to himself that he does not allow to others. Had the Kantian teaching missed what is true in these paradoxes, it would have been less true and less responsive to the paradoxical aspect of human life itself, in which man finds himself neither a brute nor a god, neither a mere particular nor a mere universal.

But, of all the misinterpretations of Kant, perhaps none is more ob-

[76] It is noteworthy that the same "paradoxes" have been found in Rousseau. Was Rousseau the father of an impersonal fascism or of democratic individualism run wild? An affirmative answer to either of these questions shows a misunderstanding of Rousseau analogous to the misunderstanding of Kant explored here.

[77] Cf. George Santayana, *Egotism in German Philosophy* (1916; 2d ed., New York, 1940), pp. 50–51.

viously wrong or more widely accepted than the accusation that Kant represents something vaguely called "Prussian philosophy," in which blind obedience to law is so esteemed as an absolute virtue that neither political nor moral freedom is allowed to be more than a name. The accusation is too ridiculous to deserve serious consideration on its own merits and should be refuted only because of its widespread acceptance.[78] But the refutation is easy: it not only separates two wills within the individual but puts each in a different person, attributing rights to one and duties to the other.[79] It forgets that all moral discipline is, for Kant, self-discipline and that self-discipline, while not the whole of morality, is a necessary condition of it. It forgets that Kant taught that all just government is self-government. The same man, by virtue of the same faculty in its positive and negative use, is both subject and legislator in the realm of ends and in the just state.

§ 11. SUMMARY

Let us pause and summarize the results of our argument, results anticipated in § 2 above, and relate it to some other concepts in Kant's ethics.

We have distinguished two meanings of will: *Wille* as practical reason, the legislative function, and *Willkür*, as the executive faculty of man.

The freedom of the former is autonomy; it gives a law to *Willkür*. This law is determined by the nature of *Wille* and not by anything else in the world, including human nature or the will of God. The moral law is a synthetic a priori statement of what a *Willkür* would necessarily do if it were exclusively rational; it is a law or imperative of duty for a *Willkür* which does not do by nature what the law

---

[78] John Dewey is not responsible for the extremes of this view, for he acknowledged Kant's "individualism" and held only that such "Prussianism" arose because "the two worlds of Kant were too far away from each other" and could be connected only through the remnants of the idealistic theory of history and the state (cf. *German Philosophy and Politics* [New York, 1915], p. 122, and the defense of Kant by Julius Ebbinghaus, "Interpretation and Misinterpretation of the Categorical Imperative," *Philosophical Quarterly*, IV [1954], 97–108. On the latter see also K. Kolenda, "Professor Ebbinghaus' Interpretation of the Categorical Imperative," *Philosophical Quarterly*, V [1955], 74–77).

[79] *Perpetual Peace*, VIII, 348 n. (Beck 11–12 n.): "With regard to the most sublime reason in the world that I can think of with the exception of God (say, the great Aeon), when I do my duty in my post as he does in his, there is no reason, under the law of equality, why obedience to duty should fall only to me and the right to command only to him." God is excepted only because of the inapplicability of the concept of duty to a holy will; but the same law applies both to man and to God.

requires. In addition to its real use in discovering or formulating the moral law, practical reason also has a merely logical use in the derivation of rules of actions either from the moral law or, in the case of prudence, from human desires and the laws of nature.

The freedom of the latter is spontaneity, the faculty of initiating a causal series in nature. It can exercise this (negative) freedom in one of two ways: (1) It can take the law of pure practical reason as the limiting condition on its maxims, out of respect for law or the rational personality that decrees it. It is then a good will, acting out of duty. If it did so without any internal obstacles, but by its own nature, it would be a holy will; struggling, as it does, against the sensuous impulses, it is at most a virtuous will. (2) It can take some other principle (maxim) posited or adopted by practical reason, in its logical use, as its formal principle. If it does this, there are two possibilities: (*a*) It may take a principle which is not opposed to the legislation of reason, and then it is a legal and sometimes a prudent will. (*b*) It may take a principle that is opposed to the law of pure practical reason, and then it is an evil will. In either case, it is a free will.

The *Willkür*, however, can fail to exercise its freedom or realize its potentiality of being free in a negative sense. Then it gives way to the importunities of sense and is a will in name only, really being an *arbitrium brutum*.[80] The pure practical reason, on the other hand, cannot fail to be free[81] and autonomous, however little effective it may be in its control of *Willkür*. However depraved *Willkür* may be, it still hears the "heavenly voice" of pure practical reason, so that even the most hardened criminal trembles before its tribunal (35, 80 [124, 172]).

§ 12. MORAL EVIL

Consider the following dilemma which has embarrassed many defenders of Kant, who have accepted the conclusion that a good will is a free will. If there is evil, it must be a result of a failure to be free. Therefore, either there is no moral evil, all evil being natural and therefore not imputable to human responsibility, or goodness of will is not equivalent to moral freedom. It is therefore concluded that when Kant asserted the existence of radical evil in human nature, in *Religion within the Limits of Reason Alone*, he was diverging from his own critical doctrine. Depending upon the reader's standpoint, this

---

[80] *Critique of Pure Reason*, A 534 = B 562.

[81] *Foundations of the Metaphysics of Morals*, 448 (67). Even theoretical reason is free in this sense, for "we cannot conceive of a reason which consciously responds to a bidding from the outside with respect to its judgments."

is regarded either as a sign of Kant's robust sense of the hard fact of moral evil, which he admitted no matter what it did to the neatness of his system, or as a regrettable failure to remain consistent with his own high teaching.

But the alleged contrariety between the teachings of the *Religion* and of the *Critique* disappears in the light of our analysis. Kant speaks of the reality of moral evil in the immediate context of the most extreme statement of the causal predictability of all human action (100 [193]), in a place where freedom to do both moral and immoral actions seems to be put to its most extreme test. He says, of an evil man, that his "actions by the uniformity of conduct exhibit a natural connection. But the latter does not render the vicious quality of the will necessary, for this quality is the consequence of freely assumed evil and unchangeable principles. This fact makes it only the more objectionable and culpable."

This is consistent with the fuller treatment in the *Religion*, and both are consistent with the summary given above in § 11. The *Religion* tells us that by the "nature of man" is understood the subjective ground of decision (of *Willkür*) which is independent of determination by the impulses, for otherwise there would be neither moral good nor moral evil. The subjective ground must itself be an act (*Aktus*) of freedom; it cannot be other than a "rule, which the *Willkür* makes for itself for the use of its freedom." The evil lies, therefore, not in a failure under the conditions of nature to exercise freedom but in a maxim that is freely adopted and is in opposition to the maxim (not of the *Willkür*, as are the impulses) of the pure practical reason.[82] This propensity to take some other maxim than the moral law as the governing principle of action can no more be explained than the opposing disposition to take the moral law. Both are there as predispositions to, not as causally determinative of, free acts which can in no way be explained.

So long as there is a *Willkür* responsive to the determinations of desire or other natural impulses, there is the constant danger of thinking that anything that seduces the *Willkür* from obedience to the moral law *ipso facto* destroys its freedom, so that the resulting evil is not morally imputable. "But the freedom of *Willkür*," he says, "has the peculiarity that it can be determined to action through no incentive except insofar as man has taken this incentive up into his maxim, i.e., made it a general rule by which he will act; only in this way can any incentive, whatever it may be, coexist with the absolute spontaneity

[82] *Religion within the Limits of Reason Alone*, VI, 21 (Greene and Hudson, 17).

of *Willkür*, i.e., with freedom."[83] The disposition to evil (or to good) is itself, as Kant says in the *Critique*, something freely chosen.[84]

It is very easy to see how the clear separation of *Wille* from *Willkür* provides a secure place for imputable evil, so much so that one could construct, from § 11, the Kantian theory of evil in its main outlines, even if we did not have the evidence from the *Religion*. When *Willkür*, in the exercise of its spontaneity, acts on maxims which are incompatible with the moral law, it does moral evil. It is only the freedom of the will as pure practical reason that is analytically connected with morality, but this will does nothing but issue orders which may or may not be obeyed. It neither sins nor does virtuous actions,[85] because it does not act at all. Only because it was believed that there was one function of will and one kind of freedom was it erroneously thought that the *Critique* identified free and moral acts. When Kant spoke of moral evil, therefore, it was natural that he should be thought to have fallen into serious inconsistency.

§ 13. FREEDOM AND CREATION

The relation of freedom to metaphysical or theological necessity is perhaps a less pressing one nowadays than that of its relation to physical necessity. But this was not so obviously the case in Kant's day, and some of his earliest discussions of freedom, in the *Nova dilucidatio*, concerned the ancient problem of reconciling human freedom with God's foresight and predestination. The classical problem of predestination in its relation to morals and its bearing upon the problem of evil fascinated Kant as a young man, and he occasionally returned to it in

---

[83] *Ibid.*, 24 (19). So far, therefore, from denying that imputable evil exists, the doctrine holds that all actions are imputable; for, so long as there is a *Willkür* at all, it is acting by maxims which are either moral or immoral. Hence there are no morally neutral acts (*ibid.*, 24 [20]). When a *Willkür* without choice surrenders to the forces of blind impulse, we should not call it *Willkür* at all, since we do not, in these circumstances, impute responsibility to the person.

[84] *Ibid.*, 25 (21); *Critique of Practical Reason*, 100 (194).

[85] Kant says "freedom of choice [*Wahl*] of maxims of action" is "absolute spontaneity" or *libertas noumenon*, and from it."one can never adduce a reason why anything against the law occurs," while freedom of *Willkür*, subjective freedom or *libertas phaenomenon*, is freedom in respect to choice [*Wahl*] of the lawful or the unlawful (*Opus postumum*, XXI, 470). If one adds to the statement about absolute spontaneity that one can never adduce a reason why anything happens in *accordance* with the law, since such transcendental freedom has no explanatory value, we have here the distinction between what Henry Sidgwick has called "neutral freedom" and "moral freedom" ("The Kantian Conception of Free Will," *Mind*, XIII [1888], 405–12).

his later works.[86] The special problem of the *Critique* concerns the possibility of freedom in a world in which the realm of nature and the realm of grace are connected in the Leibnizian manner, a manner dangerously close to the Kantian. If freedom and God's omniscience are not compatible in Leibniz, then they would not seem to be compatible in Kant either. It is this, rather than the Calvinistic form of the puzzle, that occasions Kant's discussion here.

He argues that if God is the cause of men's actions through the original creation of man's substance, then only comparative freedom exists, and morality is impossible. But though Kant is willing to grant the premise of the creation of noumena, he denies that the inference is valid. It is invalid because the syllogism contains four terms, "causation" and "creation" not being equivalent. It would be valid only if things in themselves were temporal, and if they are temporal, then even an attempt like that of Mendelssohn[87] to make God non-temporal will not save freedom. For, whatever might be the nature of God, if things in themselves are in time, God's creation of them is a temporal act and restricted to the conditions of time, which conflicts both with God's theological and metaphysical predicates and with the initiation of a new causal series in time.

But since things in themselves and, a fortiori, God are not in space and time, the relation between God and things in themselves cannot be a causal relation, though we have to think of it by analogy with causation. The causal relation holds only among phenomena. If it were ontologically real and God's creation were itself causal, then "man would be a marionette or an automaton" and only Spinozism would remain.[88] But because Kant has, on other grounds, denied the temporality of things in themselves, the relation of God to them and, a fortiori, to their temporal appearances,[89] is not one of cause.

Kant's view may be summarized by saying not only that a syllogism whose major premise contains the term "creation" and whose minor

---

[86] E.g., *Critique of Practical Reason*, 100–103 (194–96); *Religion within the Limits of Reason Alone*, VI, 144 (Greene and Hudson, 135); *Metaphysik der Sitten*, VI, 280 n.; *Perpetual Peace*, VIII, 361 n. (Beck, 24 n.); incidentally in *Critique of Pure Reason*, A 206 = B 251–52. The relation of historical determinism to freedom in history is discussed in *Idea for a Universal History* and in *Streit der Fakultäten*, VII, 41. The relation between the problem of freedom with respect to God's foresight and that of freedom in a Laplacean universe is briefly but suggestively handled in T. D. Weldon's *Kant's Critique of Pure Reason* (2d ed.; 1958), pp. 210–11.

[87] In his *Morgenstunden;* cf. *Critique of Practical Reason*, 101 (195).

[88] *Critique of Practical Reason*, 101–2 (196); on Spinozism in its relation to fanaticism, see *What Is Orientation in Thinking?* VIII, 143 (Beck, 302).

[89] Cf. *Perpetual Peace*, VIII, 361 n. (Beck, 24–25 n.).

contains "causation" is formally invalid but that if "X creates Y" and "The appearances of Y cause the appearances of Z," we can say nothing of the relation of X to the appearances of Z.

But I do not see how this meets the issue. For X is also the creator of Z. Since the appearances of Y and Z could not be different from what they are without a different noumenon underlying each[90] and since each is created by X, it is not easy to see how X can be let off so easily and exculpated for the appearances of Z.

Kant himself seems to have felt that his argument here is not entirely convincing and to have put it forward only *faute de mieux*. The last paragraph of this section (103 [197]) can be read only as evidence of such dissatisfaction.[91] As a puzzle from theology and classical rationalism, I suspect that the problem did not interest Kant at this time as much as it had earlier. The relation of God to the world is not an object of theoretical knowledge but only one of practical belief. This particular aspect of the relation does not have positive moral consequences which make it necessary for Kant to take a stand on it, and such puzzles are dismissed in the *Strife of the Faculties*.

§ 14. FREEDOM AS A POSTULATE

Freedom is the only one of the Ideas of pure reason that we can know. It is proved by the apodictic law of practical reason. All other Ideas gain reality (i.e., are known to have objects) only through their connection with it.[92] These Ideas are those of God and the immortality of the soul. They are called "postulates" because they are dependent upon the need of human reason to establish the possibility of the highest good; they are not directly necessary to morality or revealed in the fact of pure reason, and they cannot be theoretically justified.

It is a little surprising, therefore, to find Kant calling freedom in the positive sense also a postulate of pure practical reason.[93] This is to be explained in three ways. First, there is the wide latitude that Kant

---

[90] *Critique of Pure Reason*, A 556 = B 584.

[91] One of the first commentators on the *Critique* (Brastberger, *Untersuchungen über Kants Kritik der praktischen Vernunft*, p. 156), who was almost sentimentally sympathetic to and uncritical in his acclaim of Kant's book on most points, rejects Kant's solution to this problem or, rather, confesses that he cannot find what Kant's solution is. Crusius, who in so many matters concerning freedom anticipated Kant, declared the problem to be insoluble.

[92] *Critique of Practical Reason*, 4 (88). The postulates "give objective reality to the Ideas of speculative reason in general" (*ibid.*, 132 [229]). In this sense freedom may be, and is, considered a postulate.

[93] *Ibid.*, 132 (229). Elsewhere he says that it is freedom in the negative sense which is a postulate (cf. *Zum ewigen Frieden in der Philosophie*, VIII, 418).

permitted himself in using the word "postulate." The variety of its meanings will be discussed below in chapter xiii.

Second, there is the specific relation of freedom to the *summum bonum* rather than to the moral law itself. With reference to the highest good as an object of a necessary human need, whatever it is necessary to assume in order to achieve it may be considered a postulate. Though the Analytic has given better reasons to assert freedom than that it is necessary to the highest good, when the highest good is the topic of discussion, whatever we have to assume in order to show its real possibility is to that extent a postulate. We cannot conclude that the doctrine of the Analytic is in any way abandoned or even modified because what was there "deduced" is here "postulated." The doctrine of freedom as a postulate is, in fact, earlier than the deduction of freedom. In the Dialectic of the second *Critique* we hear the last echo of a doctrine developed in the *Critique of Pure Reason* which put God, freedom, and immortality on exactly the same level.[94]

Third, there is a difference in the meaning of freedom as a condition of the moral law and as a condition of the *summum bonum*. Freedom in the latter sense is an object of faith, not a *scibile*;[95] it is the faith (*Vertrauen*) in the achievability of the *summum bonum*, i.e., the belief in virtue (*Glaube an die Tugend*) as adequate to achieve the highest good. In this sense, freedom is not mere autonomy but "autarchy of will."[96]

[94] *Critique of Pure Reason*, B 395 n. (not in A). Albert Schweitzer (*Die Religionsphilosophie Kants*, chap. ii and p. 134) argued that the original plan of the second *Critique* was that it would continue the doctrine of the cosmological Ideas of the first, and in the order of their derivation in the Dialectic but that Kant then discovered the special prerogative of the Idea of freedom. This caused him to take that Idea from the Dialectic as planned and put it into the Analytic.

[95] *Critique of Judgment*, § 91.

[96] *Fortschritte der Metaphysik*, XX, 295.

XII

The "Aesthetic" of Pure Practical Reason; Commentary on Analytic, Chapter III; Part of Dialectic; and Methodology

§ I. THE PSYCHOLOGICAL AND THE ETHICAL PROBLEM

Kant has repeatedly asserted the necessity of distinguishing between the subjective, psychological factors in conduct, which can be learned through observation, and the objective a priori law or norm of morality, which can be discovered only by pure reason. The *Foundations of the Metaphysics of Morals* tried to show that this distinction is implicit in ordinary moral consciousness, however unsophisticated it may be and however little self-conscious discipline of reason may be found in it. In that work Kant attempted to give this distinction a definitive form so that the a priori principle could be discerned in its simple purity. The *Critique of Practical Reason*, in following a synthetic or progressive method, does not begin with the consciousness of duty in order to show that it has features which cannot be exhaustively explained in empirical psychological terms, but with a delineation of the formal and material elements in all willing. Only at the end of chapter i of the Analytic is the statement of the supreme principle of pure practical reason attained. It is not based upon any empirical data given by or about human nature; it is a law for rational beings generally. It is, moreover, a norm or a regulative principle for men and for any other rational beings in the world, if there are any, who are not pure rational beings. That is, it is a priori descriptive of a fully rational being and a regulative concept for a partially rational being; hence it is meant to be applied to human beings.

"Apply to" may mean two different things. It may mean that this law is applied as a norm in judging the conduct of men, being a standard of comparison between what is and what ought to be. And it may mean that one renders obedience to it, so that it is the supreme factor in the determination of choice and the conduct issuing from it. The former of these meanings is explored chiefly in the *Metaphysics of Morals*, where it lends itself to a full casuistical treatment. Except incidentally, it is only the second of the two which is studied in the *Critique of Practical Reason*. There are two separate but closely connected discussions of it, one in the chapter "The Incentives of Pure Practical Reason" and the other in the Methodology. Some corollary problems are discussed in the chapter on the resolution of the antinomy arising from the Idea of the *summum bonum*.

The problem of these chapters and sections is a singularly difficult one for Kant, because in the rest of his treatment of the moral principle he is writing about rational beings in general, and the path from a priori knowledge to a posteriori application is always (not for Kant alone) a hard one; it is one that must be trodden with exceeding care, for Kant realized here and in his other works that a mistake in the analysis of the a posteriori factors could cast doubt on the validity of the a priori features of experience that were his chief concern. In none of his works is this transition made in such a manner as to give complete satisfaction to Kant's critics, and their reluctance to accept his psychology has favored a skepticism toward his theses in pure philosophy. It is, nevertheless, a passage that must be made if pure reason is to be practical.

Man is a rational being, but he is also a being of need, impulse, and sense. He is, or may be, a free agent, but he is also a part of the mechanism of nature. His self is noumenal, but he also has an empirical character that sets him off from all other rational beings and all other empirical objects. How, then, can we describe his relation, actual and ideal, to the pure moral law? How can the moral law or his consciousness of it be a determining factor in his conduct, as it is if he can properly claim to be a moral agent?

Before venturing upon Kant's actual answer to this question, let us try to become clear as to what would constitute, in his terms, a satisfactory answer to it. Kant says that this question is equivalent to that of how the will can be free, and to that question, like all others concerning fundamental powers or faculties, no answer can be given. We cannot find any higher principle that will throw light on such facts as the sensuous character of our intuition, the practicality of reason, the fact that our reason is discursive rather than intuitive, and the freedom of the will. But we can go this far: we can explain their inexplicability and show that attempts to explain them away are not successful. Though it displaces the inexplicable mystery of man by only one step, the *Critique of Practical Reason* does attempt an explanation, in psychological terms, of how the knowledge of the moral law can be effective in the determination of conduct. "We shall not have to show a priori why the moral law supplies an incentive," because we cannot, "but rather what it effects (or, better, must effect) in the mind so far as it is an incentive" (72 [165]). It is essential that this mystery be removed from the phenomenological surface, as it were, for the thing is so puzzling that doubts of its reality can have the actual effect of reducing the effectiveness of this incentive; and if this incentive is reduced or destroyed, there is only legality—contingent accordance with the requirements of moral law—but no morality. And, as practical moral teachers, we must know what steps to take to render this incentive effective and sufficient. This is possible only if we know the mechanism of its effectiveness and in this way remove doubts that it can be effective—doubts that led Hume, for example, to regard reason as the slave of the passions instead of their master, as Kant believed it to be.

Kant has another reason for giving an extensive analysis of the moral disposition and intention, within which the consciousness of the law is effective. The proper object of moral judgment is not the law, but man. A man is a moral agent only if he meets two demands, viz., his actions must accord with the law, and they must be undertaken because the law demands them. That is, an action is moral because it is regarded as duty. We can never understand the subjective phenomena of morality or have a firm basis for either moral imputation or moral decision if we do not understand the way in which the moral law enters into consciousness and makes a clear demand upon our allegiance. If we cannot understand this, we leave the door open to those who would give simpler explanations that have the advantage of being readily comprehended but the disadvantage of being theoretically wrong and damaging to morality itself.[1]

The justification for calling the discussion of these topics "the aesthetic" is found in the analogies that Kant points out between the analytical parts of the first two *Critique*'s.[2] The division of the *Critique*'s is parallel, but the parts are in reverse order. The first begins with the sensuous givenness of representations, proceeds to study their synthesis into the consciousness of objects, and ascends, finally, to the regulative principles by which consciousness of objects is synthesized into experience of a world. The second begins with the principles

---

[1] This practical function of the philosopher, in whose "subtle investigations the public takes no interest," is alluded to in *Critique of Practical Reason*, 108 (203), and in the last sentence of the book, 163 (262).

[2] *Ibid.*, 16, 90 (102, 183); cf. above, chap. iv, § 7.

(chap. i), applies them to objects of practical reason (chap. ii), and, finally, comes to "their application to the subject and its sensuous faculty" in the chapter on "the aesthetic of pure practical reason, if I may be allowed to use, on the basis of analogy, [this term] which [is] not entirely suitable" (90 [183]). (Kant remarks that even the term "Logic" is not entirely suitable either.)

We may well consider for a moment the extent to which this term is and is not suitable. It is suitable insofar as the word "aesthetic" has general reference to the sensibility,[3] in this case to feeling as a mode of sense.[4] But it would be a mistake to expect very much similarity between the two Aesthetics. In the first *Critique*, there is a Transcendental Aesthetic having to do with the sensible conditions of a priori synthetic knowledge. Practical philosophy, however, has been excluded from transcendental philosophy,[5] and Kant is not here concerned with the manner in which the *objects* of practical reason are given to knowledge. He is, rather, involved in a study of how the subject, as a sensuous being, is affected not by the objects of pure practical reason but by its principles.

§ 2. A DIFFERENT BUT RELATED PROBLEM

It might appear that the question of this chapter has already been answered as well as Kant can answer it. For, it may be said, we are here concerned with the relation of the intelligible to the sensible nature of man, and Kant has already said that this noumenal-phenomenal distinction is the kernel of the doctrine of transcendental freedom.

Though the psychological-ethical and the phenomenal-noumenal problems are intimately related, they are not entirely the same. The doctrine of transcendental freedom was believed by Kant to be necessary to that of moral or practical freedom, but not sufficient to it. The problem of the Aesthetic is not, therefore, solved by resolving the third antinomy. Here Kant is concerned with an immanent phenomenological problem, not with one in the ontology of appearance and reality. The question is not directly How could a law of the intelligible world be reflected in the determination of events in the phenomenal? It is, rather, How can a being in the phenomenal world, through his knowledge of the law of the intelligible, control his conduct so that this law does in fact become effective? To answer this question we need to know as much about man as about the law; and a treatment of transcendental freedom cannot give us this information.

---

[3] *Critique of Pure Reason*, A 21 = B 35.   [4] Cf. above, chap. vii, § 3.

[5] *Critique of Pure Reason*, A 15 = B 29; cf. above, p. 9 f.

§ 3. SOME EARLIER ATTEMPTS AT AN ANSWER

Prior to the *Foundations of the Metaphysics of Morals*, Kant had considered the problem before us, but not until the full maturity of the critical doctrine had been reached did he appreciate the singular difficulty of any solution.

In the *Prize Essay, The Distinctness of the Principles of Natural Theology and Morals*, and under the influence of both Wolff and the English moralists, Kant stated the formal principle, "Do the most perfect thing that can be done by you," but adds, against the rationalists, that no particular obligation can be derived from this[6] "except when indemonstrable material principles of practical knowledge" are added.[7] There is, he then believed, an unanalyzable "feeling for the good" which supplies these material principles, and, though he did not say so explicitly, it is quite clear that he believed the moving force in morality to come from the moral feelings and not from the formal principle itself. Yet this essay ends on an unexpectedly tentative note: "It is still to be settled whether it is simply the cognitive faculty or whether it is feeling (the primary inner ground of the appetitive faculty) which decides the basic principles of practical philosophy." It is as if Kant, even then, was not secure in his conviction that feeling is an independent factor in morality.

In the *Observations on the Feeling of the Beautiful and the Sublime*, published the same year, Kant seems to have decided in favor of feeling as the source of moral ideas. After setting forth the necessity of universal principles in morality (since a merely good disposition is not enough), he says of the principles required: "They are not speculative rules, but the consciousness of a feeling which lives in every human breast, and which extends much farther than to the particular grounds of sympathy and complaisance. I believe I cover it when I say it is the feeling for the beauty and worth of human nature." He then explains how this feeling and its associated "broadened inclination" can control our good-natured drives and give rise to the "beauty of virtue."[8]

This is eudaemonism, and the *Dreams of a Spirit-Seer* attempts a "pneumatological" explanation[9] of. these more extensive and comprehensive social feelings, which he calls "moral," through a mechanism of the community of rational beings under psychical laws that are compared to Newton's laws which govern the unity of physical nature.

---

[6] Cf. also *Critique of Practical Reason*, 41 (130), and above, pp. 106 f.

[7] *Prize Essay*, II, 299 (Beck, 284).

[8] *Beobachtungen über das Gefühl des Schönen und Erhabenen*, II, 217.

[9] *Träume eines Geistersehers*, II, 330, 335; cf. above, p. 159, n. 68.

This is a speculative metaphysics of moral feeling, in which metaphysics is only a hypothetical extension of the type of explanation valid within empirical experience. But if we remember what "metaphysics" meant to Kant before and after 1770 and the change which came in his conception of its scope and method about this time,[10] we shall not be surprised at the developing intellectualism present in a very significant statement that Kant made in commenting upon an ethical essay by his former pupil, Marcus Herz. In 1773 he wrote: "The concept of morality must please in the highest degree, must have moving power; and though it is indeed intellectual, it must have direct relation to the basic incentives of the will."[11]

This view, not further developed at that time and, indeed, so briefly indicated as to make its full interpretation hazardous, is probably the first intimation of the doctrine of the critical writings of the 1780's. In the intervening period, Kant seems to have been so torn between two incompatible doctrines of the moral motive (if, indeed, he had time to think of them at all) that when we come to the *Critique of Pure Reason* we find him espousing each of them on a single page. Thus the necessity of rewards and punishments as a spur to morality is asserted in a passage which sounds like a religious eudaemonism:

It is necessary that the whole course of our life be subjected to moral maxims, but it is impossible that this should happen unless reason connects with the moral law, which is a mere Idea [and not yet a maxim], an operative cause which determines for such conduct as is in accord with the moral law an outcome that is in exact accordance with our supreme ends [i.e., happiness]. Thus without a God and a future world invisible to us now but hoped for, the glorious Ideas of morality are indeed objects of approval and admiration but not springs [*Triebfeder*] of purpose and of action.[12]

Yet almost immediately and with no obvious consistency, he denies that the prospect of future happiness makes the moral disposition possible. The moral disposition is one of worthiness to be happy, to which the hope of happiness is added by these "postulates"; but the desire for happiness does not generate the moral disposition.[13] The

---

[10] Cf. above, p. 7 ff.

[11] To Herz, end of 1773 (X, 145). The *Vorlesungen über Metaphysik* ([Pölitz ed., 1821], p. 242), of uncertain date, speaks of the moral feeling as that through which the motives of the understanding gain moving power. The student's lecture notes, however, even if accurately datable, cannot be depended upon to be accurate where any subtle issue is at stake, as every professor will ruefully acknowledge.

[12] *Critique of Pure Reason*, A 812–13 = B 840–41.

[13] In a similar passage in the Reflexions on his essay on the sublime and beautiful, Kant has recourse to the mysterious working of future rewards and punishments on

second of these views is the one that is to appear again and again, and the religious eudaemonism of the quoted passage is transcended, never to be asserted again. Still we look in vain in the first *Critique* for an analysis of the desire to be worthy of happiness, which is a truly moral and not eudaemonistic desire. Without such an analysis, the view of the *Critique of Pure Reason* seems to be an incompatible mixture.

For an analysis of this desire, we must turn to the celebrated Duisburg Fragment 6, written, I believe, just after the first *Critique*.[14] Here the desire for happiness is still fundamental, though here again Kant recognizes that such a desire does not *eo ipso* generate virtue. But happiness is here given a moral definition, under which it can be desired morally. Happiness is well-being only insofar as it is dependent upon our choice and not upon accidental circumstances; it is, accordingly, nothing but "well-ordered freedom." Well-ordered freedom, the exercise of which occasions self-satisfaction, is the unity of all actions under general laws and is equivalent to morality. Hence Kant concludes that morality is a necessary condition of happiness and makes it possible, but does not have happiness as its purpose. It is the a priori form of happiness, the content being contingent upon circumstance. Virtue and only virtue can bring about happiness, but it does not necessarily do so, and, even when it does, that is not the source of its worth. But to feel that we are the authors of a state of being worthy of happiness (i.e., to have its a priori condition) is itself a positive feeling of self-contentment, and *this* constitutes the human worth of morality and is a necessary factor in happiness. The inner applause is a sufficient motive and is an "intellectual pleasure" in the enjoyment of freedom.[15]

This fragment constitutes a transition from a dualistic to a monistic theory of the moral motive. Previously, except perhaps in the one sentence of the letter to Herz, the cognitive and conative factors had been kept separate, with the consequence that pure reason could not consistently be asserted to be intrinsically practical. In Fragment 6

---

the moral disposition which can remain pure even under their influence. He says: "If, however, in some supernatural way there is some influence on the purity of our nature, future rewards no longer have the character of motives" (XX, 28). This is no longer an expedient that Kant could take in the *Critique*, though the thought remains in the estimate of the purity of Christian morals and his rejection of a hedonistic interpretation of Christian motives (123 n. [220 n.]).

[14] Reflexion 7202 (Ak., XIX, 276–82; Reicke, I, 9–16).

[15] The term "intellectual pleasure" is later rejected (*Critique of Practical Reason*, 117 [213]).

the conative element is itself intellectualized[16] and formalized, and moral happiness, i.e., a happiness *in* morality and not a happiness resulting *from* it, becomes the goal. But when, in the next few years, Kant formulated the doctrine of autonomy, even moral happiness became a corollary effect and not a motive as a separate and distinct factor in moral purpose. We are now ready to study this last and most momentous change in Kant's views.

§ 4. INCENTIVES

Triebfeder is the generic name for the dynamic or conative factor in willing.[17] It may be mere impulse, as in an animal, or an interest,[18] in which the representation of some law, natural or moral, guides action. If our interest is in the object of an action, Kant has already shown that the incentive must be a sensuous desire under the principle of self-love (22 [108]). If we are interested in the action directly, it is because we find satisfaction in the law of the action, and the question is: How can a sensuous being take an interest in a pure rational principle? Or How can a rational principle itself be the incentive for a sensuous being?

In the *Foundations*, Kant distinguished between "incentive" and "objective ground of volition" or motive, as between the desire for subjective ends and that for ends valid for every rational being.[19] Consequently, he said there that the moral imperative excludes from the legislation all admixture of any interest as an incentive. By this he means that our incentives are not the author of any moral law, and this is a view from which he never subsequently departed. But the ascription of incentives only to the sensuous side of our nature, with the resulting contrast between incentive and motive, is abandoned; and though, in a sense still to be explained, all incentives are subjective, they need not be private and sensuous. Indeed, even in the *Foundations*, the Idea of the intelligible world (the moral realm) is called the "incentive,"[20] showing that the privacy of incentives is not essential to the concept. The subjectivity of incentive can thus mean two

---

[16] Josef Bohatec (*Die Religionsphilosophie Kants*, p. 141) refers to the doctrine of Fragment 6 as "intellectual eudaemonism."

[17] Cf. the discussion of the proper translation of *Triebfeder*, above, p. 90, n. 2.

[18] *Critique of Practical Reason*, 79 (172): "From the concept of an incentive comes that of an interest." Cf. also *Foundations of the Metaphysics of Morals*, 459 n. (80 n.); *Vorarbeiten zur Tugendlehre*, XXIII, 378; *Metaphysik der Sitten*, VI, 212.

[19] *Foundations of the Metaphysics of Morals*, 427 (45).

[20] *Ibid.*, 462 (83).

things: (*a*) it has a reference to the private, personal motivations of the subject, which are based on sensuous impulse, which is, at most, guided by reason, and (*b*) it refers to the workings of the moral principle, which is itself objective, upon the constitution of the human subject, and this working is the incentive which is obviously subject-conditioned as well as objectively determined. This sense of "subjective" is retained in the *Critique*, where, we are told, an incentive is "a subjective determining ground of the will whose reason does not by its nature necessarily conform to the objective law" (72 [164]). Here "subjective" merely means located in and thus in part depending upon the constitution of the subject, without implying that this subjectivity is indicative of dependence upon personal differences in sensuous desires. There is, therefore, no contradiction in saying that the objective law must be the incentive, though its role as incentive is subjective and presupposes "the sensuousness and hence the finitude of such beings" as man.[21]

The relation of the moral law to the incentive is therefore a formal distinction analogous to that between the law and the categorical imperative or the law and duty. The imperative is the law as it appears to a finite being whose will does not obey the law by nature; the imperative is the law, but in the imperative mood. Similarly, for finite sensuous beings the law appears as a constraint or necessitation, i.e., as duty, because its "is" is our "ought."[22] Contrariwise, the moral law is a dictate of pure practical reason, which, as such, has no incentive.[23] Hence incentives arise only in a being affected by sense *not* because the incentive is subjective in any pejorative meaning but because a non-sensuous rational being would, by nature and without an incentive, execute the moral law.

§ 5. DESIRE AND PLEASURE

We must, therefore, know something of the sensuous nature of man in order to understand the way in which the moral law, objective though it is, can become a subjective incentive. For this, we must turn to Kant's psychology and to the "transcendental definitions,"[24] which,

---

[21] *Critique of Practical Reason*, 76 (168). The statement "The law itself must be the incentive" is not quite accurate and must be qualified (cf. below, § 7).

[22] *Foundations of the Metaphysics of Morals*, 449, 455 (68, 75).

[23] *Vorarbeiten zur Tugendlehre*, XXIII, 378.

[24] *Erste Einleitung in die Kritik der Urteilskraft*, XX, 230 n.; *Critique of Practical Reason*, 9 n. (94 n.).

he says, are all that he needs to "borrow from psychology" for this *Critique*.

That man is a living being—indeed, that there are men in the world—affected by desires and susceptible to pleasure is an empirical fact. The relation between pleasure and desire is to be determined empirically when desire is given an empirical content (as hunger, thirst, and the like). It is essential that the psychologist not give definitions which are implicit hypotheses about matters which can be settled only empirically.[25] They must be defined in such a way as to leave open for empirical determination the relations which subsist between the defined feelings. They must be defined, he says not quite accurately,[26] only "in terms belonging to the pure understanding, i.e., categories, which contain nothing empirical." There are three such definitions:

Life is the faculty of a being by which it acts according to the laws of the faculty of desire. The faculty of desire is the faculty such a being has of causing, through its representations, the reality of the objects of these ideas. Pleasure is the representation of the agreement of an object or an action with the subjective conditions of life [9n. (94 n.)].

We have already mentioned the distinction between the lower and the higher faculty of desire.[27] The latter is not one of experiencing a subjective need which will produce pleasure only indirectly through success in bringing an object of desire into existence, but it is the faculty of desire whose object is one that can be represented only by pure reason and caused by virtue of this representation. That is, an object of the higher faculty of desire is not a thing considered *materialiter* but a thing considered formally as under a law and pleasing only because of its conformity to and generation through the law. Since only reason can represent a law, reason is the higher faculty of desire, and its a priori principle is a purposiveness which is an imperative for all actual purposing.[28]

The question of the present chapter may therefore be phrased thus: How can reason be the higher faculty of desire and not merely provide norms for judgment, *post facto?*

[25] This is in conformity to Kant's theory of the philosophical uses and dangers of definition (cf. my "Kant's Theory of Definition," *Philosophical Review,* LXV [1956], 179–91).

[26] He means not categories, but predicables (cf. *Critique of Pure Reason,* A 82 = B 108). But even this is not correct. Pleasure is an empirical, not a transcendental, predicate (*ibid.,* A 343 = B 401).

[27] Cf. above, chap. vii, § 4.

[28] *Critique of Practical Reason,* 24–25 (112); *Erste Einleitung in die Kritik der Urteilskraft,* XX, 246.

§ 6. THE GENESIS OF RESPECT

We are now ready to deal systematically with the early parts of chapter iii. Unfortunately, this is the most repetitious and least well-organized chapter in the book, and there are a number of infelicitous expressions that have seemed to many critics to be evidence of serious inconsistencies. Nevertheless, the main points are made again and again, sometimes in almost identical words and as conclusions from similar arguments, so that there is little occasion for any serious misunderstanding or for doubt as to what Kant means.

If morality is genuine, the moral law must directly determine our choice; this we are told in the first sentence (71 [164]). If it does not, some feeling or desire which is independent of the law must be the cause, and the action can at best be merely legal. In genuine morality, the moral law must be the incentive.

Why and how the moral law is such an incentive is the unanswerable and perhaps meaningless question: Why ought I be moral? But the question here is not one of the authority of the moral law; it is a question of what are the conditions, in a being like man, that make it possible for him to take an interest in the law or to have the law as his incentive. And this question, Kant thinks, can be answered a priori with the help of his transcendental definitions.

Our inclinations are not, by nature, law-abiding. The moral law, therefore, is felt as a constraint on them in a being possessed of a practical reason. Some inclinations it thwarts by disciplining them into a coherent system like that described in Fragment 6; thus selfishness is disciplined into rational self-love.[29] But one kind of inclination[30] is absolutely opposed to the moral law; it is inclination to regard one's own subjective maxims and interests as having the authority of law. This is self-conceit or moral arrogance, and it is absolutely incompatible with morality. The vision of the moral law before man strikes down his self-conceit and humbles his arrogance. It produces a feeling which is pain, under the transcendental definition of pain. What humiliates us is an object of respect. Hence we respect the moral law and have a feeling of respect for it even when we do not obey it.

The moral law occasions also a positive feeling; for the interest or

[29] Rational self-love may or may not be moral. In any event, it is not a basis for a direct duty (cf. *Critique of Practical Reason*, 93 [187], and *Religion within the Limits of Reason Alone*, VI, 45 n. [Greene and Hudson, 41 n.]).

[30] Cf. above, chap. vii, § 7, for a discussion of the two kinds of selfishness. It is hardly appropriate to refer to either as an *inclination*. It is rather a system of inclinations under a maxim. Butler rightly called it a "sentiment" in contrast to a "particular passion."

purpose of reason is the reign of moral law, and whatever accords with this interest will necessarily be associated with a feeling of pleasure or satisfaction. In the chapter before us, Kant never says explicitly that there is a pleasurable component in respect, and, indeed, he generally makes it appear more unpleasant than pleasant. But elsewhere he calls respect "negative pleasure"[31] and declares it to be the ground of a feeling of pleasure or satisfaction (116 [213]). But though there is at most an analogon of pleasure, both positive and negative effects on feeling are recognized in respect: not only are we struck down by the majesty of the moral law, we are also raised up by it to a height and destination that nothing in our natural talents can sustain. To avoid the notion that respect is a sensuous feeling passively experienced, Kant seems hesitant not only to call it pleasure but even to call it feeling; but it produces an effect on conduct that is analogous to that produced by pleasure or pain. To call it simply pleasure or pain would obscure the unique phenomenological features of respect (88 [181]).

The dissimilarity of rational and empirical grounds of determination is made recognizable through the resistance of a practically legislating reason to all interfering inclinations, which is shown in a peculiar kind of feeling which does not precede the legislation of practical reason but which is, on the contrary, first occasioned by it, as a compulsion. That is, it is revealed through the feeling of respect of a kind that no man has for any inclinations whatever, but which he may feel for the law alone [92 (185)].

But the enjoyment is unmistakable, and the only danger in recognizing it is that of subreption, of falsely locating it so as to think of it as the cause instead of as the effect of the law's determination of the will. We must recognize the inward contentment as a mode of pleasure which necessarily accompanies obedience to the law but must guard against thinking of it as the determining ground or object of the action.

The sublimity of the moral law is more than a metaphor for Kant. Not only does he use the language of the aesthetics of the sublime in describing the moral law, but he gives an analogous interpretation of the origins of the feelings of sublimity and respect. In both there is humiliation or thwarting of our sensuous nature (our perceptual faculty and imagination in the sublime, our feeling of worth in respect) which occasions a pain which, in turn, is transmuted into a kind of elation by the discovery in ourselves of a power superior to that which has humiliated us (in the sublime) and superior also to that power in us which has been humiliated (in feelings of both respect and of the sublime). But whereas a subreption necessarily occurs in the sublime feel-

---

[31] Cf. *Critique of Judgment*, § 23.

ings, so that we attribute to the object a sublimity which actually exists only in ourselves, the feeling of respect is directed to a law, which is a law of our own freedom, self-imposed and not imposed upon us from without, and to the persons, ourselves or others, who embody this law. Hence respect for the law and respect for our personality are not distinct and even competing feelings, as are the two feelings which merge in our experience of the sublime.[32]

§ 7. AN ALLEGED INCONSISTENCY

Serious inconsistencies have been alleged to be present in Kant's discussion of the incentive to morality. He states:

> The moral law should directly determine the will. If the determination of the will occurs in accordance with the moral law but only by means of a feeling of any kind whatsoever which must be presupposed in order that the law may become a determining ground of the will [71 (164)]

we have to do with legality, not morality. These are the opening sentences of chapter iii and must, because of their position, be given pre-eminent importance and weight.

Then he tells us that respect for the law is the incentive for morality,[33] that respect is not the incentive to morality but is morality itself (76 [168]), and that the law is the incentive (72 [164]).

It is regrettable that Kant was not more careful; though, had he been so, the race of Kant-commentators would have been unemployed. But it is unjust to do more than complain of his carelessness here and to allege serious and insurmountable inconsistencies where the development of the argument itself makes sometimes one and sometimes another choice of words appropriate, though the statements taken out of their context certainly seem incompatible.

In spite of what Kant says, the law *itself* is not the incentive. A law is just not the sort of thing that can be an incentive. At most, consciousness of a law can be an incentive. If the law itself were a determinant of conduct, without the intervention of consciousness (which

---

[32] Cf. *Critique of Practical Reason*, 86–87 (180); *Metaphysik der Sitten*, VI, 402–3; *Critique of Judgment*, § 27. He had previously (*Beobachtungen über das Gefühl des Schönen und Erhabenen*, 2. Abschnitt) distinguished among virtues those which are sublime from those which are beautiful, obviously following Burke, *Inquiry into the Origin of Our Ideas of the Sublime and Beautiful*, Part III, Secs. X and XI. On the long history of these aesthetic concepts in morals before Kant and in Kant's early works, see Giorgio Tonelli, "Kant: dall'estetica metafisica all'estetica psico-empirica," *Memorie della Academia delle Scienze di Torino* (1955), pp. 77–421, *passim* (use the exhaustive index).

[33] *Critique of Practical Reason*, 78 (171); at 85 (178): "respect for duty."

means, for us men, also feeling), it would not be a practical law, and men would not be free agents. Kant frequently speaks of laws' doing things, when he means that the world is such that the laws describe it (natural laws) or when he means that consciousness of the law will induce a rational being to do what the law demands.[34]

Hence we must ask: What is the nature of the consciousness of the law, such that it can be the incentive? If the *Critique* leaves any room for doubt on this, it is removed by the *Metaphysics of Morals*. There Kant says: "The respect for the law, which is, subjectively, called the moral feeling, is identical with the consciousness of one's duty."[35] We do not, therefore, have a theoretical knowledge of our duty and of our will at potential variance with it, with the subsequent addition of the feeling of respect. To know one's duty may not be, as Socrates believed, to do it. But to know what the law requires and to feel respect for it (if not actually to obey it)[36] are, for Kant, identical; even knowledge of a moral law is not aseptically theoretical. Hence a false contrast between "law" and "respect" falls away when we read for the former "consciousness of law," which is the only mode in which a practical law can be effective and yet be distinct from a natural law.

But, then, what of the opening sentences? The second sentence is often read as if Kant, when he wrote it, thought that the law must directly determine the will without any feeling intervening between the law and the decision—a view at variance with the remainder of the chapter. Yet he did not believe this even when he wrote this sentence. For though the word "presupposed" is there precisely to guard against another error (that of the moral-sense or moral-feeling school), it should also guard against the opposite error of supposing that the determination must or can be without any *subsequent* feeling. The determination of the will by law does not require any feeling which must be presupposed; that means that it does not require any feeling independent of, or prior to, the consciousness of the law. The feeling of respect, like any other feeling, need not be presupposed as something in the natural man awaiting an object which can be found only in the law; the feeling of respect presupposes the law and our consciousness

[34] Cf. *ibid.,* 29 (117), the suggestion that the law is only the self-consciousness of practical reason.

[35] *Metaphysik der Sitten,* VI, 464.

[36] Even the sinner, who transgresses the law, shows his reverence for it by trembling before its majesty (*Critique of Practical Reason,* 80 [172]). Cf. *Religion within the Limits of Reason Alone,* VI, 46–47 (Greene and Hudson, 41–42) on the reestablishment of the effectiveness of respect for the moral law, "which we have never been able to lose."

of it (or is, indeed, equivalent to the latter). The first sentence, therefore is not incompatible with, but anticipates, the later statement: "In
the subject there is no *antecedent* feeling tending to morality."[37]

§ 8.   THE MORAL FEELING

Though Kant made use of the concept of moral feeling in his precritical works, the general trend of his teaching appeared to be an
elimination of all feeling from morality. It is hard to know whether the
desiccated picture of Kant's personality as that of a *reiner Verstandes-
mensch* has led people to ignore his positive theory of the moral feeling or whether a caricature of his ethics as otherworldly has created
the false picture of the man; but the two conceptions usually go together, and they are both wrong.

Kant banished feeling from a positive position in ethics only insofar
as feeling is sensuously effected and, even as moral feeling, is put in the
false position of being the source of the rational principle. Thus he
criticizes Epicurus (115 [211]) for finding a pleasure in morality without giving a definition of morality in terms other than those of pleasure; and he regards all theories of moral sense or moral feeling as being
necessarily subsumed under the principle of self-love (38 [128]),
since all pleasure, whatever its origin, is of one and the same kind (23
[110]). He held, moreover, that any theory of moral feeling which
gave it a founding role necessarily led to subjectivism and relativism; a
man, he said, could legitimately excuse himself from a moral duty by
saying that he did not like the action demanded, if feeling is the source
of moral approbation.[38]

Nevertheless, moral feeling has a place in Kant's ethics, as is made
clear in the chapter before us; but it is an effect of the consciousness of
the moral law on sensuous feeling, not a feeling given prior to the discovery of what the law demands of us in principle and not a mystical
feeling whose source would be in some otherworldly inspiration.

The moral feeling has two components, because it is, stripped to its
essentials, the same as respect (75, 80 [168, 173]), though, as we shall
see, it contains some other feelings that are corollary to respect. But

[37] *Critique of Practical Reason,* 75 (167, 168); similarly, 23–24, 117 (110, 213). The
same point is emphasized in *Critique of Judgment,* § 29, Remark (VI, 271 [111]).
But compare the statement at *Critique of Practical Reason,* 25 (112): "Reason determines the will in a practical law directly, not through an intervening feeling of
pleasure or displeasure, even if this pleasure is taken in the law itself." It is difficult
to reconcile this statement with the others, for it suggests that pure practical reason
can determine the action without the mechanism explored in this chapter.

[38] *Lectures on Ethics,* 13, 37.

whereas in his discussions under the term "respect" Kant emphasizes the humbling of the self which is essential to the aggrandizement of the law, under the term "moral feeling" he puts more weight upon the enjoyment of the spontaneity and freedom which is felt in the moral disposition.

Before discussing this positive joy in morality, which is not explicitly included under "moral feeling" (though only the word is lacking),[39] we must turn for a moment to another description of moral feeling and then consider the concepts of duty and virtue.

In the *Metaphysics of Morals* Kant lists the predispositions, "the subjective conditions of susceptibility to the concept of duty" by virtue of which man can be obligated, even though the consciousness of them, as an influence on the mind, can only follow upon the moral law.[40] One of these is moral feeling, and here Kant's account of it varies markedly from that in the *Critique*.

The moral feeling, he says, "is the susceptibility to pleasure or pain merely from the consciousness of the agreement or conflict of our action with the law of duty."[41] And, he continues in a sentence difficult to translate, all determination of the will (*Willkür*) proceeds (*a*) from the representation of the possible action (*b*) through the feeling of pleasure or pain (through taking an interest in the action or its effect) (*c*) to the act. The aesthetic condition, the feeling, is either pathological or moral: the former if the pleasure precedes the representation of the law, the latter if it follows it and is, as it were, pleasure *in* the law.

The differences between this statement and those in the *Critique* arise from the fact that Kant is talking of two different things under the same name, under a single name that had had a long history of application to each. In the *Critique* he is discussing the feeling that a rational sensuous being has in the face of recognized duty; in the *Metaphysics* he is discussing not a feeling as a phenomenological state of consciousness, but as a potentiality, an *Empfänglichkeit*. Naturally, this must precede, logically or temporally, the actual feeling of respect. But this

---

[39] That is, in the principal discussion, *Critique of Practical Reason*, 115–18 (211–15).

[40] *Metaphysik der Sitten*, VI, 399. The others are love of one's fellows, conscience, and respect (for self). The *Critique of Judgment*, § 88, gives another listing of "mental dispositions that make for duty," viz., gratitude, obedience, and humility (submission to deserved chastisement), and in § 91 speaks of gratitude to and veneration for the unknown cause, arising from the admiration of nature and producing an effect on moral feeling. A similar thought is expressed in *Critique of Practical Reason*, 160 (258), in the anecdote about Leibniz.

[41] Similar definitions are in *Religion within the Limits of Reason Alone*, VI, 27 (Greene and Hudson, 23) and in *Lectures on Ethics*, p. 44.

statement does not conflict, except verbally, with the statement that there is "no antecedent feeling tending to morality"; it is as if one were to say in English, "A man must have feeling before he can have a feeling"—perhaps a not very lucid way of saying a simple thing, but certainly no evidence of fundamental confusion in the speaker's mind.

Yet, in spite of this, there is a difference between the analyses of the actual moral feeling (i.e., the feeling that is felt, and not the potentiality for it) as given in the *Critique* and as suggested in the *Metaphysics*. The *Metaphysics of Morals* says that the moral feeling is either pleasure or pain, pleasure if there is felt accordance with the law and pain if there is not. The *Critique*, on the other hand, says that there is something analogous to both pleasure and pain even if the action does conform to the law, because even in conformity there is the pain of humiliation arising from the thwarting or striking-down of inclination.

But there is no real inconsistency here. The *Metaphysics of Morals* makes a sharp contrast between pathological and moral pleasure and pain and discusses only the latter. Now there is no moral pain in obedience to the law; there is at most a pain arising from the thwarting of pathological feeling. But, because of the difference drawn between the two kinds of feelings, Kant can discuss one without the other in the later work. In the former, he discusses them together and thinks of pathological feeling as the material cause of moral feeling. "Sensuous feeling," he says (75 [168]), "which is the basis of all our inclinations, is the condition of the particular feeling we call respect." In the *Metaphysics of Morals* this relationship is neglected, and therefore there is missing this peculiar mixture of pleasure and plain. That he is discussing moral feeling, as actual, in a slightly different sense in the two works is shown by the fact that in the *Metaphysics* moral feeling is not equated with respect, while in the *Critique* it is.

§ 9. DUTY[42] AND PERSONALITY

In the *Foundations*,[43] Kant formulates the definition: "Duty is the necessity of an action done from respect for law." We are at last in a

---

[42] The form of the celebrated apostrophe to duty (86 [180]) may have been suggested by Rousseau's apostrophe to conscience in *Émile*, which Kant admired, On Kant's text see H. Romundt, "Vorschlag zu einer Änderung des Textes von der Kritik der praktischen Vernunft,' *Kant-Studien*, XIII (1908), 313-14, and replies by B. Bauch and P. Natorp, *ibid.*, pp. 315-16. Kant made little use of this popular trope, since it was hardly in keeping with the *Sachlichkeit* of his style. There is an apostrophe to sincerity in *Religion within the Limits of Reason Alone*, VI, 190 n. (Greene and Hudson, 178 n.).

[43] *Foundations of the Metaphysics of Morals*, 400 (16).

position to understand the full meaning of this in all its ramifications, when Kant says: "Respect for law is not the incentive to morality, but is morality itself" (76 [168]). Morality is a disposition or settled habit to act in accord with law because it is law; and one who respects law, in the sense described here, is one who acts from duty. Duty is the necessitation or constraint to an action by a law in the consciousness and conduct of a person who does not, by nature, necessarily act as the law requires. A non-sensuous rational being would not have to have any incentive (72 [164]) to such obedience, and therefore the concept of duty is not applicable to such a being; such a being would have a holy will. The "ought" of the moral imperative is an "is" for such a being.[44] But man, as a sensuous being, is "under the discipline of reason" (82 [175]) and is not endowed with a holy will. His will is at best virtuous.

Even so, man is a person and, as such, is holy. He is an end-setting being and therefore an end in himself. He has dignity and is not like a thing having only a price. Personality—that attribute which distinguishes rational beings from things—is freedom from the mechanism of nature through a capacity to be subject to laws given by itself (autonomy). An empirical self, having only negative freedom, is "subject to his own personality so far as he belongs to the intelligible world" (87 [180]). Personality is sublime, and whenever we respect any man, we respect the law of the intelligible world which he more or less adequately represents in the phenomenal world (77–78 [170]). Categorical imperatives for the empirical self are laws of the intelligible self; the "should" of the former is the "would" of the latter. While man, empirically regarded, is "unholy enough," personality and humanity in him are holy.

With this explanation of the provenance of duty, there is a significant introduction of the concept of personality. Whereas Kant had emphasized, in the first *Critique*, the impossibility of a rational psychology of the soul as substance and had made the self only an appearance —an emphasis continued in the second *Critique*—there is here and elsewhere a transition to a more metaphysical interpretation of the self not only as thought but as directly experienced as a being noumenal in character.[45] The phenomenalistic interpretation of the self, though it is, as it were, the official Kantian doctrine, shows signs here and there of being transcended in a metaphysical personalism and activism, since the spontaneity felt in self-consciousness separates man from nature. While a "metaphysics" in the classical and not in the Kantian sense seems to

[44] *Ibid.*, 449, 455 (68, 75); cf. *Critique of Judgment*, § 76.

[45] A full study of this, with a collection of relevant passages, is given in Heimsoeth's *Studien zur Philosophie Immanuel Kants*, pp. 227 ff.

be suggested by this, it is not a theoretical but a practical-dogmatic metaphysics which is involved:

> Meanwhile, we may still retain the concept of personality . . . in so far as it is merely transcendental, that is, concerns the unity of the subject, otherwise unknown to us, in the determinations of which there is a thoroughgoing connection through apperception. Taken in this way, the concept is necessary for practical employment and is sufficient for such use; but we can never parade it as an extension of our self-knowledge through pure reason.[46]

Again and again it is asserted that no theoretical use of the concept can be made, e.g., in theoretically valid arguments for immortality. But the evidence of spontaneity and our knowledge of the law of the self as noumenon certainly give a richer conception of personality than that of the transcendental unity of apperception, though the propositions in which it functions are all practical, not theoretical.

Personality, then, is not a category; it is an Idea of reason, and personality is not a given. We are persons, but no finite sensuous being is fully adequate to the Idea of personality. In human nature, considered empirically, we find at most only a "predisposition to personality," which is the capacity for respecting the moral law and making it sufficient incentive for the will.[47] When this predisposition is strengthened through practice and becomes actual and effective, there is a state of virtue and goodness of character; a good man in the empirical world is one whose law is derived from, and is followed out of respect for, the Idea of his personality in the intelligible world. Even in an evil man, one who voluntarily embraces other maxims than those conforming to the moral law, the predisposition to personality is not lost; it has only been rendered ineffective by a free choice against the demands of the moral law. Moral evil is voluntarily going against the demands of one's own personality as pure practical, legislative, reason.

§ 10. VIRTUE

Virtue is a "naturally acquired faculty of a non-holy will" (33 [121]). It is the moral disposition in conflict or, as Abbott eloquently translates it, "the moral disposition militant."[48] Without the two poles of sensuous inclination and pure rational principle, it could not arise.

---

[46] *Critique of Pure Reason*, A 365, absent from B; cf. B 431–32, absent from A.

[47] *Religion within the Limits of Reason Alone*, VI, 27–28 (Greene and Hudson, 22–23). This is identified with moral feeling in the sense of the *Metaphysik der Sitten*, VI, 399, instead of in the sense of the second *Critique* (cf. above, p. 224).

[48] *Critique of Practical Reason*, 84 (178). Abbott's translation here aptly preserves the military symbolism of the page.

We stand under the discipline of reason; we are conscripts in the moral host, taking orders, and not volunteers, acting from our individual merit. We are members of the realm of ends, but we are subjects in it and not, at first, sovereigns of it (82 [175]). In man, virtue is always defective, and virtue itself, like personality, is a mere Idea to which no perfectly adequate empirical representation can be found.[49]

In many of Kant's examples of virtue, the necessity of acting out of respect for law and not from inclination is presented as if the action had to take place without, or even always against, inclination. But this is not what the examples were chosen to illustrate, and this is no part of Kant's theory; even acting from inclination is not in itself evil, but only the taking into one's maxim of action and insubordination of sensuous incentives to rational incentives—this insubordination itself being free and spontaneous and a matter of principle—is the root of moral evil.[50]

The purpose of the examples of virtuous action can be understood only in the light of their polemical or pedagogical use. An act in which a man did what duty required of him and to which his inclination also pointed might easily appear—and certainly would appear to a man with Kant's skeptical hatred of cant—to be an action done in accordance with law *because of* his inclination. Even where inclination seems to be against the law, the mystery of the human heart is so deep that we can never be sure that we will not, upon more penetrating self-analysis, come upon "the dear self" as the real determinant.[51] But where we find the dear self in this role, there is no morality; hence the best *illustrations* of genuine morality will be found where the dear self is obviously opposed, though that does not mean, as we shall soon see, that the best morality is one in which there must be active and painful self-abnegation. Virtue does not entail a renunciation of happiness, but only a willingness "to take no account of happiness when duty is in question" (93 [186]).

But those who read Kant's examples and fail to understand the text that they were meant to illustrate have always regarded his ethics as singularly repellent and have thought that if they represent typical and most estimable virtue, then it is an ethics which they must reject.[52] Inclinations and feelings, however, have a legitimate place in Kant's ethics which is not brought out by these examples. They may even be seen as

---

[49] *Ibid.*, 127 n. (224 n.); *Critique of Pure Reason*, A 315 = B 372; *Critique of Judgment*, § 57, Remark I.

[50] *Religion within the Limits of Reason Alone*, VI, 36 (Greene and Hudson, 31).

[51] *Foundations of the Metaphysics of Morals*, 407 (24).

[52] Cf. above, p. 120, n. 20.

necessary corollaries of true virtue, since without inward resistance there is holiness of will but no virtue.[53] But human nature is not left, in the practice of virtue, with what Hegel called the "undigested lump of sour virtue in the stomach"; the rational element can be strengthened until it brings about a reformation of the natural man.[54] What would be morally indifferent or even evil before this reformation[55] can become a mark of the most complete virtue.

§ 11. MORAL SATISFACTION

We said above, in § 7, that in moral action we find a satisfaction in the experience of our own autonomous spontaneity and that this is the positive element in respect as the moral feeling.[56] Man is humiliated by his vision of the law, before whose majesty even the boldest sinner trembles (80 [172]); but he is elevated in his consciousness that this humiliation is the mark of his higher vocation, for it is humiliation of himself by himself, of his heteronomous natural being by his autonomous intelligible being (cf. 76 [169] on Fontanelle).

In morality, therefore, in the consciousness of determination by law, there is a feeling of joy, since reason's interest is being furthered (116 [212]). Freedom itself, as the exercise of moral will, thus becomes subject to enjoyment, which is not happiness but essential to it.[57] This joy, however, cannot define virtue, since it arises only from a prior consciousness of virtue, which, formally and abstractly considered, has

[53] A holy will has no incentives, no duty, and no virtue; it is only a standard or Idea by which we judge human incentives, duty, and virtue. Kant observes that the Stoic sage was believed to be so perfect that he was "elevated above duties though he propounded duties to others," but that this error arose only because the Stoics failed to conceive the law "in the same purity and rigor as does the precept of the Gospel" (*Critique of Practical Reason*, 127 n. [224 n.]).

[54] On "sweet and sour duty," cf. *Metaphysik der Sitten*, VI, 377, 391, and *Lectures on Ethics*, p. 199.

[55] Even the inclinations refined to civility have nothing stable or of absolute worth in them: "Everything good that does not grow from its connection with a morally good disposition is nothing but empty show and glittering misery" (*Idea for a Universal History*, Seventh Thesis, VIII, 26). In such judgments, Kant shows some of the passion and often uses some of the words of Rousseau.

[56] The *Critique of Judgment*, § 29, General Remark (V, 271 [111–12]), emphasizes the positive side of the moral feeling more than the second *Critique* does. In fact, the discussion of self-contentment in the second does not directly identify it as a component in the moral feeling, and the whole treatment of it is not found in the chapter on the incentives but is introduced later into the chapter on the *summum bonum*. Nevertheless, it is clear that the joy in morality is a part of it, the humiliation of natural man before the law being a necessary precondition.

[57] *Critique of Practical Reason*, 118 (215) and Fragment 6 (Reflexion 7202).

nothing to do with happiness itself. It was the fundamental logical error of the eudaemonists to recommend virtue as a source of happiness within one's self, arising from self-approbation predicated upon consciousness of virtue, without giving a criterion for approbation so that conformity to it could indeed be a source of joy. But the error of Epicurus and the moral-sense theory (38, 116 [128, 212]), already pointed out by Hutcheson and Price,[58] should not cause us to commit the opposite error of denying a positive joy to be possible in moral conduct.

Hume[59] had complained of the lack of a name for this feeling of moral well-being, and Kant, as if directly answering Hume, says:

Do we not have a word to denote a satisfaction with existence, an analogue of happiness which necessarily accompanies the consciousness of virtue, and which does not indicate a gratification, as "happiness" does? We do, and this word is "self-contentment," which in its real meaning refers only to negative satisfaction with existence in which one is conscious of needing nothing. Freedom and the consciousness of freedom, as a capacity for following the moral law with an unyielding disposition, is independence from inclinations, at least as motives determining (though not as affecting) our desiring; and, so far as I am conscious of freedom in obeying my moral maxims, it is the exclusive source of an unchanging contentment necessarily connected with it and resting on no particular feeling.[60]

That this feeling is the stronger the more purely the law is presented, is a fundamental thesis in Kant's educational theory.[61] Other impure motives may well work in the direction of legally correct action (81 [174]), but they may cloud the vision of the man for the only thing that can bring him to morality and lasting equanimity. Thus, Kant continued:

Even the feeling of sympathy and warm-hearted fellow feeling, when *preceding* the consideration of what is duty and serving as a determining ground, is burdensome even to right-thinking persons, confusing their considered maxims and creating the wish to be free of them and subject only to law-giving reason.[62]

---

58 Cf. above, p. 106.

59 *Enquiry concerning the Principles of Morals*, Appendix IV (ed. Selby-Bigge [2d ed.], p. 314).

60 *Critique of Practical Reason*, 117 (214); on contentment cf. Wolff, *Vernünftige Gedancken von Gott, der Welt und der Seele des Menschen*, § 463.

61 *Critique of Practical Reason*, 152, 157 (251, 255); cf. *Foundations of the Metaphysics of Morals*, 410-11 (27); *Über den Gemeinspruch* . . . , VIII, 288.

62 *Critique of Practical Reason*, 118 (214), italics added. Similarly, *Foundations of the Metaphysics of Morals*, 428 (46). But contrast the remarks in *Religion within the Limits of Reason Alone*, VI, 58 (Greene and Hudson, 51) on the vanity and sin of wishing to be free from all inclinations.

It was no doubt in reaction to this that Friedrich Schiller wrote:

In the Kantian moral philosophy the idea of duty is presented with a hard-
ness which frightens away all the graces and which could mislead an obtuse
mind to seek moral perfection on the path of a dour and monkish asceticism.
However much the great philosopher tried to avoid this misunderstanding,
which must have been disturbing to him above all, with his serene and free
mind, I still think that he himself gave obvious occasion to it through the
sharp and shrill contrast between the two principles which work on the will
of man—an occasion which perhaps can hardly be avoided in his theory.[63]

To this Kant replied in a passage in the *Religion* which is not in any
way inconsistent with the teaching of the *Critique*, though, if it had
been said in the *Critique*, the "occasion" would not have been so obvious:

Now if one asks, What is the aesthetic character, the temperament, so to
speak, of virtue, whether courageous and hence joyous or fear-ridden and
dejected, the answer is hardly necessary. This latter slavish frame of mind
can never occur without a hidden hatred of the law. And a heart which is
happy in the performance of its duty (not merely complacent in the recognition thereof) is a mark of genuineness in the virtuous spirit—a genuineness
even in piety, which does not consist in the self-inflicted torment of a re-
pentant sinner (a very ambiguous state of mind, which ordinarily is nothing
but inward regret at having infringed upon the rules of prudence[64]), but
rather in the firm resolve to do better in the future. This resolve, then, encouraged by good progress, must needs beget a joyous frame of mind, without which man is never certain of having really attained a love for the good,
i.e., of having incorporated it into his maxim.[65]

Let this lay the ghost of an old error. But it has often been said that
the Kantian doctrine is "false to human nature," in that it neglects or
denies the role of spontaneous feeling precisely because it puts them in

---

[63] *Über Anmut und Würde*. Note that Schiller says that this is a misunderstanding
of Kant's views and that Kant regarded Schiller as a philosophical ally, not an opponent (Cf. *Religion* . . . , VI, 23 n., first sentence [Greene and Hudson, 19 n., second sentence]). Schiller's famous verse can be regarded only as a joke and not as
presenting Schiller's real views of the Kantian philosophy. There was a point that
actually divided them, however, though it is not clearly brought out in their *Ausein-
andersetzung*, to wit, whether the collaboration of rational and sensuous elements is
essential to virtue (Schiller) or, at most, one of the duties (Kant, *Metaphysik der
Sitten*, Tugendlehre, § 48 [VI, 473]—to unite the virtues and the graces is a duty).
For perhaps the best full study of the Kant-Schiller controversy and the extensive
literature that has grown from it see Hans Reiner, *Pflicht und Neigung* (Meisenheim, 1951), pp. 28–49.

[64] On repentance see *Critique of Practical Reason*, 98 (192).

[65] *Religion within the Limits of Reason Alone*, VI, 23 n. (Greene and Hudson,
19 n.).

second place, after the rational determination.[66] It therefore seems to make impossible, as well as undesirable, demands upon the natural man. Not, perhaps, *transcendentally* impossible demands, because of Kant's doctrine that "thou canst, because thou shouldst," but demands that living men cannot be reasonably expected to acknowledge.

There are three answers to this. One is that it is an irrelevant criticism, since for Kant an ethical theory is not to be judged by the facts of human nature (about which, indeed, we know far too little and into which we surreptitiously introduce unexamined pessimistic or optimistic moral judgments according to our taste).[67] Second, as a corollary to this, we must remember that such judgments of human frailty are not alien to Kant himself. His derogatory judgments of the moral prospects of human nature and society are, in fact, sharper than those of either Aristotle or Dewey, two other great proponents of reasonable morality.[68] And, third, Kant saw the need, for us men, of supplementing the pure moral motive with others more natural to man, in spite of his warnings against this in the *Critique*, where he was examining pure practical reason. Love is the most important of these motives:

> When it is a question not merely of the representation of duty [which is the task of the *Critique*] but of its execution, if one asks about the subjective ground of action on which, if presupposed, one can at least expect what man *will* do and not what on the objective ground he *ought* to do, it is love which

[66] Dr. Johnson was no great philosopher, not even a competent one. But he was a man of solid understanding whose testimony on a point of moral judgment carries a weight it would not have had if it had issued from a degree of philosophical sophistication he neither had nor admired; thus does the wise layman sometimes serve as the impartial observer in philosophical disputes. Boswell writes: " 'Sir,' said Mr. Johnson, 'I can lay but little stress upon that instinctive, that constitutional, goodness that is not founded upon principle. I grant you that such a man may be a very good member of society. I can conceive him placed in such a situation that he is not much tempted to deviate from what is right; and so, as goodness is most eligible when there is not some strong enticement to transgress its precepts, I can conceive him doing no harm. But if such a man stood in need of money, I should not like to trust him. And even now, I should not trust Mr. Dempster with young ladies, for there is always a temptation" (*London Journal*, July 22, 1763). The same is given in slightly altered form in the *Life* ("Modern Library" ed.), p. 268; cf. also Price, *Review of the Principal Questions of Morals*, ed. D. D. Raphael (Oxford, 1948), p. 191.

[67] *Über den Gemeinspruch* . . . , *passim*, but especially VIII, 276–77.

[68] *Foundations of the Metaphysics of Morals*, 407 (23); *Idea for a Universal History*, Sixth Thesis (VIII, 23): "Out of such crooked lumber as man is made of, nothing truly straight can be builded." Similarly, *Religion within the Limits of Reason Alone*, VI, 100 (Greene and Hudson, 92).

is an indispensable supplement to the imperfection of human nature, as a free assumption of the will of another under one's own maxim.[69]

This love cannot be commanded; it is not a duty, because it is self-contradictory to require of a man that he do something out of inclination.[70] It must, therefore, be distinguished from the love which can be, and in the gospel is, commanded, which is practical love or the ready willingness to fulfil our total obligation to others. Kant, with his conviction that the true kernel of all religious truth is moral, regards this as equivalent to the love commanded by Christianity.[71]

§ 12. MORAL EDUCATION

By what course is the human race brought to a state in which the moral disposition may rise and flourish? How can the child, in a civilized state, be brought from innocence to moral maturity? These two questions are closely related, and though in the *Critique* Kant deals only with the second, the first was very much on his mind during the years immediately preceding the writing of it.

In the Age of Enlightenment, religion as the moral teacher of mankind was gradually pushed from its pre-eminent position. Though Kant esteemed religion as the moral teacher of mankind, religion was, for him, only its teacher, not its source. The great Enlightenment philosophers sought a generally naturalistic origin of morality, of which religion might be seen as only a vehicle. Lessing, Herder, Kant, and Schiller were at one in attempting a natural history of freedom, and, with it, of morality, though for Kant, at least, neither natural history nor divine revelation was adequate to explain its peculiar form and unique authority. These attempts led to their philosophies of history, in which the education of the human race is the chief theme, appearing even in the titles of some of their books.

[69] *Das Ende aller Dinge*, VIII, 337. A similar office is assigned to sympathy, which is "an impulse, planted in us by nature, to do that which the representation of duty alone would not be able to accomplish" (*Metaphysik der Sitten*, Tugendlehre, § 35). But in moral education it is better to try to weaken the inclinations than to ally them with consciousness of duty, an alliance which may indeed make for better actions but will not produce better men (Reflexion 6722; cf. *Critique of Practical Reason*, 88 [182]). Even to let other motives co-operate with the moral law is risky (*ibid.*, 72 [164]). The difference in these passages cannot be denied; but the emphasis upon a kind of moral synergism is more obvious in the practical than in the purely theoretical investigations of morals.

[70] We cannot be commanded to do anything from inclination *Critique of Practical Reason*, 83 [176] and *Das Ende aller Dinge, loc. cit.*

[71] On practical love cf. *Metaphysik der Sitten*, VI, 449, and below, p. 243, n. 13.

That the human race must advance *itself* is clearly and sharply stated by Kant:

> Nature has willed that man should, by himself, produce everything that goes beyond the mechanical ordering of his animal existence, and that he should partake of no other happiness or perfection than that which he himself, independently of instinct, has created by his own reason.

It is

> just as if she had willed that, if man ever did advance from the lowest barbarity to the highest skill and mental perfection, and thereby worked himself up to happiness (so far as it is possible on earth), he alone should have the credit and should have only himself to thank—exactly as if she aimed more at his rational self-esteem than at his well-being.[72]

There is a natural predisposition to morality in man, but not natural morality. From a state of natural innocence, men fell into evil; history is his gradual working himself out of it. The *Conjectural Beginning of Human History* treats the Book of Genesis as an allegory of this fall and its consequences: "The history of nature begins from the good, for it is the work of God; the history of freedom begins from evil, for it is the work of man."[73] The *Idea for a Universal History* traces the history of man's social arrangements, which are his measures for controlling the evils naturally arising from his "unsocial sociability" or need for, but antagonism to, his fellows. As Heraclitus said, conflict is the origin of all things; and the product is civilization and ordered state, in which man assumes the role of unselfishness, respect for others, and decency—a role which fools nobody and which is called "permitted moral pretence."[74] From it, however, true morality can arise when reason, gradually perfected as an instrument, becomes aware of its higher vocation. Thence arises the genuine interest in morality, and thereafter "moral pretence" must be combated.[75]

Assuming that genuine moral ideas have a certain currency in society, how is the child brought to recognize them and respect them? This is the problem of moral education proper. It is, for Kant, a unique and irreducible division of pedagogy, not merely because of its method,

---

[72] *Idea for a Universal History*, Third Thesis, VIII, 19–20.

[73] *Mutmasslicher Anfang der Menschengeschichte*, VIII, 115, an obvious paraphrase of the opening sentence of *Émile*.

[74] *Anthropologie in pragmatischer Hinsicht*, § 14 (VII, 152–53): "All human virtue in society is counterfeit; only a child takes it for real money. But it is better to have counterfeit coins than to have nothing in circulation; and finally they can be exchanged for hard cash, though only at considerable discount."

[75] *Critique of Pure Reason*, A 748 = B 776.

but because of Kant's moral egalitarianism. Whereas the philosophers of the Enlightenment generally were convinced that sound ethics had to be based upon knowledge and that progress in knowledge was the precondition and almost the guarantor of moral progress but, as practical men, were willing to tolerate a philosophically untenable popular morality (based on religion) as a kind of *Interims-Ethik*, Kant sharply rejected both their premises and their conclusion. Kant, more than any other philosopher of his age, respected the "ordinary moral consciousness" of the ordinary man; under the influence of his early pietism and of Rousseau, he came to regard the unshakable moral convictions of the simple and humble as the proper starting point for philosophical analysis; and philosophy, so far from being the moral teacher of mankind (8 n. [93 n.]), is given the task of defending it from its outward enemies—the philosophers of heteronomous ethics—and its internal dangers —moral fanaticism and mysticism.[76]

In this egalitarian context, even for children, education for morality is successful only when conducted in the Socratic manner. Strictly speaking, moral education is perhaps impossible, since morality is a product of a sudden inward revolution in the manner of willing[77] and each act must be regarded as if it were an entirely fresh beginning.[78] But for us men, in whom virtue is always defective, goodness is only a continuous striving after the good,[79] and this striving can be stimulated and guided.

The "Methodology of Pure Practical Reason" describes what Kant believed to be the most effective measures in this stimulation and guidance. Fundamental to all of them is his conviction that the only incentive to morality is respect for the moral law and that the more purely this law is presented, the stronger is the incentive.[80] It is a mistake, therefore, to recommend virtue on any grounds other than its intrinsic worth, for if it is recommended for its utility, there will always be smart people who can find other surer means to their advantage.[81] Equally to be avoided is "sentimental" education which inspires the child to high-flown fancies and thoughts of merit instead of duty.[82]

[76] *Critique of Practical Reason*, 70–71, 163 (162–63, 262); *Foundations of the Metaphysics of Morals*, 405 (22).

[77] *Religion within the Limits of Reason Alone*, VI, 47–48 (Greene and Hudson, 43–44).

[78] *Ibid.*, 41 (36).   [79] *Ibid.*, 47–48 (43).

[80] *Ibid.*, 48 (44); *Critique of Practical Reason*, 157, 158, 159 (255, 256, 257).

[81] Cf. *Über den Gemeinspruch* . . . , VIII, 288.

[82] *Critique of Practical Reason*, 86 (179). Kant, himself a novel-reader, warns against romancing (*ibid.*, 155, 157 [253, 255], Reflexion 7236).

Instead of persuasion and a vain attempt at instilling a moral disposition as if it were plasma that could be injected into the child's mind and heart, Kant offers the Socratic method for bringing to light the "darkly thought metaphysics of morals which dwells in the reasonableness of each man."[83] He then proposes a moral catechism, in the manner of Rousseau's *Émile*, in which the child's mind is sharpened to the intrinsic difference between moral dignity and the price of things.[84] He proposed, as a practical measure, that educators should collect historical examples for such analysis; his own example is of efforts to suborn a witness in the trial of Anne Boleyn.[85] When the child's judgment is made keen to the essentials of the action under examination, he begins to take an interest in the law of reason by which his analytical powers are exercised. Thus he is prepared for the final stage of his education. Finally, the teacher will call the pupil's attention to the "purity of will by a vivid exhibition of the moral disposition" in the examples.[86] In this way the child is to be brought to experience the contentment and self-respect that can spring only from virtue, and his "heart is freed from a burden which has secretly pressed upon it" (161 [259]).

The *Critique of Practical Reason*, "which is only preliminary," does not deal with the education for specific duties. This is a casuistical problem that Kant takes up in the *Metaphysics of Morals*, the *Lectures on Ethics*, and the *Lectures on Pedagogy*.

[83] *Metaphysik der Sitten*, VI, 376.

[84] Examples are given *ibid.*, VI, 480 ff., and in the *Vorarbeiten* to the same work, XXIII, 413–15.

[85] Warnings against examples in morality are warnings against the danger of *hysteron proteron* as well as against heteronomy and *Sturm und Drang* (cf. *Foundations of the Metaphysics of Morals*, 408–9 [25], etc.). But they are useful in moral education, because they are more effective than abstract precepts (*Anthropologie*, § 75).

[86] *Critique of Practical Reason*, 160 (259). For this "vivid exhibition" Kant quotes (158–59 [257]) Juvenal *Satires* viii. 79–84, evidently one of his favorite passages, for he used it again in *Religion within the Limits of Reason Alone*, VI, 49 n. (Greene and Hudson, 45 n.) and in *Metaphysik der Sitten*, VI, 334.

Part III

Part II

XIII

The Dialectic of Pure Practical Reason; Commentary on Dialectic, Chapters I and II (except Secs. IV and V)

§ 1. WHAT DIALECTIC IS

Both theoretical and practical reason have a dialectic and on the same grounds, viz., as reason they seek the unconditioned for all that is conditioned, but they cannot find it as an object of knowledge, though, in default of a critique, it appears that they have found it (107 [202]). Dialectic is the exposure of the illusion that the unconditioned, as required by reason, is an object of some definite and specific cognition.

The *Critique of Pure Reason* gives a full account of what dialectic is. General logic, Kant tells us there, is sometimes employed as if it were an organon for the production of knowledge instead of as a canon for the institution and evaluation of inferences among cognitions which have their source in experience.[1] As such an organon, it is an art of giving to ignorance and sophistry the appearance of truth. But instruction in such an art is beneath the dignity of philosophy; and dialectic, he says, has come to mean the criticism of the illusions arising from the sophistical art.

Transcendental logic likewise produces illusion when the categories of the understanding, which give knowledge only when related to experience, are used as an organon for knowing things in general, whether given in experience or not.[2] The transcendental illusions which arise in this way are not arbitrary and intentional, like those produced by the sophistical dialectician for forensic purposes, but arise necessarily from the inescapable, yet insatiable, requirements of thought. The conditions of all judgment are the categories, but out where experience cannot reach they are mere Ideas, rules, or maxims for the employment of our reason. Unchecked by experience, they inevitably appear to be

[1] *Critique of Pure Reason*, A 61 = B 85.

[2] *Ibid.*, A 63 = B 88.

objective truths of the highest kind, since no experience can ever refute them. They seem to be true, that is, until their illusoriness is exposed by criticism, which prevents them from deceiving us, though it cannot prevent them from arising, any more than a knowledge of the laws of light can prevent our seeing optical illusions.[3]

The master method of exposing dialectical illusion is what Kant calls the "skeptical method," which consists in "watching, or rather provoking, a conflict of assertions, not for the purpose of deciding between them, but of investigating whether the object of controversy is not perhaps a deceptive appearance."[4] The aim of the skeptical method is not skepticism but certainty, since, by exposing illusion where it exists, it will prevent it from infecting the entire organism of reason with dubiety. By restricting the pretensions of theoretical knowledge, it opens the way for the practical use of reason, and the antinomy, which destroys speculative or theoretical metaphysics about the supersensuous, is thereby the "most fortunate perplexity" into which pure reason could ever fall (107 [203]).

§ 2. THE DIALECTICAL ILLUSIONS OF PURE PRACTICAL REASON

One might well be surprised that there is a dialectic of pure practical reason. In the first *Critique* Kant says that moral philosophy does not lend itself to the skeptical method, since it can "present its principles, together with their practical consequences, one and all *in concreto*, in what are at least possible experiences, and the misunderstanding due to abstraction is avoided."[5] While the going beyond sense experience is the occasion for the theoretical dialectic, leading theory into a "chaos of uncertainty, obscurity, and instability," the power of practical judgment shows itself at its best where everything sensuous is excluded.[6] There is no need to see whether pure practical reason, like theoretical reason, "presumptuously overreaches itself"; it does not "lose itself among unattainable objects or contradictory concepts," and pure practical reason stands in need of no critique (3, 16 [87, 102]).

Yet we are promised in the Introduction a Dialectic as the exhibition and resolution of illusion in the judgments of practical reason (16 [102]). And this does not refer to the illusion that practical reason in its empirical function overreaches itself and usurps the place of pure practical reason;[7] for the section which fulfils this promise is clearly

---

[3] *Ibid.*, A 297 = B 353–54.   [4] *Ibid.*, A 423 = B 451.   [5] *Ibid.*, A 425 = B 453.

[6] *Foundations of the Metaphysics of Morals*, 404 (21).

[7] This is the sense of "dialectic" in the *Foundations* (405 [21]): from the conflict of reason with the senses a "natural dialectic arises, a propensity to argue against the stern laws of duty."

entitled "Dialectic of *Pure* Practical Reason." In this it seems to be in open conflict with the first paragraph of the Preface and the Introduction.

But practical reason is not a reason by which we *know* anything; its reality is shown by an *act*, and, so far as the question of volition is concerned, it always has "objective reality." We may say that, so far as pure practical reason is *practical*, it has no dialectic and creates no illusions because it issues no declarative statements; it only requires, inspires, guides, and judges actions which may not be real but are always possible. Still, so far as it is *reason*, it seeks the unconditioned condition for its actions and judgments and decisions, but in doing this it is theoretical reason employing "practical data."[8] Kant himself says as much in formulating the ultimate questions of philosophy. "What can I know?" is a purely speculative question. "What ought I to do?" is a purely practical one. "What may I hope?" is "at once practical and theoretical, in such a fashion that the practical serves as a clue that leads us to answer the theoretical question, and when this is followed out, to the speculative question."[9]

While the Dialectic of Pure Practical Reason is not restricted to the dialectical illusions arising from hope based upon the performance of duty, this constitutes its principal problem. All the discussions in it fit the formula that the practical as such is not dialectical and that the skeptical method is not needed in practical philosophy as such. The illusions are theoretical *illusions about morality*, not *moral illusions*. The moral illusion, which is heteronomy, has already been exposed in the Analytic (109 [205]).

Because the illusions to be exposed are theoretical, we cannot expect so much novelty here or advance beyond the first *Critique* as we found in the Analytic. Most of the problems have already been discussed in the Dialectic of the earlier *Critique,* though to some degree with a different outcome.

Explicitly, there is one illusion arising from the fact that practical reason is *reason* and therefore seeks the unconditioned. It may seek the unconditioned as the determining ground of the will in perfection or the will of God (41 [129–30]). This error has been dealt with in the Analytic. Or, when the true unconditioned condition of morality (the moral law) is given, it may seek the unconditioned as the totality of the object of pure practical reason in the concept of the highest good and seek to know it theoretically (108 [203]). This is resolved in the Dialectic.

[8] *Critique of Pure Reason*, B xxii.   [9] *Ibid.*, A 805 = B 833.

There is, however, a far more important illusion that concerns Kant in the Dialectic. This is the illusion that there is a necessary conflict between theoretical and practical reason (121 [218]) and that the first *Critique* forbade him to do what he does in the second. A major part of the Dialectic is devoted to exposing this apparent conflict of reason with itself.

§ 3. THE CONCEPT OF THE HIGHEST GOOD

The concept of the highest good (*summum bonum*) is the concept of the unconditioned for the practically conditioned, i.e., the concept of a supreme end which unites all other ends. Without it, there could be no system of ends. As a putatively individual, concrete state of affairs completely determined by its definition, it is called an Ideal and not a mere Idea or concept.[10] As a system of ends, it includes not merely the form of the will but also its objects. While the Analytic, in the doctrine of the moral good, taught that the moral good is the sole object of pure practical reason, the Dialectic does not abstract from all the diverse purposes of will but defines the condition under which they can and must be synthesized in a single system. In doing this, it requires the introduction of non-moral goods under a moral condition, and the concept of this systematic connection of distinct kinds of good is that of an a priori synthetic connection of morality as *bonum supremum* with the totality of other goods (summed up as "happiness"[11]) into a whole called the *bonum consummatum* or the complete good.

There are three important questions to ask about the *summum bonum* interpreted as *bonum consummatum:* (1) Is it the determining ground of the moral will? (2) Is there a moral necessity (duty) to seek and to promote it? (3) How is it possible? We shall deal with the first two questions in this section.

1. Is the highest good the determining ground of the moral will? Repeatedly Kant says that it is not; yet, even so, his answer is not so clear and unequivocal as one might wish. Consider the two paragraphs at the end of chapter i of the Dialectic (109-10 [204-5]). The first tells us that only the moral law is the determining ground of the moral

---

[10] *Ibid.,* A 810 = B 838, A 840 = B 868.

[11] The highest good is identified in other ways, too. It is the Kingdom of God (128 [224]), the intelligible world (132 [Abbott, 230, mistranslates this passage and does not indicate the identification of the *summum bonum* with the intelligible world]), the existence of natural beings under the moral law (*Critique of Judgment,* § 86), the moral vocation of man (*Critique of Pure Reason,* A 840 = B 868). These need not be discussed separately.

will; any other makes for heteronomy. The second tells us that "the concept of it and the Idea of its existence as possible through our practical reason are likewise the determining ground of the pure will." But this is only because the moral law is included and thought in the concept. That is, it is only the law as a necessary component of the highest good that is the determining ground.[12]

This is certainly an inept way of making one point twice; it means that the highest good is not an independent determining ground of the will in addition to or in place of one of its components. It cannot be supplementary to it and leave the purity of will undefiled; but Kant is unwilling to draw this conclusion in its full force. For, he tells us, the moral will must have an object as well as a form, and, because of the finite and sensible nature of man, the concept of the possibility of the highest good is necessary to the moral disposition, but not to the definition of duty.[13] But if the "possibility of the highest good" means anything more than its necessary condition, it is to that extent incompatible with what he has said earlier and more consistently about the lawful form of the maxim itself being the object of the moral will.[14]

---

[12] *Critique of Practical Reason*, 109 (204–5). Since the object is not defined independently of the moral law, having the highest good as an object does not *ipso facto* entail heteronomy (*ibid.*, 64 [156]). But it would entail heteronomy if it were a determining ground independently of the moral law. Hence the happiness included in the *summum bonum* may be the object, but it cannot be the determining ground, although it might yet be said that the *summum bonum* is the determining ground inasmuch as it contains the law as its own condition. This is insisted upon in *Über den Gemeinspruch* . . . , VIII, 280 n.

[13] Thus it is not possible to subject the whole course of life to moral maxims unless reason connects with the moral law an outcome in exact conformity to our supreme ends (*Critique of Pure Reason*, A 812 = B 840; cf. A 811 = B 839). The will requires the conditions of the highest good as "necessary conditions for obedience to the precept" of the moral law (*Critique of Practical Reason*, 132 [229]). "The subjective effect of the law . . . the intention to promote the practically possible highest good, at least presupposes that the latter is possible" (*ibid.*, 143 [241]). The law, which causes only respect and does not recognize the need of man "to love an object," is widened at the behoof of this need so as to take up the final moral goal of reason into its determining ground, "the synthetic enlargement of the concept of the law taking place through [reference to] the natural character of man as a being of needs who cannot be indifferent to the results of his actions" (*Religion within the Limits of Reason Alone*, 6 n. [Greene and Hudson, 6 n.]). "Reason needs to assume the highest good and its conditions to prevent the highest good and, consequently, all morality from being regarded as a mere ideal, which would be the case if the highest good, the Idea of which necessarily accompanies morality, never existed" (*What Is Orientation in Thinking?* VIII, 139 [Beck, 299]). Yet that the highest good is necessary to give "firmness and effect to the moral disposition" is denied in *Über den Gemeinspruch* . . . , VIII, 279.

[14] Cf. above, pp. 133 ff.

Kant simply cannot have it both ways. He cannot say that the highest good is a motive for the pure will, and then say that it is so only under the human limitation that man must have an object which is not exclusively moral (for there is nothing moral in happiness except insofar as its condition is worthiness to be happy, and even then the moral value lies in the worthiness, not in the enjoyment). The theory of the Analytic requires him to deny that the concept of the highest good provides an autonomous motive. While the hope for the highest good may in fact be a necessary incentive to do that to which the concept of duty would not move man, it is clear that to admit the latter human—all-too-human—fact into the determination of conduct in accord with moral norms is to surrender autonomy.

The existence or even the possibility of the *summum bonum*, therefore, cannot be held, in consistency with his settled views, to be logically or ethically necessary as a motive to genuine morality. At most, the hope for it may be psychologically necessary to a semblance of morality, perhaps to the highest semblance of it which can be attained by man; belief in its possibility may be a legitimate accompaniment of morality which is pure and autonomous. But whether such a "may" could be changed to an "is"—this is an empirical question, and no consistent answer to it seems to be found in the various parts of Kant's works.

2. What is the relation of the highest good to the moral law with respect to practice? Kant tells us that we are commanded by reason to seek to realize the highest good. If the highest good were not possible, the moral law would be null and void.[15] It is for this reason that it seems to him to be so essential to show the highest good to be possible.

Yet Kant is almost casual in introducing his readers to this command of reason. None of the formulations of the categorical imperative have had this content. In the *Metaphysics of Morals*, where he will be directly concerned with what the law requires of us, the highest good, as he developed the concept here, is not among the "ends which are also duties." And it is easy to see why this command of reason is not fully expounded: it does not exist.

Or at least it does not exist as a separate command, independent of the categorical imperative, which is developed without this concept. For suppose I do all in my power—which is all any moral decree can demand of me—to promote the highest good, what am I to do? Simply act out of respect for the law, which I already knew. I can do absolutely nothing else toward apportioning happiness in accordance with

[15] *Critique of Practical Reason*, 114 (210). This is strongly denied elsewhere, e.g., *ibid.*, 142–43 (241); *Critique of Judgment*, § 87 (V, 451 [302]).

desert—that is the task of a moral governor of the universe, not of a laborer in the vineyard. It is not *my* task; my task is to realize the one condition of the *summum bonum* which is within my power (143 n. [242 n.]); it is seriously misleading to say that there is a command to seek the highest good which is different from the command to fulfil the requirements of duty.

The two questions (p. 242) must therefore be answered in the negative. The highest good is a synthetic concept, but all the moral consequences drawn from it (as motive, as object) are drawn from one of its members (*bonum supremum*), not from both (*bonum consummatum*).

The truth of the matter is that the concept of the highest good is not a practical concept at all, but a dialectical Ideal of reason. It is not important in Kant's philosophy for any practical consequences it might have, for it has none except those drawn from the concept of *bonum supremum*. It is important for the architectonic purpose of reason in uniting under one Idea the two legislations of reason,[16] the theoretical and the practical, in a practical-dogmatic metaphysics wholly distinct from the metaphysics of morals. Reason cannot tolerate a chaos of ends; it demands the a priori synthesis of them into a system. An impartial observer cannot approve of a disparity between happiness and worthiness to be happy, but neither in nature nor in the moral law can Kant find anything except a contingent connection between them. If, therefore, we are to conceive of a system of ends, as reason requires for its own satisfaction (and not for obedience to a law which speaks with commanding authority long before its credentials are presented), then we must suppose that the highest good is possible. But we must not allow ourselves to be deceived, as I believe Kant was, into thinking its possibility is directly necessary to morality or that we have a moral duty to promote it, distinct from our duty as determined by the form and not by the content or object of the moral law.

§ 4. THE ANTINOMY OF PURE PRACTICAL REASON

If the reader accepts the conclusions that I have just drawn, he can hardly attach to an antinomy in the concept of the highest good the importance which Kant professes to find in it. Believing, however inconsistently, that the moral law stands or falls with the possibility or impossibility of the highest good,[17] Kant gives a quite exaggerated

---

[16] The assumption of the highest good is definitely assigned to theoretical reason at *Critique of Pure Reason*, A 809 = B 837, and *Critique of Judgment*, §§ 83–84; cf. also *Critique of Pure Reason*, A 839 = B 867.

[17] *Critique of Pure Reason*, A 811 = B 839; *Critique of Practical Reason*, 114 (210).

importance to the antinomy that he believes he finds. He goes so far as to say that the exposure of the "self-contradictions of the pure practical reason" compels us to undertake a critique of it (109 [204]), assigning a role to this antinomy that we have seen the theoretical antinomy actually had in the birth of the first.[18] This is no doubt a mere *façon de parler*, and when we examine the antinomy we shall find that it is really quite a poor thing, wholly unable to carry this great historical and systematic burden. We shall also find, regrettably, that Kant's usual high-quality workmanship is not much in evidence in the discussion of the antinomy.

I shall, first, give a summary presentation of Kant's argument and then see what revisions it needs in order to make it actually conform to his intentions.

The *summum bonum* is not a simple concept, as the Stoics and Epicureans believed in identifying the motives to virtue with those directed to the attainment of happiness. It is a synthetic concept with two independent components,[19] not a concept whose predicate is found by analysis. But it is an a priori concept, since reason requires a necessary connection between the two members, viz., happiness in proportion to worthiness to be happy.[20]

As a synthetic concept, the connection between the components must be that of ground and consequent. There are two possibilities: thesis—the desire for happiness must be the necessary and sufficient ground of or motive to morality; antithesis—the maxim of virtue must be the necessary and sufficient condition of happiness.[21] The first is absolutely impossible, as shown in the Analytic. The second is impossible in the world as we know it in experience, for here happiness depends upon circumstances and prudence, not upon mere intention and purity of heart. Any connection between them in this world is contingent and accidental, and this does not satisfy reason's demand for a necessary connection. Hence the connection is neither analytic nor synthetic a priori, and the concept of the highest good is therefore

[18] Cf. above, p. 25, n. 4. In *Prolegomena*, § 52a, however, he asserts the uniqueness of the theoretical antinomies.

[19] Both Stoics and Epicureans denied this, differing only in respect to what was the *analysandum* (*Critique of Practical Reason*, 112 [208]).

[20] *Ibid.*, 111, 113 (207, 209). I wish to correct the error of having omitted the word "pure" in both editions of my translation. The first sentence of the section beginning on p. 113 (207) should read: ". . . assumed by a pure practical reason. . . ."

[21] *Ibid.*, 113 (209). Note that the identification of these two antinomic propositions as thesis and antitheses is not made by Kant himself and is a matter of dispute, as pointed out later in the text.

"impossible before reason." With its exposure, the moral law, which commands that we pursue it as a necessary object, is discovered to be nugatory.

The second of the possibilities, however, is not absolutely false. It is false only under the assumption that the connection is one that must be found in accord with the laws of nature; and even then it is only subjectively false, i.e., our reason cannot conceive how it would be possible, but it cannot show that it is impossible (145 [244]). Just as the antinomy of freedom was resolved by assigning the truth of the thesis to man's supersensible nature, here it is resolved by assigning the connection between the two components to an intelligible world. Thus the *possibility* of the highest good is established,[22] if we assume that there is an intelligible world governed by a moral being with requisite power to apportion happiness in accordance with virtue.

Thus Kant. But it should be obvious that we do not have here an antinomy in any strict sense. First, in spite of his statement (109 [204]) that he is concerned with the "self-contradiction of pure practical reason," the two propositions are not contradictories. Second, each does not have an independent warrant;[23] one of them is false on its face. The whole antinomy is devised and artificial. Third, its resolution is not what one would expect from the proffered analogy to the third antinomy. For there the antithesis is vindicated in the phenomenal world and the thesis in the noumenal; here the thesis is not vindicated at all.

Even so, it is possible to reformulate the antinomy so that it better conforms to Kant's purposes. I shall give two such statements:

I. THESIS: *The maxim of virtue must be the cause of happiness.*
   ANTITHESIS: *The maxim of virtue is not the efficient cause of happiness;* happiness can result only from successful use of knowledge of the laws of nature.

---

22 *Ibid.*, 119 (215). The argument has been interrupted by a discourse on the connection between happiness and virtue not mediated by the intelligible world (pp. 115–19 [211–15]). These paragraphs might well be set apart from the rest and called a "Remark." We have already commented upon them in chap. xii. The connection between virtue and happiness in the highest good is made possible in an intelligible world of perfect beings without the mediation of God, according to the *Critique of Pure Reason*, A 810 = B 838, where it is called a "system of self-rewarding morality." But for us men this is not sufficient, or, rather, we are not sufficient to it.

23 Each proposition in an antinomy is "not merely in itself free from contradiction but finds conditions of its necessity in the very nature of reason—only that, unfortunately, the assertion of the opposite has, on its side, grounds that are just as valid and necessary" (*ibid.*, A 421 = B 449).

This is a real antinomy, since the propositions are contradictory, not contrary; each expresses an inescapable interest of reason (moral and theoretical); and each is a true formula for one of these interests. Furthermore, the resolution of this antinomy conforms to that of the third antinomy in the first *Critique*. The antithesis is and remains (unfortunately for the virtuous) true of the sensuous world; the wind is not tempered to the shorn lamb, and the rain falls on the just and the unjust alike. The thesis is false in "a system of nature which is merely the object of the senses" (115 [211]). But it may be true if there is an intelligible world in which there is a moral government distributing happiness (in the sensuous world, under natural conditions)[24] according to laws holding in the intelligible world (laws of the moral intentions of persons). Hence the pursuit of virtue does not rule out the hope, based upon the possibility, of a proportionate happiness.

Another statement of the antinomy[25] is possible, and it has the merit of keeping the *summum bonum* in the center of attention throughout.

II. THESIS: *The summum bonum is possible. Proof:* The moral law requires it.
  ANTITHESIS: *The summum bonum is not possible. Proof:* The connection between virtue and happiness is neither analytical nor synthetic a priori nor empirically given.
  RESOLUTION: The antithesis is true of the sensible world if the laws of nature have excusive sovereignty; the thesis may be true of the intelligible world because the synthetic connection of virtue (as ground) to happiness (as consequent) is not *absolutely* impossible.

In either formulation we are enabled to see that the concept of the highest good is not impossible. Kant, believing that it is morally necessary, then turns to those conditions which would make it actual if superadded to morality, which is the only one of the conditions that lies within our control and competence.[26]

---

[24] Kant says that the effect must be in the sensuous world. He therefore does not base the postulate of immortality upon the need for happiness in another world as the locus of this reward. But in this life the adjustment is not made. The four paragraphs which I have suggested should be set apart as a "Remark on a Self-rewarding System of Morality" do not speak of the moral contentment in this life as being happiness. This would suggest that the happiness in the *summum bonum* must be that of an afterlife, not under a system of nature. So, even before we are ready to take up the postulate of immortality, we run into an obscurity, the first of many we shall find in this notion (cf. below, chap. xiv, § 4).

[25] Slightly modified from a proposal by August Messer, *Kants Ethik*, p. 88.

[26] The twofold division of his task, mentioned on p. 110 (205), seems to refer to this; but this division did not actually serve to articulate the succeeding sections of the Dialectic. Perhaps Kant had intended a more extensive discussion of the postulate of freedom prior to the introduction of the other two postulates; then this division would apply.

§ 5. THE PRIMACY OF PURE PRACTICAL OVER THEORETICAL REASON

The question is: Have we a right to use concepts of reason, and to assert objects for them, which are beyond the sphere of knowledge marked off for and by theoretical reason? It is not sufficient to point out merely that the interests of practice extend beyond those of theory. Theory alone does not decide between the thesis and the antithesis of the third antinomy, and theory would leave us in a state of vacillation which could be ended, if theory were the only use of reason, by a decision forced upon us by the needs of practice.[27] This decision would indeed be a decision in favor of the thesis. The failure of theoretical reason to decide between thesis and antithesis would permit us to employ the requisite "faith" in the claims of dogmatism but could not give faith the "form of science," i.e., show its systematic rational structure.[28]

There is not now, after the Analytic's demonstration of the function of pure practical reason, any remnant of arbitrariness or irrationality left in the decision that must be made. We do not have the contrast between "reason" and "faith" but that between "theoretical reason" and "rational faith," i.e., an a priori faculty that goes beyond theory. A contrast exists, but not necessarily an opposition, because (*a*) there is only one reason with two interests, not two reasons with opposing interests (121 [217]), and (*b*) the practical does not require us to go against anything that the theoretical reason has established or can establish. Put in classical theological terms: the things of faith are beyond the things of *theoretical* reason but not beyond the things of reason *simpliciter;* and there are no valid things of faith that are against the things of theoretical reason.

Theoretical reason pushes inquiry to the farthest limits in striving to reach the unconditioned. It cannot do this by attaining knowledge of the unconditioned, but its interest is whatever furthers the exercise of this function.[29] Its true interest, therefore, is not in some special cognition, or definition, of the unconditioned but solely in the restriction of speculative folly. The interest of practical reason is the "determination of the will with respect to the final and perfect end" (120

---

[27] *Critique of Pure Reason,* A 475 = B 503.

[28] *Ibid.,* A 470 = B 498.

[29] There is an inconsistency in Kant's use of the word "interest." He identifies interest with (*a*) the end of the use of a faculty and (*b*) a principle under which its exercise is advanced. Thus, of theoretical reason, *a* is "the knowledge of objects up to the highest a priori principles," and *b* is the establishment of limits which cannot be breached by "monstrosities of reason" which interfere with its orderly progress. Its interest in sense *b* is the restriction of speculative folly (*Critique of Practical Reason,* 120, 121 [217]). The interest of theoretical reason appears to the dogmatic metaphysician to be *a;* to the critical metaphysician like Kant, it is *b*.

[216]), and whatever shows this end to be possible furthers the practical interest.

The two interests may superficially appear to be in conflict, but they are not opposed to each other if the interest of theoretical reason is not some end which it cannot achieve (knowledge of things in themselves) but only the guaranty of the orderly progress of science, and if the interest of practical reason is not presented as cognition but as determination of actions. Then judgments about what furthers the latter interest can be compatible with the former interest. These judgments will not be cognitive judgments known theoretically to be true; they will be only postulates.

The *Critique of Pure Reason* itself prepares the way for the assertion of the primacy of the practical over the theoretical interest of reason. The interest of speculative reason in the Ideas needed by pure practical reason is very small;[30] yet the Ideas needed by speculative reason for its own purpose are the same as those needed by pure practical reason;[31] and theoretical reason can present them only as problematic concepts.[32] Practical reason, if there were a conflict between it and theoretical reason, would enter the contest with the "right of possession" on its own side.[33] In the absence of opposition, the question concerns solely which maxim should be followed: to refuse stubbornly to admit any non-empirical objects (the canon of Epicurus) or to "admit certain theoretical positions" inseparably bound with a priori practical principles but going "beyond any possible insight of the speculative reason (although not contradictory to it)" (120 [216]). The doctrine of primacy prevents what is a difference from becoming an incompatibility, by establishing an order of subordination instead of co-ordination. And in this subordination the practical has primacy because "every interest is ultimately practical."[34]

If theoretical reason can be assured that these "theoretical positions" are *required* by the practical interest and exceed, but do not *conflict* with, its own interest, this primacy is assured. Kant claims that the requirement is shown by the resolution of the antinomy of practical reason and the necessity of the conception of the *summum bonum*. Sections 6–9 of this chapter of the *Critique* are devoted to the establishment of the absence of conflict.

---

[30] *Critique of Pure Reason*, A 798 = B 826.   [31] *Ibid.*, A 796 = B 824.

[32] *Ibid.*, A 796 = B 824: "Reason has a presentiment of objects which possess a great interest for it. But when it follows the path of pure speculation, in order to approach them, they fly before it."

[33] *Ibid.*, A 777 = B 805.

[34] *Ibid.*, A 816 = B 844; *Critique of Practical Reason*, 121 (218).

§ 6. THE POSTULATES OF PURE PRACTICAL REASON[35]

Kant warns us at the beginning[36] against confusing "postulate" as he uses this word in the *Critique* with the usage of the mathematician. Since the mathematician does not now mean what Kant says he meant then, his explanation, meant to clarify matters, succeeds (through no fault of his own) in making them only more obscure. It is therefore necessary to speak more fully of mathematical postulates.

In mathematics, a postulate was, for Kant and his contemporaries,[37] an indemonstrable practical (i.e., technically practical) proposition giving a rule for the synthesis of an object in intuition, when the possibility of the object is known a priori. Mathematical proof is by means of constructions of objects in intuition, and postulates are the a priori rules for such construction. For example, the following is called a postulate, what is postulated being the possibility of the action of constructing a circle: "Around the center C, with radius CA or diameter AB, to describe a circle."[38] The use of the word "postulate" in more recent mathematics differs from that in Kant's theory of mathematics and, in fact, closely resembles the meaning that it has in his moral philosophy. This is because recent mathematics has become "deductive" instead of "constructive," and a postulate is an assumption made in order that some mathematical purpose may be achieved. Thus instead of the postulate being, in the eighteenth-century manner, "To construct a parallel to a line through a point," it is now the assumption "Through a point external to a line in a plane, one and only one parallel line can exist." A postulate now differs from an axiom, if at all, only in not being intuitively certain and resembles it in being theoretical instead of practical. With the general acceptance of a game theory of mathematics, the difference between axiom and postulate is only verbal. For Kant, on the other hand, axioms differed from postulates in being both intuitively certain and theoretical rather than practical. No philosophical proposition was, for him, axiomatic.[39]

In philosophy, however, a postulate is an assertion of the possibility

---

[35] The specific postulates will be discussed in chap. xiv.

[36] *Critique of Practical Reason*, 11 n. (96 n.). Cf. *Critique of Pure Reason*, A 234 = B 287: "In mathematics a postulate means the practical proposition which contains nothing save the synthesis through which we first give ourselves an object and generate its concept...." Also *Vorlesungen über Logik*, § 38, and Reflexion 4370.

[37] Similarly, Wolff, *Philosophia rationalis sive logica*, § 269, and Baumgarten, *Acroasis logica*, § 250.

[38] Cf. Gottfried Martin, *Arithmetik und Kombinatorik bei Kant* (Itzehoe, 1938), p. 19; cf. also p. 21.

[39] *Critique of Pure Reason*, A 732 = B 760; *Prize Essay*, II, 278 ff. (Beck, 264 ff.).

or actuality[40] of an object as a corollary to the acknowledgment of a necessary law. The practical proposition is the law (or rather its associated imperative); the postulate is a theoretical proposition, but it is not a proposition that is theoretically (i.e., apodictically) certain.

Kant likewise discriminates between hypothesis and postulate.[41] Given some *X*, whether merely actual or necessary, *Y* is postulated if *Y* is known a priori to be the only condition under which *X* is known to be even possible; or *Y* is hypothesized if it is merely assumed as an explanation for *X*.[42] Sometimes Kant writes as if the difference lies in the nature of the purposes involved in the explanation of *X*. If *X* is necessary and *Y* is a priori essential to it, then *Y* is postulated; if knowledge of *X* is an arbitary (theoretical) purpose, *Y* is hypothesized, even though it is necessary to it.[43] This is Kant's meaning in saying that we must postulate, e.g., the existence of God because morality (the "*X*" of our schema) is necessary and God is necessary to it, while the existence of God is only hypothesized in natural theology or speculative metaphysics—not because the concept is any less essential there but because the purpose is arbitrary. Moreover, a hypothesis is a species of cognition which can be raised to certainty by increase in knowledge (e.g., a scientific hypothesis) or, if it is based only on a subjective need of reason (as is the hypothesis of God's existence in natural theology), it is a mere hypothesis that cannot possibly be raised to the dignity of knowledge, though it claims to be knowledge. A postulate, on the other hand, is not subject either to supplementation or correction by new facts, nor does it, when properly understood, claim to be an objective cognition. Still, it is "in degree inferior to no cognition even though in kind it is wholly different."[44]

A postulate in the *Critique of Practical Reason*, then, is "a theoretical proposition which is not as such demonstrable, but which is an inseparable corollary of an unconditionally valid practical law" (122 [219]). The law demands an action but not the acceptance of any

[40] Each is asserted in *Critique of Practical Reason*, 134 (231–32); cf. also below, p. 259, nn. 1 and 2.

[41] Also between a presupposition and a postulate: "At some future time we shall show that the moral laws do not merely presuppose the existence of a supreme being, but also, as themselves in a different connection absolutely necessary, justify us in postulating it" (*Critique of Pure Reason*, A 634 = B 662). Similarly, *Critique of Practical Reason*, 142 (240).

[42] *Ibid.*, A 633 = B 661. Accordingly, a postulate is called a "necessary hypothesis" in *Critique of Practical Reason*, 11 n. (96 n.).

[43] *Critique of Practical Reason*, 11 n. (96 n.); *What Is Orientation in Thinking?* VIII, 141 (Beck, 300–301).

[44] *What Is Orientation in Thinking?* VIII, 141 (Beck, 301).

theoretical corollary. We accept the corollary not because it is commanded but because, in putting ourselves under the moral law, "the principle which determines our judgment, while subjectively a need, is the ground of a maxim of moral assent, as a means of promoting that which is objectively (practically) necessary."[45] That is, I am commanded to seek the highest good; I can do so only under the condition, objectively, that the highest good is possible and, subjectively, that I believe it is possible; but I am not commanded to *believe* anything (144 [242]). I am commanded to do something I could not do and would not recognize that I ought to do, unless I held, without objective proof, that certain things are possible.

If, however, as we have argued in § 3, the command to seek the *summum bonum* is merely the command to do my duty, the close connection of the moral law with the postulates (with the exception of that of freedom) cannot be established. While Kant thinks that the connection is a rational one, it is, so to speak, subjectively rational, like the need to assume the existence of God in speculative metaphysics (as an object of a hypothesis). It has only "practical reality," which means merely "validity for practice" and not for knowledge. In fact, however, even this is to claim too much, for it is only because of the natural character of man that he needs any supplement (in the form of belief) for the performance of his duty.[46] In the light of this fact, it is hard to agree that Kant has met the difficult issue posed by Wizenmann (143 n. [242 n.]).

---

[45] *Critique of Practical Reason*, 146 (244). In *Zum ewigen Frieden in der Philosophie* (VIII, 418 n.; not to be confused with *Perpetual Peace*) it is said that a postulate is an imperative, commanding a certain maxim and not directed to an object. While this conforms to Kant's statement that the law (meaning the imperative) is a practical postulate (*Critique of Practical Reason*, 46 [135], denied at 132 [229]), it is not possible to reconcile this isolated statement with the full teaching of the *Critique*. Indeed, it is not possible even to reconcile this note with the teaching in the body of the essay in which it is found, according to which a postulate is a practically necessary theoretical proposition about an unknowable object.

[46] "All men could have enough [incentive to the fulfilment of their duty] if they would only hold themselves [as they ought] merely to the precept of pure reason in the law. What do they need to know of the outcome of their moral actions, which the course of the world will bring about? For them it is enough that they do their duty, though it be that this life is all and that in it happiness and worth never come together. But because of the inescapable limitations of man. . . ." (*Religion within the Limits of Reason Alone*, VI, 6 n. [Greene and Hudson, 6 n.]). See *Foundations of the Metaphysics of Morals*, 411–12 (28), where it is stated that moral philosophy abstracts, even more than theoretical philosophy, from the peculiar nature of human reason. The doctrine of the postulates is obviously at variance with this; the statement in the *Foundations* concerns the formulation of the law, not that of duty and the postulates.

The need of reason to believe in the existence of a highest good and to postulate the existence of its conditions does indeed arise from "an objective determining ground of the will," but only because of "inescapable human limitations." It is therefore not a "need of pure reason" but a need of the all-too-human reason. Yet this criticism of Kant's reply to Wizenmann does not consign Kant a place among the pragmatistic proponents of a "will to believe," since James, as a typical example, held the "right to believe" to spring from a "will to believe" precisely because pure reason could not, for him, be practical. The pragmatic need to believe rests on a failure of reason to demonstrate what we men must believe to be true if we are to be moral. In this predicament the pragmatist claims that we have the right to "consult our passional nature," whereas Kant says we consult reason, which is more than a theoretical cognitive faculty. Hence Kant has, or claims to have, a rational criterion of and motive for belief, which is lacking to the pragmatist. But, if my argument is correct, there can be no need of *pure* reason for the postulates, not because pure reason may not have some needs but because its need is exhausted in issuing the moral command. If reason is taken in the broader sense of concern with the promotion of the good under human limitations, the difference between his view and that of the pragmatists becomes chiefly verbal, and Kant answered Wizenmann no better than James answered his critics.

But let us return to Kant's text.[47] Propositions which were problematical for speculative reason are now shown to have objects (134 [232]), since, if they did not, their non-existence would render the law null and void.[48] In willing to do what duty requires, I do not know that there is a God, though I am, in a literal sense, morally certain of it; *it* is not certain, but *I* am certain.[49] In willing to do what duty requires, I act as if there were a God, or "I will that there be a God."[50] I am not thereby enabled to have any insight into the nature of God or the other conditions of the highest good; no synthetic propositions

---

[47] The argument of chap. ii, § vii, is a continuation of chap. i, § ii of the Analytic (50–57 [140–47]).

[48] "I inevitably believe in the existence of God and in a future life, since my moral principles would [otherwise] be themselves overthrown, and I cannot disclaim them without becoming abhorrent in my own eyes" (*Critique of Pure Reason*, A 828 = B 856).

[49] *Ibid.*, A 829 = B 857.

[50] *Critique of Practical Reason*, 143 (241). It is on this point that the fictionalist interpretation of Kant is based. But Kant does not meet the entrance requirements of the fictionalist school: the existence of God is not theoretically false and to be accepted only as a practical fiction.

can be made about them, for no intuition occurs to connect my concepts with their objects. Theoretical reason gains nothing by this addition, for it cannot make any use of the concepts which practical reason hands to it beyond the use it already had for them as regulative concepts (136 [233–34]). Hence the moral argument does not breach the walls that theoretical reason so solidly built between what can and what cannot be known. The task of theoretical reason with respect to these objects is and remains merely negative, a police function:[51] to prevent fanaticism, to purify them of anthropomorphic elements which would sensualize them and destroy even their moral function (141 [239]), and to ward off dogmatic attacks on them.[52]

§ 7. BELIEF AND IGNORANCE

The epistemic mode in which a postulate is held is a "faith of pure practical reason," "moral belief," or "rational belief."[53] Through this epistemic mode, Kant encompassed within philosophy what had previously been an epistemic resource outside of, or hostile to, philosophy. The faith-reason contrast before Kant was parallel to that between revealed theology and philosophy. With Kant, several kinds of faith are distinguished, and one of them is tamed and domesticated into philosophy.

Faith or belief, however rational it is, remains contrasted with knowledge. Knowledge is assent on grounds that are both objectively and subjectively sufficient; mere opinion is assent on grounds that are neither objectively nor subjectively sufficient; but faith is assent on grounds that are subjectively sufficient in spite of being objectively insufficient.[54] The subjectively sufficient grounds may be need in speculation (doctrinal belief), revelation and ecclesiastical dogma (historical belief), need for the purposes of some arbitrary use of skill (pragmatic belief), or reason's needs for the satisfaction of duty (rational belief, a belief of pure reason). The former are grounds of theoretical beliefs; the latter, of practical beliefs.[55]

[51] *Critique of Pure Reason,* B xxv.

[52] *Ibid.,* A 829 = B 857.

[53] *Critique of Practical Reason,* 126, 144, 146 (223, 242, 244); *Critique of Pure Reason,* A 828 = B 856; *What Is Orientation in Thinking?* VIII, 141 (Beck, 300); *Foundations of the Metaphysics of Morals,* 462 (83).

[54] *Critique of Pure Reason,* A 822 = B 850.

[55] *Ibid.,* A 825 = B 853; *What Is Orientation in Thinking?* VIII, 141 (Beck, 300). That the distinction between doctrinal and rational belief may have arisen in Kant's response to Hamann's version of Hume is suggested by Philip Merlan, "Hamann et les Dialogues de Hume," *Revue de métaphysique et de morale,* LIX (1954), 285–89.

The faith of pure reason is needed to "orient ourselves"[56] in the "empty space" of thought beyond experience, in that "wide and stormy ocean, the native home of illusion, where many a fogbank and many a swiftly moving iceberg give the deceptive appearance of farther shores."[57] It must be a faith in objects of practical reason, since theoretical reason, in default of intuition, gives no point of orientation. Subjective needs, which vary from man to man, have no place in the determination of these objects, for they all concern objects of experience whereof knowledge can be attained. In this, Wizenmann was correct (143 n. [242 n.]). But to be subjective does not mean to be arbitrary and contingent; "subjective" means dependent upon the nature of the subject, and this can be interpreted either a priori or a posteriori. Subjective needs require satisfaction and may be validly satisfied after knowledge has reached the end of its tether; that is one reason why it is so important to determine a priori the difference between a mere boundary and a limit of knowledge.[58] Only when we are sure that theory has been brought to a stalemate, can the resource of faith be used.

This faith cannot be commanded, and it is not essential to have it in order to be moral.[59] But to have it is to enjoy a positive moral worth,[60] and morality, though compatible with "doubtful faith," is not compatible with a dogmatic unbelief which would deny possibility to the object of pure practical reason.[61] But in no sense does faith precede morals as premise, and whatever faith contains as a surplus beyond what is needed for moral exercise is superstition and fanaticism. The history of religion is the history of the gradual replacement of historical faith by its kernel of rational faith, which the Christian religion has contained, but in a masked way.[62]

But is not faith a very paltry substitute for the kind of knowledge that the first *Critique* showed to be impossible? Not at all, Kant

[56] *What Is Orientation in Thinking?* VIII, 136 n. (Beck, 296 n.); cf. *Critique of Pure Reason*, A 475 = B 503.

[57] *Critique of Pure Reason*, A 236 = B 295; cf. also A 395–96.

[58] *Prolegomena*, § 59.

[59] *Critique of Judgment*, § 87 (V, 452 [303]). But one who does not have it must surrender a purpose he ought to have. Spinoza is Kant's example of such a truncated moral philosopher.

[60] *Fortschritte der Metaphysik*, XX, 298.

[61] *Critique of Judgment*, § 91 (V, 472 [325]).

[62] *Religion within the Limits of Reason Alone*, VI, 116, 118, etc. (Greene and Hudson, 106, 109, etc.); *Mutmasslicher Anfang der Menschengeschichte, passim; Streit der Fakultäten*, VII, 38–47.

answers. While in the precritical period he did indeed believe knowledge of the supersensible was both possible and compatible with needs of morals (though not essential to them), in the critical period he not only denied that it was possible because of the dialectical illusions but asserted this to be a victory of reason, and not merely of practical reason. For if knowledge of the supersensible were possible, it would be merely an extension of theoretical knowledge and would carry into the supersensible realm the procedures and conclusions of science in the world of nature; and this would be at most a quantitative aggrandizement of reason but would exclude a more extensive, but quite different, employment of reason—the practical. In order to give reason full scope for its development, therefore, Kant says, "I have . . . found it necessary to deny knowledge in order to make room for faith."[63]

The price paid, however, for saving morals from the dogmatism of metaphysics is ignorance, as the other side of faith. But suppose it were possible to have knowledge of the supersensuous and suppose, furthermore, that the objects I knew there were not, in fact, objects under laws of phenomena. Suppose, that is, that it were possible to establish a rational, speculative metaphysics which would *not* be a foundation for "all that unbelief, always very dogmatic, which wars with morality";[64] suppose that we had the "elevated knowledge" of God, freedom, and immortality that some boasted of and thereby gained Kant's withering contempt[65]—what then?

A theme celebrated in the Faust tradition[66] is elaborated in the last section of the Dialectic.[67]

Granted all these impossible suppositions: this knowledge, if the accession to it did not bring with it a change in our "whole nature," would change rational faith into pragmatic faith, and virtue would be impossible (146 [245]). "Most actions conforming to the law would be done from fear, few would be done from hope, none from duty. The moral worth of actions, on which alone the worth of the person and even of the world depends in the eyes of supreme wisdom, would not exist at all. The conduct of man, *so long as his nature remained*

---

[63] *Critique of Pure Reason*, B xxx. Similarly, Coleridge: the existence of God "could not be intellectually more evident without being morally less effective; without counteracting its own end by sacrificing the life of faith to the world mechanism of a worthless because compulsory assent" (*Biographia literaria*, chap. x).

[64] *Critique of Pure Reason*, B xxx.

[65] *Critique of Practical Reason*, 5 (89–90); cf. *Prolegomena*, IV, 373 n. (Beck, 122 n.).

[66] Especially Chamisso's *Faust* (1803).

[67] Cf. also *Critique of Pure Reason*, A 476 = B 504; A 801 = B 829.

as it now is, would be changed into mere mechanism, where, as in a puppet show, everything would gesticulate nicely but no life would be found in the figures" (147 [245], italics added).

Kant said, in the first *Critique*, that the moral interest was on the side of dogmatism (the side of the theses). That the thesis should be true is indeed the interest of pure practical reason; but that it should be known to be true conflicts with the moral interest under the human limitations. Kant said, as a young man, long before his moral theory was developed, "It is necessary that one be convinced of the existence of God; but not so necessary that one should prove it."[68] Now the old man discovers the deepest moral root of this Faust-like apprehension of the danger of knowledge of secrets of the other world—secrets he himself had played with when he wrote his *Dreams of a Spirit-Seer*. In the absence of knowledge, respect for law allows us a conjecture or a glimpse into the mystery;' but "God and eternity in their awful majesty" do not stand "unceasingly before our eyes" so as to blind us to our precariously human condition and to obliterate that state of mind in which we imperfect beings, naturally bent upon happiness, can exercise our autonomy. "It is therefore good that we do not know there is a God, but only believe it."[69] Against the Enlightenment's exaggeration of the saving power of knowledge, which was a securalization of pre-Enlightenment exaggeration of the faith in and knowledge of God, Kant stands between Rousseau and Goethe: "Ein guter Mensch in seinem dunklen Drange / Ist sich des rechten Weges wohlbewusst."[70] Other knowledge of the supersensible he does not need and should not have.

---

[68] *Einzig möglicher Beweisgrund* . . . , end (II, 163).

[69] Reflexion 4996; cf. *Critique of Practical Reason*, 148 (246).

[70] *Faust*, Prolog im Himmel.

XIV

The Postulates of Pure Practical Reason; Commentary on Dialectic, Chapter II, Sections IV and V; and Conclusion

§ 1. INTRODUCTION

In chapters xi and xiii it was mentioned that Kant uses the word "postulate" rather loosely and that his list of practical postulates varies from place to place. There is some diversity even within the *Critique of Practical Reason*. The possibility[1] and the actuality[2] of God, freedom, and immortality; the possibility of the *summum bonum*;[3] and the moral law itself[4] are named as postulates. But, in spite of this diversity, Kant's meaning and intention in the *Critique* are clear: the three postulates, officially and deliberately so called, are the actual freedom of the will, the immortality of the soul, and the existence of God.

We have already discussed the concept of freedom and the sense in which freedom is a postulate.[5] There remains, therefore, in this chapter to discuss only the two remaining postulates. We shall begin, however, by examining once again the concept of postulate in the light of how a postulate is "demonstrated," then examine the two postulates themselves, and conclude with a discussion of the relation between ethics and religion. The very last section comments upon Kant's conclusion to the whole work, which, though it follows the Methodology, follows smoothly upon the Dialectic.

---

[1] *Critique of Practical Reason*, 134 (232): ". . . Through the practical law, which requires the *existence* of the highest good possible in the world, there is postulated the *possibility* of those objects of pure speculative reason."

[2] *Ibid.*, next sentence: "Practical reason inexorably requires the *existence* of those objects for the *possibility* of its practically and absolutely necessary object, the highest good." *Ibid.*, 125 (221): ". . . The postulate of the *possibility* of a highest derived good (the best world) is at the same time the postulate of the *reality* of a highest original good, namely, the existence of God" (all italics supplied).

[3] Cf. the just preceding quotation.

[4] *Ibid.*, 46 (135); denied at 132 (229).   [5] In chap. xi, § 14.

Kant does not use the words "moral argument" in the second *Critique*, but it is the name by which he refers to this argument in the third. Although it is not an entirely suitable name, it has become so widely accepted that it is useless to try to reject it; but we must try to be very clear in deciding what a "moral argument" is; else we shall find the term so vague that it covers some arguments that are logically quite different from the argument first called a "moral" one.

It is universally recognized that a value-judgment or a practical proposition containing an "ought" cannot be derived by an argument from premises which are exclusively factual. Enthymemes in which this is done always require a hidden value-premise, which is omitted simply because it is thought to be obvious. Only a philosopher would object to an argument that said, "You ought to take an aspirin because you have a headache." But even he would make himself tedious if he insisted upon completing such syllogisms. Still, such an argument is not valid unless the value-premise is supplied.

A moral argument is one in which a *factual* conclusion is reached from a *value*-premise, either immediately or taken in conjunction with a factual premise.[6] Such an argument likewise is formally invalid. It cannot be expected that a philosopher of Kant's skill and stature should be guilty of such a sophomoric blunder; yet the ordinary interpretation of the moral argument attributes this nonsense to him.

Italicizing two words in Kant's definition of a postulate shows him to be aware of the danger of this kind of error, though whether he finally avoided it in its most subtle and insidious form is not a matter that can be decided by examination of a single sentence of his text. He says a postulate is "a theoretical proposition which is not *as such* demonstrable, but which is an inseparable corollary of an unconditionally valid practical law" (122 [219]). We must now examine this "*as such*."

Whether a proposition is theoretical or practical depends ultimately upon its function, not upon its formal structure or content, though we have the means, syntactic or semantic, to make these functions clear. "*A* causes *B*" is a theoretical proposition; "Since you wish to have *B*, do *A*" is a practical proposition; "*A* is a means to *B*" has some of the characteristics of both. Just as we can move from theoretical to practical propositions by supplying a practical premise (e.g., "If you want *X*, you ought to do what will lead to *X*"), it would appear that we

---

[6] If the value-term is the middle, then, of course, a factual conclusion can be validly reached from two value-premises.

might move from a practical to a theoretical proposition by supplying another premise. The only premise that would serve, however, would be a value-premise, giving a syllogism in which the value-term was the middle. We have already seen that the moral law is a theoretical proposition describing a priori how a pure rational being would act and that the categorical imperative expresses this law in imperative form (as a practical proposition) for rational beings whose will is not pure. We can easily state a syllogism from which the theoretical statement about a pure rational being can be derived from the practical imperative for us: The maxim I ought to act upon is one that a rational being would act upon; the maxim I ought to act upon is Y; therefore, Y *is* a maxim for a purely rational being.

In the Dialectic's discussion of the postulates, however, the problem is not simply one of syntactics and formal logic. We come to the following situation: Given a practical proposition, Kant argues that it can be valid, even for practice, only if a theoretical proposition is assumed and if this theoretical proposition is known to be neither demonstrable nor refutable *as such*. The necessity of practically acceding to the practical proposition, therefore, is substituted for the unavailable theoretical evidence for the theoretical proposition, and the theoretical proposition is asserted on moral grounds which are epistemologically (not psychologically) subjective, that is, on grounds which are found in a "need of reason" and not on grounds of objective evidence. The theoretical proposition supported in this way is a postulate. It is valid for no theoretical purpose; and, inasmuch as all the grounds for holding it are practical, all the consequences drawn from it must likewise be restricted to their practical bearing.

Such a derivation of the theoretical proposition contributes nothing to our knowledge of tne truth of the proposition, if truth be taken as a theoretical (i.e., cognitive) predicate. Kant, as we shall see, does not always remain within the precisely valid limits of his "proof." But he tries.

Such an argument, he correctly says, does not permit us to comprehend how the Ideas of God, freedom, and immortality (the Ideas of the objects of the postulates) are possible or are to be theoretically determined; "All that is comprehended is that [they are] postulated through the moral law and for its sake" (133 [231]). If he is correct, I cannot render obedience to the moral imperative to seek the *summum bonum* unless I believe that it is possible, and I can believe it possible only if I believe in the existence of these objects. This belief is not one growing out of a mere subjective wish for the highest good, a wish I might happen not to feel; for then the imperative to seek it would be hypothetical. Nor is the belief a hypothesis for any theoretical purpose which I confidently hold for some theoretical purpose only because I need it for this purpose and know that it cannot be refuted. It is, he says, a belief that I cannot renounce and at the same time maintain my allegiance to moral law, an allegiance I cannot surrender without becoming contemptible and hateful in my own sight.

This "cannot" is meant to refer to a transcendental impossibility—not a logical one because the relation of the moral law to the existence of God is not analytical, and not a psychological one, for many a man has in fact achieved virtue in a world in which he found no comfort and support. I use the word "transcendental" in the sense of the *Critique of Pure Reason*, to refer to the conditions of a priori synthetic propositions.[7] But the quotation just given shows that the transcendental connection is not between the moral law I accept and the objective conditions of the *summum bonum;* it is not that the acknowledgment of the moral law either requires the existence of God or justifies a theoretical knowledge of God's existence; it requires only that I *believe* in God's existence. Even if God does not exist but I only believe that he exists, the *practical* consequences for obedience to the moral law are the same. A postulate, therefore, does not have to be known to be true, it does not even have to be true, for it to serve its practical function. Kant always recognizes the first of these denials. But though he does not derive knowledge of their truth in his moral arguments, he does seem to think that he derives their truth.

If Kant's theory of postulates reduced to the very modest form in which the necessity of believing was asserted (or even proved) without raising any claim to the truth of the belief (except insofar as one cannot believe what one knows to be false), it would be of little philosophical interest. It would be interesting in a phenomenology of morals, but practical reason would not be justified by such an argument in occupying the "empty space" left by theory.

But all that Kant's argument, if otherwise valid, legitimately entails

---

[7] This is obviously wider than Kant's meaning of "transcendental," which is generally restricted to the justification of a priori synthetic knowledge, and accordingly it is denied that morals belong in transcendental philosophy (*Critique of Pure Reason* A 15 = B 29). But there seems to be no other word that indicates the sphere of these synthetic a priori theoretical judgments which are not parts of the structure of theoretical knowledge as such. Kant himself points out the resemblance between his moral philosophy and transcendental logic. He says that Wolff's general practical philosophy is to his metaphysics of morals as general logic is to transcendental logic (*Foundations of the Metaphysics of Morals,* 390 [6]). The moral argument for the existence of God is referred to as a "transcendental argument" in *Critique of Pure Reason,* A 589 = B 617; similarly in *Critique of Practical Reason,* 113 (209).

is the necessity of making certain postulations as acts, and not the truth
of the postulates thus made. But Kant does not, as I have said, restrict
his conclusions in this way. He soon regards the proof of the necessity
of the postulations as contributing, though only very little, to theory.[8]
For, he tells us, the practical argument "compels knowledge [i.e., the-
ory] to concede that there are such objects without more exactly defining them." Theory thus gains an "accession," but not an accession
that it can use in the further extension of its realm by making synthetic
a priori judgments about them; still the Ideas, which, for theoretical
reason, were objectively empty ("without objects"), are now shown
to "have objects." Since it cannot extend its knowledge of them, the
work of speculative reason on this gift from the practical is negative,
"not broadening, but purifying." But the objects are there; they are
asserted; the category of existence is applied.[9] All the disarming cau-
tions about how little is gained by theory remind one of the young
lady who excused herself for having an illegitimate baby by insisting
that the baby was very small.

How, then, does Kant justify moving from "the postulates must be
asserted" to "the postulates have objects"? He does so through the doctrine of the primacy of pure practical reason (119 ff. [216–18]). This
doctrine arises, as we have seen, from the conviction that we have not
two reasons, but one reason with two interests; that these interests are
not incompatible; and that the two interests point in the same direction,
while only one of the routes of approach to the unconditioned can actually reach its destination with a proof without flaw.

The doctrine of primacy is Kant's closest anticipation of the later
coherence theory of truth. If we cut off theoretical from practical reason and ascribe only to the former the privilege of establishing truths,

[8] The practical-dogmatic metaphysics which gains this accession is a part of
theory, yet its propositions are valid only from a practical point of view; thus it
differs both from speculative metaphysics (which is not valid at all) and from the
metaphysics of morals (which is a part of practical philosophy). Needless to say,
Kant never worked out the details of such a hybrid of theory and practice, but its
foundation lies in the point we are here examining. The moral argument for the
existence of God, he says (*Fortschritte der Metaphysik*, XX, 305), is "sufficient to
ground a theory of the supersensuous, but only as a practical-dogmatic transition
to it. It is not really a proof of God's existence absolutely (*simpliciter*), but only in
a certain respect (*secundum quid*), namely with respect to the final goal that the
moral person has and ought to have. It is related to the rationality of assuming such
a being, where the person has a right to permit an influence on his decisions to come
from an Idea that he has made according to moral principles, exactly as if he had
made it in accordance with a given object."

[9] All quotations and allusions in this paragraph refer to *Critique of Practical
Reason*, 135 (232–33); similar assertions are also on the following page.

we find (*a*) that we cannot establish a coherent self-dependent system and (*b*) that if the doctrine of postulates is left in the state of justifying only the process of postulation as a practical act but not the postulates as true, an entire area of human experience, completely rational in itself, is likewise left unfounded in any theory about the world. If, on the contrary, we say with Kant that the two can be taken together, with the inadequacy of the one complemented by the primacy of the other, we are on the way to agreeing with the later idealists in their methodology that whatever we have to believe in order to "save the appearances" is, to that extent, true, whether the "appearances" in question are empiricotheoretical or practical. Kant's *Sachlichkeit* or modesty is shown in his refusal to make any speculative use of the objects posited in this way; but I think there can be little doubt that he regarded his argument as an argument for that which was posited in this way and not merely as an argument for the necessity of this positing.

§ 3. IDEAS AND POSTULATES

The *Critique of Pure Reason* contains two quite different accounts of transcendental Ideas. According to one, the categories, when not schematized and thus putatively applied to things in themselves, are Ideas, i.e., concepts which have no adequate object in experience. According to the other, the Ideas are an original possession of reason, being its principles for the systematizing of experience, which can be undertaken only if there are concepts of unconditioned conditions. In the latter theory, the logical origin of the Ideas is to be found not in the table of judgments, which is our clue to the categories, but in the types of syllogisms that reason can use. In each theory, however, the Ideas have this in common: they are a priori necessary to reason, but, as they can have no objects of intuition corresponding to them, they are necessarily dialectical if taken as more than regulative. The dialectic is resolved, yet the necessity of the Ideas is saved by showing that they are maxims necessary to the conduct of thought, not by showing that they really do have objects. Whether they have objects remains an irresolvable problem for speculative reason; but speculative reason does not need, for its own interest, to solve this problem. It suffices speculative reason only to know that the Ideas cannot be shown to be false as cognitions and that they can be shown to be necessary as maxims.

It is the second of the two theories of Ideas that is important in Kant's practical philosophy; for the purpose of the treatment of the postulates is to show that the three Ideas derived from the second of the theories do have objects. The three Ideas in the second theory are these: the Idea of the absolute unity of the subject of experience (the soul), the Idea of the absolute unity of the series of conditions of appearances (the world), and the Idea of the absolute unity of the condition of all things in general (God).[10] Speculative metaphysics is the study of these three Ideas and the attempt to define and prove the reality of each of these objects. The *Critique of Pure Reason* examines the proofs of speculative metaphysics concerning each. The proofs of the first are listed in the chapter on Paralogisms, those of the second in that on the Antinomy, and those of the third in that on the Ideal of Pure Reason.[11] Corresponding to these Ideas, we accordingly find in the *Critique of Practical Reason* three postulates. Thereby Kant aims to show that theoretical and pure practical reason point to the same objects, but, whereas they "fly before it when it follows the path of pure speculation,"[12] they can be definitely grasped if pursued on the path of the practical.

§ 4. THE IMMORTALITY OF THE SOUL

The doctrine of the immortality of the soul was always taken seriously by Kant. But he never had much faith in theoretical arguments for it. Even when he was still traditionalistic in his rationalism, the premise for immortality was found in the "incomplete harmony between morality and its consequences in the world"; but he did not have a crudely eudaemonistic theory, for he held that it was better to base the belief on immortality upon the moral disposition rather than to base the moral disposition on a hope for future rewards.[13]

In the *Critique of Pure Reason*, Kant discovered that all synthetic a priori judgments about the soul are proved only in syllogisms which contain paralogisms. His argument, though long and complex, can be stated in its essentials very simply. The thought of the self in the transcendental unity of apperception, the "I" in the " 'I think' that must be able to accompany all of my representations," is the thought of a simple substance. But the soul, though thought of as a substance, is not given under the only condition whereby a substance can be known, viz., in time. Hence the judgment that the self is a simple substance, from which its immortality was to be derived, is not a valid synthetic a priori judgment, and no synthetic predicate can be proved of the

---

[10] *Critique of Pure Reason,* A 334 = B 391; B 395 n.; cf. *Critique of Judgment,* § 91 (V, 473 [325]).

[11] In a slightly different context, they occur, respectively, as the theses of the second, third, and fourth antinomies.

[12] *Critique of Pure Reason,* A 796 = B 824.

[13] *Träume eines Geistersehers,* II, 373.

soul. The illusion that it can be proved arises because the paralogism is not noticed whereby the major premise has to do with the pure concept of substance while in the minor premise and conclusion substance is thought of as a mode of existence in time.[14]

This theoretical argument, Kant wittily remarks, "so stands on the point of a hair that even the schools keep it from toppling only so long as they keep it spinning around like a top."[15] But the failure of the theoretical argument does not in the least prejudice "the right, nay, the necessity, of postulating a future life in accordance with the principles of the practical employment of reason."[16] Indeed, the arguments which are "serviceable for the world at large" are unaffected by this criticism, and the failure of speculative arguments is itself a valuable "hint" to turn from vain speculation in these matters to practical concerns.[17]

"The proofs serviceable to the world at large," as seen in the *Critique of Pure Reason*, are not the proofs finally acceptable to Kant in the second *Critique*. There are two. First, there is the analogical argument that every organ is suitable for its proper function and that our "human endowments" so far transcend the limits of utility in this "present life" that its proper function and destiny cannot be restricted to its corporeal existence.[18] The other is the postulation of the immortality of the soul as directly necessary to the *summum bonum*, without which "the glorious ideas of morality are indeed objects of approval and estimation, but not springs of purpose and action."[19] The first is an example of the teleological argument that Kant respected and recommended, even though he showed it to be theoretically invalid;[20] we

---

[14] The paralogism is most succinctly explained in *Critique of Pure Reason*, B 410–11. Another refutation of the argument for immortality from the simplicity of the soul is directed against Mendelssohn at B 414 ff.; still another is found in the second Antinomy, especially A 443 = B 471.

[15] *Ibid.*, B 424.   [16] *Ibid.*   [17] *Ibid.*, B 421.

[18] *Ibid.*, B 425–26; cf. A 827 = B 855. This is a doctrinal belief, not a moral belief, because its premise is a theoretical judgment about man's (moral) nature. It differs subtly but essentially from the moral argument of the second *Critique*. I have not been able to find any anticipation, in other writers, of the moral argument proper; but the doctrinal belief based upon man's moral nature, which was Platonic in inspiration, was widely accepted in the eighteenth century. It was formulated by Addison (*Spectator*, No. 111 [1711]), who said he did not remember having seen this, the "strongest" of the arguments for immortality, presented elsewhere; by Platner (*Philosophische Aphorismen*, §§ 1176–79 [1782]), by Mendelssohn (*Phaedon* [1769]), by Crusius (*Anweisung vernünftig zu leben*, Part I, Thelematologie, §§ 218–21 [1744]), and by Lessing (*Erziehung des Menschengeschlechtes*, §§ 79 ff. [1780]), all of whom had been read by Kant.

[19] *Critique of Pure Reason*, A 813 = B 841; cf. A 811 = B 839.

[20] *Ibid.*, A 623 = B 651.

shall meet it again later. The second is an argument which is incompatible with the doctrine of autonomy and disappears in deserved oblivion.[21]

Elsewhere in the first *Critique*, in a part written just before the *Critique of Practical Reason*, there is a remark that anticipates the doctrine of the second *Critique* more clearly than the other two arguments do. In the Preface to the second edition, he says that the belief in immortality is based on a "notable characteristic of our nature, never to be capable of being satisfied by what is temporal (as insufficient for the capacities of its whole calling)."[22] This seems to be an intimation of the moral argument that is to follow in a few months; but it is so much an *obiter dictum* and so closely related to the theoretical hypothesis or doctrinal belief mentioned in the previous paragraph that it may not be justified to see more than an obscure germ of the later argument in it.

But the argument of the *Critique of Practical Reason* is a model of economical lucidity. We shall restate it in numbered sentences in order to facilitate comment.

1. The highest good is a necessary object of the will.

2. Holiness, or complete fitness of intentions to the moral law, is a necessary condition of the highest good.

3. Holiness cannot be found in a sensuous rational being.

4. It can be reached only in an endless progress, and, since holiness is required, such endless progress toward it is the true object of the will.

5. Such progress can be endless only if the personality of the rational being endures endlessly.

6. The highest good can be made real, therefore, only on "the supposition of the immortality of the soul" (122 [218–19]).

First, I must comment upon statement 6. Kant says that the highest good is possible only "on the supposition of the immortality of the soul." This might mean that it is practically possible only to a being that supposes, i.e., postulates, that it is immortal. Or it might mean that it is practically possible only if the soul is immortal. In the light of what we have said above about the postulates and of Kant's own statement of the postulate that "I will . . . that my existence in this world be also an existence in a pure world of the understanding" (143 [241]), one might well prefer the second interpretation. As so often, here we have to do only with Kant's *façon de parler;* often, throughout his works, he uses such constructions as "the concept of *x*" when the argument

---

[21] Cf. *Metaphysik der Sitten,* VI, 490.

[22] *Critique of Pure Reason,* B xxxii.

permits or even requires simply "*x*." But in this passage, I think it is clear that he means something of both of the alternatives. We shall therefore reformulate statement 6 to read: "The highest good, therefore, can be made real only if the soul is immortal; and a moral being that acknowledges the law must suppose that it is immortal."

We have already commented extensively on statement 1.[23] But our criticisms of it have not touched the *nervus probandi* of this argument. For here, as shown in sentence 4, Kant is not in the least concerned, or at least not directly concerned, with the second component of the highest good. He is here dealing only with virtue and its perfection, and the argument would seemingly be unaffected by the complete omission of the second component. Why, then, does he bring in the conception of the *summum bonum* in statements 1 and 2, only to omit it in sentence 4?

I hesitate to suggest what seems to me to be the only reason, as it is almost incredible that Kant could have made such a mistake. But in default of more credible explanations, I must propose one that does not seem to have been noticed by other critics of the postulates.

Kant has, I believe, confused the "supreme condition" (*bonum supremum*)[24] of the *summum bonum*, which is virtue, with the supreme perfection of virtue, as though his definition of the *summum bonum* were the conjunction of perfect happiness with the perfection of virtue (i.e., holiness). This conception I shall call the "maximal conception of the *summum bonum*":[25] perfect blessedness under the condition of holiness. If the maximal conception is substituted for the one that Kant formally defined (110 [206]), to wit, the conception that happiness in various degrees is apportioned by the degree of virtue—a conception I shall call the "juridical conception of the *summum bonum*"—the premise necessary for the argument is supplied. Only because Kant thought of the maximal conception at this point is he able to suppose that the necessity of the *summum bonum* entails the neces-

---

[23] Above, chap. xiii, § 3.

[24] *Critique of Practical Reason*, 110 (206). Note the contradiction between this and the second sentence of 122 (218).

[25] *Ibid.*, 129 (227): greatest happiness combined in the most perfect proportion with the highest degree of moral perfection. Similarly, *Vorlesungen über Metaphysik* (Heinze ed.), p. 712: "Two things constitute the *summum bonum*—the moral perfection of the person and the physical perfection of his state." In *Critique of Pure Reason*, A 810 = B 839, the *summum bonum* is called an "Ideal of reason" and not a mere Idea or concept, and Ideal being "the concept of an individual object completely determined through the mere Idea"; hence, as *completely* determined by the definition, the supreme good is there taken in its maximal sense.

sity of holiness, which in turn is said to entail immortality. That he began with the juridical conception is shown by his statement that, granting the existence of God, the necessary relation of morality to happiness is possible in the sensuous world (115 [211]); that he changed to the maximal conception is shown in the statement in the section on Immortality that "the Infinite Being" inexorably requires holiness "in order to be true to His justice in the share He assigns to each in the highest good" (123 [219]).

Let us try to clear the air of this erroneous conception of the *summum bonum* by reformulating statements 1 and 2 into (I): There is a necessary moral imperative, "Be ye perfect." Premise 3 may stand as a sad commentary on human nature. Premise 4 suggests that perfection may be either (*a*) a state or (*b*) an endless progress toward a state, and that *a* and *b*, while different for us men, may be identical for an intellectual non-temporal intuition such as we may suppose God has. Premise 5 tells us that (4, *b*) is possible if man's duration is without end.

We may now restate the whole argument.

I. The moral imperative requires of man that he be perfect (holy).
II. No sensuous being can be in a state of perfection (holiness).
III. But in the eyes of God, continuous and unending progress toward perfection is equivalent to perfection as a state in the distributive justice of the *summum bonum*.
IV. This progress is possible only if the soul is immortal.
V. Therefore, the moral imperative (I) can be fulfilled only if the soul is immortal; and a being that acknowledges this imperative must suppose himself to be immortal.

Against this reformulation, two objections can be made. The first is that it presupposes the existence of God in Premise III, which is based on the second and weaker of the two components of the *summum bonum*. Premises I and II are compatible (assuming that Premise I is true, and a moral law is valid) only on the assumption III of an intuitive intelligence, which Kant ascribes to God; whereas God is postulated only to mediate the two components of the *summum bonum*, which is not, in fact, achieved in the sensuous world.

The second objection concerns the formulation of Premise I itself. Would it not be far simpler, we may ask, to let "perfection" mean what it does ordinarily mean, namely, a state, and then modify the alleged imperative to read: "Seek perfection"? We are told to seek the Kingdom of God, not to settle in it. This is indeed all that is clearly demanded of me, and the imperative that is so formulated demands it without in the least being "degraded from its holiness, by being made

out as lenient (indulgent) and thus compliant to our convenience."[26]
This imperative and obedience to it would meet the putative commands
of God—if it can be shown that there is a God—without the speculative
conception that what for us is an infinite progress in time is for him
a state.

Only through the substitution of the maximal for the juridical conception of the *summum bonum*, can we say that a state of holiness must
be attainable, even in infinite progress. Neither the Kantian text nor
the Christian doctrine, which Kant is here rationalizing, nor the voice
of duty itself requires the maximal conception.

What, then, is left of the postulate? Only a hope. "On the basis of
[one's] previous progress from the worse to the morally better, and of
the immutability of intention which thus becomes known to him, he
may hope for a further uninterrupted continuance of this progress,
however long his existence may last, even beyond this life."[27] This hope
need not in the least jeopardize the autonomy of the moral disposition.
If we assume that the moral condition with which life ends is unchanged on entry into another life, it is wise to act as if there is a future
life.[28] The moral disposition may inevitably engender the belief in it.
But it is not a duty to believe in it;[29] and, if my analysis is correct, Kant
has given no very good reason why one should believe in it.

It suffices, in conclusion, to point out two puzzles which are present
in Kant's theory of immortality. Presumably the soul upon death, if it
is indeed immortal, is no longer a denizen of the world of space and
time; if we say it never was, as when Kant says the acts of pure practical reason are not in time (98–99 [191–92]), we only multiply the
difficulty of the problem I am about to mention. If, I say, the soul is no
longer under the temporal condition, it is not possible to understand
what is meant by "continuous and unending progress." We can conceive of substances only under the temporal condition, and our language must be adapted to this temporal condition, even though it is
recognized that this is not justified. If we say the soul is immortal and
mean that it is eternal, we may add, "Of course our intellect can conceive of eternity only as infinite temporal duration; but eternity is not

---

[26] *Critique of Practical Reason*, 122 (219). I take this occasion to correct an error
in the first sentence of the paragraph here referred to, as it occurs in the New York
edition (p. 127) of my translation. For "toward" read "to reach."

[27] *Critique of Practical Reason*, 123 (219–20); the hope includes a hope of blessedness (*ibid.*, 123 n., 127 n., 128–29 [220 n., 224 n., 225–26]).

[28] *Das Ende aller Dinge*, VIII, 330.

[29] *Critique of Practical Reason*, 146 (244) and, in its dogmatic theological form,
Religion within the Limits of Reason Alone, VI, 128 n. (Greene and Hudson, 119 n.).

a quantum of time, but is atemporal." Very well; but we must be reminded that the premise for the eternity of the soul includes the idea of continuous change, which is a temporal and not an eternal mode.

The other puzzle concerns the happiness of the immortal soul. This puzzle is of less moment in the interpretation of the argument for immortality than in that of the argument for the existence of God, since the need for happiness as a part of the *summum bonum* enters as a condition only in the latter argument. Nevertheless, it is difficult to frame a conception of the happiness or bliss of a being no longer affected by desire, even if, in virtue, "the determination of the will directly by reason alone is the ground of the feeling of pleasure" (116 [213]). It has always been difficult to render a conception of an afterlife both intelligible and concretely attractive, even on hedonistic principles. And when these principles are denied or the conditions of their application are withdrawn from the soul in its immortality, it seems impossible to speak of happiness as a reward for virtue or as a component of the highest good for beings no longer affected by sensuous desire.

But I doubt very much that these objections to the conception of life after death would have troubled Kant. He was not concerned with any theoretical determination of the supersensuous, because it would be impossible on theoretical grounds and empty of practical significance.

§ 5. THE EXISTENCE OF GOD

In *The Only Possible Premise for a Demonstration of the Existence of God* (1764) Kant proposed an ontological argument quite different from the Cartesian form, and in Part II of that work he supplemented the ontological with a teleological argument. The ontological argument in the Cartesian form was refuted in the *Critique of Pure Reason*, but he did not consider at any later time the specific kind of ontological argument that he himself had invented; instead of being refuted, it just died a natural death along with the rest of speculative rationalistic metaphysics, for it suffered from the fundamental defect of all ontological arguments, viz., that it is not possible to know the existence of anything from mere concepts (139 [236]).

In the *Critique of Pure Reason* God is called the "Ideal of Pure Reason," not just an Idea; for God is thought of as a single individual substance and the ground of the existence and unity of all things in general. Three possible theoretical proofs are distinguished: the ontological, or proof of existence from the concept of perfection; the cosmological, or proof of the existence of a first cause from the existence of the world; and the physicoteleological, or proof from the empirical evidence of intelligent design in nature. These are the only possible proofs, for they have as their respective premises a mere concept, a concept of existence, and a concept of a specific existence. The structure of the refutation can be briefly described. The ontological argument is invalid because "God exists" is a synthetic proposition and therefore cannot be proved without intuition, but intuition of a supersensuous being is necessarily lacking. The other arguments, however, while they, as it were, lead up to the concept of God, cannot realize it without surreptitiously introducing the ontological form of argument. Hence no theoretical proof of God's existence is possible.

The teleological argument, however, is worthy of respect and remains subjectively persuasive even when its formal fallacy is revealed. It remains useful when its concept of God as the Author of design in nature is used simply as a regulative Idea for anticipating the orderliness of nature. Its use as a regulative maxim can always benefit science in the comprehension of nature and never injure it except by misuse, even when the facts discovered by its use do not bear out the expectation of teleological unity. [30] But if God as the source of order in nature is taken as an object of knowledge, as in the pretensions of natural theology, the interest of theoretical reason is infringed, since the concept of God, now taken anthropomorphically, is used "to impose ends upon nature, forcibly and dictatorially, instead of [helping us to pursue] the more reasonable course of searching for them by the path of physical investigation"—though this investigation is guided by the regulative Idea that the variety of nature is to be explained under a minimum of laws, which is rendered intelligible on the assumption of a design.[31]

Like the other Ideas, therefore, the Idea of God properly understood is a problematic one that cannot be asserted by theoretical reason but need not be asserted for the purposes of theory. Theory can use it, provided only that its possibility is guaranteed.[32] But the needs of practical

[30] *Critique of Pure Reason,* A 688 = B 716.

[31] *Ibid.,* A 692 = B 720; *Critique of Judgment,* Introduction, V.

[32] Cf. above, p. 259, nn. 1 and 2. Kant uses the word "possibility" in two senses, and thus sometimes says that the *Critique of Pure Reason* shows the Ideas to be possible and at others that it could not show them to be possible (*Critique of Pure Reason,* A 558 = B 586; *Critique of Practical Reason,* 4, 132, 145 [88, 229, 243]). "Possible" in the first usage means "logically possible," i.e., thinkable without contradiction or thinkable through the (unschematized) categories; in the second, it means "really possible," i.e., possible in the sense of the first Postulate of Empirical Thought in General (*Critique of Pure Reason,* A 218 = B 266), or having some connection with a given structure of actual experience. The sense in which the existence of God is logically possible is the same as that in which, for instance, the inhabitants of another planet are logically possible. But the real possibilities are dif-

reason build on this possibility an assertion. The first attempt to justify this has already taken place in the first *Critique.*

The reader of this commentary has already had the passage in which this attempt is made called several times to his attention; only a brief reminder of it is needed here. The *summum bonum* is not possible unless the soul is immortal and God exists—the former because in this world happiness and worthiness to be happy are not matched, and the latter because they cannot be brought into unison without a supernatural agency. The *summum bonum* is a necessary object of the will; hence it is necessary to postulate it along with its conditions. But though Kant says it is not the desire for happiness, even happiness in accord with virtue, that is the motive to morality, he nevertheless says that without the *summum bonum* and these conditions of it, "the glorious ideas of morality are indeed objects of admiration and approval, but not springs of purpose and action."[33] We postulate the existence of God "in order that through such agency effect may be given" to the moral laws.[34]

The element of reward is no longer a principal premise for the argument for immortality in the second *Critique*, but Kant does not omit it from the later argument for the existence of God.[35] Nevertheless, with

---

ferent, for the existence of God is not connected with intuitions but only with concepts. To be really possible in the sense meant in the second *Critique* is to be (*a*) logically possible and (*b*) related necessarily to some other fact (viz., the moral) whose reality is given. Thus the fact of pure reason is the practical corollary of intuition (cf. above, pp. 152 f., 172 f.) in converting mere concepts of the logically possible into cognitions that the logically possible is really possible (cf. *Critique of Practical Reason*, 66 [157]).

[33] *Critique of Pure Reason*, A 813 = B 841.

[34] *Ibid.*, A 818 = B 846, A 589 = B 617, A 634 = B 662; Reflexionen 6110, 6236.

[35] Only in *Religion within the Limits of Reason Alone*, VI, 101 (Greene and Hudson, 92) does Kant seem to have been able to argue for the existence of God exclusively from the first component of the *summum bonum*. The highest moral good, he there tells us, cannot be achieved by an isolated individual, but only in a moral commonwealth. The establishment of this moral commonwealth cannot be the work of man, who can only make himself worthy of membership in it; its actual establishment can be only by the grace of God. Virtue is worthiness to this grace (which now replaces worthiness to be happy), and the *summum bonum* is the Kingdom of God to be established by God. Hence the moral command to seek the Kingdom of God requires that such a moral legislator exist or justifies the belief and hope independently of the rewards it may contain. The last time the moral argument is given in its classical form, involving both the components of the *summum bonum* is in *Critique of Judgment*, § 87, where it is presented with only one modification. Here the natural desire of man for happiness is not taken as a prior condition for the definition of the *summum bonum*, but the existence of God is taken as the condition under which a man may morally set before himself any

the development of the theory of autonomy, there is a decisive modification of the peculiar feature of the argument of the first *Critique*. The belief in the existence of God is based upon the putative necessity of the second element in the *summum bonum* (124 [220]); but he now succeeds in explaining more fully how it can be present and not function as a motive—a matter that made the conclusion in the first *Critique* seem heteronomous, as pointed out above. Now the reason for assuming the *summum bonum* and its conditions is not that man naturally desires happiness and happiness is a component of the *summum bonum;* it is that the moral command would not be just ineffective, *it would be null and void*, if it commanded the impossible, and the *summum bonum* would be impossible (so far as human mind can comprehend it) (145 [244]) if God did not exist.

We are now ready to summarize Kant's argument for this postulate.

1. Happiness is the condition of a rational being in the world in whose whole existence everything goes according to wish and will.

2. Man's will is not the cause of nature and does not bring nature into complete harmony with the principles of his will.

3. There is, therefore, no ground in the moral law (or in nature) for expecting a necessary connection between the morality and happiness of men.

4. But such a connection, in the concept of the *summum bonum*, is postulated in the command that we ought to seek the *summum bonum*.

5. The highest good must, therefore, be possible.

6. Therefore, a cause adequate to it must be postulated.

7. Such a cause must be the Author of nature, acting through understanding and will. Such a being is God (125 [221]).

Let us begin our examination of this argument with statement 3. The disproportion of worthiness to be happy and actual happiness can be and often has been taken as evidence *against* the existence of God, at least in the sense of statement 7. How then does Kant manage to build this premise of his opponents into an argument for the existence of

---

purpose as necessary, even if the realization of it is not within his power. This purpose is not happiness desired and subsequently restricted to the moral condition of worthiness, but happiness only insofar as it is morally earned. A similar thought is in *Über den Gemeinspruch* . . . , VIII, 280 n.

Though Kant supplemented the moral argument in various ways, as we have seen, he did not renounce it (cf. George A. Schrader, "Kant's Presumed Repudiation of the Moral Argument in the *Opus postumum*," Philosophy, XXVI [1951], 228–41). That the "new" doctrines of the *Opus postumum* can be found side by side with the moral argument is shown also by Walter Reinhard, *Über das Verhältnis von Sittlichkeit und Religion bei Kant* (Bern: Haupt, 1927).

God? The answer is found not in any alleged theoretical fact or hypothesis of the kind ordinarily used to "solve" the problem of natural evil, but by the practical premise (4), viz., "Seek to realize the highest good."

We have already commented extensively on this alleged imperative.[36] We have argued that, as an imperative, it is a command only that we seek virtue, let the eschatological chips fall where they may. But Kant regards the second component of the *summum bonum* as essential because he holds an ideal of the rationality of morals. This is described at the beginning of chapter ii of the Dialectic. Happiness, he says there, is required in the *summum bonum* "not merely in the partial eyes of a person who makes himself his end but even in the judgment of an impartial reason, which impartially regards persons in the world as ends-in-themselves." (Here we meet Kant's version of the English philosophers' "disinterested observer.") "For to be in need of happiness and also worthy of it and yet not partake of it could not be in accordance with the complete volition of an omnipotent rational being, if we assume such only for the sake of argument."[37]

This seems innocent enough; but notice that it completely displaces premise 4, the practical clause of which made the argument of the second *Critique a moral* argument.[38] The alleged command to seek to establish the *summum bonum* now contributes nothing to the conception of the distribution of happiness in accord with worthiness. The argument based on this conception of the *summum bonum* as rational is a revision of the teleological argument, which is purely theoretical.

It is not, of course, a physicoteleological argument, but only an analogy to it. It is a teleological argument, based not on the moral command in question but on the moral phenomenon as requiring a designer for the adjustment of two disparate things to each other. This is not made clear in the *Critique of Practical Reason*, where the moral argument is compared with the physicoteleological to the detriment and censure of the latter (138 [236]). But it dominates the final theological sections of the *Critique of Judgment*, and the moral argument of the

36 Cf. above, pp. 244–45, 253.

37 *Critique of Practical Reason*, 110 (206). The practical consequences of this impartiality is the conception of each man as an end-in-himself; this is drawn at 131–32 (229).

38 Kant has not begged the question by this statement, as it might appear. The conception of God here is not used to establish the concept of the *summum bonum*. The conception of an impartial observer is the essential one; it follows that if there were an impartial observer with the requisite power, the *summum bonum* would be made real.

second *Critique* had already been assigned to the obscurity of a difficult footnote by the time Kant wrote the treatise on religion. The explicit formulation of the new teleological argument is given in the
Metaphysik der Sitten, in the sample of moral catechism Kant works
out. The passage is as follows:

TEACHER: When we are conscious of a good and active will through
which we hold ourselves to be worthy (or at least not unworthy) of happiness, can we base on it the certain hope of partaking of this happiness?

PUPIL: No, not on that alone. . . . Our happiness remains only a wish
that cannot be a hope unless some other power is added.

TEACHER: Has reason perhaps grounds in itself to believe in God, i.e., to
assume as real a power that apportions happiness according to desert, ordering nature and ruling the world with supreme wisdom?

PUPIL: Yes; for we see in the works of nature which we can judge such
an extensive and profound wisdom that we cannot explain it except through
the inexpressibly great art of a Creator; and from this we have reason to
promise ourselves a not less wise government as respects the moral order,
which is the highest ornament of the world; to promise ourselves that if we
do not make ourselves unworthy of happiness through trespassing against
our duty, we may also hope to participate in it.[39]

This passage is especially noteworthy. There is no discussion of the
summum bonum in the *Metaphysik der Sitten*. The proof of God's existence is an argument from design, pure and simple. As a theoretical
argument, it "always deserves to be mentioned with respect,"[40] but it
is neither theoretically coercive nor independent of the ontological argument. Yet it is, if my analysis is correct, the hidden sense of the
moral argument, since the practical premise of the moral argument—
the command to seek the whole *summum bonum*—merely calls attention to the internal heterogeneity of this concept without placing us
under any obligation to seek the second of the components.

The shift from the practical to the theoretical argument, however,
contributes nothing to the theoretical fruitfulness of the concept of
God; it may indeed lessen it. For theoretical arguments, as shown in
the first *Critique*, could lead, if they were valid, only to the cosmological concept of a cause, which is less than what is meant by God, or
they enrich the concept with anthropomorphic predicates, reasoning
by analogy.[41] These analogies, however, never lead to the superlatives

[39] *Metaphysik der Sitten*, VI, 482; cf. also *Critique of Judgment*, § 91 (V, 479
[332]), where we are told that the teleological argument is a desirable confirmation
of the moral.

[40] *Critique of Pure Reason*, A 623–24 = B 651–52.

[41] *Ibid.*, A 817 = B 845; *Critique of Practical Reason*, 140 (238).

demanded by the concept of God.[42] If the anthropomorphic elements in the physicoteleological conception are removed, nothing is left of the concept of God but the mere name.

The moral argument, paradoxical though it may seem, leads to a less anthropomorphic conception of God than that of natural theology. For all the predicates essentially attributed to God are predicates which define merely a rational being endowed with a will (131 n. [228 n.]), and these concepts are not empirical, psychological concepts. We do not need to consider the peculiar nature of human understanding or will—that the former is discursive and that the latter is sensuously affected—in the definition of moral personality, but only the canonical relation of the former to the latter.[43] This relation is the starting point for the (moral) argument for the existence of God, and this is the only essential content that the concept of God has. The only conclusions that can be drawn from the concept concern these two in their interrelations; they are all moral in their import. If we try to "sensualize" the conception of God, we weaken its moral force by mixing empirical concepts drawn from human nature with the purely rational concepts of a moral being in general.

The only valid theology, therefore, is moral theology; God is a concept belonging not to physics (or its extension, metaphysics) but to morals (138 [236]). Until the moral motive was explored, metaphysics, based on the study of nature, did not need a rational theology, and no trace of one is found before moral consideration generated it.[44] Similarly, the ultimate teleology of the world is moral, not natural. The final purpose of creation is moral; it is the *summum bonum* (130 [228]). Men serve and glorify God—in the figurative sense, the only one Kant will permit—by respect and obedience to his command.

The theological discussion in the second *Critique* ends here without developing the most interesting philosophical and ethical conclusions which are implicit in it. The theoretical interest in the concept of God is to find an absolute and sufficient ground for the unity of the world, a cause of all causes, and a purpose of all purposes. If we examine this

---

[42] *Critique of Practical Reason*, 138–39 (236–37)—an obvious echo of Hume's *Dialogues concerning Natural Religion*. The necessary anthropomorphism of the physicoteleological conception of God is described in *Critique of Pure Reason*, A 697–700 = B 725–28.

[43] *Critique of Practical Reason*, 137 (234); cf. *ibid.*, 57 (147), and *Foundations of the Metaphysics of Morals*, 411–12, 425 (28, 43).

[44] The development is placed about the time of Anaxagoras in *Critique of Practical Reason*, 140 (238), but it seems to be attributed to Christianity in *Critique of Pure Reason*, A 817 = B 845.

doctrine a moment, the transition from the penultimate to the last paragraph of Section V will not appear so sudden. Kant says: "It follows that, in the order of ends man (and every rational creature) is an end in himself."[45] But how it follows is explained only in the *Critique of Judgment*.

The third *Critique* argues that the purposive order of nature must be judged as itself without a purpose, unless we can find in it something that is an absolute purpose, under which all other purposes can be subsumed. This absolute purpose must be an autonomous will, for a good will is that by which a being can have an absolute (not relative) worth and, in reference to it, the world itself can have a final purpose, i.e., be a system consonant with and therefore admissible by reason.[46]

The purposes in the phenomenal world, under the law of nature, can thus be synthesized only by the Idea of an intelligible world in which the final purpose is a moral one, the existence of rational beings in a realm of ends.[47]

Our conception of purpose and natural mechanism is dependent upon the fact that we possess a discursive understanding; if we had an intuitive understanding, these two conceptions could be constitutively and not merely regulatively synthesized. In the regulative Idea of a complete teleological order, which is possible only if there is moral autonomy as an end in itself, the two legislations of reason—the theoretical and the practical, or nature and the realm of ends—are at last shown to be compatible with each other. Only in such a world, in which we suppose that there is a legislation for nature by a moral governor, can the necessary connection between the two elements of the *summum bonum* be thought. Without this conception, we would have to give up this conception of the *summum bonum* or suppose that it is brought about only beyond the realm of nature or that it remains a miraculous event in a world whose lawful constitution has nothing to do with moral law.[48]

It is the concept of the *summum bonum* as the final purpose of the world with its corollary concept of God that finally bridges the gap between nature and morals. Through these concepts Kant believes that he is enabled to approach most nearly the goal of a single system of

---

[45] *Critique of Practical Reason*, 131 (229). It has quite other premises, from which it follows much more clearly and convincingly, in *Foundations of the Metaphysics of Morals*, 429 (47).

[46] *Critique of Judgment*, § 86 (V, 442-43 [293-94]).

[47] *Ibid.*, and *Über den Gebrauch teleogischer Prinzipien*, VIII, 182 f.

[48] Cf. *Critique of Pure Reason*, A 816 = B 844.

philosophy[49] and to show that practical and theoretical reason are finally one and the same. The system that brings them into unison, however, exists only for reflective judgment, i.e., as a guiding maxim for the systematization of experience, not as a determinative principle from which specific natural and moral consequences can be drawn. If it were not a merely regulative principle for judgment, we should have the double absurdity of a theological physics and a theological morality.[50]

§ 6. MORALITY AND RELIGION

There is no such thing as a theological morality, i.e., a system of moral rules derived from knowledge of God. There are three reasons for this. First, we do not have the knowledge. Second, if we did have it and used it as a moral premise, the autonomy of morals would be destroyed. Third, moral laws are not dependent upon any lawgiver, as if a difference in the nature of God (or the non-existence of God) would make any difference in the determination of duty. Theological morals commits a *hysteron proteron;* for our entire concept of God, so far as it is valid, grows out of our moral conceptions.[51] Actually, of course, this is not true, for theological belief is originally historical, not rational.[52] It is based on revelation or alleged revelation and is never pure but contains historical and psychological accidents. But it contains a hidden kernel of pure rational belief, which Kant uncovers in his treatise on religion, in the *Strife of the Faculties* and the *Conjectural Beginning of Human History*.

Religion is "the recognition of all duties as divine commands, not as sanctions, i.e., arbitrary and contingent ordinances of a foreign will, but as essential laws of any free will as such."[53] They can be recognized as commands only under the assumption of a legislator, who need not be the author of the law but only thought of, in religion, as the source of our obligation to obey it. There are no duties to God,[54] certainly no

---

[49] *Ibid.*, A 840 = B 868.

[50] *Critique of Judgment*, § 91, last paragraph of book.

[51] *Foundations of the Metaphysics of Morals*, 408–9 (25); *Critique of Practical Reason*, 139 (237).

[52] Kant to Jacobi, August 30, 1789 (XI, 76): "If the gospel had not previously taught universal moral laws in their purity, pure reason would not have been able to comprehend them in such perfection; but since they are given, one can now convince anyone of their correctness and validity merely by reason."

[53] *Critique of Practical Reason*, 129 (226); cf. *Critique of Judgment*, § 91 (V, 481 [334]); *Metaphysik der Sitten*, VI, 487; *Streit der Fakultäten*, VII, 36.

[54] Against Wolff, who had divided duties into those toward self, toward others, and toward God.

duty to believe in his existence; but regarding all duties as if they were divine commands of a morally perfect and omnipotent legislator for both morals and nature connects the moral disposition with the hope for the *summum bonum* and adds, to respect for the law, dimensions of love of and adoration for God.[55]

This is not a wholly new and adventitious accommodation of Kant's moral ideas to an inherited religious tradition. His attitude toward morality, from the beginning, had a religious humility and single-mindedness, and he is here only claiming that his moral system already contains the essential elements of religion. Religion, properly understood, is nothing but the recognition of the holiness of morals, to the defense of which the whole of his ethical work had been devoted from the beginning.

Nevertheless, the definition of religion acknowledges a dimension of moral law that was taken from it by the Copernican Revolution in ethics. *Sittengesetz* and *Moralgesetz* were relatively new words in German philosophy when Kant wrote; and prior to Kant they meant a law for morality drawn from the will of God, as a supplement to natural and positive law. Kant secularized the conception of moral law, against the theonomic doctrines of both the Wolffians (e.g., Baumgarten) and the critics of Wolff (especially Crusius), and thereby erected what has been called "the first non-theological philosophical ethics since Thomasius."[56]

The definition of religion given here does not add any new substance or authority or content to the moral law. It is not a transformation of the ethical position that Kant has just gained against theonomy but a restriction, rather, of the broader claims of religion itself to have dogmas and sources of insight disconnected from the moral. The definition of religion must be taken quite literally: it is a definition of religion, not a surreptitious modification of the concept of morals.[57]

---

[55] *Metaphysik der Sitten*, VI, 227; *Religion within the Limits of Reason Alone*, VI, 6 n. (Greene and Hudson, 6 n.). Kiesewetter, one of Kant's most enthusiastic (yet singularly instructive) followers, would not have regarded this as an addition. He wrote Kant, March 3, 1790 (XI, 137): "I am convinced . . . that the fundamental principle of your moral system is perfectly harmonious with the Christian religion, perhaps even that if Christ had heard and understood you he would have said, 'Indeed, that is what I intended to say in speaking of the love [of] God.' "

[56] By Herbert Spiegelberg, *Gesetz und Sittengesetz* (Zurich and Leipzig: Niehaus, 1935), p. 252. This book gives a valuable account of the development of the concept of moral law; few studies, I think, show Kant's originality in concepts and terminology better than this account of the slow development of the notion of moral law and its differentiation from natural and divine law.

[57] *Streit der Fakultäten*, VII, 42. "Love God" and "love thy neighbor" alike have only ethical content (*Critique of Practical Reason*, 83 [175–76]). Aside from the fact

Christianity, the only true religion,[58] is also the only one that contains a true moral theory. It is not heteronomous, because it commands that we seek holiness apart from the motive for divine reward. And it does not base the knowledge of what the law commands on the acceptance of any historical dogma. But, while it is as pure as the Stoic conception, it is more realistic, in not permitting us to think that holiness (or wisdom) is humanly possible without the grace of God. And without this confession of human impotency, the moral ideal is secretly degraded to a level achievable by natural man. In the face of the sublimity of the moral law, however, humility and not Stoic pride is the only adequate response (127 n. [224 n.]).

§ 7. THE TWO AWESOME THINGS

Natural theology, arising from the contemplation of nature, is supplemented by contemplating that which is not nature; not by contemplating God, of whom we have only a "conjecture" and whom we do not see in his "awful majesty," but by harkening to the "heavenly voice of duty" in us.

The two realms of reason, the theoretical and the practical, are brought into poignant juxtaposition in the celebrated conclusion: "Two things fill the mind with ever new and increasing admiration and awe, the oftener and the more steadily we reflect on them: the starry heavens above me and the moral law within me" (161 [260]). These two had often before been represented together by Kant,[59] but never

---

that Kant's theology was moral and that of the deists was natural, this connection of morals and religion, whereby the latter contributes nothing to the content of the former, is common to both. Thus Kant says (*Streit der Fakultäten*, VII, 36) that there is no material difference (difference in object) between morality and religion, but only a formal difference; and Tindal characteristically wrote: "Acting according to the reason of things considered in themselves [is morality; religion is] acting according to the same reason considered as a rule of God" (*Christianity as Old as Creation;* quoted from Leslie Stephen, *History of English Thought in the Eighteenth Century,* I, 144).

58 *Perpetual Peace*, VIII, 367 n. (Beck, 31 n.): There can be only one true religion because there is only one true morality. Similarly, *Religion within the Limits of Reason Alone,* VI, 107 (Greene and Hudson, 98), and *Streit der Fakultäten*, VII, 36: there is only one religion, of which Christianity is the plainest (*schlichteste*) form.

59 *Allgemeine Naturgeschichte und Theorie des Himmels,* concluding paragraph; *Beobachtungen über das Gefühl des Schönen und Erhabenen,* II, 208–9; *Träume eines Geistersehers,* II, 332; *Einzig möglicher Beweisgrund . . . ,* II, 141. A similar conjunction in Seneca, one of Kant's favorite authors, has been pointed out by Vaihinger in *Ad Helviam matrem de consolatione* cap. viii (cf. "Ein berühmtes Kantwort bei Seneca?" *Kant-Studien,* II [1898], 491–93); but, as Vaihinger indicated, the Seneca passage is more like those in Kant's precritical writings than that in the *Critique*.

with the grand simplicity of this passage. That the two were deeply connected in Kant's own life of feeling, no doubt having first been joined by Kant's mother,[60] is sufficiently attested by the early biographers who knew him personally.

But there is a marked progress in this passage, not only stylistically but also philosophically; it arises from the fact that, when writing the earlier ones, Kant had not yet succeeded in sharply distinguishing between the legislations of the two realms. In his earlier works he had thought of the starry heavens as a possible abode of moral beings of a higher order than man or as the place of our souls after death. All that is now transcended in the complementary conceptions of an unmoral astronomy and a non-naturalistic ethics; all that remains of the older conception of the relation of the moral law to the natural law is the Typic. The stark contrast between the two, not some simple harmony hazarded between them, gives force to their bold contexture. What had previously been thought of as a synthesis from the standpoint of the physical object—the evidence of natural teleology, the natural origin of the moral disposition—he now sees as a synthesis of contrasts within man's own rational nature. The starry heavens seem sublime because man first feels reduced by them to impotency, only to rise above them again when he knows that his rational nature, which comprehends them, is not subdued but heightened by the magnitude and power revealed in them. He erroneously attributes a sublimity to nature which actually belongs only to his own rational being;[61] the sublimity ascribed to nature is a clue to his own superiority to nature, for we convert "respect for the idea of humanity in our own subject into respect for the object."[62] What the starry heavens awake in us only indirectly is produced directly by the contemplation of the moral law, sublime in itself, and of the moral agent who embodies the law; the humility thus induced in man is itself sublime.[63]

There is no tendency remaining now to use natural concepts in the articulation and elaboration of moral ideas or to confuse two things, to the detriment of each. But the two things are not set before us merely as a literary peroration. Even on the last pages Kant extracts

[60] In the famous statement on his reverence for his mother (Jachmann, *Immanuel Kant geschildert in Briefen an einen Freund* [1804], neunter Brief), he speaks of her as having "planted and nourished the seed of the good" and "opened [his] heart to the impressions of nature," the same combination as in the present apothegm.

[61] *Critique of Judgment*, § 26 (especially V, 256 [95]).

[62] *Ibid.*, § 27 (V, 257 [96]).

[63] *Ibid.*, § 28 (V, 264 [103]); *Critique of Practical Reason*, 117 (213); *Beobachtungen über das Gefühl des Schönen und Erhabenen*, II, 215.

a lesson of use to moral philosophy by drawing an analogy from the history of astronomy.

"Admiration and respect," he says, "can indeed excite to inquiry, but they cannot supply the want of it" (162 [261]). The consequence of passive admiration and an admixture of human wants in subsequent astronomical investigation was astrology.[64] A like undisciplined elaboration of the "noblest attribute of human nature" led, in morals and religion, to fanaticism and superstition. With the perfection of the method of scientific investigation in astronomy and physics, there was brought forth "a clear and henceforth unchangeable insight into the structure of the world" (163 [261]). Perhaps even more important, it gave a model to philosophy, to set it on the secure path of science.[65] This method he now recommends in the investigation of morals. "Science," in the sense of critically and methodically directed inquiry, is "the narrow gate that leads to wisdom."

The *Critique of Practical Reason* is meant to be the key to that narrow gate.

[64] He has drawn a similar analogy in *Prolegomena*, IV, 366 (Beck, 115): "Critique stands in the same relation to the common metaphysics of the school as . . . astronomy to the astrology of the fortune-teller."

[65] Cf. *Critique of Practical Reason*, 108 (203); *Critique of Pure Reason*, B xxiv.

Bibliography

Bibliography

I. TEXTS OF "KRITIK DER PRAKTISCHEN VERNUNFT"

Critik der practischen Vernunft von Immanuel Kant. Riga. bey Johann Friedrich Hartknoch, 1788 [*sic*]. Pp. 292. Zweyte, vierte, fünfte, und sechste Auflage[n], 1792, 1797, 1808, 1827. (Third edition not published; second edition was a double printing.) Reprint: Neueste mit einem Register vermehrte Auflage. Grätz [*sic*], 1796. Other reprints: Frankfort and Leipzig, 1791, 1795, 1803.

ROSENKRANZ, KARL, and SCHUBERT, F. W. In Vol. VIII of their edition of Kant's works. Leipzig, 1838.

HARTENSTEIN, G. In Vol. IV of his edition of Kant's works. Leipzig, 1838 (in Vol. V of the edition of 1867).

KIRCHMANN, J. H. VON. In the series "Philosophische Bibliothek." Berlin, 1869, 1870, 1882, 1897.

KEHRBACH, KARL. In the series "Reclams Universalbibliothek." Leipzig, [1878].

VORLÄNDER, KARL. In the series "Philosophische Bibliothek." Leipzig, 1906; 9th ed., 1929.

NATORP, PAUL. In *Kants Gesammelte Schriften*, Vol. V. Berlin: Königliche Preussische Akademie der Wissenschaften, 1908, 1913.

KELLERMANN, BENZION. In *Immanuel Kants Werke*. Edited by Ernst Cassirer *et al.* Vol. V. Berlin: Bruno Cassirer, 1914, 1922.

GROSS, F. In "Grossherzog Wilhelm Ernst Ausgabe" of *Kants Sämmtliche Werke*. Leipzig: Inselverlag, 1920.

WEISCHEDEL, W. In *Kants Werke*. Vol. IV. Leipzig: Inselverlag, 1957.

II. TRANSLATIONS OF THE "CRITIQUE OF PRACTICAL REASON"

Kant's Critique of Practical Reason and Other Works on the Theory of Ethics. Translated with a memoir of Kant by THOMAS KINGSMILL ABBOTT. London: Longmans, Green, 1873; 6th ed., 1909; reprinted, 1954.

Kant's Critique of Practical Reason and Other Writings in Moral Philosophy. Translated and edited, with an Introduction, by LEWIS WHITE BECK. Chicago: University of Chicago Press, 1949.

Immanuel Kant: Critique of Practical Reason. Translated, with an Introduction, by LEWIS WHITE BECK. New York: Liberal Arts Press, [1956].

Immanuelis Kantii Critica rationis practicae. In *Opera ad philosophiam criticam latine vertit Fredericus Gottlob Born, volumen tertium.* Leipzig: Impensis Engelhard Ben. Schwickerti, 1797.

French translations by JULES BARNI (Paris, 1848), FRANÇOIS PICAVET (Paris, 1888; 2d ed., 1902; reprinted with new Introduction by FERDINAND ALQUIÉ [Paris: Presses Universitaires de France, 1949]), and J. GIBELIN (Paris: Vrin, 1945).

Italian translation by FRANCESCO CAPRA (Bari, 1909; 7th ed., Florence, 1955, with Introduction by EUGENIO GARIN).

III. TRANSLATIONS OF OTHER WORKS BY KANT AS CITED IN COMMENTARY
(IN CHRONOLOGICAL ORDER)

Principiorum primorum cognitionis metaphysicae nova dilucidatio (1755). Cited as "*Nova dilucidatio*." F. E. ENGLAND, *Kant's Conception of God*, Appendix, pp. 213–52. London: Allen & Unwin, 1929.

The Distinctness of the Principles of Natural Theology and Morals (1764). Also called "*Prize Essay*." L. W. BECK, *Kant's Critique of Practical Reason and Other Writings in Moral Philosophy* (Chicago, 1949), pp. 261–85.

The Forms and Principles of the Sensible and Intelligible Worlds (1770). Cited as "*Inaugural Dissertation*." JOHN HANDYSIDE, *Kant's Inaugural Dissertation and Early Writings on Space*, pp. 35–83. Chicago and London: Open Court, 1929.

Lectures on Ethics (ca. 1780). Translated by LOUIS INFIELD. New York: Century Co., [1930].

Critique of Pure Reason (1781, 1787). Translated by NORMAN KEMP SMITH. London and New York: Macmillan Co., 1929.

Prolegomena to Any Future Metaphysics (1783). Translated by LEWIS W. BECK. New York: Liberal Arts Press, 1951.

Foundations of the Metaphysics of Morals (1785). In ABBOTT, *op. cit.* Abbott's title is *Fundamental Principles of the Metaphysics of Morals.*

What Is Orientation in Thinking? (1786). In BECK, *Kant's Critique of Practical Reason and Other Writings in Moral Philosophy*, pp. 293–305.

Critique of Judgment (1790). Translated by J. H. BERNARD (1892). New York: Hafner, 1951.

Religion within the Limits of Reason Alone (1793). Translated by THEODORE M. GREENE and HOYT H. HUDSON. Chicago: Open Court, 1934.

Perpetual Peace (1795). Translated by LEWIS WHITE BECK. New York: Liberal Arts Press, [1957]. (This translation, with Akademie pagination, is included also in BECK, *Kant's Critique of Practical Reason . . .* , pp. 306–45, but citations are to the 1957 edition.)

IV. STUDIES OF KANT

ADICKES, ERICH. "Korrekturen und Konjekturen zu Kants ethischer Schrift," *Kant-Studien*, V (1901), 207–14.

ASTER, ERNST VON. "Band V und VI der Akademie Ausgabe," *Kant-Studien*, XIV (1909), 468–76. (Review of the Natorp edition of the *Kritik der praktischen Vernunft*.)

ATTISANI, ADELCHI. *Metodo attivo e metodo speculativo nella metodica della ragion pratica di E. Kant.* Messina: Sessa, 1951.

BALLAUF, THEODOR. *Vernünftiger Wille und gläubige Liebe. Interpretationen zu Kants und Pestalozzis Werk.* Meisenheim: Anton Hein, 1957.

BARNI, JULES. *Examen des Fondements de la métaphysique des mœurs et de la Critique de la raison pratique.* Paris: Ladrange, 1851.

BECK, LEWIS WHITE. "Apodictic Imperatives," *Kant-Studien*, XLIX (1957), 7–24.

———. "Les deux concepts kantiens de vouloir dans leur contexte politique," *Annales de philosophie politique*, IV (1962), 119–37.

BENDAVID, LAZARUS. *Vorlesungen über die Critik der praktischen Vernunft.* Vienna: Stahel, 1796.

BOHATEC, JOSEF. *Die Religionsphilosophie Kants in der "Religion innherhalb der Grenzen der blossen Vernunft" mit besonderer Berücksichtigung ihrer theologisch-dogmatischen Quellen.* Hamburg: Hoffman & Campe, 1938.

BRASTBERGER, GEBHARDT ULRICH. *Untersuchungen über Kants Kritik der praktischen Vernunft.* Tübingen: Cotta, 1792.

CAIRD, EDWARD. *The Critical Philosophy of Immanuel Kant.* 2 vols. London and New York: Macmillan Co., 1899 and 1909.

CASSIRER, ERNST. *Rousseau, Kant, Goethe.* Translated by JAMES GUTMAN, P. O. KRISTELLER, and J. H. RANDALL, JR. Princeton: Princeton University Press, 1947.

COHEN, HERMANN. *Kants Begründung der Ethik.* Berlin: Dümmler, 1877.

COOK, WEBSTER. *The Ethics of Bishop Butler and Immanuel Kant.* Ann Arbor: University of Michigan, 1888.

DELBOS, VICTOR. *La Philosophie pratique de Kant.* Paris: Alcan, 1905; 2d ed., 1926.

DÖRING, A. "Kants Lehre vom höchsten Gut," *Kant-Studien*, IV (1898), 94–101.

DUNCAN, A. R. C. *Practical Reason and Morality: A Study of Immanuel Kant's Foundations for the Metaphysics of Morals.* Edinburgh: Nelson, 1957.

EISLER, RUDOLF. *Kant-Lexikon.* Berlin: Mittler, 1930.

ENGLAND, F. E. *Kant's Conception of God.* London: Allen & Unwin, 1929.

EUCKEN, RUDOLF. "Über Bildnisse und Gleichnisse bei Kant," *Zeitschrift für Philosophie und philosophische Kritik*, LXXXIII (1883), 161–93.

FACKENHEIM, EMIL. "Kant's Concept of History," *Kant-Studien*, XLVIII (1957), 391–98.

FERVERS, KARL. *Die Beziehung zwischen Gefühl und Willen bei Tetens und Kant.* Diss., Bonn, 1925.

FOUILLÉE, ALFRED. "La raison pure pratique doit elle être critiquée?" *Revue philosophique*, LIX (1905), 1–33.

GAHRINGER, ROBERT E. "The Metaphysical Aspect of Kant's Moral Philosophy," *Ethics*, XLIV (1954), 277–91.

GELFERT, JOHANNES. *Der Pflichtbegriff bei Wolff und anderen Philosophen der deutschen Aufklärung mit Rücksicht auf Kant.* Diss., Leipzig, 1907.

GRASSI, LEONARDO. *Preludi storico-attualistici alla Critica della ragion pratica.* Catania: Crisafulli, 1943.

GUÉROULT, M. "Canon de la raison pure et Critique de la raison pratique," *Revue internationale de philosophie,* VIII (1954), 333–57.

GUREWITSCH, ARON. *Zur Geschichte des Achtungsbegriffes und zur Theorie des sittlichen Gefühls.* Diss., Würzburg, 1897.

HAEGERSTROM, AXEL. *Kants Ethik im Verhältnis zu seinen erkenntnistheoretischen Grundgedanken systematisch dargestellt.* Uppsala: Almqvist & Wiksell; Leipzig: Harrassowitz, 1902.

HAEZRAHI, PEPITA. "The Avowed and Unavowed Sources of Kant's Theory of Ethics," *Ethics,* LXII (1952), 157–68.

HEGLER, ALFRED. *Die Psychologie in Kants Ethik.* Freiburg: J. C. B. Mohr, 1891.

HEIDEMANN, INGEBORG. *Spontaneität und Zeitlichkeit: Ein Problem der Kritik der reinen Vernunft.* Ergänzungsheft der *Kant-Studien,* No. 75. Cologne, 1958.

———. *Untersuchungen zur Kantkritik Max Schelers.* Diss., Cologne, 1955.

HEIMSOETH, HEINZ. *Studien zur Philosophie Immanuel Kants: Metaphysische Ursprünge und ontologische Grundlagen.* Cologne: Balduin Pick, 1956.

HENRICH, D. "Hutcheson und Kant," *Kant-Studien,* XLIX (1957), 49–69.

HÖFFDING, HARALD. "Rousseaus Einfluss auf die definitive Form der kantischen Ethik," *Kant-Studien,* II (1898), 11–21.

JODL, FRIEDRICH. *Geschichte der Ethik als philosophischer Wissenschaft.* Stuttgart and Berlin: Cotta, 1920.

JONES, WILLIAM T. *Morality and Freedom in the Philosophy of Kant.* London: Oxford University Press, 1940.

JOSTEN, CLARA. *Christian Wolffs Grundlegung der praktischen Philosophie.* Leipzig: Meiner, 1931.

KÄUBLER, BRUNO. *Der Begriff der Triebfeder in Kants Ethik.* Diss., Leipzig, 1917.

KHODOSS, CLAUDE (ed.). *Kant: La Raison pratique.* Paris: Presses Universitaires de France, 1956. (A very useful collection of texts, arranged by subject matter and with glossary.)

KIESEWETTER, JOHANN GOTTFRIED CHRISTIAN. *Über den ersten Grundsatz der Moralphilosophie . . . nebst einer Abhandlung vom Herrn Prof. Jacob über die Freiheit des Willens.* 2 vols. Berlin: Carl Massdorff, 1790, 1791.

KNOX, T. M. "Hegel's Attitude to Kant's Ethics." *Kant-Studien,* XLIX (1957), 70–81.

KRUEGER, GERHARD. *Philosophie und Moral in der kantischen Kritik.* Tübingen: J. C. B. Mohr, 1931.

LINDSAY, A. D. *Kant.* London: Oxford University Press, 1934.

LIPPMANN, E. O. VON. "Zu: 'Zwei Dinge erfüllen das Gemüt. . . ,'" *Kant-Studien,* XXXIV (1929), 259–61; XXV (1930), 409–10.

LORENTZ, P. "Über die Aufstellung von Postulaten als philosophische Methode bei Kant," *Philosophische Monatshefte,* XXIX (1893), 412–33.

MARTY, FR. "La Typique du jugement pratique pur: la morale kantienne et son application aux cas particuliers," *Archives de philosophie*, No. 1 (1935), pp. 56–87.

MELLIN, GEORG SAMUEL ALBERT. *Encyclopädisches Wörterbuch der kritischen Philosophie.* 5 vols. in 10. Züllichau and Leipzig, 1797.

———. *Kunstsprache der kritischen Philosophie oder Sammlung aller Kunstwörter derselben.* Leipzig: Fromann, 1798.

———. *Marginalien und Register zu Kants Kritik der Erkenntnisvermögen.* II. *Kritik der praktischen Vernunft.* Züllichau, 1795. Neuherausgegeben von LUDWIG GOLDSCHMITT. Gotha: Thienemann, 1902.

MENZER, PAUL. "Der Entwicklungsgang der kantischen Ethik in den Jahren 1760–1785," *Kant-Studien*, II (1897), 290–322; III (1898), 40–104.

MESSER, AUGUST. *Kants Ethik: Eine Einführung in ihre Hauptprobleme und Beiträge zu deren Lösung.* Leipzig: Veit, 1904.

———. *Kommentar zu Kants ethischen und religionsphilosophischen Hauptschriften.* Leipzig: Meiner, 1929.

MICHAELIS, CHRISTIAN FRIEDRICH. *Über die sittliche Natur und Bestimmung des Menschen: Ein Versuch zur Erläuterung über I. Kants Kritik der praktischen Vernunft.* 2 vols. Leipzig: Iohann Gottlob Beigang, 1796, 1797.

MORITZ, MANFRED. *Studien zum Pflichtbegriff in Kants kritischer Ethik.* The Hague: Nijhoff, 1951.

NAHM, MILTON C. " 'Sublimity' and the 'Moral Law' in Kant's Philosophy," *Kant-Studien*, XLVIII (1957), 502–24.

NECKIEN, FERDINAND. *Die Lehre vom Gefühl in Kants kritischer Ethik.* Diss., Leipzig, 1938.

PATON, H. J. *The Categorical Imperative: A Study in Kant's Moral Philosophy.* London: Hutchinson [1946]; Chicago: University of Chicago Press, 1948.

———. *In Defence of Reason.* London: Hutchinson, 1951. (See especially "Can Reason Be Practical?" [pp. 117–56] and "Kant's Idea of the Good" [pp. 157–77].)

PAULSEN, FRIEDRICH. *Immanuel Kant, His Life and Doctrine.* Translated by J. E. CREIGHTON and ALBERT LEFEVRE. New York: Charles Scribner's Sons, 1902.

PEACH, BERNARD. "Common Sense and Practical Reason in Reid and Kant," *Sophia* (Padova), XXIV (1956), 66–71.

PORTER, NOAH. *Kant's Ethics: A Critical Exposition.* Chicago: Griggs, 1886; 2d ed., 1894.

ROSENTHAL, GERTRUD. "Kants Bestimmung des Erziehungsziels," *Archiv für die Geschichte der Philosophie*, XXXVII (1926), 65–74.

ROSS, SIR [WILLIAM] DAVID. *Kant's Ethical Theory: A Commentary on the Grundlegung zur Metaphysik der Sitten.* Oxford: Clarendon Press, 1954.

RUGE, ARNOLD. *Die Deduktion der praktischen und der moralischen Freiheit aus den Prinzipien der kantischen Morallehre.* Hab.-Schrift, Heidelberg, 1910.

SCHILPP, PAUL ARTHUR. *Kant's Pre-critical Ethics*. Chicago and Evanston: Northwestern University Press, 1938.

SCHMIDT, KARL. *Beiträge zur Entwicklung der Kant'schen Ethik*. Marburg: Elwert, 1900.

SCHWEITZER, ALBERT. *Die Religionsphilosophie Kants in der Kritik der reinen Vernunft bis zur Religion innerhalb der Grenzen der blossen Vernunft*. Freiburg: J. C. B. Mohr, 1899.

SEIDEL, ARTHUR. *Tetens Einfluss auf die kritische Philosophie Kants*. Diss., Leipzig, 1932.

SNELL, FRIEDRICH WILHELM DANIEL. *Menon oder Versuch in Gesprächen die vornehmsten Punkte aus Kants Kritik der praktischen Vernunft zu erläutern*. Mannheim: Schwan & Götz, 1789; 2d ed., rev., 1796.

STANGE, CARL. *Die Ethik Kants: Zur Einführung in die Kritik der praktischen Vernunft*. Leipzig: Dietrich, 1920.

TEALE, A. E. *Kantian Ethics*. New York: Oxford University Press, 1951.

UNGER, RUDOLF. " 'Der bestirnte Himmel über mir': Zur geistesgeschichtlichen Deutung eines Kant-Wortes." In *Festschrift zur zweiten Jahrhundertfeier seines Geburtstages* [in Königsberg], pp. 239–63. Leipzig: Dietrich, 1924.

VIDARI, GIOVANNI. "Sguardo introduttivo alla 'Critica della ragion pratica,' " *Rivista di filosofia*, XV (1924), 223–31.

DE VLEESCHAUWER, H. J. *La Déduction transcendentale dans l'œuvre de Kant*. Paris: Leroux, 1937. (See especially Vol. III.)

VORLÄNDER, KARL. *Immanuel Kant, der Mann und das Werk*. 2 vols. Leipzig Meiner, 1924.

WEBB, C. C. J. *Kant's Philosophy of Religion*. Oxford: Clarendon Press, 1926.

WHITTEMORE, ROBERT. "The Metaphysics of the Seven Formulations of the Moral Argument," *Tulane Studies in Philosophy*, III (1954), 133–61.

WILLE, E. "Konjekturen zu Kants Kritik der praktischen Vernunft," *Kant-Studien*, VIII (1903), 467–71.

WITTE, JOHANNES. *Beiträge zum Verständnis Kants*. Berlin: Mecklenburg Verlag, 1874. (Contains one of the very few discussions of the categories in the second *Critique*, pp. 92 ff.)

WUNDT, MAX. *Kant als Metaphysiker: Ein Beitrag zur Geschichte der deutschen Philosophie im achtzehnten Jahrhundert*. Stuttgart: Enke, 1924.

ZILIAN, ERICH. *Die Ideen in Kants theoretischer und praktischer Philosophie*. Diss., Königsberg, 1927.

ZWANZIGER, JOHANN CHRISTIAN. *Commentar über Herrn Professor Kants Kritik der praktischen Vernunft; nebst einem Sendschreiben an den gelehrten Herrn Censor*. Leipzig: Hischer, 1794.

I have not been able to find a copy of Theodor Gottlieb Rätze's *Beilage zu Kants "Kritik der praktischen Vernunft"* (Chemnitz, 1794) or of C. T. Michaelis' *Zur Entstehung der Kritik der praktischen Vernunft* (Berlin, 1893). The former is listed in Benjamin Rand's *Bibliography of Philosophy*,

Psychology, and Cognate Subjects (Vol. III of Baldwin's *Dictionary of Philosophy and Psychology* [New York: Macmillan Co., 1905]), Part 1, p. 310. The latter is listed in *Friedrich Uberwegs Grundriss der Geschichte der Philosophie*, 12th ed., Vol. III, p. 716; but there is reason to believe this entry is an error.

While this book was in press, and hence too late for me to make use of them, there appeared two very instructive studies by John R. Silber of topics in the *Critique of Practical Reason:* "Kant's Conception of the Highest Good as Immanent and Transcendent" (*Philosophical Review*, LXVIII [October, 1959], 469–92) and "The Copernican Revolution in Ethics: The Good Re-examined" (*Kant-Studien*, LI [1959–60], 85–101). They are especially relevant to the issues examined in this Commentary, chap. ix, § 3, and chap. xiii, § 3, respectively.

Index of Passages Cited from *"Critique of Practical Reason"*

AKADEMIE EDITION*	ABBOTT TRANSLATION	COMMENTARY
3	87	10, 43, 44, 46, 169, 174, 175, 183, 185, 188, 240
3	88	16, 27, 46, 184
4	88	27, 28, 59, 197, 207, 272
4	89	28, 48
5	89	46, 58, 174, 257
5	90	40, 46, 58, 257
6	90	27n, 46
6	91	16, 58, 59, 166
7	92	16, 19, 57, 59, 175
7	93	174, 185, 190
8	93	46, 51, 52, 57, 112, 154, 165, 235
8	94	45, 46, 53, 59, 60
9	94	90, 217, 218
9	95	60
11	96	139, 149, 251, 252
12	97	60, 169
13	99	21
13	100	60, 104
14	100	59
15	101	32, 44, 46, 49, 92, 113
16	102	44, 46, 54, 66, 127, 211, 240
19	105	77, 164
20	106	79, 162
21	107	75, 84, 95, 117
21	108	75, 83
22	108	97, 216
22	109	38f, 93, 98
23	109	39, 93, 105
23	110	93, 95, 223
24	110	223
24	111	39, 105
24	112	218
25	112	98, 218, 223
26	113	40, 80, 99
26	114	83, 157, 198
27	114	78, 130
27	115	99, 160, 164
28	115	98, 146, 160, 161
28	116	98, 122
29	116	122, 196, 198
29	117	122, 164, 168, 169, 196, 198, 222
30	118	111, 173, 199, 200
30	119	84, 200
31	120	54, 140, 152, 165, 166, 167, 180, 182, 196, 197
32	120	166, 178
32	121	107
33	121	227
33	122	92, 122, 167, 169, 196
34	123	96, 102, 115, 118, 130, 135, 161
35	124	48, 161, 203
36	125	91, 116
36	126	116
37	127	116
38	128	66, 100, 103, 105, 106, 223, 230
38	129	66, 105, 107
40	129	103, 104
41	129	104, 241
41	130	108, 213, 241
42	131	140, 166, 195
43	132	134, 161, 166, 172, 180, 192
44	133	172
45	134	46
45	135	113
46	135	111, 253, 259
47	136	166, 167, 171, 197
48	137	46, 174, 183, 185
48	138	187
49	139	175, 188
51	141	181
52	142	21
53	143	61, 181, 182

*Akademie pagination included in Beck translations.

Index of Names and Subjects

Note.—The titles of Kant's works are not cited on the mere occasion of a reference to them or of a quotation from them; they are cited only where there is some discussion of the work in question or where the occurrence of a particular term in the particular work is of importance.

Abbott, Thomas Kingsmill, viii, xi, 90 n., 91 n., 92 n., 166 n., 177 n., 227, 242 n.
Abel, Jacob Friedrich, 57
Act, 112 ff., 119, 241
  universalizability of, 159 n., 160, 162
Action, 134, 153
Activism, 226
Actor, 30 ff., 193 ff.
Addison, Joseph, 266 n.
Aesthetic
  in *Critique of Practical Reason*, 56, 67 f., 69, chap. xii
  transcendental, 56, 67, 186, 212
Aesthetic concepts, 220, 221 n., 231; *cf. also* Beauty; Sublimity
Alleged Right To Lie, On an, 80
Almsgiving, 162
Altruism, 100
Analogies of experience, 186 n., 193
Analytic, 65 f.
  of practical reason, 53, 56, 66 ff., 78, 211
  of pure practical reason, 80, 127
  transcendental, 56, 65 f., 69, 193, 211
Anaxagoras, 277 n.
Anderson, Georg, 14 n.
Announcement of Lectures for Winter Semester 1765–66, 6 n.
Anthropology, 7, 30 n., 90
Anthropology from a Pragmatic Point of View, 54
Anthropomorphism, 255, 276 f.
Antinomy, 25, 156
  of practical reason, 16, 245 ff.
  of theoretical reason, 48, 240, 247, 265
  third, 24 ff., 174, 183 n., 184, 186 ff., 188 ff., 193, 194 ff., 200, 212, 247 ff., 249
A posteriori, 20, 84, 210
Apperception, 189
  transcendental unity of, 138, 227, 265
Appetitus, 37, 94
Applied ethics, 10 n.
"Apply to," meaning of, 209

A priori, 20, 60, 65, 118 n.
  theoretical and practical, 84
Aquinas, St. Thomas, 37 n., 184
Architectonic, viii ff., 15, 55 f., 126, 185
Aristotle, 37, 41, 135, 184, 188, 232
Astrology, 283
Aufgegeben, 186
Autarchy of will, 208
Autonomy, 11, 14, 59 n., 102, 122 ff., 151 n., 166, 168, 180, 196 ff., 216, 267, 270, 274
Aversion, faculty of, 90 n.
Awe, 281 f.

Bad will, 198 n.; *cf. also* Evil
Baeumler, Alfred, vii
Balguy, John, 41 n.
Barni, Jules, vii n., 154 n., 177 n.
Bauch, Bruno, 225 n.
Baumeister, Friedrich Christian, 94 n., 177 n.
Baumgardt, David, 200 n.
Baumgarten, Alexander Gottlob, 37 n., 90 n., 94 n., 106 n., 131 n., 177 n., 251 n., 280
Beauty, 92, 106, 132 n., 213
Beck, L. W., viii, 85 n., 103 n., 120 n., 177 n., 219 n.
Bedingung, 81
Belief, 207, 255 f., 266 n., 270; *cf. also* Faith
Bendavid, Lazarus, 150 n.
Bering, Johann, 13, 57 n.
Bernacker, Karl, 94 n.
Bernard, J. H., xi
Bestimmung, 78, 81
Bestimmungsgrund, 78, 95
Bewegungsgrund, 91 n.
Biester, Johann Erich, 57 n.
Bohatec, Josef, 216 n.
Boleyn, Anne, 236
Bonitas, 131, 132, 149 n.
Bonum consummatum, 242, 245

Brett Duval Fromson

Running
and Fighting
Working in Washington

SIMON AND SCHUSTER
NEW YORK

Copyright © 1981 by Brett Duval Fromson
All rights reserved
including the right of reproduction
in whole or in part in any form
Published by Simon and Schuster
A Division of Gulf & Western Corporation
Simon & Schuster Building
Rockefeller Center
1230 Avenue of the Americas
New York, New York 10020

SIMON AND SCHUSTER and colophon are trademarks of
Simon & Schuster
Designed by Irving Perkins and Associates
Manufactured in the United States of America

1 2 3 4 5 6 7 8 9 10

Library of Congress Cataloging in Publication Data
Fromson, Brett Duval.
Running and fighting.

1. Fromson, Brett Duval.
2. United States.   Congress—Officials and employees
—Biography.   3. Civil service—United States—
Biography.   I. Title.
JK1083.F76   328.73'07658'0924   81-9188
AACR2
ISBN 0-671-42428-9

Acknowledgment

How does one thank his family for love and intelligent criticism given over a quarter of a century? Though this paper cannot begin to do it, it can carry a small written message—a whisper of affection and gratitude.

To Dan Green, who took a chance on me, I want to say, "Thanks, I needed that." It was beginner's luck for me to work with a superb professional. There would be no book without him.

John Herman helped shape this story and then guided it through the production process. His editing greatly improved the book.

To Walter Betkowski, my always kind and hard-headed agent, I owe a special note of gratitude.

Finally, my thanks to those with whom I worked and lived during my stay in Washington, D.C. They taught me the book!

To J. T. F.

Author's Note

This story is a work of nonfiction composed from memory and memoranda. Though not an exposé, it is about the men and women who run your government and about what happens to these frail, powerful people. Politicians excepted, all names have been changed in the text.

NOT ONE word of the commencement speaker reached me. His speech was blown away by the breeze that had broken the June heat wave.

I gave my attention to the man on my left and the woman on my right. He, wearing a homemade electric-blue graduation gown that his parents must have hated, sat reading Allen Ginsberg's *Howl*. She sported the traditional black mortarboard cap but without a gown. Instead she wore gym shorts, a red T-shirt ("Support ERA"), and a pair of blue track shoes. Nervously, she adjusted her bra as the day got hotter. The three of us talked a little. He was headed for law school—"My dad's an attorney." She had chosen medical school—"Columbia Physicians and Surgeons; P&S, you know." Each of them exuded the quiet confidence of people who knew where they were going and why.

I was not so sure. I was on my way to work for the federal government in Washington, D.C. Three months earlier I had been interviewed for a position in the President's Executive Office, and one month later an assistant to the President had telephoned to offer me the job. I had said yes because that impressive voice on the other end of the telephone offered adventure.

I hoped it would measure up to my father's when he was my age. In 1943 he had left college for government service in the Office of Strategic Services, America's first civilian intelligence

11

agency, with personnel recruited from among the best in academia, business and government. As he had served the country after college, so would I. As he had shone, so would I.

With a job in the Executive Office of the President, I had hopes of whispering in great men's ears about monumental issues. I had the confidence of a young man who had never failed to meet the challenges of life in a well-to-do home and superior schools.

Coming to Washington, however, had never been a childhood ambition. I hadn't even visited it as a kid. Washington wasn't the kind of town my mother and father liked. They recalled a provincial Southern city, hot weather, no air conditioners, and bureaucrats. Partly because I knew my parents were unlikely to frequent Washington, I was pleased to be going there. I wanted it to be my world.

Neither my older sister nor my two older brothers nor any good friends (with the important exception of my girl friend Joni Simpson) had any desire to be directly involved with national politics. That I was on my way to Washington, D.C., was not, however, pure chance. Despite Vietnam, Watergate and stagflation, I retained an uncrystallized faith in democratic government.

This faith derived largely from my being raised in a small Connecticut town where "government" was a hundred familiar friends and enemies congregating at the Town Hall to argue about and then compromise on such issues as property taxes and the elementary-school budget. The only paid and permanent officials were Mrs. Runner, the town clerk; Mr. Coley, the tax assessor; and two constables. The selectmen and the members of the boards of education, finance and zoning all served without pay after their working day ended.

Malfeasance, of course, was not unknown to us in Connecticut. One summer a selectman was caught renting his dump truck to the town for three times the going rate. A constable was indicted for violating the Mann Act. Minor conflicts of interest and peccadilloes, however, never impeded the opening of school in the fall, the plowing of roads in winter, or the passage

12

of the town budget in spring. The people had a realistic view of town government; as with one's neighbors, if you didn't expect too much, on occasion you could be pleasantly surprised.

The government I grew up with worked. It was simple, because our town was simple—five thousand affluent people whose only demand on their leaders was to maintain two-acre zoning and good schools without raising land taxes too high.

I knew from school and later from college that the federal government had a more complex mandate. I saw on television and read in the newspapers about its failures and fiascos, about Vietnam and Watergate and inflation. Yet I was insulated from those troubles. The draft was ended the year I turned eighteen. Nixon resigned when I was a sophomore in college. While inflation roared out of control, my parents were supporting me financially. I was immune from the effects of poor national leadership.

So, when leaving Stanford, I was not angry with the government. Intellectually, I knew it was floundering, but that didn't bother me tremendously. I figured that it was about time for a new group of politicians and advisers to rise to the top and lead. I wanted to assist and influence the new political elite. My political views were still largely unformed, but I thought that, as a reasonably well-educated citizen, I had a responsibility to help government make more rational decisions. I saw government as a system of checks and balances that solved problems. Because the President, the members of Congress, and the many bureaucrats had blundered so, I guessed they would use all the help they could get.

My ticket to Washington was the economics I studied at Stanford. I had done well in my courses, and in the fall of my senior year my adviser in the department asked me into his office.

"What do you think about economics graduate school?" he asked.

I hadn't thought about it at all. Economics had merely been something to study. I had never wanted it as a vocation. The prospect of spending the rest of my life analyzing models of a business firm or of the national economy bored me. It sounded

13

like a dry, dry life. I respected this professor, however, so I said, "I don't know, Professor. I doubt whether I could go to economics graduate school right away."

"Well," he said, "perhaps you'd like to spend some time working on economic policy in Washington before you make any decision?"

He was sitting with his back to the window, through which I could see one of those Technicolor sunsets that stir the soul of all Easterners. It was a sign, an omen. I could almost see the opening credits projected on the horizon: *Mr. Fromson Goes to Washington.*

"Now, that's an idea," I told him.

During the spring break, I went to interview in Washington. My adviser had worked there during the Johnson administration and arranged meetings for me at four agencies within the Executive Office of the President: the Council of Economic Advisers (CEA), the Office of Management and Budget (OMB), the office of the Special Trade Commission (STR), and the Council on International Economic Policy (CIEP). Though smaller than bureaucracies like the Department of Defense or the Department of Energy, these four were physically and politically closer to the President. The CEA fed economic advice directly to him. The OMB prepared the annual budget he presented to the Congress. The STR personally represented him at all trade negotiations with foreign countries, and the CIEP was established to coordinate United States foreign economic policy for him.

I had four interviews in two days. The positions they offered required an excellent undergraduate training or a master's degree in economics. A doctorate was deemed unnecessary—"We don't need any more Ph.D.'s," they explained. "Economics in the Executive Office of the President is political economy, with the emphasis on political." My training in fiction writing interested them more than any Ph.D.

I could not have gone wrong if any of them had given me a job. Luckily, one did. A month later I was basking in the sun on the sloping roof outside my room. My eyes were closed, so I couldn't see the rolling green of the coastal foothills. A copy of John Maynard Keynes's *General Theory* and an empty beer bottle were around somewhere. I was contemplating whether yesterday or today was the most beautiful day in history.

The phone inside my room rang. Without getting up or opening my eyes, I reached a long arm through the open window and pulled the receiver off the hook.

"Hello."

An operator spoke. "This is the White House calling. Is Mr. Fromson there?"

My eyes opened wide. I sat up unsteadily, still a bit sedated. The beer bottle fell over and rolled into the copper gutter.

The operator repeated herself. "This is the White House. Is Mr. Brett Duval From—"

"Yes, I'm here."

"Please hold on. Mr. Samuel Platt will speak with you." She clicked off. A second later a man spoke.

"Brett, this is Sam Platt with CIEP. Do you want to come work for us?"

I hesitated, still groggy from too much sun.

"Well?" he asked.

"Sure."

"Great, we'll see you on the second Monday in June."

"OK."

"That a good date for you?"

"Sure, I guess so," I said, hoping commencement exercises were before that date.

"Fine, fine. See you then." He hung up.

I put the receiver back on the hook, lay down and shut my eyes again. Then I opened them a bit to admire the fiercely blue sky and said to myself, "You did it." I would be working for the most powerful person in Washington, the President of the United States. There seemed no better starting place.

The day after commencement, I left Stanford with my girl friend Joni. She had a job with a House of Representatives subcommittee that authorized legislation for United States for-

15

eign aid. I had no doubt she would do well. She had the gift of expressing her character instantly and entirely, no matter what mood she happened to be in, so that people knew immediately who they were dealing with. There was nothing phony about her. She was someone people naturally trusted. In an environment of mistrust like Washington, she would win a reputation as a fair trader.

Joni had already applied to and been accepted by the Stanford Graduate School of Business, but she had deferred for a year and was wondering "Should I go to a business school?" She may have had doubts, but I had none. She was not cut out to marry early and raise a family. As much as I did, Joni wanted to succeed in a career of her own. We considered work and romance difficult enough to balance; work and marriage seemed impossible.

In Washington Joni and I would share a house with three other young people who were friends of friends. We had only corresponded with them by letter.

Our house mates were Nicholas Sprague, son of a former United States ambassador, who worked as a lobbyist for a Washington law firm; Diana Daniels, daughter of a prominent lawyer, who was "finding herself" by waiting tables in a chi-chi Georgetown restaurant; and Charity Livingston, an upper-crust girl with Declaration of Independence signers on both sides of her family, who worked as legislative assistant for a United States Senator. Nicholas had matriculated at Yale, Diana at Harvard, and Charity at Princeton. I expected them to be more sophisticated than I. After all, I had spent four years away from Eastern society as defined by prep schools, the Ivy League, and *The New York Times* wedding page.

On our first day of work, the alarm clock went off at 7:30 A.M. At breakfast my feet tapped nervously. What had been a distant political abstraction one week earlier was now quite real.

I was in the greatest arena of politics and power, and I didn't know whether I would succeed or fail. I didn't even know what success or failure in Washington meant.

16

Summer

THE OLD EXECUTIVE OFFICE BUILDING (OEOB) is the bureaucracy's palace. Neo-Renaissance in style and rectangular in shape, it has balustrades and balconies, and lavishly decorated five-tiered granite walls that rise to a slate-shingled mansard roof a hundred feet above its next-door neighbor, the White House, tethered alongside like a dinghy to a stately man-of-war.

As I entered the OEOB, the warm wet air and cacaphony of the morning rush hour receded; inside all was cool, dry and quiet. I watched thin men in dark suits walk by on missions for the President. Unlike the Capitol or the Supreme Court Building, it has neither tourists nor casual visitors wandering in these marble halls. Part of the White House compound, this is the unpublicized bastion for most of the President's top aides.

Waiting for the beefy guard sitting behind a desk to clear me through the checkpoint was unexpectedly nerve-racking. I stood timidly while he addressed me.

"What's your name?" He didn't look up from his master list of scheduled visitors.

"Brett Fromson."

"Sign the check sheet," he said, pushing a mimeographed piece of paper across the desktop. I found my name right after Fosdick and wrote my signature. The officer of the Executive Protection Service began leafing through a circular file on his meticulously organized desk. He compared my signature with a file card I could not see. Only then did he look up at me, and not with a friendly cast to his gaze. "Have a seat over there," he ordered, pointing at a hard, wooden bench in the entrance hall.

He called over another equally large guard. They muttered to each other for some minutes glancing occasionally at me. While I sweated in my blue-and-white candy-striped seersucker suit and reminded myself that I had gotten a haircut the week before, they gave me occasional suspicious stares as if they had caught me speeding and were wondering whether I was armed. The other men in the checkpoint queue glared resentfully at this young man who was delaying them.

Had I done something wrong? Perhaps their security investigation of me had found some irregularities in my past life? I was in such a state that I even asked myself, "I did get that phone call, didn't I?"

The sergeant called me over. "Can I see some identification?" I gave him my Connecticut driver's license, my MasterCard, and my Stanford student I.D. He motioned me to come closer; I stepped forward so that my legs were flush against the desk. He asked me, "Why did you sign in with us as Brett Fromson? The official signature we have for Mr. Fromson is Brett Duval Fromson."

So that was the problem: They weren't sure I was me. Welcome to the federal bureaucracy. I explained it was a petty oversight. The sergeant suggested in no uncertain terms that from then on I sign my signature the way the government had it registered. I promised that I would. He then sent me over to the Secret Service office, where they would photograph me, fingerprint me, and issue me a security card. I followed his command and hurried down the black-and-white-checked marble corridor. I was only too pleased to let them fingerprint me; I just wanted to get in the building.

Instigated by executive order of President Nixon in 1971, CIEP had its legal basis in Public Law 93-121, approved October 4, 1973. The initial Presidential ukase was sweeping and vague.

The bill conferred no specific authority on CIEP, nor did it impose any specific requirement except the submission of an annual international economic report to the Congress from the President. Blessed with this mandate, the CIEP was whatever the President wished to make of it. Nixon had established the CIEP to tighten his control over American international economic policy the way the National Security Council (NSC) helped him with international security affairs.

The President was CIEP's official chairman. The members were the Secretaries of Treasury, State, Defense, Commerce, Agriculture, Transportation and Labor. The wide membership was designed to prevent "end-runs" on the President by Cabinet officers trying to get an informal decision without the knowledge of other bureaucrats with a stake in that particular issue.

By the time I arrived on the scene, the CIEP was no longer coordinating or even serving as the forum for international economic policy making. It had moved one step further along the bureaucratic life cycle: Birth, Adolescence, Maturity, and finally (no, not Rigor Mortis) Transmutation. Instead of letting CIEP die when he no longer wanted to use it to coordinate international economic policy, the President redefined its purpose. CIEP staff was now employed to organize the latest White House forum for economic policy, the Economic Policy Board (EPB). The EPB's membership was identical with CIEP's, except that it also included the Secretaries of Health, Education and Welfare (HEW), Housing and Urban Development (HUD), and Interior, and the Director of the OMB, the Chairman of the CEA, and the Assistant to the President for Economic Affairs. Thus, CIEP paid personnel became the EPB's unofficial staff. The President could have gone to Congress for more money, but with the November elections only five months away, he was loath to have his Executive Office scrutinized by hostile, partisan Congressmen.

After the Secret Service office was through with my fingers and face, a minor clerk phoned CIEP-EPB offices to have someone come down and pick me up. The OEOB is large, but not as

19

large as the Pentagon, so I offered to find my own way. The clerk said, "Have a seat. They're on their way." I was the only person he could boss around.

A few minutes later, a grandmotherly lady walked into the office, took one look at me, and introduced herself as Mary Byrne, "Sam Platt's secretary." Mary gently explained that Sam was waiting in his office, that we had better hurry. A long-legged twenty-one-year-old boy and a plump fifty-nine-year-old secretary strode and waddled respectively as fast as they could along the corridors and circular stairways to CIEP-EPB's third-floor suites.

No expense had been spared on plaster work; the walls were covered with intricate border designs straight from the baroque palaces of Austria. No interior feature impressed me more than the great spiraling staircases, up one of which Mary led me. The steps were hard New England granite. The banister was mahogany and smooth to the touch. The grandeur of the building bespoke not only the aesthetics of public architecture in the Victorian Era, but also, the importance of the past and present occupants of the OEOB. Before the turn of the century, the building housed three paramount bureaucracies: State, War and Navy. It was then appropriately named the State, War and Navy Building. By 1949 and the age of American global ascendancy, they had all moved to larger quarters and the building was renamed the Executive Office Building. Postwar Presidents quickly brought in personal staff to fill the space. With the further growth of the government and concomitantly the Executive Office, another building was erected to house Presidential staff in 1965; that Holiday Inn-like brick structure built on the other side of Pennsylvania Avenue became the *New* Executive Office Building, and this was renamed the *Old* Executive Office Building.

The OEOB was the building where Theodore Roosevelt, William Howard Taft, Franklin Delano Roosevelt, Henry L. Stimson, Cordell Hull and George C. Marshall had served. My awe was dimmed only by the memory that the OEOB had also been home to Richard M. Nixon's plumbers, who had sallied forth to the Watergate from their windowless rooms in the OEOB's dank basement.

By the time Mary and I arrived at Sam's three-office suite, he was already in a meeting with lobbyists from the domestic shoe industry; they were pleading for government tariff protection from lower-cost foreign shoemakers. Sam had left a note on Mary's desk asking her to show me my office and escort me to the weekly CIEP-EPB staff meeting at 10 A.M. if he was still in conference.

Digs in the OEOB are the cushiest I've seen in Washington. Proximity to the President may not necessarily mean power to influence, but it does mean comfort. My office was a snug wood-paneled 12-by-15-foot room. The royal-blue wall-to-wall carpeting was dotted with Presidential seals to remind me exactly where I was. Matching the carpet was an elegant silver-, white-and-blue–striped settee for visitors. The walls were decorated with nineteenth-century lithographs depicting wealthy burghers and their families cruising through the snow in horse-drawn sleighs. Every office in the OEOB had quaint reproductions that gave a deceptive feeling of gentility as if to mask the vulgar wielding of political and bureaucratic power that went on day after day.

I took a seat at my massive oak desk topped with gilt-edged blotter and WATS line for limitless dialing anywhere within the continental United States. As Mary brought in White House stationery, pens, pencils, and other office supplies, I swiveled in my armchair and looked out my tall draped window into one of the two OEOB inner courtyards; the President's Secretary of Energy was getting into a waiting black limousine.

I hadn't expected anything so plush, but as I learned, in Washington the President's men go first class. They quickly get used to it. My office had been unoccupied for the previous three months because the senior staffer who was to have it thought it too small. Compared to the ballrooms that his peers like Sam had, it was.

Sitting in that office with Mary waiting hand and foot on me, I felt a little uncomfortable. What had I done to deserve all this?

Since at 10 A.M. Sam's meeting with the men from the shoe industry was still in progress, Mary walked me down the hall to Room 208, a long wood-paneled chamber overlooking the Ellipse and Washington Monument. This was the site of the CIEP-EPB weekly staff meeting. The room was half-filled; principal staff members sat at the long table in the center, while junior staffers like me took chairs on the perimeter.

The boss was a corpulent older man sitting at the far end of the table. His bald head and roman nose made him look like Telly Savalas, but he was actually the Honorable William Seaman, Special Assistant to the President for Economic Affairs and Executive Director of the EPB. He had deep, fleshy furrows in his wide forehead and a glow on his bullet-shaped dome. He seemed tough. I soon discovered that he was a friend of the President and former chairman of a national accounting firm. He was another in the long line of White House assistants whose position is based on loyalty to the President, not expertise in any single field. Seaman had people like Sam to provide economic intelligence.

After Seaman briefed us on President Ford's recent summit meeting in the Caribbean with Giscard D'Estaing of France, Schmidt of West Germany, and Callaghan of Great Britain, he called on the senior staff for questions or observations.

Sitting at the table was a fairly representative sampling of the men I would meet. These were the elite bureaucrats with legal, managerial, and/or economic training who fight for the ear of the politician.

To an uninformed observer, they wouldn't have seemed at all extraordinary. These men, however, captivated me. Forget the bland smiles on their faces; forget the meek positions of their hands in their laps. These men, as much as anyone in Washington, set the government's agenda. Theirs was the power to influence the President by controlling the flow of information to him. Supported by thousands of "word processors" (a.k.a. typists), they thought of themselves not as bureaucrats but as policy makers. They wrote the "decision memoranda," those thin white sheets of paper that gave the President his policy options.

They "sat at the table" where I wanted to sit. Their power to influence was more seductive than any curve in a woman's body.

The first to speak was Steve Brawn, Deputy Assistant to the President for Economic Affairs and Seaman's second in command. He was a man I could see leading a squad of Marines up Pork Chop Hill. He had a rocklike chin and broad shoulders, behind which others could duck. Brawn had been at CIEP-EPB only two months, however, and was no larger-than-life figure. "Seems like the summit went well," he said. "That's all I have to say." Brawn was Seaman's loyal subordinate. Such an agreeable attitude was fundamental to his success in Washington; if the President should be reelected in November, only those whose loyalty was unqualified would be retained. Excepting the maids and janitors in the OEOB, no one had tenure in the Executive Office. We all served at the pleasure of the President.

Brawn didn't make waves. He flew around the country to speak in support of the President's "political vision and economic leadership." He wanted to stay in Washington longer than the twenty-two months that were the post-WWII average for Cabinet assistant secretaries; twenty-two months are not enough time to figure out the taxi zones in Washington, let alone change government policy on any important issue.

As a CIEP aide told me, "He wants to leave his mark on the government." I admired Brawn's pretensions and would try to emulate him, albeit on a smaller scale. I even picked up one of his physical mannerisms, keeping my hands on the table while I spoke and rapping the wood to emphasize points.

The other senior staff at the table were different from Brawn. They were career men, a bit shorter and with shoulders more stooped. They had seen Seamans and Brawns come and go, but they had survived. No matter what happened to the President, they would find another place in Washington to influence some other elected politician. These men were not ideologues—far from it. Listening to their friendly, sober voices, I began to understand what skills allow unelected policy makers to prosper even while the government flounders.

Ben Hayes, Seaman's personal assistant, spoke first. He was

23

thirty years old and wanted to know from Seaman "if the skies were blue, the tennis good, and the women plentiful" in the Caribbean. His question extracted the customary chuckles and smirks. Smiling genially, Hayes said, "No, seriously, the summit seems to have been a wonderful success. . . . We'll have to evaluate the ramifications of the summit negotiations before any conclusions can be drawn." Like most of his peers, Hayes wanted to avoid voicing objections in this forum; he would have written a memo to Seaman or, better yet, would have had a quiet conversation with him. Bureaucratic lobbying took place in private, not at staff meetings, where you were surrounded by rivals for Seaman's attention.

Hayes was followed by Paul English, associate director for international monetary problems. A lawyer and economist, English was known as "Mr. Memo," because he left trails of memoranda wherever he went. Producing so many memos, he always appeared to be busy; after he wrote them, they were proof that he had been busy. More importantly, however, these written messages worked gradually to convince English's superiors that his ideas were sound—"After all, look at all the documentation." In an accentless voice, English informed Seaman that he would have his memo.

Seaman then said, "Sam, what do you think?" This was aimed at a small, sturdy man whose shoetips barely reached the floor unless he sat forward in the large leather armchair. His wavy hair was cropped short and he wore a standard-issue blue Brooks Brothers summer-weight suit. I recognized him now. He was my new boss, Sam Platt.

He was the only one to ask a substantive question. He wanted to know how the Caribbean summit would affect the upcoming CIEC meetings in Paris, where representatives from the poor nations of the world were negotiating with the United States and other industrialized countries for a larger piece of the world's riches. Sam was CIEP-EPB representative to CIEC, from one acronym to another.

Seaman said that there was no change; United States policy

24

remained in opposition to the central demand of the Third World that commodity cartels be established to guarantee higher prices for their exports. Sam nodded agreement with Seaman. He had his orders. Though a Schedule-C supergrade appointee earned as much as a Congressman, Sam knew there was no room for debate with our superiors. As I would learn, we were in an election year; the President wanted political loyalty above all else.

When discussion on the summit ended, Seaman looked over at me and announced, "I'd like to introduce Brett Fromson to you. Brett will be working with Sam. Stand up, Brett, so everyone can see you." I stood up awkwardly, but tried to smile confidently. There was a brief round of applause. Sam turned around in his chair and said, "Welcome aboard, kid."

My moment of attention vanished as suddenly as it had appeared. Seaman's electronic buzzer buzzed before I had a chance to sit down. The President wanted to see him right away. Before leaving, he said, "In my absence, Steve Brawn will give you a short message. He speaks for me and most importantly for the President, so listen up." With those foreboding words, Seaman left.

The remaining men straightened up in their chairs. The tension was immediate and total. No one whispered to his neighbor. Sitting on the edge of my chair on the edge of the room, I waited to see what would happen. Brawn moved into Seaman's chair at the head of the table, put his elbows on the varnished top, and said, "Recently, there have been repeated stories in the press about dissension and confusion in the President's Administration. While we don't know who the leakers and cry-babies are, I want to remind everyone that we are in the middle of a Presidential campaign and will soon be reaching the tightest part. The President has been slipping in the polls as we all know. But the President, Mr. Seaman and I are confident that we shall still be in the White House come January. The President needs and expects your loyalty. If any of you have complaints about his policies or leadership, direct your problems to

25

me or to Bill Seaman—not the press. Let me remind you that if you can't play team ball, you don't belong here." He paused for emphasis. "That's all, gentlemen."

The meeting adjourned quickly. Most of the men headed directly for the doors. Sam lingered for a moment in conversation with Brawn and then walked over to me. My face must have betrayed some anxiety, because Sam said, "What Brawn said shouldn't concern you. This isn't the Nixon White House, and we're not the plumbers outfit. C'mon, there's work to be done."

Sam went to the daily CIA briefing. This was designed to keep him and two other senior staffers abreast of the latest political and economic intelligence useful for the success of American foreign economic policy. They reviewed information relating to wide-ranging questions like: What is the extent of Cuban and Soviet influence in the domestic affairs of Jamaica? What are the chances that the Peruvian anchovy harvest will disappear as it did in 1972–73 and endanger world fertilizer stocks? How successful is Russian oil exploration in Siberia? Which developing countries are using American economic aid to buy Sten guns and napalm instead of tractors?

I returned to my office and began reading a Council on Wage and Price Stability (CWPS) report on the structure of the United States aluminum industry. The goal of the paper was to identify whether the price of aluminum was controlled by a few private firms to the detriment of their customers and the over-all rate of inflation. The elite of big government was wondering what the elite of big business was up to.

The analysis was technical; the style pure "bureaucratese." I had not gotten more than fifteen pages into it when Sam poked his head in the doorway and asked me if I wanted to get some lunch. We descended the nearest staircase to the staff mess on the ground floor along the 17th Street side of the OEOB. The mess was a warren of small rooms whose walls were covered with Americana wallpaper. The armchairs were hard and wooden like those at a New England boarding school.

Lunch was self-serve, simple and inexpensive. Black women behind long stainless-steel counters served large portions of fried chicken or hash or roast beef for $1.50, including potatoes and vegetables, a meal that would have cost double that in the world outside the OEOB (excluding, of course, the United States Congress, home of the subsidized meal).

I ordered liver as Sam had done, and with tray in hand I followed him to a small square table. Unlike many of the grim-looking men I saw muttering to one another at nearby tables, Sam was relaxed. Mary had said that Sam was a hard worker but not humorless. Unlike many in the White House, he was not worried about every bump and grind in the polls.

Over lunch Sam suggested that I not take Washington too seriously. "There'll be ups and downs, assholes and saints. Don't let them bother you. You're young. You've got a long way to go. I worked my way up, and I didn't have a Congressman for a father-in-law."

I heard Sam, but I wasn't going to act on his admonition. I wanted to take Washington seriously. I wanted to dive right in, make it, be better than my bosses expected. Sam must have sensed my attitude, because he changed the topic of conversation to professional football. He talked about how the Washington Redskins "were going to grab the Dallas Cowboys by the short hairs and give them a good yank" in next season's games. People in political Washington like football more than any other game except politics. It's the game's exercise of raw power and deception that fascinates them, but then again perhaps it's the "team play."

As Sam and I walked back to the CIEP-EPB offices, he commented that my hair could use a trim. I told him I had been clipped only last week and that I'd never gotten a haircut more than once a month. He still suggested that I go over to the West Wing of the White House and get a haircut from Mr. Potts, the President's barber. Sam made an appointment for me, and ten minutes later I went. Potts would fit me in between the Secretary of the Treasury and the chairman of the CEA.

Mr. Potts was a short middle-aged man from the South, with

a silver pompadour and a smile like a pearly king. He welcomed me, took my jacket, sat me in the leather barber chair, and set to work. The large RCA color television was on; either the chairman of the CEA or the Secretary of the Treasury had been watching Bill Cullen and *The Price Is Right*.

Potts cut and talked, cut and talked. The President's barber had been hired as much for his ability to put high officials at ease as for his tonsorial skills. Potts spewed stories and political gossip. Massaging my scalp, he commented that I had a pretty tight scalp, tighter than the President's but not as tight as former Treasury Secretary Bill Simon, about the same as Henry Kissinger's. I assumed that was a compliment.

Potts then launched into a story about the tight-scalped, conservative Mr. Simon. As a child, he was chauffeured to and from school. Each morning and afternoon, the less privileged kids whose parents couldn't afford such transport would shout insults at him as he went by. One afternoon, Simon had the driver stop and went out to confront his detractors. Simon picked out the ringleader and beat the crap out of him. The lesson of the tale, Potts explained, was that you have to be a tough son-of-a-bitch to succeed.

I didn't know what this fable said about Simon; it was more revealing of Potts, who obviously identified with Simon's pinstriped machismo. Not surprisingly, when Potts finished with me, I looked like a full-fledged member of Young Americans for Freedom. As I entered the OEOB from the White House, the same well-fed guard who had hassled me this morning now smiled and said, "Hello, sir." When Sam saw me he commented dryly, "Now you look the part."

I didn't leave my office until 7 P.M. that evening. The study of the aluminum industry by the senior economist at the Council on Wage and Price Stability (CWPS) was slow going, and I had to finish a critique of the paper that day. My memo on it would constitute the bulk of CIEP-EPB's agency review of the paper. In Washington parlance, Sam wanted it "quick and dirty."

By 4 P.M., I understood the main thrust of the paper: six major aluminum companies directly or indirectly set prices and production levels to make entry into the industry unprofitable for new competitors. There was no assertion or documentation that these aluminum companies were in violation of federal antitrust laws. The authors of the paper did suggest, however, that because of the noncompetitive structure of the aluminum industry prices did not fall in a recession but always rose in a recovery. They added that these companies' aluminum plants were being built almost exclusively outside the country much to the United States' strategic disadvantage.

The first seven-eighths of the paper were strong, but the last eighth was weak. Actually, it was nonexistent. There was no final chapter. After an analysis that described the aluminum industry as an oligopoly serving its own interests, the authors seemed to have forgotten that perhaps the government should consider action to protect the public's interest. I called the CWPS author on the telephone and asked him if I had received an incomplete copy of the paper.

"Nope, you got the whole thing."

"Are you sure there's not another chapter?" He didn't answer at first.

Then he said dolefully, "There was once, but not anymore."

"Too controversial?"

"I can't discuss it now. I gotta go. Sorry." He hung up.

I took his warning to heart. I let the matter drop. My job was to review what was presented, not complain about what was missing. I stayed late. So did Mary.

She was a maiden secretary of the old school who had been brought up to jump whether the boss said "Jump" or not. I soon discovered that the memos I gave her were typed and returned error-free before the deadline. Each day before getting lunch for herself, she would ask Sam and me if she could bring back anything for us. Mary never complained about the work load or about Sam's smelly cigars, which I felt sure she detested. Staying late at the office when we needed evening or weekend typing

29

was nothing for her. Mary shared the special neurosis of the better public servants: When you think you're working in "the national interest," your work is never over.

By 6 P.M., I gave Mary the handwritten draft on yellow legal paper. She typed and I revised until 6:45. My four-page memo concluded in my new language of bureaucratic understatements that, "The analysis of industry behavior suggests certain areas of concern to the President. There are, however, no recommended remedies." I figured I would tell Sam about my conversation with the CWPS economist. If I wrote things down, I'd have to defend them. On my first day, I didn't want to get involved in an issue whose controversy might rub off on me. I wanted my new bosses to like me and trust me.

At seven, after Mary had left, the Secret Service security officer with the "burn bag" for unwanted classified documents entered without knocking and asked if I had anything for him. To my regret, I didn't yet have anything valuable enough to be burned. For the moment, all I needed for my trash was a wastepaper basket.

I called Joni at home. She had left work at six. "When are you leaving?" she asked.

"Right now."

"They've already got you working late?"

"Yes, but so does everyone else." I added enthusiastically, "This is where the action is."

Joni was unimpressed, perhaps because she worked for the legislative branch of government. "Great, but be home in twenty minutes if you want dinner."

It had been a fine day. Later, I would meet other young people who had been through similar first days. I recall what my housemate Charity Livingston said about her first day. "I drafted legislation in the morning, lunched with the Senator at noon, and spent the afternoon in the Senate cloakroom counting votes with the lobbyists."

By the end of that first day, we newcomers to Washington knew that we'd stay. We felt that the fate of the nation was in our hands—or a little piece of it anyway. Unlike our cousins in Manhattan whose main concern seemed to be earning enough money to pay next month's rent, we in Washington were paid $20,000-plus a year to be junior navigators on the ship of state. We had no need to compute an index for the quality of our life in Washington. [(Ambition ÷ Ideals) × (Salary + Perquisites).] Our first days took care of that in the most dramatic way.

Yet, in what way were we in Washington any different from our former classmates? None that I could tell. My father was a successful businessman like so many of theirs. Like their parents, he and my mother had raised us in wealthy exurbia and sent us to public and then private schools. Perhaps because my father had gone to Washington to join the OSS, I was fascinated by working for the government. No, that was not it; their parents also served the government during World War II. What was the difference? After my first day of work, I knew.

We may have told our friends in New York that Washington was comfortable, well-paid, or even an exciting lesson in civics, but the delectable secret we kept to ourselves was that we were the rising elite of politicians, bureaucrats, do-gooders and lobbyists who would climb to the top before the Dow hit 1,500 and would lead the government and America into the twenty-first century. Though we saw ourselves closer to the bottom of the Washington hierarchy than to the top, closer to lackey than to President, we had little doubt that it was our destiny to rise. After all we were only just out of college, and look where we were already—with other "up-to-snuff" people who would govern the longest-lived, richest and strongest democratic government of the best country on earth.

None of us knew what it would take to do well. We guessed that resilience and hard work were essential, but those are rather loose guides. We kept our questions and ambitions to ourselves. You can understand why we didn't make predictions for ourselves: What if for some unforeseeable reason we flopped? After all, there seemed to be no set criteria for a good performance. Who knew what would please our superiors? It would be bad enough to end up at age forty-five as a press flack for some second-rate bureaucracy, but to be there after having informed people that you planned on a position as the next Special Assistant to the President for the Future of Mankind and Democracy? That would be too much. Such were the nightmares of the up-and-comers.

So, each one of us learned immediately—on the first day perhaps—to dream of recognition and responsibility while we denied our dreams in front of others. We practiced self-effacement to protect ourselves.

It took me only fifteen minutes to drive home to the brick townhouse that Joni and I shared with Charity, Diana and Nicholas. Our home was tucked away safely in the Northwest section of Washington. The city is divided into quadrants: Northwest, Northeast, Southwest and Southeast. The whites live predominantly in Northwest, and the blacks everywhere else. There are some integrated neighborhoods like Capitol Hill, DuPont Circle and Columbia Road, where whites are buying and blacks selling, but as in most American cities, whites and blacks live separately. This color line is broken only by blacks who are members of the upper reaches of the federal bureaucracy. Many black professionals, the doctors and lawyers, still live in black neighborhoods north of Massachusetts Avenue and east of Rhode Island Avenue. So it was that the only dark-skinned people who lived in our neighborhood were members of the Kuwaiti Embassy across the street.

In this exclusive neighborhood, our furnished four-bedroom house rented for $500 a month. Originally, the white family that owned the house lived in it, but they had moved out to the suburbs in Virginia across the Potomac River, after the 1965 race riots. They were pleased to rent their old home to young men and women whose rent would more than pay the property taxes until the family decided to sell. The five of us were also pleased; we paid $100 per month per person.

When I arrived home that summer evening after my first day, the others were seated at the Victorian mahogany dining table finishing dinner. The lighted candles on the table and side tables cast an intimate glow over the little party. They were discussing a recent *Economist* magazine editorial on the Palestinian problem. It was a cozy, well-ordered group.

Some seconds passed before they noticed me, so intent were they on each other. I had a rare chance to observe without disturbing the moment. Nicholas, the diplomat's son, sat at the head of the table as if protocol demanded. He was dressed like me in a Brooks Brothers suit and button-down shirt. Joni, Charity and Diana sat along the sides. The far end opposite Nicholas was reserved for me. I watched Nicholas and Charity speaking to Joni and ignoring each other. Diana seemed on the verge of sleep.

Nicholas said to Joni, "There'll be no peace in the Middle East until we recognize the PLO."

"There'll be no peace in the Middle East until the PLO recognizes Israel's right to exist," Charity countered to Joni.

"If she didn't work for the Senator from California, she wouldn't give a damn about the Jews," Nicholas replied, referring to Charity in the third person.

"If his firm didn't represent Arab interests, he might give a damn about more than oil," she said with her aristocratic nose up and a condescending glance at Nicholas.

Nicholas and Charity regularly performed this way. They had known each other since childhood, through boarding school and college, and now in Washington. Like siblings, they shared an endearing rivalry. Their quarrels were a comfort to them, a source of amusement. I always waited for them to drop their poses. It was a futile wait. For them, not posing would have been the biggest pose of all.

Though Nicholas was handsome and Charity a sleek, black-silk-haired knockout, they rarely went out. Occasionally, they slept together, but they were not constant lovers. That would have been too incestuous. They did sometimes make mock romantic advances toward each other. "How can you go out with that coked-up toad," Nicholas might say to her, "when I'm available?" Charity would reply, "Why should I save myself for someone who only goes out with Midwestern girls with big breasts?" Then they would laugh.

Diana was the first to notice me. "Your hubby is home," she wise-cracked to Joni. This became Diana's nightly welcome to me. Joni and I were one of the few "couples" among our friends. We tried to play down this peculiarity. We rarely discussed our relationship. We were uncertain about the future, and we dealt with that uncertainty by ignoring it.

After dinner Charity and Diana left to play tennis. Joni, Nicholas and I adjourned to the front porch. This was soon to become a postprandial ritual. We didn't care about the sunset (we sat on the eastern side of the house); we waited only for the day to unwind. The cicadas would chirp, and over a beer, a gin-and-tonic, a joint, or nothing at all, we talked and relaxed.

That first night, we were joined by an old friend of Joni's who had just graduated from college. His name was Peter Dortmund.

Peter wasn't the sort of young man who impressed people in Washington, and he knew it. He had an insignificant job at some computer trade association. His father was no one important; he made industrial movies for IBM. Peter was shorter than most men in Washington, and he slouched. He lived across the Potomac, in Roslyn, Virginia, in a barracks-like apartment complex surrounded by interstate highways. It was the kind of shabby address many people would have tried to hide. Not Peter. "That's what I like about him," Joni said. "He's totally unpretentious."

To Nicholas' fidgety annoyance, Peter and Joni reminisced about old friends from California, where they had spent a year in school. Nicholas kept crossing and uncrossing his legs.

Joni asked Peter what his plans were. Would he stay in Washington?

"Sure, I guess so. Why not? It's a pleasant town."

Nicholas said, "That's not much of a reason for being here."

He looked at Nicholas with a smile and said, "I know."

Nicholas added, "That's what I like, a young man with drive."

34

Joni suggested a game of charades to lighten the evening. Peter and Joni were one team, Nicholas and I the other. Each team prepared titles for the other side to act out and identify. Nicholas was the first one up; I was to guess.

It always amazed me how seriously some people in Washington take charades. Nicholas was one. As he read the title on his scrap of paper, he screwed up his face and paced the porch, which was now lighted by electric bulbs.

"Let's start," said Joni. "Ready, set, go." Peter kept time with his wristwatch.

"OK," said Nicholas meaningfully to me. "Here we go." He cupped his hands together like a beggar.

I hesitated a second and he reprimanded me sharply, "It's a book."

"Right," I agreed.

Nicholas made signs with his fingers that I translated into words. "Two words, second word, two syllables, second syllable."

Nicholas put one hand on his brow as if saluting and the other on his rear end like a pennant on the stern of a boat. He smiled at me knowingly as if to say, "Anyone can get this."

"Sailor, midshipman," I shouted.

He shook his head.

"Popeye?"

"No," he said, and repeated this routine. Joni and Peter began to laugh at Nicholas. Soon I was laughing, too. Nicholas refused to try another clue.

"Time's up," Joni announced. "Three minutes. Time's up."

Nicholas said to me, "Cap and tail, you idiot. I was tugging at my cap and my other hand was a tail. Cap and tail. Cap-tail. Capital, *Kapital. Das Kapital.* God, you're hopeless."

I said, "I thought people gave one clue at a time."

He replied waspishly. "Don't you see? This was the perfect clue. The whole title all at once."

"Sorry," I said.

Nicholas said to Peter, "You gave me this one, didn't you? You probably haven't even read it."

35

"Yes, I have," Peter said.

"Well, I wrote my honors thesis on Marx," Nicholas had to add.

After the game, Peter left.

I asked Nicholas what he thought of Peter. I knew what he was going to say.

"A strange fellow," he said. Part of Nicholas wanted to feel superior to Peter—the same part that judged people by where they attended college. Nicholas, however, was not a callow snob. Before Joni went to bed, he apologized.

"I don't care if you like my friends," Joni replied. "Just don't insult them. You wouldn't act that way at work, would you? Pretend my friends are potential clients."

One morning in July after a few weeks on the job, I saw a headline in a newspaper vending machine: "Another OPEC In Bauxite?" This was the question I was attacking inside the OEOB. The President had ordered a set of secret investigations to determine whether the United States was vulnerable to commodity cartels in countries that had seen what OPEC did for the oil-laden states. The studies were called Commodity Policy Coordinating Committee (CPCC) reports.

Sam had enlisted my help on this because he was spending every other week in Paris at government meetings. He delegated to me the job of organizing the CPCC investigation into bauxite, an impure mixture of aluminum oxides necessary for the production of aluminum metal. I was ordered to assemble and analyze pertinent economic and political information.

The basic question was: Determine whether the United States is susceptible to economic or strategic blackmail by countries upon whom we are dependent for bauxite. No one in the government knew the answer. The United States government had no uniform policy of examining our vulnerability to cut-offs of such critical materials.

Our problem was political. Though we produced only 20 percent of our annual bauxite consumption, the other 80 percent was available to us. Only political embargo could create a shortage. The danger was that we imported about half of the bauxite from Jamaica, the Caribbean island whose government had at that time a close affiliation with Castro's Cuba. It must have crossed some high official's mind in the moment just before dawn that a Soviet-Cuban-backed Jamaican bauxite embargo would cripple the United States economy and embarrass the government. We would not have been so worried if the bauxite came from our ally Australia.

Since intelligence information on international politics was crucial to the problem, I received CIA and State Department cables on the internal political affairs of Jamaica and other bauxite-producing nations. The cover sheets were stamped "Classified," "Secret," or "Top Secret." I gladly accepted the information, not only because it was sometimes helpful in understanding the behavior of the foreign governments, but also because in the United States government there is prestige associated with reading memos marked "Classified," "Secret," "Top Secret." It suggests that what you're doing is sufficiently important for your bosses to have allowed you to see a bit more of the "truth" they use in making policy. Some of the documents were politically sensitive and would have caused the United States problems had they been made public; others were so innocuous that I suspected they had been classified simply to deny other bureaucrats access.

My only qualm was that I didn't know whether I had the necessary security clearance. Mary and Sam never mentioned it. I considered asking Sam, but thought better of it. After all, I knew I was no spy. If I had broached it with him, he might have been forced to take me off the project. To this day, I have no idea what clearance I did have, but that was typical of my experience in Washington; I was always slightly over my head.

Surprisingly, it was often easier to get secret intelligence on the politics of some foreign country than to obtain unclassified, mundane data on bauxite production, consumption, exports and prices. The information was available; prying it out of the mitts of government bureaucrats was often difficult.

Sam and I may have run this CPCC working group, but we

depended on lower-level bureaucrats in the executive agencies for the basic numbers on which we'd base the analysis. For us in the Office of the President, these men were not to be trusted. Though their bosses, the assistant secretaries, may have been accountable to the President, these people were not. These were men who had risen through the bureaucracy, but not by the President's beneficence; their loyalty was to the bureaucracy, not the White House.

These men were safe in their jobs but insecure in their heads. They could not be fired, but they could be isolated from the flow of important information. That was why when Sam and I called a meeting to discuss the bauxite report, all the agency representatives showed up for fear that something would happen without them. Instead nothing happened because of them. There were Sprunt and Hatch from State, Leight and Stone from Defense, Hinkamp and Skinner from Treasury, Seggerman and Sherry from Interior, and Swift and Holmes from Transportation. Fortunately, we held these meetings in an OEOB treaty room with a table thirty feet long.

Mary had placed Presidential pencils, pads and glasses, all proclaiming "The White House," in front of each man. These amenities put our guests in a better mood. This is not to say, however, that they were cooperative. Each pair was there to protect his agency's interest and his own standing in that agency, not to achieve the President's objective. For example, the men from State regularly fought with the man and woman from Treasury over who would supply Sam and me with the data on foreign bauxite production.

Sam chaired the sessions. He would delegate tasks to the agency we thought best able to get the information. They rarely refused our requests. We were generally reasonable. Our difficulty was rather that each agency representative would demand that more than one bureaucracy work on what we assigned. Inevitably a week later when the work was due for submission and review (otherwise known as "submersion and re-do"), one would telephone and complain to us that he could not meet the original deadline because another agency hadn't completed its part of the assignment. Meanwhile, Sam and I wanted to get the report to the President. With Sam in Paris so often and me being so new, the bureaucrats could resist our efforts for weeks. I would call them. They would say, "It'll be there tomorrow." I would call the next day. "It'll be there tomorrow." My house mate the lobbyist, Nicholas, finally suggested a way to apply pressure; "Call his boss and tell him the President wants to see the report tomorrow." I did that. I called an assistant secretary on the phone, or rather I had my secretary call his secretary to con him into thinking I was more important.

"Bill," I said in a deep friendly voice.

"Brett," he replied, though I had met him only once.

"The President has to have our report within forty-eight hours. Can you get your man Becker on the stick? He's been a little slow delivering it."

"Brett, Brett, don't worry," he'd say, as if we were golfing buddies. The next morning the data were delivered by messenger to me.

Sometimes it was not so simple. On the day I finished writing the report for Sam to send up to the President, I got a telephone call from one of the more dithering people attached to the task force, a man from Treasury.

He began, "Brett, I've got the figures on Jamaican bauxite production. Can you send a White House courier over to get them?"

I replied, "John, those figures were supposed to be in last week. I've already compiled them."

"Well, what are your sources? Are they official?" he asked peevishly.

"I've checked them against other sources, and they're accurate. I'd like to see your numbers, but there's no need to send a special messenger. My report has already gone to Sam. Just give me the figures over the phone so I can use them to double-check my own."

He said, "No."

"What do you mean, no?"

"If they're not going to be considered before you and Sam

send this paper to the President, then why do you need them at all? You're probably using State Department numbers anyway."

I replied, "Listen, John. If you had gotten them to me on time, you wouldn't be so unhappy. Now, if you don't want to divulge your numbers, don't."

John hung up and that was the last I heard from him. We simply worked around him. In retrospect, I should have been more conciliatory. From a political perspective, perhaps I should have said the report was still in the works and that next day delivery would be fine. I found out a month later that he had complained to Sam; he had said I was "a pain in the ass." He was right. I hadn't learned the virtue of discretion in Washington.

After four weeks' crunching numbers on bauxite exports, imports, consumption, production and prices, I determined that there could be no long-lasting embargo. The organization of bauxite producers, the International Bauxite Association (IBA), hadn't the internal political unity to maintain unilateral price hikes or embargoes; bauxite is not a scarce commodity like oil, and the IBA economies are more dependent on us to buy this bauxite than we are on them to produce. The economies of nations like Jamaica would collapse unless we bought from them, whereas we could develop other sources of bauxite in other countries, like New Guinea and Surinam.

At the end of this first month in Washington I felt good. Sam was pleased with my work. The secretaries and clerks in the OEOB's great halls said hello to me when we passed. Coming through the security checkpoints had become second nature. I walked around the building secure in the knowledge that I worked long hours at good pay for some of the important people in the nation's capital. I was impressed with myself, a typical response to working in the Old Executive Office Building, where humility is a rare commodity.

This elite subculture of which I was now a part led me deeper into Washington, into the politics that take place outside the OEOB, the White House, the Capitol, or any other public building.

40

A recent acquaintance, Bobby Peabody, asked me one day if I would help him host a fund-raiser for a moderate Democrat who was opposing the old segregationist from South Carolina, Senator Strom Thurmond. This made my decision simple. The always enthusiastic Bobby didn't have to sell me at all.

In the summer before an election, people in Washington's more affluent neighborhoods like Georgetown raise money under yellow-striped tents the way most Americans raise corn or squash. It is fertile ground for new, ambitious politicians from the provinces who need money to unseat the entrenched incumbents armed with war chests built up with contributions from local bankers, businessmen, farmers, realtors, and out-of-state special-interest groups who don't want to lose their voice in Congress. If the challenger wants to make it a fair fight, he must look elsewhere for monetary support—fall back on any hidden network he may have via family, school, college, military

41

or business to put him in touch with people who want to exchange their financial capital for political capital. The Washington fund-raiser is where needy politicians meet charitable patrons; such is philanthropy in the nation's capital.

These affairs typically are organized by Republican or Democratic party regulars, those who for ideological convictions or personal ambition are willing to spend weeks and months before the event tracking down potential contributors, sending out invitations, talking up the candidate, arranging food and drink for hundreds, and convincing someone to surrender his or her home or club to a horde of mostly dimly known persons who would probably steal the silver if given an opportunity.

Our fund-raiser was unusual in that we hosts were not yet politically active. It was more of a social affair for us. All we knew about our candidate was that he was a moderate Democrat by the name of Charles "Pug" Ravenal. He was simply the excuse for us to get together and meet a few friends of friends; there were times when I thought that Washington was such an excuse for us.

We were a homogeneous group—educated at the better schools and colleges; white as milk; from affluent or wealthy families; politically moderate; and aggressive, but rarely rude. I knew five of the eight hosts prior to the fund-raiser; we had many friends in common. It was no fluke that we had met; I wondered that it hadn't happened earlier. We were stewards to the powerful, their heirs apparent. There were a few thousand other young people in Washington doing the same thing. We helped draft the laws, write the regulations, edit the press releases, and run the public hearings. We would receive, or already were receiving, admission to America's best business, law and public-policy schools. As the barroom toast went, "We may have come to do good, but we stay to do well."

Our guest of honor Ravenal was—not surprisingly for this group—Harvard-educated. He had run for governor of South Carolina two years earlier only to have victory denied him when his fading opponent successfully sued in court to bar him from running in the general election because he had recently been domiciled outside of the state while working with a brokerage house in Manhattan. In this election, however, there were no such complications, and Ravenal was set to prove that given a fair shot at elected office, an intelligent Democrat with the backing of liberals in Washington and brokers in New York could defeat Strom Thurmond and his merry band of South Carolina businessmen and out-of-state right-wingers.

Old Strom, aged seventy-five, was looking to remain in the Senate through his eighty-first birthday or die trying. Thurmond's reelection depended not only on past constituent service, but also on his young, blond, ex-beauty-queen wife having given him two towheaded kids who could campaign with their mother as tokens of Strom's virility and inner youthfulness. You had to hand it to Strom. He had taken the standard politician's use of pretty cheerleaders to lure voters one better—he hadn't hired one; he had married one.

I could see her standing beside a beaming Strom on the campaign trail. She's dressed in a short pleated skirt, white ankle socks, two-tone bucks, and a tight white sweater with a big block "S" between her breasts. The folks in the crowd say to each other, "A man's never too old who can keep a gal like that happy." Frankly, I thought Ravenal would have a tough time defeating the Senator and the Cheerleader. He did.

Preparation for our fund-raiser went well. Invitations were mailed weeks in advance. We sent them to all our friends and acquaintances. I even sent one to my landlord. Under the direction of Bobby's mother, we deveined the celery stalks lest a guest suffer the embarrassment of celery strands hanging from his or her mouth. The day of the party, I left the OEOB by five-thirty. I drove back to the house to take a shower and change. It had been a steamy day and I had sweated up a storm while working on Capitol Hill. I could not arrive at the Peabodys' like that, not only because they would have minded, but also because this fund-raiser's success would be measured in dollar contributions to Ravenal; as a host, I literally could not afford to offend any guests.

I had never met Ravenal. So, as soon as I arrived at the Peabodys' red-brick Georgetown home, I went to say hello. He was trim, with the face and spectacles of Clark Kent, and he bore the earnest look of a fatigued politician who needed all the friends he could get. He was a bit pale, as if his new friends had already taken their pint of blood. He was, it seemed, being slowly worn down by the twenty-four-hour demands of the campaign. By election day, I thought, he would be skin, bones and smile.

I introduced myself. He connected my name with the invitation and thanked me for the help. He was not merely being considerate; he was also encouraging the troops who could raise thousands of Washington dollars for him during the sultry midsummer night. He was tense and thirsty. I got him a vodka on the rocks.

The guests began to arrive, and the mean age at the party rose from twenty-three to forty-five. The men wore conventional business suits, the women sensible summer dresses with short sleeves and crew necks. No tight jeans or satin shirts here; in Washington, clothes are uniforms, not personal expression. As I understood it from Bobby, the party was supposed to go like this: guests come; they meet friends and known political personalities supporting the candidate; everybody drinks; hosts circulate to keep bores off others' backs; people drink more and forget the day's petty hassles; candidate gives short but rousing speech; pledges roll in; exodus commences; candidate departs to catch plane home; clean-up begins; hosts go to their respective homes with sighs of relief.

It didn't quite happen that way. I spent the first part of the party engaged in loose conversations with people swimming in gin-and-tonics. The alcohol consumption, great all over Washington, proceeded at a rapid rate and accelerated when the journalists arrived. One writer from *The Atlantic Monthly* pumped me for any dope I might have on "this Ravenal character." He was openly cynical about any new politician professing political reform and personal integrity. As he drank more, his discontentment with politicians increased. "Assholes. All assholes." I changed the subject to his latest article and he

44

warmed right up. "The essence of my story is . . ." Nothing stimulated this man like his own writing and a few drinks. Unfortunately, he didn't plan to write anything on Ravenal, let alone an admiring piece. "I don't cotton to South Carolina," he said.

Inside the dainty pre-Revolutionary house, politicos palavered among the American and English antiques and filled the pastel-colored salons with cigar and cigarette smoke. Hefty men and women leaned against any available wall space and ate and drank and drank some more. It sounded like an eighteenth-century roadhouse at feeding time.

I was unsure how to raise money for the candidate. I wondered how I should talk to our guests. Should I hype the candidate? I tried that only once. It was in conversation with a sweet-looking older lady wearing a black dress and pearls. She sat on a sofa while everyone else was in the backyard listening to Ravenal's speech.

"Don't you want to hear the speech?" I asked, sitting down beside her. "He makes excellent speeches."

"I don't like speeches," she said.

"Do you know Mr. Ravenal's position on the issues?"

"I don't want to know them."

"Why?" I asked.

"If I knew them, I wouldn't give him any money. I'm only doing this for his family."

"Oh," I said. "Well, yes, I can understand that."

"Good," she said firmly.

"Can I get you a drink?" I asked.

She looked at me severely and replied, "I don't drink."

I got up from the couch. "Well, it was nice talking to you."

"Goodbye," she said.

I was chagrined to notice that Joni seemed to have great success pitching the candidate to the guests. I drew her into a corner and asked, "What is your technique?"

She smiled. "I only approach men without wedding rings, and I don't talk about Ravenal. I tell them how bad Thurmond is."

"That's it?"

"No."

"What else do you do?"

"I give them my telephone number."

"Why?" I asked skeptically.

"They might want to have lunch."

"With you?"

"Yes."

"Jesus," I said.

"It's all for the cause."

"What cause?"

"Ravenal."

"To hell with him."

Joni smiled at me and said, "How did you get to be so cute?"

I grimaced at the word *cute*. I retreated to the bar to reassert my masculinity.

There was an open bar, and the guests were making good use of it; they had paid seventy-five dollars a shot to abuse this privilege. Nicholas met me there. He came by to recapitulate the speech. "Ravenal got up on a wrought-iron chair, not a stump, and said 'you' not 'you all,' and told them how nice it was to be in Georgetown. Then he told them how he would help the nation by removing Strom from the U.S. Senate. It was not a great speech." Afterward, however, the checks flowed in, thousands of dollars' worth. Five strong drinks and one quick speech seemed to loosen the pursestrings of people who had scarcely known of Ravenal two hours earlier. From eavesdropping (which you could barely avoid doing, people spoke so loudly), I gathered that giving was in the American tradition of keeping up with the Joneses—"If George has enough confidence in this guy to give $500, the least we can do is $250. . . ." There was also, of course, the possibility that one might be backing a winner, a future friend in the Senate.

I found the scene cheaper and far more entertaining than a film or play. I enjoyed watching politicians like former Senator John Culver, Democrat from Iowa. Falstaffian in girth and louder than anyone else in the place, he held forth in the up-

46

stairs living room. Because of his pink skin, he looked like a hard-drinking man, but his hand held nothing more potent than club soda and lime juice. He got off many good statements. The one I remembered best was, "Any politician worth his salt should be prepared to lose an election and not have his world come crashing down around his head." I wondered if he had given that advice to Ravenal.

By ten o'clock, all the guests had left except the hosts and Bill and Pat, two sodden officials of a craft union that had given Ravenal a hefty contribution. Despite our hints, these two showed no intention of leaving.

"It's getting late," we said.

"I'll sleep late tomorrow."

"We have to clean up now," we said.

"We'll help you."

And on and on.

I was cajoling Pat on the patio. I turned away to say goodbye to Nicholas, and by the time I turned back to finish our disconnected conversation, Pat had passed out in the bushes. I had to get him another drink before he'd leave the shrubbery—"For my wounds." In the meantime, his associate Bill had managed to wrap the inside of his trousers' right rear pocket around the curved wrought-iron back of a small outdoor chair. "I don't know how I could have done that," he said over and over again. It took me fifteen minutes to disentangle him from the chair. Diana and Charity were in hysterics over my clumsy efforts to free Bill from the chair and elevate Pat from the bushes. "Let them stay where they are." Finally, Mrs. Peabody got Pat and Bill out the door by promising, "You can finish your drinks outside."

Pat and Bill were still on the front steps when Joni and I left at eleven o'clock. A rare Canadian cold front had passed through, sweeping the moist evening weather down toward South Carolina. Both exhilarated and tipsy, we rambled arm in arm to my car.

As I was about to start the engine, an anglicized voice called out from across the prim Georgetown street. "Pardon me, could

47

you give me a lift?" Attached to that voice was a man with big black spectacles resting on his large nose. He wore his hair short and parted neatly on one side, reminiscent of an RAF flyer. He seemed friendly, and so, after asking Joni if she minded, I said, "Come on."

This gentleman pushed off from the car he had been leaning against, and waving a lighted cigarette with great style, wandered over to my car. A comrade in drink, he needed a ride.

He opened the left rear door and lurched into the back seat. "Where are you headed?" I asked. He gave me an address that was only two blocks away. He did not introduce himself, which made me think I should know who he was. Whoever he was, he knew he didn't have the stuff to walk even that short distance. In a loud voice he announced that he was going to visit his ex-wife.

As I pulled the car in front of the correct address, my mystery passenger pulled himself up toward the front seats and very graciously asked who had done him this good turn. I introduced Joni and myself. He thanked us and introduced himself as "a former columnist and now collector and historian of Oriental art."

He then opened the right rear door to exit. Unfortunately, there was a pool of rope on that side of the car's floor that formed a coil around his left ankle. He couldn't get out. With his right foot planted on the sidewalk curb and his left in my car, he straddled the storm sewer precariously. As he held himself up with the car door, I reached back and untangled his foot from my car. (I was becoming expert at untangling people.) Free, he said, "Thanks so much, good night," and traipsed up the driveway to his destination.

I pulled over to the side of the road and asked Joni, "Do you know who that was?" To my surprise she didn't. I had to laugh. This man, who could barely extricate himself from my car, had gone from Groton School to Harvard College to Claire Chennault's Flying Tigers to writing columns with his brother Stewart that could make or break careers.

As we drove home, the stars radiant over the grand houses, I detoured so we passed the homes of Katharine Graham, Henry Kissinger and Averell Harriman. Perhaps some day they too would need a lift. All Washington seemed accessible.

At 2 P.M. one day in early August, Sam had returned from a meeting with Brawn and asked me to come to his office. I went across the suite's carpeted foyer and walked into Sam's big office with the Currier and Ives snowscape reproductions. Sam stood smoking his customary afternoon cigar and checking one of the countless memoranda that littered his hulk of a desk. He looked up briefly over his spectacles and motioned for me to sit down.

"Well," he said, "I just saw Brawn. I want you to prepare briefing materials for him on United States arms sales."

"I don't know much about that, Sam."

"Don't worry; he doesn't either. You'll learn. Anyway, Les Stein will give you whatever leads you need."

"Why does Brawn need a briefing on arms sales?"

"To address the International Management and Development Institute."

"What's that?"

"A forum for multinational companies."

"Are they meeting here in the Old Executive Office Building?" I asked.

"Yup."

"Why's that?"

"It's for the President's top men to brief these business executives on present and future government policies affecting international business—to make them feel that they're getting the same briefings we give the President. It's bullshit, but just get on with it. You work for a politician, even if he is the President. Considering that he's running for his political life this election, you should be thankful you're as insulated from domestic politics as you are," he said, smiling. "Now get out of here and get to work. Call Les Stein. He'll put you on the right track."

I never knew precisely what Les Stein did at CIEP-EPB. He was rarely in the halls or offices. Supposedly he handled "relations" with the CIA and NSC. He dressed the part in flat gray suits, white shirts, and drab blue ties. At staff meetings, he blended into the background and rarely spoke.

I went back to my office and phoned Stein. Guarded as usual, he gave me only the name and number of a Colonel Johnson at the National Security Council (NSC). In charge of international arms sales for NSC, Johnson was one of the final arbiters on United States arms policy. Stein told me that Johnson could give me all the documents and contacts necessary to prepare Brawn's briefing. That was my first and last conversation with Stein.

At the time, military sales had replaced diplomacy and economic aid as the preeminent tool of American foreign policy. As previously set forth in the Nixon Doctrine, the United States relied on sending massive military aid and private American investment into proxy countries like Iran to protect our global interests against Russian imperialism and oil embargoes. Our expectation was that these proxy countries would become dependent on us for their military and economic survival and thus dependable allies. The price for their oil and anti-Communism was reflected in figures for United States arms exports; comparing the decade of the 1970s with the 1960s, U.S. security assistance to the Near East and South Asia increased from 6.6 billion dollars to 72.4 billion dollars, or 1,100 percent. Were United States arms sales out of control? As low man on the totem pole, I hoped the answer would be "No."

I went to see Colonel Johnson. Unlike everyone else I knew in the Old Executive Office Building, Colonel Johnson wore a military uniform to work. He looked like a grandfather dressed for the Memorial Day Parade. Ushering me into his fourth-floor office that looked down on the White House's green copper roof, he asked how he could help.

After I had explained the briefing on arms sales for Brawn, Johnson granted my request for classified data on American weapons transfers abroad. On the assurance that I would return the information within the week, he gave me a few thick compendiums marked "Secret" or "Top Secret." I packed them under my arm, thanked him, and nervously headed for the door. He asked me, "You do have security clearance for these, don't you?"

Without a moment's hesitation, I answered, "Yes."

The military documents I used were not exotic. They merely indicated what weapons went to what countries. Probably, I could have done my job without any classified documents. But the stamp "Secret" or "Top Secret" assured me that the estimates on which I would base my report to Brawn were as accurate as any allowed outside the Department of Defense.

As important as the classified information were the interviews I set up with government officials. The most important was with the deputy to the assistant Secretary of State responsible for nonnuclear weapons transfers to foreign governments. In theory, he was the man who could answer all my questions—on a confidential basis. After two days' poring through the classified material, I went to meet him over at the State Department. It was an unseasonably comfortable summer day as I walked the half mile to the dull concrete building that is home for the United States State Department.

I guessed that my contact at State, Mr. Lang, was having a rough time. In the newspapers and national magazines, arms exports were reported to be running at $20 billion per year. Most were going into the politically unstable Middle East. On the telephone, I had tried to allay any fears he may have had that I was setting him and his boss up to take the political heat surrounding arms transfer. I had suggested "an informal chat." I wanted him to express the concerns he rarely acknowledged to himself. Being an unknown person from the executive office of a President in the middle of a reelection campaign, I expected that he would not trust me. I had prepared, however, an extensive series of important and unimportant questions that would eventually flush out the bits of information I needed. I thought I was being very clever.

"So what can I do for you?" Lang asked. I told him about the briefing for Brawn, and he offered to answer whatever questions he could. I began by asking about how the United States

51

government stops the introduction of sophisticated weapons into regional conflicts.

There was a pause. Then he replied crisply, "First, it is State Department policy to provide no sophisticated weapons to our allies unless their security is threatened by neighbors with more advanced weaponry."

"You mean what they would receive from the Soviet Union?" I asked.

"Yes. The Soviets were the first to export jet fighters, surface-to-air missiles, and surface-to-surface missiles."

"Then, whenever our allies come to us for a military response, we generally arm them."

"Quite often," he said with a sag in his voice. "We have no choice."

"How do we deal with the Soviets to slow the exports of arms?"

"We try to get consensus on disarmament in the U.N."

"But there's been no progress so far," I added.

"No. . . ."

"And you aren't hopeful."

"No."

"So U.S. arms policy is locked into steady escalation."

"Unless we grow less afraid of the Russians, and vice versa," he said.

"Have you ever seen regional arms escalation cease in the post-war period?"

"Rarely," he said.

"Don't most arms exports go to potentially unstable regions?"

"Every place outside Europe and the United States is unstable."

"The Middle East too?" I asked.

"Especially the Middle East."

"Yet over half of all purchases of U.S. military equipment is made by Saudi Arabia, Iran and Israel," I pointed out.

"Yes, there are risks involved in our policy."

"In developing countries like Iran and Saudi Arabia, whose

goodwill do our arms sales get? The army, of course, but who else?"

"That's a tough question to answer," he said in a soft voice.

I then asked the question that every newspaper was asking. "Isn't it potentially destabilizing to put tons of highly sophisticated and lethal weapons into the hands of regimes ruling undeveloped—possibly feudal—societies?"

"You mean Saudi Arabia or Iran?" he asked.

"Yes."

He gave me the answer he gave all the newspapers. "We have complete confidence in the stability of those governments."

"Confidence in the Shah's ability to stay in power?"

"Yes," he said firmly. "Iran and Saudi Arabia are making giant strides toward industrialization, and they are our suppliers of crude oil. We will back them regardless."

"Are there plans for evacuation of sensitive equipment and personnel from these countries in the event of armed conflict?"

"In those unlikely circumstances, we estimate that there will be sufficient time to withdraw American forces, dependents and sensitive documents from any dangerous areas," he assured me.

"Would you say that U.S. arms sales have proven an effective foreign-policy tool?" I asked.

"Over-all, yes. We are the world's most powerful military and economic nation. We have a responsibility to protect our allies."

"But arms sales can cut both ways, depending on the political stability of the client," I said.

"Yes, expanding the power of the military in new republics or democracies may endanger civilian rule and economic development. And there is the possibility these weapons could at some future date be used against us or our allies."

Our question-and-answer period went on like this until we both had enough. In the latter part, we discussed specific weaponry with the door shut. He tried to answer my inquiries. It was as if he wanted to tell the truth to someone.

"Well," I said, "thanks very much, Mr. Lang. You've been very informative."

53

"I hope so. By the way, I'd love to see what you've gleaned from our conversation, when you finish your memo."

"I'm sorry, but I can't circulate it. It will be strictly for internal use," I answered.

"Yes, I see," he said.

"Very sorry," I said.

"No problem," he said.

"Thanks again, Mr. Lang."

"No trouble at all, Mr. Fromson."

As we shook hands, I noticed his palm was sweaty, as was his shirt around the armpits. We had spoken for over two hours, yet I was so intent on the issues that I took little notice of his appearance until I said goodbye. If I were to meet Lang today, I would not recognize him.

Our conversation had been tremendously civil and disturbing. It complicated my job. I couldn't write a smooth, clean memo detailing all the virtues of arms sales. We had a policy, but no doctrine to back it up with. By being so inquisitive, I had forced myself into the uncomfortable position of the skeptic who wants to be a conformist. Now, I had to put my observations and doubts on paper for Brawn. He would not appreciate an alarmist memo from a pipsqueak.

As I approached the OEOB, I noticed its mansard roof bristled not only with the typical electronic gizmos for NSC communications, but also with dark-eyed sharpshooters. The Shah of Iran was in Washington visiting the President.

For the first time that summer, I left work confused. I went home and ran five miles through the groves of Rock Creek Park hidden in the middle of Northwest Washington. Afterward, I was exhausted but not relieved. Joni and I stayed home that night. After an unsatisfactory dinner of jellied beef consommé and dill pickles, Joni went into the living room to read Joan Didion's latest book, while I washed and dried the dishes in the kitchen. When I finished, I went into the living room, picked her up in my arms, and carried her to bed. I forgot the frustrations of the job until the radio alarm clock came on at 7 A.M., when a news broadcaster reported that the Shah and the President had announced, the night before, a new understanding to sell more American weapons to Iran.

The next day, Sam reviewed my memo before sending it up to Brawn. My draft ended:

> The U.S. government must consider the short term benefits and long term risks of foreign arm sales. For example, the immediate diplomatic and strategic benefits generated by supplying the Shah of Iran with billions of dollars of our latest, most advanced, weapons must be weighed against the probability of greater Iranian economic dislocation and more military tension in the Persian Gulf. The arms trade is a tool of U.S. foreign policy; it can cut both ways, for and against the United States and our allies.

In the circumstances, I thought that conclusion was risky. Sam encouraged me to be candid. With his backing, I even included an addendum: "For Your Information and Consideration." In it I listed all the questions that Lang could not answer satisfactorily. It was a list one page long.

The only passage Sam nixed was:

> Past U.S. actions have not always been characterized by good judgment. For example, the normal decision review channels were obviated by the previous administration when considering arms sales to the Shah of Iran. We may have supplied too many, too sophisticated weapons to an unstable regional power.

Sam thought it an impertinent judgment. He cut it "for your sake." He was trying to protect me.

He knew that in any President's executive office, we all served at the pleasure of our superiors. Seaman at the President's pleasure, Brawn at Seaman's, Sam at Brawn's, and I at the pleasure of each or all of them. My brief was sent to Brawn, who read it in private the day before his speech.

An hour before Brawn was to speak before the IMDI bigwigs,

55

I went up to the "Old State Department Library" a floor above us in the OEOB. Its upper balconies stripped of books and only collecting dust, the old library looked like the interior of a Victorian theater waiting to be torn down. I was surprised at its shabbiness. Executives of international business were gathered for their briefing on international economic policies to be given by the assistants to the President and assorted under and assistant secretaries of State and Treasury. I took a seat in the back of the room and glanced around. It was a who's who of corporate giants. There was Exxon in the corner and Union Carbide in the first row. Chase Manhattan was sitting next to General Motors.

I had been given a sleek black IMDI folding notebook with a "Top Management Report" inside. Subject: "The Management of International Corporate Citizenship." I would not have given it a second glance except that there was an article in the back under the title "Government-Business Co-operation in Iran's Socio-economic Revolution." Authors: His Imperial Majesty Mohammed Reza Pahlavi, Shahanshah Aryamehr of Iran, with His Excellency Ardeshir Zahedi and two American businessmen named Bradley and Logan.

With typical exaggeration, the Shah was discussing his "Revolution of the Shah and the People."

> Almost 15 years ago I came to the conclusion that no country can survive as a truly independent entity if its society is not based on social justice, modern technology, a strong economy and the will and power to defend itself. . . . The main philosophy behind this "Revolution of the Shah and the People" is the dignity and individual freedom of the human being. Our concept is that everyone is equal before the law.

He knew what we Americans wanted to hear. Ambassador Zahedi and the two Americans discussed what the "Revolution of the Shah and the People" meant for American business. Zahedi explained first that American business was welcome in Iran, but not with bribes. The Americans responded on cue.

56

BRADLEY: I'm glad you brought up that point. The American business system—along with business and government in many parts of the world—is in disrepute because of headlines on "bribery." Yet I know from many corporate executives that if a bribery occurs within their companies—either on the giving or receiving end—it results in instant dismissal.

LOGAN: Yes, there is a growing realignment in the U.S. business community that we cannot tolerate some of the practices that have taken place in the past.

I closed the black book. This IMDI get-together was pure public relations. We were telling fairy tales to one another. This was the last place my memorandum would be used. I never did hear what Brawn said to them. I got up and left. I ran into Nicholas on my way out.

"What are you doing in this crowd?" I asked.

"This is what I do during the day." Gesturing to the men seated, he added, "These fellows are our clients, or at least some of them." He paused. "So why are you going? Isn't your boss in charge here?"

"Well, like you say, Nicholas," I said, gesturing to the room as he had, "these fellows are not my clients. Brawn is. I just do the briefing materials. I don't have to listen to the speeches."

Nicholas, like an older brother, looked at me and said quietly, "You don't agree with policy, eh?"

"No, I just don't like wasting my time."

"Sometimes it goes that way, Brett. *C'est la vie.*"

"Right," I replied halfheartedly. "You take notes for *moi.* See you at home."

I should have stayed and listened, but I was too annoyed. With all the problems to be seriously addressed, why were we spending ourselves on this stuff? The November election, of course. Political pressures were building up on everyone, from the President down to the likes of me.

In Washington during the end of August, anyone who could afford to get away did. A city built atop swamps, Washington lay blanketed for days under layers of hot air, sweat and carbon monoxide. Walking outdoors from the air-conditioned OEOB was like entering a polluted steambath. In one stretch that month, there were nine consecutive days of health alerts.

Normally, black people made up 80 percent of Washington's population; in the month of August that figure must have increased to 95 percent. Segregation of whites from blacks in the District of Columbia is not, of course, restricted to the eighth month of the year. Segregation is a year-round practice. Busing is not an issue since the whites send their children to private and parochial schools or pay to have their kids attend public schools in nearby Maryland or Virginia. A bigger problem is the migration of young white professionals like me to black areas. We are renovating the city and thus pushing the blacks out of the core areas into the outskirts of growing suburban ghettos.

Young blacks and whites had little to do with each other. No blacks lived in my neighborhood or worked in the OEOB, except the maids and a few policemen. None were at the parties I attended, nor were they invited to play tennis at clubs like the Chevy Chase. Of course, there were young ambitious black men and women living and working around Washington, members of Washington's longstanding black middle class. I saw them in the museums and restaurants, but those in that mainstream were a minority among their own. Most young blacks who worked seemed to be employed as clerks, messengers, secretaries, telephone operators, taxi drivers, bus drivers, or road-crew laborers.

Then there were the unemployed. That summer it seemed that every other young black man was spending his time shooting the breeze with pals on the stoop or gazing at the merchandise in the store windows. Young whites like me knew they were there, but with our friends from school and jobs with important politicians, we had nothing to do with them. All of this struck me forcefully, coming as I did from a small, all-white town in Connecticut. But I thought of them particularly because I was working on youth unemployment for the President.

It was Saturday when I received a phone call from Ben Hayes, Mr. Seaman's personal aide. He asked whether we would drop by the Old Executive Office Building that night and watch the Presidential debate in Brawn's quarters with some of his friends. It sounded like fun, and I hoped that it would be an opportunity to strengthen my ties with the powers that were. So, I said "Sure."

The OEOB's formal halls were empty as Joni and I walked up to Brawn's office. Joni was a bit nervous; as we walked along the third-floor corridor so wide and impressive that a Rolls Royce would not have seemed out of place, she asked if Brawn knew there was a party going on in his palatial office. I doubted it. We went into his suite of rooms through the double wooden doors. Passing through the foyer, we entered the high-ceilinged expanse where Brawn normally presided, at that moment occupied by three other couples lounging on his government-issue American heritage reproduction furniture and drinking gin-and-tonics while a bland CBS newsman droned through the television speaker about the President, his challenger, and the future of the American political system.

Ben and his friends were slightly older than Joni and I. These men and women watching the debate were as clean-cut as they come. Actually, with the exception of Joni in her patched jeans and long straight blond hair, we all were. The women had permanents, wore lipstick, summer dresses and stockings. They smiled demurely, while the men in their button-down shirts and khaki trousers dominated conversation. They talked mostly of politics and football. Phrases like "We'll beat 'em this fall" and "Wait till next year" abounded. It was often difficult to tell whether they were discussing the Washington Redskins or Jimmy Carter.

The debate began; Ben went to the bar cart to get himself another drink and asked me to join him. As I filled my glass with ice, he asked, "Brett, how would you like to do a special project for Mr. Seaman?"

"Sure, Ben, what is it?"

"The President needs something quick and dirty on youth unemployment. Think you can come up with something in a week?"

"Sure I can, Ben, but this sounds like a Domestic Council or CEA job."

"Don't worry about them. Seaman wants some ideas of his own that the President can announce before Election Day. Can you help us?"

I wanted the assignment. In the executive office of the President, success is measured by proximity to the President, and this was one step closer. That I knew little about the issue of youth unemployment didn't stop me. In Washington you become an instant expert because the politicians demand fast answers to complicated questions. Most staffers simply try to stay one step ahead of their bosses by calling around town for help from real experts (that is, people who are two steps ahead).

The League of Women Voters Presidential debate was terribly boring. The President and his opponent labored long and well to avoid taking clear positions on important issues that could offend certain constituencies. They chanted incantations against Inflation, Unemployment, and the USSR. They understood that the trick to winning the election was to give as few people as possible a reason to vote against them. At that moment, however, I did not appreciate the beauty of their performance. I wanted to hear some proposals to solve problems like youth unemployment. Then I remembered that while I was waiting to hear from the President on that issue, he was waiting to hear from his advisers, who were waiting for Mr. Seaman, who was waiting for Ben, who was waiting for me.

At lunch on Monday, I told Sam what Ben had in mind. I felt a little guilty leaving my boss, but I thought it was time to move in the organization. "Can you spare me for a few weeks?" I asked.

"Brett, certainly I can, but are you sure you want to get involved in that domestic political stuff?"

"I think so. I want to try it."

"OK, but if I were you I'd start looking elsewhere for jobs. We'd all be smart to do that," Sam said.

"Nobody on the staff seems to be doing that," I replied.

"They're not going to until after Election Day. Once you've worked for the President with all the perquisites and powers, it gets hard to leave. Be smart. Get off the ship now."

"What are you going to do, Sam?"

"I've got some leads."

"Sam, are you going to vote for the President?" I asked.

"That's a pretty nosy question."

"Sorry," I said. As I began walking to the door, Sam called out, "The answer is no."

"Then how can you work for him?"

"Just because I wouldn't vote for a guy doesn't mean I wouldn't work for him. He's still the man at the head of the government. If I leave now, who will replace me? Who wants a job for two months?"

"I'd take it," I offered facetiously.

"Sorry," he said. "Can't have you kids running *everything* in this government."

In my new-found status as assistant to the assistant to the assistant to the President, I discovered I could call anyone for help, and he or she would show up at my office within twenty-four hours. I was amazed at the new-found power that resulted simply from saying into the telephone receiver, "Hello, I'm calling from the White House . . ."

The first person I brought to the OEOB was the top labor economist from the Brookings Institution. He resembled my former adviser in the economics department at Stanford. This time, however, the professor was coming to my office at my convenience.

As he explained, youth unemployment is less a "youth" problem than a black problem. White kids experienced initial difficulty getting a job but soon entered the regular work force as their fathers did. Not so with nonwhite youth. In the years between eighteen and twenty-five, when most people learn basic job skills and discipline, they were generally unemployed. Many of them had so little work history, they could not qualify for the unemployment rolls if they wanted to.

The United States Department of Labor reported a 50 percent black youth unemployment rate. There is no one cause for such high black youth unemployment; there are many. Some have not been taught at home or in school to read, write, or do simple arithmetic; most live in cities where lower-skilled manufacturing jobs are declining and higher-skilled white-collar jobs are increasing; they are discriminated against by employers because of their race and their lack of prior jobs; the inflation-adjusted minimum wage has made businesses more reluctant to hire low-skilled people; more women and illegal aliens have entered the job market; and finally, the economy has been growing more slowly, just as the baby boom has come of age.

Given that gloomy diagnosis, I called in the Deputy Assistant Secretary of Labor in charge of all manpower and training programs. He detailed the specific government actions designed to ameliorate the youth unemployment problem. They were mostly summer employment programs that cost $500 million a year to prevent race riots in July and August. There were also a few skill-training and remedial-reading and arithmetic programs that were funded with perhaps $100 million. The economist from Brookings had already estimated a multi*billion*-dollar effort would be required to train a generation of unskilled, unwanted young people. In short, from what the Deputy Assistant Secretary of Labor told me, I had to conclude that this was not a problem the government could solve in the two months before the election. Congress had recessed. No new programs could be funded. The best we could do was make a good-faith gesture of future commitment.

After the Labor secretary left I went to brief Ben. With the usual smile on his freckled face, he asked, "Well, what've we got?"

"Not too much, I'm afraid." I related the heart of my conversation with the economist and the secretary from Labor. I was so hard up for possible programs to expand that I mentioned one called the Self-Employment Incentive Program; it was supposed to encourage young entrepreneurs to start their own businesses.

Ben listened to my whole talk without asking one question. When he spoke it was with great enthusiasm.

"Well, I think we have something. Yes, I really like that Self-Employment Incentive Program. It's not another public-works money-waster. Gives you the feeling that people want to hear about—Self Help, Rugged Individualism, what made this country great. Grabs you, doesn't it?"

"I don't know. Where are these poor kids going to get the capital required to start up?"

"Sure it does, Brett," he continued, ignoring my question. "Sort of a youth unemployment program that everybody can get behind. A new look for youth unemployment programs—reliance on Ambition and Ingenuity. Employment Without Welfare. It's great."

"But the program isn't going to solve anything, even if we gave it a billion-dollar budget."

"Maybe not, Brett, but it's great stuff for the President. Something he can hype as another way to solve youth unemployment."

"Ben, that's what I'm telling you. It's not going to solve any problems, politics aside."

"Sure it will. Why, there must be lots of teen-agers out there who could organize house-painting companies. That's what I did on my summers home from college."

"But, Ben, these kids don't have affluent neighbors constantly fixing up their homes on the scale needed to get the unemployment rate down. This is not even a good-faith gesture."

"Brett," he said, his voice rising. "I like it. All we do is give it a good PR push. It'll make good copy. You'll see."

"Jesus Christ, Ben, is that the point?"

He stopped and looked me dead in the eye. "Right now it is, and if I were you, I wouldn't expect it to change."

I went back to my office and prepared a memorandum telling Ben all the things he wanted to hear. I was lying, but that didn't

63

stop me. My superiors' overriding desire was to give the public the impression of action and leadership. They were trying to pull the election out with last-minute public relations. I didn't mind so much their deception—people lie all the time—I minded their allegiance to this futile charade.

I stopped work on the project with that memo. Sam never asked me why I was suddenly back working for him and I was grateful. Disgusted with myself, I didn't tell Joni about the project. But even if no one else knew I had compromised myself for nothing more than closer proximity to an almost-beaten President, I knew I had acted like everyone else—conform and maybe get ahead. I was beginning to see the grubbier side of government and Washington, D.C. As long as you play team ball, they promote you and pay you well.

In the second week in September, I heard from Charity Livingston, who worked for a member of Congress from California, that there was a job at Congress' Joint Economic Committee (JEC), the group of nine Senators and nine Representatives responsible for advising the Congress on the state of the economy and economic policy. A position on the professional staff was opening up.

I went over to the Dirksen Senate Office Building one morning for a set of interviews in the JEC's offices. At 9:30 A.M. Capitol Hill was an outdoor version of Grand Central Station at rush hour as 17,000-plus employees of the Congress, 5,000-plus lobbyists, and another 54,000 tourists converged on the Capitol Building and the five marble-coated Congressional office buildings flanking it.

The corridors were jammed with frantic aides dodging clumps of tourists who wanted to know, "Where is Congressman Beano's office?" Occasionally, one of the many tall wooden doors that faced the hallways would open and a Senator would stride out into the rush of people with an assistant alongside who was trying hopelessly to give him a last-minute briefing before a public hearing or press conference or vote on the floor. The Senator would wave and smile hello to everyone, while the aide whispered directions into the politician's ear to vote yes or no on the pending bill.

Behind the doors through which the Senator had passed were his offices. The Senator probably had a five-room suite. The first door was emblazoned with the name and escutcheon of his state. Underneath, a wood-grained formica rectangle said, "Welcome." This was the reception area. If you opened that door you were met by a generally curvaceous female receptionist sitting behind a desk. Her job was primarily to give constituents passes to the Senate gallery, answer the phone, and keep cranks from disturbing the Senator or his staff.

If you opened one of the next three doors you would walk into one of three rooms with decorative molding around the high ceilings shared by four to six aides to the Senator. The noise in here would be only slightly less than in the corridor; phones would be ringing, IBM Selectric II's booming and clattering, and a few garrulous lobbyists sitting on desks waiting for a free legislative assistant. Most likely no one would ask you to leave. They'd be too busy to notice, or if they did notice you, they'd assume you were a staffer from some other office. Only if you looked like a tourist would you be sent to the receptionist. Congressional staff wage a constant war to keep tourists in the halls or public galleries. If you don't have a cause or special interest, they're not very interested in talking to you.

The fifth and final door, which has no markings and is always locked from within, leads to the Senator's personal office. Larger than the other offices, here the head man entertains important constituents, lobbyists, and his staff. Like Brawn's, this private office is furnished with one Presidential-sized desk, the flag of the Senator's home state and Old Glory, three or four armchairs, a long leather couch, some locked metal files, a wall covered with testimonials, plaques, trophies, and assorted knickknacks from constituents, and an adjoining bathroom with shower. Try to get through this door and you'll be arrested by one of the many Congressional policemen that patrol the corridors.

It was into such a suite that I went for my interview with the

JEC. At the first door, the receptionist welcomed me and then escorted me to the staff director's office. He occupied the large room behind the fifth door. John O'Hara was a stout gray-haired man who had been on the Hill since before World War II and director of the JEC for over a decade.

He read my short résumé and commented, "Very impressive, very impressive." He looked up. "Do you work quickly?"

"I think so."

"Good. Can I call this guy Sam Platt about you?"

"Of course. No problem."

"Fine. I want you to go see Barbara Plunkett. Miss Plunkett is one of the senior economists. Then see Tom Schmidt. If we hire you, he'll be your boss." That was the extent of my conversation with O'Hara.

O'Hara showed me into a large room with four desks. Miss Plunkett sat at the corner desk nearest the large window. She was a svelte woman in her thirties who wore a severely tailored red suit with a large gold pin over her left breast. I sat in an armchair facing her.

She scanned the résumé. "Well, you are a good candidate. But let me ask you, how long do you plan to stay with the committee?"

"Quite a while, ma'am."

Brushing a lock of black hair from her forehead, she said, "Call me Barbara."

We went over my training in economic theory and quantitative methods of economic analysis. Then Miss Plunkett asked, "May I ask you a question?"

"Sure."

"What do you think of me?"

"Pardon?"

"I mean what do you think of working in the same office with a woman as an equal or superior?"

"That's fine with me, ma'am."

She interjected, "Barbara, please."

"Right . . . Barbara . . . I get along fine with women at the office. No problem. None at all."

"Well, Brett, I like that, and I like you." She paused for effect. "Why don't you go see Tom Schmidt?"

I got up quickly. "Great. It was good to meet you, Miss Plunkett."

"Barbara," she reminded me with a smile.

"Right, Barbara."

"See you later, Brett."

As I walked out the door, I didn't know whether to be flattered or worried. I made a note to keep my distance from her. I had been brought up not to mix business with pleasure.

Tom Schmidt sat in the next room. He shared it with only two other people; he had half and they had half. Like O'Hara and Miss Plunkett, Schmidt read my résumé. Unlike them, however, he did so while talking on the phone. He sported a silver Vandyke beard.

"Yeah, I understand . . . No, George, we're not going to support you on the bill. . . . We'd like to but no fuckin' way . . . You don't like our attitude? . . . Tough," Schmidt said, and then he hung up. "Welcome to Capitol Hill," he said to me. "Tell me about yourself."

Just then his phone rang. Picking up the receiver he motioned me to answer. So I did. The conversation sounded like this.

"Well, Mr. Schmidt, I grew up in Connecticut—"

"Cut the crap, George, I'm not with you on the legislation—"

"At Stanford I studied—"

"You should have thought of that before, Georgie boy—"

"My work in the Office of the President has included—"

"Don't cry on the phone, George—"

"I'm a good worker who can—"

"Don't call me back today—"

"So I think I can make a solid contribution to the committee and—"

"Bye, George."

Schmidt then looked at me and asked, "Can you work fast?"

"Yes."

"Can you work weekends?"

"Yes."

"Well, if your references check out, you've got the job."

"Great."

"Listen. You'll run hearings, write a little legislation, do some legislative analysis. OK?"

"Fine." I paused before asking, "How much will I be paid?"

"Twenty thousand to start, but with all the cost-of-living adjustments and annual raises, don't worry. You also get twenty-six paid vacation days and thirteen paid sick days. Any other questions?"

"No." It sounded like heaven to me.

A day later O'Hara called me up and said, "The job is yours." That was how I got my position on Capitol Hill. My slot at CIEP-EPB had been the big break; the JEC job was a logical result of my first stroke of luck.

I hardly needed to give Sam two weeks' notice. He had already spoken with Schmidt, who called for references. Sam was very kind and congratulated me on my next step up. So did Mary. There was no farewell party for me at CIEP-EPB, but two weeks later, early October, I received an autographed photo of the President. I guessed Sam and Mary had arranged that for me. I would miss them.

Autumn

FOR THE first few moments of the Joint Economic Committee's farewell party for my predecessor, the staffers edged nervously about in the twilight that filtered through the tall, thick-paned windows of the Congressional hearing room. Drained from the day's frenzy, they exchanged stale jokes and political gossip. Forty or so people in groups of two or three spoke in low voices and stood uncomfortably under the unremitting gaze of the larger-than-life portraits of former Committee chairmen. They were waiting for the politicians to arrive and give a center to this gathering.

When Senator Humphrey bustled in through the open door way, the small groups of staff instantly broke apart and surged forward as one mass to welcome him. Having returned that afternoon from a two-week rest in Minnesota, the Senator was surprisingly slim. His skin was a warm tan color, a welcome change after the chemotherapy sessions of the prior months to kill his cancer. He boomed his "Hello, how are you?" to everyone. Secretaries and clerks, lawyers and economists, clustered around this lively man to greet his return to Capitol Hill. The ladies moved closest, giving him their sweetest smiles as if they appreciated more than the men his mortality. All of the men except one looked on from a further distance.

The man standing shoulder to shoulder with Humphrey was

Schmidt. His clear blue eyes and pink nose and cheeks gave him a cherubic appeal.

I went to the buffet table to talk with Peter Ente, the young man I was replacing on the Committee staff. Ente was blond-haired, a little older than I was, and he already had the fleshy body that often comes after college. He had piled Swedish meatballs, rumaki, guacamole, crustless tea sandwiches, chopped chicken liver, and a couple dozen melon balls on his plate. Like many people working on Capitol Hill, he ate a lot, drank a lot, smiled a lot, and talked a lot.

Chewing as he spoke, he said, "Hi, you're taking my place, aren't you?"

I said hello and introduced myself quietly.

"Don't be bashful. Won't do you any good up here on the Hill. I don't mind meeting my replacement. We're all replaceable." He was in a talkative mood after much drinking. "I've got some advice for you," he continued. "Get yourself a guardian angel and only grab issues nobody else on the staff has prior claim to. Don't be an asshole either, 'cuz nobody'll like you no matter how smart you are." He popped a few melon balls in his mouth. "And another thing. This isn't school; guys like Schmidt aren't here to teach. They're trying to hustle just like you and me." In went more melon balls. "Try to figure out what the guy on top wants and you'll go far. You won't get any of what you want unless he gets most of what he wants."

He shoveled in the remaining melon balls and thus gave me time to ask him, "Where are you going now that you're leaving the Committee?"

"The Speaker of the House's office."

"Impressive," I said.

"Yep," he said with a smile.

"How old are you anyway?" I asked.

"Twenty-five. How about you?"

"Twenty-two," I said.

"Only twenty-two. You've gotten a quick start. I hate to think where you'll be when you're my age, one foot in the grave," he said. "Look me up in three years," he added.

"Sure," I said.

"See you later," he said and chugged back to the buffet table.

I gazed at the people in the formal hearing room. The men tended to be short and talkative. Two of the men were in the corner, arm-wrestling. Right behind them, Miss Plunkett and two middle-aged secretaries discussed breast cancer, while a young man wondered to the black bartender about HHH's chances of surviving the coming session of Congress.

These people looked drab. Most had bad complexions from too much fluorescent light and sway backs from sitting all day. They reflected the exhausting pace of working for tense politicians. But I heard no one complain about his job. For people on Capitol Hill, it was an honor to work for politicians whose lives and ideas were larger than their own. As one guy said, "No matter how tired I get, I'd rather be here at 8 P.M. on a weeknight than at home eating spaghetti in front of the television."

In that hearing room, I felt no sense of fantasy or high order as I had felt in the office of the President. Rather there was the smell of sweat in the air, the sweat of many people passing through government, politics and Washington, doing the best they could to survive and maybe prosper.

In a corner, the two young Committee clerks who were arm-wrestling were joined by a third. He was a plug of a man. He had a flattop haircut and small, gray sideburns. He said something to one of the two clerks. Then he took a step back, unbuttoned his suit jacket, and positioned himself squarely in front of his subordinate. The older man put his hands on his hips.

Grinning widely, the young clerk rolled up his shirt sleeves, formed a fist of his right hand, slowly pulled back his arm into a cocked position, and punched the man right in the gut. From the side, the only sign of impact I noticed was a slight forward stoop of the chest followed by the shoulders. Then the boy stepped back and the man gave him a playful cuff on his head. The boy sat down and returned to arm-wrestling his friend. The man turned away, and walked over to the buffet table where I stood.

Not since my days in high-school locker rooms had I seen this macho ritual that begins, "C'mon, give me your best shot right here. I can take it. I can take it." No one at the party blinked an eyebrow at it; a few congratulated him.

Gnawing on a celery stick stuffed with cream cheese, the man walked up to me. He wore a French-tailored suit that looked strange on his stubby torso. This was Bob Lackey. He was a senior clerk for the Committee. For a man near fifty, his face was surprisingly unlined except for a dimple on each cheek and some small scars from adolescent acne. His eyes darted quickly in their sockets beneath bushy eyebrows and a large flat forehead.

Lackey had been with the Committee a long time, first as the lowest clerk. He was a Committee man. His loyalties were to the men who ruled it whether they were Democrats or Republicans, progressive or reactionary, idiots or geniuses.

Like so many others, Lackey had come to Washington from the rural South after World War II. National politics and government didn't interest him very much. He had come for the good salary and stayed to accumulate the petty powers that make for influence in the bureaucracy. He now had the right to oversee staff's annual leave, sick leave, hearing dates, and requests for more pens and paper. That he worked on Capitol Hill for moderate and liberal Democrats was mere accident. He had a twin brother who had served as a chief clerk in the Nixon White House.

Lackey came up to me and asked, "Well, how are you enjoying our little shindig?"

"Very much, Mr. Lackey," I said.

"That's just great. And you can call me Bob. Everybody does. I know you'll fit in well. A genius. That's what you are," he said fulsomely.

I replied, "Thank you. I hope you feel that way a year from now."

Lackey immediately changed the subject. "Who'll you be working for?" he asked.

"Schmidt," I said. At the mention of Schmidt, Lackey lit up a smile for me. He didn't have to say anything; I could see he would now treat me with a bit more respect than if I worked for some junior Republican member. For Lackey, I was a potential friend or foe and thus it made a difference to him to know, as he said, "where your bread was buttered."

"He's a great one," Lackey hurried to add. "The nineteenth member of the committee, you know. That's what they say."

I looked over his flat head at Humphrey who was still surrounded by admirers. He was talking to ten people at once and was one step ahead of them all. He looked fit. He appeared more robust than in fear-ridden 1968, when I had stood in a sea of union workers at the AVCO shipyards in Bridgeport, Connecticut, and seen incumbent Vice-President Humphrey speak mightily but too late to defeat Mr. Nixon. Now I was standing a mere ten feet from him and watching with more admiration at age twenty-two than I had at fourteen. After three months in Washington, I looked forward to working for a politician who was free to say and do what he felt was right. His was the peculiar liberation of a dying man.

I had no intention of being rude to Lackey, but it was a minute or two before I looked away from Humphrey and back to him. I didn't know whether he was insulted or not, but by the time I returned to the conversation, he was walking away.

Someone's hand wrapped around my wrist. It was Joni. She had finally gotten away from her last meeting of the day. It was now 7:30 P.M.; this was the typical ten-hour day that many people on the Hill work.

"How was your day?" I asked.

Joni had a habit of repeating questions. "My day? Fine. My mother called me twice to suggest I meet some lawyers who are from Palm Beach."

"Nothing new then."

"Nope."

"If you want to go meet some you could," I said.

"What's bothering you?" she asked.

"Nothing."

"Well, calm down then. I'm going to get a drink." We occasionally had disagreements over her meeting people that her mother approved of. I resented the fact that her parents seemed less than enthusiastic about me. They would have preferred a friend of the family, a known quantity.

Before Joni could leave, a deep voice from behind me said, "Is this a friend of yours, Brett?" It was Schmidt.

"Joni Simpson, this is Tom Schmidt."

"How do you do, Miss Simpson." Schmidt's courtly tone of voice surprised me. He normally cursed in the office.

Schmidt put his right arm on my right shoulder thus excluding Joni from the conversation. He said to her, "Joni, please excuse us for a few minutes." Having dismissed her, he took me on a tour of the empty hallways. Like most with political influence, he assumed that he could approach anyone with his sure voice and easy camaraderie.

He began. "Brett, I want to say a few things while I have time. First, you're at the bottom of the professional staff. Don't forget that as long as you're working for me. None of the people or the Committee owe you a thing. You have me and to that extent some protection. But I'm going to start you out slow. You'll do the projects I give you and later on we'll give you more independence if things go well.

"As for the members and staff, like most people in politics in Washington, they want to be stroked, so pay your superiors some respect whether they deserve it or not. You'll do better that way. Remember, you're not the star; you're the bright young aide. Your life will be more pleasant if you stick to that role.

"Think of your work here as an apprenticeship. Establish a good reputation. Then perhaps go work for another committee or for the President or perhaps back to the university for more credentials. You're an able young man and you can go a long way in Washington if you put your mind to it."

I replied, "I'll take one thing at a time." He had sketched out too many warnings and prospects for me to take it all in. The point sank in, however: Schmidt was going to help me. For that, I was grateful.

"Drop by my office tomorrow at nine. I have a project I want you to help me with," he said.

Joni was at the bar, cornered between the chips and some old guy whose belly slid over his belt. I went over to get a drink and then rescue her. At the tables stacked with iced beer, mixers, wine and hard liquor, Schmidt was talking intently to the staff director, John O'Hara. I eavesdropped on their conversation while fiddling with the ice cubes. Schmidt was questioning O'Hara.

"Who the fuck was handling that vote?"

O'Hara answered, "Brink, the Speaker's man."

"If he worked for me, he'd be shoveling snow in North Dakota right now," Schmidt spat out. "He ought to have his chops busted for blowing that vote. I could have had a hundred lobbyists inside that damned cloakroom if I thought the vote would be close. But everyone said, 'Don't worry. We've got it in the bag. We've worked a deal in the Rules Committee. The floor vote will be a snap.' " That was the Schmidt I remembered talking on the phone when he was interviewing me for the job.

Having filled my wine glass with ginger ale (something I learned to do after a month of regular party-going in D.C.), I walked away from Schmidt and O'Hara before they noticed me. Joni saw me and excused herself from her aged suitor.

"Let's go," she suggested.

"Fine with me." We walked out the door and on to the marble that covers all floors in official Washington, the Dirksen Senate Office Building included. My thoughts were concentrated on Ente, Lackey, Schmidt, and all their admonitions.

Joni asked me, "Did you enjoy the party?"

"Uh-huh," I said absent-mindedly.

She added, "The food was terrific."

"Uh-huh," I said.

"You're quite the conversationalist."

"Uh-huh," I said.

Joni continued. "Well, I had a wonderful time. I got pinched on the ass by five different old men and pounced on by three young ones."

"That's good."

We were near the staff parking lot when Joni did get my attention by saying, "Hey Brett, there's Peter." So it was. Peter Dortmund was fifty yards up 1st Street N.E. and about to hop in his copper-colored Volkswagen Rabbit. Joni shouted, "Peter, Peter." He didn't seem to hear her so she ran over to his car as he was starting the engine. I trotted after her.

"What are you doing here?" Peter asked.

"We work here," Joni replied. "What are you doing here?"

Peter said that he had dropped off a package for a friend. Joni and I invited him to come to the Tune Inn, a low-rent Capitol Hill bar, for beer and fried chicken, but Peter begged off. He explained that he wanted to develop some photographs that night. He raced away.

I asked, "Doesn't he ever see people?"

"I don't know. I'm probably his closest friend here, and I only see him once every couple of weeks. He's probably just working a few things out, that's all."

"So are the rest of us, but we still see people."

The President lost the election. It had been a close race. In the end, voters decided in favor of a new face, a new man who would put all things right. I voted for the President's opponent myself, but not because I thought he could work magic. My vote was against the President's administration. I didn't like the way they had handled the issues I knew something about, especially United States arms policy and youth unemployment. In my case, familiarity had bred contempt.

I was glad to be working for the Joint Economic Committee of Congress. In the full flush of optimism over my new job, I felt a renewal of vigor. Now that the election was over, I was certain that things would change; controversial issues would once again be forthrightly addressed. We would all see how good our government could be, how good we wanted it to be. I was beginning to hit the proper moral tone of *Mr. Smith Goes to Washington.*

I was started out fast at the JEC. At 9 A.M. the day after the farewell party for Ente, Schmidt informed me that, under his supervision, I was going to organize a hearing for Senator Humphrey on what the public thought about the government's handling of the economy. The voters were complaining. Schmidt swore that the only way I'd figure out what the hell was going on was to start doing it.

Schmidt organized my efforts very carefully. This was a "cookbook" exercise designed to teach me how to master the problems involved in running a Congressional hearing. I reported to Schmidt, not Humphrey.

My first task was to obtain from Humphrey's office a date convenient for the Senator. A phone call to his personal secretary achieved this. I took care to clear the date with O'Hara, so that there could be no conflict with other JEC hearings. Next, I had Lackey reserve a hearing room in the Dirksen Senate Office Building. After that I submitted a list of potential witnesses to Schmidt. The list included the top pollsters in the country: Richard Baxter, vice-president of the Roper Organization, Inc., New York; Michael Curtin, director of Survey of Consumer Attitudes, Institute for Social Research, University of Michigan, Ann Arbor; Jay Schmeideskamp, vice-president of the Gallup Organization, Inc.; Arthur H. White, vice-president of Yankelovitch, Skelly and White, Inc., Stamford, Connecticut; Lou Harris of Louis Harris Associates, and Patrick Caddell, the President's pollster.

Schmidt told me that Lou Harris was a "must." He had done polling for the Senator for many years. I sent letters signed by the Senator or his signature machine—(I never knew which)—inviting these men to appear. The letters gave the topic of the hearing, "An Assessment of Public Opinion and Public Expectations Concerning the Government and the Economy," the date, and the information that traveling expenses and a per diem of $50 were customarily offered to witnesses. We left their testimony to them. We wanted honest appraisals of how people felt about the government.

A week later, I telephoned each prospective witness and received oral confirmation from every office. A JEC press flack and I wrote a press release to give the electronic and print reporters advance warning of the hearing. Finally, I wrote an opening statement for Humphrey; I based this on Schmidt's editorial suggestions ("Keep it short and to the point") and on other statements Humphrey had made in public concerning the voters' dissatisfaction with their government. I submitted this statement to Schmidt for his revisions. These seven steps ate up three weeks.

Mr. Humphrey's hearing began on the fourth week. He presided from the Chairman's overstuffed brown leather swivel chair positioned at the center of the semicircular dais that stretched toward the audience. He was the literal and metaphorical fulcrum around which the hearing would swing. From my seat in a red leather armchair one foot to the left and two feet behind, I had the pleasure given to all aides of public figures—the privilege of being simultaneously voyeur and exhibitionist. I could see each bead of sweat or flake of dandruff on the main actors and was myself an object of some attention for the tourists, whose eyes could not dwell endlessly on the familiar visage of Hubert Humphrey. This feeling of watching and of being watched was something I gradually became accustomed to on Capitol Hill. Many staffers dream of sitting in their Senator's seat. Yet sitting there that first hearing day, I didn't hope for that. I was more interested in influence and observation than in emulation.

But as Humphrey raised his gavel to start the proceedings, I was slightly envious of his opportunity to chair this hearing. Schmidt and I had brought the five most discerning American pollsters for his questioning. Their broad smiling faces showed them to be only too willing to discuss what people think and feel about government. Here was Humphrey, the leading exponent of active government, with the chance to hear from the seers why the beneficiaries of progressive government were unhappy and scornful of political leaders trying their best to serve their constituents. Here was the opportunity for Humphrey, in the security of beckoning death, to accept and try to understand the growing American disdain for the activist government in which Humphrey had worked so hard, endured so much pain, and enjoyed such power.

Under the intense lights of the television crews, Humphrey banged down the gavel. He read the opening statement that I had written for him the day before. It had been concisely written before Schmidt got hold of it for final revisions. Despite his instructions to me, Schmidt added a few embellishments like "This hearing affords"; "to deal with it in terms of"; and "to be able to bring into sharp focus." These awkward phrases were what I came to accept as "governmentese," linguistic monstrosities that would have given Strunk and White nightmares. Schmidt, like so many old politicos, understood the political uses of obfuscation and ambiguity; unfortunately, he was so well versed in their uses that he could no longer write a simple sentence.

The gavel came down at 9 A.M., and the next time I looked up at a clock it was 1:30 P.M.

Schmidt sat to my left, and to his left sat assorted members of the "majority" staff. To my right, on the other side of Humphrey, sat the "minority" staffers. At that time, "majority" meant Democrat and "minority" signified Republican. The two sides are segregated to make it easier for the members, their aides, the press, and the public to follow the proceedings. Majority and minority staffs also have separate offices; as Schmidt said to me over a cup of lousy cafeteria coffee, "Separate dugouts are essential. After all, we're not playing for the same team."

When Humphrey finished his opening statement, he was still the only member of the Committee present. The other members were temporarily represented by their aides. From the audience, numbering over one hundred (excluding those who would see him on the evening news), Humphrey looked as if he had brought along more bright, young aides than he had fingers or toes. Our presence lent him an added air of authority. In Washington, aides are a measure of a politician's power and potential force. They represent more speeches, more legislation, more hearings, more deals, and especially more public exposure. For the lazier members of Congress, staff can embody the saying "why do it yourself when somebody else can do it better." This, of course, was not the case with Humphrey, who had more useful energy and ideas than his entire staff. This hearing was his idea. As he told me a minute before the gavel came down, "This hearing's a check to see how we're doing." That was the first time he ever spoke to me.

As Senator Humphrey said sardonically in his opening remarks, "There was another witness we hoped to have, Mr. Patrick H. Caddell. He indicated he might be able to be with us; in fact, he said he would, and then he had to cancel out. I hope that he is not just giving his counsel and advice to the White House. We need to hear from him over here in Congress so we can stay abreast of what is going on at the other end of Pennsylvania Avenue." This little jab at Caddell's expense was Humphrey's way of letting Schmidt know that he didn't blame Schmidt and me for having failed to get him the young hotshot of the polling world. He was also voicing his objection to being stood up.

A week before the hearings, Caddell's office had assured me that he would be at the hearing, but the afternoon before, he backed out. In Caddell's case we were competing with the President for his time; no matter how famous or powerful a Senator may be, there is only one President, and he has first claim on everyone's service. If I had still been working for the President, I doubt whether Caddell would have called me so late.

Mr. Baxter from the Roper Organization led off. It was like listening to a quarterly business report that told you which beliefs were selling and which were being dumped at discount prices. "At the end of last year Americans felt better personally about the year they had just been through than they have for some time . . . optimism was up 9 percentage points from the year before . . . 70 percent now call our political system basically sound. This contrasts with only 50 percent willing to bet on our political system three years ago. . . . What I am really saying is that, all in all, Americans are feeling better about our institutions than they were in recent years."

What, I wondered, did "feeling better about their institutions" mean? Sitting there, under the camera crews' klieg lights, I saw Schmidt wipe a drop of sweat off the tip of his nose. I looked to see whether Senator Humphrey was going to question Mr. Baxter and his sweeping assurances. I wanted Humphrey to take him on—dive in immediately and ask questions.

I quickly wrote a question for Humphrey, showed it to Schmidt for his approval, and then on one knee (the classic position for a Congressional aide) slipped the sheet of paper in front of Humphrey—"What have the voters seen their politicians, businessmen and labor leaders do recently to make the public believe our political system is basically sound?" Perhaps the new President was turning voters on? Senator Humphrey read the question but crumpled it up. He went to our next witness, Lou Harris. So much for my first attempt at influencing a Senator.

In the excitement of the moment, I had forgotten that our hearing was structured so that all witnesses would testify before any questions were asked. Before the hearing, I had argued with Schmidt for immediate follow-up questions for each witness. Schmidt overruled me; "The other witnesses would be insulted if Humphrey asked one guy a lot of questions before they even had a chance to speak. Wouldn't you feel that way if you were testifying? It'd be rude."

Schmidt was right. "Put yourself in other people's shoes and you'll make more sense," he said.

Senator Humphrey said, "All right, Mr. Harris, we will hear from you."

Harris smiled. "Let me say it is a distinct pleasure to come before your subcommittee at a time when, for the first time in ten years, I can report some rising confidence among the public in both the executive and legislative branches of the federal government."

"Would you repeat that?" asked Senator Humphrey, hamming it up. Still smiling, Harris did.

He then continued, "The Congress has gone up from 9 percent who felt they had a great deal of confidence in the people running Congress in 1976 to 18 percent this year.

"But, make no mistake about it, to a majority of the American people, times are still hard and troubled. They are having a perfectly dreadful time making ends meet and are deeply worried . . . people are prepared to take drastic steps to meet that situation, but above all else, want leadership down here in Washington, D.C., which is willing to risk unpopularity to tell people the tough medicine they have to take to do the job."

Schmidt leaned to his right and whispered in my ear, "That guy's whistlin' Dixie." He mimicked Harris, "Above all else people want leadership down here in Washington, D.C., which is willing to risk unpopularity, tell people to take bad-tasting medicine." He continued, "If we did that, we'd be out of office by the next primary. That guy's dreaming."

Harris' statement criticized us in Washington without angering the Senator. Perhaps it was because Harris was a veteran political adviser to Humphrey. But, sitting behind Humphrey, I could see the Senator tapping his feet and writing notes to himself in anticipation of the question period.

Humphrey did not take criticism of Congress lightly. He loved Congress and all its weaknesses more than anyone else. He engendered that feeling of institutional loyalty in his staff. Schmidt had it, and I was beginning to feel it build in me the more I was exposed to the irrepressible Senator from Minnesota. He truly believed in the potential goodness of democratic government. He was always telling people to "get involved."

Next up to the microphone was Mr. White of Yankelovitch, Skelly and White. I didn't remember anything he said except that "90 percent felt their own families were doing well, and 60 percent felt the country was doing well, too."

Had there been this discrepancy when my parents were my age? In the Great Depression and the Second World War, the American family's future was clearly tied to the nation's fate.

Economic depression meant nearly every family suffered some deprivation, and war sent someone from most families overseas to fight and possibly die. I knew from my parents that when things were bad for the Republic they were bad for most of its citizens. For example, in the thirties, less food was placed in front of my father, but when the Americans liberated Rome in 1944, he dined sumptuously.

Was this thread between personal and national destiny worn thin? I thought about the people I knew of my generation. In spite of inflation and slower economic growth, we are doing pretty well—starting magazines, running political campaigns, buying condominiums, discovering new subatomic particles.

We had confidence in ourselves because that was where our efforts had succeeded. We had less confidence in our society. We observed that becoming a richer person, a better-adjusted person, or a more physically attractive person is easier than ending inflation or the nuclear-arms race.

I remember a tall, boyish young man working for Senator Kennedy's judiciary subcommittee saying to me over lunch in the Dirksen cafeteria, "I don't know whether breaking up the oil companies is or isn't a good thing, but for two years it's a fascinating experience." It would be no skin off his back if Kennedy's antitrust oil legislation died; he would still go on to greater personal distinction. "I'm no idealist," he said. He could do well no matter what shape the oil industry or Senator Kennedy's legislation was in.

Perhaps it was because I was sitting so close to Humphrey, the mythic Happy Warrior, but it seemed terrible to me that so many of my generation had given up on public service to concentrate on easily gained personal success. But there was no one I could think of to blame. I was only beginning to grasp the problem.

As the next witness, Richard Curtin of the Michigan Survey, began speaking, a slim, young woman with a terrific figure came into the hearing room. She walked quickly up the side aisle toward the front, and row upon row of well-dressed men turned their heads to stare. From my vantage point it seemed that the only ones who didn't gawk were Humphrey and the witnesses facing him. If we hadn't been in the middle of a hearing there would have been at least one low whistle.

Her name was Kim Donahue, and she worked for the JEC's minority staff. Though intelligent and with more schooling than I (she was getting a master's in economics at George Washington University), she was the one fetching extra copies of the witness' testimony for the press.

Like most of the young men on the committee, she too faced superiors who wanted assistance from junior staff, not shared access to the Committee members. But for Kim there were additional difficulties—our superiors were men who had difficulty working with her. As Schmidt would later comment to me one evening over beers at the Tune Inn, "I like Kim. She's smart and hard-working, but I just can't relax around her. You can't be yourself like you can with men." I had a feeling that Schmidt would say this about all women on Capitol Hill. His idea of women in Washington encompassed only two types: the Elizabeth Rays and the Rose Mary Woods, the bad girl and the good girl—not those wanting equal professional status.

It would have been easier for Kim if she were comfortable with the guys or, conversely, if she just demanded professional responsibilities comparable to those of her male associates as Miss Plunkett did. But she did neither. She was not, however, a "born loser." They don't get staff jobs on JEC at age twenty-three. In the nine months she had been on the JEC's staff, she had written many memos to her superiors suggesting new projects that she could do; the more she wrote the less interested her superiors were in reading them. They thought she was too pushy.

As the men eyed her, she put the copies on the press table, turned and walked out the way she had come in, fast. I felt sure her luck would change. She was too smart to fail.

Mr. Curtin from the University of Michigan was speaking while Kim walked in and out. I didn't listen to him closely.

Schmidt was taking notes and passing questions to Humphrey. Senators don't like to receive too many staff questions at the same time, because they can become more distracting than useful. This was especially true for Humphrey, who always took things where he wanted to anyway. Running a hearing for Humphrey was easier than most. As I was to discover, the toughest jobs were running hearings for Senators who depended almost entirely on their staff for information and direction.

The final witness was Jay Schmiedeskamp of George Gallup's organization, the most famous American polling group. Schmiedeskamp had just returned from foreign business and had finished writing his statement in an airplane on the way to the hearing, so I hadn't expected much. When he delivered it, however, it turned out to be the day's most challenging testimony. His comments on the role of government were particularly frank.

Schmiedeskamp concluded, "As a final note, I would like to urge upon you, as I have many times before, the importance of improving consumer confidence in government, the lack of which has greatly hampered the effectiveness of the government's economic policies in recent years. In that connection, perhaps it is appropriate to note in these halls of Congress that, according to a Gallup poll in late May . . . only 40 percent said they approved of the job performance of Congress. The ball would seem to be in your court, gentlemen."

Senator Humphrey cut in quickly and loudly. "There are reasons for it, not necessarily on the basis of performance but on the basis of what I call bad public relations. It's one thing for the President to be able to command the radio and television and the press, and another thing to have 535 individual voices in the Congress of the United States with 25 or 30 of those members thinking they are leaders, presenting contrasting views, which the press readily promotes. . . ."

Angry, Humphrey continued, "I simply point out that I think there has to be a voice raised occasionally to point out that individual Congressmen . . . in most instances run stronger in their respective districts than Presidents do."

Humphrey was rolling now, the quintessentially extroverted politician who knew when to keep things simple and loud.

"I think that I know more about the views of the people in Minnesota than any pollster or any President or anybody else. I make it my business. That is why I am here on my sixth term. I didn't get here because God Almighty appointed me. I got here because I know what people are thinking in International Falls, what they are thinking about in Duluth, what they are thinking about in Rochester, Minneapolis-St. Paul, what the farmer is thinking about, what the educators are thinking about, and that is why I get over 60 percent of the vote. I don't intend to let anybody rub the Congress' nose in the dust."

While Schmiedeskamp sat slightly dumbfounded thinking that he had had no intention of rubbing anyone's nose in the dust, the right-wing Republican junior senator from Utah, Orrin Hatch, said to Humphrey, "I hate to say this, but I think you are probably a better pollster."

Breezing past Hatch's gratuitous comment, Humphrey continued:

"I know what you (Schmiedeskamp) are saying about the public-opinion polls. I read all about the perks that we get and all, this sort of jazz. . . . There isn't a very good view about the Congress because nobody writes about how hard it works, nobody —there is very little reported on that. We get reported on our mistakes and on controversy."

Schmiedeskamp, trying to get a word in edgewise, said, "My only point, sir, was that there is a need for action, and I think it would be welcomed by the American people." But Humphrey was in no mood to take his advice.

"We will get you in on this in a minute. I was doing this for several purposes. I am not running for reelection. I intend to use the next years to vent every damned thing I wanted to say, and I am going to say it," Humphrey said. He turned quickly to Schmidt and asked *sotto voce* for more ice water. The Senator hadn't yet reached his crescendo. Lackey quickly filled Humphrey's glass.

Humphrey boomed on. "I went over to the House of Representatives to testify on cancer research and the whole damned day ended up in newspaper headlines on how somebody got a free trip to Jamaica." With the mention of the word "cancer," Humphrey was instantly metamorphosed from the seasoned politician into the sacred victim. The audience began to sit up on the edges of their chairs. Here was a dying political legend in the process of apotheosis. I could feel the energy of the man radiating in all directions.

He continued.

"Really and truly, it's disgusting . . . so the cancer hearing ended up being a story on conflict of interests. Anybody involved in this program, by legislation or by illness, damn well doesn't like it. The word went out to the people that all they are doing in the cancer program is cheating on tickets to airlines—to go to Jamaica. Some little piddling pooping thing that didn't amount to a hoot . . . good God Almighty, headlines like that, when we had reports at the hearing indicating that a child who got leukemia ten years ago had a 10 percent chance to live and today has a 60 percent chance. . . . Instead what do you read about? Somebody got a ticket to go to Jamica—*pffft.* That is why Congress gets in trouble around here."

Senator Orrin Hatch added, "I hope Senator Humphrey keeps up this activism that has been noticeably lacking the past number of years with regard to this particular point. I have deep regard for him and a deep respect for him, and we ought to pay more attention to Senator Humphrey in this area."

Schmidt nudged me with his elbow and whispered, "There goes that jerk giving Humphrey his eulogy as early as possible."

I wasn't thinking about Hatch, but about Humphrey. Despite the Senator's original desire to know how the American people saw the Congress, when confronted with their criticisms, Humphrey had lashed out at the bringer of bad news—Schmiedeskamp. The pollster's call for more government action and less talk annoyed Humphrey. The Senator was annoyed that Schmiedeskamp told him again and again that he and his fellow politicians weren't doing a good job. I could hear him say to himself, "I know that."

Whether Humphrey felt some personal insecurity about his own performance, or whether he was simply protecting the institution that had been his home for so long, I didn't know. But I felt angry too. I didn't care anymore about exploring the reasons for public disenchantment with the government. I was swept away in the Senator's emotions.

All his life, Hubert Humphrey had advocated and fought for an activist federal government—exactly what Schmiedeskamp was chastising the Congress for not doing. There was Humphrey, knowing he would die soon, in a period dominated by a government in stasis and an electorate moving to the right. There would be no more Civil Rights Act for him; his beloved Full Employment and Balanced Growth Act (Humphrey-Hawkins) was considered outdated and was being gutted. Humphrey was allowed one or two outbursts to rail at the unfairness of life.

At 1:30 P.M., the Committee adjourned subject to the call of the chairman. Humphrey had finished with a rousing tirade against bankers and high interest rates. The audience clapped when he finished.

Obviously pleased with his performance, Humphrey turned to me and said, "That was a fine hearing. You did a very good job, young man." That was the payoff—a compliment from the man himself. Schmidt overheard Humphrey's comment. He saw me smiling and smiled himself. With Humphrey's seal of approval, I went up a notch in Schmidt's book, which gave me more confidence and a slightly higher standing among the staff.

That night the ABC network news did a story on our hearing. The videotape showed Humphrey, and there behind him were Schmidt and I. I looked more relaxed than I had felt. The cameraman had filmed the two of us staring to the right, where, unseen by the television audience, Kim Donahue had just walked in. To my surprise, Humphrey's eyes drifted in that direction too. I doubt, however, whether he knew that she was on the Committee staff. She didn't get the chance to run a hearing the way I had. It remains an advantage to be a man in Washington.

The pace and tension of work on Capitol Hill wore people down. The strapping staff director John O'Hara had spent twenty years here. When I met him he had to keep an oxygen tank in his office to cope with his respiratory ailments. He had the thankless job of trying to keep order among a staff of forty men and women who took orders from different members of the Committee, most of whom had their own subcommittee fiefdoms. O'Hara was impotent to control a man like Schmidt, who by virtue of his closeness with Humphrey had as much influence as he.

The staff was organized along an odd set of rules that was both anarchic and discriminatory; on the one hand, everyone tried to steal or lock up projects for themselves, while, on the other hand, if junior staffers tried this and were caught, they were assigned jobs like preparing the weekly summary of government economic indicators. In such an atmosphere of internecine feuding, people rarely let their guard down. Few Committee aides socialized after hours. That was why Schmidt surprised me when he invited Joni and me to dinner at his home. Schmidt liked to keep his distance from other staffers outside the office. He preferred politicians or staff members from other committees or from the Executive Office of the President.

I assumed that his invitation was extended as a reward for having worked well my first month on the JEC. For Schmidt could be cruel when people acted less intelligently than he expected. Two other young Committee staffers had worked for Schmidt only three weeks before asking for a reassignment within the Committee—"I couldn't take it. Nothing I did was ever quite right," they complained. Schmidt had a mean streak, but he hadn't frightened me. First, it hadn't been directed at me, and second, I didn't submit work I wasn't pleased with.

I had heard a story of Schmidt sweeping every article off the desk of a subordinate who had given him an inferior memo for the second time in a row. The person began crying; he did not stay long on the Committee. Schmidt, however, was not usually so heartless. He could be hospitable as he was the night Joni and I dined at his home.

Schmidt lived in a nineteenth-century brick town house off Massachusetts Avenue, "Embassy Row" in the local vernacular. I had expected a split-level in suburban Bethesda, Maryland.

I rang the front doorbell, and Schmidt came to the imposing wood front door. He was not wearing his usual plaid polyester suit; instead he looked comfortable in a pair of gray flannels and a tweed jacket. He welcomed Joni and me and introduced us to Marilyn, his girl friend. She was a leggy brunette in her thirties.

Schmidt showed us into the living room. The furniture was 1930s modern. From an ice bucket in the corner, he fetched an already opened bottle of German white wine. He and Marilyn had the flush of people who had begun drinking some hours earlier.

"Here's to a marvelous dinner," I said.

"To a great dinner," he replied, touching his goblet to mine. "Now, excuse Marilyn and me. We have to finish the preparations. Take a look around." It was strange seeing him so hospitable. I thought he was up to something. Did he want a favor?

Joni and I wandered around the white dining room. The room was dominated by a huge, horizontally spreading glass-cased cabinet. Wider than four Bismarcks, this Teutonic cupboard housed dozens and dozens of old intricately carved cut-crystal glasses and goblets that could have been used in Kaiser Wilhelm II's court.

Directly across the dining room, sitting on the mantel over the fireplace, was a crescent-shaped black hat with a plumed white feather. I asked, "Tom, whose hat was this?"

Schmidt walked through the short vestibule that separated his kitchen from the dining room. "Oh that. That was my grandfather's. He was the Austrian Minister of the Interior. That was one of the things my father and mother brought with them to America when they fled Austria. They took this cabinet and the dining table, too." His tone was matter of fact.

"Why did your grandfather have to flee?" Joni asked.

"Oh, he didn't leave," Schmidt chuckled. "Only my mother, my father and I left. He stayed. He was in no danger, nor for that matter was my father—but my mother and I were. You see, she was a Jew."

"How old were you when you left?" Joni asked.

"Nine when we moved from Vienna to Vienna, Texas, where my father became a professor of chemistry at Vienna College." Schmidt said with a laugh, "I've always wondered if he picked Vienna simply because of the name. A bit of the old world in the new."

Not content to leave the topic and let Schmidt's story come out in the course of the evening, Joni asked, "Do your parents still live in Texas?"

"No," Schmidt replied. "Eventually, they moved to San Francisco. But they're both dead now. He jumped off the Golden Gate Bridge, and my mother died of leukemia three years ago. That's the way I think I had always expected them to go—he, quickly in an overwhelming fit of *angst;* and she, suffering slowly." With a wave of his left arm, Schmidt referred to all the downstairs furnishings. "These are all recent bequests from them. Without these this big house would be nearly empty." Joni didn't ask any more questions. The ease with which Schmidt spoke of his parents' deaths made her uncomfortable. She thought it was unfeeling. Joni never understood Schmidt. Sometimes I didn't either.

Schmidt returned to the kitchen to help Marilyn. He asked me to open a bottle of rosé to be drunk with the appetizer. With the sole, he would open a cooled bottle of white Burgundy, with the filet mignon, a fine red Bordeaux wine. As we sat down for dinner, Schmidt put Mozart's *Magic Flute* on the stereo, and Marilyn lit the white candles on the linen-covered dining table.

The dinner was atypical for Washington; at first, there was no talk of politics or the economy. Schmidt held forth on such topics as opera ("Only Mozart's and Verdi's are worth a damn"), gluttony ("I eat too well, drink too well, and have ulcers—a regular Renaissance man"), and romance ("There are some women who make all the flowers worth it when they get into bed").

The wine went to his head. By the meat course he was trying hard to give the impression of sobriety. As he got drunker, he sat up straighter and dabbed the edges of his mouth more frequently. He was having trouble with his short-term memory and was in no condition to discuss any issue intelligently. The wine, however, seemed to liberate deeply held opinions.

He began speaking about inflation and the collapse of Germany's Weimar Republic. In his bass voice he warned, "Inflation, that is what feeds on the public's confidence in itself, in government." He quoted the annual inflation rates for each year from 1919 to the election of Hitler as chancellor. He listed the number of anti-Semitic incidents from Hitler's assumption of power to the beginning of World War II. Then he fell silent.

I saw for the first time how lonely Schmidt was. A refugee, now without parents or close friends save Marilyn, Schmidt was alone. The first time I had met him at the staff party, he had made me feel I had known him a long time, but now I began to realize that at work he showed little of himself. I was flattered that he felt comfortable enough with me to open up a bit after hours.

When we said goodnight, I felt like giving him a hug, not a handshake. Of course, I didn't. It would have made both of us uncomfortable.

The next morning Schmidt did not come to work. I called his home during the day, but there was no answer until 5:30 P.M. when Marilyn, who had returned from work, picked up the ringing phone. She said that Schmidt was in the hospital with a bleeding ulcer. "I thought this might happen," she said. I would visit him in the hospital, but I was not to see him at the office for a month.

• • •

92

The day after it became common knowledge on the Committee that Schmidt was in the hospital for an extended rest, I received a phone call at my desk.

"Fromson, JEC," I said into the receiver.

"Har yew?" the man at the other end of the line said. "I wanna speak to someone who can help me with our garbage problem."

"This is the Joint Economic Committee of Congress, sir," I said, wondering why anyone would be calling us about his garbage.

"I know that, sonny. This is the Mayor of Naples—"

"Naples?" I asked. I thought I had an escapee from a Veterans Hospital on the line.

"Naples, Texas," he said.

"Oh," I replied, still mystified.

"Listen, we used to get help from your committee when Wright Patman was chairman of the Committee. Now I've got this problem with the garbage collectors. They're bandits. They've just raised their rates by five hundred dollars a month. We need some help. This inflation's killing us."

"Sir, I'm afraid I can't give you much help. The JEC doesn't deal with constituent matters. That's what your Congressman is here for."

"I know that, but don't you think a five-hundred-dollar-a-month increase is outrageous? What the hell good is the federal government if you guys can't help us with this inflation?"

"I do think it's outrageous, sir, and I wish I could help you, but our committee has no jurisdiction over rates for hauling garbage in East Texas."

"You're a lot of help, kid," he replied. "Hope you have a rotten day."

Immediately I called Ellie, the receptionist, to find out who sent this call to me.

She explained. "It went to Lackey but he told me to switch it to you."

"Oh," I said. "I see."

I called Lackey on the intercom. "Bob, why did you send me that mayor with the garbage problem? I don't know anything about his town or the local scene. Why didn't you send him to his Congressman?"

"Well, Brett, with Schmidt out, O'Hara gave me approval to give you assignments."

"I'll be right over," I answered. I didn't want him controlling my assignments; he didn't know a thing about economics.

Lackey's desk was located in the Committee's main office, a rectangular room about 40 by 60 feet and ten feet below ground level; from the windows you could see a concrete wall and the bottoms of a few trees. This place was called the Snakepit. It was divided by assorted beige partitions into cubbyholes into which were stuffed one large Xerox machine, one receptionist, three clerks who handled requests for committee publications, one economist from the minority staff, two copy editors from the Government Printing Office, two middle-aged press flacks, the bookkeeper, Lackey, an intern or two, and a sweet Southern lady who clipped articles for a JEC member who kept her on the payroll as a favor to someone. The room's enforced intimacy made it a hotbed for gossip-mongering and backbiting.

I walked over to Lackey's desk. It was a solid old-fashioned double-drawered wooden desk. As suited Lackey's role as chief clerk, his phone had as many buttons as the receptionist's. On his desk was a brand new IBM Selectric II typewriter with an automatic correcting device. It was not plugged in, and in the month and a half that I had been on the Committee I had never seen anyone use it. Lackey had another typewriter on a stand beside his desk which he used a bit. The unused typewriter struck me as an indication of the small material objects around which Lackey's work life circled. He had to worry about all the little administrative chores everyone else hoped to avoid. He appreciated the petty and their uses. The importance of giving or withholding new desks or chairs in a bureaucracy.

Lackey was talking on the phone when I came in. He hung up. "Brett, there's a project John O'Hara and I want you to do," he said, invoking the staff director's name as protection. He reached into his top desk drawer with his scabby hand and pulled out a one-inch-thick neatly typed manuscript. On the cover page was a title, *Foundations for a National Policy to Preserve Private Enterprise in the 1980s.* The author was an assistant professor at a small college in Massachusetts. I quickly leafed through its seventy-five pages broken into chapters like "Tomorrow's Needs," "The Capital Gap Problem," "Government Regulation and the Perspective of Small Business" and, finally, "New Strategies."

"John and I," Lackey repeated, "want you to evaluate and see whether this paper is suitable for publication by the Committee."

I said, "I don't know too much about this subject, but I'll do this one project for you. When do you need it?"

"The day after tomorrow."

"I have to review the transcripts of the Humphrey hearing before the GPO (Government Printing Office) prints it, but other than that I'm free. I'll get it to John on time."

"Fine, you give it to me and I'll get it to John," he said. As I turned to leave, Lackey added, "By the way, this was written by a friend of one of the Senators so don't be too tough."

I walked away without a reply. I understood I was supposed to give it the soft touch.

Back in the relative quiet of the office I shared with Schmidt, I sat down at my desk to read the study. I wanted to review it and think about it overnight before writing the critique and recommendation.

Having recently studied in the economics department at Stanford, where the ideal was "rigorous and quantitative analysis," I was not impressed with *Foundations for a National Policy to Preserve Private Enterprise in the 1980s.* I read the study three times. The first time its arguments and documentation seemed slightly confused, the second time disturbingly inept, and the third time a complete mess.

The next day I wrote a criticism:

95

1. The author cannot write a sentence unless loaded with social-science jargon.

2. The author's assertions are unoriginal and documentation scanty. He relies on others' work to such a degree that it leaves me wondering if he could make the arguments on his own.

3. To "save free enterprise," the author suggests creating a Cabinet-level agency for small business. Why in this case more government bureaucracy is needed to "save free enterprise" is unclear. There is no indication that owners and operators of small business want this, nor does the sad experience of the scandal-ridden Small Business Administration suggest a larger bureaucracy as the answer to assisting smaller enterprises in an economy dominated by large corporations.

My final recommendation to O'Hara was: Forget this study. It was not worth rewriting. There were competent economists who could prepare a piece for the Committee without damaging our reputation as a publisher of provocative but technically sound analyses of political issues.

I had a secretary type the evaluation, sent the original to O'Hara and dropped a copy on Lackey's desk. I didn't want Lackey deleting my recommendation against publishing this report before it got to O'Hara. I wanted O'Hara to know that I was not going to write a memorandum supporting a shoddy piece of work by a crony of some Senator. If he wanted to have it published, I was in no position to stop him, but I didn't want to be the guy who gave it the Committee's seal of approval. I wasn't going to be used the way I had been on the youth-unemployment assignment downtown in the Old Executive Office Building.

At two-thirty that afternoon, Lackey stormed into my office clutching the memo like a dead bird and asking, "What in the hell is this?" He stood at the edge of my desk.

Immediately on the defensive, I replied, "Bob, I know it is a bit tough, but that paper is a disaster."

"You've got John upset about it now. Dammit, what makes you think that you know more about this than the author?"

I said loudly, "That report is trash. If you don't like my telling you what I think, then why did you ask for my opinion?"

From across the room, Dick Rosen, Senator Proxmire's staff guy on the Committee, looked up from his incredibly cluttered desk and growled, "Keep it down."

In a lower but still angry voice, Lackey said, "I told you to send this memo to O'Hara through me. If you had, I could have checked it."

"Sorry," I said disingenuously.

Lackey left and that was the last I heard of *Foundations for a National Policy to Preserve Private Enterprise in the 1980s* until April, when it appeared in my mailbox in the Snakepit unchanged except that this time it was printed and bound as an official Committee document. That was also the last time Lackey tried to supervise me. I knew that if Schmidt had been there when I argued with Lackey, he would have lectured me on the stupidity of "telling someone to go to hell unless you can put him there."

Ten minutes after Lackey walked out, Proxmire's man Rosen hung up his phone and asked me to come over to his desk. He was about fifty years old but had a baby face. The first time we met, I mistook him for a publications clerk.

Sitting in his large swivel chair, Rosen could barely see over the piles of memos, reports and magazines that buried his desktop. As usual, he was rummaging for misplaced papers; all his classified documents, however, were safely stored in the safe beside his desk. Rosen did work on defense issues for Proxmire. It was Rosen who uncovered the infamous cost overruns on the Defense Department's C-5A cargo plane and first convinced the notable "whistle blower," Ernest Fitzgerald, to testify about waste and mismanagement in the Department of Defense. Rosen was used to tilting against DOD's minions.

Rosen and I got along well, but I had not previously worked with him because of my close relationship with Schmidt. The committee staff was broken into provinces. Junior staff worked for only one superior, in my case Schmidt.

"Hey, Brett," Rosen said. "How'd you like to do a project for me while Schmidt's out?" Rosen wanted me to draft a piece of legislation for Senator Proxmire, a bill to give the Congress greater oversight on the federal government's research-and-development efforts.

As with the thousands of other bills drafted during a session of Congress, this one was preceded by a study that "established" the legislative imperative for it. The year before, the JEC had, at Proxmire's request, commissioned outside experts to tell them what was wrong with government-sponsored research and development, especially military R&D where over 60 percent of all federal R&D money was being spent, $15 billion plus. A longtime opponent of the defense establishment and its demands for more complicated and more expensive weapons systems, Proxmire wanted some legislative vehicle that would allow him to rein in DOD's supersecret, supercostly R&D programs. He had seen one too many overblown and ineffective weapons systems that he thought could have been "nipped in the bud" (a favorite Proxmire phrase) if Congress had been able to review it at the R&D stage.

Since the Joint Economic Committee has no legislative authority—that is, its members could not use it as a vehicle to introduce legislation to the floor of the House or Senate—I thought it slightly odd that I, a Committee aide, was drafting a bill. As Rosen explained to me, however, staff members of the Joint Economic Committee regularly draft legislation for the members who introduce it through other committees. For example, the noted Humphrey-Hawkins Full Employment and Balanced Growth Act had been written for Senator Humphrey by the Committee staff.

My first task in writing this legislation was to visit the Senate Counsel's office. It is with the help of this nonpartisan staff that most legislation is drafted; the House of Representatives has a similar group. I told him what I wanted to say, and he put it into legal jargon consonant with existing federal legislation and regulations. (One does not need to be a lawyer to write laws on Capitol Hill; all one needs is an idea, good or bad.)

I explained to counsel that Proxmire wanted to expand Congressional oversight of military R&D. There were many ways to do this. We chose to tie the review process to the President's Council on Wage and Price Stability (CWPS). Why CWPS? Politics, of course.

CWPS was the paper tiger the President periodically unleashed to rant against inflationary wage, price and regulatory actions. It had two hundred employees, many of whom were secretaries and clerks. CWPS could not even monitor the inflationary acts of government, of private business, or of unions. Why then was Proxmire about to burden them further with cost-benefit evaluations of federal R&D? CWPS's inclusion in the bill was determined by the fact that its authorizing legislation came out of the Senate Banking Committee, whose chairman happened to be Bill ("Golden Fleece") Proxmire. His desire for greater political leverage over the Department of Defense was making for unwieldy legislation. Rosen was delighted that we could use CWPS.

Concerned about our approach, I showed the draft bill to a private economist who specialized in R&D. This man was a former high-level official in the Office of Management and Budget. He had left the government in 1972; as he said to me, "I don't think politicians know the meaning of the word 'leadership' any more." This was a common complaint among veteran observers of Washington. I refused to buy that interpretation of the problems with government. If I had, I would never have come to Washington.

Sucking on his pipe, this former adviser to Presidents concluded that the Proxmire legislation on R&D was "misdirected," because the waste in government R&D was caused by too much time-consuming and cumbersome evaluation of projects. Our bill would add yet another bureaucratic barrier to the R&D process.

I did not know whether he was correct, or whether Rosen's belief in increased Congressional oversight was the key to improving government R&D. Yet there I was, delegated to write this bill. In retrospect, it is a bit frightening to think that each day there are probably a hundred young men and women like me on Capitol Hill making similar legislative decisions with similarly uncertain convictions about the worth of their efforts. In my case I felt singularly unprepared to write this bill, and yet I had no choice; there was no backing out of this opportunity to show my superiors I could do good work for them even if I doubted its usefulness. I did not show Rosen the consultant's criticism; I didn't think he'd want to hear it.

A few days went by before Rosen responded to my draft of the bill. When he did, he changed the legislation's direction. Instead of restricting the bill to R&D, he now proposed to expand the bill to require that *all* government agencies provide the CWPS with estimates of the impact *any new federal rule, regulation, or program* would have on the economy. Talk about monumental paper shuffling! I began to wonder whether he knew what he was doing.

This change was ridiculous. We had lost the original focus of the bill. For the CWPS to evaluate economic-impact statements for every significant government action was impossible; it would require a staff and budget the size of the Department of Commerce. With this latest change, our own bill could not have withstood the cost-benefit criteria it was establishing for the rest of the government. By hewing to the Senator's desire for more power, we were creating a little Frankenstein.

Rosen did not share my doubts; or if he did, he too was keeping them hidden. We went ahead. My doubts about the bill did not interfere with my work on it. I went on and drafted the statement that Proxmire would use when introducing the legislation on the floor of the Senate. I wrote the best defense for the bill I could. God knows it needed it. I had reconciled myself to introduction of our legislation for one simple reason. I had confidence that it would fail in the legislative process. Some Congressmen would see the folly of it; the DOD bureaucrats would lobby against it; and other Congressional committees would oppose this power grab. Very few bills introduced by a single Senator get through committee review, let alone pass on

100

the Senate floor. Coalitions, not individuals, get legislation passed.

Rosen and perhaps even Senator Proxmire may have had similar feelings, but they still introduced the bill. It was given a name, S1805; "S" stood for Senate, "1805" meant 1804 other bills had already been introduced this session of Congress. If the bill failed to pass, that was no great reflection on Proxmire. He could always blame its failure on DOD opposition, not on its own defects.

Before coming to Washington, I never thought I'd be pleased to be on the losing side. When I heard later that S1805 had died in committee, however, I smiled. I felt I had played the game well; I had done a good job for Rosen and Proxmire without committing some public disservice. I was beginning to learn patience. Unlike the time in the OEOB when I tried to tell Ben Hayes about the hypocrisy of the Self-Employment Incentive Program, this time I played along and let things take their course.

As November slipped into December, Thanksgiving into Christmas, Washingtonians began to celebrate the holidays with a vengeance. There was a rising frenzy of partying, which calmed only when the Congress recessed a day or so before Christmas. When there were still ten more shopping days till Christmas Day, Washington was a party-hopper's heaven.

Though such celebration is certainly not unique to Washington, I had never been subjected to such sustained and intensive socializing. It was as if all the parties, all the drinking, eating, smoking, kissing and fondling were one quick release of the year's accumulated tension. Through our roommates, Joni and I were invited to the more exclusive parties—that is, black tie and boarding-school education—through our jobs to countless office parties, and through college friends to drunken blowouts.

The big Christmas party scene for people our age was directly related to the homogeneous backgrounds of young people in political Washington. This notion was captured by a young woman I knew; she made it a point to know every young person in Washington whom she considered to be a somebody-in-the-making. As she said, "In Washington, a higher percentage of the population is well educated, well connected, well dressed, well spoken, and well heeled than in any other city in the country, so there simply are more people to see, to enjoy."

She had a point. In the third week of December, the population under thirty seemed to double in Washington. People—home from school, looking for next year's jobs, or just visiting friends—came from everywhere. One day that week, I walked out of the Dirksen Senate Office Building to the nearby parking lot and I met a friend from Stanford in town to interview for a fellowship at the Brookings Institution, Washington's leading think tank. A minute later in the same snow-filled parking lot, I ran into another friend of mine from Harvard who had just started working as a parking attendant. Even the car jockeys in Washington have college degrees.

While most Washington parties for young Washingtonians were arranged on the spur of the moment, there were other, more formal and exclusive social events orchestrated by the wives of the local gentry and socially active diplomats and politicians. These gatherings were justified by their organizers as mixers, where their sons and daughters could meet other budding success stories from or temporarily in Washington. Like most statements in Washington, this was only part of the truth; it ignored the compulsive need of wives of certain powerful or near-powerful men; these women felt a duty to their husbands to reaffirm the family's status in local society by having their children socialize with the offspring of other "good" families. We were also being put together to establish and reinforce the social connections that could prove useful twenty years hence, when, as assistant secretaries, Congressmen, judges and editors, we might need a favor or two from each other.

Having always celebrated Christmas with my family in the relative isolation of Weston, Connecticut, I was intrigued by the parties to which Joni and I were invited. Other than rinky-dink dancing-school cotillions at age twelve and boarding-school mixers with girls from Miss Porter's—which generally led me to jump out a window to escape the overwhelming awkwardness of the situation—I had little experience with the social gatherings of the upper class. After four years in California, however, I looked forward to these East Coast rituals as performed by the latest cohort of Washington's "best and brightest."

The most memorable meeting of the tribe was at a ball hosted by the wife of a European ambassador. Her warm, pudgy daughter Jackie had little of her mother's social interest and so compelled Charity, Diana, Nicholas and me to attend and keep her company. I went without Joni; her parents were in from Palm Beach for a visit and she spent the evening with them.

Dressed in my black dinner jacket which, in my vanity, I thought became me, I escorted Diana. We drove to a preball dinner at a country estate in what was once horse country and is today the countrified suburbia of McLean, Virginia. This house was a bit like Mt. Vernon, with white columns on a slight rise surrounded by acres of snow-covered pastures.

Diana was a husky and nervous woman. These past six months since her graduation from Harvard hadn't been particularly happy ones. She had returned to Washington, to please her parents more than anything else. They wanted Diana near them. After all, they had never really approved of her going to Cambridge in the first place. "What is wrong with Hollins, Sweetbriar, or UVA?"

Her parents were memorable for their warm Southern hospitality and antebellum racial attitudes. One fall afternoon Joni and I and Diana and a friend of hers played three sets of tennis at the Chevy Chase Club, Washington's most select country club. Afterward, we ran into Diana's parents. We chatted with them in the club's well-shaded parking area, which runs along Connecticut Avenue, a main road from Maryland's wealthy suburbs to downtown Washington.

I was standing in my whites talking to Diana's mother, when she said in her dainty Southern accent, "My, look at those boys on the street. I wonder what they're doin' here?" I turned expecting to see something unusual like seven-foot transvestites.

Instead, it was simply a foursome of black men walking on the sidewalk along busy Connecticut Avenue toward the city limits of Washington.

Mrs. Daniels wasn't through. She added, "My, they do look threatnin'."

I tried not to laugh. She reminded me of a Southern relative of mine who once said about blacks in his part of the country, "I like Nigras. Never had anything against 'em. We always treated them well. The only thing I wonder about is why after three hundred years in this country they still have that kinky hair, those broad noses, such big thick lips, and that black skin. Ya know, I don't think they *want* to change."

Diana's love life was still a series of one week affairs, the last with a first-year student at Georgetown Law; he was going to be at the ball. I hoped she would not make a scene at the party. As her escort and house mate, I would look out for her.

She and I walked into the foyer of the house where we were to dine before the ball along with thirty other young men and women. One of the five matrons chaperoning the ball showed us into a long, cozy living room filled with people my age. I knew about fifteen of them; and the rest looked vaguely familiar. We felt comfortable in the knowledge that everyone was "a friend of a friend." There was a roaring fire in the hearth at the far end of the elm-wainscoted den. I got Diana a bourbon and then walked quickly to the fireplace to warm up. A bluff middle-aged man bent over the fire poking at the logs with a blunt-tipped long brass blowpipe. He was the master of the house. He turned to me and said, "Bought this 'blowpoke' from Orvis. Couldn't get through the winter without it." The room was filled with comments like that, regarding the essential nature of L. L. Bean, boarding schools and colleges, Cuban cigars, good booze, and Washington.

I wandered into the dining room to find my table and to see whom I would be eating with. Reading the small white place cards, I knew four of the eight.

Sitting two places to my right would be Burgess White. Recently graduated from Harvard, he was caught up in the "great man" syndrome, as in "I want to be a great man in the tradition of Adams, Wilson, or Franklin Delano Roosevelt." Burgess worked as special assistant to some deputy undersecretary. From previous dinners at our house, I knew him to be supremely confident in his own talents and painfully concerned with pushing ahead in his career. His hair was always as carefully watered as Jay Gatsby's.

He was coming off a recent traumatic experience—he had failed to receive a Rhodes Scholarship to Oxford University. A former girl friend of his had split up with Burgess when it became apparent that he was looking to get married to a bright well-educated young woman who would make her contribution to man's betterment by wedding Burgess and helping him go down in American history as an important figure.

Burgess often made people around him nervous. He didn't bother me. He seemed to like me, I suppose because I was also on the fast track and possibly could be someone to know in the future. I was glad, however, not to be sitting right next to him at dinner. I didn't feel like getting pumped about what had gone on in Congress that day.

To my left there would be my house mate, Charity Livingston, "of the New York Livingstons" as she reminded me more than once. I was one of the few people who appreciated her haughtiness. It stemmed from an unusual combination of rich-kid willfulness and adult combativeness. Tall and slim, with silky black hair, she spoke whenever she wished and said whatever she wished; she could have been surrounded by a howling mob of Iranian religious fanatics and still would have defended the Shah if she felt like it. Appropriately, Charity worked for Senator Moynihan, known on Capitol Hill as the "Mouth from New York." Charity had energy that allowed her to party until 3 A.M. and still arrive at her Senator's office on time and prepared to put in a full day's work. She supplemented her diet with some cocaine, but she was not addicted to the drug. She ran more on nervous energy than anything else.

Also at the table was an acquaintance of Charity's from Capitol Hill. His name was Adrian Rubin. He was an intelligent

105

twenty-year-old anti-Russian hard-liner whom Charity had brought along to keep her company for the evening. He had landed a job on some Congressman's personal staff after having worked on his election campaign. Adrian was short and thin. His eyelashes were long and dark, his mouth pert with rather red lips. He had yet to graduate from Vassar and was, as Charity put it, "a Henry Kissinger in training."

Diana would sit next to Adrian and on her other side would be Elliot Rodman, her most recent fling. During their brief relationship of the week before last he usually arrived at our house at 11 P.M. and left by 8:30 A.M. He wasn't interested in relieving Diana's emotional distress; he was interested in relieving his own. He was a frenetic first-year law student. I didn't blame him for having stopped seeing Diana, but rather for the way he did it. He simply stopped coming by and refused to return her phone calls. He was on the run. He was here with one of Diana's close college friends on his arm. Diana had seen that and began downing the bourbons quickly.

Dinner went surprisingly well. Diana chatted politics with Burgess and Adrian; she ignored Elliot. Charity explained the intricacies of cocaine to me. The unpleasamt moment occurred during dessert, when manly Burgess said to petite Adrian, "Say, where do you work?"

"Where do *you* work?" Adrian asked antagonistically.

"I'm special assistant to the deputy undersecretary of State," Burgess replied. "Now what about you?"

Adrian hesitated and then said softly into the tablecloth, "Beano, Congressman Beano."

"You work for Peano?" Burgess asked.

"No, Beano, a freshman Congressman, a . . . a Republican."

"Oh," Burgess said coolly. "What state is he from?"

This last question was a severe blow to Adrian, and he pretended he hadn't heard the question. Like all of us to varying degrees, his self-image was dependent on the political order, and freshman Congressman Peano, Beano, or whoever, was by far inferior in the pecking order to a top man in State. It was intolerable to Adrian that he should work for a nobody, because he too became a nobody. Burgess' nasty questioning was calculated to make him feel this way, so that next time Adrian would treat Burgess with a bit more deference. None of us came to Adrian's defense, not even Charity. We found it acceptable and amusing to see him defend himself, even if he were attacked by an insufferable egotist like Burgess. It was part of the Washington scene; he had to stick up for himself.

After dinner, we drove in separate cars to the embassy for the ball. There was a uniformed Washington policeman standing on the cold sidewalk outside the neo-neoclassical concrete mansion that had been built early in the twentieth century by a button magnate and now housed the ambassador and his wife. Having guards at the door was not unusual in Washington because of all the dignitaries. There was always the fear of a politically inspired attack. The embassy was only a few hundred yards from the Islamic Center, which had been taken over the year before; and even closer to the spot in Sheridan Circle, where agents of the Chilean government had murdered two people with a bomb.

Diana and I walked past the lonely policeman and into the marble-floored foyer, where a man in black tie checked our names with the guest list. The ballroom was on an upper floor. After putting our overcoats in the coatrooms (one for men and one for ladies), we ascended the twin marble staircase that wound up past two large Belgian tapestries woven of silk and gold thread. Diana was walking fairly steadily on the smooth steps and seemed ebullient.

We older ones were joined by a hundred or more sixteen-to-twenty-year-olds. The younger people made us feel more like chaperones than guests. They mingled self-consciously at the bar ordering one drink after another. As was usual at most parties in Washington I went to, there were more women than men. Why this was so I never understood. Despite the plethora of good-looking women almost no one was dancing. A small society band from New York City played a good Noel Coward, a fair Duke Ellington, and a lousy Crosby, Stills, Nash and Young. The unwillingness of people to relax and have fun was,

107

I thought, because so many of them resented even being there. Most had been coerced into attending. I observed to Nicholas that the young men seemed too uncomfortable to ask the women to dance and the young women too tense to accept. "There are too many tired genes at this party."

He replied, "Do you have to think all the time I'm talking with you? You're a nervous strain sometimes."

"I know."

"Why can't you just accept things as they are? Life would be easier if you did."

"I doubt it."

"You frustrate me," he said. "I'm getting another drink."

I talked with various people for an hour, danced a little with Charity and Diana, and prepared to leave. I was standing at the bar having a farewell drink when I caught a glimpse of Diana across the room. She looked drunk and was leaning heavily on the shoulder of a bewildered Burgess White for support. Elliott Rodman was standing with his back to her and his hand all over his latest conquest's derriere. Diana was watching this. Her face was pale as if she suddenly realized that he had not a gram of real affection for her. I put my glass down and headed over to her. Before I could reach her, she collapsed to the marble floor. She didn't pass out, however, and got up quickly. Unfortunately, she had scraped her chin and was bleeding a little. Everyone stared at her. I could tell by their looks that they were thinking, Who is she? or, if they knew her, "God, what's happened to Diana since I knew her? Is she having a breakdown?" No one said anything, of course.

I took Diana by the elbow and ushered her down the stairs. I told her that we were going home. She didn't object. I walked into the ladies' coatroom to get her coat for her. As I did, I saw Charity introducing little Adrian to cocaine. Charity asked me if I wanted to partake. I begged off and took Diana home.

When I got home and crawled into bed, Joni asked sleepily, "How was the party?

I replied, "Stiff."

"Did you sing any Christmas carols?"

"No, it wasn't that sort of a party." A sleep-talking Joni babbled, "No Christmas carols . . . too bad . . . no carols." As I nodded off, I thought, "That party was one perquisite I could have done without."

Not all my pre-Christmas evenings were spent in such exclusive surroundings. The last evening Joni's parents were in Washington more accurately captured the range of nightly entertainment available in Washington that month.

It began with a play at the Kennedy Center for the Performing Arts, an aircraft-carrier–sized building beached along the bank of the Potomac near the Watergate complex. Theater in Washington is tremendously popular and less expensive than in New York City. Plays by famous authors with big name stars would sell out months before the opening.

The Kennedy Center brooked little experimentation. Their shows were almost exclusively those with established stars or those imported from England. The ideal Kennedy Center play would have been a comedy by Shakespeare starring Robert Redford.

At my recommendation, Joni's parents had purchased four tickets to a play about a man whose efforts to write are constantly frustrated by interruptions by visitors. It was clever, and almost the entire audience was amused by it. Joni's mother was the exception; she walked out midway in the second act when an actress removed her sweater thus exposing her breasts to the main character in an unsuccessful attempt to seduce him and further her own literary ambitions. Joni's mother's dislike of "frontal nudity of any sort" caused her to spend a large part of the play in the National Theater's lobby eating Jujubes and sipping that insipid throat-choking noncarbonated orange drink that is sold in theaters worldwide.

Since Mr. Simpson had bought the tickets on my suggestion, I felt some responsibility for the fiasco. I apologized for the play. Mrs. Simpson said, "Oh, I don't blame you. But what has happened to the theater?" My relationship with Joni's parents was based on scrupulous politeness. We were mutually skeptical

109

about the other's relationship with Joni. They saw me as an obstacle to their daughter's marrying a wealthy man from a Palm Beach family. I saw them as an interference in the life of Joni and me.

After dinner, Joni and I deposited Mr. and Mrs. Simpson at the Hay-Adams Hotel where they were staying and returned to the Ebbit Grill to have a drink and talk. The tavern was packed with the usual late-night crowd—collegiate-looking young people wearing button-down shirts, khakis and boating shoes. I told Joni about the Washington society ball I had been to the night before. After a few beers, we decided to go out somewhere in Washington where people didn't care who we worked for or what colleges we had attended or who our families were. We went to Fourteenth Street.

Fourteenth Street is to Washington what 42nd Street is to New York City, what Broadway is to San Francisco, what the Combat Zone is to Boston. The economy of the street is based on booze, sex and drugs. There are bars, sex shops, strip joints, massage parlors, and movie houses that offer films like "Naughty Girls of the Orient" and "Boys at School." The population is transient, except for the shopkeepers, policemen, pimps and prostitutes.

That full-moon night the low life was particularly low, because of the icy streets and falling snow. The snow blanket covered the spittle- and paper-littered sidewalks and made dirty Fourteenth Street seem almost pretty. The pulsating neon signs advertising sexual excitement at a discount price were drawing few customers and threw a yellowish light out into the otherwise white snow. Prostitutes were on every corner where during the Christmas season you might have expected to see a bell-ringing Santa Claus or Salvation Army Band. They wore short cloth or leather overcoats, miniskirts, and high-heeled leatherette boots.

Joni and I walked undisturbed through all this. We felt no hostility or aggression. There were no harangues from drunks. The atmosphere was calm; one of the sex shops had even decorated its window with a large pine wreath and used artificial snow to paint on the glass "Merry Christmas."

110

Slowly the snow became deeper, the action quieter. A prostitute on her way home said, "It's been a slow night." The shops were closing up. It reminded me of the America outside official Washington, of a place where people's first question is not "Who do you work for?"

On Christmas Eve, Washington was quiet and snowbound. Joni and I went skating on the frozen Chesapeake and Ohio Canal that parallels the Potomac River from Georgetown to Harper's Ferry, West Virginia. Skating along arm in arm, we glided for miles from Georgetown to the Francis Scott Key Bridge which spans the Potomac at the point where the District of Columbia ends and Maryland begins. The Old Executive Office Building, the Capitol, the CIEP, the JEC, the large embassy and Fourteenth Street all seemed far away.

As I pushed off on one skate blade and then the other, the only place that came to mind was Weston, Connecticut, and the pond at my family's home, where I had skated so often as a kid. I had never spent a Christmas away from my family. Skating with Joni on the canal that evening, however, I had no desire to be back there; I anticipated other Christmases in Weston. This first one on my own was shared with someone I loved. That pleased me immensely.

Joni and I went to a midnight church service. The carols and hymns were calming. Afterward we walked home and gave each other our presents. It was the most peaceful Christmas I could remember.

The next day we made Christmas dinner, and Peter Dortmund came over. His family was in Canada and Peter didn't bring anyone along. He had no girl friend. As Peter said, "I can't find anyone I'm really comfortable with." Having met so many women in Washington, I was surprised.

"I don't like to socialize with all of the politicos, and that's where the women are."

"Then why are you here?" I asked. "Washington is politics and all the social folderol that goes with it." Politics was my daily concern. The most important thing in my life was whether my

111

next project on the JEC would give me more authority and responsibility. I couldn't fathom a guy like Peter. He was apathetic.

Charity dropped by for dessert. She attempted to engage Peter in the sort of social chit-chat she knew so well. She wondered if they knew anyone in common. "Do you know Tizzy Ledbetter?"

"No."

"Katie Palmer?"

"No."

"Pierpont Fay?"

"Nope."

"Oh, I give up."

"Good," said Peter with a smile.

"Where did you meet Joni and Brett?"

"I met Joni in Europe."

"Europe? Do you know Ernst Duffler . . . ?"

Charity was not going to give up on Peter, now that she had another continent. She went through Germany, France and half of England before deciding that she and Peter had no friends in common. "What a fluke my meeting you," she concluded.

Winter

AFTER FOUR California "winters" at Stanford, I expected the cold and grayness of Washington's January and February to affect my disposition. To my surprise, it was a winter without chill; my work went too well for me to feel the cold.

Schmidt was recovered from his bleeding ulcer and once again helping to make me in his image. During the first week of the first session of the new Congress, he called me over to his desk. Lounging in his chair, he said, "We've got a new member on the Committee. Senator McGovern. He's interested in railroads. I want you to handle him. He's got some vague notions about using the Committee as a vehicle for investigating that screwed-up industry. Try to give them some help, some sensible direction."

"I don't know very much about railroads," I replied.

"Then learn." He paused and said, "Don't worry, neither does he or his staff." I had heard that before.

"A little of 'the blind leading the blind,' don't you think?"

"Just do it and don't be a wise ass."

So it was that I was drafted to help orchestrate the education of a United States Senator.

Most other young people in Washington were not so lucky. Take Kim Donahue for example; she was still handing out testimony at hearings and gathering data for senior staffers. So many of us were gophers. Even at the Joint Economic Committee, whose purview was everything and anything related to economics, I was the only one my age to be given authority and responsibility on a level equal to men and women ten years my senior. Schmidt saw to that.

Concommitantly with my new duties for McGovern, I received a pay increase. If other staffers resented my advancement, they said nothing about it. Everyone seemed friendly toward me. As long as I did good work and didn't trespass on another's turf, my relations with fellow Committee aides went well.

I was fighting to kill some of the arrogance that success in Washington had fostered in me. I was no longer interested in being seen as Young Man on the Way Up. That image threatened people. I took more time to "shoot the breeze" with other staffers and hear what they were doing. I had more lunches with people on the Committee staff and fewer with my elite young friends. I ate more often in the DSOB cafeteria and less at a nearby French bistro, La Ruche. I even began to have lunch with Miss Plunkett.

My earlier fears about her were unjust. At lunch she spoke of how difficult it is for people in Washington to fall in love the way they had always hoped to. "We are all under such great pressure during the day—men and women. Everyone must be so aggressive during the day, but at night most men don't want that kind of woman. The men have been working at the behest of some politician or bureaucracy, and they want someone who will make them feel important."

"They are tired," I added.

"So are the women," she said with a worn smile. "We postpone marriage. I have a dozen girl friends who under any criteria are very attractive to men. Yet not one of them has any serious relationship with a man, and they're not lesbians. Maybe it is because the work pressures in Washington are so similar and powerful?"

There was truth to what she said. Of all my friends, Charity, Diana, Nicholas, Peter and others, none had more than vest-pocket affairs. Joni and I were the only "couple," and we had

114

met before coming to Washington. If we had met in Washington, I doubt whether we would have fallen in love. We wouldn't have had the time or the energy.

With the rest of the staff friendly (even Lackey congratulated me on my new assignment and pay boost), I had to worry only about the actual task of helping McGovern investigate rail issues. Despite my lack of knowledge about railroads, I was confident of success. If I asked the right questions about railroads and government rail policy, the range of possible answers to that industry's problems would become apparent and therefore I could intelligently advise the Senator. Whatever tension I felt was not related to the size of the job or to working with a Senator; it was caused by wanting to exceed Schmidt's expectations for me.

On the fifth floor of the thick-walled Dirksen Senate Office Building, there was a corner office with windows overlooking Union Station, the central rail depot for Washington. On two walls of the spacious sitting room were etchings of nineteenth-century trains. In one, a black train rushed through a snow-covered pass and in the other a single fire-eating locomotive roared along flat steel track somewhere in the Western plains. The occupant of this office said to me in his High Plains twang, "I remember when I was a boy in South Dakota. I'd be awake at night and hear the whistles of those trains blowing through the town at night."

The remembrance was heartfelt. The speaker was Senator George McGovern. In that moment, he seemed to revisit a time when the railroads were the majestic and tyrannical conveyors of commerce and culture, a period I had only read of in history books. He was remembering the railroads as I had never known them. My childhood memories were of the bankrupt Penn Central's New Haven line trains breaking down, as if on some perverse schedule, between Darien and East Norwalk, of dilapidated cars wobbling along worn tracks. Listening to McGovern's romantic memories, I thought my first task would be to help him strip away his nineteenth-century perceptions and

115

see rail for what it was in the last quarter of the twentieth century—a public disaster.

This is not to suggest that the Senator was ignorant of the symptoms of rail's economic ill-health. He knew from his constituents in South Dakota that train derailments were occurring more frequently than ever, that at harvest time rolling stock was nowhere to be found and that the state was latticed with thousands of miles of unprofitable and thus abandoned track. What the Senator needed was someone to help him understand *why* the nation's railroads were in such disrepair and what should be done by the government to improve the situation. My job was to find the people and written sources to answer that question. My conversation and reading would significantly influence the answers the Senator would get.

Up to this point in his political career, the Senator had embraced increased federal loans to, and public ownership of, the railroads. He had recently introduced a bill to have the United States Department of Transportation build rolling stock and provide money to states to buy abandoned rights-of-way. I didn't know how many billions of dollars this proposal would cost, but I doubted that it would help the situation. His approach reflected a belief that the problem couldn't get worse if the federal government threw more money at it.

I was not alone on this project. Schmidt received weekly briefings from me on our progress, and McGovern's legislative assistant ("L.A.," in Hill parlance) for energy and transportation, Robin McIntosh, worked with me at every step. Robin was twenty-eight years old, a recent addition to the Senator's personal staff. She had been involved in South Dakota energy regulation. I liked Robin immediately; she had the face of an angel.

While in theory her responsibility was to McGovern and mine was to the Committee, in reality we served each other's interests. A happy McGovern meant a happy JEC, and vice versa. He wanted assistance from JEC staffers to pursue issues his personal aides lacked time or expertise to analyze; the Committee wanted his name and energy and influence to lend prestige to the Committee.

116

Political loyalty aside, Robin and I simply got on well. Whenever one of us dashed off recklessly in one direction, the other would gently pull us back together for a little preliminary thinking. Neither of us presumed to be the boss. Our relationship was a comfortable blend of camaraderie and competition. Robin was the only female legislative assistant I worked with on the Hill. According to the records kept by the Senate, 70–75 percent of the legislative assistants are men, and 25–30 percent are women. Having broken into the policy-making level of government (that is, nonsecretarial), Robin voiced little of the frustration I heard from my committee mate Kim Donahue. Where Kim could not get started, Robin was in the race with the rest of us.

We first met in the Dirksen Senate Office Building's dismal underground cafeteria. Since in the past ten years the number of Congressional staff has increased faster than the increase in square feet of office space, many meetings that demand some privacy are held in the cafeterias. Staff offices are simply too crowded. Lighted by the ubiquitous fluorescent tubes of office life, the Dirksen cafeteria serves cheap food thanks to taxpayer subsidies. Robin had what I soon discovered was her hourly dose of coffee while I sipped a little orange juice in the hope it might prevent a cold.

The primary challenge was to get McGovern a public hearing so that he could examine the railroad fiasco as long and as fully as he wanted. The point was not simply to study the railroads in the privacy of our offices and then quietly release our findings to the public. We wanted to stir up interest, wake people up, tell them whether the railroads were headed for a disaster that would make the Penn Central bankruptcy look like small potatoes. We also, of course, had more selfish motives. We wanted as much publicity as possible for McGovern and the Committee.

Getting McGovern his hearing was no simple task. We could not do anything without the approval of Senator Lloyd Bentsen, the phlegmatic Democrat from Texas. Bentsen was chairman of the Joint Economic Committee's Subcommittee on Economic

Growth and Stabilization, the subcommittee to which McGovern had been assigned. Without Bentsen's permission, McGovern could hold no hearing. These were the rules of the Committee.

Robin and I discussed how to obtain for McGovern his hearing without bringing Bentsen in to chair it and his man on the Committee, Jim Skaggs, to organize it. Robin had a slight look of terror when I mentioned that possibility. She was new at her job and very keen on making a good impression on McGovern. She would fail if Bentsen and Skaggs horned in on her Senator's show. McGovern would lose publicity and the freedom to study problems that interested him. She felt that Bentsen might just do that, because he was very concerned with the higher coal rates that the railroads were asking the Texas utilities to pay. A Bentsen railroad hearing would have narrowed the focus of our investigation considerably. It probably would have dealt only with the utilities' complaints that if freight rates for coal continued to increase (a new phenomenon after years of rates fixed regardless of inflation), the power companies would have to pass the additional cost to their customers. I didn't want to see that happen either. I was not looking forward to dealing with Bentsen's man Skaggs. He and Schmidt didn't like each other one bit, and I was Schmidt's protégé.

Allied in our opposition to Bentsen and Skaggs's participation, Robin and I spent a fruitless hour planning how to keep the hearing for McGovern. We considered trying to mollify Bentsen with a few witnesses to discuss coal but rejected the idea; let him do his own staff work if he was so interested. We mulled over having McGovern telephone Bentsen and ask straight out, "as a personal favor," for his own hearing but rejected that too; we didn't want the Senator to ask for favors unless absolutely necessary.

Finally, after Robin's third cup of coffee, we hit upon a decent tactic. We would schedule the hearing to be held in New York City on a day we knew McGovern had to be there as a delegate to a United Nations conference on food and famine. We would make it as inconvenient as possible for the mildly interested

Bentsen to appear. It was a neat solution if we could convince McGovern to agree. We were going to argue that it would get him better media coverage (there being fewer hearings in Manhattan than in Washington) and better witnesses (since most railroads have headquarters in New York).

The next day we lunched with McGovern in the Senators' dining room, a smaller and more elegant version of the Dirksen cafeteria. The only important distinction between the two was that they had separate kitchens, the Senators' being much better.

As is typical on Capitol Hill, most of our fellow diners were white, and the waiters and waitresses black. Thousands of black men and women work on the Hill, but of the six thousand professional aides working for the Senate, only twenty-one are black. Job discrimination is less of a problem for the members, since Congress has always exempted itself from such provisions of landmark social legislation as the 1964 Civil Rights Act. The Congressmen's argument in support of this practice is that they must have a free rein to hire staff to meet the special needs of their district or state. Considering the civil-rights legislation they have passed for everyone else in the past fifteen years, the hypocrisy of their position is outstanding. I doubt whether McGovern supported this policy of special privilege, but he was not about to rewrite the club rules.

McGovern ran the "working lunch" like a college seminar, but he was eager for us to get going. Like all politicians in Washington, McGovern was in a programmed rush from the time he got out of bed until he got back into it. Everyone ordered quickly and identically, three chef salads and iced tea.

We asked him how he wanted us to organize his hearing.

McGovern said, "I want you to know that you can investigate wherever you want. I want as accurate a picture of this industry as possible."

"Rail management, labor and government regulation?"

"Yes, even labor."

Robin and I were buoyed to hear this. It meant that Mc-

Govern had few set ideas on rail issues. It meant that we would have significant control over the forming of his hearing.

Robin suggested our hearing date to the Senator. He liked it. "Convenient," he said.

Schmidt had already told me that McGovern and Bentsen were personal friends, so I asked the Senator if he would call Bentsen to confirm things. "I think this would obviate any possible problems at the staff level." McGovern understood that Senator-to-Senator would be better than staff-to-staff and immediately agreed to the plan. Such conversations are common on Capitol Hill.

"Yes, fine, if you think so," he said.

McGovern must have called Bentsen that afternoon, because the next morning Skaggs called Schmidt to complain. "Jim," Schmidt said, "if your man wants to come, I'm sure McGovern would love to have him there. Brett told me McGovern and Bentsen resolved this." I didn't hear what Skaggs replied. There was little he could say. Robin and I had taken the onus for the decision off ourselves by letting the Senators resolve the issue. As much as we served the Senator's interest, he made our job easier by serving ours too.

Having scheduled the hearing, Robin and I began reading all the books, articles, dissertations and hearing transcripts on rail that we could get. We had two months to figure out the politics and economics of a $20-billion industry employing over 500,000 workers and paying over $2 billion in taxes. The industry's pathetic 1.26 percent rate of return on net investment aside, United States rail was still a honey pot of considerable size for its private management, unionized workers, federal regulators, and bankers. No matter how bad rail was doing, its 200,000-mile roadways and innumerable acres of land (some with large mineral and petroleum deposits) that ran alongside attracted many competing interests. We assumed that each would try to use us and McGovern for their interest.

Since Robin was often busy with energy affairs for McGovern,

120

I did much of the field work on my own. My first conversation was with a twenty-eight-year-old staff aide of a Congressional subcommittee with oversight responsibility for railroads. His name was Bill Bree. I called him on Congress' internal phone system. I figured Bree would have some useful tips on whom to talk to and where to get witnesses for the hearing. I had never met him before.

"Hello," I said. "This is Brett Fromson, Joint Economic Committee."

"What can I do for you?" Bree replied in a cheery voice.

"I'm running a hearing for McGovern on the railroads and government rail policy."

"Oh," he said with surprise. "I hadn't heard."

"Well, since you guys and your Committee are such old hands at this, I thought you might give me some advice, some idea about how to go at it."

"Very simple," he said smoothly. "Call the AAR [the Association of American Railroads, lobbyists for the railroad companies], call the UTU [the United Transportation Union, lobbyist for its members], and the ICC [the Interstate Commerce Commission, the government regulators]." Bree rattled off these acronyms like a pro. "Tell them what you want to hold hearings on and they'll get you your witnesses and testimony."

"You mean they select the witnesses?"

"Yeah, it's standard operating procedure with rail hearings we do."

I didn't know anything about what was or was not "standard operating procedure," but the McGovern hearing was not going to be run that way. I was not going to organize a forum for industry spokesmen to mouth platitudes in defense of their interests. I hoped to uncover some witnesses who would give us more than the common wisdom.

More than that, however, I was amazed at Bree's approach to a Congressional hearing. He was suggesting that the staff abdicate its responsibility to give a hearing a sense of direction. Just because McGovern had delegated his authority on the rail hearing to Robin and me did not mean we had a right to delegate that power to others and certainly not to people we neither knew nor had reason to trust.

I said to Bree, "I suppose they could reach our conclusions for us, too."

In a chummy voice he replied, "If you want them to help write the Committee report [the conclusions and recommendations for government policy], they could. We do that sometimes. It keeps everyone happier that way." There was such an air of 'you and me' about Mr. Bree.

"Thanks, but we'll get our own witnesses and draw our own conclusions."

"Look, don't get upset," he said. "Do what you want, but you're asking for trouble."

"Thanks for the advice." I said goodbye before I said something I'd later regret. I felt the less we had to do with Bree, the better off McGovern would be.

As it turned out, Bree was one to be wary of. I learned from friends on other committees that he was soon in touch with all his industry cronies about "the McGovern hearing. Stay away from them. They're unreliable. . . ." He didn't want us upsetting any of his industry clients, especially not at a public hearing. He wished to restrict the public debate to happy talk about how labor and business could work things out without anyone else poking their nose in. I didn't blame him for seeking to placate these people; he was probably doing what his bosses wanted— keep the people with election dollars and political organizations on their side.

Bree was one of the many young men I met on Capitol Hill who refused to rock any boat that might offer them eventual safety. Like most people he wanted a four-bedroom house in the suburbs and an income to beat inflation. I didn't care if that was what he wanted; I just didn't like him getting it by using his position in the government to cozy up to the special interests. I told myself that if I ever saw Bree I was going to tell him what I thought of him.

I did meet Bree later, at a reception under the crystal chandeliers of a wood-paneled hearing room in the ornate Russell Senate Office Building. I didn't know who he was until Nicholas pointed him out. Nicholas knew him from past lobbying. He was a clean-cut six-footer. He chatted diffidently with a Capitol Hill dolly—a plain but sexually attractive young woman with short blond hair, a medium-length white blouse under a blue tailored suit, and a wide, white smile. She looked up at him with her big baby blues.

He could be saying anything to her. As far as she was concerned it really wouldn't make any difference if he were charming or insolent as long as it was somebody. He could have been explaining railroad regulation. She wouldn't care. She'd look at him, and she'd sigh. This was one way of getting a husband.

I cut in. I excused myself to the young woman, introduced myself to the surprised Bree, and proceeded to tell him point blank what a two-bit hack I thought he was and why. He was stunned. His mouth was agape. The embarrassed dolly slipped away. I finished thirty seconds later, said goodbye, and returned to Nicholas, who stood at the buffet table eating carrot sticks and pretending not to know me. It was not good fortune for a lobbyist to be publicly identified with such impolitic behavior. Nicholas was so sensitive that he left the room and said he'd meet me back at the house.

I should not have done that. It was rude and unlikely to change Bree's behavior. Nicholas called me "stupid." Maybe I had had a bad day and wanted to take it out on an easy target? Perhaps I had had too much to drink? Was I merely indulging in the luxury of saying what I wanted when I wanted? Did I want to humiliate him in front of a good-looking young lady? Maybe I wanted to teach him a lesson that not all people his age were like him? I don't know. It was probably a little bit of all of these reasons. Yet, if I wasn't going to object to people like Bree at my age when I had little to lose, would I do it when I was older with more at stake? Ambitious as I was, I still thought that people in the government who sacrifice the public trust for their career ambitions deserve every rebuke they get.

• • •

123

Because Bree spread the rumor that McGovern was out to "get the rail industry," we had some initial difficulty getting witnesses for our hearing. For a solid week, Robin and I spoke with presidents and chairmen of the nation's largest railroads who were recommended by industry observers—that is, reporters, business analysts, and other Capitol Hill staffers. Yet each time, no matter how amiable our conversation, it always ended with the chief executive officer saying, "I'd be glad to speak with the Senator privately, but I don't know about testifying."

This response was due not only to Bree's whispering campaign, but also to a silent agreement among rail management to avoid dealings with government officials, at least in public. They and their Washington vice-presidents for government relations (that is, lobbyists) did meet frequently in private or at industry conferences, with members and employees of the Interstate Commerce Commission (the regulators), and with "friendly" members of Congress (that is, those who received large donations from the railroads). Whatever antagonism the titans of railroad may have felt for these officials who had presided over the demise of rail, they kept it hidden in closed-door conversations. The ICC may have allowed too few rate increases, and the pro-rail Congressmen may have given rail fewer dollars in subsidy than the truckers got to maintain their rights of way (that is, roads), but at least they didn't humiliate rail executives in public.

I began to think of the rail industry as one big unhappy family. Public airing of dirty laundry was anathema. The relationship between business and regulators was like a bad marriage; they often fought intensely in private, but divorce and public testimony was unthinkable. They were wretched, but mutually dependent on the present situation. Both feared significant change like deregulation. The ICC dreaded losing its bureaucratic fiefdom. Most railroads wondered if they could compete in a more competitive market after nearly a century of safe, if debilitating, regulation and subsidy.

So it was that Robin and I were considered interlopers by the rail family members. At each step of our search, we had to assure and reassure them that we would be fair and honest in our dealings. We had to lobby the lobbyists to get their participation. That is why I went one morning to meet with the men from the Association of American Railroads (AAR).

The AAR's lobbying headquarters were in a petite wooden house of historical demeanor on the House side of Capitol Hill. These quaint digs implicitly proclaimed, "We are nice people. Look, we work in a little colonial house, not a nasty, impersonal concrete office building. We are folks just like you." The clapboard house even had a picket fence around it.

I walked in. The atmosphere was relaxed, the space was broken into small rooms decorated with reproductions of colonial furniture and horsy wallpaper. Only the IBM typewriters and push-button telephones reminded me that this visit was business not pleasure.

As usual in Washington, a good-looking young woman greeted me. She got tea for me while I waited for the AAR's executive vice-president, Emmett Stott, and its chief Congressional lobbyist, Blaine Carson. They were both over fifty, which was typical of almost everyone I met in the rail industry. It was as if in the past quarter century no one new had been willing to join the railroads. Given the postwar decline of rail and the emergence of trucking as the dominant form of transportation (rail shipped 70 percent of freight in 1944 and 35 percent in 1978), this wasn't surprising. How many young people wanted to join a no-growth industry?

Emmett Stott, with whom I had set up the meeting, came out of his office. "Hello, Brett. C'mon in my office and let's chat. Blaine will be here in a few minutes," he said in a folksy baritone voice. Stott was tall, tanned and wrinkled. He looked as if he had just flown in from Florida. His role was to make one feel comfortable.

I sat down on a long floral-patterned couch, and Stott placed himself in a club chair in front of me. When his associate came in, he would sit to my right on the sofa so the three of us formed a right triangle with me as the locus of the right angle.

Stott began talking about fishing, specifically the joys of salt-water fishing versus fresh-water fishing. "I was just down in Florida doing some bonehead fishing," he said. I nodded. "You ever fished for bonehead?" he asked.

"No," I said.

"Well, it's wonderful." He continued on "boneheads" until Carson arrived. Carson was beefier than Stott. Carson did all the talking. He spoke in euphemisms.

"I understand that Mr. McGovern is looking into the railroads," he said, and then paused (translated, "What are you guys up to?").

"Yes, that's right. We're looking at rail and trying to see how the government can help improve its performance. We're not hunting for scapegoats."

Carson grinned like a cat. "Well, that's great, just great. We'd like to know your approach so we can be of help to you" (translated, "What the *hell* are you up to?").

"The Senator would like to have some of your member railroads testify at his hearings."

"No problem," Carson replied. "Would you like us to help you get witnesses? The AAR is here to help you" (translated, "Let us get the witnesses").

"I appreciate the offer, but we'd prefer to round up our own witnesses."

Carson's eyebrows dropped a notch. "Well, we normally assist committees with their witness lists. Our association members prefer not to be called directly. They're a bit wary about the Congress, you know" (translated, "We're not going to be dicked around in front of any reporters by some unfriendly, grandstanding Senator").

"Mr. Carson," I said. "I can assure you that Senator McGovern only wants to hear everyone's viewpoint. He would not browbeat witnesses for a few headlines." I hoped I was right.

"I'm sure that you and the Senator are honorable men," Carson continued, "but why don't you just give me the dates and places of the hearings, and I'll get you some industry representatives" (translated, "C'mon boy, play ball with us").

With a hint of sarcasm, I replied, "Mr. Carson, I'm certain

126

that you and the AAR would do a fine job, but we feel we should select our own witnesses. Certainly you can understand our position. We can't allow others to do our job for us."

Carson and I went fishing like this for a half hour or so before parting cordially. We each came away with something. I didn't have my witnesses, but at least the AAR men could see that McGovern wasn't proposing to nationalize the railroads. Whether it was this conversation that put them at ease or what, I don't know; but the AAR did eventually give us its unofficial seal of approval and gave their members permission to participate in the McGovern hearings. That, however, came after our first hearing. They wanted to size us up.

Despite McGovern's liberal Democratic voting record, the brethren of rail labor were almost as suspicious of us as their boardroom counterparts. The union leaders had much to lose by public exposure of their part in the rail debacle. In protecting their members' high wages (56 percent higher than those for all industry in the United States) and the antiquated work rules (the basis of pay for many engineers and conductors was pegged to a 1910 "100-mile day," which now took 2–3 hours), the union bosses had killed any chance for new-job creation or significant productivity increases. Their trump card was the strike threat; the effectiveness of this is demonstrated by the fact that there has not been a national strike since October 10, 1949. Management accommodated labor and then tried to pass through the increased costs via higher freight rates or by taking money allocated for track improvement to cover the higher wage bill. Management's assumption seemed to be that the government would bail them out (without nationalization, of course) and labor's premise was that whoever owned the railroads would have to pay them what they demanded or face a crippling rail strike. Both sides expected the taxpayer to pick up the tab. Up till now, the taxpayer had done that.

All the while, members of Congress and the regulators at the ICC had watched and done little. The Congressmen fought to protect the regulation that kept them in business. No one looked out for the over-all health of the industry. To protect the status quo, the industry had been betrayed by those who knew how to manipulate politics for their own interests—management, labor and government. The politics of rail and regulation made economic decline inevitable. This is so regardless of the subsidies given to competitive transport like trucks, planes and barges.

My first meeting with rail labor came in early March. McGovern and I met with Al Chesser, president of the United Transportation Union (UTU), which represents most rail laborers. The Senator and Chesser knew each other from past political campaigns. The UTU had supported McGovern in the 1968 Presidential election and in his runs for the Senate.

I flew up to New York City for the meeting on the 7 A.M. Eastern Airlines shuttle to La Guardia.

I was the second person off the plane and grabbed a taxi to the United States Delegation to the United Nations located across from the General Assembly at 46th Street and First Avenue. It was 8 A.M., and the FDR Drive along the east side of Manhattan was already jammed with traffic. So were the avenues and side streets of the area around the United Nations.

I left the cab a block away from the United States Mission. An undistinguished and stubby concrete building, it stands on the corner next to Uganda House, a taller amber-glass monument to Idi Amin's ego. The American flag atop the United States Mission, however, flies higher than Uganda House thanks to an extra-long pole.

I entered the building through bronze doors that were emblazoned with the seal of the United States. After I identified myself and my purpose, a receptionist behind a bullet-proof glass partition passed me through to the bank of elevators. An armed guard escorted me. I rode up to Senator McGovern's temporary suite. I was early, because I hoped to get an extra ten minutes of briefing time with the Senator before the labor chieftain arrived. It would allow me forty minutes with the Senator instead of thirty. Forty minutes alone with a United States Senator in the middle of the week is a generous allotment for an aide, but little time to summarize the economics of the rail industry for a busy politician who likes to ask questions.

I waited a minute in the outside office until McGovern's middle-aged traveling secretary showed me into his room. She was one of three secretaries on the Senator's personal staff. This was a small number for a Senator, but in the Senate a member's personal staff is directly linked to his state's population. South Dakota is not a major population center. McGovern, however, knew how to use his small staff to create a big impression. Beyond the basic constituent services, they legislated, investigated and publicized more on a per-staff basis than any other Senate office I knew. Because of them, George McGovern and South Dakota were better represented in the national and international media than any of the neighboring states or Senators. The only drawback to this frenetic pace was that occasionally McGovern's staff and the Senator himself shot from the hip and completely missed the target. The Senator's briefing had not always been thoroughly done and sometimes not at all. At Joint Economic Committee hearings, I had heard the Senator ask questions that would not have been uttered if an aide had explained the topic of the hearing to him. It is impossible to forget the time he turned to me at a hearing and asked in all honesty, "Is this on inflation or unemployment?" This is not to say that McGovern was alone in his occasional lapses. The daily pace of a Senator or a Representative on Capitol Hill often befuddles even the best. An active Senator like McGovern may speak to or meet with hundreds of people in one day. He cannot always know where he is, why he is there, and what he should say. That is what his staff is there for. That was why I flew to Manhattan —to make certain that McGovern was prepared to meet Chesser of the UTU and to discuss the rail labor situation. We needed Chesser as a witness.

I had set the meeting with Chesser a week earlier after approximately ten phone conversations with his secretary and personal aide. I never spoke directly with him. He was as well-insulated as a Senator, and from what people in the railroad industry said, just as powerful in his arena.

129

After waiting a minute in the outside office, I was told by McGovern's secretary to go in. I walked quietly into McGovern's chamber. The Senator was talking on the telephone. He sat in a swivel chair and stared out the window at the United Nations building and the East River, which were only two hundred yards away. "I'll try," he said into the receiver. "But I've got a one-o'clock lunch meeting at *The New York Times* with their editorial board, so I may be late. Yeah, great, good to hear from you." He hung up.

He swung around in his chair and faced me. He looks the same in person as on television. Weak chin, sparkling eyes, and a kind smile. I had never briefed him by myself and was a little nervous, but he left me no time for anxiety. "Let's get going," he said.

I explained to him that in the last ten years, rail union leaders had increased each union member's earnings by 129 percent while total employment in the railroads fell by 20 percent. In effect, the union chiefs had mortgaged future job growth in exchange for wage boosts much greater than the increase in labor productivity. I informed McGovern that this had been done with the tacit approval of the government regulators and private management, who acceded to labor's demands rather than risk a nationwide rail strike that could paralyze the economy.

McGovern said nothing. He simply nodded his head. Obviously, I wasn't telling him anything new, so I went into a discussion of work rules that impeded a return to more reliable and speedy rail service. I was in the midst of explaining the 100-mile rule when his secretary knocked urgently on the door.

"Excuse me, Senator," she said, poking her head in. "The guard in the lobby downstairs just called to say that Mr. Chesser is on his way up."

McGovern replied, "Mary, you meet him as he gets off the elevator. Tell him I'll be through here in ten minutes." Mary left. McGovern said, "Let's shut the doors and get some privacy." Before I could take the large ring notebook off my knees,

130

he was out of his chair and shutting the door to the room. Then he returned to his desk and told me to continue the briefing.

I resumed my explanation of the 100-mile rule. McGovern seemed slightly taken aback by this work rule that allowed men to earn a full day's pay for a few hours' work. I said, "Mr. Chesser disagrees with the importance of what I'm saying."

McGovern smiled gently and said in his folksy Midwestern voice, "Well, I think we should just make him feel comfortable. I don't want to scare him away from the hearing."

The Senator was explaining to me how Chesser's union had helped him with money and volunteers in the 1972 Presidential campaign, when suddenly the door was opened and in walked Al Chesser with a large assistant at his back.

Al Chesser looked like a cross between LBJ and George Meany. As I soon found out not only did he have Johnson's ears and Meany's fleshy face, but he also possessed the former President's Texas drawl and the old labor organizer's penchant for hyperbole. His assistant was close to sixty and had the demeanor of a man with tired blood. Anyone who thinks the movers and shakers of politics are half as good-looking as they are powerful has viewed too many photos of the Kennedys.

I glanced quickly at McGovern to see how I should respond. Would the Senator explain to Chesser that he hadn't yet finished his briefing or would he forget it and let Chesser have his way? There may have been a question in my mind, but there was none in McGovern's. He loosed a broad smile, got up with his hand outstretched and said, "Al, how are you?"—whereupon I shut the briefing book.

The Senator started by asking Chesser about rumors of payroll fraud in the rail industry that Robin and I had heard. The allegations were that there were "ghosts" on the payrolls of the railroads (that is, people who were paid but never showed up for work). Chesser took the question like a veteran; he said that that was a management problem, not a labor problem. He added with a smile, "We'd be fools, however, to send all the managers to the penitentiary and pretend that rail labor wears

131

a halo. But you know, Senator, that's a can of worms you might not want to open at your first hearing."

McGovern replied nicely, "Well, Al, we aren't planning to. I just wanted to see if there was any truth to the stories."

Chesser seized the floor and held it for an hour and a half. He rambled on about the labor situation without interruption. The Senator listened politely no matter what Chesser said. He didn't want to lose Chesser as a witness at the hearing. Chesser *was* the voice of rail labor. Though I disagreed with nearly every opinion Chesser spouted, I shut up throughout. He was a man for whom propaganda was fact. Double-talk and loud allegations were his forte. He painted himself and his union members as the angels of efficiency in rail when in fact they had opposed changing the 100-mile rule or reducing some freight-train crews from three to two men even though such a move had worked well for all the European railroads. He was trying to con McGovern into thinking that Chesser and the UTU were blameless for poor, high-cost rail service. He implicitly denied that management and labor and government had worked hand in hand to create the situation.

Chesser went on for an eternity, asserting everything and proving nothing. I watched McGovern closely to see if he was buying Chesser's line. The Senator would occasionally nod, and I interpreted the nods to mean that he wasn't hearing anything new. It was apparent that Chesser enjoyed talking—not just talking but babbling. McGovern seemed "antsy." He kept crossing his right leg over the left and vice versa. However, Chesser didn't want to go. Since McGovern wasn't going to ask him to hurry up, I had to. This is part of the dirty work an aide does. Senators are used to their subordinates playing "the heavy."

Chesser was seated directly under a nondescript wall clock. Therefore, I began periodically to glance at the clock and then check my wrist watch. Glance and check. Within a few minutes I had McGovern checking the clock over Chesser's head. Five minutes later, however, Chesser was still running off at the mouth. My ruse had failed. No, it hadn't. Without warning, the

132

labor paladin suddenly announced, "Well, Senator, it's been a real pleasure, but I'm sure you have other appointments."

"Oh, Al," McGovern said warmly, as if surprised the meeting would ever end. "I always have time for you." He stood up and escorted Chesser down the hall to the elevator. Chesser's aide and I followed. As the Senator pushed the down button for Chesser, he added, "You don't have to worry about the hearing. We won't be throwing any curve balls."

Chesser nodded agreement and they shook hands on it. We had him, great. It was gratifying to see the elevator doors close on Chesser and his assistant. Perhaps I should have felt outraged that McGovern had cut a deal with the labor chief to go easy on him? I didn't, however; Robin and I had another way to emphasize and publicize rail labor's contribution to the rail disaster—the white paper. This document accompanies most Congressional hearings. It is a distillation of conclusions and recommendations. It would be prepared before the hearing and distributed to the press the day of the hearing. McGovern's name would go on it to lend increased credibility. It was, in fact, a staff project. It would reflect what Robin and I had learned about railroads. McGovern would only review the final draft. Walking back to the Senator's office, he asked me, "Well, what did you think of what he had to say?"

Without hesitation, I said, "Senator, I thought it was 90 percent bullshit." I waited with some sudden fright for his response.

He looked at me with a gleam in his eye, and he said softly, "I think you're right." I knew then and there that Robin and I had carte blanche to write the white paper as we saw fit.

On the plane ride home, I thought about how McGovern, a United States Senator, had treated this union boss with such deference. Though this meeting would lead to Chesser's appearance at our hearing, it grated on me a bit that McGovern had to listen to such drivel.

Had McGovern asked so few questions of Chesser for politeness sake or because he didn't know what to ask? Robin and I had been giving him weekly briefing memoranda to keep him up to date, but who knew whether he read them? Yet for any shortcomings McGovern may have had, I knew that without his initiative, there would be no hearing, no white paper, no contribution to the public debate.

McGovern depended on us to do much of the basic thinking. I hoped Robin and I were rewarding his trust. I was learning about politicians and the role of the aide. I was settling into my job. The old nervousness and eager-beaver tension was being replaced with the harder calm of the experienced aide. Working at the frenzied pace of the bureaucracy on Capitol Hill, where people eat, sleep and drink politics, I was enjoying the special neurosis of those helping to govern the nation—the simultaneous sense of power to manipulate, responsibility to protect the public good, and unworthiness to serve.

Life at Tilden Street felt the pressures of my work on Capitol Hill. It was most evident in the minor details. After two weeks without washing, my towel smelled like buttered popcorn. I shaved every other day. I watched more TV and read fewer books. My car always seemed to be out of gas just when I had to race to the office for early-morning, late-night, or weekend work. Joni and I never left the city on weekends for visits to the country. The only excursion I remember was an afternoon we spent at Malcolm X Park.

Joni and I probably would not have gone there if Peter Dortmund had not shown up at Tilden Street one Sunday afternoon in late January and suggested a photo-taking session. Peter wanted to take photographs of Joni and me, especially of Joni. We suggested nearby Montrose Park in Georgetown, but Peter was adamant about Malcolm X Park, so off we went.

Peter was an inveterate photo-bug. He owned numerous cameras; he even had his own darkroom in the small, undistinguished one-bedroom apartment he kept in unattractive Roslyn, Virginia.

Peter had a voyeur's mentality. Unlike us and most of our friends in politics, Peter seemed to reject participation and to embrace observation. Even his job gave that impression. At the computer association he worked for, his job was to write press releases on computer innovations.

That early March afternoon, winter seemed to have ended prematurely. I saw buds on some trees. The wind was from the south and was tinged with warmth. The sculptured concrete edges of the empty rectangular reflecting pool where Joni and I sat for our portrait were hot from the sun. As he hid behind his camera taking our photo, it crossed my mind that he must have wished he was in my place next to Joni. I detected no jealousy, nothing so active or intense, but rather a silent longing for intimacy with a woman he felt comfortable with. Peter still had difficulty with women. He was good-looking, but quiet in an uncommunicative way that had none of the charms of shyness.

Peter seemed tense when not shooting us with his camera. He walked nervously in his dark leather coat. Joni and I strolled arm in arm. Soon Joni took Peter's arm too, and we were a trio. She asked him how things were going.

Something at the computer association was bothering him. He explained that there had been a break-in the week before. Some people had stolen certain computer tapes and then vandalized the machines. His employers now planned to make every employee take a lie-detector test to determine whether, as Peter said, "it was an inside job."

Joni protested that they could not make Peter take the test.

Peter replied, "It would look awfully strange if I didn't."

He was right, and I told him so. "Better to take it. Otherwise they'll get suspicious and just make your life uncomfortable."

Peter agreed. He said he'd call us on Monday after the test. He seemed more relaxed after our conversation. "I'm sure I'll pass," he joked. "I've never flunked a test before." When Charity later heard of this story, she commented, "He's the first one I'd suspect."

The next evening he phoned as promised. "I think everything went well. I haven't been arrested by the police." He was fascinated by the interrogation procedure. How they placed the interrogator behind him. How the pulse sensors were attached to his body. What questions they asked to establish a normal response—name, age, date of birth. He even mentioned the tranquil tone of voice used by the tester. I asked Peter whether he had told his family.

"No," he said. "I wouldn't want to upset them. My father's very busy right now. IBM has him down in Georgia making a film."

"I forgot—your father worked for IBM."

"Yeah."

"No wonder you work for a computer association."

"Like father, like son."

In mid-March Robin and I stumbled upon a "deep throat" in the federal government who had tales to tell about the nation's largest railroad, Conrail. He wanted to speak privately with us about payroll fraud. Evidently, his superiors didn't want to hear his observations, so he was willing to tell us. He refused to speak about it over the phone. "My phone isn't safe," he whispered into the receiver. We thought him slightly paranoid, but nonetheless agreed to meet him at a time and place of his choosing. He might substantiate the rumors we had heard.

He would not come to our office on a weekday. He wanted to meet at a bar on a Saturday at eleven in the morning. Robin couldn't make it, so I brought Schmidt as a witness to verify what was and was not said. I was not overly surprised that Conrail was the railroad under suspicion. This bastard child of the government and the bankrupt Penn Central Railroad had the most extraordinary contracts with its workers; the unions had obtained *lifetime* wage protection for any members laid off or downgraded as the railroad abandoned unprofitable operations. (Conrail's chairman, Edward G. Jordan, estimated that Conrail lost money on 30 percent of its traffic.) Lifetime employment guarantees for Conrail workers must have eliminated much of the incentive for them to show up for work.

Robin and I were excited by this stroke of luck. If at a public hearing we could expose massive corruption at the nation's larg-

136

est railroad, McGovern would grab headlines. The voters might pressure the Congress for a serious overhaul of the way railroads were regulated and operated. Our only fear was that the payroll fraud at Conrail might overshadow any discussion of regulation, poor management, antiquated work rules, and shortsighted legislation.

We had no antipathy toward Conrail. It was simply the best example of a bad situation. Conrail was also a logical target for us, since taxpayers had already put over $3,300,000,000 into subsidies for this railroad. McGovern had the right as a United States Senator to determine whether those funds were being well spent.

Schmidt and I met the informant at a bar on Capitol Hill called The Man in the Green Hat. It was a clammy, squishy day. From a cane-back chair at the bar, I watched in the mirror as a newly polished white Corvette Stingray drove up to the curb outside. Though I had never met him before, I knew it was he as soon as he got out of his car. He was the only person wearing black sunglasses on that totally overcast day. He had on a dingy blue raincoat with the lapels folded up à la James Bond.

He was in his fifties with thin legs and a beer belly. He had the weathered face of a longshoreman, not smooth like most Washington bureaucrats. He looked in the bar before entering. The only people besides Schmidt and me were some idle waiters and two older ladies who had picked the wrong day for sightseeing.

I introduced myself. He said, "You sounded a lot older on the phone, kid." I smiled, embarrassed at my age. I was getting tired of being called "kid." He looked at me and slowly shook his head. I thought to myself that he was thinking, "Jeez, they got kids up here doing a man's job."

I wanted to get going, so I said, "We hear there's a payroll problem at Conrail. Can you help us?"

He looked at me sideways and asked, "You ever heard of the LIRR?"

"Yeah. The Long Island Rail Road. Noted for running late trains."

137

"If at all," he added. "Listen. In 1972, there was a strike at the LIRR. When those men went out they were owed one week's pay. There was one tough son-of-a-bitch in management who said to those 6,800 strikers, 'If you want those paychecks, then come to a central pay window with photo identifications and you'll get your money.' Well, the LIRR union bosses said, 'No way,' because they knew what would happen if each man went to pick up his own check—the LIRR would see how many phantoms they had on the payroll. Management hung tough and refused to mail out the pay checks or give them to the gang bosses to hand out. The men had to come get 'em." He paused. "That happened over six years ago. There are over five thousand pay checks still waiting to be picked up." The man paused again, to drink his beer.

"Now, that was at the LIRR, a punk railroad compared to Conrail. The Justice Department in Philly is worried that there may be bigger wage fraud on Conrail. They've got a grand jury convened. I'd guess that Conrail could be getting ripped off for a hundred million dollars a year."

"How do you figure that?" I asked.

"Hey, I don't figure it. I know it. I've worked for the railroads. You know how Conrail distributes its pay checks to the men. Gang bosses pass them out in the yards. Conrail has over one thousand pay stations. Why, shit, GE operates on six continents and has fewer than half that number of stations."

"Fine," I said, "But what proof do you have?"

"No proof. Just indications. For example, most railroads pay out forty cents in payroll costs for every dollar of revenue; at Conrail it's sixty-three cents for every dollar. That's over fifty percent more. Conrail's work rules and wage scales are not that different from other lines. Figure it out for yourself, sonny."

"Can you give me those computations?"

"Sure, but not on DOT [Department of Transportation] stationery."

"That's OK," I said. I looked at Schmidt for approval. He nodded agreement. He was a silent partner in the conversation.

138

He was letting this be my show. I asked our informant, "How does Conrail payroll distribution work? What's the procedure?"

"You see, the guys at corporate headquarters in Philly send the pay checks to the various yard masters, who distribute them to the gang bosses, who give them to the 'tricks'—the workers, you know. You get in trouble if you open your mouth or pry too much. It's a buddy system. A guy might show up every coupla weeks to pick up his pay check and spend the rest of his time tending a bar or running his home-improvement company."

I asked, "Don't the other workers complain about this?"

"Look," he said, leaning closer. "They don't like it, but they don't want to get their heads cracked either. Nobody's dumb enough to go to the authorities."

"Doesn't management know about this?"

The man leered slightly. "They got to know. The guys running Conrail may not be too smart, but they're smart enough to figure that out. A lot of them are old union men, still have their union cards. You check this stuff out. It'll be worth your while. Go to Philly. See what the Conrail execs have to say. Ask them about fifteen thousand missing W-2 tax forms, fifteen thousand phantoms, ask about a Justice Department investigation."

The bar had been filling up with people during this half-hour conversation. Our guest was suddenly aware of the people sitting nearby; they looked at us the way people at bars always glance at others. They made him nervous, however. "I've got to go," he said curtly.

"Sure, but can we talk later?" I asked.

He got up. "Maybe."

"OK, thanks for the information."

He left quickly and carefully not bumping into any table or person. From inside, Schmidt and I watched him get in his Corvette Stingray. He drove away, back to his wife and children in the suburbs of Maryland.

"I wonder why he talked to us?" I asked.

Schmidt said, "Probably couldn't get his bosses to follow up this stuff."

"Do you think he's on the level?" I asked.

"Yeah."

"Why?"

"Did you notice how scared he was?"

"Yes, he didn't even finish his beer."

"Look at his napkin."

I did. It was shredded.

Schmidt said, "He's scared, because he's a leaker. He's taking a risk. If I were you I'd go up to Conrail in Philadelphia. See what they say. Let them deny it. But check with the Justice Department first."

"OK," I replied. "Thanks for the advice."

"That's what I'm here for," Schmidt answered.

"I appreciate everything you've done for me."

"Don't worry about it. If you do well, I do well. I'm not philanthropic."

"You want another beer?" I asked. "It's on me."

"On you? Of course," he said.

I called Conrail headquarters the next Monday and made a date for Robin and me to meet with the counsel in charge of labor affairs. I did not mention anything about payroll fraud. "We'd like to discuss work rules."

I called the Justice Department Congressional liaison and obtained the name of the attorneys in Philadelphia who handled railroad cases. Philadelphia would be the place for any federal probes into Conrail, since its headquarters are in the City of Brotherly Love. I called at lunch time, when the secretaries were out; a young lawyer answered the phone. I asked him if he or any of his peers could corroborate my information.

"Are you people looking into payroll-fraud allegations at Conrail?"

"No comment," he said.

"Can you deny it?"

"I'll get axed if I say anything."

"Then you are not denying it?"

140

"I'm not denying anything. Look, where did you get your information?"

"No comment. But thanks for the corroboration."

"Please don't call back." He explained. "My bosses are cracking down on leaks about possible grand-jury proceedings. They are supposed to be secret." He hung up.

Robin and I took the Metroliner up to Philadelphia. The train pulled out of Washington's Union Station at 6:30 A.M. The cars were clean inside, and the passengers subdued behind their morning papers. Very few of them who boarded in Washington were fat; those who got on at Baltimore and Wilmington carried more flesh and breathed more heavily. The corpulent persons from these two older cities seemed more at ease on the train, more cushioned against the jarring of steel wheels against steel tracks.

I sat by a window and drew letters on the glass fogged up by my breath. Snug in my overcoat and wishing still to be in bed, I closed my eyes. I was close to happy. I felt virtuous to have gotten up before dawn on government business which could result in revelations of wasteful and possibly criminal activities.

At Conrail headquarters in downtown Philadelphia, Robin and I met with the attorney in charge of labor affairs and with two Conrail labor negotiators. When I had spoken with the attorney on the phone, his name had seemed familiar. When I met him I knew why. He had been an assistant secretary in the prior administration. He had been in charge of youth unemployment, among other issues. I remembered his smiling face. He had exchanged his government job for a position with federally funded Conrail. I supposed Conrail had been looking for another way to keep in touch with the men in Washington who controlled its budget. Perhaps political connections, not better management skills, were this man's talent?

This lawyer was smooth. He used qualifiers like "It could be said," double negatives like "It's not that I'm not in favor of it," and vague assurances like "We'd like to be as much help as we possibly can." He impressed me as the sort of person who could look you right in the eye and lie.

141

His two subordinates, the labor negotiators, were rough. They spoke like gang bosses in a switching yard. When they wanted to hide something in our conversation, they just shut up; they did not emit soothing platitudes like their boss the attorney.

Robin and I wanted to put them at ease. We talked about all labor practices at Conrail except payroll fraud. Robin and I gave them every chance to bring the matter up. We asked about work rules, wages, benefits, et cetera. They stayed away from any discussion of payroll distribution. Robin and I had to force the issue.

I asked the lawyer, "In January of last year, a full thirteen months ago, the U.S. Department of Transportation secretly determined that your railroad was spending 40 percent more than other railroads would for labor forces of the same size. In February of last year, the Department of Transportation met with your bankers, the U.S. Railway Association, to see why Conrail's labor costs were as high as they had been for the old Penn Central. This past November an Interstate Commerce Commission analyst concluded in a since-restricted memo that Conrail was spending 50 percent more than other railroads to perform the same amount of track maintenance and repair work. Recently, we have learned that a federal grand jury investigation has been under way for months as a result of Conrail's refusal to provide the ICC with documents pertaining to an estimated fifteen thousand undeliverable W-2 payroll-tax forms. Are you aware of any such investigation, any payroll problems at Conrail, any phantom workers?"

The lawyer was taken aback. He didn't expect us to have as much information as we did. His boyish face went slightly white. He paused before saying in the unmistakably tense tone of the defensive bureaucrat, "To my knowledge, there have been no payroll problems, and I'm not aware of any investigations." I repeated my question to him. I wanted to give him another chance to condition his absolute denial. He uttered, however, the same answer.

Robin asked his two underlings the same question. Now

frightened, they backed up the lawyer. "If you're asking me, I don't know anything about that. I have heard that goes on at some railroads."

They were playing us for dummies—kids. If we in Washington knew of the grand jury, they in Philadelphia knew of it too. There was nothing more to say. Robin and I bid them goodbye and caught a train back to Washington. Though convinced that they had lied to us, I was not particularly angry. We agreed that it was unreasonable to expect corroboration from Conrail, since they were financially dependent on Congressional subsidies. They would say anything to protect those subsidies. I couldn't wait till we got them in public.

Our train was due in Washington's Union Station at 3:30 P.M. We arrived at 4:30. Robin and I had gauged McGovern's response correctly. When told the story of our meeting at Conrail and the grand-jury investigation into payroll fraud, he wanted Conrail's chairman at the hearing for close questioning. He wanted to make an example of Conrail, an example of "special interests triumphant over the public interest."

The final ten days before the hearing were as busy as a rush hour at Grand Central Station. Robin and I worked madly to set the final witness list and also to write the Senator's white paper, an overview of the rail situation and its causes. We worked from 9 A.M. to 9 P.M. We spoke with witnesses ("We have to have twenty copies of your testimony forty-eight hours in advance . . . Please be there by 8:45 A.M. so that we can introduce you to the Senator . . . You'll have twenty minutes for your statement . . . Remember, the room number is 305 . . ."). We wrote McGovern's opening statement—"There has never been a more urgent need for Congress to reevaluate the role of railroads in our national transportation network and to redefine the role of government regulation of transportation service." We drafted his press release announcing the hearings—"Senator George McGovern (D-S.D.) announced today that he will be holding a hearing on National Railroad Policy: Which Way is Up? McGovern will be holding the hearing under the auspices of the

Joint Economic Committee's Subcommittee on Economic Growth and Stabilization." We established his final witness list —"Al Chesser, President of United Transportation Union, Edward Jordan, Chairman of Conrail, and Robert Reebie, Chairman of Reebie Associates." Reebie was a consultant on rail issues who was there to give the Senator a reasonably unbiased evaluation of the industry.

We wrote a letter for McGovern's signature that assured Conrail's Jordan that he would be given fair treatment at the hearing. We didn't want him to think we were setting an ambush. After receiving this letter, Jordan phoned McGovern and promised to attend the hearing. We also scribed the Senator's white paper. This eight-page report formed the analytical base from which McGovern was to examine United States railroads. It was the product of the past six weeks of reading and interviewing and was less liberal than you might imagine.

In this report, "McGovern" called for deregulation so that railroads could make money to improve tracks and rolling stock. He argued that it was unfair and inefficient for railroads to compete for freight customers against barges and trucks who have rate-making freedom and billions of dollars in federal subsidies to finance the canals and interstate highway system they travel on.

In a surprisingly probusiness stance, we had McGovern rejecting nationalization as too large a drain on the United States Treasury, billions of dollars the government didn't have to buy up private railroads and make them into a Conrail of cosmic proportions. McGovern's paper suggested that rates should no longer be set by accountants and bureaucrats at the ICC, but by railroad marketing people, who better understood their customers' needs and their own costs. Railroads should no longer be forced by ICC to use accounting techniques that couldn't tell them whether a train route was making or losing money.

This was pretty strong stuff for a Senator like McGovern. He let us write this in his name, however, because our arguments made sense. He let us operate with little regard for partisan politics. He agreed that government policy had contributed to

144

the financial and operating ill-health of railroads. Essentially, Robin and I were arguing for wage, price and marketing decisions to be put back in the economic realm—removed from the strictly political one. The short-run political concerns of Congressmen and ICC bureaucrats had helped to create a rail system that failed to meet the nation's transportation needs. By acknowledging this, McGovern acknowledged his trust in his staff. This made Robin and me feel that our efforts had been rewarded.

Robin and I had worked smoothly together. There was little backbiting or competition by one for reward at the expense of the other. That Robin was a woman affected me little; the only difference was that we could rely on the basic attraction between men and women to keep us together when under pressure or when confused about the next step toward a successful hearing. We genuinely liked one another. I talked about this with Joni and Charity. They agreed friendship was usually an effective complement to their work on Capitol Hill, but Charity added, "It can be a problem." Joni added, "Some guys think that if you smile at them, you want to sleep with them." I wanted to know who had been making propositions to Joni.

A week before the hearing, in late March as buds began to appear on Washington's trees, Robin and I were called by an aide for Congressman Toby Moffett, Democrat from Connecticut. His aide wanted to cut a deal. Moffett had a bone to pick with Conrail over a bridge in his district that Conrail refused to use or repair. His district was losing business. In exchange for an opportunity at McGovern's hearing to interrogate Conrail's Chairman Jordan on this bridge decision, Moffett offered to give us a confidential memo issued by Conrail's bankers to private investors; it suggested that in the next five years Conrail would run a $2.3 billion deficit. This forecast was contrary to public reassurances made by Mr. Jordan to Congress that Conrail's financial prosperity was just around the corner.

Robin and I debated whether to let Moffett into McGovern's hearing. On the one hand, we wanted to use the fiery Moffett and his memo to stimulate a public debate on Conrail. We did not, however, want to share McGovern's limelight. In the end, it was not our decision. The Senator liked the Representative and wanted to give him a little added publicity. Their personal relationship overwhelmed any objections Robin or I had. We simply added Moffett to the witness list.

Four days before the hearing, I heard from our "deep throat" that Conrail's Chairman Edward Jordan had privately fired Conrail's President Richard Spence. This was tremendous news. Now we had another mystery to explore, another way to hook the media. Robin and I immediately informed the television correspondents who planned to attend the hearing. The Senator also called Jordan to make certain that he could still come. Jordan personally assured the Senator that he would. There had been a rumor in the press that we were out to "get Conrail." McGovern told Jordan our aims were more lofty than that. Jordan said that he was relieved.

The day before the hearing Robin and I flew up to New York City to prepare for the hearing. Since it was being held in Manhattan, there were many unknowns. No one knew precisely how much time it would take us and McGovern to go from our hotel to the hearing room in the Federal Building downtown. Getting a competent recording service to prepare the official transcript was an unknown challenge. Even getting the hearing-room door unlocked could be a problem. Would there be room for the television crews? These minor details took up the entire day, so that though we were staying at the St. Moritz on Central Park South, I had no time to visit friends or even window-shop along Fifth Avenue.

That night we briefed McGovern one last time. The briefing was unusual in that it was held at Orsini's, an Italian restaurant noted as much for the celebrities and power brokers it attracts as for the food it serves.

Strolling with McGovern the three blocks from the St. Moritz to Orsini's, we were stared at by every passer-by. A few said, "Hello, Senator," but most simply looked, not wanting to disturb him when his attention was already captured by his entourage of aides. Robin and I, however, were too busy trying to get the Senator a few last-minute facts to bask in our proximity to a celebrity.

I thought that McGovern looked tired. His smile was weak and his voice muted. Like most politicians, he had already had a busy day and by eight-thirty at night it was not unusual for him to be fatigued. Competent aides in Washington work hard, but competent politicians work harder. Unless asleep or in the bathroom, they are on public display all day.

Once the maître d'hôtel at Orsini's saw McGovern enter the door of his restaurant he positively exuded charm. Dressed in black tie, the gray-haired Italian ushered us to a large round table in the china-red dining room. We sat in a conspicuously elevated corner near the front of the restaurant where we could be seen by other patrons.

People stared as they had done on the sidewalk, but only one diner caught the Senator's attention. This was a white-haired gentleman in black tie who I later learned from Schmidt had been a generous supporter of McGovern in past political races. Definitely over sixty-five, the man was accompanied by a slim young blonde who was not his daughter.

That gentleman made me think of a certain aged Senator I knew of, who also had a penchant for the company of young, good-looking women. While his wife still lived, this Senator was always discreet about his affairs. Once she died, however, he lost self-control. The day before we flew up to New York, I heard from Robin that in an official Senate elevator moving from the fifth floor to the first floor this ancient Senator had ripped off the blouse of a comely friend of hers, a young receptionist. This was the same fellow I had seen falling fast asleep at a public hearing, the same man who was reputed to be fueled each day by assorted prescription drugs, the same guy who regularly padded by my office at four in the afternoon in his suit and fluffy bedroom slippers on his way to his chauffeured limousine. He was a powerful Senator, who served his constituents well. He had been returned to Congress by them for decades.

At Orsini's, McGovern and Robin and I ate pasta and veal

147

and drank a few bottles of red wine. By the time we got to briefing McGovern, everyone was having problems with his short-term memory. The briefing never got off the ground, but dinner was rousing. We traded political gossip.

It was common knowledge on the Hill that Teddy Kennedy would challenge Jimmy Carter for the Presidency. All of us at the dinner table wanted to hear McGovern say whom he would support—Kennedy or Carter. He wouldn't. There was little doubt in my mind, however, that he would support Kennedy. McGovern was not close to Carter, personally or ideologically. Though the next Senatorial election in 1980 was going to be rough for McGovern, who was being targeted for defeat by numerous right-wing, religious-interest groups, the Senator stated, "I don't want Jimmy Carter campaigning for me, and I don't plan to campaign for him."

We left Orsini's at 10:30 P.M. I fell asleep on my bed wondering if the hearing would go smoothly the next day.

The hearing was held in the Federal Building in lower Manhattan. Whereas the shined brass and marble of the Congressional buildings gave an event grandeur, the Federal Building's bleak architecture made everything seem smaller than life. The building was a flat skyscraper of moderate height in the middle of a dreary concrete plaza. It was served by slow elevators with fast doors and filled with small fluorescent-lit rooms suffering from low ceilings.

Schmidt arrived in Manhattan early that morning to monitor the hearing. He, Robin and I went by cab to the Federal Building at 7 A.M., two hours before McGovern was to gavel the hearing to order. This period of time was consumed with minor but critical tasks like finding the building's superintendent to unlock the hearing-room door, having the clerk make copies of the witnesses' statements, and buying film for a photographer to take photos of the hearing for the inevitable press releases the JEC and McGovern's office would issue. Schmidt remained in the background and observed.

The bulky television crews showed up by 8 A.M., draped electrical cable on the floor, and focused their floodlights on the places where McGovern and the witnesses were to sit. The suitably attractive television reporters arrived by 8:30 A.M. They wanted to know when Conrail's Jordan was to show up. To keep them happy, I assured them he would arrive by 9 A.M.

At 8:55 A.M., however, I was crushed by a piece of news. A fat, red-faced Conrail vice-president in charge of public affairs handed me this letter:

> DEAR SENATOR MCGOVERN: The attached press release confirms that Conrail has witnessed a significant event. The departure of Conrail's President, Mr. Richard D. Spence, requires that the responsibilities he discharged be given immediate attention in the interim in which a successor will be selected, either by myself or by other Conrail officials.
>
> I am sure you will understand why this will prevent my attendance at your hearing this morning. Mr. John L. Sweeney, vice president for Government Affairs, and Mr. Ronald M. Dietrich, vice president for law, will represent me in any capacity that you deem appropriate. Mr. Sweeney will read my statement, if you so wish, and either he or Mr. Dietrich is authorized to respond to any questions which you may have.
>
> I very much appreciate your courtesy in our telephone conversation last Wednesday, and your reassurance that the mission of the hearings was as outlined in your original invitation, not as erroneously reported in the press. Thus, I am disappointed that this sudden emergency precludes my presence.
>
> Sincerely,
> [signed]   EDWARD G. JORDAN

What were we going to do? I was too shocked to feel anger. Though I suspected that the departure of Spence was merely a weak excuse for Jordan to avoid our questioning, I was not immediately concerned with that. My main worry was McGovern. What would Robin and I say to him? How should we tell him that the man to whom he had extended his personal invitation and assurance of fair treatment had double-crossed him at the last minute? I expected that McGovern would explode, would feel that Jordan was playing him for a fool. Who would believe that story about Jordan searching for a successor? A better explanation was that Jordan didn't want to be questioned on the reasons for Spence's "departure." Did they have anything to do with the payroll fraud allegations? Was Spence the "fall guy"? These were questions he could evade by not appearing.

Robin, Schmidt and I intercepted McGovern at 8:59 A.M., before he entered the hearing room, which was filled with reporters who already had copies of the letter. The Conrail press flack had been generously distributing copies. He wanted to establish Jordan's excuses as fact.

We took McGovern into an empty nearby room to show him the letter. It was a good thing we did. I have never seen a politician as livid as the Senator was in that room. He could barely talk. First, Conrail's legal staff had lied to his staff about the existence of any payroll-fraud investigations, and now Conrail's chairman was backing out on the Senator himself after assuring him that he'd be there. His first response was to refuse to seat any Conrail flunkies at the witness table. "They don't deserve to participate," he said.

Schmidt remained silent. He was going to let Robin and me work this out. He had gotten me the assignment, but he wasn't going to do the job for me.

"Senator, wouldn't it be better to have a target for our questions?" I asked.

Robin added, "At least that way we get them out in the open. It'd make better press."

McGovern sat on a desk and contemplated this for a minute or two. On the one hand, his pride was hurt, so he wanted to deny Conrail a seat; yet by doing so he would play right into their hands—let them avoid a public discussion of the problems their railroad represented. He resolved the dilemma by saying, "All right, they can testify."

The hearing began ten minutes later than scheduled. McGovern had calmed down by then. As we sat behind him under the hot television lights, he said, "I was just advised that Mr. Edward Jordan, Chairman of Conrail, will not be with us. I will have more to say about that later on. Let me just say for the moment that I am very disappointed in Mr. Jordan's last-minute cancellation. . . . Mr. Jordan will be represented here today by Mr. Sweeney, and we will see that Mr. Jordan's prepared statement is made part of the record. But I can only say that I regard this last-minute cancellation, after assurances that Mr. Jordan would be with us today, as one in a long line of efforts and demonstrations on the part of Conrail indicating that they do not properly recognize their accountability to the Congress that has so generously subsidized their operations. . . ."

The cameras rolled when the Senator made that statement; friends later said they saw it on television. Robin and I grinned at each other over McGovern's words. It was gratifying to hear him deliver a public reprimand to the people who had been stringing us along ever since we met them. I expected fireworks from the Senator before the hearing ended. First, however, he was to get an overview on rail from Robert Reebie, the most trenchant observer of the railroad industry I had found. Robin and I had put Reebie ahead of the others as a way to rebrief the Senator on the whys and wherefores of the rail industry.

Chesser, the labor boss, testified, but he didn't say anything worth remembering. He blustered for pages of transcript, dropping platitudes left and right: "You talk about featherbedding. The most secure place for an executive today is to get to be a railroad executive." (An ironic observation given Mr. Spence's recent dismissal.) The one thing he didn't talk about at any length was labor's role in this industry. Unlike Conrail's Jordan, Chesser at least showed up; his tactic in defending his union's behavior was to testify about everyone (especially management) and everything (especially mismanagement) except organized labor.

Senator McGovern got to Mr. Sweeney at around 10:30 A.M. The first thing he did was to enter Jordan's letter, his prepared

151

statement, and the two-sentence Conrail press release on Mr. Spence's departure into the printed record. Then he leaned forward in his seat and said, "Let me just make some other comments."

With emotion and economy of words, he explained to Mr. Sweeney our concerns.

Here we have the largest single rail system in the country propped up by a massive and unending investment, and it suddenly announces the departure of the man responsible for daily operations. In a similar incident Conrail, without explanation, fired R. P. Wille, assistant vice-president for auditing, last February, shortly after the emergence of the W-2 payroll problem that we have heard about for some time.

In January 1977, a full year before Conrail found itself with 15,000 undeliverable W-2 tax forms on its hands, the Department of Transportation determined that Conrail's predecessor, Penn Central, was spending about 40 percent more than other railroads in terms of labor/cost/revenue ratios. A month later the DOT met with the U.S. Railway Association to ask whether the association had examined Conrail's labor costs to ascertain if this labor/cost/revenue ratio still prevailed. Last November, an ICC financial analyst concluded that Conrail was spending 50 percent more than other railroads to perform a given amount of track maintenance and repair work.

The Senate Appropriations Committee, which was considering a $300 million appropriation for Conrail, was not informed of Conrail's payroll problem until I found out about it earlier this month and one day before the mark-up in the legislation. It was only then Conrail submitted an agenda, a totally unidentified four-page statement to the committee, explaining the problem, and nothing but the briefest reference to a Federal Grand Jury investigation which had been underway for months as a result of Conrail's refusal to provide the Interstate Commerce Commission with documents pertaining to the payroll problem.

In fact, up to this point Conrail officials were making outright denials to my staff that they were even aware of any investigation or any payroll problems in the Conrail system. We need an explanation of why, according to Conrail's own

152

statements, you deny the continuing existence of a payroll problem after DOT, ICC, the Justice Department, and the U.S. Railroad Association were aware of this possibility.

I realize it is necessary to elect a successor to Mr. Spence. But it might be useful for the top management officer, so heavily subsidized by the taxpayer, to attend a public hearing and explain what happened. That might be a good place to begin, educating the Congress and the public as to the reasons for these abrupt changes in management . . . Please proceed, Mr. Sweeney.

The overweight man from Conrail replied, "I was not informed until the day before that there was a so-called Conrail payroll problem. First of all, it is not a payroll problem. It is a problem of undistributed W-2 forms.

"The railroads that preceded Conrail had a system under which the W-2 forms were handed out with the pay check in January of each year. And so years and years could go by without ever knowing the correct address for the employee who was receiving the check. . . .

"When the finance department decided last summer to revise that system, there was no way except by this process to update the addresses. That is why we had 14,000 undelivered W-2 forms. We have yet to find the first instance of fraud."

This appeared to be a complete refutation of the allegations. If McGovern wanted information, he'd have to dig, to detect some logical inconsistency in Sweeney's statement. He had to demand a full accounting of how the 14,000 W-2 forms were delivered; were they simply distributed by the gang bosses and yard superintendents or were correct addresses found for real workers? Sweeney hadn't said. Why had it taken nine months to deliver 14,000 W-2 payroll tax forms? Why were 600 still undelivered? McGovern had to dissect Sweeney's statement that Conrail had uncovered no payroll fraud, no ghosts. How did they search? How long? Who did the looking?

I began to write these questions, but Schmidt who sat beside

153

me gently tapped my wrist and shook his head. He leaned over and whispered in my ear, "Let him do it his way."

I was instantly drained of all energy. There was nothing for me to do. I sat back in my chair and watched.

Perhaps McGovern was tired that day, but he let Sweeney off the hook. He asked none of the questions I would have been happy to give him. Instead of grilling the go-fer from Jordan's office, he asked "If we were to grant that there is no hanky-panky in the way money is being distributed in Conrail and other parts of the rail industry—why wasn't the Congress informed of this earlier?"

He had unilaterally taken us out of the ball game. Now all Sweeney had to do was defend slow reporting. Suddenly, all focus was off payroll fraud, off labor-management complicity, and onto why busy men trying to resuscitate a railroad hadn't told Congress about a few missing tax forms. I didn't know whether the man from Conrail was lying or telling the truth, but how would we ever know, if McGovern didn't push him with tough questions?

At noon the hearing ended with a whimper. "The subcommittee recessed," as they say in the official record. McGovern, Robin, Schmidt, and I left the Federal Building together. Outside in the midday light, the Senator caught a yellow cab to LaGuardia Airport, and the three of us returned to the St. Moritz to pack up and have a drink at the hotel bar.

I complained to Schmidt that we had failed. He looked tolerantly at me. "Why—because McGovern didn't do things the way you wanted him to?"

"Yes, I thought he'd be more like the McGovern of 1972, a fighter for his position."

"Listen. He's the boss. He did it the way he wanted to. Maybe he doesn't want to fight Conrail. What can I say?" Schmidt paused. "McGovern liked the hearing. Maybe not what Jordan did to him, but he learned something. He understands railroads a little better now. Why don't you take some pleasure in having educated a United States Senator? At least now he can vote intelligently on rail bills that come to the floor."

154

I just looked at Schmidt and blew some air out between my lips. Maybe he was right. Perhaps my expectations had been too high. "I thought we could have made a difference if he had dug deeper."

"You did make a difference. A little less than you thought, that's all."

I wasn't satisfied. Government rail policy was as bad as ever. I wanted to do something that would really make people sit up and take notice. I was already thinking about another project.

First, however, I needed a holiday. Joni wanted to see her family in Palm Beach, and after two months indoors under fluorescent lights, I wanted to see the sun, so we flew to Florida for two weeks.

Peter drove Joni and me to Dulles Airport in his Volkswagen Rabbit. We were catching a night flight to Palm Beach. I sat in the back seat and listened to Joni and Peter talk. Peter was surprisingly gregarious. He said that he was soon taking a trip himself. "I want to see the country. I haven't been to most of the states." Joni encouraged him. She thought he needed a change. Joni and I checked in. Peter drove back toward Roslyn, Virginia, and his cramped apartment. That was the last time we ever saw Peter Dortmund.

At 2 A.M. we arrived at Miami International Airport. Joni's father met us at the airport. Joni nodded off to sleep in the front seat of his Cadillac Seville as he drove us to Palm Beach, but I remained awake and at attention.

On the drive home he asked me how my work had been going. I explained that I had been working for McGovern on an investigation into the railroad industry. "He probably wants to nationalize it, doesn't he?" Mr. Simpson said.

Whether from fatigue or as a joke, instead of telling him the truth—that neither I nor McGovern endorsed nationalization, I said in a serious voice, "That's right, and I'm with him." Mr. Simpson's response was quick; he stopped talking to me. Perhaps that was what I had wanted him to do.

I spent the next morning and afternoon at the Simpsons'

155

house. House is really the wrong word; compound is more apt. Situated on the upper part of a six-acre hillock, the house is not visible from any public road. A high ledge backed by barbed-wire fencing, green hedges, and six unfriendly German shepherds keep out intruders. I marveled at such defenses. As in Southern California, to have a wall around your house is an attempt to keep at bay some of the randomness of life there; in having such a perimeter there was implicit a belief that the freeways were crowded with potential Charlie Mansons. Perhaps they were.

My first morning in Palm Beach, I sat down in the breakfast room at 9 A.M. and did not leave the table until 2 P.M. My only companion was Joni's mother; Joni went to the doctor's.

Mrs. Simpson probed for five hours on such issues as abortion, ERA, religion, SALT II, big government and the Panama Canal. What did I think about the morality of "killing babies"? Wasn't ERA antifamily? Should we sign the dangerous SALT II agreement? Did I favor government meddling in family life? Would I have given away the Panama Canal that we bought and paid for? I waited for her to ask whether I believed in God. There was only one "right" answer to each question. Uncertainty was a crime. I tried to be diplomatic, to avoid confrontation with this ideologue. There was no point in being honest with her. She wished only to hear agreement with her views. I felt that she had reached a state of ideological purity reserved for the fanatic, the isolated, or the wealthy—in this case all three.

"I think I might go for a swim in the pool."

Mrs. Simpson replied, "That's fine, Brett, but let me get the dogs in their pens first." She went to have the cook lock the dogs up.

The pool and pool house (a glass-and-stone structure bigger than many American houses) were to the right of and behind the main house. I changed out of my clothes into one of the many swim trunks in the pool house. I wanted to swim miles after that breakfast grilling, but I could swim only six laps before stopping from exhaustion. I climbed out of the pool to dry

156

off only to find that I had forgotten a towel. I walked toward where the towels were. Without my spectacles, I loped behind the diving board. I stopped immediately. Two feet in front of me was a large German shepherd. His name was Striker, though I did not know this at the time.

I had never been afraid of a dog before, but this dog scared me. He didn't bark or growl or wag his tail. He just looked intently at my groin area. I knew that dog was going to bite me. From his point of view, this was a reasonable proposition. He assumed I was an intruder. He was trained to bite such people.

We stared at each other for an indeterminate period of time, three seconds or three minutes. Fright replaced any sense of time I might have had. In panic, I made the first move. I leaped for the ladder to the diving board. Striker leaped for me. I reached the ladder. Striker reached me. He bit me hard on my thigh about three inches below my rear end. Scrambling up the ladder, I yelped in pain but was able to get up without dragging Striker with me.

My first thought on reaching the relative safety of the diving board was, "I hope this isn't one of those intelligent German shepherds that can scale a ladder." Fortunately he was not. Having treed me, Striker was content to sit under a nearby tree and gloat, lapping some pool water to quench his thirst. I was humiliated. My spirits picked up, however, after I examined my injury. There was little blood, only four long red welts running across my left thigh where Striker's two lower and two upper teeth had clamped.

I could have called for help, made a dash for the pool house and the telephone, but I didn't. I couldn't face the prospect of another interrogation by any other member of the family. At least Striker wasn't asking any questions. To be honest, I also stayed quietly on the diving board because I was damned if I was going to give Striker the satisfaction of hearing my cries. At least, I could have the pretense of being the superior animal. Besides, after the Eastern winter it was reasonably pleasant to bask in the sun, even if it was on a stiff, gritty diving board.

Two hours later Joni returned. From a balcony on the house

overlooking the pool, she called out to me, "What are you doing on the board?"

I explained, "The dogs are out."

She shouted back, "Stay where you are, and I'll have someone get the dogs in." That she was not about to deal with Striker herself, reinforced my conviction that the diving board was the safest place for me.

Later I learned how the dogs had gotten out though Mrs. Simpson had assured me they were locked up. She had put the dogs in their pen, but Mr. Simpson had let Striker out.

If I were paranoid, I would say that this was his response to my facetious comments the night before on nationalization of the railroads or to my working for the big, bad government. But, of course, I'm not.

Spring

OB, Organizational Behavior, the study of how people behave in organizations and bureaucracies, public and private. It is a quiet little acronym I first heard at HBS, Harvard Business School. They may study OB at HBS, but that spring I experienced OB in D.C.

Before the last frost in early April, I flew up to Cambridge to visit my older brother Michael, who was an HBS first-year student, a harassed individual not unlike a duck, appearing calm on the surface while the feet paddle furiously underwater. Always a hard worker, Michael was studying harder than ever. His daily schedule was simple: up at six, classes all day, study till midnight. His hobby was napping. I asked what he planned to do over his spring break. "Sleep," he replied as we trod quickly alongside the frozen Charles River.

He took me to his OB class. There were about fifty people in the low-ceilinged room with amphitheater seating. The artificial light was white and harsh. It is traditional at HBS for visitors to be introduced to the class before it begins. Michael explained that I was his brother and I worked for a committee of Congress. A general murmur arose. I heard a few cutting comments about the relative inefficiency of the public sector compared to the private sector. The response didn't surprise me, although I figured these men and women might feel differently twenty

159

years hence if their companies needed loan guarantees or tariff protection from the government.

HBS uses the "case method" in teaching business to its students. These "cases" are simply incomplete stories about particular businesses. The stories have a beginning and middle, but no end. A situation is described, a crisis precipitated; the students must devise suitable resolutions.

The case that day was about a company with one division that suffered from bad employee relationships and thus poor economic performance. The professor asked certain students to analyze the company's problem and propose some strategy to improve the firm's performance.

The student analyses were cogent and incisive. Soon they had dissected the case to the satisfaction of the professor. They had more trouble, however, in devising a plan of action that would improve the corporation's financial performance while upsetting as few employees as possible. One large and outspoken male student said that the way to end the problem was to "knife problem employees in the back. Get rid of them. Make up some excuse to get 'em out."

Another student asked if such a plan was ethical, since it relied upon a superior lying to subordinates. At this the loud student shouted, "Time out, time out." He formed a t-shape with his hand like a quarterback who, in a football game, wants a break in the action. "I want to get one thing straight. When I said stick 'em in the back, I didn't mean to knife 'em . . . I didn't mean to be vindictive, but after all, they've gotta go. They're causing problems."

The class broke into unkind laughter. They criticized him for being "Machiavellian" and "out of touch with reality." As I came to learn that spring in Washington, however, he was not out of touch with reality. His "Machiavellian" attitudes are part of the regular indoctrination course for the young in government. Each of us—Peter, Joni, Nicholas, Charity, Kim and I—had seen them practiced on us, and some of us had inflicted them on others.

•   •   •

160

I returned to Washington from Cambridge on Friday night and went to the office on Saturday morning to check my mailbox, organize my desk, etc. The marble-coated Dirksen Senate Office Building was deserted. No aides rushing through the halls. No tourists, since the building was closed to the public on weekends. In my room with its basement-level windows, I was oblivious to everything except the building's hum.

Schmidt came in. He sat at his flat desk and stared out the window. He had his hands in the pockets of the cloth-lined beige windbreaker he wore. He wore old khaki trousers. He was dressed as if he were heading to the hardware store to buy some flower bulbs for the coming thaw, but there was no gay purposefulness in his face.

"What brings you here on Saturday?" I asked.

"Didn't you hear?" He looked at me with surprise.

"No. What?"

"Humphrey died."

When sad news takes me by surprise, I often say something inane. "Oh." Then I realize what was said. "I'm sorry."

"Yeah," Schmidt replied. "Well, we knew it was coming, but it hurts just the same."

"I'm glad it's finally over," I said.

"Well, I'm not." He paused. "No, I don't mean that."

Schmidt headed toward the door. "Where are you going?" I asked.

"To the rotunda. His body is lying in state."

"Would you like any company?" I asked.

"Yeah, I'd like that."

I put on my tweed jacket, and we walked via the underground tunnels that connect the Congressional office buildings with the Capitol. We did not talk. Schmidt was lost in his unhappiness, and I didn't know what to say to him except that I was sorry, and I had already said that. Though I was as close to Schmidt as anyone on the Committee, our relationship was not one of equals. I did not presume to share his deep grief. I felt little passion over Humphrey's death. It had been a long time coming.

Along with fifty to one hundred other people, Schmidt and I were herded into an ornate marble-and-granite hallway adjacent to the great dome. Most of the others were Senators and their families dressed up as if for a Presidential inauguration. I stood stiffly among them, quite frankly wondering if the Capitol police were going to kick me out once they discovered I was no VIP. Since I was with Schmidt, however, they did not. People treated Schmidt with respect. Periodically, Senators walked over to him to commiserate and offer condolences.

After a half hour of waiting, there was a flurry of activity. I drifted toward the front of the corridor's opening onto the rotunda. I saw Senator Humphrey's widow, Muriel, and his family enter the chamber to pay public homage to her husband.

For the first time, I saw the casket. It lay where I remembered President Kennedy's had lain, on a bier directly under the apex of the soaring rotunda. It was guarded by four soldiers, one from each branch of the military service, each in dress uniform. The Humphrey family was dwarfed by the vastness of the chamber and moved in slow motion toward the flag-draped burial chest. They walked to the side of the bier and stood gazing from ten feet away.

Our group was then ushered in by the uniformed police. Senators and their families shuffled in first, aides to Humphrey second. I followed Schmidt. As we went in and lined up in a row facing the casket, I heard a sudden tremendous noise—the cacophony of hundreds of camera shutters opening and closing and of light bulbs popping. I looked beyond the coffin to the other side of the domed interior; there were scores of photographers and cameramen blasting away to get a picture of us mourners.

The noise and flashing surprised me. I realized instantly that I had become part of the sad pageant. I could almost see tomorrow's newspaper photo with the caption "Loyal aides pay their respects to Senator Hubert H. Humphrey in Capitol rotunda." I looked away from the photographers in the bleachers and stared instead at the bier. After a few seconds, I could tell I was going to do something I hadn't done in years—cry.

And I did. First one eye and then the other. I looked over at Schmidt. He was not crying, only looking at the hard marble floor. I stared at the coffin. I cried because I did not feel sad. Mine were tears of guilt and confusion at thinking such a thing. It was a thought I wished to deny. Yet, after nine months in Washington, an awareness was being etched on my consciousness—the government was stale.

In youth unemployment, "make-work" jobs provided by the government failed to provide young black and Hispanic Americans with skills to get jobs in growth areas of the economy. To make matters worse, government-mandated increases in minimum wage priced these lower-skilled citizens out of the entry-level jobs that traditionally have been first steps toward economic improvement for the unskilled and unwanted.

In military defense, our research-and-development efforts were top-heavy with review boards churning out overly complicated weapons, and yet Senators wished to add more layers of bureaucracy. Likewise, in my experience at the OEOB with the strategic material bauxite, I had seen how slow and self-preserving federal bureaucrats are in their civil-service havens. So it had been in railroads, where outdated government regulation had in large part created the mess we see today; what had begun as a late-nineteenth-century response to robber barons like Leland Stanford, was perpetuated by the government fifty years too long.

I had come to Washington as a liberal, an optimist. This town was turning me into a conservative, a pessimist about government. I was losing faith. It was a disorienting feeling.

The next day, I read the Sunday *New York Times* as always. At the top of the front page was a picture of the bier and of some people standing behind it. Among the dozen were Schmidt and I. The caption read, "An honor guard stood around flag-draped coffin of Hubert H. Humphrey in Capitol rotunda as visitors paid respects." The black-and-white photograph conveyed none of the emotion I had felt. I didn't bother to clip the photo. It had all the emotional power of a picture of bored politicians watching a small parade on an overcast day.

163

Personal ambition and cumulative disenchantment with the orthodoxy of my superiors in government led me now into a major political fight; it centered on the Social Security system. The issue was social-security payroll taxes and whether to raise them. The Congress was poised to jack them up by almost $200 *billion,* the largest tax increase in the history of the nation. No one on Capitol Hill or anywhere in the government had studied the likely ramifications for Americans of this proposal. I decided I would. It was open territory, a chance to show my bosses the kind of work I thought government workers had a responsibility to do.

A project of this magnitude normally went to a senior staffer, but since no one was working on Social Security, I grabbed it and ran to Schmidt for his approval. I reminded him that at the last JEC annual hearings on the state of the economy, some witnesses had expressed concern about the rapid growth of social-security payroll taxes. He agreed to let me write a report to be published as an official JEC staff report. He spoke with O'Hara, the staff director, and O'Hara went along. I was in business. Whether the members of the JEC knew, I'm not sure. Staff-initiated projects were common in the Committee. Member approval was necessary if an aide needed large research money, but O'Hara's agreement was considered sufficient.

There was little time to waste. The vote on the social-security payroll-tax legislation was impending, only one and a half months away. I set to work.

I began by reading. First I reviewed the bare bones of the Social Security system: how it was funded; how those dollars were spent; and what the system's long-term prospects were.

Social Security is funded exclusively by payroll taxes on employees and employers. President Roosevelt committed the government to this policy in 1935. He did this less to ensure the financial foundation of the system than to guarantee it a political base. In fact, as early as 1935 it was pointed out to him by his economic advisers that payroll taxes placed a proportionately greater burden on lower-income workers than on higher-income ones. Roosevelt's response to this criticism of his regressive social-security payroll tax was unequivocal. Arthur M. Schlesinger, Jr., in his book *The Coming of the New Deal* quotes Roosevelt:

> I guess you're right on the economics, but those taxes were never a problem of economics. They are politics all the way through. We put those payroll contributions there so as to give the contributors a legal, moral, and political right to collect their pensions . . . With those taxes in there, no damn politician can ever scrap my social security program.

That was for sure. Forty-five years later, social-security financing had not changed one iota. Unfortunately, other things had. Most frighteningly, the Social Security system was in constant deficit and, unless overhauled, headed inevitably toward insolvency. The economic issues that Roosevelt chose to ignore in 1935 dictated political changes in the 1980s.

The problem was no longer to protect a fledgling government program. Social Security now had thirty-four million clients who had been promised trillions of dollars in future benefits by Congresses and Presidents who could no more renege on those promises than they could declare the Constitution invalid. As the columnist George Will wrote, "Unquestionably, Social Security's basic commitments will be met. The problem is the effect that this will have on the economy that makes Social Security—and everything else—possible."

Though the 1935 payroll tax of 1 percent on employers and employees payable on a $3,000 wage base was raised by 1979 to 6.13 percent on a wage base of $22,900, the trust funds used to finance benefits paid out to social-security recipients were estimated to run out of money by the early 1980s. As early as 1976, expenditures exceeded income by $3.2 billion. How had this happened?

Three factors were normally mentioned as the causes. First, Disability Insurance (DI is for workers who could no longer work by reason of medically determinable physical or mental

165

impairment that was expected to result in death or be of long duration) had been added to the original Social Security (Old Age and Survivors Insurance) in 1958 and then liberalized in the '60s and '70s. The increase in benefit payments for DI simply outstripped any increase in payroll taxes.

Second, the declining fertility rate in the United States foreshadowed a decline in the ratio of workers to retired persons. The falling birth rate was not, however, a cause of Social Security's present deficit. It would not be until the 1990s that this demographic doom struck the system. Today there are three workers paying taxes into Social Security for every beneficiary. By the early twenty-first century, however, there will be only two contributors for every one beneficiary.

The third major cause of Social Security's problems was a combination of the unexpectedly slow economic growth, high unemployment, and high inflation in the 1970s. Benefit and tax levels based on an inflation rate of 3 percent, a real growth rate of 4 percent, and an unemployment rate of 3.5 percent made no sense in a period of double-digit inflation, double-digit unemployment and negligible increases in economic growth and labor productivity.

When worker productivity doesn't increase, wages don't rise, and Social Security payroll-tax contributions don't grow. When unemployment swells, earned wages fall, and payroll-tax revenues begin to fall. Add to these problems the illness of inflation. As prices move up, Social Security benefit levels indexed to the Consumer Price Index are swollen. You can see why Social Security funded by payroll taxes and indexed to inflation went into deficit when real growth is 0, unemployment is 8 percent, and inflation is 10 percent.

The more I read about the Social Security, the less respect I felt for the proposed legislation before the Senate and the House of Representatives. While the Congressmen were spouting reassuring platitudes to the public about "the need to maintain the financial integrity of Social Security," they were writing legislation that could only ruin the system's long-run health.

They proposed raising payroll taxes by $186 billion. What

was wrong with that? Nothing. Except that in raising those revenues, they would further slow real economic growth, raise the unemployment rate, and increase the rate of inflation. My first task was to measure the extent of their mistakes. For this I needed a computer, an econometric model, and some assistance from the Social Security Administration (SSA).

From the SSA I needed estimates of the proposed tax increases, from the econometric model a way of simulating the economy's response to the taxes, and from the computer the capability to "run" the econometric model swiftly and accurately according to my instructions.

Like most bureaucrats, the men at the SSA were not eager to give information to an outsider. If I had been on the staff of the House Ways and Means Committee, there would have been no problem; together, the SSA and Ways and Means had written the social-security laws. These were the people who allowed federal employees to remain exempt from the taxes and contribute instead to a government pension fund that paid higher benefits than Social Security. They were the folks who had propagated the myth that Social Security was like a private pension system that earned a return on its trust fund when, in fact, the taxes paid to Social Security by workers this year are sent straight to retired persons this year like any other government transfer program. These people were used to working together to present a popular and false image of Social Security to the taxpayers. They resented people like me looking in. Such resistance only made me dig harder.

I called the administrator in charge of revenue estimates for four days without getting the data I needed. "I'm backed up with work," he'd say. "I didn't get your message. . . ." On the fifth day, I calmly but seriously threatened to come to his office in Baltimore and beat down his boss's door if he didn't send the information. "I'll be there tomorrow at 8 A.M.," I said. "OK, OK, I'll send the stuff," he replied.

Once the revenue estimates arrived, I reviewed them and then "loaded" them into the econometric model to test the hypothesis that the pending Social Security tax bill would be harm-

167

ful to the economy. The model I used consisted of an interlocking set of mathematical equations that needed to be solved simultaneously to determine the output of the entire economic system. The individual equations were estimated by empirical analysis of past relationships between economic variables. For example, one equation might specify that consumer spending is a function of changes in people's disposable income which in turn depends on taxation, as in the real economy.

When hooked up to a computer, the entire set of equations could be solved to forecast gross national product, prices and employment. I was going to solve this system *after the introduction* of additional taxation, the proposed Social Security payroll taxes. The specific model I used was built by Professor Lawrence R. Klein, of the University of Pennsylvania, winner of the 1980 Nobel Memorial Prize in Economic Science. It was not a perfect means of predicting the impact of the Social Security taxes on the American economy, but it was the best available. My only fear was that the model might understate the effect of the payroll taxes on inflation. Professor Klein's model was known to do that.

The econometric model existed, of course, only inside the memory banks of a computer. Although it took only seconds for the computer to complete a simulated decade of the American economy, I had to spend days preparing the model to run correctly. Any misspelled command guaranteed that the simulation would "blow up." At $200 a shot, I couldn't afford many such quiet explosions without exhausting the Committee's computer budget and earning the wrath of other economists, who needed money for their own projects.

Occasionally, I arrived at the office by 8 A.M. to find that the twelve hours spent the day before had produced nothing more than reams of computer paper filled with nonsensical data. Experimentation was necessary, however, and as always it was less than completely successful. Any typographical or design error in my commands to the computer could cause the simulation to abort.

Whatever the costs of my computer experiments, however,

168

they were nothing compared to the costs the economy would bear if the Congress passed their $186-billion social-security payroll-tax increase. Schmidt had told me not to worry so much whether I spent $1,000 or $2,000 on this project (the final figure was about $1,500). He said, "I don't care about that as long as you do a good job and a fast job." I appreciated Schmidt's support. I wanted to do a professional job. I had seen hack economists in Washington bend professional standards and ethics to give a Senator or a Representative the most politically convenient answer. I knew one staff member on a congressional committee who had gone so far down this road that he had built an econometric model "guaranteed to show that government revenues will increase when taxes are cut." I didn't know whether that hypothesis was right or wrong, but it wasn't scientific to design the experiment so that the desired conclusion was reached whether valid or invalid. When I expressed some doubts about his methodology, he replied, "This is Washington, not a university." Professional standards often fell before political pressures.

My work on the computer took all of March and drew me away from the other JEC staff. This project was not a group effort like running a hearing or writing a bill. I spent the time reading and thinking at my desk or communicating with the computer at a terminal. The work was solitary, the way I preferred. I did not want help from any senior staffers.

As at many Washington offices, senior staffers had a tendency to co-opt projects done by junior staff and take credit where it was not due. For example, Kim Donahue spent two months at work on a study of United States foreign aid. A senior economist had told her it would be published as a committee report and might serve as the springboard for a public hearing. None of that happened. Instead, as her mentor confided to Schmidt and me, "Kim's collected some good information. I think I can work it into a hearing I'm planning to run." With Schmidt as my protector, I didn't need any help from senior staffers to further my committee report.

During March and early April, I rarely left the Dirksen Building before dark, even though the sun was setting later and later. The Committee's computer terminal was located in the Snakepit. Every evening at 5:15 the room's clerical and secretarial personnel fled. I was left with only the computer for company. The phones would stop ringing. It was quiet. That was when I got my best work done.

After work, I was always tired. Once home, I had to take a twenty-minute shower simply to revive myself. Joni and I would go out to dinner; I tended to listen more than talk, because my mind was nearly emptied from a day of grappling with the computer and the specifics of the social-security legislation. Not surprisingly, there were often long silences at the table. "I'm not going to conduct a monologue," she'd say.

After dinner, I would watch any TV sitcom or adventure program. A book or conversation seemed too much effort. Joni hated my watching television. When she threatened to throw the set out the window, I cut my nightly hours down from three to one and a half. "You're becoming a deadhead," Joni said. Much to her chagrin, I didn't deny it.

My relations with people at the office also suffered. I withdrew into the social-security project and lost touch with the other aides, clerks and secretaries. On Fridays, I no longer spent time shooting the breeze and drinking beer with them after work in the Snakepit. The Joint Economic Committee was never as chummy a place as a Senator's office, where there is common loyalty to one boss. But even so, my aloofness was noticeable. People stopped dropping by to see if I wanted to have lunch with them. I ate rubbery chef salads at my desk. They were tasteless except for the sugary Russian dressing smothering them. I didn't care, however, what I ate or whether people did or didn't invite me out to lunch. I was pushing to get my results to the members and the public *before* the vote.

Spring had sprung. Electronic signs flashed the rising temperature on bank buildings. Hobos and bag ladies reappeared in the parks like bears after winter hibernation. Oarsmen in singles, pairs and eights stroked along the defrosted Potomac.

170

New block-long square holes were dug in the softening ground for this year's crop of office buildings. The cityscape was stirring. But I ignored everything except my work.

Two weeks before the vote on the bill, I had the ream of computer results I needed. If passed and signed into law by the President, this Social Security bill would by 1982 reduce the real Gross National Product by almost $34 billion, add a full percentage point to the rate of inflation and put 130,000 people out of work. At a time when people were complaining about "stagflation," the Congress was about to pass a bill to reduce the net earnings of workers and increase the cost of labor. What were we doing in Congress? Why hadn't anyone told the taxpayers about this?

As soon as I copied the computer results onto JEC stationery, I ran over to the House side of Capitol Hill. Selected members of the House and the Senate were meeting to hammer out minor differences in the legislation. Once this conference committee agreed on a final bill, the House and Senate would vote on it. This was my last chance to influence the legislators and their aides. I planned to give important legislative assistants my results so that their bosses would at least know the consequences of their action. I stayed away from the press, however; I had no clearance from Schmidt to publicize these numbers.

The conference committee met in the House Ways and Means hearing room under the watchful gazes of past Ways and Means chairmen, like Wilbur Mills, whose portraits hung on the high walls. Unlike the hearing I had done for Humphrey, this meeting attracted few tourists; it was wall-to-wall lobbyists with a dozen Congressional aides sitting and taking notes. The atmosphere was tense, and the air congested with cigarette smoke. I saw Nicholas and Charity. I spoke first with Nicholas.

"What are you doing here?" I asked. He was sitting near the members, so I had bent down on one knee and whispered in his ear.

"Representing some clients," he said.

"Which ones?"

"Organized labor . . . Afraid the system is going bankrupt
. . . Want higher taxes to keep the benefits coming."

"What do you think of this bill?" I asked.

"Good bill . . . It'll keep things going . . . That's all we want.
What about you?"

"The bill's a disaster . . . inflationary . . . increases unemployment . . . hurts economic growth. I've got the numbers to back
that up," I added, showing Nicholas my results.

He perused them. "So this is what you've been doing the last
month. . . . It doesn't make any difference, you know. . . .
You're pissing into the wind. . . . This bill is going to pass."
Nicholas' voice was getting louder. "Why do you want to muddy
the waters at this late date? You can't stop us." Nicholas wasn't
talking as a house mate, but as a lobbyist scared that these numbers could upset the traditional politics of social-security legislation. I was giving answers to questions his clients didn't want
asked.

His voice suddenly took on the seductive tone he used around
the house when he wanted to borrow my car. "Why don't you
give me a copy?"

"I don't have enough."

"Just one?"

"Sorry." I wasn't going to give my stuff to the opposition.
How did I know what he'd do with it? At best, he'd throw it into
a wastepaper basket. I liked Nicholas as a house mate, identified
with him as another young man in Washington, but I didn't
trust him as a lobbyist. I understood his position. He represented unionized labor. They wanted higher benefits. They preferred to have as little debate as possible on the costs of such
policy.

In rapid fire, he said quietly, "Please."

I said, "No."

"Why not?" he asked less quietly.

"Don't have enough copies."

"Do it for a friend," he said loudly.

"No."

172

"C'mon, don't be an *asshole*," Nicholas said too loudly. He realized it too late. The people around us turned to stare. The committee members looked our way. The witness stopped testifying. The chairman banged his gavel, looked directly at Nicholas and me, and warned "Staff will keep quiet or leave the room." Nicholas turned crimson, and I smiled weakly. A distinctive haughty laugh was heard from behind us. I didn't have to look to know it was Charity. I signaled to her to meet me outside in the white marble hallway. Nicholas was too embarrassed to notice my going.

Charity was amused and filled with trenchant observations like, "You wouldn't let Nicholas borrow your car again. . . . Or was it a discussion of whose turn it is to do the dishes?"

"I need to show you something," I said more seriously. "You're handling social security, aren't you?"

"Yes," she replied.

"Well, look at these numbers."

She looked. "Where did you get these?"

"They're mine."

"They're incredible," she said to me. "But what am I supposed to do with them?" I didn't know. I hadn't asked myself that question. Charity continued over my silence, "I'll show it to the Senator, but don't expect much. They just want to get this payroll-tax increase passed as soon as possible, so people will forget it before the next election."

I sighed. "OK. But at least take a copy of the numbers."

"I will, but it won't do any good."

I pressed a copy into her hand. "See what you can do."

"OK. I must go. See you at home?"

"Sure."

"Bye. Take care. You get so worked up."

"Bye," I answered. I knew my month-and-a-half's work was headed for a senatorial trash can. Yet, I approached other aides. The response was unanimous, "Thanks but no thanks." Their bosses would not be interested. "It'd be political suicide for them to vote against Social Security no matter how bad this bill is. It's

173

like voting against motherhood. They just want to get this over with," one aide said to me.

That was the attitude of all the Democrats. Reconsideration was impossible. If they were not under the mistaken impression that Social Security was going bankrupt any day now, (such dire straits were at least a year off), they were terrified of any delay in passing a $200-billion tax increase. Voters would need time to forget before the next election.

I was so desperate for an audience that I showed my work to a White House Congressional liaison. "Very disturbing," he said. "But I'm afraid it's out of our hands. We've been pushing the buttons for a delay, but nobody's listening at the other end. I don't know who's in charge here, but it isn't us. Maybe somebody is? Maybe it's just inertia? We raise payroll taxes because that's the way we've always funded Social Security," he mused. "It sure beats the political hell of controlling benefits or letting Social Security compete with other programs for general tax revenues."

I understood, but remained disappointed. There was no stopping this legislation. It seemed the time and energy and money I had spent on it was wasted. I walked back to the DSOB cafeteria and ate a lunch of meat loaf, "whipped potatoes," and chocolate pudding, a difficult task even when life was treating me well.

The day after P.L. 95-216 was signed into law by the President, Joni received a letter. It was from Peter Dortmund. The postmark was New York City. It read:

DEAR JONI,
I just spent the weekend making color 8 x 10 enlargements of you—quite nice! I'm sure Brett's just won't compare.
Just thought I'd drop a short note to let you know I'm alive, still searching for a future, and that I haven't forgotten you, one of my dearest friends. Please give my best to Brett.
                                        Love, PETER
P.S. I assume you and Brett are still together—hope I'm right.

174

Something in the letter was odd. The tone charmed, but the message was slightly ominous—". . . let you know I'm alive . . ." No, we were overreacting. It must have been a self-deprecating reference to the uneventfulness of life. ". . . still searching for a future . . ." Yes, he was just like the rest of us. We'd hear from him as soon as he had a new job. I was sure of it.

And yet, there *was* something final about Peter's letter—". . .I haven't forgotten you, one of my dearest friends . . ." This read like a goodbye. We did not know, but it was a farewell. "Please give my best to Brett. Love, PETER."

We tried to call his family's home in Hartsdale, New York. Never any answer.

Much to the surprise of Congress, voters didn't like the $186-billion tax increase. In the recess after the Social Security vote, the Senators and Representatives discovered this while visiting their states and districts. For the first time, taxpayers began to complain that the present burden of payroll taxes outweighed the future relief of retirement benefits.

Everywhere Congressmen went constituents were sure to follow, questioning their judgment.

A certain amount of carping was to be expected from workers my age, who would be the ones paying the taxes. It was not anticipated, however, that older workers and recent retirees would question our leaders. Yet, they did. They worried that continued massive increases in Social Security payroll taxation would create resentment among younger workers, a resentment that would inevitably provoke a taxpayers' rebellion and rupture Social Security's transfer of income from young to old, workers to retirees. A lobbyist for retired persons told me, "We don't want to kill the goose that lays the golden egg."

The Republicans were the first to sense the angry mood of people outside Washington. This was an opportunity for them to score political points against the Democrats. All blame was shifted to the then majority party. The Republicans portrayed themselves as a gallant minority who had tried to defend the taxpayer against the shortsightedness of government. They

175

were correct about "shortsightedness," but less than truthful about their opposition to Democratic legislation.

For the first time in years, some Republicans in the Senate and many in the House had argued on the floor against such high payroll taxes. They suggested instead raising the age of eligibility for beneficiaries; a plan that would not have applied to current retirees, only to people with time to prepare for delayed benefits. The Republican idea was also consistent with the view that productive work in old age is good for the elderly as well as society. Other Republicans offered plans to use higher income taxes instead of payroll taxes to fund the Health Insurance and Disability Insurance portions of Social Security in which there is no relationship between a person's wages while working and his benefits when disabled or retired. The logic was clear: relative to income taxes, payroll taxes lead to higher labor costs and higher prices, so why not use less inflationary taxation. In addition, payroll taxes hit lower-middle- and middle-class workers proportionately harder than the high bourgeoisie.

Most Republicans in Congress, however, voted with the Democrats or abstained from voting. How else could P.L. 95-216 have been passed in the Senate 56 to 21?

At the conference committee meeting, I had not given the Republicans my data. My work was funded by Democrats for Democrats. After the vote, however, I was impressed that the Republicans were the only ones responding to the voters with some intelligent suggestions. I heard from other Hill staffers and read in the newspapers that Republican members and a few Democrats were already pushing to revise P.L. 95-216.

This buoyed my spirits tremendously. It meant there had to be a market for my report even if it wasn't the JEC. An angry electorate would want to know the implications of P.L. 95-216. My report would further the movement for a change in Social Security policy making. With the JEC publishing my report, I would finally influence a major political debate, making the reputation I had hoped for when I first arrived in Washington. I was euphoric. That was in late April.

• • •

I visited the JEC's best economist, Tom Hamburg, to get a final quality check on my work. Though all Committee staff reports were published with a disclaimer that the opinions expressed therein were the author's alone, the Committee maintained high standards for work published under its aegis. The awful report on small business that I had reviewed for Bob Lackey six months earlier was the exception, not the rule. Hamburg checked my methodology and my written discussion of the Social Security legislation and gave them his blessing. I alerted the JEC publications clerk to be prepared for my thirty-page manuscript.

The next day, however, another economist on the committee, Will Coates, called me on the phone. "John O'Hara wants me to check your results." Coates was a baby-faced man of thirty who had worked his way up through the staff ranks from a summer intern to a senior economist. He was a prototypical staff man, competent and polite to his superiors and peers. He rarely raised his voice in a threatening manner. So when he asked to see my work, I agreed without delay.

I went to his office at the end of the day and gave Coates the one copy of the report that I had made. I kept the original with me at all times. Since the development of an anti-payroll-tax movement, I had been careful to keep the copying to a minimum. I wanted no half-baked versions floating around the Hill without the JEC imprint. I wanted to avoid embarrassing the committee via premature disclosure. When I gave Coates only one copy, however, he said that he needed another. When I asked him who else wanted a copy, he gave no direct answer except to hint that it was none of my business. He was my superior on the staff, so I walked over to the Xerox machine and made him the copy he wanted.

On my way back to my office, I wondered why, if he didn't want me to know who was going to scrutinize my paper, he didn't simply make an extra copy himself when I had left. He probably hadn't expected that I would inquire. Compliance, not resistance, was his style, the key to his rise within the JEC.

177

Since taking on Social Security, I had not been watching developments around me. Now, however, I sensed a strangeness on the Committee. Coates seemed more dominant than I had remembered; Hamburg less. I felt even odder after seeing Schmidt.

From my first day on the JEC I had turned him into a substitute father. He had insulated me from their petty bureaucratic sniping. "He's learning," Schmidt would say. I deferred only to him.

But wasn't it true that he had made me his son as much as I'd fashioned him my surrogate father? He had enjoyed my identification with him, my good work done in his name. He had my loyalty with only a few shards of rebellion thrown in. How much it was like the relationship with my real father. Those fears I'd had about Miss Plunkett—that she wanted to mix business with pleasure—had been delusions; it was with Schmidt that the real opportunity for intimacy had presented itself.

So it was naturally to him that I went after my visit with Coates. He sat at his desk listening to Mozart's *The Magic Flute* on the radio and drinking a glass of German white wine. It was unusual for him to indulge so during work hours; it was not yet 5 P.M. It was perhaps not the best time to disturb Schmidt, but I couldn't stop myself. I felt something going on over my head; I thought he could give me a clue as to what it was. I mentioned to Schmidt that my report seemed to be getting an unusually careful review.

To my surprise, he replied carelessly, "Don't get so damned upset. Pull up a chair and have a glass of wine. It's a nice Riesling that's been in the icebox all day." Schmidt popped a couple of antacid tablets and downed the rest of his glass's contents. I could tell he was a little tipsy. His normally ruddy cheeks were rosy red.

I said to him sharply, "I don't want any wine, thanks." I went sullenly to my desk.

My reply seemed to sting him. He yelled, "Don't worry so much about your friggin' report. I'll help you get it published. I'll talk to O'Hara. I'll take care of it."

178

I said, "Thanks." But for the first time, I felt stupid and angry asking Schmidt to be my protector. It was about time I took responsibility myself, time for me to stand up for my work.

The next day I heard nothing about my study from Schmidt, nor did I consider asking him any questions. I didn't phone Coates. What would I have said? "Are you worried about what my report says? Does it embarrass the Congress?" I doubted whether he would give me straight answers. I did not want to antagonize the powers-that-were with too many questions. My only desire was to have the paper printed as a JEC report.

I knew that my paper's conclusions were slightly out of step with the Democratic members of the JEC who had voted for P.L. 95-216, but I felt less uncomfortable after speaking with Kim Donahue, my compatriot on the JEC.

It was 6:30 P.M. Everyone had gone home. Hunched over my desk and still working, I sensed someone standing behind me. I looked around and saw Kim.

"Hello," I said. "What can I do for you?"

"I wanted to see your paper, the social-security piece you've been slaving away at," she replied.

"Oh, and why is that?"

"Curiosity," she said in a matter-of-fact way. "No, honestly, there's a former professor of mine from MIT visiting the Brookings Institution for a few days, and one of his specialties is social security. I thought he might like to see your paper."

"You think he would be interested?" I was flattered. "I don't know if I could release a copy."

"Don't worry," she said. "He'll just give it a quick reading. He won't let anyone else see it. You might find his comments helpful."

I considered her idea for a few seconds. Then I said, "Sure, why not? It would be good to get his criticisms. I'll make a copy on the Xerox machine in the Snakepit." I wanted an outside evaluation of the paper, something to defend myself with if Coates attacked me.

"Thanks," she said. "See you tomorrow, and, by the way,

179

Brett, don't worry about your paper being unpopular. What do you have to lose?"

"Easy for you to say," I said with a weak smile.

She laughed gently. "Well, if it matters to you. I'll still like you."

"That's wonderful, Kim. I'll remember that when they take my desk away and I need a place to do my work."

We were grinning at each other. This was the first bit of office camaraderie I'd felt in months. I appreciated her warmth toward me and her support, but I also knew it was no mistake that it was Kim who supported me; she planned to leave the Committee within a month. She was returning to get a Ph.D. in economics. "I'll be so well trained that when I come back to Washington, they'll *have* to use me."

Suddenly, it was May. My paper was still locked inside the JEC bureaucracy. I received two unexpected phone calls about what was going on. The first was from a *New York Times* reporter.

He had a flat, unemotional voice. He wanted to know all about my study.

"How did you hear about it?" I asked.

"Someone on House Ways and Means mentioned it."

"A Republican or a Democrat?"

"I don't remember. Why?"

"No reason." To my knowledge, no Republicans had seen my results. I didn't want to worry about partisan politics.

"Well, can I see a copy?" he asked.

"No," I said firmly.

"Why not?"

"Because it's not ready for public disclosure."

"You showed it to some aides, didn't you?"

"Are you a Congressional aide?"

"No, but—"

"When it's ready for the press, you'll be the first to know."

This reporter did not give up easily. He wanted a scoop, some unadulterated criticism of the social-security legislation that was the cause of so much taxpayer resentment. He was not, however, going to get that from me. I was no leaker.

In typical newspaper puffery, he said, "You know, Brett, people are awfully upset about this tax bill. It could be a big story for you."

"For you too, don't you think?" I replied.

"They're not keeping the lid on you, are they?"

I hesitated. I hadn't expected that question, and I didn't know the answer. Then I replied, "No, it's simply not ready yet."

"OK. I'll call back in a few days."

Schmidt walked into the room at this moment. I ended the telephone conversation. "Glad you called, Bob. Bye." I gave Schmidt an ingratiating stupid grin and said, "An old friend."

"That's fascinating," he replied gruffly.

The second phone call that day came in the afternoon. It was from Nicholas, my house mate. He said he was calling to give me his new extension at his office.

"How are you doing?" he asked.

"About the same as this morning at the breakfast table, Nicholas."

"Still in a dour mood, eh."

"What do you want, Nicholas?"

"How's your report coming along?"

"Fine."

"That's surprising."

"What do you mean?" I asked.

"That there are no problems with your paper."

"It's a good paper. Why should there be problems?" I replied rather defensively.

"I don't mean with the writing of the paper. I'm referring to the publishing of it. No problems there?"

"What business is it of yours?"

"None, except that I've heard about your paper from other people, Democrats, the people who pay your salary. The word I get is that you're rockin' the boat. You're embarrassing people."

"No one was bothered before. Why should they care now?"

"Because of the response of the voters. Don't tell me you didn't notice. Have the Republicans seen it?"

"Nicholas, why don't you keep out of this?"

"I'm just telling you what I've heard. Your paper is being checked out at the highest level of the Democratic leadership."

"Listen, Nicholas," I said. "I'm not worried. I don't need your rumor-mongering. Let's keep our friendship outside the office."

"Never mix business and pleasure?"

"Right. I'll see you at dinner."

I hung up the phone. I was sweating in my chair. I decided to see Schmidt and find out whether there was some graceful way to avoid a conflict between me and my bosses. But Schmidt could not see me that afternoon.

To make things worse, Will Coates phoned me to say, "Brett, I think there may be some methodological problems with your report. I think you better come over." I tried to put off the meeting until after I spoke with Schmidt, until Schmidt could help me find a safe way out of this mess. Coates, however, was insistent, so I agreed to meet with him and Tom Hamburg, the chief economist who already had OK'd my methods and results. I had the feeling that this was a setup.

We met in Hamburg's office down the hall from Schmidt's and mine. Hamburg was usually a gregarious man, but not today. I arrived before Coates. Hamburg said morosely, "Will seems to think there is some problem with the 'multiplier' in your analysis."

In economics, the "multiplier" is a word that usually refers to the change in the Gross National Product resulting from a change in government spending or taxation. For example, when the government increases taxes this will typically trim people's personal incomes reducing over-all consumer spending and thus lowering the level of economic activity as measured by the Gross National Product. While the "multiplier effect" of taxation on the economy can vary a bit depending on the number of unemployed workers and factories, over the course of four or five years the ups and downs of the economy tend to offset one another so that an average value for the multiplier is estimated by economists. In the econometric model that I had used, such an average multiplier was built in. Since my simulation was for a five-year period, an average value for the multiplier was appropriate.

Coates arrived within three minutes and began his criticism. He went through my report page by page, paragraph by paragraph. Nothing was too petty to skip. He must have spent an entire day investigating the paper. He questioned me about every number he saw and then I would explain its authenticity. This cat-and-mouse game went on for a half hour. Everyone was polite. I answered every question successfully. Hamburg said nothing. He didn't want to get involved.

Finally, Coates said in his high-pitched voice, "I want to talk about the multiplier. As I understand it, you haven't used a dynamic multiplier, one that changes with short-run fluctuations in the economy. This could skew your results, you know."

I sat there looking at Hamburg. I was waiting for him to come to my defense. After all, he had helped me design the method of analysis I had used, but he remained silent.

I said to him, "Tom, aren't you going to say anything?"

He stared uncomfortably at the linoleum floor and replied, "Well, I don't think this multiplier is too important, but Will knows this computer model better than I do, so . . ."

So I wasn't going to get any help from him, even though he was the senior economist on the Committee. From that moment on I had little doubt there were invisible hands orchestrating this scene, that the powers above were not going to speak honestly with me about my report. It was a discouraging and lonely sensation.

I was not, however, going to let Coates use some "methodological criticism" to bury my report. In cool tones, I explained to him that any variations in the multiplier would average out over the five-year period of my simulation. To prove this I had Coates wait while I called the economist who oversaw the econometric model.

As Coates and Hamburg listened from their chairs, I asked

him whether it made any difference to my results if the multiplier was held constant. His unequivocal answer was "No."

I repeated his response for Coates to hear. "It makes no difference at all to the results. That's what we thought. Thanks very much."

There wasn't much for Coates to say, and he backed off. His other criticisms were minor, so we ended the meeting within five minutes. Coates was disgruntled. I felt triumphant, having defeated a Ph.D. economist in an economic argument. I wasn't going to be stifled that easily. This was a preliminary skirmish in what seemed to be a war between me and my own bureaucracy. I didn't want a fight. I couldn't win the fight. But if that was how it had to be . . . I was scared, but in retrospect, the fear produced in me more resolve to fight than to run. I was not enervated. I was angry.

For the next week, despite the tremendous public outcry about the social-security tax hikes, neither my bosses nor I mentioned my report or when it would be released. I dragged myself through those tense, empty days. I was neither receiving nor soliciting new projects. I didn't believe they would ignore this issue, this paper, and their promises to publish it for the public and press. But as Friday rolled away, I realized that that was exactly what they were going to do—give me the old silent treatment, hope I would give up. So on Monday of the next week, I did something I had been trying to avoid, confront Schmidt about all this.

I went in to Schmidt that morning, confident that he would help me. I didn't know whom else to turn to. Schmidt was the "nineteenth member" of the JEC, my guardian.

"Good morning," I said.

"Morning," Schmidt replied from his swivel chair.

"Do you have a few minutes?"

"Yeah, sure." Schmidt leaned back in his chair and took off his glasses. I pulled a small chair over to his desk and sat down.

"What's the problem?" he asked, as if he had no idea. "You still going out with that cute blonde or has she left you?"

"Joni's fine. That's not exactly what I wanted to talk about."

"OK, shoot," he said calmly.

"It's about the social-security study, about getting it published the way you and O'Hara had said."

"Uh-huh," Schmidt replied.

"Well, I think I did a good job, and I think people have a right to see the study. That tax bill is the number-one voter complaint."

"Sure, I think it would be the best thing for the public to see it."

In a slightly heated voice I added, "It's been gone over with a fine-tooth comb by Hamburg and Coates; they haven't been able to stick any technical pins in it."

"I didn't know they had tried," Schmidt said with surprise. "You think they're trying to kill the study?" He was playing with me.

I continued. "No one has said as much, but that's my impression. It's been a week since the going-over, yet I haven't heard a thing about my going to the GPO. The publications clerk keeps saying to me, 'I gotta have some advance notice before you drop it on me. When's it going to be?' All I can say is, 'Soon, Hal.' I don't like being in that position. I've waited pretty patiently, but now I want to know what's going on."

Schmidt spoke in a mocking voice. "That's what you want—to know what's going on. Well, I'll tell you. It's simple. A well-educated boy like you should be able to figure this out. Your paper is not going to be published. If you're smart, you'll drop it. That's the way things are. I'm sorry."

I heard what he said, but I did not accept it. I asked the one question he didn't want to hear. "Why?"

He lost patience with me. "Brett," he said in a raised voice, "for such a smart boy, you're very stupid."

"Listen," I said angrily, "I know social security is politically sensitive. No one on the Committee has to endorse my paper, just let it be printed. I thought the Committee was supposed to advise the Congress to the best of its ability."

"Dammit, Brett, you're not the one to be telling me or O'Hara or anyone on this Committee what to do. Remember what I told you when I hired you—you're low man on the totem pole, and you can't open your mouth every time you feel the need to. We're not your parents." That last rebuke stung me. He saw that and softened his tone. "Brett, your report is good, damn good. But it's embarrassing to us, to our members who voted for that blasted social-security-tax bill." Sadder now, Schmidt added, "We're not bastards trying to fuck you over. I'd like to help you, but I can't. I'm not in a position to, with Humphrey gone. I don't suppose you've noticed, being so wrapped up in your own work, but I don't swing the same weight as I used to. Dick Skaggs, Bentsen's man, is the guy now, and he's not going to help you. I don't think he particularly likes you. I probably wouldn't if I were him. You cut him out of the railroad hearing and now this." Schmidt stopped, but I was too angry to keep quiet.

"Well, why didn't you tell me when I began that this was a taboo project?"

"It wasn't taboo. It's just that your timing is off. The voters are pissed off about the tax increase, and the leadership doesn't want any more of an issue on its hands than it's already got. They don't need more bad publicity—your report, for instance. Perhaps in a few months, it might be fine to publish, but dammit, there's nothing Hamburg, Coates, or I can do for you. Get that through your head."

"So you know for sure that my paper won't be released."

"Listen, go ask O'Hara or Skaggs if you don't believe me. I'm not in charge, so stop giving me shit." He paused and then added, "I can't protect you anymore. Look, I've got an appointment, so I'll see you later." He got up. I did too. Schmidt walked out. I went back to my desk.

If it's possible to have an epiphany in Washington, D.C., I had one right then at my desk. It was physical as much as anything else. Suddenly my stomach was no longer in knots. I wasn't tapping my feet nervously like a chicken. My hand no longer seemed intent upon scratching my head. I simply sat there and knew. There was nothing to be confused or worried about. As far as Schmidt was concerned, I was on my own. He would not buck the system. He was washed up on the Committee. It was every man for himself. I was free to do whatever I wanted. As former President Nixon would have said, "It is all *perfectly* clear." As much as Schmidt was finished, so was our relationship. I was calm, considering . . .

I was sitting there, feeling surprisingly good, when my phone rang. The reporter from *The New York Times* was calling again. This time I knew exactly what to say.

"What can I do for you?" I asked cheerfully.

He was taken aback. "Is this Brett Fromson?"

"This is he."

"Have you finished your study?"

"Yes."

"Can I get a copy?"

"You can't."

"Why not?"

"It isn't being released to the press."

"Is there pressure from above?"

"You could say that—off the record, of course."

"Can't I get a copy?"

"Why should you get one?"

"I could get your report into the *Times*."

"But I don't like you. Why should I do you a favor?"

"Do yourself a favor."

"Call back tomorrow. Maybe then. Bye." Click. I truly enjoyed that conversation. I wasn't going to give my report away cheaply. I now understood the political value of my information.

I felt inspired. I felt tingles up and down my back as if feathers were stroking my spine. I almost skipped over to O'Hara's office. I would do what Schmidt had suggested—ask O'Hara.

Now that I knew the answer, I wasn't afraid to ask the question. If they could have their fun with me, I could have some fun at their expense. I was almost giddy.

O'Hara was in his office, the only private one on the Committee. Fortunately, the threshold was not being guarded by O'Hara's secretary, Mathilda, whose main task in life was to keep people out.

I poked my head in the open doorway. O'Hara was sitting reading the *The New York Times* at the far end of the rectangular room. He was leaning back in his armchair and looked as if he was already retired. He didn't notice me until I said, "John." He looked up. "Could I talk to you for a minute?" I asked.

He was tense. "Yes, uh, come on in."

I sat down on his deep leather couch as if I owned it. "John, do you remember my Social Security paper?"

"Of course I do," he said seriously.

"What do you think of it?"

"It's good, of course, but . . ."

"John, did I ever give you a copy of it?"

"No, but—"

"I didn't recall giving you one, but go on. Sorry."

"Well, as I was saying, it is very good but Will Coates says he has some technical problems with it."

"Oh, technical." I said.

O'Hara was turning a little red. "I don't know myself—"

"But Coates has some technical problems," I said for him.

"Yes, that's it," he replied, to reassure himself.

"Did you know that Coates and I have already discussed 'his problems'? Did you know that the man who built the econometric model I used supports my methods?"

"Oh. Well, uh, I didn't." O'Hara twisted uncomfortably in his swivel chair. "It's not for political reasons," he added.

"I never said it was, John," I said, as if that had never even crossed my mind. "Political? I'm sure you wouldn't do that. After all, John, you had me spend two months working on this study. Social security is a hot issue. Nobody else on the Hill has done a study like mine. If the Committee can't influence the debate on social security, what can it do? We can't authorize legislation. We have a responsibility to get the best information out to the Congress, the press, the public. . . . I know politics wouldn't enter into it."

"That's right," he said.

"I knew you would feel that way," I added. "Do you think I should change my methodology?"

"I don't think you have to do that. After all, the bill has become law."

"That's what I think too, John. Why change the methodology? It's not that important, is it?"

"No, not really."

"We don't really need to publish the information, do we?"

"I don't think so." He was looking at me strangely, as if to see whether I was feverish. But there was no sweat on my brow. O'Hara was the one perspiring.

I got up. "See you later, John. I think I understand things." I walked out smoothly, with composure.

The next morning, I was again at my desk and Schmidt was at his, when Kim Donahue bustled into the room. This was her last week on the Committee staff. "Have you seen today's *New York Times?*" she asked loudly. She passed without a glance at me and went straight to Schmidt. I stood up and followed. She began reading aloud from a story in the first section of the *Times* written by the man who had called me and with whom I had had the "off-the-record" conversation.

"Listen to this," she said to Schmidt. " 'Sources close to the Joint Economic Committee report a study sharply critical of the recent Social Security tax bill is being suppressed because its publication would prove embarrassing to the Democratic leadership.' I wonder where they got that story. Brett, did you see this?"

"No," I replied.

Not a second later Schmidt asked, "Brett, did you talk to this guy?"

I looked Schmidt right in the eye and said, "Not me." That was the first time I had ever lied to him.

He didn't believe me. I had every motive to have committed this "crime." Yet he did not question my "No." He knew I would be as honest with him as the Committee had been with me. He said in a hard voice, "No, I didn't think you had. I wonder which SOB gave him his information."

"Why don't you call and ask," I suggested.

Schmidt looked at me and said, sarcastically, "Right."

"Right," I replied.

Whatever warmth there had been between us died with that word "Right." At that moment, I didn't care. I was playing by their rules now. I was tired of being jerked around.

Schmidt left. I walked back to my desk. As Kim came by on her way out the door she stopped.

"Brett," she said with a coy smile, "my professor really liked your paper."

I looked up at her sharply. "Why did you come in here and read that?"

"He was going to see it anyway."

"Why didn't you show it to me first?"

"I guess I wanted to see how you'd react."

"Well, how did I do?"

"You're playing it right. Give them a taste of their own medicine."

I didn't say anything. As Kim turned to go out the door, she added, "Don't worry, I won't tell."

I said to her, "You don't have anything to tell." Kim nodded and got out.

My first thought was, "Now they'll have a harder time keeping this paper quiet." The public value of my paper had gone up because of voters' protests, so I had raised the cost to the JEC of suppressing it.

I had been cocky with O'Hara and now hard with Schmidt, but I couldn't sustain those feelings at every moment. After Kim left I felt hot and woozy. Any revenge I might get could not soothe my aloneness. Events did not, however, give me time to wallow in self-pity.

My phone rang. This time it was a reporter from the *Chicago Sun-Times*.

"Hello, this is Susan Majors," she said in a pleasant telephone voice.

"Fromson, JEC. What can I do for you?" I said while drawing a maze on a pad of paper.

"I'd like to talk with you about the social-security study you've done."

I didn't bother to ask how she knew. "What do you want to know?"

"I'd like to see a copy."

"If you want a copy, ask John O'Hara, the staff director. Tell him I told you I'm not authorized to give anyone a copy."

"Can't you talk about this study? What's going on?"

I didn't want to be honest with her. I was playing a different game. I couldn't afford to let loose. "Be calm," I told myself. I would play this out calmly. I would not lose control. "Call me back after you talk to O'Hara." Who knew, perhaps he would feel compelled to go public now that the press was sniffing around. I hoped I had indirectly pressured him into releasing the study.

No matter what I said, I still wanted my superior's approval. In Washington, everyone wants to be approved of by someone else. The politicians want to be loved by special-interest groups, senior aides want to be loved by the politicians, and the young aides want to be loved by anyone on top.

O'Hara's approval never came. The woman from the *Chicago Sun-Times* called back within five minutes.

"What did O'Hara say?" I asked.

"I asked him if I could get a copy, and he said, 'No.' So I asked him why, and he said, 'You know perfectly well why.' I asked him if it was a political squeeze, and he said, 'You don't expect me to answer that question.' So it's up to you. Can I get a copy?"

She was asking me to "leak," to put the Committee's interest behind the public's and mine. I had little doubt that my superiors on the Committee objected to leaking "on principle." I had seen them sacrifice principles, however, when it served their interests.

Ms. Majors of the *Chicago Sun-Times* got her copy of the study.

The next day the lead headline of the *Chicago Sun-Times* front page was "SOCIAL SECURITY BILL TO PUT 130,000 OUT OF WORK." The story spread fast on the AP and UPI wires. Within twenty-four hours, every large and small newspaper in America was reporting on my study. The media play it received was much bigger than I could ever have guessed. Congressmen's aides from every region of the country called our office for a copy of this report that they had read about in the home-town papers. Even my father clipped an article on it from the Boston papers and sent it my way.

I referred all requests for copies to O'Hara. Let him deal with the public the Committee had so wanted to keep uninformed. He capitulated, of course, and authorized distribution of the report. Within days, the report had generated a wave of anger among taxpayers. Congressional hearings were held to look into rolling back the payroll taxes. My report was used to criticize the hastily passed P.L. 95-216.

I had finally made the splash I had wanted. This was the best piece of work I had done, a first-rate job—better than my efforts on bauxite, youth unemployment, government R&D, or railroads. No one on the Committee, however, congratulated me. Not that I expected them to. No one cussed me out either, at least not to my face. Like most people who cross the bureaucracy, I was not given a public dressing-down. Rather, I was quietly shunned. No one wanted to be associated with a troublemaker. That day I sure as hell didn't receive any invitations to lunch.

And that's the way it stayed. Only things got worse. While people on the Committee kept their distance, I got progressively more tired. I could not maintain the angry enthusiasm that had fortified me in the fight to make the paper public. That moment of successful rebellion had passed; I still had to show up each day. No work came my way except petty tasks like preparing weekly updates on the economy for the Committee members— "This week, the Consumer Price Index rose 0.5% . . ."

These last days of May should have been glorious. The dog days of summer hadn't hit yet. The days were sunny and breezy under pale-blue skies. All the prettiest girls seemed to have shed their bulky winter coats and wool skirts for cotton dresses lightly cinched at the waist. Joni never looked better. I never felt more discouraged.

Joni and I hadn't discussed my work in the past month. She had brought it up often, but I always stopped the conversation. "I'm doing some work on Social Security," I'd say. My work on the Hill was no longer chewed over at dinner. I'd talk about anything except that. I didn't want to bring the tensions home to Joni. My pride kept them inside. I would rather run for fifteen miles in Rock Creek Park. Nor did I want to discuss my work in front of Charity and Nicholas; I didn't trust them to keep quiet.

In the last days of May, however, I had to speak with Joni. The pressure was extreme. My chest was always tight, and I knew there was nothing wrong with my heart. It was a Friday night and we were alone in the house on Tilden Street. As we sat on the couch, I said, "I think I'm going to quit the Committee."

"Are you kidding?"

"No." I said. "I'll give notice tomorrow."

"I don't believe it. You're putting me on, aren't you. Brett Fromson, Mr. Success, wants to leave? Bullshit."

"I do."

"Why?" she asked suspiciously. I could tell she still didn't believe me.

I explained what had happened so she would understand that it was no joke. "Things won't be any different a month or a year from now. After this mess, the JEC's no place for me. Schmidt's finished, and I'm the Benedict Arnold of the Committee."

"Maybe they'll fire you. Then you won't have to quit." She laughed.

"Fire me? This is the government. They don't fire people here. Besides, I do good work. What can they get me on? 'Causing embarrassment to the Committee?' No, they'll just do what they're already doing—ostracize me. I'm not going to be able to win back their trust. I'm barely twenty-three years old. Why should I bang my head against their wall? I'm not going to knock it down."

"Well, why don't you go work for another member of Congress or another committee or even for the administration?" Joni asked.

"What's the point? I came to Washington to work on economic policy. There's no better place for that than the Joint Economic Committee. I've worked in the Executive Office of the President. I know what positions there are for people my age. You think I'd have greater freedom there? Don't be ridiculous," I said condescendingly. Then I stopped. I realized that Joni knew the facts of life in Washington as well as I did. She simply didn't want me to leave Washington. She and I hadn't thought about marriage. We had made no permanent commitment. But neither had we considered separating. Quite suddenly our cozy and glamorous Washington life seemed to be collapsing. The transiency of it was uncomfortably apparent.

Joni said with a frail laugh, "You quit the Committee. You leave D.C. I quit work. I go to business school. No more Tilden Street. No more Capitol Hill. No more Schmidt. No more Diana. No more Charity. No more Nicholas. No more Peter. No, I'll see him again with or without Washington. He's not part of politics."

"I'm sorry," I said. "I have to leave the Committee. If I don't, I won't respect myself."

I gave notice the next day. It took me a half hour to find Schmidt. I wanted to tell him I was leaving, before I informed O'Hara or anyone else. He knew me better than anyone else on the JEC, and he cared more. He was having a rough time too.

194

Now that Humphrey was dead, Schmidt was not consulted. He was drinking wine before noon.

Schmidt was still civil to me, but we rarely spoke. He must have known it was coming, because, when I told him, he showed no surprise. Nor did he ask me why. He offered me a glass of wine, and we toasted the future.

"What are your plans?" I asked.

"I don't know. I'll probably find a place in some agency downtown. I've got friends. There's always a place for an old hack like me."

That was the last real conversation we had. There was much I wanted to explain to him, but he turned cold after this talk. I had tried to find myself in him without losing myself in him. That was impossible.

After seeing Schmidt, I gave my resignation to O'Hara.

"You know, Brett," he said kindly, "when I lose a young fellah like you, I always feel like I've lost a son. I'm always sorry to see you young guys go."

His sentiments were genuine. Today he was saying goodbye as an older man; in the social-security incident last month, he had acted in his role as staff director to save his ass. I understood the difference.

"My leaving seems the best thing to do, John."

"Yeah," he said. "I guess so."

"What are your plans?" I asked. O'Hara looked tired and was breathing heavily.

"I guess I'll stay with the Committee as long as I can."

"Yeah, that sounds good," I said. "John," I continued, "I know I didn't always do what you wanted me to but—" I stopped. I realized I was beginning to apologize for my behavior and that no apologies were necessary.

He could have handled the situation better by being honest with me. I could have had the foresight to see the potential danger of criticizing the policies of those people who employed me. He had been frightened that I was causing trouble for him, and I had been impatient and willful. Conflict was inevitable. No need to apologize. Cleaner without it.

"Take care, John."

"You too, Brett."

By my last week, the story of my social-security project had spread throughout the Committee and been suitably distorted. As opposed to men like O'Hara, some staffers tried to ride me before I left. Loyal to the bureaucracy and not privy to the details of the affair, they found it easy to cast me as the villain, the betrayer of the Committee. Bob Lackey went out of his way to antagonize me. He kept telling the Senate Superintendent's Office that they could remove my typewriter. For two days running, I had to explain to delivery men, "This typewriter is still in use. I haven't left yet."

Lackey had somehow come into possession of the file on Social Security that contained all my data upon which the study had been based. When packing up my files, I discovered he had it and politely asked him for it. He refused to hand it over. He said it was government property. I had no idea whose property it was legally, but in light of the Committee's disavowal of my report I considered it more mine than theirs.

I went to see O'Hara to ask for his help, but his secretary, Mathilda, wouldn't let me in. "He's too busy to see you," she said flatly. I had been in Washington long enough to know any insistence would be futile. I had become taboo.

I never saw O'Hara. On a Saturday afternoon Joni and I went to the Dirksen Building to remove my belongings. Except for the policeman at the door, the only person I ran into was Senator Moynihan, who said "Hello" as I left with my last box.

Joni was sitting in the front passenger seat of my overladen Fiat. After putting the box in, I said, "I'll be right back. I forgot something."

I ran back inside the building, through the set of bronze doors, past the drowsy guard down the marble corridor, and into the Snakepit to Lackey's desk. I opened the bottom file drawer. My Social Security file had to be in here somewhere.

I had not yet found it when Lackey walked in. He had probably come to use the Committee's WATS line to call one of his relatives as everyone did on the weekends. He saw me and yelled, "What the hell are you doing? Get out of there."

"I'm getting my file," I said, and just then I found it.

He frightened me momentarily, but only momentarily. For as Lackey rushed toward me, he ran into the corner of a desk with the soft, lower part of his knee. The pain rushed through his body faster than he could say "Ow." He started hobbling around in a small circle near the door swearing, "That's breaking and entering, breaking and entering."

I looked at him quizzically. "You want me to call a doctor?"

"No, goddamit," he complained. "Give me that file."

"No," I said, taking a step backward.

"Give it to me."

"No."

"Give it to me." The two of us sounded like six-year-olds.

This was too ludicrous for me. I started laughing. "Come and get it."

"Give it to me," he said. I shook my head. I began backing up further. He limped toward me. "That's Committee property," he said.

He continued to follow me around the partition that separated the reception area from the back space. As soon as he came around the left side of the dummy wall, I ran around the right side to the door. He chugged after me crying, "You can't."

I was out the door and into the corridor before he could stop me. Lackey gave up. As I walked quickly away he shouted, "Make sure the Committee gets your keys and turn in your Senate I.D." He was a petty Committee man to the bitter end. I couldn't resist giving him the finger and a big grin.

I left through the DSOB's southwestern exit, straight into the spring afternoon's fading light. When I sat down in the driver's seat of the Fiat, Joni asked me what I had forgotten.

Tapping the rufous-colored file, I said, "I had to get the Social Security file. Why should they keep what they never wanted."

As we drove home through Rock Creek Park, I felt good. I was glad not to be involved in Washington's contest for political influence and power. I drove away from Capitol Hill and away from the White House. I felt freer than I had felt in a year. Whatever disillusionment drifted around me could not seep in; I could accept what had happened, roam, grow, and sleep well through many nights.

Epilogue

THAT WAS the last time I ever visited the Committee's offices in the DSOB. I stayed in Washington for some months living on the pay I received from the Committee in lieu of vacation days never taken. I spent much of my time trying to understand what had happened. I didn't look for a new job. I didn't go directly to business school. I began to write, a passion forgotten since my sophomore year at Stanford.

I began writing out of anger. I was growing angry at myself and at the government. Angry at myself for having left, and angry at the government for having no place for people like me. The more I wrote, however, the more distinctly I saw that it had been inevitable. I wanted to prosper within the political bureaucracy of Washington, but I was unwilling to accept the authority of men like Schmidt and O'Hara and to end up rewarded as they were. The rules of the game were clear: Put private or bureaucratic interests first, the public interest second. That is how the system works. The notion of a "coherent system of government" that works to "represent the people" is malarkey. What the government in Washington provides is service to a heterogeneous group of political constituencies in return for their support.

I had watched the President cater to the Shah of Iran in return for oil and anti-Communism; I had seen the JEC publish a shoddy study of small business to please a member who wanted a favor for a friend; I had watched a Senator write legislation on government research and development to increase his committee's fiefdom; I had watched government rail policy protect bad management, strong unions, and old bureaucrats in exchange for political support to certain Congressional committee members and their aides; and finally, with social security, I had watched my own bosses endorse bad public policy and then try to stifle criticism of their endorsement to avoid temporary political embarrassment.

This awareness, however, was not what angered me the most. Just because I did not fit in, didn't mean I thought the government couldn't work. Leaders in the top positions could fight industry special interests, bureaucratic passivity and political cowardice. If the President had pushed more skillfully and forcefully for an alternative to social-security payroll taxes, perhaps the taxpayers would not have to pay $186 billion in the next years without any guarantee that social security won't run out of money.

What exasperated me was that I was in no position to change the situation. That had to come from the top. When impatient upstarts try to do it, they are squashed; young people going to Washington should try to remember that. I hope that not all of them will. Occasionally, someone has to tell the emperors of Washington they have no clothes on. But he should not expect to be thanked. It is easier to go along and get along. I am certain that a new cadre of young men and women (some patient, some not) will replace those who, like me, have left. I wish them the best of luck. Short of that, they had better have a decent sense of humor.

At 8:30 A.M. some months after I had left the Committee and before I left Washington, I heard the front doorbell ring. Everyone else was too busy getting ready for work to answer it, so I walked down the stairs in my bathrobe to see who it was. The front door was paned with glass. I looked through it. "Oh God, Moonies." My recognition was instantaneous. The dull glint in the eyes. The neat short-sleeved shirts. The phony smiles.

200

I am generally unpleasant throughout the morning. At 8:30 A.M., however, I'm worse, and when I discover two Moonies at the door I'm worst of all. In one motion I opened the door and asked nastily, "Are you Moonies?"

They hesitated. One looked at the other, who replied, "Well, uh, we're members of the Unification Church of—"

"You're Moonies. I don't like Reverend Moon. I don't like his two-bit cult. I don't like what you do to people."

The one in charge replied, "Let's talk. Maybe you'll change your mind."

I looked at him and said, "You're standing on my paper." He was momentarily confused. "You're standing on my newspaper," I repeated, pointing to the ground. His sneakers were crumpling my *Washington Post*. He backed off. I shut the door and they didn't ring again.

I sat in an armchair in the living room to read the paper. My interest was piqued by a small story buried in the lower left-hand part of the front page. *FBI Discloses How Soviet Spy Switched Sides.*

> FBI officials surfaced a Soviet intelligence colonel at an elaborate news conference yesterday to explain how they turned him into a "double agent." Colonel Rudolph Albert Dortmund . . . described his 11-year-long mission of collecting political intelligence and arranging secret exchanges of information with other Soviet intelligence operatives while he was posing as a freelance photographer in the suburbs of New York City . . . Hartsdale, N.Y.

I quickly got out of my chair and ran to the stairwell. "Joni, come here. Peter, Peter's father is a spy, a Russian spy. Listen to this."

> Dortmund began his career with the KGB while serving in the military in a Soviet bloc country in Eastern Europe. He was infiltrated to West Germany, then Canada, and finally in 1968 to the United States. He apparently was identified "a number of years ago"—the FBI wouldn't be more specific—when an-

201

other spy under diplomatic cover was followed to a drop site and Dortmund showed up a short time later.

When confronted by the FBI, he chose to cooperate rather than face prosecution. He was said to be particularly anxious to prevent the KGB from training his teenage son as a spy too.

Joni had stood until this. She slumped down on the couch. "Peter? A spy?"

"They didn't say that," I replied. "I wouldn't be surprised though." Joni didn't try to defend her friend. She was thinking what I was thinking: Peter must have known. He was no dummy.

"He must have," Joni agreed.

"This explains that letter he sent you and why we could never reach him at his family's house."

"Do they say where Peter is?"

I read to the end. " 'When the Dortmund family left its home in Westchester County five months ago, they told neighbors they were going to Guatemala.' "

"Guatemala?" Joni asked.

"Wait, there's more. 'Instead, according to the FBI, they will be relocated with a new identity somewhere in the United States.' I don't think you'll hear from Peter again."

"God."

"Let's go to the library."

"Why?"

"I want to see *The New York Times*. I want to know if Peter was a spy. I want to know. Don't you?"

Joni hesitated and said, "Yes. I guess I do."

We drove in the Fiat to the Georgetown Branch of the District of Columbia's public library. The reading room was filled with retired government people leafing through newspapers and magazines. We disturbed every one of them. "Do you have today's *Times*? Do you have today's *Times*?" Finally, we found the elderly gentleman who did. "We have to look at it for a moment," I said. "It's urgent. Please."

We searched the index for the story. "It's on page A16," Joni said. I flipped to page 16. There was no story on that page—only a full-page ad for IBM, Mr. Dortmund's employer.

Joni and I stared at one another. "Reread the index. Maybe we have the wrong page."

Joni did. "A16."

"That's impossible." But it wasn't. There was only a full-page IBM advertisement.

"Maybe this edition is different from the New York one. Maybe the story is in the local edition." We drove home and called a friend in New York City to check. There was a story in her copy of the *Times*. She read from it. " '. . . no KGB agents had been caught as a result of Colonel Dortmund's conversion . . . American officials said that the operation was ended because of a growing fear that the KGB suspected Col. Dortmund's cooperation with American intelligence officials. Another factor, they said, was that Colonel Dortmund's son, also a former spy, had been ordered to return to Moscow for advanced training, with no guarantee that he could come back to the United States.' "

Peter, a spy? Is this why he had been so anxious about taking the lie-detector test at work? Is this why he had so many cameras and a sophisticated darkroom? Is this why he was in Washington?

All those times I had wondered why he was in Washington when politics seemed unimportant to him. Now it made more sense if he had been engaged in espionage. There is no better place to collect political intelligence on the United States and foreign governments than Washington, D.C. How many of Peter's friends from Georgetown and elsewhere circulated in political and diplomatic circles? Are there better places to communicate with Russian spy masters? How many Russian agents and accomplices work under the control of the embassy in Washington? More than any other United States city.

So Peter was a spy. So what? Did it mean that his friendship with Joni was fake? No, I doubt that. He did care for her. We never spoke about politics or the government. Peter asked no questions about Joni's job or mine. I think we were an escape for him, a break from the aloneness and anxiety of his father's occupation into which he slipped.

Did he slip or was he pushed? We will never know. My guess is that he was a young man engulfed by a situation over which he had no control. Perhaps he wanted to emulate his father? Perhaps he was convinced by ideological arguments to serve for the glory of Communism? Perhaps he hoped to gain some power by serving that regime?

How different were such motives from my reasons for coming to Washington to work for the United States government? Did he respect his father as I did mine? Did he believe in Communism as I did in democracy? Did he want "success" in service to a government the way I had wanted success?

There was one major difference between us. He, far more than I, was a victim of his participation in politics and government. I could walk away from Washington and write a book about the experience; Peter was stripped of his identity and hidden away nameless from the KGB by our FBI.

He was a spy or perhaps only a fledgling spy. He got what he deserved, some may say. Perhaps so. What interests me is not his culpability; that is unknowable. I only observe the powerful effect government work had on his life. I would love to speak with Peter—to understand what happened to him in Washington.

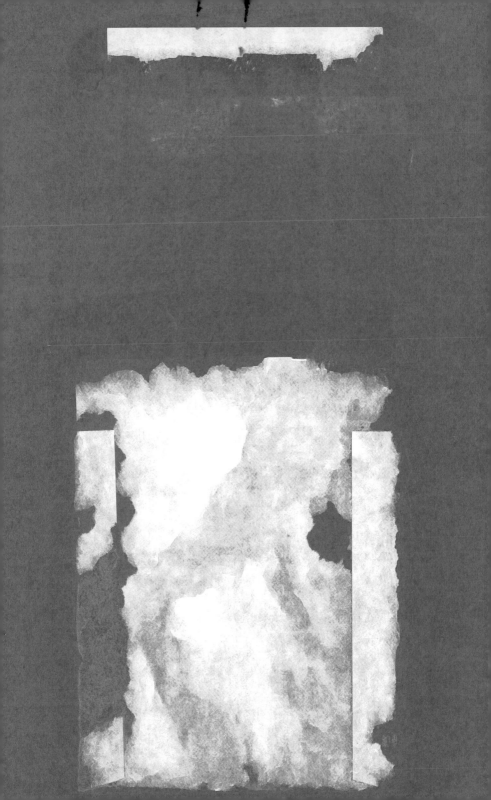